MASTERPIECES
OF
HEBREW LITERATURE

OTHER BOOKS BY CURT LEVIANT

Novels

The Yemenite Girl
Passion in the Desert
The Man Who Thought He Was Messiah
Partita in Venice
Diary of an Adulterous Woman
*Ladies and Gentlemen, the Original Music of the Hebrew Alphabet and
    Weekend in Mustara* (two novellas)
A Novel of Klass

Translations from Yiddish with Introductions

Stories and Satires, by Sholom Aleichem
Old Country Tales, by Sholom Aleichem
Some Laughter, Some Tales, by Sholom Aleichem
From the Fair, the Autobiography of Sholom Aleichem
The Song of Songs, by Sholom Aleichem
The Agunah, by Chaim Grade
The Yeshiva, by Chaim Grade
The Yeshiva, Volume II: Masters and Disciples, by Chaim Grade
The Seven Little Lanes, by Chaim Grade
The Jewish Government and Other Stories, by Lamed Shapiro
The Heart-Stirring Sermon and Other Stories, by Avraham Reisen
More Stories from My Father's Court, by Isaac Bashevis Singer
The Jewish Book of Fables, by Eliezer Shtaynbarg

Translated and Edited Texts from Hebrew with Introductions

King Artus, a Hebrew Arthurian Romance of 1279
The Golem and the Wondrous Deeds of the Maharal of Prague, by
    Yudl Rosenberg

MASTERPIECES

OF

HEBREW LITERATURE

Selections from 2000 years of Jewish Creativity

Edited and with introductions by

CURT LEVIANT

2008 • 5768
Philadelphia

JPS is a nonprofit educational association and the oldest and foremost publisher of Judaica in English in North America. The mission of JPS is to enhance Jewish culture by promoting the dissemination of religious and secular works, in the United States and abroad, to all individuals and institutions interested in past and contemporary Jewish life.

The Jewish Publication Society
2100 Arch Street, 2nd floor
Philadelphia, PA 19103
www.jewishpub.org

Design and Composition by Varda Graphics

Manufactured in the United States of America

08 09 10 11 12   10 9 8 7 6 5 4 3 2 1

ISBN: 978-0-8276-0880-1 (cloth)
ISBN: 978-0-8276-0881-8 (paperback)

Library of Congress Cataloging-in-Publication Data:
Masterpieces of Hebrew literature : selections from 2000 years of Jewish creativity / edited and with introductions by Curt Leviant.
     p. cm.
  Includes bibliographical references.
  ISBN 978-0-8276-0881-8 (alk. paper)—ISBN 978-0-8276-0880-1 (cloth) 1. Hebrew literature—Translations into English. I. Leviant, Curt.
  PJ5059.E1L4 2008
  892.4'08--dc22
                        2008022791

JPS books are available at discounts for bulk purchases for reading groups, special sales, and fundraising purchases. Custom editions, including personalized covers, can be created in larger quantities for special needs. For more information, please contact us at marketing@jewishpub.org or at this address: 2100 Arch Street, Philadelphia, PA 19103.

פאר די טייערע
קינדער
מיט ליבע

לילדים היקרים
באהבה

Contents

ACKNOWLEDGMENTS

Special thanks are due to the following publishers and holders of copyright for their kind permission to reprint the copyrighted material included in this volume.

Academy for Jewish Research, N.Y.: Maimonides, Epistle to Yemen, tr. B. Cohen.

Beacon Press, Boston: *Faith and Knowledge*, ed. N. N. Glatzer.

Columbia University Press, N.Y.: *Chronicle of Ahimaaz*, ed. M. Salzman; *The Book of Delight*, Joseph Zabara, tr. Moses Hadas; *Fables of a Jewish Aesop,* tr. Moses Hadas.

Edinburgh University Press, Edinburgh: *Jewish Religious Polemic*, ed. O. S. Rankin.

Philipp Feidheim, N.Y.: Maimonides, *Book of Knowledge*, tr. M. Hyamson; Bahya, *Duties of the Heart*, tr. M. Hyamson.

Harper and Row, N.Y.: *The Island Within*, Ludwig Lewisohn.

Holt, Rinehart & Winston, Inc.: *Memoirs of My People*, ed. Leo W. Schwarz.

Jewish Publication Society, Philadelphia: *Mekilta,* ed. J. Lauterbach; *A Treasury of Responsa*, ed. Solomon Freehof; *Post-Biblical Hebrew Literature*, ed. B. Z. Halper; *Ethical Wills*, ed. Israel Abrahams; *Mesillat Yesharim*, tr. M. Kaplan; *Selected Poems of Moses ibn Ezra*, tr. S. Solis-Cohen; *Selected Poems of Jehuda Halevi*, tr. Nina Salaman.

Jacob L. Kadushin, *Jewish Code of Jurisprudence.*

Jacob R. Marcus, *The Jew in the Medieval World.*

Oxford University Press, London: *Apocrypha and Pseudepigrapha*, ed. R. H. Charles; *The Mishnah*, tr. H. Danby.

Rabbinical Assembly of America-The United Synagogue, N.Y.: *Sabbath and Festival Prayer Book*, ed. Morris Silverman.

V. E. Reichert, tr. *The Fourteenth Gate.*

Routledge and Sons, Ltd., London: *Jewish Travellers*, ed. E. N. Adler.

Schocken Books, N.Y.: *Hebrew Poems from Spain*, tr. David Goldstein.

Shapiro and Vallentine, London: *Pentateuch with Rashi's Commentary*, ed. A. M. Silbermann.

Soncino Press, London: *The Babylonian Talmud: Tractate Berakoth*, tr. Maurice Simon; *Midrash Rabbah*, tr. S. M. Lehrman; *The Zohar*, tr. Harry Sperling and Maurice Simon.

University of Chicago Press, *The Apocrypha*, tr. Edgar Goodspeed.

Preface

This one-volume anthology was prepared for the reader who seeks (but has hitherto been unable to find) a comprehensive introduction to the more than two-thousand-year mainstream of postbiblical creativity. Some compilations have concentrated on special periods, such as talmudic, medieval or modern, and have offered brief excerpts—often no more than isolated passages—of larger works; others have focused only on belletristic material. However, *Masterpieces of Hebrew Literature* is the first volume in English, we believe, to attempt an in-depth portrait of the range of a literature, covering the major periods from the Apocrypha to the early 19th century, and presenting substantial selections of the important genres, many of them anthologized for the first time. In addition, brief introductions are provided to place the author and his work in proper perspective.

Literature in Hebrew offers a spectrum of possibilities, encompassing the many genres used throughout the centuries by Jews writing in Hebrew—the most important of which are included here, and without which no survey of Hebrew literature can be complete. Along with the expected fiction and poetry, there are legal, ethical, and midrashic works; travelogs, responsa and biblical commentary; history, chronicles, and letters; fables and prayers. The literary tradition seen in this anthology was created, interestingly enough, not in one land, but via one people writing in dispersion; whether composed in Palestine, Babylonia, North Africa, Spain, Italy, Germany, France or Russia, a common language and literary and religious heritage bind the disparate works, even though some were influenced by outside cultures.

The reader should be cautioned that only the barest sampling of an infinitely rich literature is provided in *Masterpieces of Hebrew Literature*. The book could be expanded a thousandfold and still not begin to do justice to the whole range of literature in Hebrew. The problem in an anthology of this sort is the vast amount of material available, and because selecting the works is to a degree a matter of personal preference, the contents can always be questioned. If, on balance, this work inspires the reader to explore Hebrew literature independently, it will surely have served its purpose.

Apocrypha

In the diversified Apocryphal literature we find examples of wisdom literature—a popular branch of writing in the Middle East—such as The Wisdom of Ben Sira and The Wisdom of Solomon; religious poetry and prayer, as in The Song of the Three Children; history, as in the Books of the Maccabees; and fictional narrative in The Story of Susanna, Judith, and Tobit.

The books of the Apocrypha (known in Hebrew as *Sefarim Hitzonim,* the "Outside Books") were officially placed outside the Biblical canon. But the ban in no way diminished their popularity, as may be seen by the somewhat hyperbolic statement of R. Akiba (2nd century C.E.): "Whoever reads the Outside Books loses his share in the World-to-Come." A thoroughly stringent remark not at all typical of Akiba's gentle demeanor, the intent may have been to warn the reader against accepting these books on the same level as Holy Writ.

The prohibition notwithstanding, the books of the Apocrypha were read and copied, and their influence, whether through direct quotes or indirect suggestion, was felt in various Midrashim, legends, and ancient liturgic poetry.

Hebraic in spirit and variegated in their subject matter, the Apocrypha, in Greek translation, was kept by the Church for two millenia as part of its sacred writ, and linked with what Christians term the Old Testament. Only in the past generation have all the books of the Apocrypha been retranslated into the original Hebrew from the Greek.

1

Precise dating of these works is a difficult task, but it can be stated that the books range from about the fourth century B.C.E. to the first century C.E. These books thus bridge the two major ancient periods of Hebrew literature, the Biblical and the Mishnaic, and offer massive evidence of the continuity of Hebraic literary creativity. The books, almost certainly all written by Jews, were composed mostly in Hebrew and Aramaic (related to Hebrew much as Portuguese is related to Spanish), and have survived only in translation—with one striking exception—The Wisdom of Ben Sira.

As a unit, the Apocrypha offers us many insights into the social, religious and intellectual life of the Jews during the several hundred years after the close of the Biblical canon.

The Wisdom of Ben Sira

The author of The Wisdom of Ben Sira—he is the only known author in a literature that is generally anonymous—was (as we learn in 50:27) Jeshua ben Eleazar ben Sira. From his descriptions and his sophisticated knowledge of both the secular and the religious world, we can assume that he lived in Jerusalem. He was familiar with, and enthralled by the Temple service; educated in Hebrew letters and no doubt in Greek as well; travelled in the Middle East and saw its Jewish communities. In brief, the author of The Wisdom of Ben Sira, sometimes called Ecclesiasticus, was an observant yet worldly Jew who had a perceptive insight into human nature.

The style displayed in Ben Sira, written c. 180 B.C.E., extends back to the wisdom literature of the Bible, which includes Proverbs, Ecclesiastes, Job, and several of the Psalms; it is an expression of pragmatic wisdom in epigrammatic form, accenting intelligence, religious devotion and ethical behavior. Recorded without any special order or plan, the book has many topics including relations between parents and children, the individual and God, free choice, wisdom, women, ritual sacrifice, commerce, good and evil attributes, divine justice, man's religious obligations and his tribulations.

Despite the ban on the Outside Books, and the specific Talmudic statement (Sanhedrin 100b) that Ben Sira is one of the forbidden books, Ben Sira is often quoted by the Talmudic sages who translated his Hebrew into Aramaic, the then current vernacular in Palestine. So respected was Ben Sira that his sayings were graced by the anonymous phrase used for Biblical citations, "It is written," or, "it is stated."

Ben Sira is closely modelled on the Book of Proverbs, especially the latter's chapters 1–9, and 30–31. Parallelism and thought completion dominate the construction of the two-verse line as it does the Biblical verses. The author's stylistic preferences include verses in the form of a question, epigrams that begin with the words "there is," and second phrases beginning with "because." In addition to the Biblical influences in verse structure, the language of Ben Sira echoes the Biblical voice. Many of Ben Sira's verses are fine variations of Biblical verses; in others he takes a Biblical word or image and utilizes it in a new fashion. The imitative use of Biblical diction points to the artificial style selected by the author. Ben Sira lived at a time when Mishnaic, not Biblical, Hebrew was current, and the Biblical rhetoric with its parallelism is a learned artifice in literary creativity—analogous to a contemporary writer who purposely chooses to imitate the style of the Elizabethan or eighteenth century writers of fiction.

Since 1896 about two-thirds of the original Hebrew version of Ben Sira has been discovered. During the historic Masada excavations (1964) under the direction of Yigal Yadin, five more chapters of the original Hebrew were discovered (Chapters 39–43), which represent the oldest of all extant Hebrew manuscripts of Ben Sira. However, there is no one manuscript that comprises the entire original Hebrew version.

The Story of Susanna

The story of Susanna and the Elders is not mentioned in the Talmud or the Midrash, but seems to have been popular in the Middle Ages. The *Chronicles of Jerahmeel* (twelfth century) contains this story with a slight variation, and Nachmanides (1194–1270) refers to it in his *Commentary on the Torah;* another version appears in a manuscript of *Yosippon,* a tenth century Hebrew chronicle based on Josephus.

The Story of Susanna, composed *c.* 90 B.C.E., is a Jewish version of two popular Middle Eastern folktales. One parallel is found in the legend of Ali Chosda (in the *Arabian Nights),* wherein a youngster stands up to correct an injustice perpetrated in a court of law; in Susanna it is young Daniel who instructs the court how to cross-examine each witness separately and thus proves that they perjured themselves. The second version is the folk motif wherein desire-laden elders persecute a modest young woman who subsequently triumphs over her false accusers.

Aside from the finely compressed fictive form which gives Susanna a place in Hebrew literature on its artistic merits alone, the story's purpose, too, was to accent divine justice and the correct procedures for human courts of law.

The Song of the Three Children

The popular Book of Daniel has three additions in the Apocrypha: The Song of the Three Children, The History of Susanna, and Bel and the Dragon (the latter not included in this anthology).

The Song of the Three Children, probably composed c. 165 B.C.E., the era of the Maccabean revolt, is based on a story in Daniel: Hananiah, Mishael and Azariah (the Bible gives their Babylonian names as Shadrach, Meshach and Abednego) refuse to obey King Nebuchadnezzar's command to bow down to him, and are ordered to be thrown into the fiery furnace. Not only are they unharmed, but a fourth figure appears at their side in the flames.

The Song is an extended paean of glory to God. Like the closing verse of Psalm 150 it calls upon the entire creation to praise the Lord; and like Psalm 148 it catalogues the forces of nature and summons them to praise their Creator. Scholars feel that one reason for the creation of the Song is that the folk did not like the idea that Nebuchadnezzar praised the Lord (in the Bible) while the three witnesses of God's miracle remained silent.

The original language of this work is widely held to be Hebrew, a view shared by the Church Fathers as well. Many expressions in the Greek read as though they had been translated from the Hebrew; in fact, some verses and expressions are sourced in the Bible, especially the Psalms.

The Song of the Three Children has three parts: the prayer in the fiery furnace; details on the kindling of the fire and the manner in which the three youths were saved; and the extended Psalm-like hymn with which the Song concludes.

As an addition to the Book of Daniel, the Song should be placed in chapter 2 of Daniel, between verses 23 and 24.

The Book of Tobit

The Book of Tobit is a fine example of narrative art containing all the age-old elements of good fiction: plot, suspense and interesting protagonists. Moreover, it is replete with Jewish values: Tobias' father, Tobit, performs all the *mitzvot* connected with the Temple in Jerusalem; he observes the dietary laws, fulfills the precept of burying the dead (even though proscribed by the regime). In a speech that is reminiscent of Polonius' charge to his son Laertes—both Tobit and *Hamlet* utilize a standard element in Greek romances— Tobit teaches his son moral values. This speech contains the earliest mention in Jewish literature of what was eventually called the Golden Rule, later cited in the Talmud by the sage Hillel: "That which is hateful to you, do not do to anyone."

Despite this positive Jewish outlook, the Book of Tobit shared the fate of many other Apocryphal works—it is completely ignored by Talmudic literature, Philo and Josephus.

The narrative, composed approximately 175 B.C.E., contains many folkloristic elements, some of which appear in Persian literature, especially the *Story and Wisdom of Ahikar* (fifth century B.C.E.). However, despite the borrowing, the author of Tobit thoroughly Judaizes his version. Although the skeleton of the tale is sourced in Persian and other folklores, the spirit is Jewish, for the national, religious, and moral values of the Jews (occasionally, there are even some variations on Biblical verses) fill the book.

Since some fragments of the Book of Tobit in Hebrew and Aramaic were found in the Qumran caves in the Judean desert, the assumption is that the work was written in Palestine, and most scholars agree that its original language was Hebrew.

Another Hebrew version of the Tobit story may be found in the *Book of Delight* (see page 405).

THE WISDOM OF BEN SIRA

1. All wisdom comes from the Lord,
And remains with him forever.
The sand of the seas, and the drops of rain,
And the days of eternity—who can count them?
The height of the heavens, and the breadth of the earth,
And the deep, and wisdom—who can track them out?
Wisdom was created before them all,
And sound intelligence from eternity.
To whom has the source of wisdom been revealed?
And who knows her devices?
There is but one who is wise, a very terrible one,
Seated upon his throne;
The Lord himself created her;
He saw her and counted her,
And poured her out upon all he made;
Upon all mankind, as he chose to bestow her;
But he supplied her liberally to those who loved him.

To fear the Lord is a glory and a ground of exultation;
A joy, and a crown of ecstasy.
To fear the Lord delights the heart,
And brings gladness and joy and long life.
The man who fears the Lord will have a happy end,
And be blessed in the day of his death.

To fear the Lord is the source of wisdom,
And she was created with the faithful in the womb.
She has built her nest among men as a foundation from eternity,
And among their posterity she will be held in trust.
To fear the Lord is to be satisfied with wisdom,
For she intoxicates them with her fruits.
She will fill all their houses with desirable things,
And their storehouses with her produce;
To fear the Lord is a crown of wisdom,
Making peace and perfect health flourish.
He beheld her and counted her;
He rained down understanding and sound knowledge,

And increased the glory of those who possessed her.
To fear the Lord is the root of wisdom,
And her branches are long life.
     Unrighteous anger can never be excused,
For the weight of a man's anger drags him down.
A patient man will control himself for a while,
And afterward joy will break out.
He will repress his words for a time,
And the lips of many will tell of his understanding.
In the storehouses of wisdom there are wise proverbs,
But godliness is a detestation to the irreligious.
If you desire wisdom, keep the commandments,
And the Lord will supply you with her liberally.
For to fear the Lord is wisdom and education,
And faith and meekness win his approval.
Do not disobey the fear of the Lord,
And do not approach it with a divided heart.
Do not be a hypocrite in the mouths of men,
And take heed to your own lips.
Do not exalt yourself, or you may fall,
And bring disgrace upon yourself;
And the Lord will reveal your secrets
And prostrate you before all the congregation,
Because you did not come to the fear of the Lord,
But your heart was full of deceit.

2. My child, if you come to serve the Lord,
Prepare yourself to be tried.
Set your heart right and be firm,
And do not be hasty when things go against you;
Hold fast to him, and do not forsake him,
So that you may be honored when your life ends.
Accept whatever happens to you,
And be patient in humiliating vicissitudes.
For gold is tested with fire,
And men who are approved must be tested in the furnace of humiliation.
Have faith in him, and he will help you;
Make your ways straight, and put your hope in him.
     You who fear the Lord, wait for his mercy,
And do not turn aside, or you will fall.
You who fear the Lord, have faith in him,

And you will not lose your reward.
You who fear the Lord, hope for his blessings,
And for everlasting joy and mercy.
Look at the generations of antiquity and see,
Who that put his trust in the Lord was ever put to shame?
Or who that continued to fear him was ever forsaken?
Or who that called upon him was overlooked by him?
For the Lord is merciful and has pity,
And forgives sins and delivers in times of affliction.
Alas for cowardly hearts and palsied hands!
And for a sinner who follows two paths!
Alas for a faint heart, for it does not believe;
Therefore it will not be protected.
Alas for you, who have lost your steadfastness!
What will you do when the Lord visits you?
Those who fear the Lord will not disobey his words,
And those who love him will keep his ways.
Those who fear the Lord will seek his favor,
And those who love him will be filled with the Law.
Those who fear the Lord will prepare their hearts,
And will humble their souls before him.
"Let us fall into the Lord's hands,
And not into the hands of men."
For as his majesty is,
So is his mercy also.

3. Listen to me, your father, children,
And act in such a way that you may be preserved.
For the Lord has glorified the father above his children,
And he has established the rights of the mother over her sons.
He who provides for his father atones for his sins,
And he who shows his mother honor is like a man who lays up treasure.
He who provides for his father will be gladdened by his children,
And will be heard on the day that he prays.
He who shows his father honor will have a long life,
And he who listens to the Lord will refresh his mother,
And will serve his parents as his masters.
Honor your father in word and deed,
So that his blessing may attend you.
For a father's blessing establishes the houses of his children,
But a mother's curse uproots their foundations.

Do not glorify yourself by dishonoring your father,
For your father's disgrace is no glory to you.
For a man's glory arises from honoring his father,
And a neglected mother is a reproach to her children.
My child, help your father in his old age,
And do not grieve him, as long as he lives.
If his understanding fails, be considerate,
And do not humiliate him, when you are in all your strength.
Charity given to a father will not be forgotten,
And will build you up a further atonement for your sins.
When you are in trouble, you will be remembered;
Like frost in sunshine your sins will melt away.
He who deserts his father is like a blasphemer,
And he who angers his mother is cursed by the Lord.

4. My child, do not defraud the poor man of his living,
And you will be loved by men whom God accepts.
The greater you are, the more you must practice humility,
And you will find favor with the Lord.
For the Lord's power is great,
And he is glorified by the humble-minded.
Do not seek for what is too hard for you,
And do not investigate what is beyond your strength;
Think of the commands that have been given you,
For you have no need of the things that are hidden.
Do not waste your labor on what is superfluous to your work,
For things beyond man's understanding have been shown you.
For many have been led astray by their imagination,
And a wicked fancy has made their minds slip.
  It will go hard with an obstinate heart at the end,
And the man who loves danger will perish through it.
An obstinate heart will be loaded with troubles,
And the irreligious man will add one sin to another.
There is no cure for the misfortune of the proud,
For a wicked plant has taken root in him.
An intelligent man's mind can understand a proverb;
And a wise man desires a listening ear.
As water will quench a blazing fire,
So charity will atone for sin.
He who returns favors is remembered afterward,
And when he totters, he will find a support.

My child, do not defraud the poor man of his living,
And do not make the eyes of the needy wait.
Do not pain a hungry heart,
And do not anger a man who is in want.
Do not increase the troubles of a mind that is incensed,
And do not put off giving to a man who is in need.
Do not refuse a suppliant in his trouble,
And do not avert your face from the poor.
Do not turn your eyes away from a beggar,
And do not give anyone cause to curse you,
For if he curses you in the bitterness of his spirit,
His creator will hear his prayer.
Make yourself beloved in the congregation,
And bow your head to a great personage;
Listen to what a poor man has to say,
And give him a peaceful and gentle answer.
Rescue a man who is being wronged from the hand of the wrongdoer,
And do not be faint-hearted about giving your judgment.
Be like a father to the fatherless,
And take the place of a husband to their mother.
Then you will be like a son of the Most High,
And he will show you more than a mother's love.

Wisdom makes her sons exalted,
And lays hold of those who seek her.
Whoever loves her loves life,
And those who seek her early will be filled with joy.
Whoever holds her fast will win glory;
The Lord will bless every house he enters.
Those who serve her serve the Holy One,
And the Lord loves those who love her.
Whoever obeys her will judge the heathen,
And whoever attends to her will dwell in security.
If he trusts in her, he will possess her,
And his descendants will retain possession of her.
For at first she will go with him in devious ways,
She will bring fear and cowardice upon him,
And torment him with her discipline,
Until she can trust in his soul,
And test him with her judgments.
Then she will come straight back to him again, and make him glad,
And reveal her secrets to him.
If he wanders off, she will forsake him,

And hand him over to his downfall.
　Watch your opportunity and guard against evil,
And do not have to feel shame for your soul.
For there is a shame that brings sin,
And there is a shame that is glory and favor.
Show regard for no one at the expense of your soul,
And respect no one, to your own downfall.
Do not refrain from speaking when it is needed;
For wisdom is known through speech,
And instruction through the spoken word.
Do not contradict the truth,
But feel shame for your want of education.
Do not be ashamed to confess your sins,
And do not try to force back the current of a river.
Do not make yourself a bed for a fool,
And do not show partiality for a ruler;
Contend for the truth to the death,
And the Lord will fight for you.
Do not be rash in speech,
And slothful and slack in action.
Do not be like a lion at home,
And unreasonable with your servants.
Do not stretch your hand out to receive,
But close it when you should repay.

5. Do not set your heart on your money,
And do not say, "It is enough for me."
Do not follow your soul and your strength
And pursue the desires of your heart.
Do not say, "Who can have power over me?"
For the Lord will certainly take vengeance.
Do not say, "I sinned, and what happened to me?"
For the Lord is long-suffering.
As for atonement, do not be unafraid
To add one sin to another,
And do not say, "His mercy is great,
He will make atonement for the multitude of my sins."
For mercy and wrath are both with him,
And his anger will rest upon sinners.
Do not put off turning to the Lord,
And do not postpone it from day to day;
For the Lord's wrath will suddenly come forth,

And in the time of vengeance you will perish.
    Do not set your heart on unrighteous gain,
For it will be of no benefit to you in the time of misfortune.
Do not winnow in every wind,
And do not follow every path;
That is what the deceitful sinner does.
Be steadfast in your understanding,
And let what you say be one.
    Be quick to hear,
And make your reply with patience.
If you possess understanding, answer your neighbor,
But if you do not have it, keep your hand over your mouth!
Both glory and disgrace come from speaking,
And a man's tongue is his downfall.
    Do not be known as a whisperer,
And do not set an ambush with your tongue,
For shame rests upon the thief,
And evil condemnation on the double-tongued.
Do not be ignorant in great matters or in small,
And do not prove an enemy instead of a friend;
For an evil name incurs disgrace and reproach;
So does a sinner who is double-tongued.

    6. Do not exalt yourself in your soul's designs,
So that your soul may not be torn in pieces like a bull;
If you eat up your leaves, you will destroy your fruit,
And leave yourself like a dried-up tree.
A wicked heart will destroy its possessor,
And fill his enemies with malignant joy.
Sweet speech makes many friends,
And a polite tongue multiplies courtesy.
Let those who are at peace with you be many,
But let your advisers be one in a thousand.
If you make a friend, make one only after testing him,
And do not be in a hurry to confide in him.
There are friends who are so when it suits their convenience,
Who will not stand by you when you are in trouble.
And there are friends who turn into enemies,
And reveal quarrels to your discredit.
And there are friends who will sit at your table,
But will not stand by you when you are in trouble.
They will make themselves at home, as long as you are prosperous,

And will give orders to your servants;
If you come down in the world, they will take sides against you,
And hide themselves from your presence.
Separate yourself from your enemies,
And beware of your friends.
A faithful friend is a strong protection;
A man who has found one has found a treasure.
A faithful friend is beyond price,
And his value cannot be weighed.
A faithful friend is a life-giving medicine,
And those who fear the Lord will find it.
The man who fears the Lord will make genuine friendships,
For to him his neighbor is like himself.

    My child, from your youth up cultivate education,
And you will keep on finding wisdom until you are gray.
Approach her like a man who plows and sows,
And wait for her abundant crops.
For in cultivating her, you will toil but little,
And soon you will eat her produce.
She seems very harsh, to the undisciplined,
And a thoughtless man cannot abide her.
She will rest on him like a great stone to test him,
And he will not delay to throw her off.
For wisdom is what her name implies,
And to most men she is invisible.

    Listen, my child, and accept my opinion,
And do not refuse my advice.
Put your feet into her fetters,
And your neck into her collar.
Put your shoulder under her and carry her,
And do not weary of her chains;
Come to her with all your heart,
And follow her ways with all your might.
Inquire and search, and she will be made known to you,
And when you have grasped her, do not let her go.
For at last you will find the rest she gives,
And you will find her turning into gladness.
Her fetters will become your strong defense,
And her collars a splendid robe.
She wears gold ornaments,
And her chains are purple thread;
You will put her on like a splendid robe,

And put her on your head like a victor's wreath.
   My child, if you wish, you can be educated,
And if you devote yourself to it, you can become shrewd.
If you love to hear, you will receive,
And if you listen, you will be wise.
Take your stand in the throng of elders;
Which of them is wise? Attach yourself to him.
Be willing to listen to every godly discourse,
And do not let any wise proverbs escape you.
If you see a man of understanding, go to him early,
And let your feet wear out his doorstep.
Think about the statutes of the Lord,
And constantly meditate on his commandments.
He will strengthen your mind,
And the wisdom you desire will be given you.
For the practice of it is not beneficial.

   7. Do no evil, and evil will not overtake you.
Avoid what is wrong, and it will turn away from you.
My son, do not sow among the furrows of iniquity,
And you will not reap them seven fold.
Do not ask the Lord for pre-eminence,
Or the king for a seat of honor.
Do not justify yourself in the sight of the Lord,
Or show off your wisdom before the king;
Do not seek to be made a judge,
Or you may not be able to put down wrongdoing;
Or you may show partiality to a man of influence,
And put a stumbling block in the way of your own uprightness.
Do not sin against the multitude of the city,
And do not throw yourself down in the throng.
Do not repeat a sin,
For with even one offense you are not innocent.
Do not say, "He will consider the number of my offerings,
And when I sacrifice to the Most High God, he will accept it."
Do not be discouraged about your prayers,
And do not fail to give to charity.
Do not laugh at a man when he is in bitterness of spirit;
For there is one who can humble and can exalt!
Do not sow a lie against your brother,
Or do such a thing to your friend.

Do not consent to utter any lie,
Do not indulge in idle talk in the throng of elders,
And do not repeat yourself when you pray.
Do not hate hard work,
Or farming, which was created by the Most High.
Do not be counted in the crowd of sinners;
Remember that wrath will not delay.
Humble your heart exceedingly,
For fire and worms are the punishment of the ungodly.
    Do not exchange a friend for an advantage,
Or a real brother for the gold of Ophir.
Do not fail a wise, good wife,
For her favor is worth more than gold.
Do not ill-treat a servant who does his work faithfully,
Or a hired man who is devoting his life to you.
Let your soul love an intelligent servant;
Do not defraud him of his freedom.
If you have cattle, look after them,
And if they are profitable to you, keep them.
If you have children, discipline them,
And from their youth up bend their necks.
If you have daughters, look after their persons,
And do not look too favorably upon them.
If you give your daughter in marriage, you will have done a great thing,
But bestow her on a man of understanding.
If you have a wife after your own heart, do not cast her out,
But do not trust yourself to one whom you hate.
    Honor your father with your whole heart,
And do not forget the pangs of your mother.
Remember that it was of them you were born,
And how can you requite them for what they have done for you?
Honor the Lord with all your soul,
And revere his priests.
Love him who made you with all your strength,
And do not forsake his ministers.
Fear the Lord and honor the priest,
And give him his portion, as you were commanded,
The first fruits, and the sin offering, and the gift of the shoulders,
And the sacrifice of consecration, and the first fruits of holy things.
    Stretch out your hand to the poor also,
That your blessing may be accomplished.
A present pleases every man alive,

And in the case of the dead, do not withhold your kindness.
Do not be wanting to those who weep,
But mourn with those who mourn.
Do not hesitate to visit a man who is sick,
For you will be loved for such acts.
In all that you say remember your end,
And you will never commit a sin.

8. Do not quarrel with a powerful man,
Or you may fall into his hands.
Do not contend with a rich man,
Or he may outweigh you.
Gold has been the destruction of many,
And perverted the minds of kings.
Do not quarrel with a garrulous man,
And do not add fuel to the fire.
Do not make sport of an uneducated man,
Or you may dishonor your own forefathers.
Do not reproach a man when he turns from his sin;
Remember that we are all liable to punishment.
Do not treat a man with disrespect when he is old,
For some of us are growing old.
Do not exult over a man who is dead;
Remember that we are all going to die.
Do not neglect the discourse of wise men,
But busy yourself with their proverbs;
For from them you will gain instruction,
And learn to serve great men.
Do not miss the discourse of old men,
For they learned it from their fathers.
For from them you will gain understanding,
And learn to return an answer in your time of need.
Do not kindle the coals of a sinner,
Or you may be burned with the flame of his fire.
Do not start up before an insolent man,
So that he may not lie in ambush for what you say.
Do not lend to a man who is stronger than you,
Or if you do, act as though you had lost it.
Do not give surety beyond your means,
And if you give surety, regard it as something you will have to pay.
Do not go to law with a judge;

For in view of his dignity they will decide for him.
Do not travel with a reckless man,
So that he may not overburden you.
For he will do just as he pleases,
And you will perish through his folly.
Do not have a fight with a hot-tempered man,
And do not travel across the desert with him,
For bloodshed is as nothing in his eyes,
And where there is no help, he will strike you down.
Do not take counsel with a fool,
For he will not be able to keep the matter secret.
Do not do a secret thing before a stranger,
For you do not know what he will bring forth.
Do not open your heart to every man,
And do not accept a favor from him.

9. Do not be jealous about the wife of your bosom,
And do not teach her an evil lesson, to your own hurt.
Do not give your soul to a woman,
So that she will trample on your strength.
Do not meet a prostitute,
Or you may fall into her snares.
Do not associate with a woman singer,
Or you may be caught by her wiles.
Do not look closely at a girl,
Or you may be entrapped in penalties on her account.
Do not give yourself to prostitutes,
So that you may not lose your inheritance.
Do not look around in the streets of the city,
And do not wander about the unfrequented parts of it.
Avert your eyes from a beautiful woman,
And do not look closely at beauty that belongs to someone else.
Many have been led astray by a woman's beauty,
And love is kindled by it like a fire.
Do not ever sit at table with a married woman,
And do not feast and drink with her,
Or your heart may turn away to her,
And you may slip into spiritual ruin.
   Do not forsake an old friend,
For a new one is not equal to him.
A new friend is new wine;

When it grows old, you will enjoy drinking it.
Do not envy the glory of a sinner;
For you do not know what disaster awaits him.
Do not share in the satisfaction of ungodly men,
Remember that until death they will not be found upright.
Keep far from a man who has the power of life and death,
And you will have no suspicion of the fear of death.
If you do approach him, do not offend him,
So that he may not take away your life.
Understand that you are striding along among traps,
And walking on the city battlements.
As far as you can, guess at your neighbors,
And take counsel with those who are wise.
Let your discussion be with men of understanding,
And all your discourse about the Law of the Most High.
Make upright men your companions at table,
And your exultation be over the fear of the Lord.
It is for the skill of the craftsmen that a piece of work is commended,
And a ruler of the people must be wise in what he says.
A talkative man is dreaded in his city,
And a man who is rash in speech is hated.

10. A wise judge will instruct his people,
And the rule of a man of understanding is well ordered.
Like the judge of a people are his officers,
And like the governor of a city are all who live in it.
An uneducated king ruins his people,
But a city becomes populous through the understanding of its rulers.
Authority over the earth is in the hands of the Lord,
And in due time he will set over it one who will serve his purpose.
A man's prosperity is in the hands of the Lord,
And he makes his glory rest on the person of the scribe.
Do not get angry with your neighbor for any misdeed,
And do not gain your end by acts of violence.
Pride is detested in the sight of the Lord and of men,
And injustice is wrong in the sight of both.
Sovereignty passes from one nation to another
Because of injustice and violence and greed for money.
Why are dust and ashes proud?
For while a man is still alive, his bowels decay;
There is a long illness—the doctor makes light of it;
A man is a king today, and dead tomorrow.

For when a man dies,
Reptiles, animals, and worms become his portion.
    A man begins to be proud when he departs from the Lord,
And his heart forsakes his Creator.
For pride begins with sin,
And the man who clings to it will rain down abominations.
For this reason, the Lord brings unheard-of calamities upon them,
And overturns them utterly.
The Lord tears down the thrones of rulers,
And seats the humble-minded in their places.
The Lord plucks up nations by the roots,
And plants the lowly in their places.
The Lord overturns heathen countries,
And destroys them down to the foundations of the earth.
He takes some of them away, and destroys them,
And makes the memory of them cease from the earth.
Pride was not created for men,
Nor fierce anger for those who are born of women.
    What is an honorable posterity? A human posterity!
What is an honorable posterity? Men who fear the Lord.
What is a base posterity? A human posterity!
What is a base posterity? Men who break the commandments.
Among his brothers, their leader is honored,
And those who fear the Lord are honored in his eyes.
Rich, and distinguished, and poor alike—
Their glory is the fear of the Lord.
It is not right to slight a poor man who has understanding,
And it is not proper to honor a sinful man.
Prince, judge, and ruler are honored,
But none of them is greater than the man who fears the Lord.
Free men will wait on a wise servant,
And the intelligent man will not object.
Do not parade your wisdom when you are at work,
And do not commend yourself when you are in need;
It is better to work and have plenty of everything,
Than to go about commending yourself but in want of bread.
My child, glorify your soul with meekness,
And show it such honor as it deserves.
Who can justify a man who sins against his own soul?
And who can honor a man who disgraces his own life?
A poor man is honored for his knowledge,

And a rich man is honored for his wealth.

If a man is honored in poverty, how much more will he be in wealth?

And if a man is dishonored when he is rich, how much more will he be when he is poor?

THE STORY OF SUSANNA

There once lived in Babylon a man named Joakim. He married a wife named Susanna, the daughter of Hilkiah, a very beautiful and pious woman. Her parents also were upright people and instructed their daughter in the Law of Moses. Joakim was very rich, and he had a fine garden adjoining his house; and the Jews used to come to visit him because he was the most distinguished of them all.

That year two of the elders of the people were appointed judges—men of the kind of whom the Lord said,

"Lawlessness came forth from Babylon, from elders who were judges, who were supposed to guide the people."

These men came constantly to Joakim's house, and all who had cases to be decided came to them there. And it happened that when the people left at midday, Susanna would go into her husband's garden and walk about. So the two elders saw her every day, as she went in and walked about, and they conceived a passion for her. So their thoughts were perverted and they turned away their eyes, so as not to look up to heaven or consider justice in giving judgment. They were both smitten with her, but they could not disclose their pain to each other, for they were ashamed to reveal their passion, for they desired to have relations with her, and they watched jealously every day for a sight of her. And they said to one another,

"Let us go home, for it is dinner-time."

So they went out of the garden and parted from one another; then they turned back and encountered one another. And when they cross-questioned one another as to the explanation, they admitted their passion. Then they agreed together upon a time when they would be able to find her alone.

Now it happened, as they were watching for an opportunity, that she went in one day as usual with no one but her two maids, and wished to bathe in the garden, as it was very hot. And there was no one there except the two elders who had hidden themselves and were watching her. And she said to her maids,

"Bring me olive oil and soap, and close the doors of the garden, so that I can bathe."

And they did as she told them, and shut the doors of the garden, and went out at the side doors to bring what they had been ordered to bring, and they did not see the elders, for they were hidden. And when the maids went out, the two elders got up and ran to her and said,

"Here the doors of the garden are shut, and no one can see us, and we are in love with you, so give your consent and lie with us. If you do not, we will testify against you that there was a young man with you, and that was why you dismissed your maids."

And Susanna groaned and said,

"I am in a tight place. For if I do this, it means my death; but if I refuse, I cannot escape your hands. I had rather not do it and fall into your hands than commit sin in the Lord's sight!"

Then Susanna gave a loud scream, and the two elders shouted against her. And one of them ran and opened the garden doors. And when the people in the house heard the shouting in the garden, they rushed through the side doors to see what had happened to her. And when the elders told their story, her slaves were deeply humiliated, for such a thing had never been said about Susanna.

The next day, when the people came together to her husband, Joakim, the two elders came, full of their wicked design to put Susanna to death. And they said before the people,

"Send for Susanna, the daughter of Hilkiah, Joakim's wife."

And they did so. And she came, with her parents and her children, and all her relatives. Now Susanna was accustomed to luxury and was very beautiful. And the lawbreakers ordered her to be unveiled, for she was wearing a veil, so that they might have their fill of her beauty. And the people with her and all who saw her wept. And the two elders stood up in the midst of the people and laid their hands on her head, and she wept and looked up to heaven, for her heart trusted in the Lord. And the elders said,

"As we were walking by ourselves in the garden, this woman came in with two maids, and shut the doors of the garden and dismissed her maids, and a young man, who had been hidden, came to her, and lay down with her. And we were in the corner of the garden, and when we saw this wicked action, we ran up to them, and though we saw them together, we could not hold him, because he was stronger than we, and opened the doors and rushed out. But we laid hold of this woman and asked her who the young man was; and she would not tell us. This is our testimony."

Then the assembly believed them, as they were elders of the people and judges, and they condemned her to death. But Susanna uttered a loud cry, and said,

"Eternal God, you who know what is hidden, who know all things before they happen, you know that what they have testified to against me is false, and here I am to die when I have done none of the things they have so wickedly charged me with."

And the Lord heard her cry, and as she was being led away to be put to death, God stirred up the holy spirit of a young man named Daniel, and he loudly shouted,

"I am clear of the blood of this woman."

And all the people turned to him and said,

"What does this mean, that you have said?"

And he took his stand in the midst of them and said,

"Are you such fools, you Israelites, that you have condemned a daughter of Israel without any examination or ascertaining of the truth? Go back to the place of trial. For these men have borne false witness against her."

So all the people hurried back. And the elders said to him,

"Come, sit among us and inform us, for God has given you the right to do so."

And Daniel said to them,

"Separate them widely from one another, and I will examine them."

And when they were separated from each other, he called one of them to him, and said to him,

"You ancient of wicked days, how your sins have overtaken you, that you committed before, making unjust decisions, condemning the innocent and acquitting the guilty, although the Lord said, 'You shall not put an innocent and upright man to death.' So now, if you saw this woman, tell us, Under which tree did you see them meet?"

He answered,

"Under a mastic tree."

And Daniel said,

"You have told a fine lie against your own life, for already the angel of God has received the sentence from God, and he will cut you in two."

And he had him removed and ordered them to bring in the other. And he said to him,

"You descendant of Canaan and not of Judah, beauty has beguiled you, and desire has corrupted your heart! This is how you have been treating the daughters of Israel, and they yielded to you through fear, but a daughter of Judah would not endure your wickedness. So now tell me, Under which tree did you catch them embracing each other?"

And he said,

"Under a liveoak tree."

And Daniel said to him,

"You have also told a fine lie against your own life! For the angel of God is waiting with his sword to saw you in two, to destroy you both."

And the whole company uttered a great shout and blessed God who saves those who hope in him. And they threw themselves upon the two elders, for Daniel had convicted them out of their own mouths of having borne false witness, and treated them as they had wickedly planned to treat their neighbor; they obeyed the Law of Moses and killed them. And innocent blood was saved that day.

And Hilkiah and his wife praised God for their daughter Susanna and so did Joakim her husband and all her relatives, because she had done nothing immodest. And from that day onward, Daniel had a great reputation in the eyes of the people.

THE SONG OF THE THREE CHILDREN

And they walked about in the midst of the fire, singing hymns to God and blessing the Lord. And Azariah stood still and uttered this prayer; in the midst of the fire he opened his mouth and said,

"Blessed are you, Lord God of our forefathers, and worthy of praise!
Your name is glorified forever!
For you are upright in all that you have done;
All your works are true, and your ways straight,
And all your judgments are true.
The sentences that you passed were just
In all that you have brought upon us,
And upon Jerusalem, the Holy City of our forefathers.
For in truth and justice you have brought all these things upon us because
    of our sins.
For we have sinned and done wrong in forsaking you,
We have sinned grievously in everything, and have disobeyed your
    commands;
We have not observed them or done
As you commanded us to do, for our own good.
All that you have brought upon us, and all that you have done to us,
You have done in justice.
You have handed us over to enemies without law, to hateful rebels,
And to a ruthless king, the most wicked in all the world,
Yet we cannot open our mouths.
Shame and disgrace have overtaken your slaves and your worshipers.
For the sake of your name, do not surrender us utterly;
Do not cancel your agreement,
And do not withdraw your mercy from us,
For the sake of Abraham whom you loved,
And for the sake of Isaac, your slave,
And for the sake of Israel, your holy one,
To whom you spoke, and promised
That you would make their descendants as many as the stars of heaven,
Or the sand that is on the seashore.
For, Master, we have become fewer than all the heathen,

And we are humiliated everywhere, because of our sins.
And now there is no prince, or prophet, or leader,
No burnt offering, or sacrifice, or offering, or incense;
No place to make an offering before you, or to find mercy.
But may we be accepted through a contrite heart and a humble spirit,
As though it were through whole burnt offerings of rams and bulls,
And through tens of thousands of fat lambs.
So let our sacrifice rise before you today,
And fully follow after you,
For those who trust in you will not be disappointed.
So now we follow you with all our hearts; we revere you
And seek your face. Do not disappoint us,
But deal with us in your forbearance
And your abundant mercy.
Deliver us in your wonderful way,
And glorify your name, Lord;
May all who do your slaves harm be disgraced;
May they be put to shame and lose all their power and might,
And may their strength be broken.
Let them know that you are the Lord God alone,
Glorious over the whole world."

Now the king's servants who threw them in never ceased feeding the furnace fires with naptha, pitch, tow, and faggots, and the flame streamed out above the furnace for forty-nine cubits (seventy-three feet). It even spread, and burned up those Chaldeans whom it found about the furnace. But the angel of the Lord came down to join Azariah and his companions in the furnace, and drove the fiery blaze out of the furnace, and made the middle of the furnace as though a moist wind was whistling through it, and the fire did not touch them at all, or harm or trouble them.

Then all three, as with one mouth, praised, glorified, and blessed God in the furnace, and said,

"Blessed are you, Lord God of our forefathers,
    And to be praised and greatly exalted forever.
And blessed is your glorious, holy name,
    And to be highly praised and greatly exalted forever.
Blessed are you in the temple of your holy glory,
    And to be highly praised and greatly glorified forever.
Blessed are you who sit upon winged creatures, and look into the depths,
    And to be praised and greatly exalted forever.
Blessed are you on your kingly throne,

And to be highly praised and greatly exalted forever.
Blessed are you in the firmament of heaven,
   And to be praised and glorified forever.

Bless the Lord, all you works of the Lord,
   Sing praise to him and greatly exalt him forever.
Bless the Lord, you heavens,
   Sing praise to him and greatly exalt him forever.
Bless the Lord, you heavens,
   Sing praise to him and greatly exalt him forever.
Bless the Lord, you angels of the Lord,
   Sing praise to him and greatly exalt him forever.
Bless the Lord, all you waters above the heaven,
   Sing praise to him and greatly exalt him forever.
Bless the Lord, all you powers,
   Sing praise to him and greatly exalt him forever.
Bless the Lord, sun and moon;
   Sing praise to him and greatly exalt him forever.
Bless the Lord, you stars of heaven,
   Sing praise to him and greatly exalt him forever.
Bless the Lord, all rain and dew,
   Sing praise to him and greatly exalt him forever.
Bless the Lord, all you winds,
   Sing praise to him and greatly exalt him forever.
Bless the Lord, fire and heat,
   Sing praise to him and greatly exalt him forever.
Bless the Lord, cold and warmth,
   Sing praise to him and greatly exalt him forever.
Bless the Lord, dews and snows,
   Sing praise to him and greatly exalt him forever.
Bless the Lord, nights and days,
   Sing praise to him and greatly exalt him forever.
Bless the Lord, light and darkness,
   Sing praise to him and greatly exalt him forever.
Bless the Lord, ice and cold,
   Sing praise to him and greatly exalt him forever.
Bless the Lord, frosts and snows,
   Sing praise to him and greatly exalt him forever.
Bless the Lord, lightnings and clouds,
   Sing praise to him and greatly exalt him forever.
Let the earth bless the Lord,
   Sing praise to him and greatly exalt him forever.

Bless the Lord, you mountains and hills,
   Sing praise to him and greatly exalt him forever.
Bless the Lord, all things that grow on the earth,
   Sing praise to him and greatly exalt him forever.
Bless the Lord, seas and rivers,
   Sing praise to him and greatly exalt him forever.
Bless the Lord, you springs,
   Sing praise to him and greatly exalt him forever.
Bless the Lord, you whales and all the things that move in the waters,
   Sing praise to him and greatly exalt him forever.
Bless the Lord, all you wild birds,
   Sing praise to him and greatly exalt him forever.
Bless the Lord, all you animals and cattle,
   Sing praise to him and greatly exalt him forever.
Bless the Lord, you sons of men,
   Sing praise to him and greatly exalt him forever.
Bless the Lord, O Israel,
   Sing praise to him and greatly exalt him forever.
Bless the Lord, you priests of the Lord,
   Sing praise to him and greatly exalt him forever.
Bless the Lord, you slaves of the Lord,
   Sing praise to him and greatly exalt him forever.
Bless the Lord, spirits and souls of the upright,
   Sing praise to him and greatly exalt him forever.
Bless the Lord, you who are holy and humble in heart,
   Sing praise to him and greatly exalt him forever.
Bless the Lord, Hananiah, Azariah, and Mishael,
   Sing praise to him and greatly exalt him forever.
For he has rescued us from Hades and saved us from the hand of death,
And delivered us from the burning fiery furnace;
   From the midst of the fire he has delivered us.
Give thanks to the Lord, for he is kind,
   For his mercy endures forever.
Bless him, all you who worship the Lord, the God of gods,
   Sing praise to him and give thanks to him,
   For his mercy endures forever."

THE BOOK OF TOBIT

The story of Tobit, the son of Tobiel, the son of Hananiel, the son of Aduel, the son of Gabael, of the stock of Asael, of the tribe of Naphtali, who in the days of Shalmaneser, king of Assyria, was carried into captivity from Thisbe, which is to the south of Kedesh Naphtali in Galilee above Asher.

I, Tobit, walked all the days of my life in ways of truth and uprightness. I did many acts of charity for my brothers and my nation who were taken to the land of the Assyrians, to Nineveh, with me. And when I was in my own country, in the land of Israel, when I was young, the whole tribe of my forefather Naphtali revolted from the house in Jerusalem, which had been chosen from all the tribes of Israel for all the tribes to offer sacrifice in, and in which the temple of the dwelling of the Most High had been dedicated and built for all ages.

So all the tribes which had revolted with it would offer sacrifice to the heifer Baal. But I alone went many a time to Jerusalem for the festivals, as the Scripture commands all Israel in an everlasting decree, taking with me the first fruits and the tenth parts of my crops and my first shearings, and I would give them to the priests, the sons of Aaron, at the altar. A tenth part of all my produce I would give to the sons of Levi, who officiated at Jerusalem, and another tenth I would sell, and go and spend the proceeds in Jerusalem each year, and a third tenth I would give to those to whom it was fitting to give it, as Deborah my grandmother had instructed me—for I was left an orphan by my father.

When I became a man, I married Hannah, who was of the stock of our family, and by her I had a son, Tobias. And when I was carried into captivity to Nineveh, all my brothers and relatives ate the food of the heathen, but I kept myself from eating it, because I remembered God with all my heart. And the Most High gave me favor and standing with Shalmaneser, and I became his buyer. I made a journey to Media, and deposited ten talents of silver with Gabael, the brother of Gabrias, in Ragae, in Media. But when Shalmaneser died, his son Sennacherib became king in his place, and the highways were unsafe, so that I could no longer travel to Media.

In the times of Shalmaneser I used to do many acts of charity for my brothers. I would give my bread to the hungry and my clothes to the naked, and if I saw one of my people dead and thrown outside the wall of Nineveh, I would bury him. And if Sennacherib the king killed anyone who had come as a fugitive from Judea, I buried them secretly, for he killed many in his anger, and their bodies were looked for by the king and could not be found. But one of the Ninevites went and informed the king about me, that I was burying them, and I hid, and when I learned that I was being sought for, to be put to death, I was frightened and escaped. Then all my property was seized, and nothing was left me but my wife Hannah and my son Tobias.

Before fifty days had passed, his two sons killed him, and fled into the mountains of Ararat, and Esarhaddon his son became king in his place. He appointed Ahiqar, my brother Hanael's son, to have charge of all the accounting of his kingdom and all its administration. And Ahiqar asked for me, and I went to Nineveh. Ahiqar was cupbearer and keeper of the signet and had charge of administration and of the accounts; Esarhaddon appointed him second to himself, and he was my nephew.

When I reached my home and my wife Hannah was restored to me, and Tobias my son, at the Harvest Festival, which is the feast of the Seven Weeks, a good dinner was prepared for me, and I sat down to eat. And I saw the abundance of food, and I said to my son,

"Go and bring any poor man of our brothers whom you can find, who remembers the Lord, and I will wait for you."

And he came back and said,

"Father, one of our race has been strangled and thrown out in the bazaar!"

Then before I tasted anything I rushed out and brought him into a room until the sun set. Then I returned and washed myself and ate my food in sadness; and I remembered the prophecy of Amos, as he said,

Your feasts will be turned into sorrow,
And all your good cheer into lamentation.

And I wept aloud.

And when the sun was set, I went and dug a grave and buried him. And my neighbors laughed at me and said,

"He is not yet afraid of being put to death for doing this. He ran away, and here he is burying the dead again."

That same night, after I had buried him, I returned, and as I was ceremonially defiled, I lay down to sleep by the wall of the courtyard, with my face uncovered, and I did not know that there were sparrows in the wall above me, and, as my eyes were open, the sparrows' droppings fell into my eyes and produced white films on them; and I went to the physicians, and they could not help me. But Ahiqar supported me for two years, until he went to Elymais.

Then my wife Hannah found employment at women's work, and sent the work back to its owners, and they paid her wages, and gave her a kid besides. But when she came home to me, the kid began to bleat. And I said to her,

"Where did this kid come from? Is it stolen? Give it back to its owners, for we have no right to eat anything that is stolen."

But she said to me,

"It was given me as a gift, in addition to my wages."

But I would not believe her, and told her to give it back to its owners, and I blushed for her. Then she answered and said to me,

"And where are your charities? Where is your uprightness? Of course you know everything!"

Then I was grieved, and wept, and I prayed sorrowfully.

On that very day, it happened to Sarah, the daughter of Raguel, in Ecbatana in Media, that she too was reproached by her father's maids, because she had been married to seven husbands, and the wicked demon Asmodeus had killed them before they had been with her as is customary with wives. They said to her,

"Do you not know that you strangle your husbands? You have already had seven, and you have not borne the name of one of them. Why do you torment us? If they are dead, go after them! May we never see son or daughter of yours!"

When she heard these things, she was deeply hurt, and wished to hang herself, but she said,

"I am my father's only child; if I do this, it will disgrace him, and I will bring his old age down to the grave in sorrow."

And she prayed by her window, and said,

"Blessed are you, O Lord, my God, and blessed be your holy and honored name forever; may all your works bless you forever. And now, Lord, I turn my face and my eyes to you; command me to be released from the earth and to hear reproach no more. You know, Lord, that I am innocent of any sin with man; I have never defiled my name, or the name of my father, in the land of my captivity. I am my father's only child; he has no other child to be his heir. He has no brother near him or nephew whom I should keep myself to marry. I have already lost seven husbands; why must I live any longer? And if it is not your pleasure to kill me, command that some regard be had for me, and some pity be shown me, and that I no more may have to listen to reproach."

And the prayer of both of them was heard in the presence of the glory of the great Raphael, and he was sent to cure them both; for Tobit, to remove the white films, and to give Sarah, the daughter of Raguel, to Tobit's son Tobias, as his wife, and to bind Asmodeus, the wicked demon, because Tobias was entitled to possess her. So at the same time, Tobit went into his house, and Sarah, the daughter of Raguel, came down from her upstairs room.

On that day Tobit remembered the money that he had deposited with Gabael in Ragae in Media. And he said to himself,

"I have asked for death; why should I not call my son Tobias, to explain to him before I die?"

So he called him, and said,

"My boy, when I die, bury me, and do not neglect your mother; provide for her as long as you live; do what is pleasing to her, and do not grieve her in anything. Remember, my boy, that she faced many dangers for you before your birth, and when she dies, bury her beside me in one grave. All your life, my boy, remember the Lord, our God; do not consent to sin and transgress his commands. Act uprightly all your life, and do not walk in the ways of wrongdoing.

"For if you do right, prosperity will attend your undertakings. To all who act uprightly, give charity from your property, and do not let your eye begrudge what you give to charity. Do not turn your face away from any poor man, and God's face will not be turned away from you. Give to charity in proportion to what you have; if you have little, do not be afraid to give sparingly to charity, for then you will lay up a good treasure for yourself against a day of adversity; for charity will save you from death, and keep you from going down into darkness. Charity is a good offering in the sight of the Most High for all who give it.

"My boy, beware of any immorality. First, take a wife who is of the stock of your forefathers; do not marry an alien, who does not belong to your father's tribe, for we are the sons of the prophets. Remember, my boy, that Noah, Abraham, Isaac, and Jacob, our forefathers of old, all married wives from among their kindred, and were blessed in their children, and their posterity will possess the land. Now, my boy, love your kindred, and do not disdain your brothers and the sons and daughters of your people and refuse to marry one of them. For such disdain leads to ruin and great distress, and worthlessness brings loss and great want, for worthlessness is the mother of famine. The wages of any man who works for you, you must not retain overnight, but you must pay him immediately. If you serve God, you will be rewarded. Take care, my boy, in all that you do, and be well disciplined in all your conduct. Do not do to anyone else what you hate. Do not drink wine to the point of intoxication; drunkenness must not go with you on your way. Give some of your bread to the hungry and of your clothes to the naked. Give all your surplus to charity, and do not let your eye begrudge what you give to charity. Scatter your bread on the graves of the upright, but do not give to sinners.

"Ask advice of every wise man, and do not think lightly of any useful advice. Always bless the Lord God, and ask him to make your ways straight and your paths and plans prosper. For no heathen nation possesses understanding, but the Lord gives all good things, and he humbles whomever he pleases, as he chooses.

"Now, my boy, remember my commands; do not let them be blotted from your mind. And now I must inform you of the ten talents of silver that I deposited with Gabael, son of Gabrias, in Ragae in Media. Do not be afraid, my boy, because we have become poor. You are well off, if you fear God and refrain from any sin, and do what is pleasing in his sight."

Then Tobias answered and said to him,

"Father, I will do all that you have commanded me. But how can I get the money, when I do not know him?"

So he gave him the receipt, and said to him,

"Seek out a man to go with you, and I will pay him wages, as long as I live; so go and get the money."

And he went to look for a man, and found Raphael, who was an angel, though Tobias did not know it. And he said to him,

"Can I go with you to Ragae in Media, and do you know that region?"

And the angel said to him,

"I will go with you, for I know the way, and I have stayed with our brother Gabael."

And Tobias said to him,

"Wait for me, and I will tell my father."

And he said to him,

"Go, and do not delay."

And he went in and said to his father,

"Here I have found a man who will go with me."

And he said,

"Call him to me, so that I may find out what tribe he belongs to and whether he is a reliable man to go with you."

So he called him, and he came in, and they greeted each other. And Tobit said to him,

"Brother, to what tribe and to what family do you belong? Inform me."

And he said to him,

"Are you in search of a tribe and family, or a hired man to go with your son?"

And Tobit said to him,

"I only want to learn your connections and your name, brother."

And he said,

"I am Azariah, the son of Hananiah the older, one of your kinsmen."

And he said to him,

"Welcome, brother! Do not be angry with me for trying to learn your tribe and your family; you are a kinsman of mine, and come of a fine, good lineage. For I came to know Hananiah and Jathan, the sons of Shemaiah the older, when we used to travel to Jerusalem together to worship and offer our first-born cattle and the tenths of our produce, for they did not go astray when our brothers did; you come of a fine stock, brother. But tell me what wages I am to give you; a drachma a day and your expenses and my son's? And I will add to your wages besides, if you come back safe and sound."

So they agreed on these terms. And he said to Tobias,

"Get ready for the journey, and farewell."

So his son made his preparations for the journey, and his father said to him,

"Go with this man, and God who lives in heaven will prosper your journey, and let his angel go with you."

And they both went out to start, and the boy's dog followed them.

And his mother Hannah wept, and she said to Tobit,

"Why have you sent our child away? Is he not our walking-stick when he goes in and out before us? Do not let money be added to money, but let it be as dirt in comparison with our child. For while the Lord lets us live, that is enough for us."

And Tobit said to her,

"Do not be troubled, my sister. He will come back safe and sound, and your eyes will see him. For a good angel will go with him, and he will have a prosperous journey, and will come back safe and sound."

So she stopped crying.

And they went on their way and came toward evening to the river Tigris and there they spent the night. And the boy went to wash himself, and a fish jumped out of the river and would have swallowed the boy. But the angel said to him,

"Take hold of the fish!"

And the boy seized the fish and threw it up on the land. And the angel said to him,

"Cut the fish up, and take its heart and liver and gall and keep them safe."

And the boy did as the angel told him, and they cooked the fish and ate it. And they both traveled on until they drew near Ecbatana. And the boy said to the angel,

"Brother Azariah, what are the liver and heart and gall of the fish good for?"

And he said to him,

"As for the heart and the liver, if anyone is troubled with a demon or an evil spirit, you must make a smoke of them before the man or the woman, and they will be troubled no more. And as for the gall, if you rub it on a man who has white films over his eyes, he will be cured."

When they approached Ragae, the angel said to the boy,

"Brother, we will stop today with Raguel, for he is your relative. He has an only daughter, named Sarah. I am going to tell him to give her to you in marriage, for you have a right to have her, for you are her only relative, and she is beautiful and sensible. So now if you will listen to me, I will speak to her father, and when we come back from Ragae, we will perform the marriage. For I know that by the law of Moses Raguel cannot marry her to anyone else under pain of death, for it is your right and no one else's to possess her."

Then the boy said to the angel,

"Brother Azariah, I have heard that this girl has been given in marriage to seven husbands and they all perished in the bridal chamber. Now I am my father's only child, and I am afraid that if I go in, I will die like the others, for a demon is in love with her, and he harms only those who approach her. So I am afraid that I would die and bring my father's and my mother's life to the grave in sorrow over me; and they have no other son to bury them."

And the angel said to him,

"Don't you remember the commands your father gave you, about your taking a wife from your own relatives? Now you must listen to me, brother, for she must be your wife, and don't be concerned about the demon, for she will be given to you tonight to be your wife. And when you go into the bridal chamber, you must take some of the ashes of the incense, and put on them some of the heart and the liver of the fish, and make a smoke, and the demon will smell it and will flee and never come back. And when you go up to her, you must both rise up and cry out to the merciful God, and he will save you and have mercy on you. Have no fear, for she was destined for you from the beginning, and you will save her, and she will go home with you, and I suppose you will have children by her."

When Tobias heard this, he loved her, and he became deeply attached to her.

When they arrived at Ecbatana, they went to the house of Raguel, and Sarah met them and welcomed them, and they greeted her, and she took them into the house. And Raguel said to Edna his wife,

"How much this young man resembles my cousin Tobit!"

And Raguel asked them,

"Where are you from, brothers?"

And they said to him,

"We belong to the sons of Naphtali who are in captivity in Nineveh."

And he said to them,

"Do you know our kinsman Tobit?"

And they said,

"We do."

And he said to them,

"Is he well?"

And they said,

"He is alive and well."

And Tobias said,

"He is my father!"

Then Raguel sprang up and kissed him, and he wept, and blessed him, and said to him,

"You are the son of that fine, good man!"

And when he heard that Tobit had lost his eyesight, he was grieved, and wept, and his wife Edna and his daughter Sarah wept too. And they welcomed them warmly, and they slaughtered a ram from the flock, and set food before them in abundance.

Then Tobias said to Raphael,

"Brother Azariah, speak about the things you talked of on our journey, and let that matter be settled."

So he communicated the matter to Raguel, and Raguel said to Tobias,

"Eat, drink and be merry, for you have the right to take my child. But I must reveal the truth to you. I have given my child to seven husbands, and whenever they approached her, they died the same night. Still, for the present be merry."

And Tobias said,

"I will eat nothing here until you make a binding agreement with me to do this."

Then Raguel said,

"Take her at once according to the ordinance; you are her relative, and she belongs to you; and the merciful God will give you the greatest prosperity."

And he called in his daughter Sarah, and he took her by the hand and gave her to Tobias to be his wife, and said,

"Here, take her according to the law of Moses, and take her back to your father."

And he gave them his blessing. And he called in Edna his wife, and he took a scroll and wrote an agreement, and they put their seals to it. Then they began to eat.

Then Raguel called Edna his wife aside and said to her,

"My sister, get the other bedchamber ready, and take her into it."

And she did as he told her, and took her into it, and she wept. And she let her daughter weep on her shoulder, and she said to her,

"Courage, my child! The Lord of heaven and earth show you favor instead of this grief of yours! Courage, my daughter!"

When they had finished supper, they took Tobias in to her. And as he went, he remembered what Raphael had said, and took the ashes of the incense and put the heart and the liver of the fish on them and made a smoke. And when the demon smelled the smoke, he fled to the farthest parts of Upper Egypt, and the angel bound him there. When they were both shut in together, Tobias got up from the bed and said,

"Get up, my sister, and let us pray that the Lord will have mercy upon us."

And he began to say,

"Blessed are you, God of our forefathers, and blessed be your holy and glorious name forever. Let the heavens and all your creation bless you. You made Adam and gave him his wife Eve as a helper and support, and from them came the human race. You said, 'It is not good that the man should be alone; let us make him a helper like himself.' Now, Lord, it is not because of lust that I take my sister here, but in truth. Have mercy on me, and let me grow old with her."

And she said "Amen" with him; and they both slept all night.

And Raguel got up and went and dug a grave, for he said,

"Perhaps he will die too."

Then Raguel went into his house and said to his wife Edna,

"Send one of the maids and let them see whether he is alive, and if he is not, let us bury him without letting anyone know."

And the maid opened the door and went in, and found them both asleep. And she came out and told them that he was alive. Then Raguel blessed God, and said,

"Blessed are you, O God, with every pure and holy blessing! Let your saints and all your creation bless you, and let all your angels and your chosen people bless you forever. You are blessed because you have had mercy on two only children; Lord, show them mercy; grant that they may live to the end in health, with gladness and mercy."

Then he ordered his servants to fill up the grave. And he made them a marriage feast that lasted fourteen days. And Raguel swore to him before the days of the marriage feast were over that he must not leave until the fourteen days of the marriage feast were past, and then he should take half of Raguel's property and return in safety to his father. "The rest," he said, "will be yours when I and my wife die."

And Tobias called Raphael and said to him,

"Brother Azariah, take with you a servant and two camels, and go to Gabael, in Ragae in Media, and get me the money and bring him to the marriage feast. For Raguel has sworn that I must not leave, and my father is counting the days, and if I delay long, he will be greatly grieved."

So Raphael went and spent the night with Gabael, and gave him the receipt, and he brought out the bags with their seals unbroken, and gave them to him. And they got up early in the morning together, and came to the marriage feast; and Tobias blessed his wife.

Now his father Tobit was counting each day. And when the days required for the journey were past and they did not come back, he said,

"Is it possible that they have been disappointed? Or is Gabael perhaps dead, and there is no one to give him the money?"

And he was greatly distressed. And his wife said to him,

"The child has perished; that is why he has taken so long."

And she began to bewail him, and said,

"Do I not care, my child, because I let you go, you light of my eyes?"

And Tobit said to her,

"Be quiet, have no concern; he is all right."

And she said to him,

"Be quiet, do not deceive me; my child has perished."

And every day she would go down the road by which he had left, and in the daytime she refused to eat, and through the night she never ceased to bewail her son Tobias until the fourteen days of the marriage feast, which Raguel had sworn he must spend there, were over.

Then Tobias said to Raguel,

"Let me go, for my father and my mother are giving up all hope of ever seeing me again."

But his father-in-law said to him,

"Stay with me, and I will send to your father, and they will explain to him about you."

And Tobias said,

"No, send me to my father."

Then Raguel got up and gave him his wife Sarah and half of his property, slaves and cattle and money. And he blessed them as he let them go, and said,

"The God of heaven will give you prosperity, my children, before I die."

And he said to his daughter,

"Respect your father-in-law and your mother-in-law, they are now your parents. Let me hear a good report of you."

And he kissed her. And Edna said to Tobias,

"May the Lord of heaven bring you back safely, dear brother, and grant that I may see your children by my daughter Sarah, so that I may be glad before the Lord. Here I solemnly entrust my daughter to you; do not hurt her feelings."

After that, Tobias set off, praising God, because he had prospered him on his journey, and he blessed Raguel and his wife Edna.

He went on until they approached Nineveh. And Raphael said to Tobias,

"Do you not know, brother, how you left your father? Let us run ahead, before your wife, and get the house ready. But take the gall of the fish in your hand."

So they went, and the dog went along after them.

And Hannah sat looking down the road for her boy. And she saw him coming, and she said to his father,

"Here comes your son, and the man who went with him!"

And Raphael said,

"I know that your father will open his eyes; so you rub the gall on his eyes, and he will feel the sting and will rub them, and remove the white films, and he will see you."

And Hannah ran to meet them and fell on her son's neck and said to him,

"Now that I have seen you, my child, I am ready to die."

And they both wept. And Tobit came out to the door, and he stumbled, and his son ran up to him and he took hold of his father and sprinkled the gall on his father's eyes, saying,

"Courage, father!"

And when his eyes began to smart, he rubbed them, and the white films scaled off from the corners of his eyes. And when he saw his son, he fell on his neck and wept, and said,

"Blessed are you, O God, and blessed is your name forever, and blessed are all your holy angels. For though you have flogged me, you have had mercy on me; here I can see Tobias, my son."

And his son went in rejoicing, and told his father the wonderful things that had happened to him in Media.

So Tobit went out rejoicing to meet his daughter-in-law, at the gate of Nineveh. And those who saw him go were amazed, because he had received his sight. And Tobit gave thanks before them, because God had had mercy on him. And when Tobit came up to Sarah his daughter-in-law, he blessed her, saying,

"Welcome, daughter! Blessed is God, who has brought you to us, and blessed are your father and your mother."

And there was rejoicing among all his brothers in Nineveh. And Ahiqar and Nasbas his nephew came, and Tobias' marriage feast was held for seven days, with great gladness.

Then Tobit called his son Tobias and said to him,

"My child, see to the wages of the man who went with you, for we must give him more."

And he said to him,

"Father, I can afford to give him half of what I brought back, for he has brought me back to you safe and sound, and he cured my wife and he brought me the money, and besides he has cured you."

And the old man said,

"It is due him."

And he called the angel and said to him,

"Accept half of all that you brought back."

Then he called them both and said to them in private,

"Bless God and give thanks to him. Ascribe majesty to him, and before all the living acknowledge how he has dealt with you. It is a good thing to bless God and exalt his name, declaring God's works and doing them honor, so do not be slow to give him thanks. It is wise to keep a king's secret, but the works of God should be gloriously revealed. Do good, and evil will not overtake you. Prayer is good if accompanied with fasting, charity, and uprightness. A little with uprightness is better than much with wickedness. It is better to give to charity than to lay up gold. For charity will save a man from death; it will expiate any sin. Those who give to charity and act uprightly will have their fill of life; but those who commit sin are the enemies of their own lives. I will not conceal anything from you; as I said, it is wise to keep a king's secret, but the works of God should be gloriously revealed. So now, when you and your daughter-in-law Sarah prayed, I brought the remembrance of your prayer before the Holy One. And when you buried the dead, I was still with you. And when you did not shrink from getting up and leaving your dinner to go and lay out the dead, your good deed did not escape me, but I was with you. So God sent me to cure you and your daughter-in-law, Sarah. For I am Raphael, one of the seven holy angels, who offer up the prayers of God's people and go into the presence of the glory of the Holy One!"

And they were both confounded, and fell on their faces, for they were terrified. And he said to them,

"Do not be afraid; peace be with you. Bless God forever. For not through any favor on my part but by the will of God I came to you. Therefore bless him forever. All these days that I appeared to you, I did not eat or drink, but you beheld a vision. Now give thanks to God, for I must go up to him who sent me, and you must write all that has happened on a scroll."

And when they got up, they no longer saw him. And they acknowledged the great, wonderful doings of God, and how the angel of the Lord had appeared to them.

Then Tobit wrote a prayer of rejoicing, and said,

"Blessed be God who lives forever, and blessed be his kingdom,
For he flogs, and he has mercy,
He takes men down to Hades, and he brings them up,
And there is no one who can escape his hand.
Give thanks to him, Israelites, before the heathen,
For he has scattered you among them.
Show his majesty there;
Exalt him in the presence of every living being,
For he is our Lord and God,
He is our father forever.
He will flog us for our wrongdoing,
And he will show mercy again and gather us from all the heathen
Wherever you are scattered.
If you turn to him with all your heart,
And with all your soul, to act truly in his sight,
Then he will turn to you,
And he will not hide his face from you.
See how he will deal with you,
And give him thanks with your full voice.
Bless the Lord of Righteousness
And exalt the King of the Ages.
In the land of my captivity I give him thanks,
And I show his might and his majesty to a nation of sinners:
'Turn to him, you sinners, and do what is right in his sight;
Who knows but he will be pleased with you, and show you mercy?'
I exalt my God,
My soul exalts the king of heaven,
And exults in his majesty.
Let all men speak and give him thanks in Jerusalem.
O Jerusalem, the holy city,
He will flog you for the doings of your sons,

And again he will have mercy on the sons of the upright.
Give thanks to the Lord in goodness,
And bless the King of the Ages,
That his tent may be rebuilt in you with joy.
May he make glad in you those who are captives,
And the miserable may he love in you,
To all generations, forever.
Many nations will come from afar to the name of the Lord God,
Bearing gifts in their hands, gifts for the king of heaven.
Generations of generations will bring you exultation.
Cursed be all who hate you!
Blessed forever shall be all who love you.
Rejoice and exult in the sons of the upright,
For they will be gathered together, and they will bless the Lord of the
    upright.
Blessed are those who love you!
They will rejoice in your peace.
Blessed are those who grieved over all your stripes,
For they will be glad about you, when they see all your glory,
And they will rejoice forever.
Let my soul bless God, the great King,
For Jerusalem will be built of sapphire and emerald,
And her walls of precious stones,
And her towers and battlements of pure gold;
And the streets of Jerusalem will be paved with beryl and ruby and
    stones of Ophir,
And all her lanes shall say 'Hallelujah,' and shall utter praise, saying,
'Blessed be God, who has raised you up forever.' "

And Tobit ended his thanksgiving. He was fifty-eight years old when he lost his sight, and eight years later he recovered it; and he gave to charity and continued to fear the Lord his God and to give thanks to him. And when he had grown very old, he called his son and his son's sons to him and said to him,

"My child, take your sons; here I have grown old and will soon depart this life. Go to Media, my child, for I firmly believe what Jonah the prophet said about Nineveh, that it will be destroyed, but in Media there will be peace, rather than here, for a while, and that our brothers will be scattered from the good land over the earth, and Jerusalem will be desolate, and the house of God in it will be burned down, and will be desolate for a time; and then God will have mercy on them again, and bring them back to their land; and they will build the house, though not as it was before, until the times of that age are passed. And afterward they will return from the places of their captivity and rebuild Jerusalem in splendor, and the house of God will be rebuilt in it gloriously, for all generations forever, as the prophets said of it. And all the heathen will turn to fear the Lord God in truth, and they will bury their idols, and all the heathen will bless the Lord. And his people will thank God, and the Lord will uplift his people, and all who love the Lord God in truth and uprightness will rejoice and show mercy to our brothers. And now, my child, leave Nineveh, for what the prophet Jonah said will surely happen. But keep the law and the ordinances, and be merciful and upright, so that you may prosper. Bury me properly and my wife beside me. And do not live any longer in Nineveh. My child, see what Haman did to Ahiqar, who had brought him up—how he plunged him from light into darkness and how he requited him! Yet Ahiqar was saved and the other was recompensed and disappeared in darkness himself. Manasseh gave to charity, and escaped the fatal snare which Haman set for him, but Haman fell into the trap and perished. See, my children, what charity can do, and how uprightness can save!"

As he said this, he breathed his last there in his bed. He was a hundred and fifty-eight years old; and they gave him a splendid funeral.

When Hannah died, he buried her beside his father. Then Tobias went back with his wife and his sons to Ecbatana, to Raguel his father-in-law. And he reached an honored old age, and he gave his father-in-law and his mother-in-law splendid funerals, and he inherited their property and his father Tobit's. And he died in Ecbatana in Media, at the age of a hundred and twenty-seven. But before he died he heard of the destruction of Nineveh, which Nebuchadnezzar and Ahasuerus had captured. So before he died he rejoiced over Nineveh.

Pseudepigrapha

The Pseudepigrapha refers to that branch of the Apocryphal literature which was anonymously written but attributed to a famous personality of the past in order to gain greater acceptance. This process is not new in Jewish literature—even the Bible contains some examples of attributed authorship. For instance, Ecclesiastes is traditionally ascribed to King Solomon, but a close study of its language, diction and style indicates that it was written long after King Solomon's death.

The Testament of the Twelve Sons, written between 137 and 107 B.C.E., is a representative example of pseudepigraphic literature. It asserts the traditional values of Torah ethics and ideals of Israel as found in most ancient Hebrew literature; contains material that later influenced Christianity; and provides (especially in the Testament of Joseph) prime source material for the Joseph story which has intrigued writers and readers for millenia. The author, with keen psychological insight, probes the souls of the tribal fathers and assumes that the sale of Joseph is the traumatic experience in their lives; hence many of them deal with this incident in their testaments.

The Testament also reflects the tradition of ethical wills which are seen in the Torah (the blessings of Jacob and Moses), and adumbrate a literary genre that flourished in the Middle Ages (see "Ethical Wills"). Moreover, the midrashic quality of Biblical exposition and expansion is also found here—and so in this book many early Hebrew genres blend.

An easily noticeable structure is common to all the testaments. The tribal patriarch narrates his life story, confesses his sins and the moral failures unique to him, then suggests to his sons that they learn from his misdeeds and lead a moral life. He then prophesies about the end of days and divine judgment.

Although Christian scribes later interpolated some material into the Testament—especially in reference to the salvation of the world by Jesus—the book is written within the framework of Jewish law and tradition by a Jew who believed in the Torah, in sacrifices, and in the ultimate salvation of Israel. Although the complete manuscripts that have survived are in Greek, Armenian and Slavonic, the work was undoubtedly composed originally in Hebrew (even in the Greek the Hebrew idioms and phrases are recognizable). Some Hebrew and Aramaic fragments of the Testament were discovered early in the twentieth century.

The testaments are skillfully variegated in content. Zebulun regrets the Joseph incident, but places the blame on Simeon, Dan and Gad. Gad, on the other hand, readily admits his chief failing—hatred—and warns his children to excise this passion from their midst. In combining for the first time two ancient Torah commandments: "Thou shalt love the Lord thy God" (Deut. 6:5) and "Thou shalt love thy neighbor as thyself" (Lev. 19:18), Gad's Testament influenced New Testament thought (see Math. 23:37–40, and Mark 12:28–31) which makes much use of this double commandment.

The few Biblical verses devoted to the Joseph-Potiphar's-wife incident become, in the Testament of Joseph, the subject of short story material: narrative, psychological detail and dialogue add flesh to a skeletal outline. The erotic elements of the game between mistress and servant are developed here, as are the passionate woman's guiles and wiles. A comparison of chapter 37 of Genesis with the Joseph section clearly reveals the literary skills, inventiveness and insights of the author of the Testament. Further development of this story may be found in the *Book of Yashar* (see page 369).

THE TESTAMENT OF THE TWELVE SONS

THE TESTAMENT OF ZEBULUN

The copy of the words of Zebulun, which he enjoined on his sons before he died in the hundred and fourteenth year of his life, two years after the death of Joseph. And he said to them:

Hearken to me, ye sons of Zebulun, attend to the words of your father. I, Zebulun, was born a good gift to my parents. For when I was born my father was increased very exceedingly, both in flocks and herds, when with the straked rods he had his portion. I am not conscious that I have sinned all my days, save in thought. Nor yet do I remember that I have done any iniquity, except the sin of ignorance which I committed against Joseph; for I covenanted with my brethren not to tell my father what had been done. But I wept in secret many days on account of Joseph, for I feared my brethren, because they had all agreed that if any one should declare the secret, he should be slain. But when they wished to kill him, I adjured them much with tears not to be guilty of this sin.

For Simeon and Gad came against Joseph to kill him, and he said unto them with tears: "Pity me, my brethren, have mercy upon Jacob our father: lay not upon me your hands to shed innocent blood, for I have not sinned against you. And if indeed I have sinned, chastise me, my brethren, but lay not upon me your hand, for the sake of Jacob our father."

And as he spoke these words, wailing as he did so, I was unable to bear his lamentations, and began to weep, and was troubled. And I wept with Joseph, and my heart sounded, and the joints of my body trembled, and I was not able to stand. And when Joseph saw me weeping with him, and them coming against him to slay him, he fled behind me, beseeching them.

But meanwhile Reuben arose and said: "Come, my brethren, let us not slay him, but let us cast him into one of these dry pits, which our fathers digged and found no water. For this the Lord forbade that water should rise up in them, in order that Joseph should be preserved." And they did so, until they sold him to the Ishmaelites.

For in his price I had no share, my children. But Simeon and Gad and six other of our brethren took the price of Joseph, and bought sandals for themselves and their wives and their children, saying: "We will not eat of it, for it is the price of our brother's blood, but we will assuredly tread it under foot, because he said that he would be king over us, and so let us see what will become of his dreams." . . .

And after he was sold my brothers sat down to eat and drink. But I, through pity for Joseph, did not eat, but watched the pit, since Judah feared lest Simeon, Dan, and Gad should rush off and slay him. But when they saw that I did not eat, they set me to watch him, till he was sold to the Ishmaelites. And when Reuben came and heard that while he was away Joseph had been sold, he rent his garments, and mourning, said: "How shall I look on the face of my father Jacob?" And he took the money and ran after the merchants, but as he failed to find them he returned grieving. But the merchants had left the broad road and marched through the Troglodytes by a short cut.

Reuben was grieved, and ate no food that day. Dan therefore came to him and said: "Weep not, neither grieve; for we have found what we can say to our father Jacob. Let us slay a kid of the goats, and dip in it the coat of Joseph; and let us send it to Jacob, saying: Is this the coat of thy son?"

And they did so. For they stripped off from Joseph his coat when they were selling him, and put upon him the garments of a slave. Now Simeon took the coat, and would not give it up, for he wished to rend it with his sword, as he was angry that Joseph lived and that he had not slain him. Then we all rose up and said unto him: "If thou givest not up the coat, we will say to our father that thou alone didst this evil thing in Israel." And so he gave it unto them, and they did as Dan had said.

And now, my children, I bid you to keep the commands of the Lord, and to show mercy to your neighbours, and to have compassion towards all, not towards men only, but also towards beasts. For all this thing's sake the Lord blessed me, and when all my brethren were sick, I escaped without sickness, for the Lord knoweth the purposes of each. Have, therefore, compassion in your hearts, my children, because even as a man doeth to his neighbour, so also will the Lord do to him. For the sons of my brethren were sickening and were dying on account of Joseph, because they showed not mercy in their hearts; but my sons were preserved without sickness, as ye know. And when I was in the land of Canaan, by the sea-coast, I made a catch of fish for Jacob my father; and when many were choked in the sea, I continued unhurt.

I was the first to make a boat to sail upon the sea, for the Lord gave me understanding and wisdom therein. And I let down a rudder behind it, and I stretched a sail upon another upright piece of wood in the midst. And I sailed therein along the shores, catching fish for the house of my father until we came to Egypt.

And through compassion I shared my catch with every stranger. And if a man were a stranger, or sick, or aged, I boiled the fish, and dressed them well, and offered them to all men, as every man had need, grieving with and having compassion upon them. Wherefore also the Lord satisfied me with abundance of fish when catching fish; for he that shareth with his neighbour receiveth manifold more from the Lord. For five years I caught fish and gave thereof to every man whom I saw, and sufficed for all the house of my father. And in the summer I caught fish, and in the winter I kept sheep with my brethren.

Now I will declare unto you what I did. I saw a man in distress through nakedness in wintertime, and had compassion upon him, and stole away a garment secretly from my father's house, and gave it to him who was in distress. Do you, therefore, my children, from that which God bestoweth upon you, show compassion and mercy without hesitation to all men, and give to every man with a good heart. And if ye have not the wherewithal to give to him that needeth, have compassion for him in mercy. I know that my hand found not the wherewithal to give to him that needed, and I walked with him weeping for seven furlongs, and I yearned towards him in compassion.

Have, therefore, yourselves also, my children, compassion towards every man with mercy, that the Lord also may have compassion and mercy upon you. Because also in the last days God will send His compassion on the earth, and wheresoever He findeth mercy He dwelleth in him. For in the degree in which a man hath compassion upon his neighbours, in the same degree hath the Lord also upon him. And when we went down into Egypt, Joseph bore no malice against us. To whom taking heed, do ye also, my children, approve yourselves without malice, and love one another; and do not set down in account, each one of you, evil against his brother. For this breaketh unity and divideth all kindred, and troubleth the soul, and weareth away the countenance.

Observe, therefore, the waters, and know when they flow together, they sweep along stones, trees, earth, and other things. But if they are divided into many streams, the earth swalloweth them up, and they vanish away. So shall ye also be if ye be divided. Be not ye, therefore, divided into two heads, for everything which the Lord made hath but one head, and two shoulders, two hands, two feet, and all the remaining members. For I have learnt in the writing of my fathers, that

Ye shall be divided in Israel,
And ye shall follow two kings,
And shall work every abomination.
And your enemies shall lead you captive,
And ye shall be evil entreated among the Gentiles,
With many infirmities and tribulations.

And after these things ye shall remember the Lord and repent,
And He shall have mercy upon you, for He is merciful and compassionate.
And He setteth not down in account evil against the sons of men,
Because they are flesh, and are deceived through their own wicked deeds.

And after these things shall there arise unto you the Lord Himself, the
light of righteousness,

And ye shall return unto your land.
And ye shall see Him in Jerusalem, for His name's sake.

And again through the wickedness of your works shall ye provoke Him
                    to anger,
And ye shall be cast away by Him unto the time of consummation.

And now, my children, grieve not that I am dying, nor be cast down in
that I am coming to my end. For I shall rise again in the midst of you, as
a ruler in the midst of his sons; and I shall rejoice in the midst of my tribe
as many as shall keep the law of the Lord, and the commandments of
Zebulun their father. But upon the ungodly shall the Lord bring eternal
fire, and destroy them throughout all generations. But I am now hastening
away to my rest, as did also my fathers. But do ye fear the Lord our God
with all your strength all the days of your life. And when he had said
these things he fell asleep, at a good old age. And his sons laid him in a
wooden coffin. And afterwards they carried him up and buried him in
Hebron, with his fathers.

THE TESTAMENT OF GAD

The copy of the testament of Gad, what things he spake unto his sons,
in the hundred and twenty-fifth year of his life, saying unto them:
Hearken, my children, I was the ninth son born to Jacob, and I was
valiant in keeping the flocks. Accordingly I guarded at night the flock;
and whenever the lion came, or the wolf, or any wild beast against the
fold, I pursued it, and overtaking it, I seized its foot with my hand and
hurled it about a stone's throw, and so killed it.
Now Joseph my brother was feeding the flock with us for upwards of
thirty days, and being young, he fell sick by reason of the heat. And he
returned to Hebron to our father, who made him lie down near him, because
he loved him greatly. And Joseph told our father that the sons of Zilpah
and Bilhah were slaying the best of the flock and eating them against the
judgement of Reuben and Judah. For he saw that I had delivered a lamb
out of the mouth of a bear, and put the bear to death; but had slain the
lamb, being grieved concerning it that it could not live, and that we had
eaten it. And regarding this matter I was wroth with Joseph until the day
that he was sold. And the spirit of hatred was in me, and I wished not
either to hear of Joseph, or see him, because he rebuked us to our faces
saying that we were eating of the flock without Judah. For whatsoever
things he told our father, he believed him.
I confess now my sin, my children, that often I wished to kill him,
because I hated him from my heart. Moreover, I hated him yet more for
his dreams; and I wished to lick him out of the land of the living, as an ox
licketh up the grass of the field.

And Judah sold him secretly to the Ishmaelites.

Thus the God of our fathers delivered him from our hands, that we should not work great lawlessness in Israel.

And now, my children, hearken to the words of truth and righteousness, and all the law of the Most High, and go not astray through the spirit of hatred, for it is evil in all the doings of men. Whatsoever a man doeth the hater abominateth him: and though a man worketh the law of the Lord, he praiseth him not; though a man feareth the Lord, and taketh pleasure in that which is righteous, he loveth him not. He dispraiseth the truth, he envieth him that prospereth, he welcometh evil-speaking, he loveth arrogance, for hatred blindeth his soul; as I also then looked on Joseph.

Beware, therefore, my children, of hatred; for it worketh lawlessness even against the Lord Himself. For hatred worketh with envy also against them that prosper: so long as it heareth of or seeth their success, it always languisheth.

For as love would quicken even the dead, and would call back them that are condemned to die, so hatred would slay the living, and those that had sinned venially it would not suffer to live. For the spirit of hatred worketh together with the law of God in long-suffering unto the salvation of men.

Hatred, therefore, is evil, for it constantly mateth with lying, speaking against the truth; and it maketh small things to be great, and causeth the light to be darkness, and calleth the sweet bitter, and teacheth slander, and kindleth wrath, and stirreth up war, and violence and all covetousness; it filleth the heart with evils and devilish poison.

These things, therefore, I say to you from experience, my children, that ye may drive forth hatred, which is of the devil, and cleave to the love of God. Righteousness casteth out hatred, humility destroyeth envy. For he that is just and humble is ashamed to do what is unjust, being reproved not of another, but of his own heart, because the Lord looketh on his inclination. He speaketh not against a holy man, because the fear of God overcometh hatred. For fearing lest he should offend the Lord, he will not do wrong to any man, even in thought.

These things I learnt at last, after I had repented concerning Joseph. For true repentance after a godly sort destroyeth ignorance, and driveth away the darkness, and enlighteneth the eyes, and giveth knowledge to the soul, and leadeth the mind to salvation. And those things which it hath not learnt from man, it knoweth through repentance. For God brought upon me a disease of the heart; and had not the prayers of Jacob my father succoured me, my spirit would surely have departed. For by the things a man transgresseth, by the same also is he punished. Since, therefore, my heart was set mercilessly against Joseph, in my heart too I suffered mercilessly, and was judged for eleven months, for so long a time as I had been angry against Joseph.

And now my children, I exhort you, love ye each one his brother, and put away hatred from your hearts, love one another in deed, and in word, and in the inclination of the soul. For in the presence of my father I spake peaceably to Joseph; and when I had gone out, the spirit of hatred darkened my mind, and stirred up my soul to slay him.

Love ye one another from the heart; and if a man sin against thee, speak peaceably to him, and in thy soul hold not guile, and if he repent and confess, forgive him.

But if he deny it, do not get into a passion with him, lest catching the poison from thee he take to swearing and so thou sin doubly. Let not another man hear thy secrets when engaged in legal strife, lest he come to hate thee and become thy enemy, and commit a great sin against thee; for ofttimes he addresseth thee guilefully or busieth himself about thee with wicked intent. And though he deny it and yet have a sense of shame when reproved, give over reproving him. For he who denieth may repent so as not again to wrong thee; yea, he may also honour thee, and fear and be at peace with thee. And if he be shameless and persist in his wrong-doing, even so forgive him from the heart, and leave to God the avenging.

If a man prospereth more than you, do not be vexed, but pray also for him, that he may have perfect prosperity. For so it is expedient for you. And if he be further exalted, be not envious of him, remembering that all flesh shall die, and offer praise to God, who giveth things good and profitable to all men.

Seek out the judgements of the Lord, and thy mind will rest and be at peace. And though a man become rich by evil means, even as Esau, the brother of my father, be not jealous but wait for the end of the Lord. For if He taketh away from a man wealth gotten by evil means He forgiveth him if he repent, but the unrepentant is reserved for eternal punishment. For the poor man, if free from envy he pleaseth the Lord in all things, is blessed beyond all men, because he hath not the travail of vain men. Put away, therefore, jealousy from your souls, and love one another with uprightness of heart.

Do ye also therefore tell these things to your children, that they honour Judah and Levi, for from them shall the Lord raise up salvation to Israel. For I know that at the last your children shall depart from Him, and shall walk in all wickedness, and affliction and corruption before the Lord.

And when he had rested for a little while, he said again:

My children, obey your father, and bury me near to my fathers. And he drew up his feet, and fell asleep in peace. And after five years they carried him up to Hebron, and laid him with his fathers.

THE TESTAMENT OF JOSEPH

The copy of the testament of Joseph. When he was about to die he called his sons and his brethren together, and said to them:

My brethren and my children,
Hearken to Joseph the beloved of Israel;
Give ear, my sons, unto your father.
I have seen in my life envy and death,
Yet I went not astray, but persevered in the truth of the Lord.
My brethren hated me, but the Lord loved me:
They wished to slay me, but the God of my fathers guarded me:
They let me down into a pit, and the Most High brought me up again.
I was sold into slavery, and the Lord of all made me free:
I was taken into captivity, and His strong hand succoured me.
I was beset with hunger, and the Lord Himself nourished me.
I was alone, and God comforted me.
I was sick, and the Lord visited me.
I was in prison, and my God showed favour unto me;
In bonds, and He released me;
Slandered, and He pleaded my cause;
Bitterly spoken against by the Egyptians, and He delivered me;
Envied by my fellow-slaves, and He exalted me.

And this chief captain of Pharaoh entrusted to me his house. And I struggled against a shameless woman, urging me to transgress with her; but the God of Israel my father delivered me from the burning flame. I was cast into prison, I was beaten, I was mocked; but the Lord granted me to find mercy in the sight of the keeper of the prison.

For the Lord doth not forsake them that fear Him,
Neither in darkness, nor in bonds, nor in tribulations, nor in necessities.
For God is not put to shame as a man,
Nor as the son of man is he afraid,
Nor as one that is earth-born is He weak or frightened.

But in all those things doth He give protection,
And in divers ways doth He comfort,
Though for a little space He departeth to try the inclination of the soul.
In ten temptations He showed me approved,
And in all of them I endured;
For endurance is a mighty charm,
And patience giveth many good things.

How often did the Egyptian woman threaten me with death! How often did she give me over to punishment, and then call me back and threaten me, and when I was unwilling to company with her, she said to me: "Thou shalt be lord of me, and all that is in my house, if thou wilt give thyself unto me, and thou shalt be as our master."

But I remembered the words of my father, and going into my chamber, I wept and prayed unto the Lord. And I fasted in those seven years, and

I appeared to the Egyptians as one living delicately, for they that fast for God's sake receive beauty of face. And if my lord were away from home, I drank no wine; nor for three days did I take my food, but I gave it to the poor and sick. And I sought the Lord early, and I wept for the Egyptian woman of Memphis, for very unceasingly did she trouble me, for also at night she came to me under pretense of visiting me.

And because she had no male child she pretended to regard me as a son.

And for a time she embraced me as a son, and I knew it not; but later, she sought to draw me into fornication. And when I perceived it, I sorrowed unto death; and when she had gone out, I came to myself, and lamented for her many days, because I recognized her guile and her deceit. And I declared unto her the words of the Most High, if haply she would turn from her evil lust.

Often, therefore, did she flatter me with words as a holy man, and guilefully in her talk praise my chastity before her husband, while desiring to ensnare me when we were alone. For she lauded me openly as chaste, and in secret she said unto me: "Fear not my husband; for he is persuaded concerning thy chastity: for even should one tell him concerning us, he would not believe."

Owing to all these things I lay upon the ground, and besought God that the Lord would deliver me from her deceit. And when she had prevailed nothing thereby, she came again to me under the plea of instruction, that she might learn the word of God.

And she said unto me: "If thou willest that I should leave my idols, lie with me, and I will persuade my husband to depart from his idols, and we will walk in the law of thy Lord."

And I said unto her: "The Lord willeth not that those who revere Him should be in uncleanness, nor doth He take pleasure in them that commit adultery, but in those that approach Him with a pure heart and undefiled lips." But she held her peace, longing to accomplish her evil desire. And I gave myself yet more to fasting and prayer, that the Lord might deliver me from her.

And again, at another time she said unto me: "If thou wilt not commit adultery, I will kill my husband by poison; and take thee to be my husband."

I therefore, when I heard this, rent my garments, and said unto her: "Woman, revere God, and do not this evil deed, lest thou be destroyed; for know indeed that I will declare this thy device unto all men." She therefore, being afraid, besought that I would not declare this device. And she departed soothing me with gifts, and sending to me every delight of the sons of men.

And afterwards she sent me food mingled with enchantments. And when the eunuch who brought it came, I looked up and beheld a terrible man giving me with the dish a sword, and I perceived that her scheme was to beguile me. And when he had gone out I wept, nor did I taste that or any other of her food. So then after one day she came to me and observed the food, and said unto me: "Why is it that thou hast not eaten of the food?"

And I said unto her: "It is because thou hast filled it with deadly enchantments; and how saidst thou: 'I come not near to idols, but to the Lord alone.' Now therefore know that the God of my father hath revealed unto me by His angel thy wickedness, and I have kept it to convict thee, if haply thou mayest see and repent.

"But that thou mayest learn that the wickedness of the ungodly hath no power over them that worship God with chastity, behold I will take of it and eat before thee."

And having so said, I prayed thus: "The God of my fathers and the angel of Abraham, be with me", and ate.

And when she saw this she fell upon her face at my feet weeping; and I raised her up and admonished her. And she promised to do this iniquity no more.

But her heart was still set upon evil, and she looked around how to ensnare me, and sighing deeply she became downcast, though she was not sick.

And when her husband saw her, he said unto her: "Why is thy countenance fallen?"

And she said unto him: "I have a pain at my heart, and the groanings of my spirit oppress me", and so he comforted her who was not sick.

Then, accordingly seizing an opportunity, she rushed unto me while her husband was yet without, and said unto me: "I will hang myself, or cast myself over a cliff, if thou will not lie with me."

And when I saw the spirit of Belial was troubling her, I prayed unto the Lord, and said unto her: "Why, wretched woman, are thou troubled and disturbed, blinded through sins? Remember that if thou kill thyself, Asteho, the concubine of thy husband, thy rival, will beat thy children, and thou wilt destroy thy memorial from off the earth."

And she said unto me: "Lo, then thou lovest me; let this suffice me: only strive for my life and my children, and I expect that I shall enjoy my desire also."

But she knew not that because of my lord I spake thus, and not because of her. For if a man hath fallen before the passion of a wicked desire and become enslaved by it, even as she, whatever good thing he may hear with regard to that passion, he receiveth it with a view to his wicked desire.

I declare, therefore, unto you, my children, that it was about the sixth hour when she departed from me; and I knelt before the Lord all day, and all the night; and about dawn I rose up, weeping the while and praying for a release from her. At last, then, she laid hold of my garments, forcibly dragging me to have connexion with her.

When, therefore, I saw that in her madness she was holding fast to my garment, I left it behind, and fled away naked.

And holding fast to the garment, she falsely accused me, and when her husband came he cast me into prison in his house; and on the morrow he scourged me and sent me into Pharaoh's prison.

And when I was in bonds, the Egyptian woman was oppressed with grief, and she came and heard how I gave thanks unto the Lord and sang praises in the abode of darkness, and with glad voice rejoiced, glorifying my God that I was delivered from the lustful desire of the Egyptian woman.

And often hath she sent unto me saying: "Consent to fulfil my desire and I will release thee from thy bonds, and I will free thee from the darkness." And not even in thought did I incline unto her. For God loveth him who in a den of wickedness combines fasting with chastity, rather than the man who in kings' chambers combines luxury with license. And if a man liveth in chastity, and desireth also glory, and the Most High knoweth that it is expedient for him, He bestoweth this also upon him. How often, though she were sick, did she come down to me at unlooked for times, and listened to my voice as I prayed! And when I heard her groanings I held my peace. For when I was in her house she was wont to bare her arms, and breasts, and legs, that I might lie with her; for she was very beautiful, splendidly adorned in order to beguile me. And the Lord guarded me from her devices.

Ye see, therefore, my children, how great things patience worketh, and prayer with fasting. So ye too, if ye follow after chastity and purity with patience and prayer, with fasting in humility of heart, the Lord will dwell among you, because He loveth chastity. And wheresoever the Most High dwelleth, even though envy, or slavery, or slander befalleth a man, the Lord who dwelleth in him, for the sake of his chastity not only delivereth him from evil, but also exalteth him even as me. For in every way the man is lifted up, whether in deed, or in word, or in thought. My brethren knew how my father loved me, and yet I did not exalt myself in my mind: although I was a child, I had the fear of God in my heart; for I knew that all things would pass away. And I did not raise myself against them with evil intent, but I honoured my brethren and out of respect for them, even when I was being sold, I refrained from telling the Ishmaelites that I was a son of Jacob, a great and mighty man.

Do ye also, my children, have the fear of God in all your works before your eyes, and honour your brethren. For every one who doeth the law of the Lord shall be loved by Him. And when I came to the Indocoloitae with the Ishmaelites, they asked me, saying: "Art thou a slave?" And I said that I was a home-born slave, that I might not put my brethren to shame.

And the eldest of them said unto me: "Thou art not a slave, for even thy appearance doth make it manifest." But I said that I was their slave. Now when we came into Egypt they strove concerning me, which of them should buy me and take me. Therefore it seemed good to all that I should remain in Egypt with the merchant of their trade, until they should return bringing merchandise.

And the Lord gave me favour in the eyes of the merchant, and he entrusted unto me his house. And God blessed him by my means, and increased him in gold and silver and in household servants. And I was with him three months and five days.

And about that time the Memphian woman, the wife of Pentephris, came down in a chariot, with great pomp, because she had heard from her eunuchs concerning me. And she told her husband that the merchant had become rich by means of a young Hebrew, and they say that he had assuredly been stolen out of the land of Canaan. Now, therefore, render justice unto him, and take away the youth to thy house; so shall the God of the Hebrews bless thee, for grace from heaven is upon him.

And Pentephris was persuaded by her words, and commanded the merchant to be brought, and said unto him: "What is this that I hear concerning thee, that thou stealest persons out of the land of Canaan, and sellest them for slaves?"

But the merchant fell at his feet, and besought him, saying: "I beseech thee, my lord, I know not what thou sayest."

And Pentephris said unto him: "Whence, then, is the Hebrew slave?" And he said: "The Ishmaelites entrusted him unto me until they should return." But he believed him not, but commanded him to be stripped and beaten. And when he persisted in this statement, Pentephris said: "Let the youth be brought."

When I was brought in, I did obeisance to Pentephris (for he was third in rank of the officers of Pharaoh). And he took me apart from him and said unto me: "Art thou a slave or free?" And I said: "A slave." And he said: "Whose?" And I said: "The Ishmaelites'." And he said: "How didst thou become their slave?" And I said: "They bought me out of the land of Canaan." And he said unto me: "Truly thou liest." And straightaway he commanded me to be stripped and beaten.

Now the Memphian woman was looking through a window at me while I was being beaten, for her house was near, and she sent unto him saying: "Thy judgement is unjust; for thou dost punish a free man who hath been stolen, as though he were a transgressor." And when I made no change in my statement, though I was beaten, he ordered me to be imprisoned, until, he said, the owners of the boy should come.

And the woman said unto her husband: "Wherefore dost thou detain the captive and well-born lad in bonds, who ought rather to be set at liberty, and be waited upon?" For she wished to see me out of a desire of sin, but I was ignorant concerning all these things. And he said to her: "It is not the custom of the Egyptians to take that which belongeth to others before proof is given." This, therefore, he said concerning the merchant. "But as for the lad, he must be imprisoned."

Now after four and twenty days came the Ishmaelites; for they had heard that Jacob my father was mourning much concerning me. And they came and said unto me: "How is it that thou saidst that thou wast a slave? and lo, we have learnt that thou art the son of a mighty man in the land of Canaan, and thy father still mourneth for thee in sackcloth and ashes."

When I heard this my heart melted and I desired greatly to weep, but I restrained myself, that I should not put my brethren to shame. And I said unto them: "I know not, I am a slave." Then, therefore, they took counsel to sell me, that I should not be found in their hands. For they feared my father, lest he should come and execute upon them a grievous vengeance. For they had heard that he was mighty with God and with men. Then said the merchant unto them: "Release me from the judgement of Penti-phris." And they came and requested me, saying: "Say that thou wast bought by us with money, and he will set us free."

Now the Memphian woman said to her husband: "Buy the youth, for I hear that they are selling him."

And straightway she sent a eunuch to the Ishmaelites, and asked them to sell me. But since the eunuch would not agree to buy me at their price he returned, having made trial of them, and he made known to his mistress that they asked a large price for their slave.

And she sent another eunuch, saying: "Even though they demand two minas, give them, do not spare the gold; only buy the boy, and bring him to me."

The eunuch therefore went and gave them eighty pieces of gold, and he received me; but to the Egyptian woman he said: "I have given a hundred."

And though I knew this, I held my peace, lest the eunuch should be put to shame.

Ye see, therefore, my children, what great things I endured that I should not put my brethren to shame. Do ye also, therefore; love one another, and with longsuffering hide ye one another's faults. For God delighteth in the unity of brethren, and in the purpose of a heart that takes pleasure in love. And when my brethren came into Egypt they learnt that I had returned their money unto them, and upbraided them not, and comforted them. And after the death of Jacob my father I loved them more abundantly, and all things whatsoever he commanded I did very abundantly for them. And I suffered them not to be afflicted in the smallest matter; and all that was in my hand I gave unto them. And their children were my children, and my children as their servants; and their life was my life, and all their suffering was my suffering, and all their sickness was my infirmity. My land was their land, and their counsel my counsel. And I exalted not myself among them in arrogance because of my worldly glory, but I was among them as one of the least.

If ye also, therefore, walk in the commandments of the Lord, my chil-dren, He will exalt you there, and will bless you with good things for ever and ever. And if any one seeketh to do evil unto you, do well unto him, and pray for him, and ye shall be redeemed of the Lord from all evil. For behold, ye see that out of my humility and long-suffering I took unto wife the daughter of the priest of Heliopolis. And a hundred talents of gold were given me with her, and the Lord made them to serve me. And He gave me also beauty as a flower beyond the beautiful ones of Israel, and He preserved me unto old age in strength and in beauty, because I was like in all things to Jacob.

I know that after my death the Egyptians will afflict you, but God will avenge you, and will bring you into the land that He promised to your fathers. But ye shall carry up my bones with you; for when my bones are being taken up thither, the Lord shall be with you in light, and Belial shall be in darkness with the Egyptians.

And carry ye up Zilpah your mother, and nigh to Bilhah by the Hippodrome lay her near Rachel.

And when he had said these things he stretched out his feet and died at a good old age. And all Israel mourned for him, and all Egypt with great mourning.

And when the children of Israel went out of Egypt, they took with them the bones of Joseph, and they buried him in Hebron with his fathers, and the years of his life were one hundred and ten years.

Josephus — The Jewish War

Joseph ben Matthias (37–100 C.E.), later known as Flavius Josephus, was a prolific historian and enigmatic personality over whom controversy—was he or was he not a traitor?—still rages. His works, virtually the sole source for the history of Israel during the period of the Second Temple, include the *Jewish War* written soon after the events and published 75–79; *Jewish Antiquities,* composed between 73–93, a history of the Jews from the time of Abraham to the Babylonian exile, in whose rhetorical embellishments and homiletic expansions the literary skills of the Hellenist and the Jew are combined; the *Life,* appended to the *Jewish Antiquities,* which is the only extant Jewish autobiography of the period; and his last work, *Against Apion,* an inspired tract defending Jews and Judaism against Apion's now lost anti-Semitic vilification. The latter volume, too, is unique, for it is the first known defense of Judaism and Jewish morality and culture against one of its highly literate traducers.

Since there are no extraneous sources for Josephus' life but his own autobiography, we must take his word for facts about himself. Born of a priestly family in Jerusalem, as a young man Josephus successfully carried out an official mission to Rome to redeem some captive priests, and later, at the inception of the Jewish revolt, was given command of the Galilee, although he doubted whether Israel could be freed in this manner from Roman rule.

From this point in Josephus' personal history begin the questionable acts which have puzzled generations of readers. When his fortress Jotpata was defeated after a seven-week battle, he and forty others fled to a cave where—like the defenders of Masada whom Josephus has immortalized—they all decided to commit suicide. But Josephus, deceptive in his casting of lots, arranged that he would be among the last, and he convinced the only other remaining soldier to surrender to the Romans. Josephus was then taken to Rome, where he was befriended by the authorities, and then returned to Palestine with Titus. At the walls of Jerusalem during the lengthy siege, he urged his fellow Jews to give up the struggle. After being an eyewitness to the capture of Jerusalem and the destruction of the Temple, he returned once more to Rome. The irony in his passionate description of the fall of Jerusalem in the *Jewish War* is that the writer, now bearing the Roman name, Flavius Josephus, wrote it in Rome while sitting in the royal palace under the patronage of Vespasian and Titus, the general whose armies set the Temple aflame. In Rome, Josephus commenced his literary labors that were to occupy him for a lifetime, and was never again to set foot in his homeland.

The first edition of the *Jewish War* was written originally "in the language of his fathers"; most scholars assume that it was Aramaic, although everyone agrees that Josephus knew Hebrew. This first draft of the *Jewish War,* whose purpose was to enable the Jews in Babylonia and its environs to possess a chronicle of the times, is not extant; but Josephus' second version has captivated readers in the original Greek, as well as in Latin and other translations, for nearly 2000 years.

Divided by Josephus into seven books—further divisions into chapters and sections were done later by others—the first is a quick resumé of Jewish history during the Hellenistic and Roman periods, while the remaining six books chronicle the Jewish War against Rome between 67–70. Soon after its composition the book became well-known; the Church Fathers made extensive use of it, and in a fourth-century Latin translation the *Jewish War* was circulated in all of Western Europe.

Although full of sympathy for Jewish suffering, the work is written from a Roman viewpoint, a fact which is not surprising, given the patronage and the reception that Flavius Josephus had in Rome. He conceals Roman excesses and their antipathy toward Jews, and asserts that only criminal elements among the Jews wanted the war and not the majority of the population—facts which even official Roman military historians contradict.

Josephus' Greek works were not preserved by the Jews but by the Church. He is not mentioned in Talmudic or midrashic literature, but the popular tenth-century Hebrew *Yosippon* did provide a direct link between the author and his people.

The *Jewish War* excels as a literary document in which Josephus' talent as a colorful writer and recreator of moods, people and movement is evident. The section included here is not only typical of Josephus' rhetoric, but is also a testimony, at least in part, to his accuracy as a historian. In the recent excavations at Masada, Josephus' descriptions were proven to be almost always exact. In fact, the archeologist Yigal Yadin juxtaposes in his *Masada* certain modern technical observations with pertinent passages from Josephus—thus enabling the reader to see for himself that Josephus' remarks in his preface that he aims for truth and accuracy cannot be totally discounted. For all the negative evaluation of his personality and his occasionally sycophantic historiography, the "Masada" section alone, with its enormous symbolic impact on Jewish history and modern Israel, surely redeems Josephus of all his faults.

THE FALL OF MASADA

BOOK VII, CHAPTER VIII

Concerning Masada and those Sicarii who kept it; and how Silva betook himself to form the siege of that citadel. Eleazar's speeches to the besieged.

When Bassus was dead in Judea, Flavius Silva succeeded him as procurator there; when he saw that all the rest of the country was subdued in this war, and that there was but one stronghold only that was still in rebellion, he got all his army together that lay in different places, and made an expedition against it. This fortress was called Masada. It was one Eleazar, a potent man, and the commander of these Sicarii, that had seized upon it. He was a descendant of that Judas who had persuaded many of the Jews, as we have formerly related, not to submit to the taxation when Cyrenius was sent into Judea to make one; for then it was that the Sicarii got together against those that were willing to submit to the Romans, and treated them in all respects as if they had been their enemies, both by plundering them of what they had, by driving away their cattle, and by setting fire to the houses: for they said, that they differed not at all from foreigners, by betraying, in so cowardly a manner, that freedom which the Jews thought worthy to be contended for to the utmost, and by owning that they preferred slavery under the Romans before such a contention.

Now, this was in reality no better than a pretence, and a cloak for the barbarity which was made use of by them, and to colour over their own avarice, which they afterwards made evident by their own actions; for those that were partners with them in their rebellion, joined also with them in the war against the Romans; yet went they farther lengths in their impudent undertakings against them: and when they were again convicted of dissembling in such their pretences, they still more abused those that justly reproached them for their wickedness. And indeed that was a time most fertile in all manner of wicked practices among the Jews, in so much that no kind of evil deeds were then left undone; nor could any one so much as devise any bad thing that was new, so deeply were they all infected, and strove with one another in their single capacity, and in their communities, who should run the greatest lengths in impiety towards God, and in unjust actions towards their neighbours; the men of power oppressing the multitude, and the multitude earnestly labouring to destroy the men of power.

The one part were desirous of tyrannizing over others, and the rest of offering violence to others, and of plundering such as were richer than themselves. They were the Sicarii who first began these transgressions, and first became barbarous towards those allied to them, and left no words of reproach unsaid, and no works of perdition untried, in order to destroy those whom their contrivances affected.

Yet did John demonstrate by his actions, that these Sicarii were more moderate than he was himself, for he not only slew all such as gave good counsel to do what was right, and treated them as the most bitter enemies that he had among all the citizens; but, he filled his entire country with ten thousand instances of wickedness, such as a man who was already hardened sufficiently in his impiety towards God, would naturally do: for the food was unlawful that was set upon his table, and he rejected those purifications that the law of his country had ordained: so that it was no longer a wonder if he, who was so mad in his impiety towards God, did not observe any rules of gentleness and common affection towards men. Again, what mischief was there which Simon the son of Gioras did not do? or from what kind of abuses of free men did those abstain who had set him up for a tyrant? What friendship or kindred were there that did not make them more bold in their murders? for they looked upon the doing of mischief to strangers only as a work beneath their courage, but thought barbarity towards their nearest relations would be a glorious demonstration thereof.

The Idumeans also strove with these men, which should be guilty of the greatest madness; for they [all], vile wretches as they were, cut the throats of the high priests, that so no part of a religious regard to God might be preserved; they thence proceeded to destroy utterly the last remains of a political government, and introduced the most complete scene of iniquity in all instances that were practicable; under which scene, that sort of people that were called Zealots grew up, and who indeed corresponded to the name; for they imitated every wicked work; nor if history suggested any evil thing that had formerly been done, did they avoid zealously to pursue the same; and although they gave themselves that name from their zeal for what was good, yet was it an ironical description of the evil deeds done by them in their brutal nature, or because they thought the greatest mischiefs to be the greatest good.

Accordingly they all met with such ends as God deservedly brought upon them in way of punishment, for all such miseries have been sent upon them as man's nature is capable of undergoing, till the utmost period of their lives, and till death came upon them in various ways of torment; yet might one say justly that they suffered less than they had done, because it was impossible they could be punished according to their deserving. But to make a lamentation according to the deserts of those who fell under these men's barbarity, this is not a proper place for it: I therefore now return again to the remaining part of the present narration.

For now it was that the Roman general came, and led his army against

Eleazar and those Sicarii who held the fortress Masada together with him; and for the whole country adjoining he presently gained it, and put garrisons into the most proper places of it: he also built a wall quite round the entire fortress, that none of the besieged might easily escape: He also set his men to guard the several parts of it. He also pitched his camp in such an agreeable place as he had chosen for the siege, and at which place the rocks belonging to the fortress did make the nearest approach to the neighbouring mountain, which yet was a place of difficulty for getting plenty of provisions: for it was not only food that was to be brought from a great distance [to the army], and this with a great deal of pain to those Jews who were appointed for that purpose, but water was also to be brought to the camp, because the place afforded no fountain that was near it. When therefore Silva had ordered these affairs beforehand, he fell to besieging the place; which siege was likely to stand in need of a great deal of skill and pains, by reason of the strength of the fortress, the nature of which I will now describe.

There was a rock, not small in circumference, and very high. It was encompassed with valleys of such vast depth downward, that the eye could not reach their bottoms: they were abrupt, and such as no animal could walk upon, excepting at two places of the rock, where it subsides, in order to afford a passage for ascent, though not without difficulty. Now, of the ways that lead to it, one is that from the lake Asphaltitis, towards the sunrising, and another on the west, where the ascent is easier: the one of these ways is called the *Serpent,* as resembling that animal in its narrowness and its perpetual windings; for it is broken off at the prominent precipices of the rock, and returns frequently into itself, and lengthening again by little and little, hath much ado to proceed forward; and he that would walk along it must first go on one leg and then on the other: there is also nothing but destruction, in case your feet slip; for on each side there is a vastly deep chasm and precipice, sufficient to quell the courage of everybody by the terror it infuses into the mind. When, therefore, a man hath got along this way for thirty furlongs, the rest is the top of the hill, not ending at a small point, but in a plain upon a mountain top.

Upon this top, Jonathan the high priest first of all built a fortress, and called it *Masada*; after which the rebuilding of this place employed the care of king Herod to a great degree: he also built a wall round about the entire top of the hill, seven furlongs long: it was composed of white stone; its height was twelve, and its breadth eight cubits; there were also erected upon that wall, thirty-eight towers, each of them fifty cubits high; out of which you might pass into lesser edifices, which were built on the inside, round the entire wall; for the king reserved the top of the hill, which was of a fat soil, and better mould than any valley for agriculture, that such as committed themselves to this fortress for their preservation, might not even there be quite destitute of food, in case they should ever be in want of it from abroad.

Moreover, he built a palace therein at the western ascent; it was within and beneath the walls of the citadel, but inclined to its north side. Now the wall of this palace was very high and strong, and had at its four corners towers sixty cubits high. The structure also of the edifices, and of the cloisters, and of the baths, was of great variety, and very costly; and these buildings were supported by pillars of single stones on every side: the walls and also the floors of the edifices were paved with stones of several colours. He also had cut many and great pits, as reservoirs for water, out of the rocks, at every one of the places that were inhabited both above and round about the palace, and before the wall: and by this contrivance he endeavoured to have water for several uses as if there had been fountains there.

Here was also a road digged from the palace, and leading to the very top of the mountain, which yet could not be seen by such as were without [the walls]; nor indeed could enemies easily make use of the plain roads: for the road on the east side, as we have already taken notice, could not be walked upon, by reason of its nature; and for the western road, he built a large tower at its narrowest place, at no less a distance from the top of the hill than a thousand cubits; which tower could not possibly be passed by, nor could it be easily taken. Nor indeed could those that walked along it without any fear, such was its contrivance, easily get to the end of it; and after such a manner was this citadel fortified both by nature and by the hands of men, in order to frustrate the attacks of enemies.

As for the furniture that was within this fortress, it was still more wonderful on account of its splendour and long continuance; for here was laid up corn in large quantities, and such as would sustain men for a long time. Here was also wine and oil in abundance, with all kinds of pulse and dates heaped up together: all which Eleazar found there, when he and his Sicarii got possession of the fortress by treachery. These fruits were also fresh and full ripe, no way inferior to such fruits newly laid in, although they were little short of an hundred years from the laying in these provisions, [by Herod,] till the place was taken by the Romans; nay indeed when the Romans got possession of those fruits that were left, they found them not corrupted all that while; nor should we be mistaken, if we supposed that the air was here the cause of their enduring so long: this fortress being so high, and so free from the mixture of all terrene and muddy particles of matter.

There was also found here a large quantity of all sorts of weapons of war, which had been treasured up by that king, and were sufficient for ten thousand men: there was cast iron, and brass, and tin, which shew that he had taken much pains to have all things here ready for the greatest occasions; for the report goes how Herod thus prepared this fortress on his own account, as a refuge against two kinds of danger; the one for fear of the multitude of the Jews, lest they should depose him, and restore their former kings to the government: the other danger was greater and more terrible, which arose from Cleopatra queen of Egypt, who did not conceal her intentions, but spoke often to Antony, and desired him to cut off Herod, and entreated him to bestow the kingdom of Judea upon her. And certainly it is a greater wonder that Antony did never comply with her commands in this point, as he was so miserably enslaved to his passion for her than that Herod should have expected him to comply. So the fear of these dangers made Herod rebuild Masada, and thereby leave it for the finishing stroke of the Romans in this Jewish war.

Since therefore the Roman commander Silva had now built a wall on the outside, round about this whole place, as we have said already, and had thereby made a most accurate provision to prevent any one of the besieged running away, he undertook the siege itself, though he found but one single place that would admit of the banks he was to raise; for behind that tower which secured the road that led to the palace, and to the top of the hill, from the west, there was a certain eminency of the rock, very broad and very prominent, but three hundred cubits beneath the highest part of Masada: it was called the *White Promontory*.

Accordingly Silva got upon that part of the rock, and ordered the army to bring earth; and when they fell to that work with alacrity and abundance of them together, the bank was raised, and became solid for two hundred cubits in height. Yet was not this bank thought sufficiently high, for the use of the engines that were to be set upon it; but still another elevated work of great stones compacted together was raised upon that bank: this was fifty cubits, both in breadth and height. The other machines that were now got ready, were like to those that had been first devised by Vespasian, and afterwards by Titus, for sieges.

There was also a tower made of the height of sixty cubits, and all over plated with iron, out of which the Romans threw darts and stones from the engines, and soon made those that fought from the walls of the place to retire, and would not let them lift up their heads above the works. At the same time Silva ordered that great battering ram which he had made to be brought thither, and to be set against the wall, and to make frequent batteries against it, which, with some difficulty broke down a part of the wall, and quite overthrew it.

However, the Sicarii made haste, and presently built another wall within that, which should not be liable to the same misfortune from the machines with the other: it was made soft and yielding, and so was capable of avoiding the terrible blows that affected the other. It was framed after the following manner: They laid together great beams of wood lengthways, one close to the end of another, and the same way in which they were cut: there were two of these rows parallel to one another, and laid at such a distance from each other as the breadth of the wall required, and earth was put into the space between those rows. Now, that the earth might not fall away upon the elevation of this bank to a greater height, they farther laid other beams over across them, and thereby bound those beams together that lay lengthways.

This work of theirs was like a real edifice; and when the machines were applied, the blows were weakened by its yielding, and as the materials by such concussion were shaken closer together, the pile by that means became firmer than before. When Silva saw this, he thought it best to endeavour the taking of this wall by setting fire to it: so he gave order that the soldiers should throw a great number of burning torches upon it: accordingly, as it was chiefly made of wood, it soon took fire and when it was once set on fire, its hollowness made that fire spread to a mighty flame.

Now at the very beginning of this fire, a north wind that then blew proved terrible to the Romans; for by bringing the flame downward, it drove it upon them, and they were almost in despair of success, as fearing their machines would be burnt: but after this, on a sudden the wind changed into the south, as if it were done by Divine Providence, and blew strongly the contrary way, and carried the flame, and drove it against the wall, which was now on fire through its entire thickness. So the Romans, having now assistance from God, returned to their camp with joy, and resolved to attack their enemies the very next day; on which occasion they set their watch more carefully that night, lest any of the Jews should run away from them without being discovered.

However, neither did Eleazar once think of flying away, nor would he permit anyone else to do so: but when he saw their wall burned down by the fire, and could devise no other way of escaping, or room for their farther courage, and setting before their eyes what the Romans would do to them, their children and their wives, if they got them into their power, he consulted about having them all slain. Now, as he judged this to be the best thing they could do in their present circumstances he gathered the most courageous of his companions together, and encouraged them to take that course by a speech which he made to them in the manner following:

"Since we, long ago, my generous friends, resolved never to be servants to the Romans, nor to any other than to God himself, who alone is the true and just Lord of mankind, the time is now come that obliges us to make that resolution true in practice. And let us not at this time bring a reproach upon ourselves for self-contradiction, while we formerly would not undergo slavery, though it were then without danger, but must now, together with slavery, choose such punishments also, as are intolerable; I mean this upon the supposition that the Romans once reduce us under their power while we are alive. We were the very first that revolted from them, and we are the last that fight against them; and I cannot but esteem it as a favour that God hath granted us, that it is still in our power to die bravely, and in a state of freedom, which hath not been the case of others, who were conquered unexpectedly.

"It is very plain that we shall be taken within a day's time, but it is still an eligible thing to die after a glorious manner, together with our dearest friends. This is what our enemies themselves cannot by any means hinder, although they be very desirous to take us alive. Nor can we propose to ourselves any more to fight them, and beat them. It had been proper indeed for us to have conjectured at the purpose of God much sooner, at the very first, when we were so desirous of defending our liberties, and when we received such sore treatment from one another, and worse treatment from our enemies, and to have been sensible that the same God, who had of old taken the Jewish nation into his favour, had now condemned them to destruction; for had he either continued favourable, or been but in a lesser degree displeased with us, he had not overlooked the destruction of so many men, or delivered his most holy city to be burnt and demolished by our enemies.

"To be sure we weakly hoped to have preserved ourselves, and ourselves alone, out of the whole Jewish nation still in a state of freedom, as if we had been guilty of no sins ourselves against God, nor been partners with those of others; we also taught other men to preserve their liberty. Wherefore, consider how God hath convinced us that our hopes were in vain, by bringing such distress upon us in the desperate state we are now in, and which is beyond all our expectations; for the nature of this fortress, which was in itself unconquerable, hath not proved a means of our deliverance; and even while we have still great abundance of food, and a great quantity of arms, and other necessaries more than we want, we are openly deprived by God himself of all hope of deliverance; for that fire which was driven upon our enemies did not of its own accord turn back upon the wall which we had built: this was the effect of God's anger against us for our manifold sins, which we have been guilty of in a most insolent and extravagant manner with regard to our own countrymen; the punishments of which let us not receive from the Romans, but from God himself, as executed by our own hands; for these will be more moderate than the other.

"Let our wives die before they are abused, and our children before they have tasted of slavery; and after we have slain them, let us bestow that glorious benefit upon one another mutually, and preserve ourselves in freedom, as an excellent funeral monument for us. But first let us destroy our money and the fortress by fire; for I am well assured that this would be a great grief to the Romans, that they shall not be able to seize upon our bodies, and shall fail of our wealth also: and let us spare nothing but our provisions; for they will be a testimonial when we are dead, that we were not subdued for want of necessaries, but that, according to our original resolution, we have preferred death before slavery."

This was Eleazar's speech to them. Yet did not the opinions of all the auditors acquiesce therein: but although some of them were very zealous to put his advice in practice, and were in a manner filled with pleasure at it, and thought death to be a good thing, yet had those that were more effeminate a commiseration for their wives and families; and when these men were especially moved by the prospect of their own certain death, they looked wistfully at one another, and by the tears that were in their eyes, declared their dissent from his opinion.

When Eleazar saw these people in such fear, and that their souls were dejected at so prodigious a proposal, he was afraid lest perhaps these effeminate persons should by their lamentations and tears enfeeble those that heard what he had said courageously; so he did not leave off exhorting them, but stirred up himself, and recollecting proper arguments for raising their courage, he undertook to speak more sublimely to them, and that concerning the immortality of the soul.

So he made a lamentable groan, and fixing his eyes intently on those that wept, he spake thus: "Truly I was greatly mistaken, when I thought to be assisting brave men who struggled hard for their liberty, and such as were resolved either to live with honour, or else to die: I find that you are such people as are no better than others, either in virtue or in courage, and are afraid of dying, though you be delivered thereby from the greatest miseries, while you ought to make no delay in this matter, nor to await anyone to give you a good advice; for the laws of our country, and of God himself, have from ancient times, and as soon as ever we could use our reason, continually taught us, and our forefathers have corroborated the same doctrine by their actions, and by their bravery of mind, that it is life that is a calamity to men, and not death; for this last affords our souls their liberty, and sends them by a removal into their own place of purity, where they are to be insensible of all sorts of misery; for while souls are tied down to a mortal body, they are partakers of its miseries; and really to speak the truth, they are themselves dead; for the union of what is divine to what is mortal, is unsuitable.

"It is true, the power of the soul is great, even when it is imprisoned in a mortal body: for by moving it after a way that is invisible, it makes the body a sensible instrument, and causes it to advance farther in its actions, than mortal nature could otherwise do. However, when it is freed from that weight which draws it down to the earth and is hung on to it, and obtains its own proper place, it does then become a partaker of that blessed power, and those abilities, which are then every way incapable of being hindered in their operations. It continues invisible, indeed, to the eyes of men, as does God himself; for certainly it is not itself seen, while it is in the body; for it is there after an invisible manner, and when it is freed from it, it is still not seen. It is this soul which hath one nature, and that an incorruptible one also; but yet is it the cause of the change that is made in the body; for whatsoever it be which the soul touches, that lives and flourishes, and from whatsoever it is removed, that withers away and dies: such a degree is there in it of immortality.

"Let me produce the state of sleep as a most evident demonstration of the truth of what I say; wherein souls, when the body does not distract them, have the sweetest rest depending on themselves, and conversing with God, by their alliance to him; they then go everywhere, and foretell many futurities beforehand. And why are we afraid of death, while we are pleased with the rest that we have in sleep? And how absurd a thing is it to pursue after liberty while we are alive, and yet to envy it to ourselves where it will be eternal?

"We, therefore, who have been brought up in a discipline of our own, ought to become an example to others of our readiness to die. Yet, if we do stand in need of foreigners to support us in this matter, let us regard those Indians who profess the exercise of philosophy; for these brave men do but unwillingly undergo the time of life, and look upon it as a necessary servitude; and make haste to let their souls loose from their bodies: nay, when no misfortune presses them to it, nor drives them upon it, these have such a desire of a life of immortality, that they tell other men beforehand that they are about to depart; and nobody hinders them, but everyone thinks them happy men, and gives them letters to be carried to their familiar friends [that are dead]; so firmly and certainly do they believe that souls converse with one another in the [other world].

"So when these men have heard all such commands that were to be given them, they deliver their body to the fire, in order to their getting their soul a separation from the body in the greatest purity; and die in the midst of hymns of commendation made to them; for their dearest friends conduct them to their death more readily than do any of the rest of mankind conduct their fellow-citizens when they are going a very long journey, who at the same time weep on their own account, but look upon the others as happy persons, as so soon to be made partakers of the immortal order of beings.

"Are not we, therefore, ashamed to have lower notions than the Indians? and by our own cowardice to lay a base reproach upon the laws of our country, which are so much desired and imitated by all mankind? But put the case that we had been brought up under another persuasion, and taught that life is the greatest good which men are capable of, and that death is a calamity: however, the circumstances we are now in ought to be an inducement to us to bear such calamity courageously, since it is by the will of God, and by necessity that we are to die; for it now appears that God hath made such a decree against the whole Jewish nation, that we are to be deprived of this life which [he knew] we would not make a due use of.

"For do not you ascribe the occasion of our present condition to yourselves, nor think the Romans are the true occasion that this war we have had with them is become so destructive to us all: these things have not come to pass by their power, but a more powerful cause hath intervened, and made us afford them an occasion of their appearing to be conquerors over us. What Roman weapons, I pray you, were those, by which the Jews at Caesarea were slain? On the contrary, when they were no way disposed to rebel, but were all the while keeping their seventh day festival, and did not so much as lift up their hands against the citizens of Caesarea, yet did those citizens run upon them in great crowds, and cut their throats, and the throats of their wives and children, and this without any regard to the Romans themselves; who never took us for their enemies till we revolted from them.

"But some may be ready to say, that truly the people of Caesarea had always a quarrel against those that lived among them; and that when an opportunity offered itself, they only satisfied the old rancour they had against them. What then shall we say to those of Scythopolis, who ventured to wage war with us on account of the Greeks nor did they do it by way of revenge upon the Romans, when they acted in concert with our countrymen. Wherefore you see how little our good will and fidelity to them profited us, while they were slain, they and their whole families, after the most inhuman manner, which was all the requital that was made them for the assistance they had afforded the others. For that very same destruction which they had prevented the Greeks of Scythopolis from suffering at our hands, did they suffer themselves from them, as if they had been ready to be the actors against them.

"It would be too long for me to speak at this time of every destruction brought upon us: for you cannot but know, that there was not any one Syrian city, which did not slay their Jewish inhabitants, and were not more bitter enemies to us than were the Romans themselves: nay, even those of Damascus, when they were able to allege no tolerable pretence against us, filled their city with the most barbarous slaughters of our people, and cut the throats of eighteen thousand Jews, with their wives and children. And as to the multitude of those that were slain in Egypt, and that with torments also, we have been informed they were more than sixty thousand. Now these being indeed in a foreign country, and so naturally being unable to oppose their enemies, were killed in the manner forementioned: but as for all those of us who have waged war against the Romans, in our own country, had we not sufficient reason to have sure hopes of victory?

"For we had arms, and walls and fortresses so prepared as not to be easily taken, and courage not to be moved by any dangers in the cause of liberty, which encouraged us all to revolt from the Romans. But then, these advantages sufficed us but for a short time, and only raised our hopes, while they really proved to be the origin of our miseries; for all we had hath been taken from us, and all hath fallen under our enemies, as if these advantages were only intended to render their victory over us the more glorious, and were not disposed for the preservation of those by whom these preparations were made. And as for those that are already dead in the war, it is reasonable we should esteem them blessed, for they are dead in defending, and not in betraying their liberty; but as to the multitude of those that are now under the Romans, who would not pity their condition? and who would not make haste to die, before he would suffer the same miseries with them?

"Some of them have been put upon the rack, and tortured with fire and whippings, and so died. Some have been half devoured by wild beasts, and yet have been reserved alive to be devoured by them a second time, in order to afford laughter and sport to our enemies; and such of those as are alive still, are to be looked on as the most miserable, who being so desirous of death, could not come at it. And where is now that great city, the metropolis of the Jewish nation? which was fortified by so many walls round about, which had so many fortresses and large towers to defend it, which could hardly contain the instruments prepared for the war, and which had so many ten thousands of men to fight for it?

"Where is this city that was believed to have God himself inhabiting therein? It is now demolished to the very foundations, and hath nothing but that monument of it preserved, I mean the camp of those that have destroyed it, which still dwells upon its ruins; some unfortunate old men also lie upon the ashes of the temple, and a few women are there preserved alive by the enemy, for their bitter shame and reproach. Now, who is there that revolves these things in his mind, and yet is able to bear the sight of the sun, though he might live out of danger? Who is there so much his country's enemy, or so unmanly, and so desirous of living, as not to repent that he is still alive? And I cannot but wish that we had all died, before we had seen that holy city demolished by the hands of our enemies, or the foundations of our holy temple dug up after so profane a manner.

"But since we had a generous hope that deluded us, as if we might perhaps have been able to avenge ourselves on our enemies on that account, though it be now become vanity, and hath left us alone in this distress, let us make haste to die bravely. Let us pity ourselves, our children, and our wives, while it is in our own power to shew pity to them: for we were born to die, as well as those were whom we have begotten: nor is it in the power of the most happy to avoid it. But for abuses, and slavery, and the sight of our wives led away after an ignominious manner, with their children, these are not such evils as are natural and necessary among men; although such as do not prefer death before those miseries, when it is in their power so to do, must undergo even them, on account of their own cowardice.

"We revolted from the Romans with great pretensions to courage, and when, at the very last, they invited us to preserve ourselves, we would not comply with them. Who will not, therefore, believe that they will certainly be in a rage at us, in case they can take us alive? Miserable will then be the young men, who will be strong enough in their bodies to sustain many torments; miserable also will be those of elder years, who will not be able to bear those calamities which young men might sustain.

"One man will see his wife outraged, or will be obliged to hear the voice of his son implore help of his father; when his hands are bound. But while our hands are still at liberty, and have a sword in them, let them then be subservient to us in our glorious design: let us die before we become slaves under our enemies, and let us go out of the world, together with our children, and our wives, in a state of freedom.

"This it is that our laws command us to do; this it is that our wives and children crave at our hands; nay, God himself hath brought this necessity upon us, while the Romans desire the contrary, and are afraid lest any of us should die before we are taken.

"Let us therefore make haste, and instead of affording them so much pleasure, as they hope for in getting us under their power, let us leave them an example which shall at once cause their astonishment at our death, and their admiration of our hardiness therein."

CHAPTER IX

How the people that were in the fortress were prevailed on by the words of Eleazar, two women and five children only excepted, and all submitted to be killed by one another.

Now as Eleazar was proceeding on this exhortation, they all cut him off short, and made haste to do the work, as full of an unconquerable ardour of mind, and moved with a demoniacal fury. So they went their ways, as one still endeavouring to be before another, and as thinking that this eagerness would be a demonstration of their courage and good conduct, if they could avoid appearing in the last class; so great was the zeal they were in to slay their wives and children, and themselves also. Nor indeed, when they came to the work itself, did their courage fail them, as one might imagine it would have done, but they then held fast the same resolution, without wavering, which they had upon the hearing of Eleazar's speech, while yet everyone of them still retained the natural passion of love to themselves and their families, because the reasoning they went upon appeared to them to be very just, that they were doing what was best to those that were dearest to them: for the husbands tenderly embraced their wives, and took their children into their arms, and gave the longest parting kisses to them, with tears in their eyes.

Yet at the same time did they complete what they had resolved on, as if they were assisted by the hands of strangers; and they had for their comfort, the thought in doing this execution, of the miseries they were to suffer from their enemies. Nor was there at length anyone of these men found that scrupled to act his part in this terrible execution, but everyone of them dispatched his dearest relations. Miserable men indeed were they whose distress forced them to slay their own wives and children with their own hands, as the lightest of those evils that were before them.

So they being not able to bear the grief they were under for what they had done any longer, and esteeming it an injury to those they had slain, to live even the shortest space of time after them, they presently laid all they had upon an heap, and set fire to it. They then chose ten men by lot out of them, to slay all the rest: everyone of which laid himself down by his wife and children on the ground, and threw his arms about them, and they offered their necks to the stroke of those who by lot executed that melancholy office: and when these ten had, without fear, slain them all, they made the same rule for casting lots for themselves, that he whose lot it was should first kill the other nine, and after all should kill himself.

Accordingly, all these had courage sufficient to be no way behind one another in doing or suffering; so, for a conclusion, the nine offered their necks to the executioner, and he who was the last of all took a view of all the other bodies, lest perchance some or other among so many that were slain should want his assistance to be quite dispatched, and when he perceived that they were all slain, he set fire to the palace, and with the great force of his hand ran his sword entirely through himself, and fell down dead near to his own relations. So these people died with this intention, that they would leave not so much as one soul among them all alive to be subject to the Romans.

Yet there was an ancient woman, and another who was of kin to Eleazar, and superior to most women in prudence and learning, with five children who had concealed themselves in the underground conduits through which drinking-waters passed, and were hidden there when the rest were intent upon the slaughter of one another. Those others were nine hundred and sixty in number, the women and children being withal included in that computation. This tragedy took place on the fifteenth day of the month Xanthicus [Nisan] (May 2, 72).

Now for the Romans, they expected that they should be fought in the morning, when accordingly they put on their armour, and laid bridges of planks across from their banks, to make an assault upon the fortress, which they did; but saw nobody as an enemy, but a terrible solitude on every side with a fire within the palace, as well as a perfect silence. So they were at a loss to guess at what had happened.

At length they made a shout, as if it had been at a blow given by the battering ram, to try whether they could bring anyone out that was within; the women heard this noise, and came out of their underground cavern, and informed the Romans what had been done, as it was done, and the one of them clearly described all both what was said, and what was done, and the manner of it; yet did they not easily give their attention to her, disbelieving in the magnitude of the deed: they also attempted to put the fire out, and quickly cutting themselves away through it, they came within the palace, and so met with the multitude of the slain, but could take no pleasure in the fact, though it were done to their enemies. Nor could they do other than wonder at the courage of their resolution, and the immoveable contempt of death which so great a number of them had shewn, when they went through with such an action as that was.

Mishnah

The Mishnah and the Gemara, component parts of the Talmud, have been traditionally called *Torah sheh-b'al peh,* or the Oral Law. During the centuries that the oral tradition had been developing among the Jews in Palestine and Babylonia it was considered sacrilege to write down the common usages and the discussions, enactments and laws of the rabbis—for nothing was to compete with the sanctity of the Written Law, the Torah. When the Mishnah was redacted in 200 C.E. by Rabbi Judah ha–Nasi, it was to a degree a revolutionary step. As the body of oral material grew too weighty for even those of prodigious memory—and it must be remembered that with a lack of books memory was perforce keener—various schools (like that of Rabbi Akiba and Rabbi Meir) began to keep notes of discussions, for internal purposes only and not for publication. These notes eventually were the point of transition from nonwriting to writing of the Oral Law, and Rabbi Judah made full use of this written material. His code also brought uniformity at a time when many schools were utilizing their own private collections of laws.

The Mishnah is divided into six principal divisions, or orders:

1. "Seeds," laws pertaining to agriculture.
2. "Festivals," laws of the Sabbath and the holidays.
3. "Women," laws concerning marriage and divorce.
4. "Damages," civil and criminal laws.
5. "Sacred Things," laws about the Temple and sacrifices.
6. "Purifications," laws of things clean and unclean.

Each order has about ten tractates, which are subdivided into chapters and paragraphs. References to the Mishnah are made by tractate, chapter and paragraph. Thus, if one wished to refer to the opening lines of *Pirke Avot,* one would cite *Avot* 1:1.

The Mishnah is written in a terse, lucid Hebrew that reflects contemporary usage (first and second centuries C.E.) in Palestine, a language that differs strikingly from Biblical Hebrew in vocabulary, syntax, and idiom. By the time the Mishnah was written, Palestine had already come under the influence of its Greek and Roman conquerers and the stamp of these languages is imprinted to a degree in Mishnaic Hebrew.

The redactor of the Mishnah was Judah ha-Nasi (135–210), a descendant of Hillel, who succeeded his father Simeon ben Gamaliel as Patriarch. With the completion of this lifetime task Rabbi Judah, the chief rabbinic authority of his generation, had contributed to Judaism one of the books that molded the development of Judaism and gave it its most comprehensive legal compilation.

In sum, the Mishnah is a commentary and extension of the Torah statutes, as in turn the Gemara is a discussion and extended commentary upon the Mishnah. With the cessation of Jewish hegemony in Palestine in 70 C.E., and the growing number of exilic communities, the Mishnah served as a cohesive force in the development of Judaism, a spiritual substitute for a no longer viable political center. The Mishnah, too, serves as the core for the two Talmuds, the Babylonian (Talmud *Bavli)* and the Palestinian or Jerusalem (Talmud *Yerushalmi*), which base their differing discussions on exactly the same Mishnaic text.

The laws of the Mishnah were considered as sacred as the Torah, as is indicated by the opening of the *Pirke Avot:* the direct and unbroken link between Moses and the rabbinic sages. Although statements in the Mishnah were not always based directly on Scriptural authority—accepted usages, unwritten practises, oral traditions, as well as logical extensions of sacred writ, deducible rules and exegesis are the presumed link between the Torah, Jewry's basic constitution, and the Mishnah.

Owing to his stature as Patriarch, Rabbi Judah's Mishnah was immediately accepted as the authoritative code—but, because of Judaism's continually developing institutions, not as a permanent corpus of law.

Even at the time of its compilation the Mishnah was dealing with practises no longer current. The Temple had been destroyed for more than a century, yet the laws dealt with it as though it were in existence (*c.f.*, the entire fifth order, "Sacred Things"). Here, and in other places, the fusion of past and present showed the hope for eventual national restoration; and moreover, played an important part in developing a sense of nationhood and peoplehood among Jews scattered in various corners of the world.

In the Mishnah Rabbi Judah collected the *halakhot* (laws) passed down through many generations—laws that had partly been preserved in private scrolls and in memories of countless scholars. Seeking to have his Mishnah serve as a compilation, not as an authoritative code of law, he arranged it and systematized it; recorded divergent views, even if they were in the minority; and occasionally offered his own ruling.

Pirke Avot is an anthology of rabbinic maxims, and is the oldest compilation of ethical statements of the Mishnah. It is the only tractate without halakhic (legal) content, but is composed solely of epigrams and moral teachings attributed to generations of sages.

The treatise is the most popular in Talmudic literature. Ever since Gaonic times (seventh to eleventh centuries) it has been studied on the six Sabbath afternoons between Passover and Shevuot. (The sixth chapter, not originally a part of *Pirke Avot*, was added in order to have a sixth unit for the sixth Sabbath). *Avot* is included in the Siddur of the Ashkenazic rite; thus it has become available to the average Jew who could easily understand its clear and concise Mishnaic Hebrew. *Avot* has been published in many editions and with many commentaries and translations.

The two main topics of *Rosh Hashana* are:

1) the Jewish New Year and the sanctification of the new month—so crucial for establishing the precise date of the holidays, and

2) the blowing of the *shofar,* the ram's horn.

The Mishnah colorfully depicts the manner in which the new moon was proclaimed, and who may be a witness and who may not (a dice player, for instance, may not); it also describes vividly a famous conflict between the sages, and its peaceful resolution.

In their respective accents on ethical and legal-historical material, both *Pirke Avot* and *Rosh Hashana* are typical of the spirit of the Mishnah.

PIRKE AVOT (ETHICS OF THE FATHERS)

1. 1. Moses received the Law from Sinai and committed it to Joshua, and Joshua to the elders, and the elders to the Prophets; and the Prophets committed it to the men of the Great Synagogue. They said three things: Be deliberate in judgement, raise up many disciples, and make a fence around the Law.

2. Simeon the Just was of the remnants of the Great Synagogue. He used to say: By three things is the world sustained: by the Law, by the [Temple-]service, and by deeds of loving-kindness.

3. Antigonus of Soko received [the Law] from Simeon the Just. He used to say: Be not like slaves that minister to the master for the sake of receiving a bounty, but be like slaves that minister to the master not for the sake of receiving a bounty; and let the fear of Heaven be upon you.

4. Jose b. Joezer of Zeredah and Jose b. Johanan of Jerusalem received [the Law] from them. Jose b. Joezer of Zeredah said: Let thy house be a meeting-house for the Sages, and sit amid the dust of their feet and drink in their words with thirst.

5. Jose b. Johanan of Jerusalem said: Let thy house be opened wide and let the needy be members of thy household; and talk not much with womankind. They said this of a man's own wife, how much more of his fellow's wife! Hence the Sages have said: He that talks much with womankind brings evil upon himself and neglects the study of the Law and at the last will inherit Gehenna.

6. Joshua b. Perahyah and Nittai the Arbelite received [the Law] from them. Joshua b. Perahyah said: Provide thyself with a teacher and get thee a fellow[-disciple]; and when thou judgest any man incline the balance in his favour.

7. Nittai the Arbelite said: Keep thee far from an evil neighbour and consort not with the wicked and lose not belief in retribution.

8. Judah b. Tabbai and Simeon b. Shetah received [the Law] from them. Judah b. Tabbai said: Make not thyself like them that would influence the judges; and when the suitors stand before thee let them be in thine eyes as wicked men, and when they have departed from before thee let them be in thine eyes as innocent, so soon as they have accepted the judgement.

9. Simeon b. Shetah said: Examine the witnesses diligently and be cautious in thy words lest from them they learn to swear falsely.

10. Shemaiah and Abtalion received [the Law] from them. Shemaiah said: Love labour and hate mastery and seek not acquaintance with the ruling power.

11. Abtalion said: Ye Sages, give heed to your words lest ye incur the penalty of exile and ye be exiled to a place of evil waters, and the disciples that come after you drink [of them] and die, and the name of Heaven be profaned.

12. Hillel and Shammai received [the Law] from them. Hillel said: Be of the disciples of Aaron, loving peace and pursuing peace, loving mankind and bringing them nigh to the Law.

13. He used to say: A name made great is a name destroyed, and he that increases not decreases, and he that learns not is worthy of death, and he that makes worldly use of the crown shall perish.

14. He used to say: If I am not for myself who is for me? and being for mine own self what am I? and if not now, when?

15. Shammai said: Make thy [study of the] Law a fixed habit; say little and do much, and receive all men with a cheerful countenance.

16. Rabban Gamaliel said: Provide thyself with a teacher and remove thyself from doubt, and tithe not overmuch by guesswork.

17. Simeon his son said: All my days have I grown up among the Sages and I have found naught better for a man than silence; and not the expounding [of the Law] is the chief thing but the doing [of it]; and he that multiplies words occasions sin.

18. Rabban Simeon b. Gamaliel said: By three things is the world sustained: by truth, by judgement, and by peace, as it is written, *Execute the judgement of truth and peace* [Zech. 8:16].

2. 1. Rabbi said: Which is the straight way that a man should choose? That which is an honour to him and gets him honour from men. And be heedful of a light precept as of a weighty one, for thou knowest not the recompense of reward of each precept; and reckon the loss through [the fulfilling of] a precept against its reward, and the reward [that comes] from transgression against its loss. Consider three things and thou wilt not fall into the hands of transgression: know what is above thee—a seeing eye and a hearing ear and all thy deeds written in a book.

2. Rabban Gamaliel the son of R. Judah the Patriarch said: Excellent is study of the Law together with worldly occupation, for toil in them both puts sin out of mind. But all study of the Law without [worldly] labour comes to naught at the last and brings sin in its train. And let all them that labour with the congregation labour with them for the sake of Heaven, for the merit of their fathers supports them and their righteousness endures for ever. And as for you, [will God say,] I count you worthy of great reward as though ye [yourselves] had wrought.

3. Be heedful of the ruling power for they bring no man nigh to them save for their own need: they seem to be friends such time as it is to their gain, but they stand not with a man in his time of stress.

4. He used to say: Do his will as if it was thy will that he may do thy will as if it was his will. Make thy will of none effect before his will that he

may make the will of others of none effect before thy will.

5. Hillel said: Keep not aloof from the congregation and trust not in thyself until the day of thy death, and judge not thy fellow until thou art come to his place, and say not of a thing which cannot be understood that it will be understood in the end; and say not, When I have leisure I will study: perchance thou wilt never have leisure.

6. He used to say: A brutish man dreads not sin, and an ignorant man cannot be saintly, and the shamefast man cannot learn, and the impatient man cannot teach, and he that engages overmuch in trade cannot become wise; and where there are no men strive to be a man.

7. Moreover he saw a skull floating on the face of the water and he said unto it, Because thou drownedst they drowned thee and at the last they that drowned thee shall be drowned. He used to say: The more flesh the more worms; the more possessions the more care; the more women the more witchcrafts; the more bondwomen the more lewdness; the more bondmen the more thieving; the more study of the Law the more life; the more schooling the more wisdom; the more counsel the more understanding; the more righteousness the more peace. If a man has gained a good name he has gained [somewhat] for himself; if he has gained for himself words of the Law he has gained for himself life in the world to come.

8. Rabban Johanan b. Zakkai received [the Law] from Hillel and from Shammai. He used to say: If thou hast wrought much in the Law claim not merit for thyself, for to this end wast thou created. Five disciples had Rabban Johanan b. Zakkai, and these are they: R. Eliezer b. Hyrcanus, and R. Joshua b. Hananiah, and R. Jose the Priest, and R. Simeon b. Nathaniel, and R. Eleazar b. Arak. Thus used he to recount their praise: Eliezer b. Hyrcanus is a plastered cistern which loses not a drop; Joshua b. Hananiah—happy is she that bare him; Jose the Priest is a saintly man; Simeon b. Nathaniel is fearful of sin; Eleazar b. Arak is an ever-flowing spring. He used to say: If all the Sages of Israel were in the one scale of the balance and Eliezer b. Hyrcanus in the other, he would outweigh them all. Abba Saul said in his name: If all the Sages of Israel were in the one scale of the balance and with them Eliezer b. Hyrcanus, and Eleazar b. Arak was in the other, he would outweigh them all.

9. He said to them: Go forth and see which is the good way to which a man should cleave. R. Eliezer said, A good eye. R. Joshua said, A good companion. R. Jose said, A good neighbour. R. Simeon said, One that sees what will be. R. Eleazar said, A good heart. He said to them: I approve the words of Eleazar b. Arak more than your words, for in his words are your words included. He said to them: Go forth and see which is the evil way which a man should shun. R. Eliezer said, An evil eye. R. Joshua said, An evil companion. R. Jose said, An evil neighbour. R. Simeon said, He that borrows and does not repay. He that borrows from man is as one that borrows from God, for it is written, *The wicked borroweth and payeth not again but the righteous dealeth graciously and*

giveth [Ps. 37:21]. R. Eleazar said, An evil heart. He said to them: I approve the words of Eleazar b. Arak more than your words for in his words are your words included.

10. They [each] said three things. R. Eliezer said: Let the honour of thy fellow be dear to thee as thine own, and be not easily provoked, and repent one day before thy death; and warm thyself before the fire of the Sages, but be heedful of their glowing coals lest thou be burned, for their bite is the bite of a jackal and their sting the sting of a scorpion and their hiss the hiss of a serpent, and all their words are like coals of fire.

11. R. Joshua said: The evil eye and the evil nature and hatred of mankind put a man out of the world.

12. R. Jose said: Let the property of thy fellow be dear to thee as thine own; and fit thyself for the study of the Law, for [the knowledge of] it is not thine by inheritance; and let all thy deeds be done for the sake of Heaven.

13. R. Simeon said: Be heedful in the reciting of the *Shema* and in the *Tefillah;* and when thou prayest make not thy prayer a fixed form, but [a plea for] mercies and supplications before God, for it is written, *For he is gracious and full of compassion, slow to anger, and plenteous in mercy, and repenteth him of the evil* [Joel 2:13]; and be not wicked in thine own sight.

14. R. Eleazar said: Be alert to study the Law and know how to make answer to an unbeliever, and know before whom thou toilest and who is thy taskmaster who shall pay thee the reward of thy labour.

15. R. Tarfon said: The day is short and the task is great and the labourers are idle and the wage is abundant and the master of the house is urgent.

16. He used to say: It is not thy part to finish the task, yet thou art not free to desist from it. If thou hast studied much in the Law much reward will be given thee, and faithful is thy taskmaster who shall pay thee the reward of thy labour. And know that the recompense of the reward of the righteous is for the time to come.

3. 1. Akabya b. Mahalaleel said: Consider three things and thou wilt not fall into the hands of transgression. Know whence thou art come and whither thou art going and before whom thou art about to give account and reckoning. 'Whence thou art come'—from a putrid drop; 'and whither thou art going'—to the place of dust, worm, and maggot; 'and before whom thou art about to give account and reckoning'—before the King of kings of kings, the Holy One, blessed is he.

2. R. Hanina the Prefect of the Priests said: Pray for the peace of the ruling power, since but for fear of it men would have swallowed up each other alive. R. Hananiah b. Teradion said: If two sit together and no words of the Law [are spoken] between them, there is the seat of the scornful, as it is written, *Nor sitteth in the seat of the scornful* [Ps. 1:1]. But if two sit together and words of the Law [are spoken] between them, the Divine

Presence rests between them, as it is written, *Then they that feared the Lord spake one with another: and the Lord hearkened, and heard, and a book of remembrance was written before him, for them that feared the Lord, and that thought upon his name* [Mal. 3:16]. Scripture speaks here of 'two'; whence [do we learn] that if even one sits and occupies himself in the Law, the Holy One, blessed is he, appoints him a reward? Because it is written, *Let him sit alone and keep silence, because he hath laid it upon him* [Lam. 3:28].

3. R. Simeon said: If three have eaten at one table and have not spoken over it words of the Law, it is as though they had eaten of the sacrifices of the dead [Ps. 106:28], for it is written, *For all tables are full of vomit and filthiness without God* [Is. 28:8]. But if three have eaten at one table and have spoken over it words of the Law, it is as if they had eaten from the table of God, for it is written, *And he said unto me, This is the table that is before the Lord* [Ez. 41:22].

4. R. Hananiah b. Hakinai said: He that wakes in the night or that walks alone by the way and turns his heart to vanity, is guilty against his own soul.

5. R. Nehunya b. Ha-Kanah said: He that takes upon himself the yoke of the Law, from him shall be taken away the yoke of the kingdom and the yoke of worldly care; but he that throws off the yoke of the Law, upon him shall be laid the yoke of the kingdom and the yoke of worldly care.

6. R. Halafta b. Dosa of Kefar Hanania said: If ten men sit together and occupy themselves in the Law, the Divine Presence rests among them, for it is written, *God standeth in the congregation of God* [Ps. 82:1]. And whence [do we learn this] even of five? Because it is written, *And hath founded his group upon the earth* [Am. 9:6]. And whence even of three? Because it is written, *He judgeth among the judges* [Ps. 82:1]. And whence even of two? Because it is written, *Then they that feared the Lord spake one with another: and the Lord hearkened, and heard* [Mal. 3:16]. And whence even of one? Because it is written, *In every place where I record my name I will come unto thee and I will bless thee* [Ex. 20:24].

7. R. Eleazar b. Judah of Bartotha said: Give unto him what is his for thou and what thou hast are his; and it is written in [the Scripture concerning] David, *For all things come of thee, and of thine own have we given thee* [I Chron. 29:14].

8. R. Jacob said: If a man was walking by the way and studying and he ceased his study and said, 'How fine is this tree!' or 'How fine is this ploughed field!' the Scripture reckons it to him as though he was guilty against his own soul.

9. R. Dosethai b. Yannai said in the name of R. Meir: He that forgets one word of his study, the Scripture reckons it to him as though he was guilty against his own soul, for it is written, *Only take heed to thyself, and keep thy soul diligently, lest thou forget the words which thine eyes saw* [Deut. 4:9]. Could this be even if his study was too hard for him? Scrip-

ture says: *And lest they depart from thy heart all the days of thy life;* thus he is not guilty against his own soul unless he sits and puts them away from his heart.

10. R. Hanina b. Dosa said: He whose fear of sin comes before his wisdom, his wisdom endures; but he whose wisdom comes before his fear of sin, his wisdom does not endure. He used to say: He whose works exceed his wisdom, his wisdom endures; but he whose wisdom exceeds his works, his wisdom does not endure.

11. He used to say: He in whom the spirit of mankind finds pleasure, in him the spirit of God finds pleasure; but he in whom the spirit of mankind finds no pleasure, in him the spirit of God finds no pleasure. R. Dosa b. Harkinas said: Morning sleep and midday wine and children's talk and sitting in the meeting-houses of the ignorant people put a man out of the world.

12. R. Eleazar of Modiim said: If a man profanes the Hallowed Things and despises the set feasts and puts his fellow to shame publicly and makes void the covenant of Abraham our father, and discloses meanings in the Law which are not according to the *Halakah,* even though a knowledge of the Law and good works are his, he has no share in the world to come.

13. R. Ishmael says: Be swift [to do service] to a superior, and kindly to the young, and receive all men cheerfully.

14. R. Akiba said: Jesting and levity accustom a man to lewdness. The tradition is a fence around the Law; tithes are a fence around riches; vows are a fence around abstinence; a fence around wisdom is silence.

15. He used to say: Beloved is a man for he was created in the image [of God]; still greater was the love in that it was made known to him that he was created in the image of God, as it is written, *For in the image of God made he man* [Gen. 9:6]. Beloved are Israel for they were called children of God; still greater was the love in that it was made known to them that they were called children of God, as it is written, *Ye are the children of the Lord your God* [Deut. 14:1]. Beloved are Israel, for to them was given the precious instrument; still greater was the love, in that it was made known to them that to them was given the precious instrument by which the world was created, as it is written, *For I give you good doctrine; forsake ye not my Law* [Prov. 4:2].

16. All is foreseen, but freedom of choice is given; and the world is judged by grace, yet all is according to the excess of works [that be good or evil].

17. He used to say: All is given against a pledge, and the net is cast over all living; the shop stands open and the shopkeeper gives credit and the account-book lies open and the hand writes and every one that wishes to borrow let him come and borrow; but the collectors go their round continually every day and exact payment of men with their consent or without their consent, for they have that on which they can rely; and the judgement is a judgement of truth; and all is made ready for the banquet.

18. R. Eleazar b. Azariah said: If there is no study of the Law there is no seemly behaviour, if there is no seemly behaviour there is no study of the Law; if there is no wisdom there is no fear [of God], if there is no fear [of God] there is no wisdom; if there is no knowledge there is no discernment, if there is no discernment there is no knowledge; if there is no meal there is no study of the Law, if there is no study of the Law there is no meal. He used to say: He whose wisdom is more abundant than his works, to what is he like? To a tree whose branches are abundant but whose roots are few; and the wind comes and uproots it and overturns it, as it is written, *He shall be like a tamarisk in the desert and shall not see when good cometh; but shall inhabit the parched places in the wilderness* [Jer. 17:6]. But he whose works are more abundant than his wisdom, to what is he like? To a tree whose branches are few but whose roots are many; so that even if all the winds in the world come and blow against it, it cannot be stirred from its place, as it is written, *He shall be as a tree planted by the waters, and that spreadeth out his roots by the river, and shall not fear when heat cometh, and his leaf shall be green; and shall not be careful in the year of drought, neither shall cease from yielding fruit* [Jer. 17:8].

19. R. Eleazar Hisma said: [The rules about] Bird-offerings and the onset of menstruation—these are essentials of the *Halakoth;* but the calculations of the equinoxes and gematria are but the savoury dishes of wisdom.

4. 1. Ben Zoma said: Who is wise? He that learns from all men, as it is written, *From all my teachers have I got understanding* [Ps. 119:99]. Who is mighty? He that subdues his [evil] nature, as it is written, *He that is slow to anger is better than the mighty, and he that ruleth his spirit than he that taketh a city* [Prov. 16:32]. Who is rich? He that rejoices in his portion, as it is written, *When thou eatest the labour of thy hands happy shalt thou be, and it shall be well with thee* [Ps. 128:2]. *Happy shalt thou be*—in this world; *and it shall be will with thee*—in the world to come. Who is honoured? He that honours mankind, as it is written, *For them that honour me I will honour, and they that despise me shall be lightly esteemed* [I Sam. 2:30].

2. Ben Azzai said: Run to fulfil the lightest duty even as the weightiest, and flee from transgression; for one duty draws another duty in its train, and one transgression draws another transgression in its train; for the reward of a duty [done] is a duty [to be done], and the reward of one transgression is [another] transgression.

3. He used to say: Despise no man and deem nothing impossible, for there is not a man that has not his hour and there is not a thing that has not its place.

4. Levitas of Jabneh said: Be exceeding lowly of spirit, for the hope of man is but the worm. R. Johanan b. Baroka said: He that profanes the name of Heaven in secret shall be requited openly: in profaning the Name it is all one whether it be done unwittingly or wantonly.

5. R. Ishmael his son said: He that learns in order to teach is granted the means to learn and to teach; but he that learns in order to perform is granted the means to learn and to teach, to observe and to perform. R. Zadok says: Keep not aloof from the congregation, and make not thyself like them that seek to influence the judges. Make them not a crown wherewith to magnify thyself or a spade wherewith to dig. And thus used Hillel to say: He that makes worldly use of the crown shall perish. Thus thou mayest learn that he that makes profit out of the words of the Law removes his life from the world.

6. R. Jose said: He that honours the Law is himself honoured by mankind; and he that dishonours the Law shall himself be dishonoured by mankind.

7. R. Ishmael his son said: He that shuns the office of judge rids himself of enmity and theft and false swearing; and he that is forward in giving a decision is foolish, wicked, and arrogant.

8. He used to say: Judge not alone, for none may judge alone save One. And say not, 'Receive ye my opinion', for it is for them to choose and not for thee.

9. R. Jonathan said: He that fulfils the Law in poverty shall in the end fulfil it in wealth; and he that neglects the Law in wealth shall in the end neglect it in poverty.

10. R. Meir said: Engage not overmuch in business but occupy thyself with the Law; and be lowly in spirit before all men. If thou neglectest the Law many things neglected shall rise against thee; but if thou labourest in the Law He has abundant reward to give thee.

11. R. Eliezer b. Jacob says: He that performs one precept gets for himself one advocate; but he that commits one transgression gets for himself one accuser. Repentance and good works are as a shield against retribution. R. Johanan the Sandal-maker said: Any assembling together that is for the sake of Heaven shall in the end be established, but any that is not for the sake of Heaven shall not in the end be established.

12. R. Eleazar b. Shammua said: Let the honour of thy disciple be as dear to thee as thine own and as the honour of thy companion, and the honour of thy companion as the fear of thy teacher, and the fear of thy teacher as the fear of Heaven.

13. R. Judah said: Be heedful in study, for an unwitting error in study is accounted wanton transgression. R. Simeon said: There are three crowns: the crown of the Law, the crown of the priesthood, and the crown of kingship; but the crown of a good name excels them all.

14. R. Nehorai said: Wander afar to a place of the Law; and say not that it will follow after thee or that thy companions will establish it in thy possession; and lean not upon thine own understanding.

15. R. Yannai said: It is not in our power to explain the well-being of the wicked or the sorrows of the righteous. R. Mattithiah b. Heresh said: Be first in greeting every man; and be a tail to lions and be not a head to jackals.

16. R. Jacob said: This world is like a vestibule before the world to come: prepare thyself in the vestibule that thou mayest enter into the banqueting hall.

17. He used to say: Better is one hour of repentance and good works in this world than the whole life of the world to come; and better is one hour of bliss in the world to come than the whole life of this world.

18. R. Simeon b. Eleazar said: Appease not thy fellow in the hour of his anger, and comfort him not while his dead lies before him, and question him not in the hour of his vow, and strive not to see him in the hour of his disgrace.

19. Samuel the Younger said: *Rejoice not when thine enemy falleth, and let not thine heart be glad when he is overthrown, lest the Lord see it and it displease him, and he turn away his wrath from him* [Prov. 24:17].

20. Elisha b. Abuyah said: He that learns as a child, to what is he like? To ink written on new paper. He that learns as an old man, to what is he like? To ink written on paper that has been blotted out. R. Jose b. Judah of Kefar ha-Babli said: He that learns from the young, to what is he like? To one that eats unripe grapes and drinks wine from his winepress. And he that learns from the aged, to what is he like? To one that eats ripe grapes and drinks old wine. Rabbi said: Look not on the jar but on what is in it; there may be a new jar that is full of old wine and an old one in which is not even new wine.

21. R. Eleazar ha-Kappar said: Jealousy, lust, and ambition put a man out of the world.

22. He used to say: They that have been born [are destined] to die, and they that are dead [are destined] to be made alive, and they that live [after death are destined] to be judged, that men may know and make known and understand that he is God, he is the Maker, he is the Creator, he is the Discerner, he is the Judge, he is the Witness, he is the Complainant, and it is he that shall judge, blessed is he, in whose presence is neither guile nor forgetfulness nor respect of persons nor taking of bribes; for all is his. And know that everything is according to the reckoning. And let not thy [evil] nature promise thee that the grave will be thy refuge: for despite thyself wast thou fashioned, and despite thyself wast thou born, and despite thyself thou livest, and despite thyself thou diest, and despite thyself thou hereafter give account and reckoning before the King of kings of kings, the Holy One, blessed is he.

5. 1. By ten Sayings was the world created. And what does the Scripture teach thereby? Could it not have been created by one Saying? But this was to requite the ungodly which destroy the world that was created by ten Sayings, and to give a goodly reward to the righteous which sustain the world that was created by ten Sayings.

2. There were ten generations from Adam to Noah, to show how great was his longsuffering, for all the generations provoked him continually until he brought upon them the waters of the Flood. There were ten genera-

tions from Noah to Abraham, to show how great was his longsuffering, for all the generations provoked him continually until Abraham our father came and received the reward of them all.

3. With ten temptations was Abraham our father tempted, and he stood steadfast in them all, to show how great was the love of Abraham our father.

4. Ten wonders were wrought for our fathers in Egypt and ten at the Sea. Ten plagues did the Holy One, blessed is he, bring upon the Egyptians in Egypt and at the Sea. With ten temptations did our fathers tempt the Holy One, blessed is he, in the wilderness, as it is written. *Yet have they tempted me these ten times and have not hearkened to my voice* [Num. 14:22].

5. Ten wonders were wrought for our fathers in the Temple: no woman miscarried through the smell of the flesh of the Hallowed Things; and no flesh of the Hallowed Things ever turned putrid; and no fly was seen in the shambles; and the High Priest never suffered a pollution on the Day of Atonement; and the rains never quenched the fire of the woodpile [on the altar]; and no wind prevailed over the pillar of smoke; and never was a defect found in the *Omer* or in the Two Loaves or in the Shewbread, [and the people] stood pressed together yet bowed themselves at ease; and never did serpent or scorpion do harm in Jerusalem; and no man said to his fellow, *The place is too strait for me* [Is. 49:20] that I should lodge in Jerusalem.

6. Ten things were created on the eve of Sabbath between the suns at nightfall: the mouth of the earth, the mouth of the well, the mouth of the she-ass, the rainbow, and the manna and the rod and the Shamir, the letters and the writing and the Tables [of stone]. Some say also: The evil spirits and the sepulchre of Moses and the ram of Abraham our father. Some say also: The tongs made with tongs.

7. There are seven marks of the clod and seven of the wise man. The wise man does not speak before one that is greater than he in wisdom; and he does not break in upon the words of his fellow; and he is not hasty in making answer; he asks what is relevant and makes answer according to the *Halakah;* and he speaks on the first point first and on the last point last; and of what he has heard no tradition he says, 'I have not heard'; and he agrees to what is true. And the opposites of these are the marks of the clod.

8. Seven kinds of retribution come upon the world for seven classes of transgression. If some give tithe and some do not give tithe, there comes famine from drought: some suffer hunger while some have enough. If [all] resolved that they would not give tithe there comes famine from tumult and drought. And if they will not set apart Dough-offering there comes an all-consuming famine. Pestilence comes upon the world because of crimes deserving of the death-penalties enjoined in the Law that are not brought before the court; and because of [the transgressions of the laws of] the

Seventh Year produce. The sword comes upon the world because of the delaying of justice and the perverting of justice; and because of them that teach the Law not according to the *Halakah*.

9. Noisome beasts come upon the world because of false swearing and the profaning of the Name. Exile comes upon the world because of idolatry and incest and the shedding of blood; and because of [neglect of the year of] the Release of the land. At four periods pestilence increases: in the fourth year and in the seventh year and in the year after the seventh year, and at the end of the Feast [of Tabernacles] every year. 'In the fourth year'—because of [neglect of] Poorman's Tithe in the third year; 'in the seventh year'—because of [neglect of] Poorman's Tithe in the sixth year; 'in the year after the seventh year'—because of [transgressing the laws of] Seventh Year produce; 'and at the end of the Feast of [Tabernacles] every year'—because of wrongfully withholding the dues of the poor.

10. There are four types among men: he that says, 'What is mine is mine and what is thine is thine'—this is the common type, and some say that this is the type of Sodom; [he that says,] 'What is mine is thine and what is thine is mine'—he is an ignorant man; [he that says,] 'What is mine is thine and what is thine is thine own'—he is a saintly man; [and he that says,] 'What is thine is mine, and what is mine is mine own'—he is a wicked man.

11. There are four types of character: easy to provoke and easy to appease—his loss is cancelled by his gain; hard to provoke and hard to appease—his gain is cancelled by his loss; hard to provoke and easy to appease—he is a saintly man; easy to provoke and hard to appease—he is a wicked man.

12. There are four types of disciple: swift to hear and swift to lose—his gain is cancelled by his loss; slow to hear and slow to lose—his loss is cancelled by his gain; swift to hear and slow to lose—this is a happy lot; slow to hear and swift to lose—this is an evil lot.

13. There are four types of almsgivers: he that is minded to give but not that others should give—he begrudges what belongs to others; he that is minded that others should give but not that he should give—he begrudges what belongs to himself; he that is minded to give and also that others should give—he is a saintly man; he that is minded not to give himself and that others should not give—he is a wicked man.

14. There are four types among them that frequent the House of Study: he that goes and does not practise—he has the reward of his going; he that practises but does not go—he has the reward of his practising; he that goes and also practises—he is a saintly man; he that neither goes nor practises—he is a wicked man.

15. There are four types among them that sit in the presence of the Sages: the sponge, the funnel, the strainer, and the sifter. 'The sponge'—which soaks up everything; 'the funnel'—which takes in at this end and lets out at the other; 'the strainer'—which lets out the wine and collects the

lees; 'the sifter'—which extracts the coarsely-ground flour and collects the fine flour.

16. If love depends on some [transitory] thing, and the [transitory] thing passes away, the love passes away, too; but if it does not depend on some [transitory] thing it will never pass away. Which love depended on some [transitory] thing? This was the love of Amnon and Tamar. And which did not depend on some [transitory] thing? This was the love of David and Jonathan.

17. Any controversy that is for God's sake shall in the end be of lasting worth, but any that is not for God's sake shall not in the end be of lasting worth. Which controversy was for God's sake? Such was the controversy of Hillel and Shammai. And which was not for God's sake? Such was the controversy of Korah and all his company.

18. He that leads the many to virtue, through him shall no sin befall; but he that leads the many to sin, to him shall be given no means for repentance. Moses was virtuous and he led the many to virtue; the virtue of the many depended on him, as it is written, *He executed the justice of the Lord and his judgements with Israel* [Deut. 33:21]. Jeroboam sinned and he led the many to sin; the sin of the many depended on him, as it is written, *For the sins of Jeroboam which he sinned and wherewith he made Israel to sin* [I Kings 15:30].

19. He in whom are these three things is of the disciples of Abraham our father; but [he in whom are] three other things is of the disciples of Balaam the wicked. A good eye and a humble spirit and a lowly soul— [they in whom are these] are of the disciples of Abraham our father. An evil eye, a haughty spirit, and a proud soul—[they in whom are these] are of the disciples of Balaam the wicked. How do the disciples of Abraham our father differ from the disciples of Balaam the wicked? The disciples of Abraham our father enjoy this world and inherit the world to come, as it is written, *That I may cause those that love me to inherit substance and that I may fill their treasuries* [Prov. 8:21]. The disciples of Balaam the wicked inherit Gehenna and go down to the pit of destruction, as it is written, *But thou, O God, shalt bring them down into the pit of destruction; bloodthirsty and deceitful men shall not live out half their days* [Ps. 55:23].

20. Judah b. Tema said: Be strong as the leopard and swift as the eagle, fleet as the gazelle and brave as the lion to do the will of thy father which is in heaven. He used to say: The shameless are for Gehenna and the shamefast for the garden of Eden. May it be thy will, O Lord our God and the God of our fathers, that the Temple be built speedily in our days, and grant us our portion in thy Law with them that do thy will.

21. He used to say: At five years old [one is fit] for the Scripture, at ten years for the Mishnah, at thirteen for [the fulfilling of] the commandments, at fifteen for the Talmud, at eighteen for the bride-chamber, at twenty for pursuing [a calling], at thirty for authority, at forty for discernment, at fifty for counsel, at sixty for to be an elder, at seventy for grey

hairs, at eighty for special strength, at ninety for bowed back, and at a hundred a man is as one that has [already] died and passed away and ceased from the world.

22. Ben Bag-Bag said: Turn it and turn it again for everything is in it; and contemplate it and grow grey and old over it and stir not from it for than it thou canst have no better rule.

23. Ben He-He said: According to the suffering so is the reward.

6. KINYAN TORAH: [These things] have the Sages taught in the language of the Mishnah. Blessed is he that made choice of them and their Mishnah!

1. Rabbi Meir said: He that occupies himself in the study of the Law for its own sake merits many things, and, still more, he is deserving of the whole world. He is called friend, beloved [of God], lover of God, lover of mankind; and it clothes him with humility and reverence and fits him to become righteous, saintly, upright, and faithful; and it keeps him far from sin and brings him near to virtue, and from him men enjoy counsel and sound knowledge, understanding and might, for it is written, *Counsel is mine and sound knowledge, I am understanding, I have might* [Prov. 8:14]. And it gives him kingship and dominion and discernment in judgement; to him are revealed the secrets of the Law, and he is made like to a never-failing spring and like to a river that flows ever more mightily; and he becomes modest, long-suffering, and forgiving of insult; and it magnifies him and exalts him above all things.

2. R. Joshua b. Levi said: Every day a divine voice goes forth from mount Horeb, proclaiming and saying, "Woe to mankind for their contempt of the Law!" For he that occupies himself not in the study of the Law is called 'reprobate' *(NaZuF)*, as it is written, *As a golden ring in the snout* (*Nezem Zahab b'aF*) *of a swine, so is a fair woman without discretion* [Prov. 11:22]. And it is written, *And the tables were the work of God, and the writing was the writing of God, graven* (haruth) *upon the tables* [Ex. 32:16]. Read not *haruth* but *heruth* (freedom), for thou findest no freeman excepting him that occupies himself in the study of the Law; and he that occupies himself in the study of the Law shall be exalted, for it is written, *From Mattanah to Nahaliel, and from Nahaliel to Bamoth* [Num. 21:19].

3. He that learns from his fellow a single chapter or a single *Halakah* or a single verse or a single expression or even a single letter, must pay him honour, for so we find it with David, king of Israel, who learned only two things from Ahitophel, but called him his teacher, his companion, and his familiar friend; for it is written, *But it was thou, a man mine equal, my companion and my familiar friend* [Ps. 55:13]. And is there not here an inference from the less to the greater?—if David king of Israel, who learned but two things from Ahitophel, called him his teacher, his companion, and his familiar friend, how much more then must he that learns from his fellow a single chapter or a single *Halakah* or a single verse or a single

expression or even a single letter pay him honour! And 'honour' is naught else than 'the Law', for it is written, *The wise shall inherit honour* [Prov. 3:35], and *The perfect shall inherit good* [Prov. 28:10]; and 'good' is naught else than 'the Law', for it is written, *For I give you good doctrine; forsake ye not my Law* [Prov. 4:2].

4. This is the way [to get thee knowledge] of the Law. Thou shalt eat bread with salt *and thou shalt drink water by measure* [Ezek. 4:11], and on the ground shalt thou sleep and thou shalt live a life of trouble the while thou toilest in the Law. If thou doest thus, *Happy shalt thou be and it shall be well with thee* [Ps. 128:2]; *happy shalt thou be*—in this world; *and it shall be well with thee*—in the world to come.

5. Seek not greatness for thyself and covet not honour. Practise more than thou learnest; and crave not after the tables of kings, for thy table is greater than their table and thy crown than their crown; and faithful is thy taskmaster who shall pay thee the reward of thy labour.

6. Greater is [learning in] the Law than priesthood or kingship; for kingship is acquired by thirty excellences and the priesthood by twenty-four; but [learning in] the Law by forty-eight. And these are they: by study, by the hearing of the ear, by the ordering of the lips, by the understanding of the heart, by the discernment of the heart, by awe, by reverence, by humility, by cheerfulness; by attendance on the Sages, by consorting with fellow-students, by close argument with disciples; by assiduity, by [knowledge of] Scripture and Mishnah; by moderation in business, wordly occupation, pleasure, sleep, conversation, and jesting; by longsuffering, by a good heart, by faith in the Sages, by submission to sorrows; [by being] one that recognizes his place and that rejoices in his lot and that makes a fence around his words and that claims no merit for himself; [by being one that is] beloved, that loves God, that loves mankind, that loves well-doing, that loves rectitude, that loves reproof, that shuns honour and boasts not of his learning, and delights not in making decisions; that helps his fellow to bear his yoke, and that judges him favourably, and that establishes him in the truth and establishes him in peace; and that occupies himself assiduously in his study; [by being one] that asks and makes answer, that hearkens and adds thereto; that learns in order to teach and that learns in order to practise; that makes his teacher wiser, that retells exactly what he has heard and reports a thing in the name of him that said it. Lo, thou hast learnt that he that tells a thing in the name of him that said it brings deliverance unto the world, for it is written, *And Esther told the king thereof in Mordecai's name* [Esth. 2:22].

7. Great is the Law, for it gives life to them that practice it both in this world and in the world to come, as it is written, *For they are life unto those that find them, and health to all their flesh* [Prov. 4:22]; and it says, *It shall be health to thy navel and marrow to thy bones* [Prov. 3:8]; and it says, *She is a tree of life to them that lay hold upon her, and happy is everyone that retaineth her* [Prov. 3:18]; and it says, *For they shall be a chaplet of*

grace unto thine head, and chains about thy neck [Prov. 1:9]; and it says, *She shall give to thine head a chaplet of grace, a crown of glory shall she deliver to thee* [Prov. 4:9]; and it says, *For by me thy days shall be multiplied and the years of thy life shall be increased* [Prov. 9:11]; and it says, *Length of days is in her right hand; in her left hand are riches and honour* [Prov. 3:16]; and it says, *For length of days, and years of life, and peace, shall they add to thee* [Prov. 3:2].

8. R. Simeon b. Judah in the name of R. Simeon b. Yohai said: Beauty and strength and riches and honour and wisdom and old age and grey hairs and children are comely to the righteous and comely to the world, for it is written, *The hoary head is a crown of beauty; it shall be found in the way of righteousness* [Prov. 16:31]; and it says, *The glory of young men is their strength and the beauty of old men is the hoary head* [Prov. 20:29]; and it says, *The crown of the wise is their riches* [Prov. 14:24]; and it says, *Children's children are the crown of old men; and the glory of children are their fathers* [Prov. 17:6]; and it says, *Then the moon shall be confounded and the sun ashamed; for the Lord of hosts shall reign in mount Zion and in Jerusalem, and before his elders shall be glory* [Is. 24:23]. R. Simeon b. Menasya said: These seven qualities which the Sages, have reckoned as comely to the righteous were all of them fulfilled in Rabbi and in his sons.

9. R. Jose b. Kisma said: I was once walking by the way and a man met me and greeted me, and I returned his greeting. He said to me, 'Rabbi, from what place are thou?' I answered, 'I come from a great city of Sages and scribes.' He said to me, 'If thou wilt dwell with us in our place I will give thee a thousand thousand golden *denars* and precious stones and pearls.' I answered, 'If thou gavest me all the silver and gold and precious stones and pearls in the world I would not dwell save in a place of the Law.' And thus it is written in the Book of Psalms by David, king of Israel, *The Law of thy mouth is better unto me than thousands of gold and silver* [Ps. 119:72]. Moreover at the time of a man's departure, neither silver nor gold nor precious stones nor pearls go with him, but only [his knowledge of] the Law and good works; for it is written, *When thou walkest, it shall lead thee; when thou sleepest, it shall watch over thee; and when thou awakest it shall talk with thee* [Prov. 6:22]. *When thou walkest it shall lead thee*—in this world; *when thou sleepest, it shall watch over thee*—in the grave; *and when thou awakest, it shall talk with thee*—in the world to come. And it says, *The silver is mine, and the gold is mine, saith the Lord of hosts* [Haggai 2: 8].

10. Five possessions did the Holy One, blessed is He, take to Himself in his world; and these are they: the Law is one possession, and the heaven and earth are one possession, Abraham is one possession, Israel is one possession, and the Temple is one possession. Whence [do we learn this of] the Law? Because it is written, *The Lord possessed me in the beginning of his way, before his works of old* [Prov. 8:22]. Whence [do we learn this of] heaven and earth? Because it is written, *The heaven is my throne, and*

the earth is my footstool; what manner of house will ye build unto me and what place shall be my rest [Is. 66:1]? And it says, *O Lord, how manifold are thy works! In wisdom hast thou made them all: the earth is full of thy riches* [Ps. 104:24]. Whence [do we learn this of] Abraham? Because it is written, *And he blessed him, and said, Blessed be Abram of God Most High, possessor of heaven and earth* [Gen. 14:19]. Whence [do we learn this of] Israel? Because it is written, *Till thy people pass over, O Lord, till the people pass over which thou hast gotten* [Ex. 15:16]. And it says, *Unto the saints that are in the earth, and the excellent in whom is all my delight* [Ps. 16:3]. Whence [do we learn this of] the Temple? Because it is written, *The place, O Lord, which thou hast made for thee to dwell in; the sanctuary, O Lord, which thy hands have established* [Ex. 15:17]. And it says, *And he brought them to the border of his sanctuary, to this mountain, which his right hand had gotten* [Ps. 78:54].

11. Whatsoever the Holy One, blessed is he, created in his world, he created it only for his glory, as it is written, *Everything that is called by my name and that I have created, I have formed it, yea, I have made it* [Is. 43:7]. And it says, *The Lord shall reign for ever and ever* [Ex. 15:18]. R. Hananiah b. Akashya said: The Holy One, blessed is he, was minded to grant merit to Israel; therefore hath he multiplied for them the Law and commandments, as it is written, *It pleased the Lord for his righteousness' sake to magnify the Law and make it honourable* [Is. 42:21].

ROSH HA-SHANA (FEAST OF THE NEW YEAR)

1. 1. There are four 'New Year' days: on the 1st of Nisan is the New Year for kings and feasts; on the 1st of Elul is the New Year for the Tithe of Cattle (R. Eleazar and R. Simeon say: The 1st of Tishri); on the 1st of Tishri is the New Year for [the reckoning of] the year [of foreign kings], of the Years of Release and Jubilee years, for the planting [of trees] and for vegetables; and the 1st of Shebat is the New Year for [fruit-]trees (so the School of Shammai, and the School of Hillel say: On the 15th thereof).

2. At four times in the year is the world judged: at Passover, through grain; at Pentecost, through the fruits of the tree; on New Year's Day all that come into the world pass before him like legions of soldiers, for it is written, *He that fashioneth the hearts of them all, that considereth all their works* [Ps. 33:15]; and at the Feast [of Tabernacles] they are judged through water.

3. Because of six New Moons do messengers go forth [to proclaim the time of their appearing]: because of Nisan, to determine the time of Passover, because of Ab, to determine the time of the Fast; because of Elul, to determine the New Year; because of Tishri, to determine aright the set feasts; because of Chislev, to determine the time of [the feast of] the Dedication; and because of Adar, to determine the time of Purim. And while

the Temple still stood they went forth also because of Iyyar, to determine the time of the Lesser Passover.

4. Because of two New Moons may the Sabbath be profaned: [the New Moon] of Nisan and [the New Moon] of Tishri, for on them messengers used to go forth to Syria, and by them the set feasts were determined. And while the Temple still stood the Sabbath might also be profaned because of any of the New Moons, to determine aright the time of the offerings.

5. Whether [the New Moon] was manifestly visible or not, they may profane the Sabbath because of it. R. Jose says: If it was manifestly visible they may not profane the Sabbath because of it.

6. Once more than forty pairs [of witnesses] came forward, but R. Akiba in Lydda restrained them. Rabban Gamaliel sent to him [saying], 'If thou restrainest the multitude thou wilt put a stumbling-block in their way for the future'.

7. If a father and his son saw the new moon they may [both] go [to bear witness]; not that they can be included together [as a valid pair of witnesses], but that if one of them is found ineligible the other may be included to make a pair with some other [witness]. R. Simeon says: A father and his son, and any that are near of kin, are eligible to bear witness about the new moon. R. Jose said: Once Tobiah the Physician saw the new moon in Jerusalem, together with his son and his freed slave; and the priests accepted him and his son but pronounced his freed slave ineligible. And when they came before the court they accepted him and his slave but declared his son ineligible.

8. These are they that are ineligible: a dice-player, a usurer, pigeon-flyers, traffickers in Seventh Year produce, and slaves. This is the general rule: any evidence that a woman is not eligible to bring, these are not eligible to bring.

9. If a man saw the new moon but could not walk, he may be taken on an ass [on the Sabbath] or even on a bed; and if any lie in wait for them they may take staves in their hands. If it was a far journey they may take food in their hands, since for a journey enduring a night and a day they may profane the Sabbath and go forth to bear witness about the new moon, for it is written, *These are the set feasts of the Lord, even holy convocations which ye shall proclaim in their appointed season* [Lev. 23:4].

2. 1. If the witness was not known [to the judges] another was sent with him to testify of him. Beforetime they used to admit evidence about the new moon from any man, but after the evil doings of the heretics they enacted that evidence should be admitted only from them that they knew.

2. Beforetime they used to kindle flares, but after the evil doings of the Samaritans they enacted that messengers should go forth.

3. After what fashion did they kindle the flares? They used to take long cedar-wood sticks and rushes and oleaster-wood and flax-tow; and a man bound these up with a rope and went up to the top of the hill and set light

to them; and he waved them to and fro and up and down until he could see his fellow doing the like on the top of the next hill. And so, too, on the top of the third hill.

4. And from what place did they kindle the flares? From the mount of Olives [they signalled] to Sarteba, and from Sarteba to Agrippina, and from Agrippina to Hauran, and from Hauran to Beth Baltin. They did not go beyond Beth Baltin, but there the flare was waved to and fro and up and down until a man could see the whole exile before him like a sea of fire.

5. There was a large courtyard in Jerusalem called Beth Yaazek, where all the witnesses assembled, and there the Court examined them. And they prepared large meals for them so that they might make it their habit to come. Beforetime they might not stir thence the whole day; but Rabban Gamaliel the Elder ordained that they might walk within two thousand cubits in any direction. And not these, only, but a midwife that comes to help a delivery, or any that comes to rescue from a burning house or ravaging troops, or from a river-flood or a fallen house; they, too, are deemed to be people of the city and may move within two thousand cubits in any direction.

6. How do they examine the witnesses? The pair which comes first they examine first. They bring in the elder of the two and say to him, 'Tell us how thou sawest the moon: facing the sun or turned away from it? to the north or to the south? how high was it? to which side was it leaning? and how broad was it?' If he said, 'Facing the sun', he has said naught. Afterward they bring in the second witness and examine him. If their words are found to agree their evidence holds good. The other pairs of witnesses were asked [only] the main points, not because there was need of them, but that they should not go away disappointed and that they might make it their habit to come.

7. The chief of the court says, 'It is hallowed!' and all the people answer after him, 'It is hallowed! it is hallowed!' They acclaim it as hallowed whether it appeared at its proper time or not. R. Eliezer b. Zadok says: If it did not appear at its proper time they need not acclaim it as hallowed, since Heaven has hallowed it already.

8. Rabban Gamaliel had pictures of the shapes of the moon on a tablet and on the wall of his upper chamber. These he used to show to the unskilled and say, 'Didst thou see it on this wise or on that?' It once happened that two came and said, 'We saw it in the east in the morning and in the west in the evening'. R. Johanan b. Nuri said: They are false witnesses. But when they came to Jabneh Rabban Gamaliel accepted their evidence. And two others came and said, 'We saw it at its expected time, yet in the night of the added day it did not appear'; and Rabban Gamaliel accepted their evidence. R. Dosa b. Harkinas said: 'They are false witnesses: how can they say of a woman that she has given birth if the next

day her belly is between her teeth!' R. Joshua said to him, 'I approve thy words'.

9. Rabban Gamaliel sent to him [saying], 'I charge thee that thou come to me with thy staff and thy money on the Day of Atonement as it falls according to thy reckoning'. R. Akiba went to R. Joshua and found him sore perplexed. He said to him, 'I can teach thee [from Scripture] that whatsoever Rabban Gamaliel has done is done [aright], for it is written, *These are the set feasts of the Lord, even holy convocations, which ye shall proclaim* [Lev. 23:4]. Whether in their proper season or not in their proper season I know none other "set feasts" save these'. R. Joshua then went to R. Dosa b. Harkinas and said to him, 'If we come to inquire into [the lawfulness of the decisions of] the court of Rabban Gamaliel, we shall need to inquire into [the decisions of] every court which has arisen since the days of Moses until now, for it is written, *Then went up Moses and Aaron, Nadab and Abihu, and seventy of the elders of Israel* [Ex. 24:9]. And why are the names of the elders not expressly set forth if not to teach that every three [judges] which have risen up as a court over Israel are like to the court of Moses!' He took his staff and his money in his hand and went to Jabneh to Rabban Gamaliel on the day which fell according to his reckoning on the Day of Atonement. Rabban Gamaliel stood up and kissed him on the head and said to him, 'Come in peace, my master and my disciple!—"my master" in wisdom and "my disciple" in that thou hast accepted my words'.

3. 1. If the court itself and all Israel had seen the new moon and the witnesses had been examined, yet night fell before they could proclaim 'It is hallowed!' then it is an intercalated month. If the court alone saw it, two [of them] should stand up and bear witness before them, and then they may say, 'It is hallowed! it is hallowed!' If it was seen by three who [themselves] make up the court, two [of them] must stand up and set [two] of their fellows beside the single [other judge] and bear witness before them, and then they may say, 'It is hallowed! it is hallowed!' For no single person can be deemed trustworthy in himself.

2. All *shofars* are valid save that of a cow, since it is a 'horn'. R. Jose said: But are not all *shofars* called by the name 'horn'? for it is written, *When they make a long blast with the ram's horn* [Josh. 6:5].

3. The *shofar* [blown in the Temple] at the New Year [was made from the horn] of the wild goat, straight, with its mouthpiece overlaid with gold. And at the sides [of them that blew the *shofar*] were two [that blew upon] trumpets. The *shofar* blew a long note and the trumpets a short note, since the duty of the day fell on the *shofar*.

4. [The *shofars*] on days of fasting were rams' horns, rounded, with their mouthpiece overlaid with silver. And between them were two [that blew upon] trumpets. The *shofar* blew a short note and the trumpets a long

note, since the duty of the day fell on the trumpets.

5. The Year of Jubilee is like to the New Year in the blowing of the *shofar* and in the Benedictions. R. Judah says: At the New Year they use rams' horns and at the Years of Jubilee wild goats' horns.

6. A *shofar* that has been split and stuck together again is not valid. If the broken pieces of a *shofar* have been stuck together again it is not valid. If a hole had been made in it and it was stopped up again, if it hinders the blowing it is not valid, but if it does not, it is valid.

7. If the *shofar* was blown in a cistern or in a cellar or in a large jar, and a man heard the sound of the *shofar,* he has fulfilled his obligation; but if he heard only an uncertain noise he has not fulfilled his obligation. So, too, if a man was passing behind a synagogue, or if his house was near to a synagogue, and he heard the sound of the *shofar,* or the reading of the *Megillah,* if he directed his heart he has fulfilled his obligation, but if he did not he has not fulfilled his obligation. Though one may have heard and another may have heard, the one may have directed his heart and the other may not have directed his heart.

8. *And it came to pass when Moses held up his hand that Israel prevailed, and when he let down his hand Amalek prevailed* [Ex. 17:11]. But could the hands of Moses promote the battle or hinder the battle!—it is, rather, to teach thee that such time as the Israelites directed their thoughts on high and kept their hearts in subjection to their Father in heaven, they prevailed; otherwise they suffered defeat. After the like manner thou mayest say, *Make thee a fiery serpent and set it upon a standard, and it shall come to pass that every one that is bitten when he seeth it shall live* [Num. 21:8]. But could the serpent slay or the serpent keep alive!—it is, rather, to teach thee that such time as the Israelites directed their thoughts on high and kept their hearts in subjection to their Father in heaven, they were healed; otherwise they pined away. A deaf-mute, an imbecile, or a minor cannot fulfil an obligation on behalf of the many. This is the general rule: any on whom an obligation is not incumbent cannot fulfil that obligation on behalf of the many.

4. 1. If a Festival-day of the New Year fell on a Sabbath they might blow the *shofar* in the Holy City but not in the provinces. After the Temple was destroyed Rabban Johanan b. Zakkai ordained that they might blow it wheresoever there was a court. R. Eliezer said: Rabban Johanan b. Zakkai ordained it so only for Jabneh. They replied: It is all one whether it was Jabneh or any other place wherein was a court.

2. In this also Jerusalem surpassed Jabneh in that they could blow the *shofar* in any city that could see Jerusalem and that could hear [the *shofar* in Jerusalem] and that was near, and that was able to come; but at Jabneh they could blow it only in the court.

3. Beforetime the *Lulab* was carried seven days in the Temple, but in the provinces one day only. After the Temple was destroyed, Rabban

Johanan b. Zakkai ordained that in the provinces it should be carried seven days in memory of the Temple; also [he ordained] that on the whole of the Day of Waving it should be forbidden [to eat of new produce].

4. Beforetime they used to admit evidence about the new moon throughout the day. Once the witnesses tarried so long in coming that the levites were disordered in their singing; so it was ordained that evidence could be admitted only until the afternoon offering. And if witnesses came from the time of the afternoon offering onwards, then this day was kept holy and also the morrow was kept holy. After the Temple was destroyed Rabban Johanan b. Zakkai ordained that they might admit evidence about the new moon throughout the day. R. Joshua b. Karha said: Rabban Johanan b. Zakkai ordained this also that wheresoever the chief of the court might be, witnesses should go only to the place of assembly.

5. As for the order of the Benedictions a man recites 'the Fathers', 'Power', and 'the Hallowing of the Name', and combines with them the Sovereignty verses; but he does not then sound the *shofar*; [he then recites] 'the Hallowing of the Day' and sounds the *shofar*; [he then recites] the Remembrance verses and sounds the *shofar*; [he then recites] the *Shofar* verses and sounds the *shofar*; then he recites the Benedictions, 'the [Temple-]Service', and the 'Thanksgiving' and the Benediction of the Priests. So R. Johanan b. Nuri. R. Akiba said to him: If he does not sound the *shofar* at the Sovereignty verses why does he make mention of them? but, rather, he recites 'the Fathers', 'Power', and 'the Hallowing of the Name', and combines the Sovereignty verses with the 'Hallowing of the Day', and sounds the *shofar;* [he then recites] the Remembrance verses and sounds the *shofar;* [he then recites] the *Shofar* verses and sounds the *shofar;* and then he recites the Benedictions, 'the [Temple-]Service', and the "Thanksgiving' and the Benediction of the Priests.

6. They may not recite less than ten Sovereignty verses, ten Remembrance verses, or ten *Shofar* verses. R. Johanan b. Nuri says: If he recites three of each he has fulfilled his obligation. They may not make mention of any Remembrance, Sovereignty, or *Shofar* verses that record divine chastisement. They begin with [verses from] the Law and end with [verses from] the Prophets. R. Jose says: If a man ended with [verses from] the Law he has fulfilled his obligation.

7. When a man passes before the Ark [to lead the prayer] on a Festival-day of the New Year [not he but] the second blows the *shofar*; but at the times when the *Hallel* is recited he first recites the *Hallel*.

8. For the sake of a *shofar* for the New Year none may pass beyond the Sabbath limit, or clear away a heap of stones, or climb a tree or ride on cattle or swim on the water; nor may one cut it, whether in a fashion that transgresses the rules of the Sabbath rest or that transgresses a negative command [in the Law]; but if he wished to pour water or wine therein he may pour it. They should not hinder children from blowing the *shofar*, but should engage with them in this until they learn [how to blow];

but he that is engaged in practice has not fulfilled his obligation, nor has he fulfilled his obligation that hears another engaged in practice.

9. The manner of blowing the *shofar* is three blasts thrice repeated. A sustained blast is three times the length of a quavering blast, and a quavering blast is three times the length of an alarm blast. If a man blew the first blast, then prolonged the second blast equal to two, that is reckoned to him only as one blast. If a man had recited the Benedictions and was then assigned a *shofar*, he should blow thrice a sustained, a quavering, and another sustained blast. Like as the agent of the congregation is bound [to say the daily *Tefillah*] so is each person bound. Rabban Gamaliel says: The agent of the congregation fulfils the obligation that rests upon the many.

Talmud

The Talmud is the most seminal work in the development of post-Biblical Jewry; it is the text that has molded Jewish religious and social attitudes and shaped the life and thoughtways of a people in exile. The Talmud is composed of the Mishnah and the Gemara (completion, or teaching), which is an explication and amplification of the discussions of the Mishnah during the approximately three hundred years following the redaction of the Mishnah. Although there is only one Mishnah, there are two Talmuds, the Babylonian and the Palestinian. Of the two, the former is the better known and the more widely printed. Although there are Hebrew passages, the language of both Talmuds is basically Aramaic.

The Gemara is classically divided into its two components— halakha (legal material) and aggada (nonlegal material). The halakha contains laws, statutes, obligatory practises, all discussions that pertain to legal principles. The aggada includes items of an ethical, historical, biographical, folkloristic and anecdotal nature.

The traditional order of the Babylonian Talmud is a passage of the Mishnah, followed by a usually longer discussion in the Gemara. Since the first printed edition of the Babylonian Talmud (1520–1523, by Daniel Bomberg, a gentile printer in Venice), the pagination of the Babylonian Talmud has remained fixed. References to passages are by tractate and folio page (a or b). For instance, the Talmud selections here begin with Berakhot 30b.

The Talmud, like the Mishnah, is not an attempt at codification of Jewish law. Rather, it is an anthology of views, discussions, and opinions not only of Mishnaic material which it presumably treats, but of dozens of related, or even nonrelated, topics. Owing to its encyclopedic range and compressed style— much of it is verbatim, "shorthand" notes taken during discussion—the Talmud cannot be read: it must be studied. The link between one idea, one remark and another may be tenuous, until the association of thoughts is noticed. Rather than a linear development, then, the thoughts progress in staircase fashion—one leading to another—until eventually the discussion comes home again with some thematic connection.

The growth of the Gemara is similar to that of the Mishnah. About twenty years after the redaction of the Mishnah (200 C.E.), Abba Areka, a Babylonian sage, returned from Palestine and brought back with him the Mishnah. In Babylonian academies he and Samuel expounded the Mishnah; they compared it to other halakhic statements not included therein, asked questions and proposed answers. These comments and those of their disciples were collected and preserved by word of mouth for generations until, like the Mishnah, these too were collected and edited. The Talmud was finally redacted by Rav Ashi (352–427), a task to which he devoted thirty years, editing two tractates a year. At his death his son continued the gigantic task. In the year 500 C.E. the Talmud was declared officially closed.

It is difficult to ascribe any one literary genre to the Talmud, for it does not fit any one literary category. The Talmud deals with the individual and society, with man's behavior at home, at work, in the synagogue and in the market place; it deals with ceremonies and rituals from birth through marriage and death. In sum, it is an epitome of rabbinic Jewish thought and feeling over several centuries. No history of the Jews during the first few centuries of the "common era" can be written without reference to the Talmud.

Berakhot (benedictions, or blessings), is the first of eleven tractates that comprise the order "Seeds," which deals mainly with the Torah's agricultural laws. *Berakhot* is the only tractate in "Seeds" for which there is Gemara commentary. *Berakhot* deals with all sorts of benedictions, the time and order of prayers, and the laws concerning the recitation of the *Shema Yisrael* ("Hear O Israel"—the Jew's fundamental declaration of faith). In typically Talmudic fashion, integrated with the legal discussions is the aggadic material which reflects the cultural setting of Babylonian and Palestinian Jews—their daily life, work, prayers and even (in chapter nine) their dreams. Whereas chapter four discusses the times of the various services and whether or not they are obligatory, chapter five accents man's spiritual preparation for prayer and its efficacy.

BERAKHOT

CHAPTER V

MISHNAH. ONE SHOULD NOT STAND UP TO SAY TEFILLAH SAVE IN A REVERENT FRAME OF MIND. THE PIOUS MEN OF OLD USED TO WAIT AN HOUR BEFORE PRAYING IN ORDER THAT THEY MIGHT CONCENTRATE THEIR THOUGHTS UPON THEIR FATHER IN HEAVEN. EVEN IF A KING GREETS HIM [WHILE PRAYING] HE SHOULD NOT ANSWER HIM: EVEN IF A SNAKE IS WOUND ROUND HIS HEEL HE SHOULD NOT BREAK OFF.

GEMARA. What is the [Scriptural] source of this rule?—R. Eleazar said: Scripture says, *And she was in bitterness of soul* [I Sam. 1:10]. But how can you learn from this? Perhaps Hannah was different because she was exceptionally bitter at heart! Rather, said R. Jose son of R. Hanina: We learn it from here: *But as for me in the abundance of Thy lovingkindness will I come into Thy house, I will bow down toward Thy holy temple in the fear of Thee* [Ps. 5:8]. But how can we learn from this? Perhaps David was different, because he was exceptionally self-tormenting in prayer! Rather, said R. Joshua b. Levi, it is from here: *Worship the Lord in the beauty of holiness* [Ps. 29:2]. Read not *hadrath* [beauty] but *herdath* [trembling]. But how can you learn from here? Perhaps I can after all say that the word *'hadrath'* is to be taken literally, after the manner of Rab Judah, who used to dress himself up before he prayed! Rather, said R. Nahman b. Isaac: We learn it from here: *Serve the Lord with fear and rejoice with trembling* [Ps. 2:11]. What is meant by *'rejoice with trembling'?*—R. Adda b. Mattena said in the name of Rab: In the place where there is rejoicing there should also be trembling.

Abaye was sitting before Rabbah, who observed that he seemed very merry. He said: It is written, *And rejoice with trembling?*—He replied: I am putting on *tefillin.* R. Jeremiah was sitting before R. Zera who saw that he seemed very merry. He said to him: It is written, *In all sorrow there is profit* [Prov. 14:23]?—He replied: I am wearing *tefillin.* Mar the son of Rabina made a marriage feast for his son. He saw that the Rabbis were growing very merry so he brought a precious cup worth four hundred *zuz* and broke it before them, and they became serious. R. Ashi made a marriage feast for his son. He saw that the Rabbis were growing very merry, so he brought a cup of white crystal and broke it before them and they became serious. The Rabbis said to R. Hamnuna Zuti at the wedding of Mar the son of Rabina: Please sing us something. He said to them: Alas for us that we are to die! They said to him: What shall we respond after you? He said to them: Where is the Torah and where is the *mizwah* that will shield us!

R. Johanan said in the name of R. Simeon b. Yohai: It is forbidden to a man to fill his mouth with laughter in this world, because it says, *Then will our mouth be filled with laughter and our tongue with singing* [Ps. 126:2]. When will that be? At the time when *'they shall say among the nations, The Lord hath done great things with these'* [Ps. 126:3]. It was related of Resh Lakish that he never again filled his mouth with laughter in this world after he heard this saying from R. Johanan his teacher. . . .

Our Rabbis taught: One should not stand up to say *Tefillah* while immersed in sorrow, or idleness, or laughter, or chatter, or frivolity, or idle talk, but only while still rejoicing in the performance of some religious act. Similarly a man before taking leave of his fellow should not finish off with ordinary conversation, or joking, or frivolity, or idle talk, but with some matter of *halachah.* For so we find with the early prophets that they concluded their harangues with words of praise and comfort; and so Mari the grandson of R. Huna the son of R. Jeremiah b. Abba learnt: Before taking leave of his fellow a man should always finish with a matter of *halachah,* so that he should remember him thereby.

So we find that R. Kahana escorted R. Shimi b. Ashi from Pum Nahara to Be-Zinyatha of Babylon, and when he arrived there he said to him, Sir, do people really say that these palm trees of Babylon are from the time of Adam?—He replied: You have reminded me of the saying of R. Jose son of R. Hanina. For R. Jose son of R. Hanina said: What is meant by the verse, *Through a land that no man passed through and where no man dwelt* [Jer. 2:6]? If no one passed, how could anyone dwell? It is to teach you that any land which Adam decreed should be inhabited, and any land which Adam decreed should not be inhabited is not inhabited. R. Mordecai escorted R. Shimi b. Abba from Hagronia to Be Kafi, or, as some report, to Be Dura.

Our Rabbis taught: When a man prays, he should direct his heart to heaven. Abba Saul says: A reminder of this is the text, *Thou wilt direct their heart, Thou wilt cause Thine ear to attend* [Ps. 10:17]. It has been taught: Such was the custom of R. Akiba; when he prayed with the congregation, he used to cut it short and finish in order not to inconvenience the congregation, but when he prayed by himself, a man would leave him in one corner and find him later in another, on account of his many genuflexions and prostrations.

R. Hiyya b. Abba said: A man should always pray in a house with windows, as it says, *Now his windows were open* [Dan. 6:11].

I might say that a man should pray the whole day? It has already been expressly stated by the hand of Daniel, *And three times,* etc. [Ibid.]. But perhaps [this practice] began only when he went into captivity? It is already said, *As he did aforetime* [Ibid.] I might say that a man may pray turning in any direction he wishes? Therefore the text states, *Toward Jerusalem* [Ibid.]. I might say that he may combine all three *Tefillahs* in one. It has already been clearly stated by David, as is written, *Evening and morning and at noonday* [Ps. 55:18]. I might say that he should let his voice be heard in praying? It has already been clearly stated by Hannah, as is said, *But her voice could not be heard* [I Sam. 1:13]. I might say that a man should first ask for his own requirements and then say the *Tefillah?* It has been clearly stated by Solomon, as is said, *To hearken unto the cry and to the prayer* [I Kings 8:28]: 'cry' here means *Tefillah,* 'prayer' means [private] request. A [private] request is not made after 'True and firm', but after the *Tefillah,* even the order of confession of the Day of Atonement may be said. It has also been stated: R. Hiyya b. Ashi said in the name of Rab: Although it was laid down that a man asks for his requirements in 'that hearkenest unto prayer', if he wants to say something after his prayer, even something like the order of confession on the Day of Atonement, he may do so.

R. Hamnuna said: How many most important laws can be learnt from these verses relating to Hannah [I Sam. 1:10 ff.]! *Now Hannah, she spoke in her heart:* from this we learn that one who prays must direct his heart. *Only her lips moved:* from this we learn that he who prays must frame the words distinctly with his lips. *But her voice could not be heard:* from this, it is forbidden to raise one's voice in the *Tefillah. Therefore Eli thought she had been drunken:* from this, that a drunken person is forbidden to say the *Tefillah. And Eli said unto her, How long wilt thou be drunken,* etc. R. Eleazar said: From this we learn that one who sees in his neighbour [31*b*] something unseemly must reprove him. *And Hannah answered and said, No, my lord.* 'Ulla, or as some say R. Jose b. Hanina, said: She said to him, Thou art no lord in this matter, nor does the holy spirit rest on thee, that thou suspectest me of this thing.

Some say, She said to him: Thou art no lord, [meaning] the *Shechinah* and the holy spirit is not with you in that you take the harsher and not the more lenient view of my conduct. Dost thou not know that *I am a woman of sorrowful spirit: I have drunk neither wine nor strong drink.* R. Eleazar said: From this we learn that one who is suspected wrongfully must clear himself. *Count not thy handmaid for a daughter of Belial;* a man who says the *Tefillah* when drunk is like one who serves idols. It is written here, *Count not thy handmaid for a daughter of Belial,* and it is written elsewhere, *Certain sons of Belial have gone forth from the midst of thee* [Deut. 13:14]. Just as there the term is used in connection with idolatry, so here. *Then Eli answered and said, Go in peace* [I Sam. 1:17]. R. Eleazar said: From this we learn that one who suspects his neighbour of a fault which he has not committed must beg his pardon; nay more, he must bless him, as it says, *And the God of Israel grant thy petition* [Ibid.].

And she vowed a vow and said, O Lord of Zebaoth [*Hosts*] [I Sam.

1:11]. R. Eleazar said: From the day that God created His world there was no man called the Holy One, blessed be He, *Zeboath* [hosts] until Hannah came and called Him *Zebaoth*. Said Hannah before the Holy One, blessed be He: Sovereign of the Universe, of all the hosts and hosts that Thou hast created in Thy world, is it so hard in Thy eyes to give me one son? A parable: To what is this matter like? To a king who made a feast for his servants, and a poor man came and stood by the door and said to them, Give me a bite, and no one took any notice of him, so he forced his way into the presence of the king and said to him, Your Majesty, out of all the feast which thou hast made, is it so hard in thine eyes to give me one bite?

If Thou wilt indeed look [Ibid.]. R. Eleazar said: Hannah said before the Holy One, blessed be He: Sovereign of the Universe, if Thou wilt look, it is well, and if Thou wilt not look, I will go and shut myself up with someone else in the knowledge of my husband Elkanah, and as I shall have been alone they will make me drink the water of the suspected wife, and Thou canst not falsify Thy law, which says, *She shall be cleared and shall conceive seed* [Num. 5:28]. Now this would be effective on the view of him who says that if the woman was barren she is visited. But on the view of him who says that if she bore with pain she bears with ease, if she bore females she now bears males, if she bore swarthy children she now bears fair ones, if she bore short ones she now bears tall ones, what can be said? As it has been taught: *'She shall be cleared and shall conceive seed':* this teaches that if she was barren she is visited. So R. Ishmael. Said R. Akiba to him, If that is so, all barren women will go and shut themselves in with someone and she who has not misconducted herself will be visited! No, it teaches that if she formerly bore with pain she now bears with ease, if she bore short children she now bears tall ones, if she bore swarthy ones she now bears fair ones, if she was destined to bear one she will now bear two. What then is the force of *'If Thou wilt indeed look'?*—The Torah used an ordinary form of expression. . . .

But wilt give unto Thy handmaid a man-child [I Sam. 1:11]. What is meant by *'a man-child'*? Rab said: A man among men; Samuel said: Seed that will anoint two men, namely, Saul and David; R. Johanan said: Seed that will be equal to two men, namely, Moses and Aaron, as it says, *Moses and Aaron among His priests and Samuel among them that call upon His name* [Ps. 99:6]; the Rabbis say: Seed that will be merged among men. When R. Dimi came [from Palestine] he explained this to mean: Neither too tall nor too short, neither too thin nor too corpulent, neither too pale nor too red, neither overclever nor stupid.

I am the woman that stood by thee here [I Sam. 1:26]. R. Joshua b. Levi said: From this we learn that it is forbidden to sit within four cubits of one saying *Tefillah*. . . .

Now Hannah, she spoke in her heart [I Sam. 1:13]. R. Eleazar said in the name of R. Jose b. Zimra: She spoke concerning her heart. She said before Him: Sovereign of the Universe, among all the things that Thou hast created in a woman, Thou hast not created one without a purpose, eyes to see, ears to hear, a nose to smell, a mouth to speak, hands to do work, legs to walk with, breasts to give suck. These breasts that Thou hast put on my heart, are they not to give suck? Give me a son, so that I may suckle with them. . . .

And the Lord spoke unto Moses, Go, get thee down [Ex. 32:7]. What is meant by *'Go, get thee down'?* R. Eleazar said: The Holy One, blessed be He, said to Moses: Moses, descend from thy greatness. Have I at all given to thee greatness save for the sake of Israel? And now Israel have sinned; then why do I want thee? Straightway Moses became powerless and he had no strength to speak. When, however, [God] said, *Let Me alone that I may destroy them* [Deut. 9:14], Moses said to himself: This depends upon me, and straightway he stood up and prayed vigorously and begged for mercy. It was like the case of a king who became angry with his son and began beating him severely. His friend was sitting before him but was afraid to say a word until the king said, Were it not for my friend here who is sitting before me I would kill you. He said to himself, This depends on me, and immediately he stood up and rescued him.

Now therefore let Me alone that My wrath may wax hot against them, and that I may consume them, and I will make of thee a great nation [Ex. 32:10]. R. Abbahu said: Were it not explicitly written, it would be impossible to say such a thing: this teaches that Moses took hold of the Holy One, blessed be He, like a man who seizes his fellow by his garment and said before Him: Sovereign of the Universe, I will not let Thee go until Thou forgivest and pardonest them.

And I will make of thee a great nation, etc. R. Eleazar said: Moses said before the Holy One, blessed be He: Sovereign of the Universe, seeing that a stool with three legs [i.e., the three patriarchs] cannot stand before Thee in the hour of Thy wrath, how much less a stool with one leg! And moreover, I am ashamed before my ancestors, who will now say: See what a leader he has set over them! He sought greatness for himself, but he did not seek mercy for them! . . .

Remember Abraham, Isaac and Israel Thy servants, to whom Thou didst swear by Thyself [Ex. 32:13]. What is the force of *'by Thyself'?* R. Eleazar said: Moses said before the Holy One, blessed be He: Sovereign of the Universe, hadst Thou sworn to them by the heaven and the earth, I would have said, Just as the heaven and earth can pass away, so can Thy oath pass away. Now, however, Thou hast sworn to them by Thy great name: just as Thy great name endures for ever and ever, so Thy oath is established for ever and ever.

And saidst unto them, I will multiply your seed as the stars of heaven and all this land that I have spoken of etc. [Ex. 32:13]. *"That I have spoken of'?* It should be, 'That *Thou* has spoken of'!—R. Eleazar said: Up to this point the text records the words of the disciple, from this point the words of the master. R. Samuel b. Nahmani, however, said: Both are the words of the disciple, only Moses spoke thus before the Holy One, blessed be He: Sovereign of the Universe, the things which Thou didst tell me to go and tell Israel in Thy name I did go and tell them in Thy name; now what am I to say to them?

Because the Lord was not able [yekoleth] [Num. 14:16]. It should be *yakol!* R. Eleazar said: Moses said before the Holy One, blessed be He: Sovereign of the Universe, now the nations of the world will say, He has grown feeble like a female and He is not able to deliver. Said the Holy One, blessed be He, to Moses; Have they not already seen the wonders and miracles I performed for them by the Red Sea? He replied: Sovereign of the Universe, they can still say, He could stand up against one king, He cannot stand up against thirty. R. Johanan said: How do we know that in the end the Holy One, blessed be He, gave Moses right? Because it says, *And the Lord said, I have pardoned according to thy word* [Num. 14:20]. It was taught in the school of R. Ishmael: *According to thy word:* the nations of the world will one day say, Happy is the disciple to whom the master gives right!

But in very deed, as I live [Num. 14:21]. Raba said in the name of R. Isaac: This teaches that the Holy One, blessed be He, said to Moses: Moses, you have revived Me with your words.

R. Simlai expounded: A man should always first recount the praise of the Holy One, blessed be He, and then pray. Whence do we know this? From Moses; for it is written, *And I besought the Lord at that time* [Deut. 3:23 ff.], and it goes on, *O Lord God, Thou hast begun to show Thy servant Thy greatness and Thy strong hand; for what god is there in heaven and earth who can do according to Thy works and according to Thy mighty acts,* and afterwards is written, *Let me go over, I pray Thee, and see the good land* etc.

(Mnemonic: Deeds, charity, offering, priest, fast, lock, iron). [32 *b*] R. Eleazar said: Prayer is more efficacious even than good deeds, for there was no-one greater in good deeds than Moses our Master, and yet he was answered only after prayer, as it says, *Speak no more unto Me,* and immediately afterwards, *Get thee up into the top of Pisgah.*

R. Eleazar also said: Fasting is more efficacious than charity. What is the reason? One is performed with a man's money, the other with his body.

R. Eleazar also said: Prayer is more efficacious than offerings, as it says, *To what purpose is the multitude of your sacrifices unto Me* [Isa. 1:11], and this is followed by, *And when ye spread forth your hands* [Isa. 1:15]. R. Johanan said: A priest who has committed manslaughter should not lift up his hands [to say the priestly benediction], since it says [in this context], '*Your hands are full of blood*'.

R. Eleazar also said: From the day on which the Temple was destroyed the gates of prayer have been closed, as it says, *Yea when I cry and call for help He shutteth out my prayer* [Lam. 3:8]. But though the gates of prayer are closed, the gates of weeping are not closed, as it says, *Hear my prayer, O Lord, and give ear unto my cry; keep not silence at my tears* [Ps. 39:13]. Raba did not order a fast on a cloudy day because it says, *Thou hast covered Thyself with a cloud so that no prayer can pass through* [Lam. 3:44]

R. Eleazar also said: Since the day that the Temple was destroyed, a wall of iron has intervened between Israel and their Father in Heaven, as it says, *And take thou unto thee an iron griddle, and set it for a wall of iron between thee and the city* [Ez. 4:3].

R. Hanin said in the name of R. Hanina: If one prays long his prayer does not pass unheeded. Whence do we know this? From Moses our Master; for it says, *And I prayed unto the Lord* [Deut. 9:26], and it is written afterwards, *And the Lord hearkened unto me that time also* [Deut. 9:19]. But is that so? Has not R. Hiyya b. Abba said in the name of R. Johanan: If one prays long and looks for the fulfilment of his prayer, in the end he will have vexation of heart, as it says, *Hope deferred maketh the heart sick* [Prov. 13:12]? What is his remedy? Let him study the Torah, as it says, *But desire fulfilled is a tree of life* [Ibid.]; and the tree of life is nought but the Torah, as it says, *She is a tree of life to them that lay hold on her* [Prov. 3:18]—There is no contradiction: one statement speaks of a man who prays long and looks for the fulfilment of his prayer, the other of one who prays long without looking for the fulfilment of his prayer. R. Hama son of R. Hanina said: If a man sees that he prays and is not answered, he should pray again, as it says, *Wait for the Lord, be strong and let thy heart take courage; yea, wait thou for the Lord* [Ps. 27:14].

Our Rabbis taught: Four things require to be done with energy, namely, [study of] the Torah, good deeds, praying, and one's worldly occupation. Whence do we know this of Torah and good deeds? Because it says, *Only be strong and very courageous to observe to do according to all the law* [Josh. 1:7]: 'be strong' in Torah, and 'be courageous' in good deeds. Whence of prayer? Because it says, *'Wait for the Lord, be strong and let thy heart take courage, yea, wait thou for the Lord'.* Whence of worldly occupation? Because it says, *Be of good courage and let us prove strong for our people* [2 Sam. 10:12].

But Zion said, The Lord hath forsaken me, and the Lord hath forgotten me [Isa. 49:14]. Is not 'forsaken' the same as 'forgotten'? Resh Lakish said: The community of Israel said before the Holy One, blessed be He: Sovereign of the Universe, when a man takes a second wife after his first, he still remembers the deeds of the first. Thou hast both forsaken me and forgotten me! The Holy One, blessed be He, answered her: My daughter, twelve constellations have I created in the firmament, and for each constellation I have created thirty hosts, and for each host I have created thirty legions, and for each legion I have created thirty cohorts, and for each cohort I have created thirty maniples, and for each maniple I have created thirty camps, and to each camp I have attached three hundred and sixty-five thousands of myriads of stars, corresponding to the days of the solar year, and all of them I have created only for thy sake, and thou sayest, Thou hast forgotten me and forsaken me!

Can a woman forsake her sucking child ['ullah] [Isa. 49:15]? Said the Holy One, blessed be He: Can I possibly forget the burnt-offerings [*'olah*] of rams and the firstborn of animals that thou didst offer to Me in the wilderness? She thereupon said: Sovereign of the Universe, since there is no forgetfulness before the Throne of Thy glory, perhaps Thou wilt not forget the sin of the Calf? He replied: *'Yea, "these" will be forgotten'.* She said before Him: Sovereign of the Universe, seeing that there is forgetfulness before the Throne of Thy glory, perhaps Thou wilt forget my conduct at Sinai? He replied to her: *'Yet "the I" will not forget thee'.* This agrees with what R. Eleazar said in the name of R. Oshaia: What is referred to by the text, *'yea, "these" will be forgotten'?* This refers to the sin of the Calf. *'And yet "the I" will not forget thee':* this refers to their conduct at Sinai.

The pious men of old used to wait an hour. On what is this based? —R. Joshua b. Levi said: On the text, *Happy are they that dwell in Thy house* [Ps. 84:5]. R. Joshua b. Levi also said: One who says the *Tefillah* should also wait an hour after his prayer, as it says, *Surely the righteous shall give thanks unto Thy name, the upright shall sit in Thy presence* [Ps. 140:14]. It has been taught similarly: One who says the *Tefillah* should wait an hour before his prayer and an hour after his prayer. Whence do we know [that he should wait] before his prayer? Because it says: *'Happy are they that dwell in Thy house'.* Whence after his prayer? Because it says, *'Surely the righteous shall give thanks unto Thy name, the upright shall dwell in Thy presence'.* Our Rabbis taught: The pious men of old used to wait for an hour and pray for an hour and then wait again for an hour. But seeing that they spend nine hours a day over prayer, how is their knowledge of Torah preserved and how is their work done? [The answer is] that because they are pious, their Torah is preserved and their work is blessed.

Even if a king greets him he should not answer him. R. Joseph said: This was meant to apply only to Jewish kings, but for a king of another people he may interrupt. An objection was raised: If one was saying *Tefillah* and he saw a robber coming towards him or a carriage coming towards him, he should not break off but curtail it and clear off!— There is no contradiction: where it is possible for him to curtail [he should curtail, otherwise he should break off].

Our Rabbis taught: It is related that once when a certain pious man was praying by the roadside, an officer came by and greeted him and he did not return his greeting. So he waited for him till he had finished his prayer. When he had finished his prayer he said to him: Fool! is it not written in your Law, *Only take heed to thyself and keep thy soul diligently*

[Deut. 4:9], and it is also written, *Take ye therefore good heed unto your souls* [Deut. 4:15]? When I greeted you why did you not return my greeting? If I had cut off your head with my sword, who would have demanded satisfaction for your blood from me? He replied to him: Be patient and I will explain to you. If, [he went on], you had been standing before an earthly king and your friend had come and given you greeting, would you have returned it? No, he replied. And if you had returned him greeting, what would they have done to you? They would have cut off my head with the sword, he replied. He then said to him: Have we not here then an *a fortiori* argument: If [you would have behaved] in this way when standing before an earthly king who is here today and tomorrow in the grave, how much more so I when standing before the supreme King of kings, the Holy One, blessed be He, who endures for all eternity? Forthwith the officer accepted his explanation, and the pious man returned to his home in peace.

Even if a snake is wound round his foot he should not break off. R. Shesheth said: This applies only in the case of a serpent, but if it is a scorpion, he breaks off. An objection was raised: If a man fell into a den of lions [and was not seen again] one cannot testify concerning him that he is dead; but if he fell into a trench full of serpents or scorpions, one can testify concerning him that he is dead!—The case there is different, because on account of his crushing them [in falling] they turn and bite him. R. Isaac said: If he sees oxen [coming towards him] he may break off; for R. Oshaia taught: One should remove from a *tam* ox [an ox that has not gored before] fifty cubits, and from a *mu'ad* [one which has gored 3 times] ox out of sight. It was taught in the name of R. Meir: If an ox's head is in a [fodder] basket, go up to a roof and kick the ladder away. Samuel said: This applies only to a black ox and in the month of Nisan, because then Satan is dancing between his horns [i.e., full of high spirits and mischief in the spring].

Our Rabbis taught: In a certain place there was once a lizard which used to injure people. They came and told R. Hanina b. Dosa. He said to them: Show me its hole. They showed him its hole, and he put his heel over the hole, and the lizard came out and bit him, and it died. He put it on his shoulder and brought it to the Beth ha-Midrash and said to them: See, my sons, it is not the lizard that kills, it is sin that kills! On that occasion they said: Woe to the man whom a lizard meets, but woe to the lizard which R. Hanina b. Dosa meets!

Midrash

Midrash (explication, or commentary) dealt originally with an exegetical formulation of rules; that is, taking a Torah verse, expounding upon it beyond its literal meaning, and deriving a subsidiary statute which might be applicable to a contemporary situation. Thus the Midrash continued the process of interpretation and oral commentary that originated early in Jewish history. In Ezra 7:11 we read that Ezra "had set his heart to seek (*lidrosh*, root *d-r-sh*, same as in Mi*drash*) the law of the Lord and to do it, and to teach in Israel statutes and ordinances."

There are two basic types of Midrash, the Midrash Halakha (legal) and the Midrash Haggadah (homiletic). The intent of the former is to interpret scriptural words, phrases, and verses, and thus to derive new laws, and to establish a connection via exegesis between common practise and Torah verses. The Midrash Haggadah, on the other hand, is basically homiletic, sermonic, folkloristic, bordering on fiction and rich in fantasy, and less binding than halakha; its purpose was to heighten man's religious and ethical behavior. In a famous confrontation between Nachmanides and Fra Paulo (see the *Disputation with Paulo Christiani*, page 417), Nachmanides nonplussed his opponent by stating that Midrash Haggadah was intrinsically imaginative and was not binding upon Jews. The Midrash Haggadah often quotes discourses or sermons of rabbis who, like modern preachers, waged an eternal battle against a slumbering audience—hence the occasionally startling remarks which were no doubt intended to snap the congregation out of drowsy lethargy.

Whereas the intent of halakhic Midrash is juridical, the aim of haggadic Midrash is ethical and religious instruction. A variation upon Scripture, the Midrash gives free reign to its imagination and cites material not only from the Bible but from other sources as well. Haggadah (aggada is the Aramaic term) was considered important even in ancient times, as may be seen in the midrashic statement: "If you wish to know Him at whose word the world came into being, then learn Haggadah, for through it you will know the Holy One Blessed be He, and follow his ways." (*Sifre* to Deut. 11:22).

The *Mekilta*, one of the most ancient midrashim, originated in the school of Rabbi Ishmael (first and second centuries C.E.), and is a commentary on approximately thirteen chapters of Exodus (12:1–23:19, 31:12–17, 35:1–3). It treats almost all the statutes as well as some sections of narrative, often using the parable as its chief literary form. Actually, the *Mekilta* is a combination of the two basic types of midrashim, with the haggadic character slightly outweighing that of the halakhic.

One of the leading works in the category of Midrash Haggadah is the *Midrash Rabbah,* expositions on the Pentateuch and the Five Megillot (Song of Songs, Lamentations, Esther, Ecclesiastes and Ruth) that usually follow the scriptural text verse by verse. The Midrash likes to establish links between passages and between characters in the Bible, often supplying inventive stories; it fills the gap in the normally terse narrative and rounds out a story where only the barest hints are given. The portion included here is from *Exodus Rabbah*, composed in the latter part of the seventh century.

MEKILTA

CHAPTER V [EXODUS 20:2]

I Am the Lord Thy God. Why were the Ten Commandments not said at the beginning of the Torah? They give a parable. To what may this be compared? To the following: A king who entered a province said to the people: May I be your king? But the people said to him: Have you done anything good for us that you should rule over us? What did he do then? He built the city wall for them, he brought in the water supply for them, and he fought their battles. Then when he said to them: May I be your king? They said to him: Yes, yes. Likewise, God. He brought the Israelites out of Egypt, divided the sea for them, sent down the manna for them, brought up the well for them, brought the quails for them. He fought for them the battle with Amalek. Then He said to them: I am to be your king. And they said to Him: Yes, yes.

Rabbi says: This proclaims the excellence of Israel. For when they all stood before mount Sinai to receive the Torah they all made up their mind alike to accept the reign of God joyfully. Furthermore, they pledged themselves for one another. And it was not only concerning overt acts that God, revealing Himself to them, wished to make His covenant with them but also concerning secret acts, as it is said: "The secret things belong to the Lord our God and the things that are revealed," etc. [Deut. 29:28]. But they said to Him: Concerning overt acts we are ready to make a covenant with Thee, but we will not make a covenant with Thee in regard to secret acts lest one of us commit a sin secretly and the entire community be held responsible for it.

Another Interpretation: *I Am the Lord Thy God.* When the Holy One, blessed be He, stood up and said: "I am the Lord thy God," the earth trembled, as it is said: "Lord, when Thou didst go forth out of Seir, when Thou didst march out of the field of Edom, the earth trembled" [Judg. 5:4]. And it goes on to say: "The mountains quaked at the presence of the Lord," [ibid. v. 5]. And it also says: "The voice of the Lord is powerful; the voice of the Lord is full of majesty," etc. [Ps. 29:4] up to: "And in his palace every one says: 'Glory!'" [ibid., v. 9]. And their houses even were filled with the splendor of the Shekinah. At that time all the kings of the nations of the world assembled and came to Balaam the son of Beor. They said to him: Perhaps God is about to destroy His world by a flood. He said to them: Fools that ye are! Long ago God swore to Noah that He would not bring a flood upon the world, as it is said: "For this is as the waters

110

of Noah unto Me; for as I have sworn that the waters of Noah should no more go over the earth" [Isa. 54:9]. They then said to him: Perhaps He will not bring a flood of water, but He may bring a flood of fire. But he said to them: He is not going to bring a flood of water or a flood of fire. It is simply that the Holy One, blessed be He, is going to give the Torah to His people. For it is said: "The Lord will give strength unto His people," etc. [Ps. 29:11]. As soon as they heard this from him, they all turned back and went each to his place.

And it was for the following reason that the nations of the world were asked to accept the Torah: In order that they should have no excuse for saying: Had we been asked we would have accepted it. For, behold, they were asked and they refused to accept it, for it is said: "And he said: 'The Lord came from Sinai'," etc. [Deut. 33:2].

He appeared to the children of Esau the wicked and said to them: Will you accept the Torah? They said to Him: What is written in it? He said to them: "Thou shalt not murder" [ibid. 5:17]. They then said to Him: The very heritage which our father left us was: "And by thy sword shalt thou live" [Gen. 27:40].

He then appeared to the children of Amon and Moab. He said to them: Will you accept the Torah? They said to Him: What is written in it? He said to them: "Thou shalt not commit adultery" [Deut. 5:17]. They, however, said to Him that they were all of them children of adulterers, as it is said: "Thus were both the daughters of Lot with child by their father" [Gen. 19:36].

Then He appeared to the children of Ishmael. He said to them: Will you accept the Torah? They said to Him: What is written in it? He said to them: "Thou shalt not steal" [Deut. 5:17]. They then said to Him: The very blessing that had been pronounced upon our father was: "And he shall be as a wild ass of a man: his hand shall be upon everything" [Gen. 16:12]. And it is written: "For, indeed, I was stolen away out of the land of the Hebrews" [ibid. 40:15]. But when He came to the Israelites and: "At His right hand was a fiery law unto them" [Deut. 33:2], they all opened their mouths and said: "All that the Lord hath spoken will we do and obey" [Ex. 24:7]. And thus it says: "He stood and measured the earth; He beheld and drove asunder the nations" [Hab. 3:6].

R. Simon b. Eleazar says: If the sons of Noah could not endure the seven commandments enjoined upon them, how much less could they have endured all the commandments of the Torah! To give a parable. A king had appointed two administrators. One was appointed over the store of straw and the other was appointed over the treasure of silver and gold. The one appointed over the store of straw was held in suspicion. But he used to complain about the fact that they had not appointed him over the treasure of silver and gold. The people then said to him: "Reka!" (good-for-nothing!) If you were under suspicion in connection with the store of straw how could they trust you with the treasure of silver and gold! Behold it is a matter of reasoning by the method of kal vahomer: If the sons of Noah could not endure the seven commandments enjoined upon them, how much less could they have endured all the commandments of the Torah!

Why was the Torah not given in the land of Israel? In order that the nations of the world should not have the excuse for saying: Because it was given in Israel's land, therefore we have not accepted it. Another reason: To avoid causing dissension among the tribes. Else one might have said: In my territory the Torah was given. And the other might have said: In my territory the Torah was given. Therefore, the Torah was given in the desert, publicly and openly, in a place belonging to no one. To three things the Torah is likened: To the desert, to fire, and to water. This is to tell you that just as these three things are free to all who come into the world, so also are the words of the Torah free to all who come into the world.

Who Brought Thee Out of the Land of Egypt. Out of the House of Bondage. They were slaves to kings. You interpret it to mean that they were servants of kings. Perhaps it is not so, but means that they were slaves of servants? When it says: "And redeemed you out of the house of bondage, from the hand of Pharaoh king of Egypt" [Deut. 7:8], it indicates that they were servants of kings and not servants of slaves. Another Interpretation: *Out of the House of Servants.* Out of the house of worshipers, for they worshiped idols.

CHAPTER VI [EXODUS 20:3-6]

Thou Shalt Not Have Other Gods Before Me. Why is this said? Because it says: "I am the Lord thy God." To give a parable: A king of flesh and blood entered a province. His attendants said to him: Issue some decrees upon the people. He, however, told them: No! When they will have accepted my reign I shall issue decrees upon them. For if they do not accept my reign how will they carry out my decrees? Likewise, God said to Israel: "I am the Lord thy God, thou shalt not have other gods—I am He whose reign you have taken upon yourselves in Egypt." And when they said to Him: "Yes, yes," He continued: "Now, just as you accepted My reign, you must also accept My decrees: 'Thou shalt not have other gods before Me.' " R. Simon b. Johai says: What is said further on: "I am the Lord your God," [Lev. 18:2] means: "I am He whose reign you have taken upon yourselves at Sinai," and when they said: "Yes, yes," He continued: "Well, you have accepted My reign, now accept My decrees: 'After the doings of the land of Egypt,' etc." [ibid. v. 3]. What is said here: "I am the Lord thy God who brought thee out from the land of Egypt," means: "I am He whose reign you have taken upon yourselves," and when they said to Him: "Yes, yes," He continued: "You have accepted My reign, now accept My decrees: 'Thou shalt not have other gods.' "

Thou Shalt Not Have. Why is this said? Because when it says: "Thou shalt not make unto thee a graven image," etc. [v. 4], I know only that it is forbidden to make any. But how do I know that it is forbidden to keep one that has already been made? Scripture says: "Thou shalt not have other gods," etc.

Other Gods. But are they gods? Has it not been said: "And have cast their gods into the fire; for they were no gods" [Isa. 37:19]? What then does Scripture mean when it says: "Other gods"? Merely those which others called gods. . . .

Before Me. Why is this said? In order not to give Israel an excuse for saying: Only those who came out from Egypt were commanded not to worship idols. Therefore, it is said: "Before Me," as much as to say: Just as I am living and enduring for ever and for all eternity, so also you and your son and your son's son to the end of generations shall not worship idols.

Thou Shalt Not Make unto Thee a Graven Image. He shall not make one that is engraven. But perhaps he may make one that is solid? Scripture says: "Nor any manner of likeness." He shall not make a solid one. But perhaps he may plant a plant as an idol for himself? Scripture says: "Thou shalt not plant thee an Ashera" [Deut. 16:21]. He shall not plant a plant for an idol to himself. But perhaps he may make an idol of a tree? Scripture says: "Of any kind of tree" [ibid.]. He shall not make an idol of a tree. But perhaps he may make one of stone? Scripture says: "Neither shall ye place any figured stone," etc. [Lev. 26:1]. He shall not make an idol of stone. But perhaps he may make one of silver or of gold? Scripture says: "Gods of silver or gods of gold ye shall not make unto you" [Ex. 20:20]. He shall not make an idol of silver or of gold. But perhaps he may make one of copper, iron, tin, or lead? Scripture says: "Nor make to yourselves molten gods" [Lev. 19:4]. He shall not make for himself any of these images. But perhaps he may make an image of any figure? Scripture says: "Lest ye deal corruptly, and make you a graven image, even the form of any figure" [Deut. 4:16]. He shall not make an image of any figure. . . .

Thou Shalt Not Bow Down unto Them nor Serve Them. Why is this said? Because it says: "And hath gone and served other gods" [Deut. 17:3], which means that one becomes guilty for the act of serving by itself and for the act of bowing down by itself. You interpret it thus. But may it not mean that one is guilty only if he both serves and bows down? Scripture however says here: "Thou shalt not bow down unto them nor serve them," declaring that one becomes guilty for the act of serving by itself and for the act of bowing down by itself.

Another Interpretation: *Thou Shalt Not Bow Down to Them.* Why is this said? Because it says: "He that sacrificeth unto the gods save unto the Lord only shall be utterly destroyed" [Ex. 22:19], from which we have heard the penalty for it, but we have not heard the warning against it. Therefore it says here: "Thou shalt not bow down to them." And it also says: "Thou shalt bow down to no other god" [ibid. 34:14].

For I the Lord Thy God Am a Jealous God. Rabbi says: A God above jealousy. I rule over jealousy, but jealousy has no power over Me. I rule over slumber, but slumber has no power over Me. And thus it says: "Behold, He that keepeth Israel doth neither slumber nor sleep" [Ps. 121:4].

Another Interpretation: *For I the Lord Thy God Am a Jealous God.* Zealously do I exact punishment for idolatry, but in other matters I am merciful and gracious.

A certain philosopher asked R. Gamaliel: It is written in your Torah: "For I the Lord thy God am a jealous God." But is there any power in the idol that it should arouse jealousy? A hero is jealous of another hero, a wise man is jealous of another wise man, a rich man is jealous of another rich man, but has the idol any power that one should be jealous of it?

R. Gamaliel said to him: Suppose a man would call his dog by the name of his father, so that when taking a vow he would vow: "By the life of this dog." Against whom would the father be incensed? Against the son or the dog?

Said the philosopher to him: Some idols are worth while.

What makes you think so? asked R. Gamaliel.

Said the philosopher: There raged a fire in a certain province but the temple of the idol in it was saved. Was it not because the idol could take care of itself?

Said R. Gamaliel to him: I will give you a parable: To what is this comparable? To the conduct of a king of flesh and blood when he goes out to war. Against whom does he wage war, against the living or against the dead?

The philosopher then said: Indeed, only against the living. Then he said again: But if there is no usefulness in any of them, why does He not annihilate them?

Said R. Gamaliel to him: But is it only one object that you worship? Behold you worship the sun, the moon, the stars and the planets, the mountains and the hills, the springs and the glens, and even human beings. Shall he destroy His world because of fools? "Shall I utterly consume all things from off the face of the earth? Saith the Lord" [Zeph. 1:2].

The philosopher also said to him: Since it causes the wicked to stumble, why does God not remove it from the world?

But R. Gamaliel continued saying: Because of fools? If so, then since they also worship human beings: "Shall I cut off man from off the face of the earth?" [ibid., v. 3].

Visiting the Iniquity of the Fathers upon the Children. When there is no skip, but not when there is a skip. How is this? The wicked son of a wicked father, who in turn also was the son of a wicked father. R. Nathan says: A destroyer the son of a destroyer, who in turn was the son of a destroyer. When Moses heard this word: "And Moses made haste, and bowed his head toward the earth, and worshipped" [Ex. 34:8]. For he said: God forbid! In Israel there is no case of a wicked son of a wicked father who in turn was also the son of a wicked father. One might think that just as the measure of punishment extends over four generations, so also the measure of rewarding the good extends only over four generations. But Scripture says: "Unto thousands." But: "Unto thousands" I might understand to mean the minimum of "thousands," that is, two thousand [people,] but it also says: "To a thousand generations" [Deut. 7:9]— generations unsearched and uncounted.

Of Them that Love Me and Keep My Commandments. "Of them that love Me," refers to our father Abraham and such as are like him. "And keep My commandments," refers to the prophets and the elders. R. Nathan says "Of them that love Me and keep My commandments," refers to those who dwell in the land of Israel and risk their lives for the sake of the commandments. . . .

CHAPTER VII [EXODUS 20:7–11]

Thou Shalt Not Take the Name of the Lord Thy God in Vain. Swearing falsely was also included in the general statement which says: "Or if any one swear clearly with his lips" [Lev. 5:4]. Behold, this passage here singles it out from the general statement, making the punishment for it severer but at the same time exempting it from carrying with it the obligation of bringing a sacrifice. One might think that just as it is exempt from the obligation of bringing a sacrifice it is also exempt from the punishment of stripes. But Scripture says: "Thou shalt not take the name of the Lord Thy God," etc. It has been exempted only from carrying with it the obligation of bringing a sacrifice, but not from carrying with it the penalty of stripes.

Remember the Day of the Sabbath to Keep it Holy. "Remember" and "observe" [Deut. 5:12] were both spoken at one utterance. . . . This is a manner of speech impossible for creatures of flesh and blood. For it is said: "God has spoken one utterance which we have heard as two," etc. [Ps. 62:12]. And it also says: "Is not My word like as fire? saith the Lord; and like a hammer that breaketh the rock in pieces?" [Jer. 23:29]. *Remember* and *observe.* Remember it before it comes, and observe it after it has gone. . . . Eleazar b. Hananiah b. Hezekiah b. Garon says: "Remember the day of the Sabbath to keep it holy," keep it in mind from the first day of the week on, so that if something good happens to come your way fix it up for the Sabbath. R. Isaac says: You shall not count the days of the week in the manner in which others count them. But you should count them with reference to the Sabbath.

To Keep It Holy. To consecrate it with a benediction. On the basis of this passage the sages said: At the entrance of the Sabbath we consecrate it by reciting the sanctification of the day over wine. From this I know only about the "sanctification" for the day. Whence do we know that the night also requires a "sanctification?" It is said: "Ye shall keep the

Sabbath," etc. [Ex. 31:14]. So far I know only about the Sabbath. How about the holidays? Scripture says: "These are the appointed seasons of the Lord," etc. [Lev. 23:4].

Six Days Shalt Thou Labour and Do All Thy Work. But is it possible for a human being to do all his work in six days? It simply means: Rest on the Sabbath as if all your work were done. Another Interpretation: Rest even from the thought of labor. And it says: "If thou turn away thy foot because of the Sabbath," etc. [Isa. 58:13] and then it says: "Then shalt thou delight thyself in the Lord," etc. [ibid. v. 14].

But the Seventh Day Is a Sabbath unto the Lord Thy God. Why is this said? Because it says: "Whosoever doeth any work in the sabbath day, he shall surely be put to death" [Ex. 31:15]. We have thus heard the penalty but we have not heard the warning. Therefore it says here: "But the seventh day is a sabbath unto the Lord thy God, in it thou shalt not do any manner of work." I thus know only the penalty for and the warning against work on Sabbath during the daytime. How do I know that there is also a penalty for and a warning against work during the night time of the Sabbath? It says: "Everyone that profaneth it shall surely be put to death" [Ex. 31:14]. From this however we only learn about the penalty. But we have not heard any warning. Scripture says: "But the seventh day is a sabbath unto the Lord thy God." Now there would be no purpose in saying "a sabbath" [instead of "a Sabbath day"] except to include the nighttime in the warning. These are the words of R. Ahai the son of Josiah.

Thou nor Thy Son nor Thy Daughter. That is, the minors. Perhaps it is not so but means the grown ups? You must reason: Have they not already been forewarned themselves? Hence what must be the meaning of: "Thou nor thy son nor thy daughter"? The minors.

Nor Thy Man-Servant nor Thy Maid-Servant. That is, children of the Covenant. You interpret it to mean children of the Covenant. Perhaps it is not so but refers to the uncircumcised slave? When it says: "And the son of thy handmaid and the stranger may be refreshed" [Ex. 23:12] behold, the uncircumcised slave is there spoken of. Hence whom does Scripture mean when it says here: "Nor thy man-servant nor thy maid-servant"? Those who are children of the Covenant.

Nor Thy Stranger. Meaning the righteous proselyte. Perhaps it is not so but means the resident alien? When it says: "And the stranger" [Ex. 23:12], behold, it speaks there of the resident alien. Hence what does it mean by saying here: "Thy stranger?" The righteous proselyte.

For in Six Days the Lord Made Heaven and Earth, the Sea, and All that In Them Is. This tells that the sea is equal to all the other works of creation.

And Rested on the Seventh Day. And is He subject to such a thing as weariness? Has it not been said: "The Creator of the ends of the earth fainteth not, neither is weary" [Isa. 40:28]? And it says: "He giveth power to the faint" [ibid. v. 29]. And it also says: "By the word of the Lord were the heavens made," etc. [Ps. 33:6]. How then can Scripture say: "And rested on the seventh day?" It is simply this: God allowed it to be written about Him that He created His world in six days and rested, as it were, on the seventh. Now by the method of *a fortiori* you must reason: If He, for whom there is no weariness, allowed it to be written that He created His world in six days and rested on the seventh, how much more should man, of whom it is written: "But man is born unto trouble" [Job 5:7], rest on the seventh day.

Wherefore the Lord Blessed the Sabbath Day and Hallowed It. He blessed it with the manna and hallowed it by the manna.—These are the words of R. Ishmael. R. Akiba says: He blessed it with the manna and hallowed it by prescribing a benediction for it. R. Isaac says: He blessed it with the manna and declared it holy by the verdict upon the wood-gatherer [Num. 15:35]. R. Simon the son of Johai says: He blessed it with the manna and hallowed it by the lights. R. Simon the son of Judah of Kefar Akko says in the name of R. Simon: He blessed it with the manna and hallowed it by the shining countenance of man's face. In this sense it is said: "Wherefore the Lord blessed the sabbath day and hallowed it."

CHAPTER VIII [EXODUS 20:12–14]

Honour Thy Father and Thy Mother. I might understand it to mean only with words but Scripture says: "Honour the Lord with thy substance," etc. [Prov. 3.9]. Hence it must mean, with food and drink and with clean garments.

Another Interpretation: *Honour Thy Father.* . . . Rabbi says: The honoring of one's father and mother is very dear in the sight of Him by whose word the world came into being. For He declared honoring them to be equal to honoring Him, fearing them equal to fearing Him, and cursing them equal to cursing Him. It is written: "Honour thy father and thy mother," and correspondingly it is written: "Honour the Lord with thy substance" [Prov. 3:9]. Scripture thus puts the honoring of one's parents on an equality with honoring God. It is written: "Ye shall fear every man his mother and his father" [Lev. 19:3], and correspondingly it is written: "Thou shalt fear the Lord thy God" [Deut. 6:13]. Scripture thus puts the fear of one's father and mother on an equality with the fear of God. It is written: "And he that curseth his father or his mother shall surely be put to death" [Ex. 21:17], and correspondingly it is written: "Whosoever curseth his God," etc. [Lev. 24: 15]. Scripture thus puts the cursing of one's father and mother on an equality with the cursing of God. Come and see the rewards for obeying these two commandments. It is said: "Honour the Lord with thy substance . . . so shall thy barns be filled with plenty," etc. [Prov. 3:9–10]. And it says: "Honour thy father and thy mother that thy days may be long." "Thou shalt fear the Lord thy God" [Deut. 6:13]. And it promises in reward: "But unto you that fear My name shall the sun of righteousness arise with healing in its wings'" [Mal. 3:20]. It also says: "Ye shall fear every man his mother and his father, and ye shall keep My sabbaths" [Lev. 19:3]. Now what is promised as a reward for keeping the Sabbath? "If thou turn away thy foot because of the sabbath . . . then shalt thou delight thyself in the Lord," etc. [Isa. 58:13–14].

Rabbi says: It is revealed and known before Him by whose word the world came into being that a man honors his mother more than his father because she sways him with persuasive words. Therefore in the commandment to honor He mentions the father before the mother. And it is revealed and known before Him by whose word the world came into being that a man is more afraid of his father than of his mother because he teaches him the Torah. Therefore in the commandment to fear He mentions the mother before the father. Where something is imperfect Scripture seeks to make it complete. Perhaps, however, it means that the one preceding in this text should actually have precedence over the other, but there is a teaching against this in the passage: "Ye shall fear every man his mother and his father," [Lev. 19:3], where the mother precedes. Scripture thus declares that both are equal, the one as important as the other. . . .

Thou Shalt Not Murder. Why is this said? Because it says: "Whoso sheddeth man's blood," etc. [Gen. 9:6]. We have thus heard the penalty for it, but we have not heard the warning against it; therefore it says here: "Thou shalt not murder."

Thou Shalt Not Commit Adultery. Why is this said? Because it says: "Both the adulterer and the adulteress shall surely be put to death" [Lev. 20:10]. We have thus heard the penalty for it but we have not heard the warning against it; therefore it says here: "Thou shalt not commit adultery."

Thou Shalt Not Steal. Why is this said? Because it says: "And he that stealeth a man and selleth him" [Ex. 21:16]. We have thus heard the penalty for it but we have not heard the warning against it; therefore it says here: "Thou shalt not steal." Behold then this is a warning against stealing persons. . . .

Thou Shalt Not Bear False Witness against Thy Neighbor. Why is this said? Because it says: "Then shall ye do unto him as he purposed to do unto his brother" [Deut. 19:19]. We have thus heard the penalty for it but we have not heard the warning against it; therefore it says here: "Thou shalt not bear false witness," etc.

How were the Ten Commandments arranged? Five on the one tablet and five on the other. On the one tablet was written: "I am the Lord thy God." And opposite it on the other tablet was written: "Thou shalt not murder." This tells that if one sheds blood it is accounted to him as though he diminished the divine image.

To give a parable: A king of flesh and blood entered a province and the people set up portraits of him, made images of him, and struck coins in his honor. Later on they upset his portraits, broke his images, and defaced his coins, thus diminishing the likeness of the king. So also if one sheds blood it is accounted to him as though he had diminished the divine image. For it is said: "Whoso sheddeth man's blood . . . for in the image of God made He man" [Gen. 9:6].

On the one tablet was written: "Thou shalt have no other god." And opposite it on the other tablet was written: "Thou shalt not commit adultery." This tells that if one worships idols it is accounted to him as though he committed adultery, breaking his covenant with God. For it is said: "Thou wife that committest adultery, that takest strangers instead of thy husband" [Ezek. 16:32]. And it is also written: "And the Lord said unto me: Go yet, love a woman beloved of her friend and an adulteress," etc. [Hos. 3:1]. On the one tablet was written: "Thou shalt not take." And opposite it on the other tablet was written: "Thou shalt not steal." This tells that he who steals will in the end also swear falsely. For it is said: "Will ye steal, murder and commit adultery and swear falsely" [Jer. 7:9].

And it is also written: "Swearing and lying, and killing, and stealing, and committing adultery" [Hos. 4:2]. On the one tablet was written: "Remember the Sabbath day to keep it holy." And opposite it on the other tablet was written: "Thou shalt not bear false witness." This tells that if one profanes the Sabbath it is as though he testified in the presence of Him by whose word the world came into being that He did not create the world in six days and did not rest on the seventh day. But he who keeps the Sabbath does testify in His presence that he did create the world in six days and did rest on the seventh, as it is said: "Ye are my witnesses, saith the Lord" [Isa. 43:10].

On the one tablet was written: "Honour thy father," etc. And opposite it on the other tablet was written: "Thou shalt not covet thy neighbour's wife." This tells that he who covets will in the end beget a son who may curse his real father while giving filial honor to one who is not his father. It was for this that the Ten Commandments were arranged five on one tablet and five on the other. These are the words of R. Hananiah, the son of Gamaliel. But the other sages say: All the ten were written on each of the two tablets. For it is said: "These words . . . and He wrote them upon two tablets of stone," etc. [Deut. 5:19]. . . .

Thou shalt Not Covet. Rabbi says: One passage says: "Thou shalt not covet" and one passage says: "Thou shalt not desire" [Deut. 5:18]. How are both these passages to be maintained? Behold the latter one is a prohibition against seeking opportunity to benefit by encouraging the adulterer.

Thou Shalt Not Covet Thy Neighbour's House. This is a general statement. *Nor His Manservant, nor His Maid-Servant, nor His Ox, nor His Ass,* are specific. Now a general statement followed by a specific statement cannot include more than the specific statement. When it says however: *Nor Anything that is Thy Neighbour's,* it again makes a general statement. . . .

MIDRASH RABBAH

CHAPTER I (EXODUS)

18. AND PHARAOH CHARGED ALL HIS PEOPLE [1, 22]. R. Jose b. R. Hanina said: He decreed against his own people too. And why was this? Because his astrologers told him, "The mother of Israel's saviour is already pregnant with him, but we do not know whether he is an Israelite or an Egyptian." Then Pharaoh assembled all the Egyptians before him and said: "Lend me your children for nine months that I may cast them in the river," as it is written: EVERY SON THAT IS BORN, YE SHALL CAST INTO THE RIVER [ib. 22]. It does not say "every son who is an Israelite," but "every son," whether he be Jew or Egyptian. But they would not agree, saying: "An Egyptian son would not redeem them; he must be an Hebrew."

YE SHALL CAST INTO THE RIVER. Why did they decree that they should cast them into the river? Because the astrologers foresaw that Israel's saviour would be smitten by means of water, and they thought that he would be drowned in the water; but, as we know, it was only on account of the well of water that the decree of death was pronounced upon him, as it is said: Because ye believed not in Me [Num. 20:12]. The Rabbis say: They took deep counsel so that God should not exact retribution from them through water. They knew that God repays measure for measure, and they were confident that He would no longer bring a flood upon the world, so they decided to drown them. AND EVERY DAUGHTER YE SHALL SAVE ALIVE; what need did Pharaoh have to save the girls? What they said in fact was: "Let us kill the males so that we may take unto ourselves the females for wives," for the Egyptians were steeped in immorality.

19. AND THERE WENT A MAN OF THE HOUSE OF LEVI [2:1]. Where did he go? R. Judah, the son of R. Zebina, said: He followed his daughter's advice. It was taught: Amram was the leading man of his generation; AND TOOK TO WIFE A DAUGHTER OF LEVI. It does not say "he took her back," but HE TOOK, proving, said R. Judah, the son of Zebina, that he went through a marriage ceremony with her. He placed her on the bridal litter, Miriam and Aaron dancing before them and the angels saying: As a joyful mother of children [Ps. 113:9].

A DAUGHTER OF LEVI. Is it possible that she was 130 years old and could still be called A DAUGHTER? For did not R. Hama b. Hanina say it was Jochebed; and she was conceived on the way, and was born between the walls, as it is said: And the name of Amram's wife was Jochebed, the daughter of Levi, who was born to Levi in Egypt [Num. 26:59], which we explain to mean that her birth took place in Egypt, but not her conception, and yet she is called DAUGHTER?—This shows, said R. Judah, son of R. Zebina, that the symptoms of youth came back to her.

20. AND THE WOMAN CONCEIVED AND BORE A SON [2:2].
R. Judah said: Her giving birth is compared to her pregnancy; just as her
pregnancy was painless so was her giving birth—a proof that righteous
women were not included in the decree pronounced on Eve. AND WHEN
SHE SAW HIM THAT HE WAS A GOODLY CHILD—TOB. It was
taught: R. Meir says: His name was "Tob." R. Josiah says: His name was
Tobiah. R. Judah says: He was fit for prophecy. Others say: He was
born circumcised. The sages say: When Moses was born the whole house
became flooded with light; for here it says: AND SHE SAW HIM THAT
HE WAS A GOODLY CHILD, and elsewhere it says: And God saw the
light, that it was good [Gen. 1:4].

AND SHE HID HIM THREE MONTHS [Ex. ib.]. [This was possible]
because the Egyptians counted from the time he took her back, when she
was already three months pregnant with him. AND WHEN SHE COULD
NO LONGER HIDE HIM [2:3]. How was this? Because the Egyptians
went about from house to house, where they thought a babe had been born,
taking with them a small Egyptian child and making him cry, so that the
Israelitish baby might hear his cry and cry with him. Hence doth it say:
Take us the foxes, the little foxes, that spoil the vineyards [S.S. 2:15].

21. SHE TOOK FOR HIM AN ARK OF BULRUSHES [2:3]. Why
of bulrushes? R. Eleazar said: Because the money of the righteous is dearer
to them than their persons. Why? Because they do not commit robbery.
R. Samuel b. Nahman explained: because a soft thing can withstand the
pressure of both soft and hard elements. AND SHE DAUBED IT WITH
SLIME AND WITH PITCH. It was taught: Slime within and pitch without, so that this righteous child should not inhale an evil smell.

AND SHE PUT THE CHILD THEREIN, AND LAID IT IN THE
FLAGS (SUF) BY THE RIVER'S BRINK [ib.]. R. Eleazar says: It was
the Red Sea, because the Red Sea (yam suf) reaches as far as the Nile.
R. Samuel b. Nahman says: It was a kind of reed, as in the reeds and flags
[suf] shall wither [Isa. 19:6]. Why did they cast him into the river? So
that the astrologers might think that he had already been cast into the
water, and would not search for him.

22. AND HIS SISTER STOOD AFAR OFF [2:4]. Why did Miriam
stand afar off? R. Amram in the name of Rab said: Because Miriam
prophesied, "My mother is destined to give birth to a son who will save
Israel"; and when the house was flooded with light at the birth of Moses,
her father arose and kissed her head and said: "My daughter, thy prophecy
has been fulfilled." This is the meaning of: And Miriam the prophetess,
the sister of Aaron, took a timbrel [Ex. 15:20]; "The sister of Aaron,"
but not of Moses?—She is so called because in fact she said this prophecy
when she was yet only the sister of Aaron, Moses not having been born yet.
Now that she was casting him into the river, her mother struck her on the
head, saying: "My daughter, what about thy prophecy?" This is why it
says: AND HIS SISTER STOOD AFAR OFF, to know what would be

the outcome of her prophecy. The Rabbis interpreted the whole verse as referring to the Holy Spirit. AND SHE STOOD, hinting at: And the Lord came, and stood [I Sam. 3:10]. HIS SISTER, hinting at: Say unto wisdom: Thou art my sister [Prov. 7:4]. FROM AFAR, hinting at: From afar the Lord appeared unto me [Jer. 31:3]. TO KNOW WHAT WOULD BE DONE TO HIM, hinting at: For the Lord is a God of knowledge [I Sam. 2:3].

23. TO BATHE IN THE RIVER [2:5]. To cleanse herself from the idols of her father's palace. AND HER MAIDENS WALKED ALONG. R. Johanan said, the expression "walked" here means, walking to meet death, as it is said: Behold, I am at the point to die [Gen. 25:32]. They said to her: "Your Highness, it is the general rule that when a king makes a decree, his own family will obey that decree even if everyone else transgresses it; but you are flagrantly disobeying your father's command?" Whereupon Gabriel came and smote them to the ground.

AND SHE SENT HER HANDMAID TO FETCH IT. . . . The Rabbis say that Pharaoh's daughter was leprous and went down to bathe, but as soon as she touched the ark she became healed. For this reason did she take pity upon Moses and loved him with an exceeding love.

24. AND SHE OPENED IT, AND SAW IT [2:6]. It does not say "And she saw," but AND SHE SAW IT. This is because, said R. Jose b. Hanina, she saw that the Shechinah was with him; that is, the IT refers to the Shechinah which was with the child. AND BEHOLD A BOY THAT WEPT. Why is he called both child and boy? To show that though he was only a child, his voice sounded like that of a boy: so said R. Judah. Whereupon R. Nehemiah said to him: If this be so, you are thrusting a blemish upon Moses our teacher, peace be upon him. The fact is that this is to teach us that his mother arranged a youthful bridal canopy for him in the ark.

THAT WEPT. He was weeping, saying: "I may never see again my sister who is waiting for me." Another explanation of AND BEHOLD A BOY THAT WEPT is, that though he was a child, he behaved like a grown-up boy. Gabriel came and smote Moses so that he should cry and she (the princess) be filled with pity for him. AND SHE HAD COMPASSION ON HIM; when she saw that he was crying, she had pity on him. AND SAID: THIS IS ONE OF THE HEBREWS' CHILDREN. What did she recognise in him? She saw, said R. Jose, son of R. Hanina, that he was circumcised.

What did she mean by THIS IS ONE OF THE HEBREWS' CHILDREN? This one had to fall in the river, not another; and when they had cast Moses into the river, the decree was rescinded. This is in accordance with R. Eleazar's explanation of the text: And when they shall say unto you: Seek unto the ghosts and the familiar spirits, that chirp and that mutter [Isa. 8:19]—they see and do not know what they see, they murmur and do not know what they murmur. They foresaw that Israel's deliverer would be punished through water, so they decreed "Every son that is born," etc., and as soon as Moses had been cast into the water, they said: "Their saviour has already been cast into the water"; the decree was therefore immediately canceled.

Little did they know that he was only to be punished on account of the waters of Meribah. . . .

26. AND THE CHILD GREW [2:10]. She suckled him only for twenty-four months, and you say: AND THE CHILD GREW? This is to teach you that he grew abnormally. AND SHE BROUGHT HIM UNTO PHARAOH'S DAUGHTER. Pharaoh's daughter used to kiss and hug him, loved him as if he were her own son and would not allow him out of the royal palace. Because he was so handsome, everyone was eager to see him, and whoever saw him could not tear himself away from him. Pharaoh also used to kiss and hug him, and Moses used to take the crown of Pharaoh and place it upon his own head, as he was destined to do when he became great. It was this which God said to Miriam: Therefore have I brought forth a fire from the midst of thee [Ezek. 28:18], and even so did the daughter of Pharaoh bring up him who was destined to exact retribution from her father.

The magicians of Egypt sat there and said: "We are afraid of him who is taking off thy crown and placing it upon his own head, lest he be the one of whom we prophesy that he will take away the kingdom from thee." Some of them counselled to slay him and others to burn him, but Jethro was present among them and he said to them: "This boy has no sense. However, test him by placing before him a gold vessel and a live coal; if he stretch forth his hand for the gold, then he has sense and you can slay him, but if he make for the live coal, then he has no sense and there can be no sentence of death upon him."

So they brought these things before him, and he was about to reach forth for the gold when Gabriel came and thrust his hand aside so that it seized the coal, and he thrust his hand with the live coal into his mouth, so that his tongue was burnt, with the result that he became slow of speech and of tongue. AND SHE CALLED HIS NAME MOSES—From here you can infer how great is the reward of those who perform kind acts; for although Moses had many names, the name by which he is known throughout the Torah is the one which Bithia, the daughter of Pharaoh, called him, and even God called him by no other name.

27. AND IT CAME TO PASS IN THOSE DAYS, WHEN MOSES WAS GROWN UP [2:11]. Moses was twenty years old at the time; some say forty. "When Moses was grown up." Does not everyone grow up? Only to teach you that he was abnormal in his growth. AND HE WENT OUT UNTO HIS BRETHREN. This righteous man went out on two occasions and God recorded them one after the other. And he went out on the second day [ib. 13]—these were the two occasions. AND HE LOOKED ON THEIR BURDENS [ib. 11]. What is the meaning of AND HE

LOOKED? He looked upon their burdens and wept, saying: "Woe is me for you; would that I could die for you." There is no labour more strenuous than that of handling clay, and he used to shoulder the burdens and help each one.

R. Eleazar, son of R. Jose the Galilean, said: He saw great burdens put upon small people and light burdens put upon big people, and a man's burden upon a woman and a woman's burden upon a man, and the burden which an old man could carry on a youth, and of a youth on an old man. So he left his suite and rearranged their burdens, pretending all the time to be helping Pharaoh.

God then said to him: "Thou hast put aside thy work and hast gone to share the sorrow of Israel, behaving to them like a brother; well, I will also leave those on high and below and only speak with thee." Hence it is written: And when the Lord saw that he turned aside to see [ib. 3:4]; because God saw that Moses turned aside from his duties to look upon their burdens, He called unto him out of the midst of the bush [ib.].

28. Another interpretation of AND HE LOOKED ON THEIR BURDENS: He saw that they had no rest, so he went to Pharaoh and said: "If one has a slave and he does not give him rest one day in the week he dies; similarly, if thou wilt not give thy slaves one day in the week rest, they will die." Pharaoh replied: "Go and do with them as thou sayest." Thereupon Moses ordained for them the Sabbath day for rest.

AND HE SAW AN EGYPTIAN SMITING A HEBREW. What did he see? R. Huna in the name of Bar Kappara said: Israel was redeemed from Egypt on account of four things, one being because they did not change their names. Whence do we know that they were not suspect of adultery? Because there was only one immoral woman and the Bible published her name, as it is said: And his mother's name was Shelomith, the daughter of Dibri [Lev. 24:11].

The Rabbis said: The taskmasters were Egyptians but the officers were Israelites, one taskmaster being appointed over ten officers and one officer over ten Israelites. The taskmasters used to go to the officers' houses early in the morning to drag them out to work at cockcrow. Once an Egyptian taskmaster went to a Jewish officer and set eyes upon his wife who was beautiful without blemish. He waited for cockcrow, when he dragged the officer out of his house and then returned to lie down with the woman who thought that it was her husband, with the result that she became pregnant from him.

When her husband returned, he discovered the Egyptian emerging from his house. He then asked her: "Did he touch you?" She replied: "Yes, for I thought it was you." When the taskmaster realised that he was caught, he made him go back to his hard labour, smiting him and trying to slay him.

When Moses saw this, he knew by means of the Holy Spirit what had happened in the house and what the Egyptian was about to do in the field;

so he said: "This man certainly deserves his death, as it is written: And he that smiteth any man mortally shall surely be put to death [ib. 17]. Moreover, since he cohabited with the wife of Dathan he deserves slaying, as it is said: Both the adulterer and the adulteress shall surely be put to death" [ib. 20:10]. Hence does it say: AND HE LOOKED THIS WAY AND THAT WAY [2:12], namely, he saw what he did to him [Dathan] in the house and what he intended doing to him in the field.

29. AND WHEN HE SAW THAT THERE WAS NO MAN [2:12]—for he saw that the smitten man would no longer live. R. Judah said: He saw THAT THERE WAS NO MAN who would be zealous for God and slay him. R. Nehemiah says: He saw that there was none who would mention over him God's name and slay him. The Sages said: He saw that there was no hope that righteous persons would arise from him or his off-spring until the end of generations.

When Moses saw this, he took counsel with the angels and said to them: "This man deserves death." They agreed; hence it says: AND WHEN HE SAW THAT THERE WAS NO MAN to say a good word for him. AND HE SMOTE THE EGYPTIAN. With what did he slay him? R. Abyathar said: With the fist; and others say that he took a clay shovel and cracked his skull. The Rabbis say that he pronounced God's name against him and thus slew him, for it is said: Sayest thou to kill me? [ib. 14].

AND HID HIM IN THE SAND; as only Israelites were there, who are likened to sand, he hid him in their presence. He said unto them: "You are compared to sand, and just as sand when taken from one place to another emits no sound, so must this thing be hidden between you, that nothing be heard of it." You will thus find that the thing was only heard of through the Hebrews, as it is said: AND HE WENT OUT THE SECOND DAY, AND BEHOLD, TWO MEN OF THE HEBREWS WERE STRIVING TOGETHER [ib. 13]. This refers to Dathan and Abiram, whom he calls "striving" on account of their subsequent record; for it was they who said this thing; it was they who left over of the Manna; they it was who said: Let us make a captain, and let us return into Egypt [Num. 14:4]. It was they who rebelled at the Red Sea.

Another explanation of STRIVING is that they intended to slay one another; as it says: When men strive together one with another [Deut. 25:1], and R. Eleazar said: The verse speaks of a strife involving death. AND HE SAID TO HIM THAT DID THE WRONG, WHEREFORE WILT THOU SMITE THY FELLOW. It does not say: "Wherefore hast thou smitten?" but WHEREFORE WILT THOU SMITE? To teach us that from the moment one lifts up his hand to smite his fellow, though he has not yet smitten him, he is called wicked. THY FELLOW, who is as wicked as thou art; this tells us that both were wicked.

30. AND HE SAID: WHO MADE THEE A RULER AND JUDGE OVER US? [ib. 14]. R. Judah said: Moses was twenty years old then. They said to him: "You are not yet fit to be a judge and ruler over us, for

only a man of forty possesses full understanding." R. Nehemiah says: He was forty years old, and they said to him: "You are certainly a man, but not fit to be a ruler and judge over us." The Sages say that they said to him: "Are you not the son of Jochebed? Then why do they call you the son of Bithiah? You seek to become a ruler and judge over us; very well, we will divulge what you have done to the Egyptian." SAYEST THOU TO KILL ME. It does not say "thou seekest," but THOU SAYEST, implying that he just pronounced the Tetragrammaton over the Egyptian and slew him. When he heard this, he was afraid of being informed against.

AND HE SAID: SURELY THE THING IS KNOWN. R. Judah, son of R. Shalom, said in the name of R. Hanina the Great, and our Sages quoted it in the name of R. Alexandri: Moses was meditating in his heart, "Wherein have Israel sinned that they should be enslaved more than all the nations?" When he heard these words, he said: "Tale-bearing is rife among them, and how can they be ripe for salvation?" Hence SURELY THE THING IS KNOWN—now I know the cause of their bondage.

31. NOW WHEN PHARAOH HEARD [ib. 15]. Dathan and Abiram informed against him. He SOUGHT TO SLAY MOSES. Pharaoh sent for a sword that had no equal and struck him ten times upon his neck, but the neck of Moses became like an ivory pillar and he could not harm him, as it is said: Thy neck is as a tower of ivory [S.S. 7:5]. AND MOSES FLED FROM THE FACE OF PHARAOH. Said R. Jannai: Is it possible for a man to escape from a king? No; but when they seized Moses and condemned him to be beheaded, an angel from heaven descended in the form of Moses; and while they seized the angel, meanwhile Moses escaped.

R. Joshua b. Levi said: All the counsellors who sat before Pharaoh became some mute, others deaf, and others blind. When he said to the mute: "Where is Moses?" there was no reply. When he spoke to the deaf, they did not hear; to the blind, they did not see. This is what God said to Moses: "Who hath made man's mouth?" [Ex. 4:11], namely, who made a mouth unto Pharaoh that he should say: "Bring Moses to the scaffold to be slain." "Or who maketh a man mute?" "Who made the chiefs (counsellors) mute, deaf and blind that they should not fetch thee to him? And who made thee clever enough to escape? Is it not I, the Lord? [ib.]. I was with thee, and today, I stand by thee."

CHAPTER II (EXODUS)

5. AND THE ANGEL OF THE LORD APPEARED UNTO HIM (3, 2). It is written: I sleep, but my heart waketh [S.S. 5:2]. I am asleep as regards the commandments, but my heart is awake to do them. My undefiled—tamathi [ib.]—because they attached themselves (nithtamemu) to Me at Sinai and said: "All that the Lord had spoken will we do, and obey" [Ex. 24:7]. R. Jannai said: Just as in the case of twins (te'omim),

if one has a pain in his head the other feels it also, so God said, as it were: "I will be with him in trouble" [Ps. 91:15]. Another explanation: What does "I will be with him in trouble" mean? When they are in any trouble, they will call upon none but the Lord; in Egypt—and their cry came up unto God [Ex. 2:23]; by the sea—and the children of Israel cried out unto the Lord [ib. 14:10], and numerous examples like these. It says: In all their affliction He was afflicted [Isa. 63:9]. God said to Moses: "Do you not realise that I live in trouble just as Israel live in trouble? Know from the place whence I speak unto you—from a thorn-bush—that I am, as it were, a partner in their trouble." . . .

OUT OF THE MIDST OF THE BUSH. A heathen once asked R. Joshua b. Karhah: Why did God choose a thorn-bush from which to speak to Moses? He replied: Were it a carob tree or a sycamore tree, you would have asked the same question; but to dismiss you without any reply is not right, so I will tell you why. To teach you that no place is devoid of God's presence, not even a thorn-bush.

IN A FLAME OF FIRE. At first an angel acted as intermediary and stood in the centre of the fire, and afterwards the Shechinah descended and spoke with him from the midst of the thorn-bush. R. Eliezer said: Just as the thorn-bush is the lowliest of all trees in the world, so Israel were lowly and humble in Egypt; therefore did God reveal Himself to them and redeem them, as it is said: And I am come down to deliver them from Egypt [ib. 8]. R. Jose said: Just as the thorn-bush is the prickliest of all trees and any bird that goes into it does not come out unscathed, so was the servitude of Egypt more grievous before God than all other servitudes in the world, as it is said: And the Lord said: I have surely seen (raoh raithi) the affliction of My people [ib. 7].

Why does it say "seen" twice? Because after drowning them in the river, they immured them in a building. It is as if one took a stick and smote therewith two men, so that both received the lash and knew its sting. So was the pain and servitude of Israel revealed and known to Him at Whose word the world came into being, for it is said: For I know their pains [ib.].

R. Johanan said: Just as one makes of thorns a fence for a garden, so Israel is a fence to the world. Moreover, just as the thorn-bush grows near any water, so Israel grew only in virtue of the Torah that is called water, as it is said: Ho, every one that thirsteth, come ye for water [Isa. 55:1]. Further, just as thorns grow in the garden and by the river, so Israel participates both in this world and the world to come. Also, just as the thorn-bush produces thorns and roses, so among Israel are there righteous and wicked.

R. Phinehas b. Hama the priest said: Just as when a man puts his hand into a thorn-bush he does not at first feel it, but when he takes it out it scratches, so when Israel came into Egypt nobody perceived them, but when they went out, they departed with signs and wonders and battle.

R. Judah b. Shalom said: Just as a bird does not feel when it flies into a thorn-bush, but when it flies out its wings are torn to pieces, so when Abraham came to Egypt nobody noticed him, but when he departed, the Lord smote Pharaoh with plagues.

Another explanation of FROM THE MIDST OF A BUSH, is given by R. Nahman, son of R. Samuel b. Nahman. Some trees produce one leaf, some two or three; the myrtle, for instance, produces three because it is called a thick tree [Lev. 23:40], but the thorn-bush has five leaves. God said to Moses: "Israel will be redeemed for the sake of Abraham, Isaac, and Jacob and for thy sake and the sake of Aaron." FROM THE MIDST OF A BUSH—God hinted to him that he would live 120 years—the numerical value of the letters comprising the word.

AND HE LOOKED, AND BEHOLD, THE BUSH BURNED WITH FIRE. From this they derived that the heavenly fire shoots out branches upwards, burns but does not consume, and is black in colour; whereas fire used here below does not branch upwards and is red and consumes but does not burn. Why did God show Moses such a symbol? Because he (Moses) had thought to himself that the Egyptians might consume Israel; hence did God show him a fire which burnt but did not consume, saying to him: "Just as the thorn-bush is burning and is not consumed, so the Egyptians will not be able to destroy Israel."

Further, because when God spoke to Moses, the latter was unwilling at first to desist from his work, He therefore showed him this thing, so that he might turn his face to see and speak with Him. Hence you find at first: AND THE ANGEL OF THE LORD APPEARED UNTO HIM; and yet Moses did not go to see what it was. As soon as Moses stopped his work and went to see, straightaway God called unto him [3:4].

6. AND MOSES SAID: I WILL TURN ASIDE NOW, AND SEE [3:3]. R. Johanan said, Moses took five steps then, as it is said: "I will turn aside now, and see." R. Simeon b. Lakish said: He simply turned his face to see, as it is said: And when the Lord saw that he turned aside to see. When God saw this, He said: This man is worthy to tend Israel. R. Isaac said: What is the meaning of: HE TURNED ASIDE (SAR) TO SEE? God said: "This man is downcast (sar) and troubled at seeing Israel's affliction in Egypt, he is accordingly, worthy of being their shepherd." Immediately, "God called unto him out of the midst of the bush."

AND HE SAID: MOSES, MOSES. . . . R. Simeon b. Johai taught: What does MOSES, MOSES mean? It is an expression of love and exhortation. Another interpretation of MOSES, MOSES: it was he who taught the Torah in this life, and he will teach it in the next. For Israel will in the time to come go to Abraham and say to him: "Teach us Torah"; and he will reply: "Go to Isaac who studied more than I did," and Isaac will say: "Go to Jacob who waited more upon scholars than I did." Jacob will reply: "Go to Moses who has learnt the law from God Himself," as it is written: They go from strength to strength, every one of them appeareth before Elohim in Zion [Ps. 84:8]. "Elohim" here refers to Moses, as it says: Behold I have given thee as a god (elohim) unto Pharaoh. R. Aba b. Kahana said that he whose name is repeated will inherit both worlds.

AND HE SAID: HERE AM I—here am I for priesthood and royalty. God said to him: "You are standing in the place of the pillar of the world." Abraham said: "Here am I" and you say "Here am I." Moses wished to have priests and kings descending from him, but God said: DRAW NOT NIGH THITHER [3:5], that is, your sons will not offer up sacrifices, for the priesthood has already been allotted to your brother Aaron. THITHER (HALOM) refers to kingship, for it says: That Thou hast brought me thus far—halom [2 Sam. 7:18], and it also says: Is there yet a man come-hither—halom [1 Sam. 10:22]. Thus God said to him: Kingship is already assigned to David. Yet even so, Moses obtained both—priesthood, in that he ministered during the seven days of consecration, and kingship, as it says: And he was a king in Jeshurun [Deut. 23:5].

PUT OFF THY SHOES. Wherever the Shechinah appears one must not go about with shoes on; and so we find in the case of Joshua: Put off thy shoe [Josh. 5:15]. Hence the priests ministered in the Temple, barefooted.

The Siddur

The Siddur (literally, order [of prayers]) takes its place with the Bible, the Talmud and the Zohar as one of the classic works of Judaism—perhaps the most often used text of Hebrew literature.

The Siddur assumes man's belief in God and his need to worship, a basic theme that finds infinite expression and variation in the hundreds of prayers included in the Siddur. Prayer is evident in the earliest layer of Jewish history, and examples appear in the three major sections of the Bible (Torah, Prophets and Writings): for example, Abraham pleading for Sodom (Gen. 18:22–32), Hannah in the Tabernacle (I Sam. 2:1–10), and Jonah in the belly of the great fish (Jonah 2:1–9). One Biblical book, Psalms, is basically composed of prayers.

Despite the frequency of prayers in the Bible, it was only after the close of the Talmud (500 C.E.) that prayers were first collected in formal fashion, for the prohibition against writing down the Oral Law applied to prayers as well. There are individual meditations quoted in the Talmud, and extensive discussions and regulations concerning various prayers. However, the precise origin of formal prayer is obscure. (In Daniel 6:11 we read that Daniel faced Jerusalem and "kneeled . . . three times a day and prayed," and Psalm 55:18 refers to prayer "evening, morning and noon," thus giving a precedent for the thrice-daily services.) Organized prayer evolved as a substitute for the no longer extant sacrifices at the Temple in Jerusalem. Prayer and the development of the synagogue (in Babylonia) even prior to the destruction of the Second Temple was to a degree the salvation of Judaism. For even with its central religious and national shrine gone, Judaism was able to continue.

In the Siddur, anonymous declarations and by-lines of famous personalities intermingle. In addition to sections of the Bible, passages from the Mishnah and Talmud were added to the Siddur to enable the average person to study a minimum of sacred texts. Later, individual *piyyutim* (liturgical poems) and prayers were included in the Siddur, which absorbed contributions from all centers of Jewry. The Siddur, then, is actually an anthology, a treasury of folk creativity that spans nearly 4000 years and many geographic locales. The *Shema* ("Hear O Israel"), the most ancient, and most important, prayer in the Siddur, goes back to the times of Moses; the *Shemoneh Esrey* ("Silent Devotion"), the nucleus of every service, is more than two thousand years old. The Mishnah (see Rosh Hashanah 4:5, page 95) mentions several blessings in its discussion of the Rosh Hashanah service, and the Talmud discusses the *Tefillah* [prayer] another name for the "Silent Devotion." In contrast, the prayer for the State of Israel stems from 1948.

The three basic *minhagim* (rites, customs of service) are the Sephardic, Ashkenazic and Italian, among which there is little difference except for an occasional divergence in order and style of prayers and some hymns which may appear in one *minhag* and not in another. Whether a Jew prays in India, Yemen, North Africa, Europe, America, *etc.*, remarkably enough he finds the same basic service.

By the time the first prayerbooks were formulated, the Jews were no longer a nation with their own homeland but already a nation in Diaspora. Nevertheless, despite their dispersion, Hebrew remained the language of prayer, partly because of the Jews' eternal hope of national revival, and partly because all Jews were supposed to pray in one language. Although Hebrew is the language of Jewish prayer, some prayers (among others, the Kaddish and Kol Nidre) are in Aramaic; in the Sephardic rite Ladino is occasionally used; in the Ashkenazic rite Yiddish is used in one instance—in a phrase introducing the public recitation of "Grace After Meals."

The Siddur is responsible for the continuing awareness of the Jews' national ideals, including the use of Hebrew and the desire to return to Zion. Other recurring themes—despite the gap of millenia between the oldest and newest prayers—are the welfare of the Jewish people, the rebuilding of Jerusalem, the abolition of evil, the spread of peace, and the return of God's presence to Israel. Prayers rarely request material benefits; rather, they stress redemption, forgiveness, health, and gratitude to God. Since prayer is in the name of the entire people, it is almost always phrased in the plural; however, some private meditations, originally composed by the sages, appear in the singular.

The earliest extant Siddur is that of Rabbi Amram Gaon of the Sura Academy in Babylonia (875). The next in age and importance is the Siddur of Saadya Gaon, head of the Sura Academy from 928–942. Other early compilations were those of Maimonides (the Sephardic rite), Rashi, and Rashi's pupil, Rabbi Simcha, whose *Mahzor Vitry* served as the foundation of the Ashkenazic rite. These early Siddurim not only contained cycles of prayers and *piyyutim,* but also laws and customs connected with the services.

The first printed Siddur, published in 1486 in Rome,   was among the first printed Hebrew books; its translations are innumerable, and it was early rendered into the languages of major Jewish centers—Italian (1538), Spanish (1552), Yiddish (1562) and English (1738).

FROM THE PRELIMINARY MORNING SERVICE

ADON OLAM

Lord of the world, the King supreme,
Ere aught was formed, He reigned alone.
When by His will all things were wrought,
Then was His sovereign name made known.

And when in time all things shall cease,
He still shall reign in majesty.
He was, He is, He shall remain
All-glorious eternally.

Incomparable, unique is He,
No other can His Oneness share.
Without beginning, without end,
Dominion's might is His to bear.

He is my living God who saves,
My Rock when grief or trials befall,
My Banner and my Refuge strong,
My bounteous Portion when I call.

My soul I give unto His care,
Asleep, awake, for He is near,
And with my soul, my body, too;
God is with me, I have no fear.

YIGDAL (DANIEL BEN JUDAH OF ROME, 14TH CENTURY)

The living God O magnify and bless,
Transcending time and here eternally.

One Being, yet unique in unity;
A mystery of Oneness, measureless.

Lo! form or body He has none, and man
No semblance of His holiness can frame.

Before Creation's dawn He was the same;
The first to be, though never He began.

He is the world's and every creature's Lord;
His rule and majesty are manifest,

And through His chosen, glorious sons expressed
In prophecies that through their lips are poured.

Yet never like to Moses rose a seer,
Permitted glimpse behind the veil divine.

This faithful prince of God's prophetic line
Received the Law of Truth for Israel's ear.

The Law God gave, He never will amend,
Nor ever by another Law replace.

Our secret things are spread before His face;
In all beginnings He beholds the end.

The saint's reward He measures to his meed;
The sinner reaps the harvest of his ways.

Messiah He will send at end of days,
And all the faithful to salvation lead.

God will the dead again to life restore
In His abundance of almighty love.

Then blessed be His name, all names above,
And let His praise resound forevermore.

MISHNAH PEAH 1:1; TALMUD SABBATH 127A

In the fulfillment of the following mitzvot, no fixed measure is imposed: leaving the corner of the field for the poor, the gift of the first-fruits, the pilgrimage offering at the sanctuary on the three festivals, deeds of loving-kindness and the study of the Torah. With regard to the fulfillment of the following mitzvot, a man enjoys their fruit in this life while the principal remains for him to all eternity: honoring one's father and mother, performing deeds of lovingkindness, attending the house of study morning and evening, hospitality to wayfarers, visiting the sick, dowering the bride, attending the dead to the grave, devotion in prayer and the making of peace between man and his fellow; but the study of the Torah is equivalent to them all.

TALMUD BERAKOTH 60B

O my God, the soul with which You did endow me is pure. You did create it and fashion it; You did breathe it into me and You preserved it within me. You will restore it to me in the life to come. So long as the breath of life is within me, I will give thanks unto You, O Lord my God and God of my fathers, Master of all works, Lord of all souls. Blessed are you, O Lord, who restore life to mortal creatures.

EL ADON (8TH CENTURY)

The Lord is Master over all His works;
Blessed is He, acclaimed by every living thing.

His greatness and His goodness fill the universe,
While knowledge and discernment compass Him about.

The Lord, exalted over all the celestial host,
Above the heavenly Chariot in radiance adorned.

Purity and justice stand before His throne,
Kindness and compassion before His glory go.

The luminaries which the Lord has wrought are good,
With wisdom, knowledge and discernment were they made.

Endowed with might, endowed with everlasting power,
They govern all the world.

In splendor, lustrously their brightness radiates,
Their brilliance beautiful throughout the universe.

In rising they rejoice, in setting they exult,
Awesomely fulfilling their Creator's will.

Glory and honor do they give unto His name;
In joyous songs of praise His kingdom they acclaim.

God called unto the sun and it shone forth in light,
He looked, and then He formed the figure of the moon.

The heavenly host, the constellations give His praise,
And all celestial beings of the heavenly throne
Attribute honor, greatness, glory [to God].

    With abounding love have You loved us, O Lord our God, with exceed-
ing compassion have You revealed Your mercy unto us. O our Father, our
King, for the sake of our fathers who trusted in You and whom You did
teach the laws of life, be also gracious unto us and teach us. O our Father,
compassionate Father, have mercy upon us and imbue us with the will to
understand, to discern, to hearken and to learn, to teach and to obey, to
practice and to fulfill in love all the teachings of Your Torah. Deepen our
insight into Your Torah, and make our hearts cleave to Your commandments. Grant us singleness of purpose to love and revere Your name so
that we may never suffer humiliation. Because we have faith in Your holy,
great and revered name, may we rejoice in Your saving power. O gather
us in peace from the four corners of the earth, and restore us triumphantly
to our homeland, for You are the God who worketh salvation. You have
chosen us from among all peoples and tongues by bringing us near unto
You in faithfulness that we might lovingly give thanks unto You and proclaim Your unity. Blessed are You, O Lord, who in love has chosen Your
people Israel.

DEUTERONOMY 6:4–9

        Hear, O Israel: the Lord our God, the Lord is One.
        Blessed be His glorious kingdom for ever and ever.

You shall love the Lord your God with all your heart, with all your soul, and with all your might. And these words which I command you this day shall be in your heart. You shall teach them diligently unto your children, speaking them when you sit in your house, when you walk by the way, when you lie down, when you rise up. And you shall bind them for a sign upon your hand, and they shall be for frontlets between your eyes. And you shall write them upon the door posts of your house and upon your gates.

THE SILENT DEVOTION (FOR SABBATH MORNINGS)

O Lord, open my lips and my mouth shall declare Your praise.

Blessed are you, O Lord our God and God of our fathers, God of Abraham, God of Isaac, and God of Jacob, mighty, revered and exalted God. You bestow lovingkindness and possess all things. Mindful of the patriarchs' love for You, You will in Your love bring a redeemer to their children's children for the sake of Your name.

O King, Helper, Redeemer and Shield! Blessed are you O Lord, Shield of Abraham.

You, O Lord, are mighty forever. You call the dead to immortal life for You are mighty in deliverance.

You sustain the living with lovingkindness, and in great mercy call the departed to everlasting life. You uphold the falling, heal the sick, set free those in bondage, and keep faith with those that sleep in the dust. Who is like unto You, Almighty King, who decree death and life and brings forth salvation?

Faithful are You to grant eternal life to the departed. Blessed are You, O Lord, who calls the dead to life everlasting.

Holy are You and holy is Your name and unto You holy beings render praise daily. Blessed are You, O Lord, the holy God.

(KEDUSHAH

We sanctify Thy name on earth even as it is sanctified in the heavens above, as described in the vision of Thy Prophet:
And the seraphim called one unto another saying:
Holy, holy, holy is the Lord of hosts,
The whole earth is full of His glory.
Whereupon the angels in stirring and mighty chorus rise toward the seraphim and with resounding acclaim declare:
Blessed be the glory of God from His heavenly abode.
From Thy heavenly abode, reveal Thyself, O our King, and reign over

us, for we wait for Thee. O when wilt Thou reign in Zion? Speedily, even in our days, do Thou establish Thy dwelling there forever. Mayest Thou be exalted and sanctified in Jerusalem, Thy city, throughout all generations and to all eternity. O let our eyes behold the establishment of Thy kingdom, according to the word that was spoken in the inspired Psalms of David, Thy righteous anointed:

The Lord shall reign forever. Thy God, O Zion, shall be Sovereign unto all generations. Hallelujah!

Unto all generations we will declare Thy greatness and to all eternity we will proclaim Thy holiness. Our mouth shall ever speak Thy praise, O our God, for Thou art a great and holy God and King. Blessed art Thou, O Lord, the holy God.)

Moses rejoiced in the gift of his portion, for Thou didst call him a faithful servant. A diadem of glory didst Thou place upon his head when he stood before Thee on Mount Sinai. In his hand he brought down the two tablets of stone upon which was engraved the command to observe the Sabbath, as it is written in Thy Torah:

The children of Israel shall keep the Sabbath and observe it throughout their generations as an everlasting covenant. It is a sign between Me and the children of Israel forever; for in six days the Lord made heaven and earth, and on the seventh day He ceased from work and rested.

This precious blessing of the Sabbath, O Lord our God, Thou didst not grant to the heathens of the earth, nor didst Thou, O our King, bestow it upon idolaters, nor can the unrighteous enjoy its rest. But Thou didst give it in affection to Israel Thy people, the seed of Jacob, whom Thou didst love. May the people who sanctify the seventh day be sated and delighted with Thy bounty. For Thou didst find pleasure in the seventh day, and didst sanctify it, calling it the desirable of days, in remembrance of creation.

Our God and God of our fathers, accept our rest. Sanctify us through Thy commandments, and grant our portion in Thy Torah. Give us abundantly of Thy goodness and make us rejoice in Thy salvation. Purify our hearts to serve Thee in truth. In Thy loving favor, O Lord our God, grant that Thy holy Sabbath be our joyous heritage, and may Israel who sanctifies Thy name, rest thereon. Blessed art Thou, O Lord, who hallowest the Sabbath.

O Lord our God be gracious unto Thy people Israel and accept their prayer. Restore the worship to Thy sanctuary and receive in love and favor the offerings and supplication of Israel. May the worship of Thy people Israel be ever acceptable unto Thee.

O may our eyes witness Thy return to Zion. Blessed art Thou, O Lord, who restorest Thy divine presence unto Zion.

We thankfully acknowledge Thee, O Lord our God, our fathers' God to all eternity. Our Rock art Thou, our Shield that saves through every generation. We give Thee thanks and we declare Thy praise for all Thy tender care. Our lives we trust into Thy loving hand. Our souls are ever in Thy charge; Thy wonders and Thy miracles are daily with us, evening, morn and noon. O Thou who art all-good, whose mercies never fail us, Compassionate One, whose lovingkindness never cease, we ever hope in Thee.

For all this, Thy name, O our King, shall be blessed and exalted for ever and ever.

May all the living do homage unto Thee forever and praise Thy name in truth, O God, who art our salvation and our help. Blessed be Thou, O Lord, Beneficent One, unto whom our thanks are due.

Reader

Our God and God of our fathers, bless us with the threefold blessing written in the Torah of Moses, Thy servant, and spoken by Aaron and his sons, Thy consecrated priests:

Reader	Congregation
May the Lord bless thee and keep thee;	So may it be His will.
May the Lord make His countenance to shine upon thee and be gracious unto thee;	So may it be His will.
May the Lord turn His countenance unto thee and give thee peace.	So may it be His will.

Grant peace, well-being and blessing unto the world, with grace, lovingkindness and mercy for us and for all Israel, Thy people. Bless us, O our Father, all of us together, with the light of Thy presence; for by that light Thou hast given us, O Lord our God, the Torah of life, lovingkindness and righteousness, blessing and mercy, life and peace. O may it be good in Thy sight at all times to bless Thy people Israel with Thy peace.

Blessed art Thou, O Lord, who blessest Thy people Israel with peace.

O Lord,
Guard my tongue from evil and my lips from speaking guile,
And to those who slander me, let me give no heed.
May my soul be humble and forgiving unto all.
Open Thou my heart, O Lord, unto Thy sacred Law,
That Thy statutes I may know and all Thy truths pursue.
Bring to naught designs of those who seek to do me ill;
Speedily defeat their aims and thwart their purposes
For Thine own sake, for Thine own power,
For Thy holiness and Law.
That Thy loved ones be delivered,
Answer us, O Lord, and save with Thy redeeming power.

May the words of my mouth and the meditation of my heart be acceptable unto Thee, O Lord, my Rock and my Redeemer. Thou who establishest peace in the heavens, grant peace unto us and unto all Israel. Amen.

May it by Thy will, O Lord our God and God of our fathers, that the Temple be speedily rebuilt in our day and grant our portion in Thy Torah. There we will serve Thee with awe as in the days of old and as in former times. Then shall the offering of Judah and Jerusalem be pleasing to the Lord, as in the days of old and as in former times.

MEDITATION (17TH CENTURY)

Lord of the universe, fulfill the wishes of my heart for good. Grant my request and my petition; make me worthy to do Thy will with a perfect heart; and keep me strong to resist temptation. O grant our portion in Thy Torah. Make us worthy of Thy divine presence. Bestow upon us the spirit of wisdom and understanding, the spirit of counsel and might, the spirit of knowledge and the fear of the Lord. May it be Thy will, O Lord our God and God of our fathers, that I may be worthy to perform good deeds in Thy sight, and to walk before Thee in the way of the upright. Sanctify us by Thy commandments, that we may merit on earth a life of goodness and health and be worthy of life eternal. Guard us from evil deeds and from evil times that may threaten the world. May lovingkindness surround him who trusts in the Lord. Amen.

ALENU (CA. 13TH CENTURY)

It is for us to praise the Lord of all, to proclaim the greatness of the Creator of the universe, for He hath not made us like the pagans of the world, nor placed us like the heathen tribes of the earth; He hath not made our destiny as theirs, nor cast our lot with all their multitude.

We bend the knee, worship and give thanks unto the King of kings, the Holy One, blessed be He.

He stretched forth the heavens and laid the foundations of the earth. His glory is revealed in the heavens above, and His might is manifest in the loftiest heights. He is our God; there is none else. In truth He is our King, there is none besides Him; as it is written in His Torah; Know this day, and consider it in thy heart that the Lord is God in the heavens above and on the earth beneath; there is none else [Deut. 4:39].

We therefore hope in Thee, O Lord our God, that we may soon behold the glory of Thy might, when Thou wilt remove the abominations from the earth and when all idolatry will be abolished. We hope for the day when the world will be perfected under the kingdom of the Almighty, and all mankind will call upon Thy name; when Thou wilt turn unto Thyself all the wicked of the earth. May all the inhabitants of the world perceive and know that unto Thee every knee must bend, every tongue vow loyalty.

Before Thee, O Lord our God, may they bow in worship, giving honor unto Thy glorious name. May they all accept the yoke of Thy kingdom and do Thou rule over them speedily and forevermore. For the kingdom is Thine and to all eternity Thou wilt reign in glory; as it is written in Thy Torah: The Lord shall reign for ever and ever [Ex. 15:18]. And it has been foretold: The Lord shall be King over all the earth; on that day the Lord shall be One, and His name One [Zech. 14:9].

KADDISH

Magnified and sanctified be the name of God throughout the world which He hath created according to His will. May He establish His kingdom during the days of your life and during the life of all the house of Israel, speedily, yea, soon; and say ye, Amen.

May His great name be blessed for ever and ever.

Exalted and honored be the name of the Holy One, blessed be He, whose glory transcends, yea, is beyond all praises, hymns and blessings that man can render unto Him; and say ye, Amen.

WELCOMING THE SABBATH
L'CHA DODI
(Rabbi Shlomo Alkabets, c. 1550)

Come, my friend, to meet the bride; let us welcome the Sabbath.

"Observe" and "Remember [the Sabbath]", in a single utterance, the One God proclaimed to us. The Lord is One, and his name is One, for renown, glory and praise.

Come, my friend, to meet the bride; let us welcome the Sabbath.

Come, let us go to meet the Sabbath, for it is a source of blessing. From the beginning it was ordained; last in creation, first in thought.

Come, my friend, to meet the bride; let us welcome the Sabbath.

Sanctuary of our King, royal city, arise! Come out of your ruins. Long enough have you dwelt in the valley of tears! He will have compassion on you.

Come, my friend, to meet the bride; let us welcome the Sabbath.

Shake off your dust, arise! Put on your garments of glory, my people. Draw near to my soul, and redeem it through the son of Jesse, of Bethlehem.

Come, my friend, to meet the bride; let us welcome the Sabbath.

Awaken, awaken, for your light has come; arise and shine! Awake, awake, chant a song; the glory of the Lord is revealed upon you.

Come, my friend, to meet the bride; let us welcome the Sabbath.

Be not ashamed, be not confounded. Why are you downcast? Why do you moan? Within you the oppressed of my people shall be sheltered; the city will be rebuilt on its ruins.

Come, my friend, to meet the bride; let us welcome the Sabbath.

Your spoilers shall be spoiled, and banished shall be all who would devour you. Your God will rejoice over you as a bridegroom rejoices over his bride.

Come, my friend, to meet the bride; let us welcome the Sabbath.

Your borders shall extend to the right and the left, and you shall revere the Lord. Through the descendant of Perez we shall rejoice and be glad.

Come, my friend, to meet the bride; let us welcome the Sabbath.

Come in peace, crown of the Lord, come with joy and cheerfulness; amidst the faithful of the chosen people, come O bride; come O bride.

Come, my friend, to meet the bride; let us welcome the Sabbath.

SABBATH AND FESTIVALS
FROM THE EVENING SERVICE

Reader
Bless the Lord who is to be praised.

Congregation and Reader
Praised be the Lord who is blessed for all eternity.

Praised be Thou, O Lord our God, Ruler of the universe, who with Thy word bringest on the evening twilight, and with Thy wisdom openest the gates of the heavens. With understanding Thou dost order the cycles of time and variest the seasons, setting the stars in their courses in the sky, according to Thy will. Thou createst day and night, rolling away the light before the darkness and the darkness before the light. By Thy will the day passes into night; the Lord of heavenly hosts is Thy name. O ever-living God, mayest Thou rule over us forever. Blessed be Thou, O Lord, who bringest on the evening twilight.

With everlasting love hast Thou loved the house of Israel, teaching us Thy Torah and commandments, Thy statutes and judgments. Therefore, O Lord our God, when we lie down and when we rise up, we will meditate on Thy teachings and rejoice forever in the words of Thy Torah and in its commandments, for they are our life and the length of our days. Day and night will we meditate upon them. O may Thy love never depart from us. Blessed be Thou, O Lord, who lovest Thy people Israel.

KIDDUSH (*c. several centuries* B.C.E.)

Praised art Thou, O Lord our God, King of the universe, who createst the fruit of the vine.

Praised art Thou, O Lord our God, Ruler of the universe, who hast sanctified us through Thy commandments and hast taken delight in us. In love and favor Thou hast given us the holy Sabbath as a heritage, a reminder of Thy work of creation, first of our sacred days recalling our liberation from Egypt. Thou didst choose us from among the peoples and in Thy love and favor didst sanctify us in giving us Thy holy Sabbath as a joyous heritage. Blessed art Thou, O Lord our God, who hallowest the Sabbath.

GRACE AFTER MEALS

Blessed are You, O Lord our God, King of all the world, Who feeds the entire world with goodness, with grace, with kindness, and with mercy. You give food to all men, for your kindness lasts eternally. Because of your great goodness we have never lacked food; may it never fail us, because of Your great name. For You serve and assist all creatures, and provide food for all You have created.

Blessed are You, O Lord, Who gives food to everyone.

We thank You, O Lord our God because for all time you gave our fathers a land that is pleasant, goodly, and spacious; and because You brought our fathers forth from a land of slavery. We also thank You for Your sign on our bodies, for the Torah You taught us, for the laws You made known to us, for the life, grace, and kindness you have granted us, and for the food You are always providing us every day, every season, every hour.

For all this, O Lord our God, we thank and bless You. May Your name be blessed forever and ever by all that live—just as it is written in the Torah: Eat and be satisfied and then bless the Lord your God for the good land He gave you. Blessed are You, O Lord, for the land and for the food You have given us.

Show mercy, O Lord our God, to Israel Your people, Jerusalem Your City, Zion in which Your glory rules, the kingdom of the house of David, and the noble and sacred house that bears Your name. O God, our Father, feed and support us, and relieve us of all our troubles. We pray to You, O God, never to leave us in need of the help and gifts of flesh-and-blood men, but let us rely only upon Your helping hand, which is always full and open. Thus may we never feel shame over our lot in life.

(On Sabbath

Please, O Lord, give us strong souls because of Your commandments, especially that of the holy Sabbath, the day that is great and sacred before You. May we have our rest on that day, in loving harmony with Your will. We ask Your favor in granting us rest that is not disturbed, without grief or sorrow. O God, let us see the comforting of Zion, the rebuilding of your holy city Jerusalem. For You are our Lord Who will always give us saving and consolation.)

We pray that You rebuild Jerusalem, the holy city, soon, in these very days. Blessed are You, O Lord, Who in mercy will build Jerusalem anew. Amen.

Blessed are You, O Lord our King, King of all the world, our Father, our Creator, our Shepherd, Who was worshiped by our father Jacob, for having dealt kindly with us in days past, for treating us today with kindness, and for the goodness You will yet show to us, in former days, in this day, and in days to come. You are the giver of all things good, granting us love and kindness and mercy and prosperity and blessing and consolation and support and a peaceful life. May we never lack of the good things granted by God.

He Who is merciful over all will rule over us forever. He shall be blessed in heaven and on earth. He shall be praised in all ages, and glorified and honored eternally. May He grant us an honorable livelihood. May he break the yoke pressing on the neck of Israel, and lead us all upright to the Holy Land. May he send down many blessings on this house, and on the table at which we have eaten. May He send us the prophet Elijah, who will bring us good tidings and consolation.

Those having their meal at the table of their parents say

May He Who is merciful to all bless my honored father and mother, with all their household, their children, and all that belongs to them.

Those having their meal at their own table say

May He Who is merciful to all bless me, my wife, my children and all that belongs to us.

Those having their meal at another's table say

May He Who is merciful to all bless the master of this house, his wife, their children, and all that belongs to them—just as our forefathers Abraham, Isaac, and Jacob were blessed in their various ways. Thus may He bless us all perfectly, while we say Amen.

For the sake of all of them and ourselves may heaven bring to us eternal peace, with all the blessings of righteous living. And may we find favor and understanding in the sight of God and man.

(On Sabbath

May He Who is merciful to all let us fully accept the Sabbath day, for the everlasting life of ourselves and our people).

May He Who is merciful to all make us worthy of the coming of the

Messiah, and of the World-to-Come. He will give all help to this king who will some day come to us, as He showed kindness to David and his decendants, from whom the Messiah will come. We pray that the Lord Who brings peace to his holy places will also grant peace to us and all Israel. Amen.

Honor the Lord, you who consider yourselves His holy ones. Those who honor Him will not suffer want. Even the mighty lion must often suffer hunger; but men who seek the Lord will never lack anything that is good. Give thanks to the Lord, for He is good; His kindness endures forever. You open your hand, O God and in favor supply living beings with all they need.

Blessed is the man who trusts God. Men have been young and grown old; but in all that time they have not seen good men forsaken, or their children lacking bread. For the Lord gives strength to His people; he blesses His people with peace.

A PRAYER FOR THE STATE OF ISRAEL (1948)

Our Father in heaven, the Rock of Israel and its Redeemer, bless the State of Israel, the onset of our salvation. Protect it with the wings of your love, and spread over it the canopy of peace. Send Your light and Your truth to its leaders, officers and advisors, and direct them with Your good counsel.

Strengthen the hand of the defenders of our holy land; grant them salvation, our God, and crown them with victory. Bestow peace unto the land and eternal joy to its inhabitants.

Remember our brethren, the entire house of Israel, in all the lands of their dispersion, and speedily lead them upright to Your city, Zion, and to Jerusalem, Your dwelling place; as it is written in the Torah of Your servant, Moses: "Even if your outcasts are at the ends of the world, the Lord your God will bring you to the land that your fathers possessed, and you shall possess it." [Deut. 30:4–5]

Unite our hearts to love and revere Your name, and to observe all the teachings of Your Torah. Appear in all Your majestic glory unto all the inhabitants of Your world, and let each living soul declare: "The Lord, God of Israel, is King, and his kingdom is supreme." Amen, selah.

The Travels of Eldad the Danite

Eldad's travelogue (880), with its romantic and hopeful description of the Ten Lost Tribes—a perenially intriguing motif—became one of the most widely copied manuscripts of the Middle Ages, and, with the introduction of printing, one of the most popular books. Eldad, who claimed to have come from East Africa, visited Bagdad and Kairawan (North Africa); from the *Epistle of Hasdai ibn Shaprut* (see p. 164) we learn that he also visited Spain. Eldad introduced himself as a Jew from the tribe of Dan, which lived independently and had its own government, and declared that the Ten Tribes survived in various parts of Africa and the Near East.

With his detailed account of the Sons of Moses who lived idyllically beyond the Sambatyon, a legendary river that cast stones every day of the week but Sabbath, Eldad is the first writer to introduce into world literature the notion of a utopia. He very likely collected various legends and wove them into a credible tale which eventually encouraged a Jewry in exile—indeed that may have been his original purpose. The existence of the Ten Tribes, independent and free, particularly lifted the spirits of exilic Jewry under Christendom, for it contradicted the Christian theological notion that the Jews are in a permanent state of subjugation for having denied Jesus. The Jews, then, were able to point with pride that Jewish sovereignty indeed existed, as it did, exclusive of legend, among the Falashas of Ethiopia and the Khazars (see *Epistle of Hasdai ibn Shaprut*).

The Hebrew of Eldad's readable narrative is not quite rabbinic, but closer to Biblical diction. Eldad claimed to have spoken only Hebrew; but his manuscript contains peculiar words unknown to speakers of Hebrew and some Arabisms which indicate that he came from an Arab land and spoke Arabic. Along with his travelogue Eldad brought with him ritual rules which differed from the Talmud and which caused such consternation in Kairawan that its Jewish community sent a letter requesting the opinion of Gaon Zemach in Babylonia. Some of Eldad's rituals are mentioned by various scholars, including Rashi and Maimonides' son, Abraham.

The romance of Eldad the Danite was not only read by generations of Jews, but was translated into Arabic, Latin, Yiddish and German. Its first publication in Hebrew was in 1480, in Mantua, shortly after the printing of the first Hebrew book in 1475 *(Pentateuch with Rashi's Commentary)*—another measure of the popularity of Eldad's narrative.

THE TRAVELS OF ELDAD THE DANITE

In the name of the Lord God of Israel! May the name of our Lord the King of kings be praised who chose Israel from all the nations and gave us the law of truth and planted eternal life in our midst, the law of the upright to live thereby. Our brethren, sons of the captivity, be of good courage and strengthen your hearts to perform the law of our God in due season, for whensoever Israel doeth the law of the omnipresent, no nation and no tongue can rule over them. Peace be with you our brethren, sons of the captivity, and peace to Jerusalem, the city of our glory, the place of the Temple of our God which has been destroyed and the place of the kingdom of the house of David and Judah, who wrought justice and righteousness, and the place of the Holy of Holies. Peace to all the elders of Israel, and to the faithful in the law of God and to its interpreters, its priests and Levites and all the tribes of Israel and Judah great and small. May the Lord strengthen your hearts in the Law and in the true prophet Moses, our teacher, the servant of the Lord!

And now we shall tell our brethren, the tribes of Jeshurun, of Eldad the Danite, who relates all this, how he went forth in all the countries after being separated from the tribe of Dan and the Lord miraculously saved him in many places and from many troubles, which passed over him, till he came to this land, so that he might go and tell all the children of Israel, who are scattered in Israel, matters concerning him, that he might bring you good tidings of comfort and speak good words to your heart.

And this was my going forth from the other side of the rivers of Ethiopia.

I and a Jew of the tribe of Asher entered a small ship to trade with the shipmen and behold, at midnight, the Lord caused a great and strong wind to arise and the ship was wrecked. Now the Lord had prepared a box and I took hold of it and my companion seeing this also took hold of that box, and we went up and down with it, until the sea cast us among a people called Romranos who are black Ethiopians, tall, without garment or clothing upon them, cannibals, like unto the beasts of the field.

And when we came to their country they took hold of us and, seeing that my companion was fat and healthy and pleasing, slaughtered and ate him, and he cried, "Alas for me that I have been brought to this people and the Ethiopians will eat my flesh," but me they took, for I was sick on board ship, and they put me in chains until I should get fat and well, and they brought before me all kinds of good but forbidden food, but I ate nothing and I hid the food, and when they asked me if I had eaten I answered, yes I had eaten.

And I was with them a long time until the Lord, blessed be He, performed a miracle with me, for a great army came upon them from another place, who took me captive, but they spoiled and killed them and took me along with the captives.

And those wicked men were fire worshippers and I dwelt with them four years, and behold, every morning they made a great fire and bowed down and worshipped it. And they brought me to the province of Azania.

And a Jew, a merchant of the tribe of Issachar, found me and bought me for thirty-two gold pieces and brought me back with him to his country. They live in the mountains of the seacoast and belong to the land of the Medes and Persians. They fulfil the command "the book of this law shall not depart from thy mouth." The yoke of sovereignty is not upon them but only the yoke of law. Among them are leaders of hosts but they fight with no man. They only dispute as to the law, and they live in peace and comfort and there is no disturber and no evil chance. They dwell in a country ten days journey by ten days, and they have great flocks and camels and asses and slaves, but they do not rear horses.

They carry no weapons, except the slaughter's knife, and there is not among them any oppression or robbery and, even if they should find on the road garments or money, they would not stretch forth their hand to take it. But near them are wicked men, fireworshippers, who take their own mothers and sisters to wife, but them they do not hurt. They have a Judge, and I asked about him and they said his name was Nachshon, and they practice the four death penalties according to the law, and they speak Hebrew and Persian.

And the sons of Zebulun are encamped in the hills of Paron and reach to their [i.e. Issachar's] neighborhood and pitch tents made of hairy skins which come to them from the land of Armenia, and they reach up to the Euphrates, and they practice business and they observe the four death penalties inflicted by the court.

And the tribe of Reuben is over against them behind Mount Paron, and there is peace and brotherhood and companionship between them, and they go together to war and make roads and divide the spoils amongst themselves, and they go on the highroads of the Kings of Media and Persia and they speak Hebrew and Persian, and they possess scripture and Mishna, Talmud, and Haggadah, and every Sabbath they read the law with accents, the text in Hebrew and the interpretation [Targum] thereof in Persian.

And the tribe of Ephraim and half tribe of Manasseh are there in the mountains over against the city of Mecca, the stumbling block of the Ishmaelites. They are strong of body and of iron heart. They are horsemen, and take the road and have no pity on their enemies, and their only livelihood comes of spoil. They are mighty men of war. One is match for a thousand.

And the tribe of Simeon and the half tribe of Manasseh live in the country of the Babylonians six months' journey away, and they are the most numerous of all of them, and they take tribute from five and twenty kingdoms and some Ishmaelites pay them tribute.

And in our country we say that it is a tradition among us that ye are the sons of the captivity, the tribe of Judah and the tribe of Benjamin under the dominion of the heathen in an unclean land, who were scattered under the Romans who destroyed the Temple of our God, and under the Greeks and the Ishmaelites, may their sword pierce their heart and may their bows be broken!

We have a tradition from father to son that we, the sons of Dan, were aforetime in the land of Israel dwellers in tents and among all the tribes of Israel there were none like us men of war and mighty of valour. And, when Jeroboam, the son of Nebat, who caused Israel to sin and made two golden calves, arose over them, the kingdom of the house of David was divided and the tribes gathered together and said, "Come and fight against Rehoboam and against Jerusalem." They answered, "Why should we fight with our brothers and with the son of our Lord David, King of Israel and Judah? God forbid!" Then said the elders of Israel, "You have not in all the tribes of Israel mighty ones like the tribe of Dan." At once they said to the children of Dan, "Arise and fight with the children of Judah." They answered, "By the life of Dan our father, we will not make war with our brothers and we will not shed blood."

At once we children of Dan took swords and lances and bows, and devoted ourselves to death to go forth from the land of Israel, for we saw we could not stay, "Let us go hence and find a resting place, but if we wait until the end they will take us away." So we took heart and counsel to go to Egypt to destroy it and to kill all its inhabitants. Our prince said to us, "Is it not written, ye shall not continue to see it again for ever? How will you prosper?" They said, "Let us go against Amalek or against Edom or against Ammon and Moab to destroy them and let us dwell in their place." Our princes said, "It is written in the law that the Holy One, blessed be He, has prevented Israel from crossing their border."

Finally we took counsel to go to Egypt, but not by the way that our fathers went and not to destroy it, but only to go there to cross the River Pishon [Lower Nile] to the land of Ethiopia and behold, when we came near to Egypt, all Egypt was afraid and sent to us asking, "Is it war or peace?" and we said, "For peace; we will cross your country to the River Pishon, and there we will find a resting place," and behold, they did not believe us, but all Egypt stood on guard until we crossed their country and arrived in the land of Ethiopia.

We found it a good and fat land, and, in it, fields, enclosures, and gardens. They could not restrain the children of Dan from dwelling with them, for they took the land by might and, behold, though they wished to kill them all, they had to pay tribute to Israel, and we dwelt with them many years, and increased and multiplied greatly and held great riches.

Afterwards Sennacherib, King of Assyria, arose and took the Reubenites and the Gadites and the half tribe of Manasseh captive, and took them to Halah and Habor and the River Goazan, and the cities of Media. And Sennacherib arose a second time and took captive the tribe of Asher and the tribe of Naphtali and led them to the land of Assyria, and, after the death of Sennacherib, three tribes of Israel, being Naphtali, Gad, and Asher, journeyed on their own to the land of Ethiopia and encamped in the wilderness until they came to their border, a twenty days' journey, and they slew the men of Ethiopia, and unto this very day, they fight with the children of the kingdoms of Ethiopia.

And these tribes, being Dan, Naphtali, Gad, and Asher, dwell in the ancient Havilah, where gold is, and they trusted in their Maker, and the Lord helped them. These tribes placed their hands on the neck of their enemies and every year they make war with the seven kingdoms and seven countries. The names of these kingdoms are Tussina, Kamti, Kuba, Tariogi, Takula, Karma, and Kalom, and they are on the other side of the rivers of Ethiopia. These four tribes have gold and silver and precious stones, and much sheep and cattle and camels and asses, and they sow and they reap, and they dwell in tents, and, when they will, they journey and encamp in tents, from border to border, two days by two days' journey, and in the place where they encamp there is no place where the foot of man enters, but they encamp in a place of fields and vineyards.

And their King's name is Uzziel and the name of their great prince Elizaphan, of the children of Aholiab, of the tribe of Dan, and their banner is white and written thereon in black is, "Hear, O Israel, the Lord our God is one God," and when they seek to go out to war the crier calls with the sound of the trumpet, and the lord of the hosts comes and the armies go forth one hundred and twenty thousand with small white bannerettes.

Every three months, a different tribe goes out to war, and the tribe remains three months away, and all that they bring from the spoil of their enemies they divide among their own tribe. But the descendants of Samson, of the tribe of Dan, are superior to all. They never run away, for that were a great shame to them. They are numerous as the sands of the sea, and have no employment but war and, whensoever they fight, they say it is not good for mighty men to flee, let them die young, but let them not flee, let them strengthen their heart unto God, and several times they say and cry all of them together, "Hear, O Israel, our God is one God," and then they all take heed.

And thus they do until their three months are over and then they return and they bring all their spoil to King Uzziel, and he divides it with all Israel, and this is their statute from King David until this day, and King Uzziel takes his share and the King gives a share to all the wise men, sages of the law, dwellers in tents, and afterwards all take their portion, and the lord of the host his share. Thus they do in the three months when Naphtali goes out, and in the three months when Gad goes out, and so Asher; all of them until twelve months are completed, and then they repeat in succession.

As to the tribe of Moses our teacher, on whom be peace, the righteous servant of God whose name is called with us the tribe of *Janus,* for he fled from idolatry and clove to the fear of God, the sea surrounds them, three months' journey by three months. They dwell in glorious houses and fine buildings and castles, and train elephants for themselves in their times of joy. No unclean thing is to be found with them, no unclean fowl, no unclean beast, no unclean cattle, no flies, no fleas, no lice, no foxes, no scorpions, no serpents, and no dogs. All these were in the idolatrous land, where they had been in servitude. They had only sheep, oxen, and fowls, and their sheep bring forth twice a year. They sow seed twice a year; they sow and they reap and they have gardens, olives, pomegranates and figs, and all kinds of beans, cucumbers and melons, onions, garlic, barley and wheat, and from one comes forth a hundred.

They are of perfect faith and their Talmud is all in Hebrew, and thus they learn, "Thus taught us our Rabbis, from the mouth of Joshua the son of Nun, from the mouth of our father Moses, from the mouth of the Almighty." But they know not the Rabbis, for these were of the Second Temple and they did not reach them.

And they can speak only the Holy tongue and they all take ritual baths and never swear. They cry out against him that takes the name of God in vain, and say that by the sin of cursing your sons would die young. But they are long lived and live a hundred or 120 years and no son dies in his father's lifetime, and they reach three or four generations, and they sow and reap themselves, for they have no manservants or maidservants, and they are all equal, and do not shut their houses at night for that would be shame to them, and a young man goes with the flocks ten days' journey and fears neither robbers nor ghosts. They are all Levites, and have not among them either Priest or Israelite, and they abide in the sanctity of Moses our teacher, the servant of the Lord.

Moreover, they see no man and no men see them except these four tribes, who dwell on the other side of the rivers of Ethiopia. There is a place where these can see each other and speak if they cry out, but the River Sambation is between them, and they tell, "Thus it happened to us in war time," and they tell all Israel what happened to them. When they want anything important, they have a kind of pigeon known among them and they write their letters and fasten them to the wings or to the feet of the pigeon, and these cross the River Sambation and the pigeons come to their Kings and their Princes.

They also have very many precious stones and silver and gold, and they sow flax and they rear cochineal and make pleasant garments without end and are five times as numerous as those that came out of Egypt, for they are innumerable. The breadth of that river is 200 cubits bowshot, and the river is full of large and small stones and the sound of them rumbles like a great storm, like a tempest at sea and, in the night, the sound of it is heard a day's journey and they have with them six wells and they all unite into one lake and therefrom they irrigate their land, and therein are clean edible fish.

The river runs and the stones and sand rumble during the six working days, but on the seventh day it rests and is tranquil until the end of Sabbath. And on the other side of the river, on the side where the four tribes dwell, is a fire which flames on Sabbath and no man can approach within a mile.

And this is my name, Eldad ben Mahali ben Ezekiel ben Hezekiah ben Aluk ben Abner ben Shemaiah ben Hater ben Hur ben Elkanah ben Hillel ben Tobias ben Pedath ben Ainon ben Naaman ben Taam ben Taami ben Onam ben Gaul ben Shalom ben Caleb ben Omram ben Damain ben Obadiah ben Abraham ben Joseph ben Moses ben Jacob ben Kappur ben Ariel ben Asher ben Job ben Shallum ben Elihu ben Ahaliab ben Ahisamach ben Hushim ben Dan ben Jacob our father, on whom be peace and on all Israel.

These letters this Lord Eldad sent to Spain in the year 43 (883), and this Lord Eldad was full of law and commandments and, if a man sits with him from morning until evening, he does not cease to converse on the law in the Holy tongue and his words are sweeter than honey and the honeycomb. May the Lord give him a good reward in his world and in the world to come.

Here endeth the Book of Eldad the Danite.

Nathan ha-Bavli

The Exilarch, civil leader of Babylonian Jewry and a descendant of the Davidic royal line, and the Gaon, its spiritual leader, were the two most important personages in Babylonia, recognized even by the ruling authorities. In his vivid account of the installation of the Exilarch and the accompanying service, Nathan ha-Bavli gives details about the Gaon, the jurisdiction of the Exilarchate, and the customs of the academies. Nathan, a tenth-century historian and contemporary of philosopher Saadya Gaon, probably did not write his account in Babylonia. The scholarly supposition is that it was composed for the Jews of Kairawan, an important Jewish center in North Africa, who wanted information about their brethren. There are extant a Hebrew and an Arabic version of Nathan ha-Bavli's report, which, with its ancient order of the liturgy serves as a good corollary text to the Siddur.

THE INSTALLATION OF AN EXILARCH

When the community agreed to appoint an exilarch, the two heads of the academies, with their pupils, the heads of the community, and the elders assembled in the house of a prominent man in Babylon, one of the great men of the generation, as, for instance, Netira, or a similar man. That man in whose house the meeting took place was honored thereby, and it was regarded as a mark of distinction; his esteem was enhanced, when the great men and the elders assembled in his house.

On Thursday they assembled in the synagogue, blessed the exilarch, and placed their hands on him. They blew the horn, that all the people, small and great, might hear. When the people heard the proclamation, every member of the community sent him a present, according to his power and means. All the heads of the community and the wealthy members sent him magnificent clothes and beautiful ornaments, vessels of silver and vessels of gold, each man according to his ability. The exilarch prepared a banquet on Thursday and on Friday, giving all kinds of food, and all kinds of drinks, and all kinds of dainties, as, for instance, different kinds of sweetmeats.

When he arose on Sabbath morning to go to the synagogue, many of the prominent men of the community met him to go with him to the synagogue. At the synagogue a wooden pulpit had been prepared for him on the previous day, the length of which was seven cubits, and the breadth of which was three cubits. They spread over it magnificent coverings of silk, blue, purple, and scarlet, so that it was entirely covered, and nothing was seen of it. Under the pulpit there entered distinguished youths, with melodious and harmonious voices, who were well-versed in the prayers and all that appertains thereto.

The exilarch was concealed in a certain place together with the heads of the academies, and the youths stood under the pulpit. No man sat there. The precentor of the synagogue would begin the prayer, "Blessed be He who spoke," and the youths, after every sentence of that prayer, would respond: "Blessed be He." When he chanted the Psalm of the Sabbath day [Ps. 92], they responded after him: "It is good to give thanks unto the Lord." All the people together read the "verses of song," [Ps. 145, 150] until they finished them.

The precentor then arose, and began the prayer "The breath of all living," and the youths responded after him: "Shall bless Thy name"; he chanted a phrase, and they responded after him, until they reached the "Kedusha," which was said by the congregation with a low voice, and by the youths with a loud voice. Then the youths remained silent, and the precentor alone completed the prayer up to "He redeemed Israel."

All the people then stood up to say the Eighteen Benedictions. When the preceptor, repeating these Benedictions, reached the "Kedusha," the youths responded after him with a loud voice: "The Holy God." When he had completed the prayer, all the congregation sat down. When all the people were seated, the exilarch came out from the place where he was concealed. Seeing him come out, all the people stood up, until he sat down on the pulpit, which had been made for him. Then the head of the Academy of Sura came out after him, and after exchanging courtesies with the exilarch, sat down on the pulpit. Then the head of the Academy of Pumbeditha came out, and he, too, made a bow, and sat down at his left.

During all this time the people stood upon their feet, until these three were properly seated: the exilarch sat in the middle, the head of the Academy of Sura at his right, and the head of the Academy of Pumbeditha at his left, empty places being left between the heads of the academies and the exilarch. Upon his place, over his head, above the pulpit, they spread a magnificent covering, fastened with cords of fine linen and purple.

Then the precentor put his head under the exilarch's canopy in front of the pulpit, and with blessings that had been prepared for him on the preceding days he blessed him with a low voice, so that they should be heard only by those who sat around the pulpit, and by the youths who were under it. When he blessed him, the youths responded after him with a loud voice; "Amen!" All the people were silent until he had finished his blessings.

Then the exilarch would begin to expound matters pertaining to the biblical portion of that day, or would give permission to the head of the academy of Sura to deliver the exposition, and the head of the academy of Sura would give permission to the head of the academy of Pumbeditha. They would thus show deference to one another, until the head of the academy of Sura began to expound. The interpreter stood near him, and repeated his words to the people. He expounded with awe, closing his eyes, and wrapping himself up with his tallith, so that his forehead was covered.

While he was expounding, there was not in the congregation one that opened his mouth, or chirped, or uttered a sound. If he became aware that anyone spoke, he would open his eyes, and fear and terror would fall upon the congregation. When he finished his exposition, he would begin with a question, saying: "Verily, thou needest to learn." And an old man who was wise, understanding, and experienced would stand up, and make a response on the subject and sit down. Then the precentor stood up, and recited the Kaddish. When he reached the words, "during your life and in your days," he would say: "During the life of our prince the exilarch, and during your life, and during the life of all the house of Israel."

When he had finished the Kaddish, he would bless the exilarch, and then the heads of the academies. Having finished the blessing, he would stand up and say: "Such and such a sum was contributed by such and such a city and its villages;" and he mentioned all the cities which sent contributions for the academy, and blessed them. Afterwards he blessed the men who busied themselves in order that the contributions should reach the academies. Then he would take out the Book of the Law, and call up a priest, and a Levite after him.

While all the people were standing, the precentor of the synagogue would bring down the Book of the Law to the exilarch, who took it in his hands, stood up, and read in it. The heads of the academies stood up with him, and the head of the academy of Sura translated it to him. Then he would give back the Book of the Law to the precentor, who returned it to the Ark. When the precentor reached the Ark, he sat down in his place, and then all the men sat down in their places. After the exilarch the instructors read in the Book of the Law, and they were followed by the pupils of the heads of the academies; but the heads of the academies themselves did not read on that day, because someone else preceded them.

When the Maftir read the last portion, a prominent and wealthy man stood near him, and translated it. This was a mark of distinction and honor for that man. When he finished reading, the precentor again blessed the exilarch by the Book of the Law, and all the readers who were experienced and well-versed in the prayers stood round the Ark, and said: "Amen!" Afterwards he blessed the two heads of the academies, and returned the Book of the Law to its place. They then prayed the additional prayer, and left the synagogue.

Hasdai ibn Shaprut

Hasdai ibn Shaprut (915–975) was like many other leading medieval Jewish figures a physician by profession and a writer by avocation. He was court physician and advisor to Caliph Abd ar-Rahman III in Cordova, Spain, and fulfilled several important diplomatic missions. Until the advent of Hasdai, Spanish Jewry had been dependent for guidance in halakhic matters upon Babylonia, then still the great center of Jewish culture and learning. By virtue of his wealth, Hasdai invited sages from Babylonia, North Africa and Southern Italy to Spain, supported them, established academies and provided them with libraries; in addition, he was also patron to local scholars and Hebrew grammarians.

Hasdai is best known for the letter (*c.* 960) that he sent to the King of the Khazars, a people on the banks of the Volga in Russia who had accepted Judaism. Influenced by Jews who migrated from Persia and Babylonia, the Khazars converted to Judaism in the ninth century. One hundred years later, news of this thriving Jewish kingdom reached Spain and gladdened its Jewry, for they thought that the Khazars were of the Ten Lost Tribes. Hasdai's joy in learning of an independent Jewish nation is representative of the people of Israel's age-old yearning to hear of Jews who are not subjugated, but free (see the *Travels of Eldad the Danite* and the *Travel Diary of David Reubeni*). Hasdai ibn Shaprut's attempt to establish contact with Joseph, King of the Khazars, succeeded when two Jewish diplomats came to Spain from Khazaria and received Hasdai's letter to the Jewish king. Both Hasdai's letter and the king's reply contain valuable information about the last years of this kingdom. In 969—nine years after the letter was written—this now legendary nation was defeated in a war waged by the prince of Russia.

THE EPISTLE OF R. HASDAI,
SON OF ISAAC (OF BLESSED MEMORY)
TO THE KING OF THE KHAZARS

I, Hasdai, son of Isaac, son of Ezra, belonging to the exiled Jews of Jerusalem, in Spain, a servant of my Lord the King, bow to the earth before him and prostrate myself towards the abode of your Majesty, from a distant land. I rejoice in your tranquility and magnificence, and stretch forth my hands to God in Heaven that He may prolong your reign in Israel. But who am I? and what is my life that I should dare to indite a letter to my Lord the King and to address your Majesty?

I rely, however, on the integrity and uprightness of my object. How, indeed, can an idea be expressed in fair words by those who have wandered, after the honour of the kingdom has departed; who have long suffered afflictions and calamities, and see their flags in the land no more? We, indeed, who are of the remnant of the captive Israelites, servants of my Lord the King, are dwelling peacefully in the land of our sojourning (for our God has not forsaken us, nor has His shadow departed from us).

When we had transgressed He brought us into judgment, cast affliction upon our loins, and stirred up the minds of those who had been set over the Israelites to appoint collectors of tribute over them, who aggravated the yoke of the Israelites, oppressed them cruelly, humbled them grievously and inflicted great calamities upon them. But when God saw their misery and labour, and that they were helpless, He led me to present myself before the King, and has graciously turned His heart to me, not because of mine own righteousness, but for His mercy and His covenant's sake. And by this covenant the poor of the flock were exalted to safety, the hands of the oppressors themselves were relaxed, they refrained from further oppression, and through the mercy of our God the yoke was lightened.

Let it be known, then, to the King my Lord, that the name of our land in which we dwell is called in the sacred tongue Sefarad, but in the language of the Arabs, the indwellers of the land, Alandalus [Andalusia], the name of the capital of the kingdom, Cordova. The length of it is 25,000 cubits, the breadth 10,000. It is situated at the left of the sea [Mediterranean] which flows between your country and the great sea [Atlantic], and compasses the whole of your land.

Between this city and the great sea beyond which there is no farther habitable territory, are nine astronomical degrees; the sun advances one degree on each day, according to the opinion of the astronomers; each degree contains 66 miles and two parts of a mile, each mile consists of 3,000 cubits; so that those nine degrees make 600 miles. From that great sea [Atlantic] the whole distance as far as Constantineh [Constantinople] is 3,1000 miles; but Cordova is 80 miles distant from the shore of the sea which flows into your country [Mediterranean].

I have found in the books of the wise men that the land of Khazar is 60 degrees longitude, making 270 miles [from Constantinople]. Such is the journey from Cordova to Constantineh. Before, however, I set forth an account of it I will also premise the measure of the length of its limits. Your servant is not ignorant that the least of the servants of my Lord the King is greater than the wise men of our country; but I am not teaching, only recording.

According to mathematical principles we have found that the distance of our city from the Equator is 38 degrees, that of Constantineh 44, of your boundaries 47. I have been induced to state these facts because of my surprise that we have no account of your kingdom, and I think this is only due to the great distance of our kingdom from the realm of my Lord the King.

But I recently heard that two men, inhabitants of our land, had arrived at the dwelling place of my Lord of King, one of them called Rabbi Judah, son of Meir, son of Nathan, a prudent and learned man, the other R. Joseph Haggaris, also a wise man (happy they, and blessed their lot, whose fortune it was to see the glorious majesty and splendour of my Lord the King, as well as the state and condition of his servants and ministers), I thought that it was easy in the sight of God in his great mercy to do a wonder to me also, and to make me, too, worthy of seeing the majesty and royal throne of my Lord, and to enjoy his gracious presence. I shall inform my Lord the King of the name of the King who reigns over us. His name is Abd er-Rahman . . . Nor can any of the kings who went before be compared with him.

The extent of Spain which is under the sovereignty of Abd ar-Rahman, the Amir al-Muminim (to whom God be propitious) is 16 degrees, making 1,100 miles. The land is rich, abounding in rivers, springs, and aqueducts; a land of corn, oil, and wine, of fruits and all manner of delicacies; it has pleasure gardens and orchards, fruitful trees of every kind, including the leaves of the tree upon which the silkworm feeds, of which we have great abundance.

In the mountains and woods of our country cochineal is gathered in great quantity. There are also found among us mountains covered by crocus and with veins of silver, gold, copper, iron, tin, lead, sulphur, porphyry, marble, and crystal. It produces besides what is called in the Arabic language *lulu*. Merchants congregate in it, and traffickers from the ends of the earth, from Egypt and adjacent countries, bringing spices, precious stones, splendid wares for kings and princes, and all the desirable things of Egypt.

Our king has collected very large treasures of silver, gold, precious things, and valuables such as no king has ever collected. His yearly revenue I have heard, is about 100,000 gold pieces, the greater part of which is derived from the merchants who come hither from various countries and islands; and all their mercantile transactions are placed under my control.

Praise be to the beneficent God for his mercy towards me! Kings of the earth, to whom His magnificence and power are known, bring gifts to him, conciliating his favour by costly presents, such as the King of the Germans, the King of the Gebalim, who are as-Saglab, the King of Constantineh, and others. All their gifts pass through my hands, and I am charged with making gifts in return. Let my lips express praise to the God in Heaven who so far extends his loving kindness towards me without any merit of my own, but in the fulness of his mercies.

I always ask the ambassadors of these monarchs about our brethren the Israelites, the remnant of the captivity, whether they have heard anything concerning the deliverance of those who have pined in bondage and had found no rest. At length mercantile emissaries of Khorasan told me that there is a kingdom of Jews who are called Khazars, and between Constantineh and that country is a sea voyage of 15 days by land, many nations dwell between us and them.

But I did not believe these words, for I thought that they told me such things to procure my goodwill and favour. I was, therefore, hesitating and doubtful till the ambassadors of Constantineh came with presents and a letter from their king to our king, whom I interrogated concerning this matter.

They answered me, "It is quite true; there is in that place a kingdom Alcusari, distant from Constantineh a fifteen days' journey by sea, but many peoples are scattered through the land; the name of the king now reigning is Joseph; ships sometimes come from their country to ours bringing fish, skins, and wares of every kind; the men are our brethren and honoured by us; there is frequent communication between us by embassies and mutual gifts; they are very powerful; they maintain numerous armies, which they occasionally engage in expeditions." This account inspired me with hope, wherefore I bowed down and adored the God of Heaven.

I now looked about for a faithful messenger whom I might send into your country in order that I might know the truth of this matter and ascertain the welfare of my Lord and his servants our brethren. The thing seemed impossible to me, owing to the very great distance of the locality, but at length by the will and favour of God, a man presented himself to me named Mar Isaac, the son of Nathan. He put his life into his hand and willingly offered to take my letter to my Lord the King. I gave him a large reward, supplying him with gold and silver for his own expenses and those of his servants, and with everything necessary.

Moreover, I sent out of my own resources a magnificent present to the King of Constantineh, requesting him to aid this my messenger in every possible way, till he should arrive at that place where my Lord resides. Accordingly this messenger set out, went to the King and showed him my letter and presents. The King, on his part, treated him honourably, and detained him there for six months, with the ambassadors of my Lord the King of Cordova.

One day he told them and my messenger to return, giving the latter a letter in which he wrote that the way was dangerous, that the peoples through whom he must pass were engaged in warfare, that the sea was stormy and could not be navigated except at a certain time. When I heard this I was grieved even to death, and took it very ill that he had not acted according to my orders and fulfilled my wishes.

Afterwards I wished to send my letter by way of Jerusalem, because persons there guaranteed that my letter should be dispatched from thence to Nisibis, thence to Armenia, from Armenia to Berdaa, and thence to your country. While in this state of suspense, behold ambassadors of the King of Gebalim arrived, and with them two Israelites; the name of one was Mar Saul, of the other Mar Joseph. These persons understood my perplexity and comforted me, saying, "Give us your letter, and we will take care that it be carried to the King of the Gebalim, who for your sake will send it to the Israelites dwelling in the land of the Hungarians, they will send it to Russ, thence to Bulgar, till at last it will arrive, according to your wish, at its destination."

He who tries the heart and searches the reins knows that I did none of these things for the sake of mine own honour, but only to know the truth, whether the Israelitish exiles, anywhere form one independent kingdom and are not subject to any foreign ruler. If, indeed I could learn that this was the case, then, despising all my glory, abandoning my high estate, leaving my family, I would go over mountains and hills, through seas and lands, till I should arrive at the place where my Lord the King resides, that I might see not only his glory and magnificence, and that of his servants and ministers, but also the tranquillity of the Israelites. On beholding this my eyes would brighten, my reins would exult, my lips would pour forth praises to God, who has not withdrawn his favour from his afflicted ones.

Now, therefore, let it please your Majesty, I beseech you, to have regard to the desires of your servant, and to command your scribes who are at hand to send back a reply from your distant land to your servant and to inform me fully concerning the condition of the Israelites, and how they came to dwell there.

Our fathers told us that the place in which they originally settled was called Mount Seir, but my Lord knows that Mount Seir is far from the place where you dwell; our ancestors say that it was, indeed, persecution, and by one calamity after another, till at length they became fixed in the place where they now dwell. The ancients, moreover, inform us that when a decree of fierce persecution was issued against the Jews on account of their transgressions, and the army of the Chaldeans rose up furiously against them, they hid the Book of the Law and the Holy Scriptures in a certain cave. For this reason they prayed in a cave and taught their sons to pray there morning and evening.

At length, however, through distance of time and days, they forgot, and lapsed into ignorance as to the meaning of this cave and why they prayed in it; while they still continued to observe the custom of their fathers, though ignorant of the reason for it. After a long time there came a certain Israelite who was desirous of knowing the true meaning of this custom, and when he entered the cave he found it full of books, which he brought out. From that time they resolved to study the Law.

This is what our fathers have related to us as it was handed down from ancient times. The two men who came from the land of Gebalim, Mar Saul and Mar Joseph, after pledging themselves to forward my letter to my Lord the King, told me; "About six years ago there came to us a wise and intelligent Israelite afflicted with blindness, his name was Mar Amram, and he said that he was from the land of the Khoz, that he dwelt in the King's house, ate at his table, and was held in honour by him." On hearing this I sent messengers to bring him to me, but they did not find him, yet this very circumstance confirmed my hope.

Wherefore I have written this epistle to your Majesty, in which I submissively entreat you not to refuse my request, but to command your servant to write to me about all these things, viz., what is your State? what is the nature of your land? what tribes inhabit it? what is the manner of the government, how kings succeed one another—whether they are chosen from a certain tribe or family or whether sons succeed their fathers, as was customary among our ancestors when they dwelt in their own land?

Would my Lord the King also inform me as to the extent of his country, its length and breadth? what walled cities and what open towns it has; whether it be watered by artificial or natural means and how far his dominion extends, also the number of his armies and their leaders? Let not my Lord take it ill, I pray, that I enquire about the number of his forces ("May the Lord add unto them," etc.).

My Lord sees that I enquire about this with no other object than that I may rejoice when I hear of the increase of the holy people. I wish, too, that he would tell me of the number of the provinces over which he rules, the amount of tribute paid to him, if they give him tithes, whether he dwells continually in the royal city or goes about through the whole extent of his dominions, if there are any islands in the neighborhood, and if any of their inhabitants conform to Judaism? if he judges his own people himself or appoints judges over them? how he goes up to the house of God? with what peoples he wages war? whether he allows war to set aside the observance of the Sabbath? what kingdoms or nations are on his borders? what are their names and those of territories? what are the cities near to his kingdom called Khorasan, Berdaa, and Bab al Abwab? in what way their caravans proceed to his territory? how many kings ruled before him?

what were their names, how many years each of them ruled and what is the current language of the land?

In the time of our fathers there was among us a certain Israelite, an intelligent man, who belonged to the tribe of Dan, who traced his descent back to Dan, the son of Jacob. He spoke elegantly and gave everything its name in the holy language. Nor was he at a loss for any expression. When he expounded the Law he was accustomed to say, "Thus has Othniel, son of Kenaz, handed down by tradition from the mouth of Joshua, and he from the mouth of Moses who was inspired by the Almighty."

One thing more I ask of my Lord, that he would tell me whether there is among you any computation concerning the final redemption which we have been awaiting so many years, whilst we went from one captivity to another, from one exile to another. How strong is the hope of him who awaits the realization of these events. And oh! how can I hold my peace and be restful in the face of the desolation of the house of our glory and remembering those who, escaping the sword, have passed through fire and water, so that the remnant is but small.

We have been cast down from our glory, so that we have nothing to reply when they say daily unto us, "Every other people has its kingdom, but of yours there is no memorial on the earth." Hearing, therefore, the fame of my Lord the King, as well as the power of his dominions, and the multitude of his forces, we were amazed, we lifted up our head, our spirit revived, and our hands were strengthened, and the kingdom of my Lord furnished us with an argument in answer to this taunt. May this report be substantiated; for that would add to our greatness.

Blessed be the Lord of Israel who has not left us without a kinsman as defender nor suffered the tribes of Israel to be without an independent kingdom. May my Lord the King prosper for ever. . . .

THE ANSWER OF JOSEPH, KING OF THE TOGARMI, TO HASDAI, THE HEAD OF THE CAPTIVITY, SON OF ISAAC, SON OF EZRA, THE SPANIARD, BELOVED AND HONORED BY US.

Behold, I inform you that your honoured epistle was given to me by R. Jacob, son of Eleazar, of the land of Nemez (Germany). We were rejoiced by it, and pleased with your discretion and wisdom, which we observed in it. I found in it a description of your land, its length and breadth, the descent of its sovereign, Abd ar-Rahman, his magnificence and majesty; and how, with the help of God, he subdued to himself the whole of the East, so that the fame of his kingdom spread over the whole world, and the fear of God seized upon all kings.

You also told us that had it not been for the arrival of those ambassadors from Constantineh, who gave an account of the people of our kingdom, and of our institutions, you would have regarded all as false, and would not have believed it. You also inquired concerning our kingdom and descent, how our fathers embraced the laws and religion of the Israelites, how God enlightened our eyes and scattered our enemies; you also desired to know the length and breadth of our land, the nations that are our neighbours, such as are friendly and hostile; whether our ambassadors can go to your land to salute your eminent and gracious king, who draws the hearts of all men to love him and contract friendship with him, by the excellence of his character, and the uprightness of his actions, because the nations tell you that the Israelites have no dominion and no kingdom.

If this were done, you say, the Israelites would derive great benefit from it, their courage would be reawakened, and they would have an answer and occasion for priding themselves in reply to such as say to them, "There are no Israelites remaining to have a kingdom or dominion." We shall therefore, delighting in your wisdom, answer you with respect to each of these particulars, concerning which you have asked us in your letter.

We had already heard what you have written concerning your land, and the family of the king. Among our fathers there had been mutual intercourse by letters, a thing which is written in our books and is known to the elders of our country. We shall now inform you of what happened to our fathers before us, and what we shall leave as an inheritance to our children.

You ask, also, in your epistle of what people, of what family, and of what tribe we are. Know that we are descended from Japhet, through his son Togarma. We have found in the genealogical books of our forefathers that Togarma had ten sons; we are the issue of Cusar, the seventh. God gave them fortitude and power to carry on wars with many and powerful nations, so that they expelled them from their country and pursued them in flight as far as the great river Runa [Danube?], where the conquerors live to this day, near Constantineh; and thus the Cusars took possession of their territory.

After some ages another king rose up, named Bulan, who was a wise God-fearing man. He expelled wizards and all idolaters from the land, and trusted in God alone. An angel appeared to him in a dream, saying to him, "Bulan, God has sent me to you, saying to you, 'I have heard your prayers and entreaties, I will bless you, I will multiply you and establish your kingdom for ever. I will also deliver all your enemies into your hand. Come, rise up in the morning, and pray unto the Lord.'" And Bulan did so.

The angel of the Lord appeared to him the second time, and said to him, "I have seen your ways, your works are pleasing to me, and I know that you will walk before me with all your heart. I will give you precepts, statutes, and judgments. If you observe my precepts, statutes, and judgments, I will bless you and multiply you." He answers and says to the angel, "Thou Lord, hast known the thoughts of my heart, thou hast searched and knowest that I put all my trust only in thee. But the people subject to my rule are unbelievers; I know not whether they will trust me. If I have found favour in thine eyes, and if thou wilt vouchsafe thy mercy to me, appear to their prince and leader, so that he may assist me."

God did so, in accordance with his wish, and appeared to that prince in a dream. And that man rose early and narrated to the king what had happened to him. The king, having assembled all his princes and ministers, and the whole of his people, told them all these things. They were pleased, accepted the divine rule, and sought protection under the wings of the Almighty.

Then the angel appeared to him the third time, saying to him, "Lo, the heaven and the heaven of heavens do not contain me, yet build thou a house to my name." The king answered, "O Sovereign of the Universe, shame overwhelms me in thy presence, I have not silver and gold to do this as it is right, and as I should wish." And this answer was given "Be strong and of good courage; take with you all your hosts and arise, go into the land Dariel, and into the land Erdevil, and behold, I will put the fear and the terror of you into their hearts, and I will deliver them into your hand. I have destined for you two treasures, one of silver, and another of gold. I will be with you, I will keep you in all your ways, whithersoever you go, that you shall acquire wealth, and return in safety, and build a house to my name." The king believed, and did as he was commanded. Returning in peace, he consecrated the wealth which he had acquired to God, and out of it constructed a tabernacle, ark, candlestick, table, altar, and sacred vessels, which are preserved and remain with me to this day.

When these things were finished the fame of him went forth into all the land, so that by reason of it the Byzantine and the Mohammedan sovereigns sent envoys to him with great riches and many presents, adding some of their wise men with the object of converting them to their own religion. But the king being wise sent for a learned Israelite. He brought the followers of the different religions together, that they might enter into a discussion of their respective doctrines. Each of them refuted, however, the arguments of his opponents, so that they could not agree. When the king saw this he spake thus to the Christian and Mohammedan priests, "Go home, and I will send for you again on the third day."

On the following day he sent to the Christian priest, and said to him, "I know that the Christian ruler is greater than all others, and that his religion is excellent, nor does your religion displease me, but I ask you to tell me the truth; which of these two is better, that of the Israelites or that of the Mohammedans?" The priest answered him, "May my Lord the King prosper for ever. Know that there is truly no religion in the whole world to be compared with the religion of the Israelites, for God chose Israel out of all peoples, called them his first-born son, wrought among them great miracles and signs, brought them forth from the slavery of Pharaoh, and made them to pass through the sea on dry land, drowned their enemies in the sea, rained down manna upon them, brought water for them out of the rock, gave them the law out of the midst of fire, assigned them the possession of the land of Canaan, and built for them a sanctuary that He might dwell among them. But after they sinned against Him, He was angry and cast them away from his face, scattering them throughout all regions of the earth. Were it not for this there would be no religion in the world like the religion of the Israelites." The king answered him, "Thus far you have told me your opinion; know that I will honor you."

On the second day the king sent for the Mohammedan Kadi, whom he also consulted, and to whom he said, "Tell me the truth, what is the difference between the religion of the Israelites and that of the Edomites? which of them is the better?" The Kadi answered and said to him, "The religion of the Israelites is the better, and is altogether true: they have the law of God, just statutes and judgments; but because they sinned and acted perversely towards Him, He was wroth with them, and delivered them into the hands of their enemies. What is the religion of the Christians? They eat all things unclean, and bow themselves to the work of their hands." The king answered him, "Thou hast told me the truth, therefore I will honour thee."

On the following day, having assembled all his princes and ministers, and the whole of his people, he said to them, "I ask you to choose for me the best and truest religion." They began to speak, without, however, arriving at any result. Thereupon the king said to the Christian priest, "Of the religions of the Israelites and Mohammedans, which is to be preferred?" The Christian priest answered, "The religion of the Israelites." He then asked the Mohammedan Kadi, "Is the religion of the Israelites, or that of the Christians the better?" The Kadi answered, "The religion of the Israelites is preferable." Upon this the king said, "You both confess that the religion of the Israelites is the best and truest, wherefore I choose the religion of the Israelites, which is that of Abraham. God Almighty will assist my purpose: the gold and silver which you promised to give me He can give me without labour. Depart now in peace to your land."

Henceforth Almighty God was his helper, and strengthened him, and he was circumcised, and all his servants. This being done, the king sent and called certain of the wise men of Israel, who explained to him the law and the precepts. Hence we have this excellent and true religion to the present day, praise be to God for ever. From the time our fathers entered under the wings of the Divine Majesty, He humbled before us all our enemies, subjecting all peoples that are round about us; nor has any been able to stand before us to this day: all are tributary to us by the hands of the kings of the Christians and the Mohammedans.

After these things one of his descendants, Obadiah by name, a pious and good man, ascended the throne. He strengthened the kingdom and firmly established religion, built synagogues and colleges, sent for many of the wise men of Israel and rewarded them with much gold and silver. They explained to him the Bible, Mishna, Talmud, and the order of divine service. This king feared God, and loved the law and the precepts.

He was succeeded by Hezekiah, his son; next to him was Manasseh, his son; next to him was Chanuka, brother of Obadiah; next, Isaac, his son; afterwards, his son Zebulon; then his son Manasseh; then his son Nissi; then his son Menahem; then his son Benjamin; then his son Aaron: and I, Joseph, am the son of this Aaron. We are all members of the same royal house, nor could any stranger occupy the throne of our ancestors. May it be the gracious will of Him who appoints all kings that our kingly line remain true to His laws and precepts.

As to your question concerning the extent of our land, its length and breadth, know that it is situated by the banks of a river near the sea of Georgia, towards the region of the East, a journey of four months. Near that river dwell very many populous tribes: there are hamlets, towns, and fortified cities, all of which pay tribute to me. From thence the boundary turns towards Georgia; and all those who dwell by the sea-shore, a month's journey, pay tribute to me. On the South side are fifteen very populous tribes, as far as Bab-al-Abuab, who live in the mountains. Likewise the inhabitants of the land of Bassa, and Tagat, as far as the sea of Constantineh, a journey of two months; all these give me tribute. On the Western side are thirteen tribes, also very numerous, dwelling on the shores of the sea of Constantineh; and thence the boundary turns to the North as far as the great river called Jaig. These live in open unwalled towns, and occupy the whole wilderness [steppe] as far as the boundary of the Jugrians; they are numerous as the sand of the sea, and all are tributary to me. Their land has an extent of four months' journey distant. I dwell at the mouth of the river, and do not permit the Russians, who come in ships, to enter into their country, nor do I allow their enemies who come by land to penetrate into their territory. I have to wage grievous wars with them; for if I would permit them they would lay waste the whole land of the Mohammedans as far as Bagdad.

Moreover, I notify to you that I dwell by the banks of the river, by the grace of God, and have in my kingdom three royal cities. In the first the queen dwells with her maids and attendants. The length and breadth of it is fifty square parasangs [about four miles], together with its suburbs and adjacent hamlets. Israelites, Mohammedans, Christians, and other peoples of various tongues dwell therein. The second, together with the suburbs, comprehends in length and breadth, eight square parasangs. In the third I reside with the princes and my servants, and all my officers. This is a small city, in length and breadth three square parasangs; the river flows within its walls.

The whole winter we remain within the city, and in the month of Nisan [March] we leave this city, and each one goes forth to his fields and gardens to cultivate them. Each family has its own hereditary estate. They enter and dwell in it with joy and song. The voice of an oppressor is not heard among us; there are no enmities nor quarrels. I, with the princes and my ministers, then journey a distance of twenty parasangs to the great river Arsan, thence we make a circuit till we arrive at the extremity of the province. This is the extent of our land, and the place of our rest. Our country is not frequently watered by rain; it abounds in rivers and streams, having great abundance of fish; we have many springs; the land is fertile and rich; fields, vineyards, gardens, and orchards are watered by rivers; we have fruit-bearing trees of every kind, and in great abundance.

This too I add, that the limit of our land towards the Eastern region is twenty parasangs' journey, as far as the sea of Georgia; thirty, towards the South; forty, towards the West. I dwell in a fertile island, and, by the grace of God, I dwell in tranquillity.

With reference to your question concerning the marvellous end [i.e., the restoration of the Jews to their former glory by the Messiah. Cf. Dan. 12:6], our eyes are turned to the Lord our God, and to the wise men of Israel who dwell in Jerusalem and Babylon. Though we are far from Zion, we have heard that because of our iniquities the computations are erroneous; nor do we know aught concerning this. But if it please the Lord, He will do it for the sake of His great name; nor will the desolation of His house, the abolition of His service, and all the troubles which have come upon us, be lightly esteemed in His sight. He will fulfil His promise, and "the Lord whom ye seek shall suddenly come to His temple, the messenger of the Covenant whom ye delight in: behold he shall come saith the Lord of Hosts" [Mal. 3:1]. Besides this we only have the prophecy of Daniel. May God hasten the redemption of Israel, gather together the captives and dispersed, you and I, and all Israel that love His name, in the lifetime of us all.

Finally, you mention that you desire to see my face. I also long and desire to see your honoured face, to behold your wisdom and magnificence. Would that it were according to your word, and that it were granted me to be united with you, so that you might be my father and I your son. All my people would pay homage to you: according to your word and righteous counsel we should go out and come in. Farewell.

Hebrew Poetry —
The Golden Age of Spain

Samuel ha-Nagid

Samuel ha-Nagid (993–1056) of Cordova, Spain, the author of more than 1700 poems, was among the first Hebrew poets to write secular verse. A student at one of the talmudic academies founded by Hasdai ibn Shaprut, Samuel ha-Nagid not only wrote on matters of Talmud and halakha, but was also interested in Hebrew language and grammar, and after becoming vizier to the King of Granada, led his armies in battle. Samuel ha-Nagid is one of the finest composers of wine songs in Hebrew literature and one of the rare poets of Hebrew martial verse. Utilizing meter and rhyme, Samuel wrote nature and love poetry, and songs of friendship—models that were popular in Arabic poetry; he also composed dirges, liturgies and poems brimming with deep Jewish nationalism.

The versatile Samuel was a statesman, diplomat, general and a patron of and a contributor to Jewish learning, whose poetry and erudition were praised by Muslims and Jews alike. His three works, based on Biblical books, are *Ben Tehillim* (Psalms), his most oft-quoted composition, *Ben Mishley* (Proverbs), and *Ben Kohellet* (Ecclesiastes), each of which are modelled respectively on prayer, proverbs and philosophic wisdom. He also assembled a collection of halakhic decisions, wrote books on Hebrew grammar and language, and a treatise, *Introduction to the Talmud,* which deals with the methodology and technical terms of the Talmud.

Prior to Samuel ha-Nagid, Hebrew poetry was mainly religious and liturgical in character. With Samuel, however, the Golden Age (eleventh to the end of the twelfth century), the most fertile period of Hebrew creativity between Biblical times and the modern renaissance of Hebrew letters, comes into full fruition.

Solomon ibn Gabirol

With the flourishing of Solomon ibn Gabirol (1020–1056[?]), who lived during the lifetime of his illustrious predecessor and patron, Samuel ha-Nagid, the Golden Age reached one of its heights. Little information about his life is available, but his evidently autobiographical poems offer some facts. Born in Malaga, he was raised in Saragossa, a center of Jewish learning. Like others in Spain ibn Gabirol received an extensive secular as well as Jewish education. He was well-versed in the Bible, had a perfect command of Hebrew grammar, and studied Arabic, Arabic poetry and philosophy—all of which aided him in mastering the strict forms imposed by the Arabic prosody that Hebrew had adopted. Orphaned early in his life, ibn Gabirol suffered constantly from tuberculosis. At twenty-eight he left his home town owing to a continuing conflict between him and the town fathers (his pointed satire angered the pillars of the community), and he moved to Granada where his patron was Samuel ha-Nagid.

Ibn Gabirol wrote secular and sacred poems. In his secular poetry, wherein he utilized all the techniques of meter, rhyme and alliteration, the poet bemoans his fate and describes the injustice in life, the pain of illness and poverty, and nature poems that are usually linked to the poet's spiritual state. The secular poems are personal (if the personal can be distinguished from the conventional elements), perhaps somewhat romantic, and formalized according to the prevailing Arabic models. In expressing the attitude of the individual poet versus the world, these poems are to a degree comparable to the nineteenth century English romantic school of poetry. Not as widely known as his sacred poems (which were preserved in the prayer books of the Ashkenazim and Sephardim), ibn Gabirol's secular poetry was discovered by scholars in recent generations.

Whereas in the secular poetry, ibn Gabirol stands as individual *qua* individual, in the sacred poetry the *persona* assumes the guise of a collective entity, representing the national spirit of the people of Israel. In his outpouring to God he addresses not only the universal Creator, but also the God of the Three Patriarchs, the God of Israel who revealed himself at Sinai. These poems, in which generations of Jews saw an expression of their own longing, epitomized the sorrow and pain of centuries of exile, and the people's expectation of salvation.

Besides being a poet, ibn Gabirol was also a philosopher, the first to introduce neo-Platonism into Europe. His Arabic text, preserved only in its Latin translation, *Fons Vitae,* strongly influenced the Christian scholastics of the Middle Ages. Since the author's name was not mentioned in the work, readers thought that it was written by an Arab or a Christian philosopher, and discovered only in the middle of the nineteenth century that *Fons Vitae* was a lost work by the famed Jewish poet, Solomn ibn Gabirol.

Ibn Gabirol's longest poetic work, *The Kingly Crown,* is a hymn of glory to God, describing the universe and its Creator, and concluding with a personal confession and prayer. Written in rhymed couplets, the poem contains many lines that are mosaics of Biblical verses, and is included in the High Holiday prayers of the Sephardim and Ashkenazim.

Moses ibn Ezra

Moses ibn Ezra (1070–1139) was born in Granada, Spain, to a wealthy and famous family whose scions contributed much to Jewish culture. Thoroughly acquainted with Arabic and Hebrew knowledge, ibn Ezra knew Greek and Latin, and had a liberal general education. In his youth he began to write poetry, wine and nature songs and lyrics of passionate love. Since the Song of Songs—an earthy poem of love that was subsequently interpreted as a love song between Israel and God—Hebrew poetry had not seen verses bristling with such eros.

As with Solomon ibn Gabirol, the poet's personal life also influenced Moses ibn Ezra's poetry. Ibn Ezra was in love with his niece, and the ensuing disappointment when his family forbade the marriage is evident in much of his melancholy-laden poetry. Unfortunately, there was no fairy-tale, happily-ever-after ending. His niece married someone else, and Moses ibn Ezra roamed Cain-like over many lands until his death, not even heeding his love's death-bed plea—she died in childbirth—that he give up his wandering and return home.

As ibn Ezra grew older he wrote only sacred poetry—a phenomenon noticeable in other poets of the Middle Ages: old age and fear of heaven (or of hell) drove Boccaccio, Chaucer and Petrarch to renounce their early secular works and made them turn to sacred writings. Taking stock of his life, Moses ibn Ezra felt that he had sinned in his youth and that he should return to God; hence he devoted himself solely to liturgical poetry and penitential hymns, composing more than three hundred of the latter. Herein he accents the vanity of life on earth and warns his readers not to follow a meretricious life of worldly pleasure.

From a technical point of view, ibn Ezra's poetry is sophisticated. He imitated the most difficult Arabic models of rhymed poetry and even added to the complexities of the form. When he abandoned secular poetry and its rather conventional forms, the poet's feelings—released from the shackles of strict poetic discipline—were given freer reign; nevertheless, even in his liturgic poetry he did not completely give up meter and rhyme, and still made skilful use of poetic technique.

Judah Halevi

Judah Halevi (1085–1142) was born in Toledo in Christian Spain, but was educated in the Arab sector. He studied Arabic, Greek philosophy and medicine—the only liberal profession that a Jew in the Middle Ages could freely practise without compromising his faith—and also studied at the yeshiva of Rabbi Isaac Alfasi (see his responsum, page 280).

Early in his career Judah Halevi wrote poetry whose themes were similar to that of Moses ibn Ezra. In keeping with the literary conventions of the day, some poems praised the Spanish beauties, others were love songs describing the poet's pain at departing from his beloved. Other secular verses were devoted to wedding songs, which were very likely written for specific occasions, and songs of wine and friendship. The latter, a prevalent type in Arabic poetry which Hebrew poets imitated, has its parallels in Western literature in the songs of friendship of Elizabethan poetry, notably in the sonnets of Shakespeare. Another point of comparison with English poetry occurs in some of the secular poems where the religious and erotic elements fuse, with images and themes reminiscent of metaphysical poets like John Donne.

Later in life Judah Halevi turned from secular verse to poems that expressed the Jew's national and religious feelings, and many of which in time were chanted as prayers. In his nationalistic poetry, Judah Halevi no longer sang the conventional songs that declared the Jew's agony in exile. Considering this a negativistic approach, the poet wrote of Zion not as a messianic dream but as a realistic entity. For the first time in post-Biblical Hebrew poetry the chief leitmotif was the immediate return to Zion—based not on supernatural events at the end of days, but on the personal decision to leave the Diaspora and come to the Land of Israel.

Although Jews had long expressed these thoughts in their poetry and prayers, no one had seriously raised the idea of a return to Zion. In Judah Halevi's poetry, however, the return is not a mere conventional utterance, but a patriotic call to action. He feels that the only salvation for Israel would be the return to the Land of Israel, to settle it and rebuild it. Only in this manner —by the return of the Children of Israel to the Land of Israel— can the Jews purify themselves of the degradation of exile.

Toward the end of his life, Judah Halevi finally realized by his own action the dream of *aliya* that he held for the entire people, stopping on his way to visit various Jewish communities. His call for emigration of all fellow Jews went unheeded, but he, as it were representing all of Jewry, returned to Zion. Popular tradition has it that upon reaching the gates of Jerusalem and bending down to kiss its dust, he was trampled by an Arab horseman and died at the foot of the Holy City.

Judah Halevi also wrote a philosophic-theological text called *The Kuzari,* which in dramatic form outlines the historic, national and spiritual heritage of Israel, and continues the call for national revival that he began in his poetry.

Judah Halevi's poetry is replete with Biblical diction; he utilized the language of the Torah, the prophets and the Psalms, in combination with his own original rhetoric. In his metaphors, variegated themes, dramatic quality and innumerable forms, Judah Halevi is the chief exponent of the renaissance of Hebrew poetry—the Golden Age—in Spain.

SAMUEL HA-NAGID

In Praise of Wine

Red in appearance, sweet to the taste,
Vintage of Spain, yet renowned in the East,
Feeble in the cup, but, once up in the brain,
It rules over heads that cannot rise again.

The mourner, whose blood is mixed with his tears—
The blood of the grape demolishes his fears.
Friends, passing the cup from hand to hand,
Seem to be gambling for a precious diamond.

An Invitation

My friend, tell me,
When shall I pour you my wine?
The cry of the cock woke me,
And sleep has deserted my eyes.

Come out and see the morning light
Like a scarlet thread in the East.
Make haste, give me a cup,
Before the dawn starts to rise,

Of spiced pomegranate juice
From the perfumed hand of a girl,
Who will sing songs. My soul
Revives and then dies.

The Power of the Pen

Man's wisdom is at the tip of his pen,
His intelligence is in his writing.
His pen can raise a man to the rank
That the sceptre accords to a king.

Man Runs towards the Grave

Man runs towards the grave,
And rivers hasten to the great deep.
The end of all living is their death,
And the place in time becomes a heap.
Nothing is further than the day gone by,
And nothing nearer than the day to come,
And both are far, far away
From the man hidden in the heart of the tomb.

The Old Man's Warning

You laugh at me, now that you are young,
Because you see me old, and grey-haired.
I am an old man, but I have seen workmen
Make a coffin and a bier for a young lad.

The Hour in which I am

She said to me: "Rejoice, that God has brought you
To the age of fifty in this world." She was not aware
That there is no difference to me between my days
That have passed and what I hear of the days of Noah.
There is nothing for me in the world but the hour in which I am.
It lasts but a moment, and, like a cloud, is no more.

Two Bouts of Woe

Consider how shameful rejoicing is,
Since it comes between two bouts of woe.
You wept when you came into this world,
And another will mourn you when you go.

I Look up to the Sky

I look up to the sky and the stars,
And down to the earth and the things that creep there.

And I consider in my heart how their creation
Was planned with wisdom in every detail.
See the heavens above like a tent,
Constructed with loops and with hooks,
And the moon with its stars, like a shepherdess
Sending her sheep into the reeds;
The moon itself among the clouds,
Like a ship sailing under its banners;
The clouds like a girl in her garden
Moving, and watering the myrtle-trees;
The dew-mist—a woman shaking
Drops from her hair to the ground.
The inhabitants turn, like animals, to rest,
(Their palaces are their stables);
And all fleeing from the fear of death,
Like a dove pursued by the falcon.
And these are compared at the end to a plate
Which is smashed into innumerable sherds.

God's Assurance

On a day of danger and distress I remember your message.
You are good, and there is justice in your mouth and your heart.
I remember the message which comes to console me
When sorrow appears. I put faith in your help.
When your servant in his youth lay asleep in his bed, you sent
Seraphim to tell him of your great goodness.
They sat down beside me, and then Michael said:
"This is God's message who pleads your cause:
'On the day that you cross waters of sorrow I am with you.
When the enemy draws near, the rivers will not drown you.' "

And Gabriel, too, his companion, who has heard
Of your chariot, and all that surrounds you, said to me:
"When you walk into the fire, it shall not burn you.
I shall speak to the flames, and they will never destroy you."
This is the message on which I rely like a sword in the hand.
I see swords before me. I trust in your sword.

A Message to his Son, Joseph, on the Raising of the Siege of Lorca

Send a carrier-pigeon, although she cannot speak,
With a tiny letter attached to her wings,
Sweetened with saffron-water, perfumed with frankincense.
And when she rises to fly away, send with her another,
So that, should she meet an eagle, or fall into a snare,
Or fail to make haste, the second will speed away.
And when she comes to Joseph's house, she will coo on the roof-top.
When she flies down to his hand, he will rejoice in her, like a song-bird.
He will spread out her wings, and read a letter there:
"Know, my son, that the cursed band of rebels has fled,
Scattered among the hills like chaff from a windswept field,
And among the byways like sheep astray with no shepherd.
They looked to defeat their enemy but they did not see it.
As we went to destroy them, at that very hour they fled.
They were slaughtered, falling upon each other at the crossing.
Their designs against the barred, walled city were frustrated.
They were humiliated like thieves caught in the act.
They covered themselves with ignominy as with a garment.
Calamity attached itself to them like the skin of one's face.
They drank contempt from the beaker, and found the cup made them drunk.

In my heart there was the pain of a woman bearing her first child,
And God put balm upon it, like rain in the drought.
Then my eyes were brightened, and my enemies plunged in gloom.
I sing with a joyful heart, and they utter only laments.
The voice of gladness is in my house, and theirs hears bitter weeping.

To you, my rock and my tower, to you my soul sings.
When I was in trouble, my plaint was laid before you.
My son, put your heart in the glorious hand of my God.
Arise, sing my song in the full assembly of the people.
And make it an amulet to be bound on your hand,
And let it be written with pen of iron in your heart."

War

War at first is like a young girl
With whom every man desires to flirt.
And at the last it is an old woman.
All who meet her feel grieved and hurt.

Israel, Arise

Terminate your reign, wicked queen.
Sarah, the despised, rule over your enemies.
Gazelle of Senir, your slumber has been long
On your bed of pain. Awake, arise.
Raise yourself; there is reward for your righteousness.
Cure yourself; there is balm for your injuries.

The Wounded Lion

At times of distress, strengthen your heart,
Even if you stand at death's door.
The lamp has light before it is extinguished.
The wounded lion still knows how to roar.

SOLOMON IBN GABIROL

An Apple for Isaac

My lord, take this delicacy in your hand.
Perceive its scent. Forget your longing.
On both sides it blushes, like a young girl
At the first touch of my hand on her breast.
An orphan it is without father or sister,
And far away from its leafy home.
When it was plucked, its companions were jealous,
Envied its journey, and cried aloud:
"Bear greetings to your master, Isaac.
How lucky you are to be kissed by his lips!"

In the Morning I Look for You

In the morning I look for you,
My rock and my tower.
I lay my prayers before you,
That day and night are in me.

Before your greatness, I stand,
And am unnerved,
Because your eye will see
The thoughts that are in me.

What is it that the heart
Or the tongue can do,
And what power is there
In the spirit that is in me?

But I know you are pleased
With the songs that men make,
And so I shall praise you
While the divine soul is in me.

Epitaph on the Death of Rabbi Yekuthiel

Behold the sun deep-red towards evening time
As if enveloped in a crimson mantle,
It traverses the corners of the north and south,
And covers their borders with purple hangings;
But me, like the earth, it has left naked,
While it tarries and reposes under the shadow of the night.
Look! How the heavens are darkened,
As if covered with sackcloth for the death of Yekuthiel!

To a Friend

Did you not swear, my friend, to beware of treachery,
And are you not wearied of acting in the dark?
I delighted in you, but you washed my love
From your heart, as if with nitre and soap.
I longed for you, like one who thirsts and hopes
For the rain of Heaven; and, behold, there is fire and brimstone!

Prayer

My thoughts inquired often with astonishment
"To which of the celestial planets art thou running?"
"To the God of my life," replied I, "the delight of my longings,
My soul and my flesh wait for Him and pant after Him,
My Joy and my Portion, my Cup and my Maker,
Whom when I remember and mention, I feel
That nothing is more fitted for my soul's happiness
Than blessing the name of the Eternal God.

From "The Royal Crown"

1.

My God, I know that my iniquity
  Is heavier than my feeble words express,
And to recount my trespasses to Thee
  Doth memory fail, for they are numberless.

Yet some do haunt my mind, but these, indeed,
  Are as a drop of water from my sea
Of sin, whose roaring billows may recede,
  And by confession, calm'd and silenced be.
  O Thou in Heaven, pray list, and pardon me.

Thy precepts have I scorned, Thy Law transgressed,
  Rejecting from my wayward heart Thy word;
Slander I spake, and in my truant breast
  Lurked vice indulgent, therefore have I erred.

Falsehood and pride and violence combined
  To dog my steps and lead them far astray;
When men have counsel ask'd, oft did I blind
  Their eyes with fraud, and evil counsel say.

I have rebelled, blasphemed, yea, scorned and lied;
  I have revolted and perversely done;
I have betrayed and stiffnecked did abide,
  Defiant strove Thy just rebuke to shun.

How have my deeds been sinful, weak and vile,
  My ways corrupt and errant from Thy path,
Daring Thy precepts with deluding wile,
To merge beneath the tempest of Thy wrath.

Though great the sorrows that o'erwhelm my brow,
  These sorrows issue from Thy righteous hand
Where mercy ever dwelleth; hence I bow
  And court the shaft that sped at Thy command.

My God, I mourn, for self-accusers rise:
  "Thou hast Thy Maker grievously defied,
Hast acted graceless folly in His eyes
  For mercies, when His judgment bade Him chide."

Thou needest no service at my humble hand,
  Yet gavest me life and bless'd my happy birth;
Thy spirit bade my budding soul expand,
  To blossom on Thy fair and wondrous earth.

And Thou hast reared me with a father's care,
  Strengthen'd my limbs and nursed the tender child
Lulled on my mother's gentle bosom, where
  Thine all-protecting wing and blessing smiled.

And when I grew and all erect could stand,
  Thou did'st enfold me in Thy fostering arms
Guiding my tott'ring steps with Thy right hand
  To manly strength, which scorneth all alarms.

The ways of wisdom did'st Thou then command
  To shield my heart 'gainst sorrow and distress,
Conceal'd within the shadow of Thy hand,
  When fear and wrath did all the land oppress.

How many an unseen danger have I pass'd!
  Before the wound the balm is yet prepared;
A remedy before the spear is cast,
  The foeman vanquished before the war's declared.

Heedless I placed my head 'twixt lion's teeth,
  And thou to rescue me their jaws did'st break;
When sickness held me with her heel beneath,
  Thy heav'nly balsam came for pity's sake.

And when Thy judgment thunder'd in the storm
   Thy favour armed Thy servant against its blow;
When death assailed him in pale famine's form,
   Thy halo veiled him in a saving glow.

When plenty reigned my share of wealth I won,
   But when I roused with provocation sore
Thy wrath, as doth a father to his son,
   Thou did'st chastise, that l should sin no more.

Then unto Thee I cried in dire distress,
   My soul immortal with Thee favour found,
Thy mercy shed in Thy benign excess
   A perfect faith, within my heart, profound.

Among the foolish who blaspheme Thy name
   With clamour loud, Thou hast not cast my lot;
Among erring ones who against Thy word exclaim,
   Thy laws deriding, number'd I am not.

Of visage fair are they, yet foul deceit
   Lurketh like leprous spots deep sunk within;
Though, on the surface smiling ripples meet,
   Beneath are billows wild, and black as sin:

A vessel, filled to brim with shame and woe,
   Varnished with glitt'ring waters to allure,
Distilled of malice, virtue's direst foe
   Its touch unclean, defilement to the pure.

I am unworthy of the saving love
   Thou hast to me Thy servant ever shown,
So must I waft my song of praise above,
   And unto Thee my gratitude make known.

My soul, Thy gift divine, was pure as light;
   Alas! no more, my sin hath stain'd its crest.
I wrestled with the Evil Sense in might,
   But all too weak I sank—yet not to rest.

Contrite, Thy saving pardon I entreat,
   I feel Thy glory flood my yearning soul;
Vanquished proud sin is helpless at my feet,
   And I, Thy servant, reach Thy radiant goal.

From "The Royal Crown"

2.

Wondrous are thy works, O Lord of hosts,
And their greatness holds my soul in thrall.
Thine the glory is, the power divine,
Thine the majesty, the kingdom thine,
Thou supreme, exalted over all.

Thine is the throne in heavenly heights sublime,
The hidden dwelling-place all worlds above,
The existence from the shadow of whose light
Springs every living thing, of which aright
We say, that in its shade we live and move.

Thine the two worlds, that thou dost hold apart,
The first for work, the next for heavenly rest;
Thine the reward, which thou hast treasured there
Wrought for the righteous ones, with loving care,
Because thou hast beheld and known it blest.

Thou art One, the first great cause of all,
Thou art One and none can penetrate,
Not even the wise in heart, the mystery
Of thy unfathomable Unity;
Thou art One, the infinitely great.

Thou dost exist, but not the hearing ear,
Or seeing eye can reach thee; what thou art
And how and wherefore is to us unknown.
Thou dost exist, but through thyself alone,
King, in whose power no other has a part.

Thou dost exist; thou wast ere time began,
Pervading all, when there was yet no space.
Thou dost exist: thy mystery, concealed
Far from men's sight lies ever unrevealed,
Deep, deep, where none can find its dwelling-place.

Thou livest, but not with the twofold life
Of soul and mind: soul of the soul art thou.
Thou livest, and eternal joy shall bless,
At the end of days, those whom thy graciousness
To penetrate thy mystery will allow.

Thou art mighty, and of all thy works
There is none whose power to thine comes nigh.
Thou art mighty, and thy boundless power
Makes thee pardon, even in the hour
Of thy wrath, man's sore iniquity.

Thou art light: pure souls shall thee behold,
Save when mists of evil intervene.
Thou art light, that, in this world concealed,
In the world to come shall be revealed;
In the mount of God it shall be seen.

Thou art God, and all whom thou hast formed
Serve and worship thee in love and fear;
Nor aught lessens it thy majesty
That they worship others besides thee,
For they all would fain to thee draw near.

Yet like blind men from the path they stray,
While they seek the great King's road to gain.
In destructive pits and snares they lie,
Ever deeming their desire is nigh,
Though they toil and labour all in vain.

But thy servants move with open eyes,
On the straight path ever travelling,
Nor to right or left on either hand
Turn they till within the court they stand
Leading to the palace of the King.

Thou art God, and thy Divinity
And thy Unity the world uphold.
Thou art God, eternal, one, divine:
Thus in thee thy attributes combine,
Indivisible, yet manifold.

Thou art wise, and at thy side hast reared
Wisdom, fount of life, thy first-born son.
Thou art wise: this universal frame
At thy mighty word to being came,
When to aid or counsel thee was none.

Thou didst span the heaven's vast canopy
And the planets' shining tent uprear,
In thy hand dost thou, O Lord of might,
All creation's utmost ends unite,
Gathered as one whole from sphere to sphere.

MOSES IBN EZRA
SONGS OF WANDERING

When the Morning of Life Had Passed

When the morning of life had passed as a shadow,
And the path of my years was shortened,
Exile called to me: "O thou, that dwellest at ease, arise!"
At the sound of his voice, mine ears tingled;
I arose, with shaken heart,
To go forth, a wanderer—
And my children cried unto God!

But they are the fount of my life—
How shall I exist without them,
And the light of mine eyes be not with me?

Fate has led me to a land
Wherein my mind is bewildered and my thoughts confused—
To a people rude of speech and obscure in word;
Before the insolence of their gaze, my face is cast down.
Oh, when will God call unto me, "Go free!"
That I may escape from them—if only by the skin of my teeth!

The Dove That Nests in the Tree Top

The young dove that nests in the tree top
In the garden of spices—
Whereof should he lament?
The brooks deny him not their waters,
The palm-bough is a shade unto his head;
His nestlings disport before him,
And he teaches them his song.

Mourn, little dove, mourn for the wanderer,
And for his children, that are far away,
With none to bring them food.
He sees no one that has seen their faces,
None can he ask of their welfare, save wizards and mutterers.

Grieve for him, little dove, and bemoan his exile;
Display not before him gladness and song.

Oh, lend him thy wings,
That he may fly unto his loved ones
And rejoice in the dust of their land!

Wrung with Anguish

Wrung with anguish,
  My heart complains;
Each chamber mourning
  The other's hurt.
Like a bird in flight
  My life-span seems—
My years its wings,
  Their feathers, days.
In all my years,
  In all their days,
I have reached but a shadow
  Of my desires.
My mind is wearied,
  My strength decays;
I stumble and fall
  In the morass of age.
What now are my sayings?
  Or what my thoughts?
What is my wisdom?
  Or what mine art?
More swift than shadows
  My three-score years;
Faster they rushed
  Than a racing steed.
From the day of man's birth
  Till his time shall come,
Is but from kneading
  To rising of dough!

SONGS OF FRIENDSHIP

Sorrow Shatters My Heart

Sorrow shatters my heart;
And men distress it with blame,
Because it follows love.

They censure it for its delight in the beautiful friend,
And because it loves him, even as its own soul;
They rebuke it for the abundance of its tears
When it thinks and speaks of him.

They impute to him a blemish,
In that his face, bright as day,
Is framed about with the blackness of night.

Wherefore my heart swears by the life of Love,
That it will not listen to his detractors;
But the flame of its affection
It will hide in its innermost chamber, even from the loved one,
That his heart may not be lifted up in pride.

Fate Has Blocked the Way

Fate has blocked the way to the garden of friendship
That my heart may not find rest therein;
He has shut it out with estrangement,
As with bolted doors,
That it may not tend its plants
To bring them to blossom.

Though enemies rage, I will knock upon the doors;
In the face of the envious, will I enter the portals.
Locks will I shatter with the power of speech,
With the songs of my lips, I will break bolts in sunder.
And if nettles spring up,
I will persuade my heart that they are sprigs of balsam;
If bitter upon my palate be their must,
I will go dancing and shouting,
As one that is wild with the joy of spiced wine.

If its dews be drops from the streams of brimstone,
I will pretend that they are crumbs of ice.
For by the humility of my spirit,
I would fain restore my banished heart
To its place in the heart of the loved one.
Like a gentle shower will I enter therein,
As a stream of oil into its hidden recesses.
Then shall I walk through the darkness
Unto the light of my friend,
And he will no longer withhold from me his shining.
I will hope to eat of the fruits of the garden of his love—
The aftergrowth, if the first fruits be denied me.

Go now, O my song,
Take my message to my beloved—
For truly, song is a faithful messenger.

O Brook

O brook, whose hurrying waters go
To the far land that holds my friend,
By thee, my greeting let me send;
And if thy waves seem red as blood,
Tell him my tears have stained thy flood;
The mingled drops of eye and heart,
For exile, and for love, they flow—
Exile and love, that rend the frame
Of them who dwell from friends apart.

O brook, bespeak him tenderly;
Fill thou his heart with thought of me,
So that usurper may not claim
My place therein.
                    Make him to know
That for his ransom I would give
What years I yet may have to live—
Or if my life be all too little worth,
That which I hold most precious upon earth.

OF WINE AND THE DELIGHTS
OF THE SONS OF MEN

Winter Hath Vanished

Winter with its rains hath vanished,
Vanished with its trampling horses,
With the tumult of its riders;
Now the sun—his law fulfilling
In his circling of the heavens—
Comes again unto the ram's head,
As a king comes to his table.

On their heads the hills are binding
Turbans of bright flowers; the valley,
Gay in mantle of green grasses,
Sends forth to regale our senses
Spicy odors, as of incense
She had treasured in her bosom
Through the days of chill and gloom.

Fetch the cup—for joy it throneth
In the heart, and drives out sorrow—
With my tears assuage its burning,
For the wine is wroth, and flameth.

Guard thee against Fate; like venom
With a little honey mingled,
Are his gifts. Yet should he bring thee
Good at morn, accept, enjoy it;
Knowing surely, that ere nightfall
Into evil will he turn it.

Drink with day till he departeth,
Till the sun o'erlay his silver
With the hues of ruddy gold;
Drink with night until she leave thee—
Flying fast—a shape of blackness,
And the roseate hand of morning
Stretcheth out to seize her heel.

Drink Deep, My Friend

Drink deep, my friend, and pass the cup to me,
My heart from crushing sorrows to set free;
And if I die before thy face, do thou
Revive me quickly with thy minstrelsy.

Bring Me the Cup

Bring me the cup, what time the shadows lengthen,
And the sun kisses the hands of darkness.
Doth it seem pallid like a sick man?
Know that when it is filled, its aspect changes,
And it becomes ruddy, like the face of an ardent lover.
Verily my wine is a stripling without sword or spear,
But he shall put to flight the host of my sorrows.

The Garden Dons a Coat of Many Hues

The garden dons a coat of many hues;
The mead a broidered carpet hath unrolled;
The woods are brave in chequered mantles—Now
A wondrous scene may every eye behold:

The newborn flowers acclaim the newborn Spring,
And forth to meet his coming, gaily throng;
High, at their head, on sovereign throne is borne
The rose—the flowrets' queen—queen of my song.

From prisoning leaves she bursts, and casts aside
Her captive garb, in royal robes to shine.
I drink to her! Nor heaven forgive the wretch—
If such there be—who spares his choicest wine!

THE WORLD AND ITS VICISSITUDES

The World is like a Woman of Folly

The world is like a woman of folly,
Vain are her pomp and glory;
She speaks sweet words, but verily
Under her tongue is a snare.
O brother of wisdom, frustrate her cunning;
Turn thou her glory into shame.
Hasten, and send her from thee forever—
Her bill of divorcement in her hand!

Princes

Princes, on account of their great power, consider themselves mountains
Firmly based on the pillars of the earth;
But the storms of time upset them as in a moment,
And in their place throw up mountains of trouble.

Man

Man in the midst of the world is like a weaver,
And his days are but a thread.
Alas, the day that his web is finished
There is no more hope for his life.

Only in God I Trust

Only in God I trust. To Him, my prayer
    Ascends continually;
The secret of my soul I will not bare
    For man to see.
What help for mortal lies in mortals' power?
    What succor unto one despised
Can issue from the lips of them unprized?

Earth's favor, spurn. 'Tis she, with her own hands,
    Brings low her tower,
And she that turns her precious gifts to naught.

Of children twain to bed hath she been brought;
  Within her womb, again,
  The one is lying;
And on her back, the other crawls in pain—
  The dead, the dying.

LITURGICAL POEMS

God Hangs the World on Nothing

God hangs the world on nothing,
Like a cluster He suspends it, without cord—
It shall wear out like a mouldering rag,
But never shall His power wane.
He knows, He reveals, the hidden thoughts
Of the upright and of them that do evil—
The thoughts of man, that are vanity.

Without eye, but in my flesh,
I behold my Maker;
And I am conscious that I am of little worth,
And that my end is nothingness;
That my wit is small,
While my evil inclination is girded with sharp weapons.
For this do I sprinkle my blood
Like the waters of a fountain;
And I walk like one in a daze,
Drunken, but not with wine—
Prey unto pain and anguish,
Brother of grief and of woe.

There is no health in my bones,
Because of my sins;
In my flesh and my body, there is no wholeness,
Because of my suffering;
For this do I mingle blood-drops with my tears.
But what shall I do,
When I stand up to render account of my deeds,
On the day when my iniquity and my guilt
Come forth to meet me?
To whom shall I flee,
With whom shall I take refuge

When they testify against me
That after vanity have I walked on earth?

Oh, reawaken, call to life again,
The love of former days for Thy gazelle!
Scarred by the lion's teeth,
Torn by the talons of the lioness,
She hears again the soul-affrighting roar—
She sees again the cruel jaws agape
To drink her blood—

Bitterly do I grieve!
For Israel—fruitful vine,
That by wild beasts is trampled and devoured;
For Judah—ship that drives to dreadful wreck,
Upon the sea of exile tempest-tossed,
Rudderless, anchorless, and the captain lost!

Trembling We Seek the House of Prayer

Trembling, we seek the house of prayer
To confess our iniquities,
And to recite the vicissitudes of our lives
With all that has befallen us.
Oh, that the Rock of our salvation
Would come forth to meet us,
To deliver our souls from death
And to grant us life!

What shall we say—
For we are smitten by our own illdoing;
And our sins are like veils upon our faces,
Hiding from us our Maker!
Yea, we are like cattle
That would make the world their manger;
Like jackals, panting for the scent of their delights.

But this day, bowed low,
We hasten to the house of God, our Refuge—
For our feet are swift to run after Him
In the time of their distress.
They that have forgotten God,
Where is their gold?

Where are the jewels of their adornment?
Is there any among them that shall live,
Seeing that their origin is of the dust?
When the hand of Death is raised against them,
Shall their treasures aught avail?

Foolishly they imagined that from the lion's corpse
Honey would drip upon their hands;
And they bore not in mind their latter end—
Now, therefore, do they bear their shame.

Bethink Thee, O God! Bethink Thee, and shine forth!
Oh, cease from Thine anger
Against them that fear the day of Thy judgment,
And grant them peace.
For unto Thee they yearn,
But there is none to intercede for them.
And though they have done wickedly before Thee,
Yet justify the mortals that lament their trespasses.
Oh, make known that Thou hast accepted them
And hast forgiven their sins!

Through All My Days and My Years

Through all my days and my years
Has my heart throbbed with anguish;
I will lift up mine eyes to God,
Like the laborer that is hoping for his wage,
And my meditations shall teach me
How I may abide upon His threshold,
In the shadow of His tent,
    To Behold the graciousness of the Lord,
    And to seek Him early in His temple.

Desolate are all the heavens of my joy,
They are rolled together as a scroll;
And because of my dishonor,
The waters of the streams of my grief
Pour forth in torrents.
Traitors within my breast prey upon my heart;
Folly and willfulness have builded my paths;
The fear of my Creator they esteem but lightly,
    And the bidding of my evil desire,
    They are swift to do.

Now will I earnestly implore God's help;
For in my sinfulness I wander about,
To go down in sorrow to the grave.
Therefore do I bring the freewill offerings of my lips
To redeem therewith my soul;
And with my tears do I seek to purify
A heart fearfully polluted—
　　To avert the chastisement of its folly,
　　And to lighten the burden of its yoke.

Awake, pure soul, and return O Shulamite!
Although thou art not like unto Him,
Yet from the glory of God wast thou hewn out;
Shut up in the prison of the flesh,
Oh, how dost thou thirst for the Glorious One!
For the earth is accursed,
Therein is not friend or fellow.
All her inhabitants are banded together
To hold fast to deceit,
That they may keep alive them that speak wickedly
And put to death them that proclaim justice.
　　And Fate takes up his parable:
　　"Woe unto him who increases that which avails him not!"

JUDAH HALEVI

Where Shall I Find Thee?

　　O Lord, where shall I find thee?
All-hidden and exalted is thy place;
　　And where shall I not find thee?
Full of thy glory is the infinite space.

　　　Found near-abiding ever,
He made the earth's ends, set their utmost bar;
　　Unto the nigh a refuge,
Yea, and a trust to them who wait afar.
　　Thou sittest throned between the cherubim,
　　Thou dwellest high above the cloud-rack·dim.
Praised by thine hosts and yet beyond their praises
　　　For ever far exalt;
The endless whirl of worlds cannot contain thee,
　　　How then one heaven's vault?

And thou, withal uplifted
Over man, upon a mighty throne apart,
    Art yet for ever near him,
Breath of his spirit, life-blood of his heart.
   His own mouth speaketh testimony true
   That thou his Maker art alone; for who
Shall say he hath not seen thee? Lo! the heavens
    And all their host aflame
With glory, show thy fear in speech unuttered,
    With silent voice proclaim.

    Longing I sought thy presence,
Lord, with my whole heart did I call and pray,
    And going out toward thee,
I found thee coming to me on the way;
   Yea, in thy wonders' might as clear to see
   As when within the shrine I looked for thee.
Who shall not fear thee? Lo! upon their shoulders
    Thy yoke divinely dread!
Who shall forbear to cry to thee, that givest
    To all their daily bread?

    And can the Lord God truly—
God, the Most High—dwell here within man's breast?
    What shall he answer, pondering—
Man, whose foundations in the dust do rest?
   For thou art holy, dwelling amid the praise
   Of them who waft thee worship all their days.
Angels adoring, singing of thy wonder,
    Stand upon heaven's height;
And thou, enthroned overhead, all things upholdest
    With everlasting might.

Back My Soul

Back, my soul, into thy nest;
   Earth is not for thee;
Still in heaven find thy rest;
   There thou canst be free.

Strive not for this world's command,
   Look to what thou hast.
Thou amidst the angels' band
   Sharest the great repast.

   Demean thee before the majesty
   Of him who reigneth there,
And in a lordly company
   Be thou the courtier.

God's Still with Me

God's still with me when I go out
Whether with courage or with doubt.
My mind is still on God intent
And to his constant goodness bent.
And God will keep me glad at heart
When with my earthly goods I part,
And greater fortune to me bring
As all my gains from me I fling:
And in this timber's swelling mass
Cause me through oceans safe to pass,
And make its motion wings for me
Like storks that fly across the sea:
And give me power to hear the deep
Moan music in his troubled sleep,
The perfect image of my soul
Reflecting in his mighty whole.
And in his rage discern the fire
That seethes the cauldron of the mire,
And makes the sea an emblem fit
Of hell's confusion, and the pit:
Secure amid an Aryan crew
That to strange seas their course pursue
Where rude barbarian pirate war
Emerges from a hidden shore:
Nor daunted by the fishy breed
That mock our vessel's puny speed
Nor by sea-monsters' hideous glare,
That watch us for a dainty fare.
Courageous still when mastering pains

Shall loose the framework of my reins,
And prospect of relief delude
With feeble strain that brings no good.
I see before me sore distress
With never a crust my soul to bless:
But sweet upon my tongue the while
God's name my hunger shall beguile.

I shall not have one anxious thought
When all my labour falls to nought,
And poverty becomes my lot
And grim misfortune leaves me not.
Yea, should that greatest loss befall
Which touches me most near of all,
Of her to whom my soul is tied,
Sole offspring of a father's pride:
Serene in mind, should loss proceed
One further step my heart to bleed,
And rob me of my house's stay,
Sole theme of all my fancy's play.
The dear descendant of my flesh,
Whose play still keeps my feeling fresh,
I can forget him, though he be
In name and nature one with me.
For this and every blow of fate
Thy saving love will compensate,
And find a better home for me
In joyful service unto thee;
And make me of thy chosen band
Attentive, quick to thy command.
Even shouldst thou call for sacrifice
Of life-blood as thy favour's price.
Content to sink into the grave
If in thy land a part I have;
For then in truth this would be mine,
A witness sure that I am thine.

The Lord is My Portion

Servants of time—lo! these be slaves of slaves;
   But the Lord's servant hath his freedom whole.
Therefore when every man his portion craves,
   "The Lord God is my portion," saith my soul.

Song of the Oppressed

Yea, with my whole heart, and with all my might,
    Lord, I have loved thee! Openly, apart,
Thy name is with me; shall I go alone?
    He is my Love; shall I dwell solitary?
He is my lamp; how shall my light be quenched?
    How shall I halt, and he a staff for me?
Men have despised me—knowing not my shame
    For thy name's glory, is my glorious pride.
Fount of my life! I bless thee while I live,
    And sing my song to thee while being is mine!

A Longing

To meet the fountain of true life I run;
Lo! I am weary of vain and empty life!
To see my king's face is mine only strife;
Besides him have I fear or dread of none.
O that a dream might hold him in its bond!
I would not wake; nay, sleep should never depart.
Would I might see his face within my heart!
Mine eyes would never yearn to look beyond.

A Love Song

Let my sweet song be pleasing unto thee—
    The incense of my praise—
O my Beloved that art flown from me,
    Far from mine errant ways!
But I have held the garment of his love,
Seeing the wonder and the might thereof.
    The glory of thy name is my full store—
Enough for all the pain wherein I strove:
    Increase my sorrow: I will love thee more!
      Marvellous is thy love!

Wedding Song

Rejoice, O young man, in thy youth,
And gather the fruit thy joy shall bear;
   Thou and the wife of thy youth,
Turning now to thy dwelling to enter there.

Glorious blessings of God, who is One,
   Shall come united upon thine head;
   Thine house shall be at peace from dread,
Thy foes' uprising be undone.
   Thou shalt lay thee down in a safe retreat;
   Thou shalt rest, and thy sleep be sweet.
In thine honour, my bridegroom, prosper and live.
   Let thy beauty arise and shine forth fierce;
   And the heart of thine enemies God shall pierce.
And the sins of thy youth will he forgive,
   And bless thee in increase and all thou shalt do
   When thou settest thine hand thereto.

And remember thy Rock, Creator of thee,
   When the goodness cometh which he shall bring
   For sons out of many days shall spring,
And even as thy days thy strength shall be.
   Blessed be thou when thou enterest
   And thy going out shall be blest.

With the perfect and wise shall thy portion lie,
   So thou be discreet where thou turnest thee;
   And thine house shall be builded immovably,
And "Peace" thou shalt call; and God shall reply;
   And peace shall be thine abode; and sealed
   Thy bond with the stones of the field.
Thy glory shall rise, nor make delay;
   And thee shall he call and choose; and thy light,
   In the gloom, in the darkness of the night,
Then shall break forth like the dawn of day;
   And out from the shining light of the morn
   Shall the dew of thy youth be born.

To Rabbi Moses Ibn Ezra

How can I find rest when thou art gone!
Thou movedst, and the heart of all thy people is moved!
Were it not for the consoling hope of thy return,
The day of separation would separate me from the living.
Lo, the mountains of Bathar shall bear witness
That the clouds of my heart and the light of my eye is obscured.
Thou light of the west, return to thy sphere!
Be again the seal on every heart, the bracelet on every arm.
Thou pure tongue, why shalt thou dwell among the stammerers?
Or why shall the dew of Hermon drop down upon Gilboa.

Spring

Behold the earth which but yesterday,
Like a babe, sucked the winter rains
From the breast of suckling clouds;
Behold, how like a bride's soul,
Shut up in dismal Winter's nights
It panteth for bright days of Spring's love
And languishes for the time of affection
In Summer's congenial embrace,
So salutary and healing to the wounded heart!
When she, the virgin earth, is newly clad
With fragrant beds of flowers
Fine linen with broidered work of the lilies
Changing her beautiful robes every day,
For still more finished and lovely raiments,
Distributing garments in her circuit around her,
Transforming with every day the colours of plants
Now turning white and pale,
Then her cheeks blushing red,
Like the bride kissing her beloved.
When I remember the beauty of her blooming days
Methinks she robbed the stars of heaven.
When in the early morning we visited
The paradise of her plants, her young vine
She kissed with the flames of love,
Her hand touches the icy snow,

Though it burneth like fire in her bowels.
From earthen vessels she rises like the sun.
We bring near vessels of Shoham,
And she is poured out.
Under the shades round her garden he walks.
She laughs at the cries of many;
She rejoices; and the tear on her cheek is a drop
Like a bdellium thrown from a necklace;
She rejoices at the voice of the crane
Like the shoutings over new wine.
She fondly listens to the cooing of the dove
And indulgeth in sweet council,
She chants at the covering of her leaves,
Like the damsel at her new gown
She dances and skips like her with joy!
O how my soul longs for those morning breezes
In which she embraces her fragrant friend.
Satiated with joy she wields the myrtle,
The odour of which keeps the lovers aloof,
Whilst the myrtle branch rises and doubles,
The branch of the palm tree at the singing of the bird
Shakes hand with its fellow branch,
Shaking and bowing down before the face of Isaac
With whose name the universe laughs,
And she says, Behold, God hath made me to laugh,
Because for Isaac's sake I spoke
Though no one answered my speech;
I praise his excellence, and the ear
That listens approves and justifies.
The name of all princes is an inheritance of God,
Good and evil;
But his name is good undivided.

How pleasant is it to my ear when it hears
My soul busily occupied with his memory.
But when she sees her likeness—
All praises cease—and silence redoubles praise.
Thus, Prince Isaac! my tongue shall speak clearly,
Shall chant songs unceasingly.
When I shall make a covenant with thee
For all the days of my life,

It shall never be silent from thy praise.
Why should I anticipate thy years,
Is not thy soul ornamented with every virtue?
In thee the virtues have pitched their tent,
And wisdom's camp is gathered within thee,
Thy soul has satisfied the present age with understanding,
And bequeathed a goodly portion to their posterity,
For she has found her nest in thy heart,
And she played and delighted herself with thee.
Therefore, be fruitful and multiply,
Cause thy seed to inherit the spirit of benevolence,
And bequeath unto them thy helping hand,
See children's children to thy children,
And pour the dew of mercy over their generations.

The Physician's Prayer

My God, heal me and I shall be healed;
Let not Thine anger be kindled against me so that I be consumed.
My medicines are of Thee, whether good
Or evil, whether strong or weak.
It is Thou who shalt choose, not I;
Of Thy knowledge is the evil and the fair.
Not upon my power of healing I rely;
Only for Thine healing do I watch.

My Heart Is in the East

My heart is in the east, and I in the uttermost west—
How can I find savour in food? How shall it be sweet to me?
How shall I render my pledges and vows, while yet
Zion lieth beneath the fetter of Edom, and I in Arab chains?
A trifle would it seem to me to leave all the good things of Spain—
Seeing how precious it would be to behold the dust of the desolate sanctuary.

To Zion

Hast thou no greeting for thy captive sons,
Poor remnant of thy flock, who seek thy weal?
"Peace to thee, far and near!" Lift up thy voice
Through all thy region—west, east, north, and south!
And "Peace" to me, Hope's prisoner, who sheds
His tears like Hermon's dew, and only longs
That they might fall (where dews fall) on thy hills.
Thy woe-gone state I wail with jackal cry,
But, should I dream captivity restored,
I am a harp, to echo forth thy songs.
For Bethel and Peni-êl how I yearn!
For Mahanaim, and each trysting-spot
Where angels met thy pure saints of old:

There the Shekinah neighboured close with thee,
And He that formed thee set thy open gates
Hard by the open gates of highest heaven.
The glory of the Lord thy only light!
Not sun, or moon, or stars that lightened thee!
May it be mine to shed my life-blood there,
Where on thy sons God's spirit first was shed.
Thou home of kingship! throne of God!—Ah! woe,
That slaves now sit upon thy lordly thrones!
Oh, might I range through spots where seer and sage
Received for thee the unveiled speech of God!
Oh, had I wings, that I might fly afar,
And soothe the serried cares of this poor heart
Amid the serried range of Bether's hills,
I'd fall upon my face upon thy soil,
I'd find sweet pleasure in thy very stones,
And cherish to my heart thy merest dust;
Much more when standing by my fathers' graves,
Lost in deep wonder, there where Hebron holds
The dearest of thy sepulchres.
I pass, in thought, through forest and through field;
I stand in awe by Gilead and the hills
Which tower round thy borders—Nebo first—
Mount Nebo and Mount Hor—most sacred they,
Where two great Lights, thy lights and teachers shone.

Thy very air breathes life into the soul!
Thy smallest dust more sweet than sweetest myrrh!
Thy streams run honey from the dripping rocks!
How sweet it were to walk with naked foot
Through ruins that were once God's oracles!
Here thy ark was treasured, here thy cherubim
Once dwelt within this inmost shrine of thine.
I shave my head—cast down its beauty's crown,
And curse the fate that, in an unclean land,
Profanes the beauty of thy Nazarites.
What pleasure can I find in food or drink,
While those that are but dogs can rend thy lions?
How can the light of day gladden mine eyes,
That see crows gnaw the carcass of thine eagles?
Oh, cup of woe! Give pause! Give breathing-space!
My reins and soul are full of bitterness.
I think on Samaria—I drink thy cup;
On Jerusalem—then I drain its dregs.

O Zion, perfect beauty, grace, and love
Of old thou bindest on thee—yea, the souls
Of sages, too, are bound up in thy life.
These gladden in thy weal, these wail thy woe,
These weep thy ruin. Still, from captive pit,
Towards thee they yearn, and towards thy sacred gates
Each from his place they bow them down in prayer.
Thy bleating flocks, though captive and dispersed
From mount to hill, can ne'er forget thy Fold:
Still to thy skirts they cling and strive to climb
Up to the stately palm-growth of thy breasts.
Shinar and Patros? Can *they* match thy state?
Their vanities thy Urim and thy Thummim?
Thy Princes—Prophets—Levites—Minstrels?
To each of these what can the world compare?
The diadem of every worldly throne
Must change and pass away—thy wealth remains;
Thy crown of consecration is for aye;
Thy God desires thee for His Throne. Ah, blest
Is he whom God shall choose and draw him nigh
That he may dwell forever in thy Courts;
And blessed he who waits till he attain

To see thy light mount up, thy Dawn break forth,
To witness peace upon thy chosen ones,
To gladden in thy joy as thou return
Unto the vigour of thine ancient youth.

Jerusalem

Oh, fairest joy of Earth,
Thou City of the King,
For thee my soul is homesick,
A banished Westerling!
Compassion stirs my heart
When calling back the past;
Thy Glory that is captive!
Thy beauty that is waste!
Oh, had I wings of eagles
I'd seek thee, nor refrain
Till tears had poured upon thee
And watered thee like rain:
I'd seek thee, though thy King
Is now no more in thee,
Though dragon, asp, and scorpion,
Take place of Gilead's tree;
Thy very stones I'd cherish
And lovingly embrace,
Sweeter to me than honey
Thy broken clods should taste.

The Voyage

Thine is my soul, O God. In hope or fear
To Thee it bows and yields incessant praise.
In Thee I joy when carried to and fro;
To Thee give thanks in all my pilgrimage.
When the ship spreads her storklike wings to fly,
When deep makes roar to lower deep, and moans—
As if it learned that sorrow from my heart—
It makes the ocean like a caldron seethe;
It makes the deep sea like a wizard's pot.
When teeming creatures seem to ban the ship,
Sea-monsters waiting for their coming meal!
A time of anguish like to first-born throes
With children at the birth—no strength to bear!
Should I lack food?—the sweetness of Thy name

Is in my mouth the best delicacy.
Nor shall I care for buying or for building,
For "get or gain," or any loss that happens;
I even learn to leave my daughter dear,
The darling of my soul, though she to me
Is dear as only child can only be.
I can forget her son—That rends my heart!
No poem comes without the thought of him!
Fruit of my body! child of my delight!
Can Judah by Judah be forgot!
Yet this I count but dross for love of Thee;
That I might come within Thy gates with praise;
There would I stay and reckon this my heart
As a whole-offering on Thine Altar bound.
I'd make my grave within Thy Holy Land
There to remain, a witness to my love.

The Earth in Spring

Then, day by day, her broidered gown
   She changes for fresh wonder;
A rich profusion of gay robes
   She scatters all around her.
From day to day her flowers' tints
   Change quick, like eyes that brighten,
Now white, like pearl, now ruby-red,
   Now emerald-green they'll lighten.
She turns all pale; from time to time
   Red blushes quickly cover her;
She's like a fair, fond bride that pours
   Warm kisses on her lover.
The beauty of her bursting spring
   So far exceeds my telling,
I think sometimes she pales the stars
   That have in heaven their dwelling.

A Prayer

O God! before Thee lies my whole desire,
Although it find no utterance on my lips.
One moment of Thy will—then let me die!
Ah, would that this request of mine might come!

The rest of life I would yield up to Thee,
And sleep the sleep that should be sweet to me.
Absent from Thee, my very life is death,
But could I cleave to Thee, then death were life.
But I know not the wherewithal to come,
Or what should be my service and my work.
Teach me Thy ways, O Lord,
And from my folly's bondage bring me home.
Teach me while yet I have some power left
To make amends, and spurn not mine affliction.
Ere that day comes when I must be a burden,
When my last end lies heavy on mine end,
And I must bow, unwilling, while slow waste
Consumes my strength, too weary to uprise;
And so I go whither my fathers went,
Dwelling where they themselves are dwelling now.
Stranger am I and pilgrim on this earth,
Only beneath the sod my heritage!
So far my youthful days have had their will.
Ah! when shall I myself, too, have *my* will?
That world which he hath set within my heart
He hath refused to let me seek as end.
How can I serve my Maker while I am
Bound by my evil, slave of my desires?
How shall I aim at any high emprise,
That are to-morrow sister to the worm?
How should my heart gladden at any good,
Whereas I know not what may happen to-morrow?
The days and nights are busily engaged
In wasting me away, till I be gone!
One half of me they scatter to the winds,
The other half they bring again to dust.
What shall I say? My evil tracks me down,
A stern foe from the cradle to the grave.
What share have I in time, except Thy will?
If Thou be not my lot, what lot have I?
Spoiled of all merit, robbed and naked left,
Thy righteousness alone must cover me.
Yet why should I tell out my prayer in words?
O God, before Thee lies my whole desire!

Bahya ibn Pakuda

The details pertaining to the life of Bahya are rather scanty. He was a representative of the triumph of the opus over the personality—a typical medieval view shared by Jews and Christians that the product of a man's thought is more important than the man himself. The only known biographical points concerning Bahya are that he was a *dayan* (rabbinic judge) who lived in Saragossa, Spain, toward the end of the eleventh century (this information is provided in Judah ibn Tibbon's translation of 1161).

Bahya's *Duties of the Heart* is a milestone in the history of Jewish thought. Appearing about 150 years before Maimonides' *Guide to the Perplexed,* Bahya's book, with its intent to deepen the religious spirit of Jewry, became one of the most popular and authoritative ethical treatises in the history of Hebrew literature. Although it was written originally in Arabic, it became known in its Hebrew translation, and appeared in dozens of editions.

Bahya divides man's duties into those which are performed physically, and hence, visible; and those that are performed inwardly, and are invisible. Among the former are ceremonial laws; among the latter—faith, and the avoidance of ill-will and grudges. Although few works of Hebrew literature are devoid of ethical content, there had been no comprehensive, systematic text dealing with the duties of the mind and heart. As Bahya stated in his Preface, it is this lacuna that he attempted to fill.

Bahya's work is far removed from an all-embracing philosophical system—indeed, it accents feeling rather than thought—but its author is an optimist who feels that the world was created for man and that he is its central feature. Bahya draws most deeply from those texts of the Jewish tradition that are saturated with ethical teachings—the Bible, Talmud and Midrash—and is also strongly influenced by Saadya Gaon (892–942), whose *Book of Doctrines and Beliefs* and *Commentary on the Bible* he urges his readers to consult. Relying on the sages' comment that "anyone who says something clever, even if he is of the gentiles, is considered wise," Bahya also mentions Aristotle, whose works he knew indirectly through Arab thinkers, and in his desire to bring forth practical ethics, utilizes Arabic sayings and epigrams attributed to Mohammed and the New Testament. Bahya, who had mastered philosophy, mathematics, natural science, as well as traditional Jewish learning, felt that every shred of learning would intensify man's love for God, perfect his character, and thus improve his conduct and his relations with his fellow human beings.

Bahya's straightforward style and simple diction, his occasional use of rhymed sentences and little prayers at the end of a chapter, his personal appeals to the reader (he apologizes for telling him what to do), his use of parables and frequent references to the Bible—undoubtedly helped make *Duties of the Heart* a popular book. Oft reprinted, Bahya's work was translated into Yiddish and Ladino, thus serving the Ashkenazic and Sephardic communities. The masses termed Bahya "the Saint," the only Jewish thinker to be so labeled. In Yiddish, the work earned for him the love of European Jewry who ranked his book alongside of the Talmud, Midrash and Zohar. With Rashi's *Commentary,* the Siddur and Eldad's *Travels, Duties of the Heart* was one of the early Hebrew books printed (1489).

DUTIES OF THE HEART

THIRD TREATISE

On the service of God, expounding various grounds for the obligation to assume the service of God, blessed be He.

INTRODUCTION

Having, in the previous treatises, expounded the obligation of whole-heartedly acknowledging the unity of God and the obligation of examining the various modes of His benefits to mankind, we have next to indicate what a human being's conduct should be, once the foregoing has become clear to him—and that is to assume the obligation of the service of God, as reason would require from a beneficiary to his benefactor. It is proper to open this treatise with an exposition of the various kinds of benefits human beings render each other, and the corresponding obligations of gratitude. We shall then ascend to the consideration of what we owe to the exalted Creator in praise and thanksgiving for His abounding kindness and great goodness to us.

We assert, as a truth generally recognized, that if anyone benefits us, we are under an obligation of gratitude to him in accordance with his intent to help us. Even if he actually falls short, owing to some mishap which prevents his benefiting us, we are still bound to be grateful to him, since we are convinced that he has a benevolent disposition towards us and his intention is to be of use to us. On the other hand, should we obtain any benefit through one who had no such intention, the duties of gratitude to that person would cease and we are under no such obligation.

When we consider the benefits human beings render each other, we find that these fall into five classes: (1) a father's beneficence to his child; (2) a master's to his servant; (3) a wealthy man's beneficence to the poor for the sake of heavenly reward; (4) the beneficence rendered by human beings to each other in order to gain a good name, honour and temporal reward; and (5) the powerful man's beneficence to the weak, induced by pity for the latter and sympathy with his condition.

Let us now consider the motive in each of the classes mentioned: Is it disinterested, the sole aim being to help the beneficiary, or is it not so? First, a father's beneficence to his child: It is obvious that the father's

motive in this is to further his own interest. For the child is a part of the
father, whose chief hope is centered in his offspring. Do you not observe
that in regard to its food, drink, clothing and in warding off all hurt from
it, a father is more sensitive about his child than about himself? To secure
ease for it, the burden of toil and weariness is lightly borne by him—the
feelings of tenderness and pity for their offspring being naturally implanted
in parents. Nevertheless, the Torah and reason impose upon children the
duty of serving, honouring and revering their parents, as Scripture saith:
"Ye shall, everyone, revere his father and his mother" [Lev. 19:3]; "Hear,
O my son, the instruction of thy father and forsake not the law of thy
mother" [Prov. 1:8]; further "A son honoureth his father, and a servant
his master" [Malachi 1:6]. [And these duties are enjoined] notwithstanding
that the father is impelled by a natural instinct and the benefaction comes
from God, while the parent is only the agent.

The kindness of a master to his servant: It is obvious that the master's
intent is to improve his property by an outlay of capital, since he needs his
servant's work, and his sole motive is to further his own interest. Nevertheless, the Creator, blessed be He, imposes upon the servant the duties of
service and gratitude, as it is said, "A son honoureth his father and a
servant his master" [Malachi 1:6].

The rich man's beneficence to the poor man for the sake of a heavenly
reward: He is like a merchant who acquires a great and enduring pleasure
which he will enjoy at the end of a definite time by means of a small, perish-
able and inconsiderable gift which he makes immediately. So the rich man
only intends to win glory for his soul at the close of his earthly existence
by the benefaction which God entrusted to him, in order to bestow it upon
anyone who will be worthy of it. Yet it is generally recognized that it is
proper to thank and laud a benefactor. Even though the latter's motive
was to gain spiritual glory hereafter, gratitude is, nevertheless, due to him,
as Job said: "The blessing of him that was ready to perish came upon me"
[Job 29:13]; and further, "If his loins have not blessed me, when he
warmed himself with the fleece of my sheep" [Job 31:20].

Kindness men show each other for the sake of praise, honour and
temporal rewards: This is as if one were to deposit an article in another's
care or entrust him with money, because of the depositor's apprehension
that he may need it later on. Although, in benefiting another person, the
aim is to further his own interests, the benefactor is nevertheless entitled
to praise and gratitude for his kindness, as the wise king said, "Many court
the generous man, and everyone is a friend to him that giveth gifts" [Prov.
19:6]; and he also said, "A man's gift maketh room for him and bringeth
him before great men" [Prov. 18:16].

The kindness of one who has compassion on a poor man for whom he
is sorry: The benefactor's motive is to get rid of his own distress that

results from depression and grief for the one he pities. He is like one who cures a pain which has attacked him by means of the bounties that the Lord bestowed upon him. Nevertheless, he is not to be without due praise, as Job said, "Could I see any perish for want of clothing or any poor without covering? Did not his loins bless me, when he warmed himself with the fleece of my sheep?" [Job 31:19–20].

From what has here been advanced, it is clear that anyone who bestows benefits on others has first his own interest in mind—either to secure an honourable distinction in this world, or hereafter, or relieve himself of pain, or improve his material substance. Yet all these considerations do not absolve the beneficiaries of their duty of praising, thanking, respecting and loving their benefactors and making them some return. And this, despite that the benefit was only loaned to the benefactors; that they were obliged to dispense it, as we have pointed out; and that their beneficence is not permanent, their generosity not prolonged, and their benevolence is mixed with the intent either to further their own interest or ward off injury. How much more then does a human being owe service, praise and gratitude to Him who created the benefit and the benefactor, whose beneficence is un-limited, permanent, perpetual, without any motive of self-interest, or purpose of warding off injury, but only an expression of grace and loving-kindness emanating from Him towards all human beings.

We should furthermore bear in mind that a human being who renders a kindness to another in any of the modes above specified is not superior to the person whom he benefits, except in some casual detail, while in their humanity and essential characteristics they are alike and akin to one another, in substance and form, in physical conformation and figure [or mentality—Gen. 1:26] in their natures and in a larger part of what happens to them.

Nevertheless, the beneficiary, as we have set forth, is under an obligation of service to his benefactor. And if we thought that the beneficiary was extremely defective and imperfect in his physical conformation, figure and appearance, [we would conclude that] the obligation of service on his part would be so much the greater. So also, if we should deem the benefactor the best and most perfect of all beings, while the beneficiary was the most defective of all things and the weakest of all creatures, reason would require that the service to the benefactor should be increased to an infinite degree.

Following this analogy, when we investigate the relation of the Creator, blessed be He, to human beings, we will find that the Creator, blessed be He, is infinitely exalted and glorified above everything existing, above all that can be apprehended by the senses or conceived by the intellect as has been expounded in the first treatise of this book; and that a human being, in comparison with other species of animals, is the most defective and weakest of them all.

This can be demonstrated in three respects:

(1) In respect to his infancy and early childhood: For we find that other species of living creatures are stronger than he is, better able to endure pain and move independently, and do not trouble their progenitors in their period of growth to the same extent as a human being does.

(2) In respect to the filth and foulness within the human body and the similar appearance of exudations on its external surface when one has neglected to wash and cleanse himself for a length of time, as also in respect to the state of the body after death—the effluvium of a human corpse being more noisome than that of the carcasses of other creatures, and a human being's ordure more offensive than that of other creatures.

(3) In respect to a human being's helplessness resulting from an injury to his brain, when he loses the rational faculty which God bestowed upon him and which constitutes his superiority to the other creatures that are irrational. For at such times he is stupider and more senseless than other animals. He may inflict serious injuries on himself and even kill himself. Most animals, too, we find, possess an apprehension of what will be to their advantage, and show an ingenuity in obtaining their food, while many intellectual men fall short in this regard, not to speak of one who has lost his senses.

When we concentrate our thoughts on the greatness of the Creator, exalted be He, on His infinite might, wisdom and plenitude of resources; and then turn our attention to a man's weakness and deficiency, in that he never attains perfection; when we consider his poverty and lack of what he needs to supply his wants and then investigate the numerous bounties and favours which the Creator has bestowed on him; when we reflect that the Creator has created man as he is with deficiencies in his very being—poor and needing for his development all requisites which he can only obtain by exerting himself—this too proceeding from the Creator's mercy to him, so that he may know himself, study his conditions and cleave, under all circumstances, to the service of God, and so receive for it a recompense in the world to come, for the attainment of which he was created, as we have already set forth in the second treatise of this book—how much indeed then does a human being owe to the blessed Creator, in service, thanksgiving and continuous praise, in view of the demonstration already given of the obligation of praise and gratitude that human beings owe to each other for favours rendered them.

Should anyone be so foolish as to contest this obligation of a human being towards the Creator—when he examines and closely studies the subject, and candidly acknowledges the truth to himself, the sleeper will surely awake, the negligent will be aroused, the ignorant will investigate, the intelligent will comprehend the demonstration of the obligatory character of the service of God, the proofs for which are so clear, the evidence of which is so manifest, and the indications are so true; as the prophet (peace be unto him) said concerning one who neglects to reflect upon the obligation of the service of God, "Do ye thus requite the Lord, O foolish people and unwise?" [Deut. 32:6].

Thus the obligation to assume the service of God, incumbent on human beings in view of the bounties He continually bestows on them, has been demonstrated.

In dealing with the subject matter of this treatise, we have now to expound ten topics:

(1) the necessity of arousing men to God's service, and the methods to be employed to this end;

(2) the need for each of these methods;

(3) definition of the service [of God]; its divisions and degrees;

(4) the form which the Torah takes to arouse us; its divisions; and the excellencies which men attain through knowledge of the Torah and comprehension of its contents.

(5) the way in which the exercise of our reasoning faculties prompts us in this regard, set forth in the form of questions and answers;

(6) the various classes of obligations to the service of God, corresponding to the various kinds of benefits received, and their divisions;

(7) exposition of the minimum of service which the recipient of any benefit owes to the benefactor;

(8) the difference in the views of the learned in regard to [the problem of] necessity and [divine] justice, and which of these views is nearer the truth;

(9) the mystery of the purpose for which the human species was created on earth, compendiously set forth;

(10) an account of the use we should make of all our capacities, each in its right place.

CHAPTER I.

Arousing man to God's service and the various methods of doing so are necessary on the following grounds. The understanding and the faculty of perception impress on human beings the duty of serving God. But between the time when the benefits that man receives and the time when he has sufficient intelligence to realize the services he should render in return for them, a long period intervenes. Hence, calling attention to the external acts and inward faith which make the service of God complete, is a duty, so that a human being should not be without religion up to the time when his mental powers have become fully developed.

This stimulation is twofold. One of them is inherent in the mind, implanted in the human faculty of cognition, innate from the beginning of his existence. The other is acquired by instruction in the divine law which the prophet imparts to human beings, so as to teach them the mode of service which it is their duty to render to the Creator, blessed be He.

CHAPTER II.

Both methods of calling attention to the service of God are necessary because the innate urge is deficient in three respects; and we are therefore obliged to strengthen it by religious instruction.

First, man is made up of diverse entities, natures conflicting and mutually antagonistic. These entities are his soul and his body. The Creator has implanted in his soul qualities and forces which make him yearn for things, the use of which will promote his physical well-being, so that he will develop vigour to populate the earth, in order that the race may continue while individuals perish. This quality is the desire for bodily pleasures common to all living creatures that propogate their species.

The Creator has also engrafted in the human soul other qualities and forces, which, if he uses them, will make him loathe his position in this world and yearn to separate himself from it. This is the desire for perfect wisdom. Since, however, bodily pleasures come to a man's soul first, already in early youth, and the attachment to them is, from the outset, strong, great and extremely urgent, the desire for sensual pleasure overcomes his other faculties, and even predominates over the intellect, for the sake of which man was created. And so his spiritual sight fails and the indications of his desirable qualities disappear.

Man therefore needs external means, by the aid of which he may resist his despicable instinct—the lust for animal enjoyments—and revitalize the marks of his noblest endowment—the intellect. These aids are the contents of the Torah, whereby God, through His messengers and prophets, taught His creatures the way to serve Him.

Secondly, the intellect is a spiritual entity, originating in the higher, spiritual world. It is a stranger in this world of gross material bodies. Sensual lust in man is the product of natural forces and of a combination of his physical elements. Its foundation and root are in this world. Food gives it strength. Physical pleasures add to its vigour, while the intellect, because it is a stranger here, stands without support or ally, and all are against it.

Hence it follows that it must become weak and that it needs an external means to repel the mighty power of lust and overcome it. The Torah is the remedy for such spiritual maladies and moral diseases. The Torah therefore prohibits many kinds of food, apparel, sexual relations, certain acquisitions and practices, all of which strengthen sensual lust; it also exhorts us to use those means which will resist lust and are its opposites.

These are prayer, fasting, almsgiving, kindness; by which the intellectual faculties are revived and man is aided in this world and for the world to come, as David said: "Thy word is a lamp to my feet and a light to my path" [Ps. 119:105]; "For the commandment is a lamp and the law is light" [Prov. 6:23]; "I saw that wisdom is preferable to folly as light is preferable to darkness" [Eccles. 2:13].

Third, the sensual desire, constantly enforced by bodily nourishment, never ceases working by day or night. The intellect, on the other hand, is only called into activity to help one gratify his passions. Now it is well-known that organs which are constantly exercised in accordance with their nature, improve and become more efficient, while those that are less frequently used deteriorate and become inefficient.

It logically follows therefore that the sensual desire would become stronger because it is continually exercised, while the intellectual faculty would weaken, because it is so seldom used, and so little for its proper purpose. Hence the need of something, the acquisition of whose truth demands neither the use of man's physical organs nor the indulgence of his passions but only the exercise of his intellect, freed from the pre-dominance of lusts.

This aid is the Torah, the study of which will make the intellect stronger, purer, more luminous, and will drive away from man the folly that masters his soul and keeps him from seeing things as they really are and placing them in their proper relations. As the Psalmist says, "The law of the Lord is perfect, restoring the soul; the testimony of the Lord is faithful, making wise the simple; the ordinances of the Lord are right, rejoicing the heart; the commandment of the Lord is pure, enlightening the eyes" [Ps. 19:8–9].

From what has been said, it is clearly established how necessary it is that a human being should be aroused to the service of God by the Torah, which includes rational precepts as well as those accepted on authority, so that through these we may rise to the service of God which, our reason demonstrates, is man's duty and the main purpose for which the human species has been called into existence in this world.

CHAPTER III.

Definition of the Service of God; exposition of its parts; the merits of each of these parts.

Service may be defined as a beneficiary's submission to his benefactor, expressed in rendering some benefit within his power to the latter in return for the favor received. This submission is of two kinds. The first is submission induced by fear, hope, necessity or compulsion. The second is submission arising from a sense of duty, from the conviction that it is right to aggrandize and exalt the person to whom submission is rendered.

Of the first kind is that submission to God which has been induced by an external stimulus, as we have mentioned, and the obligation of which arises from expectation of reward or fear of punishment in this world and the next. But the second kind is the submission which arises from an inward urge in the mind, innate in the nature of a human being in whom body and soul are joined together. Both kinds of submission are praiseworthy and lead to salvation in the life hereafter, the world of eternal rest. But one of these leads to the other and is a step by which we ascend to it. The former is the submission induced by the study of the Torah. The submission which is induced by the urge of the understanding and based on rational demonstrations is nearer to God and more acceptable on seven grounds:

First, The service [of God] induced by study of the Torah may be entirely devotional and directed to the Supreme. It may, however, be hypocritical; the aim may possibly be to obtain praise for it and honour among one's fellowmen, since the service is rooted in, and founded on, hope [of reward] and fear [of punishment]. But the service of God induced by the intellectual urge is wholly and solely devoted to God. No hypocrisy is mingled with it, nor any false pretense for the sake of self-glorification, since this service is not founded on hope or fear, but is based on wisdom and knowledge of what service a creature owes to the Creator.

Secondly, service of God induced by the Torah is only rendered as the result of hope of reward or fear of punishment; but the service urged by the understanding comes from willingness of the soul and its desire to strive with all its might to serve its God for His own sake, as a result of knowledge and comprehension. For the soul will freely give all it has, provided it is convinced that what it gives is exceeded in value by what it receives in exchange, and this [boon] is that God is pleased with it.

Third, the service due to the urge of the Torah is manifested in external good deeds rather than in inward thoughts and feelings, hidden in the heart. But in the service prompted by the understanding, that which is hidden in the heart is many times as much as what is seen in the external activity of the bodily limbs. This service includes the duties of the heart.

Fourth, the service prompted by Torah is to be regarded as an introduction to the service prompted by the understanding. The former is like seed planted in the ground. The study of the Torah is as tillage is to the soil—ploughing and clearing it. The aid that comes from God is like the rain that waters the field. And the fruit that is produced and brought forth is what remains in the heart—the service of God for His sake only, and not prompted by hope [of reward] or fear [of punishment]. So our wise men have exhorted us, "Be not like servants who minister to their master upon the condition of receiving a reward . . . and let the fear of Heaven be upon you." [Ethics of the Fathers 1:3].

Fifth, the commandments of the Torah are limited. They are a known number, 613 precepts. But the duties imposed by the understanding are almost infinite, for a person daily increases his knowledge of them; and the more his faculty of perception develops and the more he comprehends God's beneficences, mighty power and sovereignty, the more will a man humble himself before Him. Hence you find that David (peace be upon him) besought God to arouse him to the knowledge of these duties and remove the curtain of folly from his eyes; as it is said, "Open Thou mine eyes that I may behold wondrous things out of Thy law." [Ps. 119:18]; "Teach me, O Lord, the way of Thy statutes . . ." [ibid. 119:33]; "Incline my heart unto Thy testimonies, and not to covetousness" [ibid. 119:36].

Furthermore, it is said "To all perfection have I seen an end; but Thy commandment is exceedingly broad" [ibid. 119:96]; that is to say, our obligation of service to Thee for Thy continual benefits to us is without limit because there is no limit to the varieties of Thy bounties to us. It is also related of some ascetics that they spent the whole of their lives in penitence. Each day they were moved to renewed repentance, because every day their recognition of God's greatness increased, and they realized how much they had fallen short in the fulfilment of their obligation of service in the past, as David said, "Day communicates knowledge unto day . . ." [Ps. 19:2]. Furthermore, it is said, "Streams of water run down mine eyes, because they keep not Thy laws." [Ps. 119:136].

Sixth, the service enjoined by the Torah is within the range of a human being's capacity. Provided he is intent upon it and sets about it, it is not withheld from any one who seeks to fulfil it. But the service prompted by the understanding can only be performed by one who makes a great effort and with the help of God, since human power is insufficient to attain it. Hence you find that David repeatedly supplicates God in Psalm 119 to give him this aid.

Seventh, when service is only derived from the Torah, a person can never be sure that he will not stumble. For in that kind of service, the force of evil passion is always lurking in ambush, waiting for the time when he will neglect it. But when the service is prompted by the understanding, a man can be sure that he will not stumble and sin, for the soul is attracted to service of God only after physical lust has been overcome and the intellect has obtained the victory over it, and controls it according to the soul's will and desire. Hence, this type of service affords a guarantee against stumbling, and one who has attained it, is guarded from sin, as Scripture saith, "There shall no evil happen to the righteous" [Prov. 12:21].

It is necessary, however, that I should expound some of the advantages of instruction in the Torah, as these occur to me. The grounds that necessitate the urge of the Torah to service of God are also seven.

First, man is composed of soul and body. Among his tendencies there are some that tempt him to surrender himself to physical pleasures, indulge in low desires, and break the restraining bonds of reason. There are also other tendencies that will make him abhor the world and renounce society, because of reverses that he has sustained and continued troubles and sorrows that have befallen him, and so he would turn to the higher spiritual life. Neither of these plans is commendable. The latter [if generally followed] would bring about destruction of the social order. The former would lead to his ruin in this world and in the next. The exalted Creator, in His compassion and infinite goodness to man, favoured him with a means by which he may improve his condition and direct aright his ways, leading to happiness here and hereafter.

This means, which points out the middle road between reason and physical desire, is the Torah which is faithful, preserves righteousness outwardly and inwardly, keeps man away from his lusts in this world and reserves for him his recompense at his latter end, as Scripture saith, "Incline thine ear and hear the words of the wise . . . for it is a pleasant thing if thou keep them within thee. . . . That thy trust may be in the Lord, I have made known to thee. . . . Have I not written for thee excellent things in counsels and knowledge, that I might make thee know the certainty of the words of truth, that thou mightest answer the words of truth to them that send [enquiries] unto thee" [Prov. 22: 17–21].

Second, the intellectual urge to the service of God does not lead to the recognition of active obligations such as prayer, fasting, almsgiving, tithing, deeds of benevolence. Nor does one thereby attain knowledge of the terms of punishments incurred by one who is negligent in service. In all this, there is need of a stand and definiteness in the way set forth by the Torah and the prophet's instruction, so that by their combination the Divine purpose may be achieved in orderly fashion—that purpose being the service of God (exalted be He), as it is said, "And God made it, so that man should fear before Him" [Eccles. 3:14]; that is to say, God gave us a law to teach us His service.

Third, the intellectual urge cannot comprehend equally all who are under the obligation of service, because some human beings are of limited intelligence, while some are superior in apprehension. But the urge of the Torah applies equally to all who have reached the status subjecting them to this service, even though they vary in their understanding of it, as we have noted at the close of the first treatise of this book. It sometimes also happens that a person falls short in some duties and exceeds in others. The intellectual stimulus varies in different individuals in accordance with their capacity of apprehension.

But the urge of the Torah is not subject to variation. Its obligation is the same for the child, the youth, the one advanced in years and the old man, the wise and the foolish, even though the resulting practice varies in different classes of individuals. And so Scripture says in regard to the comprehensive character of the instruction of the Torah for all the people, "Gather the people together, men and women, and children, and the stranger that is within thy gate [that they may hear and that they may learn and fear the Lord your God . . .]" [Deut. 31:12]. Further, it is said, ". . . thou shalt read this law before all Israel in their hearing." [Deut. 31:11].

Fourth, it is recognised that the obligations of human beings to render service are proportionate to the degrees of benefits conferred upon them. In every period there have been events which occasioned one people to be singled out from all other peoples for special benefits that God bestowed on it. It follows that individuals belonging to that people are on that account under special obligation to render additional service to the Creator beyond that required of other peoples.

There is no way of determining by the intellect alone what this service should be. Thus God chose us from among other nations by bringing us out of the land of Egypt, dividing the Red Sea and conferring other benefits subsequently, too well known to be mentioned. Furthermore, the exalted Creator specially distinguished us from all other nations by giving us a religion for which we are under an obligation of gratitude to Him; and, in return for our acceptance of this religion, He has assured us a recompense in this world and in the next—an abundance of grace and goodness, emanating from Him, that is indescribable.

All this can only be clearly made known to us by the Torah, as Scripture saith, "Ye have seen what I did unto the Egyptians and how I bore you on eagles' wings, and brought you unto Myself. Now, therefore, if ye will obey My voice indeed, and keep My covenant [then ye shall be a treasure unto Me above all people] and ye shall be unto Me a kingdom of priests and a holy nation" [Ex. 19:4–6].

Fifth, the stimulus of the Torah is a preparation for, and introduction to that of the intellect, the reason being that a man in his youth needs training and guidance, and restraint from yielding to his passion, till the time comes when his understanding has become strong and firm. So, too, some women and frivolous men do not follow the intellectual lead, because its control over them is weak and loose. This condition made it necessary to provide guidance of a medium character which they can endure and which will not be impossible for them to stand.

Hence, the instructions of the Torah turn about hope and fear—the poles of its axis. Whoever does not fall short in fulfilling the obligations of this service belongs to the class of the truly pious and is worthy of reward in this world and in the next. But one who rises from this stage to the service of God, induced by reason, reaches the degree of the prophets and the elect of the Supreme—the saints. His recompense here on earth is joy in the sweetness of the service of the Lord, as the prophet said, "Thy words were found, and I did eat them; and Thy word was unto me the joy and rejoicing of mine heart; for I am called by Thy name, O Lord God of hosts" [Jeremiah 15:16]; furthermore, "The righteous shall be glad in the Lord and trust in Him; and all the upright in heart shall glory" [Ps. 64:11].

Furthermore, "Light is sown for the righteous, and gladness for the upright in heart" [Ps. 97:11]. His reward in the world to come will consist in his attaining the highest illumination which we are unable to describe or picture, as it is said, "If thou wilt walk in my ways and if thou wilt keep my charge, . . . I will give thee a place to walk among these that stand by"

[Zechariah 3:7]; further, "How great is Thy goodness which Thou hast laid up for them that fear Thee, which Thou hast wrought for them that trust in Thee before the children of men" [Ps. 31:20]. Furthermore, "Eye hath not seen, O God, beside Thee, what He will do for one that waiteth for Him" [Isaiah 64:3].

Sixth, the Torah includes prescriptions, the obligation of which reason cannot explain, namely, those precepts which we obey on the ground of traditional authority as also certain principles that lie at the root of rational precepts. This is because the people to whom the Torah was given were at that period in such a condition that animal lusts dominated them and they were too weak in their knowledge and perceptive faculties to apprehend many of the rational precepts.

The Torah, therefore, used one method only for the rational precepts and for those resting on authority. The people were exhorted in the same way in regard to both classes of duties. An individual whose understanding and perception are strong, will exert himself and undertake the obligation of fulfilling them on both grounds—that they are rational and authoritative. And one whose intellect is too weak to perceive their rational ground will accept them because the Torah exhorts him, and will treat them as authoritative precepts. Thus all classes will be benefited, as it is said, "Its ways are ways of pleasantness, and all its paths are peace" [Prov. 3:17].

Seventh, we come to the Torah through a human intermediary [Moses] by whom were shown signs and demonstrations equally perceived by all the people with their senses, the evidence of which they could not deny. Hence, the message which he brought with him in the name of God was demonstrated to them through the senses as well as the intellect. The demonstration through the senses was an addition to the intellectual stimulus which human beings naturally possess. Whoever considers God's bounties, bestowed upon him, in common with all other human beings, will faithfully accept the special obligation to obey the precepts that are binding on his people, on the authority of the Torah and are not binding on other peoples.

And when one considers God's bounties to him, by which his tribe has been distinguished from the remaining tribes of his people, such as, priesthood or the levitical degree, he will faithfully accept the obligation to fulfill precepts by which God has distinguished his class. Hence you find twenty-four priestly dues. Analogously, anyone whom God has distinguished by special favours beyond those enjoyed by other human beings, should undertake a special service not incumbent on them, striving at the same time, according to his capacity and conception, to fulfill the duties in the obligation of which he is included with them and thanking God, blessed be He, for the bounty with which God specially favoured him. Thus will he insure its continuance and increase, and will also receive his reward in the world to come. A person should not behave like the one of whom it is said, "And silver I gave her in abundance and gold which they prepared for Baal" [Hosea 2:10].

One who falls short in the special service which he has to render for the bounty with which he has been specially favoured, will be induced to fall short in the service specially incumbent upon his tribe and afterwards in that incumbent upon his people, and at last he will renounce the Torah altogether. Not accepting the Torah, he will not even accept the obligation enjoined by the faculty of reason with which he is endowed, and its monition, and he loses the character of a rational creature; the cattle understand how to improve their condition better than he does, as it is said, "The ox knoweth his owner, and the ass his master's crib; but Israel doth not know; my people doth not consider" [Isaiah 1:3]. Such a person's fate will be like that of one, concerning whom it is said, "But the wicked shall perish and the enemies of the Lord shall be as the fat of lambs, they shall be consumed, into smoke shall they be utterly consumed" [Ps. 37:20].

Rashi

Rabbi Shlomo ben *Isaac* (1040–1105), or more commonly, Rashi (the custom of creating a name by initials was common among Jews), was the greatest medieval commentator on the Torah and the Talmud, and one of the most influential personalities in the history of Judaism during the past thousand years. After studying in academies in Worms, Mainz and Speyer (Germany), Rashi returned to his native Troyes (France) in 1065 and founded his own academy. He soon became famous for his commentaries and received questions from all parts of France and Germany. Although he was the rabbi and teacher of the Jewish community in his city, he received no salary for these duties—as was customary in his time—but earned his living by being a vintner in the busy commercial center of Troyes. There, during the times of the fairs, he came into contact with people from all parts of Europe; from them he gathered worldly knowledge and practical information which aided him in writing his commentaries.

One of Rashi's goals was to explicate the Babylonian Talmud so that a student would be able to understand it without consulting other commentaries. In this gigantic task Rashi made use of earlier works and notes from his studies at the academies. Always direct, never casuistic or complicated, with simple vocabulary and terse style, his commentary on the Talmud gained immediate and widespread acceptance.

Up to the time of Rashi, the midrashic-homiletic interpretation of the Pentateuch had been popular. Rashi, however, intended to offer a direct explication of the text; and his commentary contains the same stylistic penchant for brevity as does his Talmud commentary. Rashi familiarized himself with all the existing traditions of explication, Ashkenazic, Italian, Babylonian and Palestinian. He often included passages from the Midrash in his work, in effect anthologizing them for the reader who otherwise had no access to this literature. Rashi's commentary on the Torah, the most popular treatise in Hebrew literature, was the first Hebrew book printed. (*Rashi's Commentary to the Pentateuch*, Reggio, Italy, 1475).

Not only did Rashi's text spread throughout Ashkenazic Jewry, but even in Spain he was praised by its leading scholars. Moreover, his impact on Christian explicators of the Bible was profound. A famous Christian exegete, Nicolas de Lyra (fourteenth century) constantly quotes Rashi, and the King James Version (1611), the most famous of English translations of the Bible, made much use of Rashi.

To aid his readers in understanding a difficult word (Rashi occasionally coined words of his own), he used the vernacular, now called Old French, of which more than 3000 words appear in his writings. Interestingly enough, Rashi is the source for the oldest layer of Old French, for there are no extant French documents from the eleventh century. Since the words are transliterated in Hebrew, they also indicate pronunciation, which is otherwise usually problematic. Modern Rashi texts are to a degree trilingual: the basic Hebrew, the Old French words, and their Yiddish translation.

COMMENTARY ON THE PENTATEUCH

GENESIS 37:1-35

1. AND JACOB DWELT—After it [Scripture] has described for you the settlements of Esau and his descendants in a brief manner—since they were not distinguished and important enough that it should be related in detail how they settled down and that there should be given an account of their wars and how they drove out the Horites [see Deut. 2:12]—it explains clearly and at length the settlements made by Jacob and his descendants and all the events which brought these about, because these are regarded by the Omnipresent as of sufficient importance to speak of them at length. Thus, too, you will find that in the case of the ten generations from Adam to Noah it states "So-and-so begat so-and-so," but when it reaches Noah it deals with him at length. Similarly, of the ten generations from Noah to Abraham it gives but a brief account, but when it comes to Abraham it speaks of him more fully. It may be compared to the case of a jewel that falls into the sand: a man searches in the sand, sifts it in a sieve until he finds the jewel. When he has found it he throws away the pebbles and keeps the jewel.

Another explanation of AND JACOB DWELT: The camels of a flax-dealer once came into a city laden with flax. A blacksmith asked in wonder where all that flax could be stored, and a clever fellow answered him, "A single spark caused by your bellows can burn up all of it." "So, too, when Jacob saw [heard of] all these chiefs whose names are written above he said wonderingly, "Who can conquer all these?" What is written after the names of these chieftains?—and in this may be found the reply to Jacob's question: These are the generations of Jacob—Joseph. For it is written [Obad 1:18] "And the house of Jacob shall be a fire and the house of Joseph a flame, and the house of Esau for stubble: one spark issuing from Joseph will burn up all of these (descendants of Esau).

2. THESE ARE THE PROGENY OF JACOB—And these are an account of the generations of Jacob: these are their settlements and the events that happened to them until they formed a permanent settlement. The first cause is found in the narrative, "Joseph being seventeen years old, etc. etc."—it was through this incident that it came about that they went down to Egypt. This is the real explanation of the text and in it each statement finds its proper setting. The Midrash, however, explains that by the words, "These are the progeny of Jacob—Joseph", Scripture regards all Jacob's sons as secondary to Joseph for several reasons: first, the whole purpose of Jacob in working for Laban was only for Rachel, Joseph's mother, (and all his children were born only in consequence of this); then, again, Joseph's facial features bore a striking resemblance to those of Jacob. Further, whatever happened to Jacob happened to Joseph: the one was hated, the other was hated; in the case of the one his brother wished to

kill him so, too, in the case of the other, his brethren wished to kill him. Many such similarities are pointed out in Bereshith Rabbah (ch. 84).

Another comment on this verse is: AND HE ABODE—Jacob wished to live at ease, but this trouble in connection with Joseph suddenly came upon him. When the righteous wish to live at ease, the Holy One, blessed be He, says to them: Are not the righteous satisfied with what is stored up for them in the world to come that they wish to live at ease in this world too! AND HE, BEING A LAD—His actions were childish: he dressed his hair, he touched up his eyes so that he should appear goodlooking. WITH THE SONS OF BILHAH—meaning that he made it his custom to associate with the sons of Bilhah because his brothers slighted them as being sons of a hand-maid; therefore he fraternised with them.

THEIR EVIL REPORT—Whatever he saw wrong in his brothers, the sons of Leah, he reported to his father: that they used to eat flesh cut off from a living animal, that they treated the sons of the hand-maids with contempt, calling them slaves, and that they were suspected of living in an immoral manner. With three such similar matters he was therefore punished. In consequence of his having stated that they used to eat flesh cut off from a living animal Scripture states, [v. 31] "And they slew a he-goat" after they had sold him and they did not eat its flesh while the animal was still living. And because of the slander which he related about them that they called their brothers slaves—[Ps. 105:17] "Joseph was sold for a slave." And because he charged them with immorality [Gen. 39:7] "his master's wife cast her eyes upon him, etc." [Gen. R. 84].

THEIR REPORT—The word always means [in Old French *parleriz;* Engl. *gossip*]: whatever he could speak bad about them he told to his father.

3. THE SON OF HIS OLD AGE—because he was a wise son to him" —all that he had learnt from Shem and Eber he taught him [ib.]. Another explanation of his old age—his facial features were similar to Jacob's.

4. AND THEY COULD NOT SPEAK PEACEABLY TO HIM—from what is stated to their discredit we may infer something to their credit: they did not speak one thing with their mouth having another thing quite different in their hearts [ib.].

7. BINDING SHEAVES—Understand it as the Targum renders it: were binding bundles, i.e. sheaves. Similar is [Ps. 126:6] "bearing its sheaves". Similarly in Mishnaic Hebrew we have [Bab. Mets. 22b] "and he takes the sheaves and makes public proclamation".

8. AND FOR HIS WORDS—for the evil report about them which he used to bring to their father.

10. AND HE TOLD IT TO HIS FATHER AND TO HIS BRETHREN—After he had related it to his brothers (see v. 9) he again related it to his father in their presence. AND HIS FATHER REBUKED HIM— because he was arousing hatred against himself by relating the dream.

SHALL WE INDEED COME—"Is not your mother long since dead?" He did not, however, understand that the statement really alluded to Bilhah who had brought him up as though she were his own mother [Gen. R. 84]. Our Rabbis inferred from here that there is no dream but has some absurd incidents [Ber. 55b]. Jacob's intention in pointing out the absurdity of Joseph's mother, who was dead, bowing down to him was to make his sons forget the whole matter so that they should not envy him, and on this account he said to him, "Shall we indeed come etc."—meaning, just as it (the fulfillment of the dream) is impossible in the case of your mother so the remainder of the dream is absurd.

11. OBSERVED THE MATTER—He awaited and looked forward to the time when this would come to pass.

13. HERE AM I—An expression denoting humility and readiness: he was zealous to perform his father's bidding, although he was aware that his brothers hated him [ib.].

14. FROM THE VALE OF HEBRON—But was not Hebron situated on a hill, as it is said [Num. 13:22] "And they went up into the South and they came unto Hebron" why then does it state that Jacob sent him from the (emek) the vale, the deep part of Hebron? But the meaning is that Jacob sent him in consequence of the necessity of bringing into operation the profound (amuka) thought of the righteous man who was buried in Hebron—in order that there might be fulfilled that which was spoken to Abraham when the Covenant was made "between the parts" [cf. 15:13], "thy seed shall be a stranger etc."

AND HE CAME TO SHECHEM—A spot foredestined to be the scene of misfortunes: there the sons of Jacob sinned (by selling Joseph), there Dinah was maltreated, there the kingdom of the House of David was divided, as it said [1 Kings 12:1]. "And Rehoboam went to Shechem etc." [Sanh. 102a].

15. AND A MAN FOUND HIM—This was the angel Gabriel (Tanch.) as it is said, [Dan. 9:21] and the man Gabriel".

17. THEY HAVE JOURNEYED HENCE—they have departed from all feeling of brotherhood [ib.]. LET US GO TO DOTHAN—"let us go to seek some legal (datoth) pretexts to put you to death." According to the literal sense, however, it is the name of place, and Scripture never really loses its literal sense.

18. AND THEY CONSPIRED—they became filled with plots and craft directed toward him.

20. AND WE SHALL SEE WHAT WILL BECOME OF HIS DREAMS—R. Isaac said, this verse calls for a homiletic explanation. The Holy Spirit said this latter part of the text. They say "let us slay him", and Scripture (i.e. the Holy Spirit) breaks in upon their words concluding them by saying, "and we shall see what will become of his dreams": we shall see whose words will be fulfilled—yours or mine. For it is impossible that they

should have said, "and we shall see what will become of his dreams", for as soon as they would kill him his dreams would be of no effect [Gen. R. 84].

22. THAT HE MIGHT DELIVER HIM [OUT OF THEIR HAND]— The Holy Spirit (Scripture) bears witness for Reuben that he said this only for the purpose of saving his brother—that he would come afterwards and draw him up from there. He thought, "I am the first-born and the chief among them, and blame will attach to no one but myself" [ib.].

23. HIS GARMENT—this means his shirt. THE LONG SLEEVED GARMENT—this was the garment that his father had given him additional to those of his brothers [ib.]

24. AND THE PIT WAS EMPTY, THERE WAS NO WATER IN IT—Since it states, "the pit was empty", do I not know that "there was no water in it"? What then is the force of "there was no water in it"? Water, indeed it did not contain, but there were serpents and scorpions in it [Sabb. 22a].

25. AND THEIR CAMELS WERE BEARING etc.—Why does Scripture specially announce what they were laden with? It is to tell you how great is the reward of the righteous: it is not usual for Arabs to carry anything but naphtha and itran (tar) which are evil-smelling, but for this one (Joseph, the righteous) it was specially arranged that they should be carrying fragrant spices so that he should not suffer from a bad odour.

26. WHAT PROFIT—just as the Targum renders it. AND CONCEAL HIS BLOOD—this signifies that we hide the fact of his death (for they had not shed his blood, but had cast him into a pit to die).

28. AND THERE PASSED BY MIDIANITES—This was another caravan: Scripture indicates that he was sold several times. AND THEY DREW UP—the sons of Jacob drew up JOSEPH FROM THE PIT, and they sold him to the Ishmaelites, and the Ishmaelites to the Midianites and the Midianites into Egypt [Gen. R. 84].

29. AND REUBEN RETURNED—When Joseph was sold he had not been present, for it was his day (his turn) to go to attend to his father. Another explanation is: he had not sat with them at the meal because he was occupied with his sack-cloth and fast in penitence for having disturbed his father's couch [ib.].

30. WHITHER SHALL I GO?—Whither can I flee from my father's grief?

31. A KID OF THE GOATS—its blood resembles that of a human being.

33. AN EVIL BEAST HATH EATEN HIM—The spirit of prophecy was enkindled within him, for these words may be taken to mean that at some future time Potiphar's wife would attack him. Why did not the Holy One, blessed be He, make known to him (Jacob) that he was still living? Because they had placed under a ban and a curse anyone of them who would make it known, and they made the Holy One, blessed be He, a party

with them to this agreement (Tanch.) Isaac, however, knew that he was living, but he thought, "How dare I reveal it since the Holy One, blessed be He does not wish to reveal it" [Gen. R. 84].

34. MANY DAYS—twenty-two years—from the time he left him until Jacob went down to Egypt. For it is said, [v. 2] "Joseph was seventeen years old" when all these events happened, and he was thirty years old when he stood before Pharoah; seven years of plenty and two years of famine had passed by the time Jacob came to Egypt—making in all 22 years. These correspond to the 22 years during which Jacob had not practised the duty of honouring his parents (that is, the period during which he did not reside with them and attend to their needs) [Meg. 17a]: viz., the twenty years he stayed in Laban's house and the two years on the journey when he was returning from Laban's house—one and a half years at Succoth and six months at Bethel. This is what he meant when he said to Laban [31:41], "These twenty years that I have been in thy house are for me"—the responsibility for them lies upon me and sometime I shall be punished for a period equal to them.

35. AND ALL HIS DAUGHTERS—R. Judah said: a twin-sister was born with each of Jacob's sons and they each took a step-sister to wife (It was these daughters who comforted Jacob). R. Nehemiah said: their wives were Canaanite women and not their step-sisters; what is meant then "by all his daughters"? His daughters-in-law, for a person does not hesitate to call his son-in-law his son and his daughter-in-law his daughter. BUT HE REFUSED TO COMFORT HIMSELF—A person does not accept consolation for one living whom he believes to be dead, for with regard to the dead it is decreed that he be forgotten from the heart, but it is not so decreed with regard to the living [Gen. R. 84]. MOURNING INTO THE GRAVE—According to the literal meaning it means "the grave"—whilst I am still in a state of mourning I shall be interred (i.e. even to the day of my burial I shall mourn) and I shall not be comforted all my life. The Midrash explains it to refer to Gehinnom. "This omen has been given me by God: if none of my sons die during my lifetime I may be assured that I shall not see Gehinnom" (Tanch.). THUS HIS FATHER WEPT FOR HIM—His father refers to Isaac: he wept for Jacob's trouble, but he did not mourn for he knew that Joseph was alive [Gen. R. 84].

GENESIS 39:1–22

1. AND JOSEPH WAS BROUGHT DOWN—Scripture now reverts to the original subject, and consequently it states "Joseph had been brought down to Egypt" before the events last mentioned; it interrupted it only in order to connect the account of the degradation of Judah [Gen. 38:1] with that of the sale of Joseph, thus suggesting that it was on account of him [i.e. Joseph—Judah's part in the sale of Joseph—] that his brothers degraded him from his high position. A further reason why this narrative

of Judah and Tamar is interpolated here is to place in juxtaposition the story of Potiphar's wife and the story of Tamar, suggesting that just as this woman (Tamar) acted out of pure motives so also the other (Potiphar's wife) acted out of pure motives, for she foresaw by her astrological speculations that she was destined to be the ancestress of children by Joseph—but she did not know whether these children were to be hers or her daughter's [ib.].

3. THAT THE LORD WAS WITH HIM—the name of God was a familiar word in his mouth [Gen. R. 86].

6. AND HE KNEW NOT AUGHT HE HAD—he paid no attention to anything. SAVE THE BREAD—this means his wife, but Scripture uses here a euphemism [ib.] [cf. Joseph's own words in verse 9.] AND JOSEPH WAS OF BEAUTIFUL FORM—As soon as he saw that he was ruler [in the house] he began to eat and drink and curl his hair. The Holy One, blessed be He, said to him, "Your father is mourning and you curl your hair! I will let a bear loose against you".

9. AND SIN AGAINST GOD—The "Sons of Noah" were subject to the command which forbade immorality [Sanh. 56b].

10. TO LIE BY HER—even without sinning. TO BE WITH HER, in the world to come [Gehinnom].

11. AND IT CAME TO PASS ON A CERTAIN DAY—This means as much as "and it came to pass when a certain distinguished day arrived" —a day of merriment, a day of their sacred feast when they all went to the temple of their idols,—she said, "I shall find no day fitting to associate with Joseph as this day". She therefore told her attendants I am sick and cannot go to the temple (Tanch.). TO DO HIS WORK—Rab and Samuel differ as to what this means. One hold that it means, his actual house-work; the other that it means to associate with her, but a vision of his father's face appeared to him and he resisted temptation and did not sin as is stated in Treatise Sota (36b).

14. SEE, HE HATH BROUGHT IN UNTO US—This is an elliptical phrase: "he hath brought in to us" without stating plainly who brought him in. She was referring to her husband. A HEBREW—is one who came from the other side of the river Euphrates, being at the same time of the sons of Eber.

16. HIS MASTER—Joseph's master [not the master or owner of the garment].

17. The sentence means: the Hebrew servant whom thou hast brought unto us came to me to have his sport with me.

19. AND IT CAME TO PASS WHEN HIS LORD HEARD etc.— She said this when he was alone with her, caressing her. This is what she meant by "things like these did thy servant do to me"—caresses such as these. 21. AND CAUSED HIM TO FIND FAVOUR—so that he was liked by all who saw him.

22. HE WAS THE DOER OF IT—understand this as the Targum does: it was done at his command.

EXODUS 20:1–20

1. AND GOD SPAKE—The word God is a term for a judge. Since there are chapters in the Torah of such a character that if a person observes the commands contained therein he will receive a reward and if he never observed them at all he will not receive punishment on their account, one might think that the Ten Commandments are also of such a character (that no punishment will follow upon the infringement of them); therefore Scripture expressly states, "God spake"—God Who is Judge, exacting punishment. ALL THESE WORDS—This statement [that God spake all these words] tells us that the Holy One, blessed be He, said all these words in one utterance, something that is impossible to a human being to do—to speak in this manner. Now if this be so, why does Scripture again say the first two Commandments? But the explanation is that He repeated and expressly uttered each of these two commandments by itself. TO SAY—This expression teaches us that they answered to that which required the reply "Yea" by "Yea" and to that which required the reply "Nay" by "Nay."

2. WHO HAVE BROUGHT THEE OUT OF THE LAND OF EGYPT—That act of bringing you out is alone of sufficient importance that you should subject yourselves to Me. Another explanation: because He had revealed Himself to them at the Red Sea as a mighty man of war and here He revealed Himself as a grey-beard filled with compassion, as it is stated in connection with the Giving of the Law, [24:10] "and there was under His feet as it were a brick-work of sapphire", which is explained to mean that this [the brick-work] was before Him at the time of their bondage; "and there was as the essence of heaven" [i.e. joy and gladness] when they had been delivered, thus the Divine Glory changed according to circumstances—therefore He stated here: Since I change, appearing in various forms, do not say, "There are two divine Beings"; it is I Who brought you forth from Egypt and Who appeared to you at the Sea.

Another explanation: because they then heard many voices, as it is said [v. 15] "the people heard the voices"—voices coming from the four cardinal points and from the heavens and from the earth—therefore God said to them, "Do not say there are many Deities."—Why did God say in the singular, "Thy God," (as though speaking to one person alone)? To afford Moses an opportunity to speak in defence of Israel at the incident of the golden calf. This is exactly what he did say, [32:11] "Wherefore, O Lord, doth Thy wrath glow against Thy people," for not to them didst Thou give the command, "There shall be to thee no other gods" but to me alone!

OUT OF THE HOUSE OF SLAVES—This means, from the house of Pharaoh where ye were slaves to him. Or perhaps it only says "from the house of slaves" in the sense of a house belonging to slaves so that the words imply that they were slaves to slaves (a most abject form of slavery)!

But elsewhere it states, [Deut. 7:8] "He redeemed thee from the house of slaves, from the hand of Pharaoh, king of Egypt," so that you must now admit that they were slaves of the king and not slaves to slaves, and the meaning is: from the house where you were slaves.

3. THERE SHALL NOT BE UNTO THEE [OTHER GODS]—Why is this said? Does not the preceding verse state: I—and no other—shall be thy God? But since it states immediately after this, "Thou shalt not make unto thee [any graven image etc.]" I might say that I have only a prohibition that one may not make such gods; whence could I know that one may not retain an idol that has already been made? Perhaps there is no such law! Therefore it states here: "there shall not be unto thee" [thou shalt not have other gods].

OTHER GODS—which are not gods, but others have made them gods over themselves. It would not be correct to explain this to mean "gods other than Me," for it would be blasphemy of the Most High God to term them gods together with Him. Another explanation of Other Gods: they are so called because they are other [i.e., strange] to those who worship them; these cry to them but they do not answer them, and it is just as though the god is another [a stranger] to the worshipper, one who has never known him at all. BEFORE ME—i.e., so long as I exist; and these apparently superfluous words are added in order that you may not say that no one received any command against idolatry except that generation which went forth from Egypt [Mekilta].

4. A GRAVEN IMAGE—it is so called because it is chiselled out. OR ANY LIKENESS, i.e., the likeness of any thing THAT IS IN THE HEAVENS.

5. A JEALOUS GOD—He is jealous to exact punishment, and does not pass over His rights by pardoning idolatry. Wherever the expression *jealous* occurs it signifies in [old] French *emportement* [Engl. *zeal,*]—determining to exact punishment. OF THEM THAT HATE ME—This must be explained in the same sense as the Targum takes it: when they follow the example of the evil doings of their ancestors [Sanh. 27b]; and He stores up the mercy which a person does to give a reward for it to the thousand generations of that person's descendants. It follows, therefore, that the measure of rewards is greater than the measure of punishment in the proportion of one to five hundred, for the former is threatened only to four generations whilst the latter is bestowed upon thousands.

7. IN VAIN—for no valid reason, idly. If one takes an oath declaring something, the nature of which is evident to be different from what it is: e.g., swearing about a stone pillar that it is of gold.

8. This word REMEMBER which opens this commandment here and "observe" which opens it in Deut. [5:12] were spoken in one utterance. Similar is, [31:14] "Everyone that profaneth it [the Sabbath] shall surely be put to death," which apparently is in contradiction with [Num. 28:9] "And on the Sabbath day [ye shall offer] two lambs," a command necessi-

tating actions which, if done for any other purposes on the Sabbath, would involve a profanation of that day. Similar is, [Deut. 22:11] "Thou shalt not wear a garment of two kinds [as of woollen and linen together]" and [ib. 12] "Thou shalt make thee tassels," for the performance of which command wool and linen may be employed in combination. Similar is [Lev. 18:16] "The nakedness of thy brother's wife [the prohibition of marriage with her], and [Deut. 25:5] "her husband's brother shall come unto her" [he shall marry her].—This is the meaning of what is said [Ps. 62:12] "One thing did God speak, these two things did we hear" [Mekilta]. REMEMBER—This word expresses the verbal action without any reference to a particular time (the infinitive), similar to [Is. 22:13] "to eat and to drink"; [2 Sam. 3:16] "to go and to weep"; and the following is its meaning: take care to remember always the Sabbath day—that if, for example, you come across a nice article of food during the week, put it by for the Sabbath.

9. [SIX DAYS SHALT THOU LABOUR] AND DO ALL THY WORK—When the Sabbath comes it should be in thy eyes as though all thy work were done [completed], so that thou shouldst not think at all about work.

10. THOU AND THY SON AND THY DAUGHTER—these latter mean the young children. Or perhaps this is not so, but it means your adult children? But you must admit that these have already been placed under this prohibition [by the word "Thou," because the performance of this command is obligatory upon all adults to whom it was addressed]. Therefore these words must be intended only to admonish the adults [implied in the term "Thou"] about the Sabbath rest of their young children [to impose upon the parents the obligation of enforcing the Sabbath rest upon them]. This is the meaning of what we have learnt in a Mishna, [Sabb. 16:6] A minor who is about to extinguish a fire—we do not permit him to do this because his observance of the Sabbath is a duty imposed upon you.

11. AND HE RESTED ON THE SEVENTH DAY—If one may say so, He recorded that He rested to teach from this an inference a fortiori as regards a human being whose work is performed only by labour and toil—that he should rest on the Sabbath day. HE BLESSED . . . AND SANCTIFIED IT—He blessed it through the Manna by giving a double portion on the sixth day—"double bread"; and He sanctified it through the Manna in that on it none fell. THAT THY DAYS MAY BE LONG—If thou honourest them they will be long, and if not, they will be shortened—for the words of the Torah may be explained as concise statements: from what is included in a positive statement we may infer the negative and from what is included in a negative statement we may infer the positive.

13. THOU SHALT NOT COMMIT ADULTERY—The term "adultery," is technically only applicable to the case of a married woman, as it is said, [Lev. 20:10] [. . . the wife of his neighbour], the adulterer and the adulteress shall surely be put to death," and it further states, [Ezek. 16:32]

"The woman that committeth adultery, that taketh strangers instead of her husband." THOU SHALT NOT STEAL—Scripture here is speaking about a case of one who steals human beings, whilst the command [Lev. 19:11] "Ye shall not steal" speaks about a case of one who steals money [another person's property in general]. Or perhaps this is not so, but this speaks about the case of one who steals money and the other about the case of one who steals human beings! You must, however, admit that the rule applies: a statement must be explained from its context. How is it in regard to, "Thou shalt not murder" and "Thou shalt not commit adultery"? Each, speaks of a matter for which one becomes liable to death by sentence of the court; similarly, "Thou shalt not steal," must speak of a matter for which one becomes liable to death by sentence of the court, and this is not so in the case of theft of money but only in that of kidnapping.

15. AND ALL THE PEOPLE SAW—This statement teaches us that there was not a blind person amongst them. And whence may we learn that there was not a mute person amongst them? Because it states [19:8] "And all the people answered." And whence may we learn that there was not a deaf person amongst them? Because it states [24:7] "We will do and we will hear." [THEY] SAW THE SOUNDS—they saw that which should be heard—something which is impossible to see on any other occasion. THE SOUNDS which issued from the mouth of the Almighty. THEY MOVED—The root denotes trembling. AND THEY STOOD AFAR OFF—they moved back, startled, twelve miles, a distance equal to the length of their camp, and ministering angels came and assisted them—to bring them back, as it is said [Ps. 68:13] "The angels of the God of Hosts made them move on, move on."

17. IN ORDER TO TRY YOU—signifies in order to exalt you in the world—that you may obtain a great name amongst the nations because He has revealed Himself to you in His glory. AND THAT HIS FEAR MAY BE [BEFORE YOUR FACES]—Through the fact that you see that He is feared and dreaded, you will know that there is none beside Him and you will therefore fear Him and not sin.

18. [AND MOSES] STEPPED NEAR TO THE THICK CLOUD—within the three divisions—darkness, cloud and thick cloud, as it is said [Deut. 4:11] "And the mountain burned with fire unto the midst of the heaven, with darkness, clouds and dark clouds."

19. THUS THOU SHALT SAY—in this language. YE HAVE SEEN—There is a difference between what a person himself sees and what others relate to him, for what others relate to him sometimes his heart is divided in its opinion so that he does not believe. THAT I HAVE SPOKEN [TO YOU] FROM HEAVEN—But another verse states [19:20] "And the Lord came down upon Mount Sinai," and thus the two verses appear to be contradictory! There now comes a third verse and harmonises them: [Deut. 4:36] "Out of heaven He made thee hear His voice that He might instruct thee; and upon the earth He showed thee His great fire"—His glory was in the heavens but His fire and His power were upon the earth.

LEVITICUS 19:10–18

10. [NEITHER SHALT THOU COLLECT] THE FALLEN GRAPES OF THY VINE YARD—i.e., the single berries of the grapes which fall to the ground during the grapegathering [and belong to the poor]. I AM THE LORD YOUR GOD—the Judge Who am certain to punish if necessary and Who for the neglect of these duties will exact from you nothing less than your souls, as it is said [Prov. 22:22, 23] "Rob not the poor . . . for the Lord will plead their cause [and spoil the soul of those that spoiled them]".

11. YE SHALL NOT STEAL—This is a warning addressed to him who steals money [the property of his fellowman], but the law "Thou shalt not steal" which is contained in the Ten Commandments is a warning addressed to him who steals a human being. For this is what is learnt from the context, because it must be a matter for which one becomes liable to death by sentence of the court, [since the preceding laws in the Ten Commandments are of this character, which is the case with kidnapping and not with theft of money].

NEITHER SHALL YE DEAL FALSELY [WITH ONE ANOTHER] —Since Scripture has stated [Lev. 5: 21, 22] "If a man sin . . . and deny unto his neighbour a charge, or a deposit . . . or has found that which was lost and denieth it," that he shall pay the principal and add a fifth part more thereto, we have there mention only of the punishment he incurs; whence do we derive the prohibition [i.e., where is it forbidden]? From Scripture's statement here "neither shall ye deal falsely."

NEITHER SHALL YE LIE [ONE TO ANOTHER]—Since Scripture has stated [5:22] "If a soul sin . . . and deny unto his neighbour a charge or a deposit . . . and sweareth falsely" that he shall pay the principal and shall add the fifth part more thereto, we have there mention only of the punishment he incurs; whence do we derive the prohibition to lie? From Scripture's statement here "ye shall not lie one to another." YE SHALL NOT STEAL, NEITHER DEAL FALSELY, NEITHER LIE, NEITHER SWEAR [ONE TO ANOTHER]—If you steal you will in the end come to deny it, then you will lie [in order to back up your first denial], and ultimately you will swear falsely.

AND YE SHALL NOT SWEAR BY MY NAME [TO A LIE]—Why is this stated at all [how does the particular form of words used here tell us more than is contained in the Third Commandment]? Since it is said [Ex 20:7] "Thou shalt not take the name of the Lord thy God in vain," I might have inferred that one is not liable except he swore by the "Proper Name" of the Lord. Whence do I know that all names that are descriptive of God's attributes [Adonay, Rachum, Chanun etc.] are included in this prohibition? Because Scripture states "ye shall not swear by My Name to a lie," thus implying by any Name I have.

13. THOU SHALT NOT WRONG [THY FELLOWMAN]—This refers to one who withholds the wages of an hired servant. UNTIL THE

MORNING—Scripture speaks here of a person hired for day-work whose departure from work is at sunset. The time for drawing his wages is therefore the whole night (and the law is not infringed provided he pays it before the moment of day break). In another passage [Deut. 24:14] it states, "the sun shall not go down upon it [the man's wages]." There, however, it is speaking of one hired for night-work the end of whose period of work is at daybreak, therefore the time for drawing his wages is the whole day (but it must be done before sunset). The reason why he has the whole night or whole day to pay the wages is because the Torah gives the employer one half of the astronomical day to endeavour to obtain the money he requires for paying the wages.

14. THOU SHALT NOT EXECRATE THE DEAF—I have here only the law that one must not execrate the deaf: whence do I know that any person is included in this prohibition and that the meaning is, Thou shalt not execrate even the deaf? Because Scripture states [Ex. 22:27] "Thou shalt not curse anyone among thy people." But if this be so why does Scripture say DEAF and does not use some more general expression? It does so in order to offer an analogy: What is the case with the deaf? He is one who cannot hear your curse and therefore cannot feel aggrieved, but he has the characteristic of being a living person! The same applies to all living, thus excluding a dead person, who though he cannot hear and feel aggrieved, is not living.

THOU SHALT NOT PUT A STUMBLING BLOCK BEFORE THE BLIND—This implies: "Give not a person who is blind" in a matter an advice which is improper for him. Do not say to him: "Sell your field and buy from the proceeds of the sale an ass," the fact being that you are endeavouring to circumvent him and to take it (the field) from him. BUT THOU SHALT BE AFRAID OF THY GOD—Because in this case it is not given to human beings to know whether the intention of this man [the offender] was for the advantage or the disadvantage of the person whom he advised, and he thus might be able to evade the responsibility by saying: "I meant it for the best," Scripture therefore states with reference to him: "But thou shall be afraid of thy God" Who is cognisant of thy secret thoughts. Similarly in all actions where it is given only to the heart of him who does it to know the motive that prompts him and where other people had no insight into it, Scripture states, "But be afraid of thy God!"

15. YE SHALL NOT DO INJUSTICE IN JUDGMENT—This teaches us that the judge who perverts judgment is called an "unjust person," hateful and detested, doomed to destruction, and an abomination. He is rightly called thus for the unjust person is called by Scripture "abomination," as it is said [Deut. 25:16] "For all that do [such things] all that do injustice are an abomination unto the Lord thy God." THOU SHALT NOT RESPECT THE PERSON OF THE INDIGENT—i.e., thou shalt not say, "This is a poor man, and the rich man has in any case the duty of supporting him; I will find in favour of him [the poor man] and he will consequently obtain

some support in a respectable fashion. NOR HONOUR THE PERSON OF THE MIGHTY—thou shalt not say, "This is a rich man, or, this man is of noble descent, how can I possibly put him to shame and be witness to his shame? There is punishment for such a thing!" It is for this reason that Scripture states, "thou shalt not honour the person of the mighty. IN RIGHTEOUSNESS SHALT THOU JUDGE THY COMPANION—Take this as the words imply: strict right. Another explanation is: Judge thy fellow man with an inclination in his favour.

16. THOU SHALT NOT GO ABOUT AS A TALEBEARER—I say that because all those who sow discord between people and all who speak slander go into their friends' houses in order to spy out what evil they can see there, or what evil they can hear there so that they may tell it in the streets—they are called talebearers which is the same as "people who go about spying"; *espiement* in [old] French.

A proof of my statement is the fact that we do not find anywhere the term talebearer used in Scripture except in connection with the expression "to go." Examples are: the phrase here, and in Jer. 6:28, "[They are all] walking as spies: they are brass and iron." But as for any other expressions for "slander," the verb "go" is not used with them. Examples are [Ps. 101:5] "whoso privily slandereth his neighbour"; [ib. 120:2] "false tongue"; [ib. 12:4] "the tongue that speaketh proud things [slander]." For this reason I say that this expression means "going about and spying out."

In a similar sense we have [2 Sam. 19:28] "He spied against thy servant (to my lord)" which implies, "he spied me out with subtlety in order to speak evil about me to my lord." Similar is [Ps. 15:3]: "he has not spied out in order to have evil on his tongue." Similarly, the trader, "Rochel", is one who goes round and searches for [spies out] all kinds of merchandise; and so also the seller of perfumes which women use to make themselves nice is also called "rochel," because he constantly goes about in the villages. And its translation in the Targum has the same meaning as [Dan. 3:8] "and they slandered the Jews"; and as [Ber. 58a] "he slandered him to the king."

It seems to me that people had the custom to eat a little snack in the house of him who listened to their slanderous words, and this served as the final confirmation that his [the slanderer's] statements were well founded and that he would maintain the truth of them. It is the manner of all who go about slandering to wink [cf. Prov. 6:13] with their eyes and to suggest their slanderous statements by innuendoes in order that others who happen to hear them should not understand them.

NEITHER SHALT THOU STAND AGAINST THE BLOOD OF THY FELLOW—witnessing his death, you being able to rescue him: if, for instance, he is drowning in the river or if a wild beast or a robber is attacking him. I AM THE LORD—Who am faithful in paying reward to those who obey My commandments and Who am certain to punish those who transgress them.

17. [THOU SHALT IN ANY WISE REBUKE THY COMPANION]

AND NOT BEAR A SIN ON ACCOUNT OF HIM—i.e., though rebuking him thou shalt not expose him to shame [lit., make his face grow pale] in public, in which case you will bear sin on account of him.

18. THOU SHALT NOT AVENGE—If one says to another "Lend me your sickle," and he replies, "No," and the next day the latter says to the former, "Lend me your hatchet," and he retorts, "I am not going to lend it to you, just as you refused to lend me your sickle"—this is avenging. And what is "bearing a grudge"? If one says to another, "Lend me your hatchet," and he replies "No!" and on the next day he says to him, "Lend me your sickle," and he replies: "Here it is: I am not like you, because you would not lend me"—this is called "bearing a grudge" because he retains enmity in his heart although he does not actually avenge himself [Siphra; Yoma 23a]. THOU SHALT LOVE THY FELLOW MAN AS THYSELF—Rabbi Akiba said: "This is a fundamental principle of the Torah."

The Chronicle of Ahimaaz

The *Chronicle of Ahimaaz,* written by Ahimaaz ben Paltiel (1017–1060), depicts the history of a family in Southern Italy and provides information about the social status of that Jewry. The author, born in Capua, traces his pedigree back two hundred years—very likely from notes and traditions that had been passed down through the generations. The chronicle-memoir, (1054) reveals how the Jews communicate with their coreligionists, travel freely, rise to high positions, honor visiting sages, and are influenced by the literary traditions of the surrounding cultures. The *Chronicle* sheds light on the early Jewish settlement of various towns in Southern Italy, now (with the exception of Naples) almost completely devoid of Jews. It also shows the tolerance to Jews in Italy, a country that throughout its long history was exceptional in its attitude toward Jews. Despite the tragedy of occasional upheavals and invasions, there is little in the *Chronicle* that indicates that the Jews were victims of continual oppression.

In addition to its value as a historic and social document, the *Chronicle of Ahimaaz*—also called the *Book of Genealogies* by its author—contains many popular stories, beliefs and superstitions. Among the Jewish folkloristic elements mentioned are demons, the magic use of God's name, a dead man who prays, revivification of the dead, a cessation of the celestial cycle, and various bits of astrological lore. One folk motif recognizable from world literature is the metamorphosis of a man into a mule, which appears in the *Golden Ass* of Aupelius and, in modern times, in *Pinocchio*. The *Chronicle* also has the first recorded instance of the legend of the Wandering Jew. However, in line with the rather unreliable historiography of the day, the author draws no distinction between legend and history.

The unifying element in Ahimaaz ben Paltiel's account is his excellence as a storyteller. He has psychological insight, a sense of humor, and the skill to build a narrative and bring it to a successful conclusion; indeed, the various anecdotes in his *Chronicles* are constructed along novelistic lines. Ahimaaz's work is written in rhymed prose, a style favored by Jewish writers under the Muslim orbit—but since it is composed of brief rhymed phrases and lines, a modern translation must choose to render the work in prose.

A BOOK OF GENEALOGIES

In the name of the Lord, we will begin and finish [our task]. My help [cometh] from the Lord.

In the name of the Lord of Lords that doeth wonders I will write a book of genealogies.

In the name of Him that dwelleth in the heavens of splendor, I will begin to tell the story, diligently to investigate, arrange and present a collection of the traditions of my forefathers, to unfold them in proper order, to explain them with notes, to trace without confusion the genealogy whose parts must be collected like stubble.

With praise, I will glorify Him that dwelleth in heaven; that, in His grace and justice, safely guided my ancestors who came forth with the exiles that were spared in Jerusalem, and delivered them from destruction, children and elders, young and old, for the sake of His great mercy and the merit of the fathers of old. At all times they were protected by the God of heaven; shield and buckler has He even been to my forefathers, and so may He continue to be to their children to the last generation.

Now, with great care, I will set down in order the traditions of my fathers, who were brought on a ship over the Pishon [Euphrates or Po], the first river of Eden, with the captives that Titus took from the Holy City, crowned with beauty. They came to Oria; they settled there and prospered through remarkable achievements; they grew in number and in strength and continued to thrive. Among their descendants there arose a man eminent in learning, a liturgical poet and scholar, master of the knowledge of God's law, distinguished for wisdom among his people. His name was Rabbi Amittai. And he had a number of amiable and worthy sons, intelligent and learned men . . . The first of them was R. Shephatiah, zealous in the pursuit of wisdom; the second, R. Hananeel, engaged in the study of the Law of God which Jekutiel [Moses] delivered; the third, Eleazar who was devoted to [the Law] given in the third [month]. In the days of these good men there came from Bagdad, from our beloved ones, an esteemed man of distinguished family, an illustrious scholar, warding off wrath from the descendants of those that sleep in Hebron; he was as of the [favored] flock unto the Almighty King.

Before Aaron left his native land, his father had a mill by which he supported himself. It was turned by a mule. A lion fell upon the mule and killed it, while Aaron was out of the room. When he returned he could not find the mule, so he put the lion in its place, and fastened him to the mill to turn the grinding stones. When his father saw what he had done, he approached him and exclaimed, "What hast thou done? Thou hast put in the lion: thou hast humiliated him and broken his strength. God made him king and intended him to walk erect, and thou hast forced him into thy service, to work for thee. Now, as God liveth, thou shalt not remain with me, thou shalt go into exile, wandering by day and by night, for three years thou shalt suffer punishment for this offense. At the end of that time return to thy native land, and the Lord thy God will accept thee."

He came to Jaffa. There he found ships on every hand. He said to the sailors, "Comrades and friends, in the name of God I come to you. I will go with you, and, with the favor of Him that dwelleth in light, will control fate, so that by the help of the awe-inspiring God, the ship on which we sail may not be overtaken by enemies or storm wind."

He went in and took his place among them. At the hour for sleep they reached the city of Gaeta. There Aaron came upon a Jew, a Sephardi, who befriended him and proffered the hospitality of his home. At meal time the Sephardi did not eat, though the day was the Sabbath, sacred unto God. The master, surprised at his conduct, said:

"Today is the Sabbath unto the awe-inspiring One, why dost thou not delight thyself with that which is called a delight?"

The unhappy man answered, "Oh my master, do not urge me, for I am very sad, I am grieving for my son who has been taken from me for my many sins; I do not really know whether he is alive or dead."

The master then said to him in words of tenderness, "Observe the Sabbath properly, then show me the streets and lanes in which he used to come and go. If he be still alive, I will restore him to thee, and if dead, I will surely tell thee." The next day he did not delay. Together they went to the house of their friends that his son had frequently visited, and there they found a woman, an accursed sorceress, practicing her sorcery. She had changed the boy into a mule and had bound him to the mill stones, to make him grind as long as he lived.

When the sage saw him, he recognized him and understood, and said to the father, "See, thy son, whom thou hast thought dead, is restored to thee." He then spoke to the woman, and rebuking her, said, "Why art thou not overwhelmed with shame, since thou art caught in the net? Give back to the father his son, his own flesh."

The wicked woman was crestfallen; she did not give heed to his words and did not answer him either gently or harshly. Thereupon the good man took hold of the mule, led him out, transformed him, gave him his original form, and restored him to his father. The master turned in praise to his Maker. Together they uttered praise to their God, their Creator. . . .

From that city Aaron journeyed onward and went to Oria. There he found tents [of study], set up by the rivers, planted and thriving like trees by the waters, schools established, rooted like cedars growing at the side of flowing streams. There contending and flourishing in the pursuit of study, masters in public discourse and of learned discussion of the Law, were the distinguished scholars, the genial brothers, my ancestors, the sons of R. Amittai, R. Shephatiah and R. Hananeel, both of them true servants of God, zealously extolling the God of Israel, fervently invoking Him, declaring His praise and holiness: like the company of angels acknowledging the might and dominion of the King of kings. Among them Aaron established his home. His wisdom streamed forth, his learning flourished there. He revealed great powers, and gave decisions of the law like those which were given when the Urim were in use, when the Sanhedrin held court, and the law of Sota was valid [cf. Numbers 5:11-31]. He extended his influence, he founded a seat of learning to take the place of that which had been on the ground of the temple, where the foundations of the ark had been laid. . . .

By the grace of Him that hath formed the earth by His power, that forgiveth iniquity and sin, I will make mention of the incident that occurred at Venosa. There was a man who had come from the land of Israel, profoundly learned in the law of God, a master of wisdom. He remained in Venosa for some time. Every Sabbath he would give instruction and expound the Law before the community of the people of God. The master would lead with a discourse on the selected portion of the law, and R. Silanus would follow with his elucidation.

One day, the men of the villages came in wagons to the city; they began to quarrel among themselves. Some women came out of their houses, with the long staves used for raking the oven and charred by the fire; with these the men and women beat one another. R. Silanus, in a mistaken spirit of levity, resolved to make use of the incident, and committed a great wrong. He sought out the passage of the scriptural portion that the sage was to expound on that Sabbath, erased two lines of it and, in their stead, wrote the above story. This is what R. Silanus inserted, "The men came [to the city] in wagons; the women came from their houses, and beat the men with staves."

On the Sabbath, as the sage came upon the words, he stopped reading and all speech failed him. He looked at the letters and studied, examined and pondered and went over them several times and finally, in his simplicity, read them, and gave as part of the instruction the words that he found written there.

Then R. Silanus, in mocking laughter, said to all assembled there, "Listen to the discourse of the master on the quarrel that occurred among you yesterday, when the women beat the men, when they struck them with oven staves and drove them off on every hand." When the master realized what had been done he became very faint and pale; he hurried to his associates who were in the school engaged in study, and told them of the sorrowful experience he had just had. All of them were deeply pained and distressed, and they denounced R. Silanus the wise.

He remained in ban a number of years, until R. Ahimaaz arrived there on his pilgrimage, and, in his wisdom, annulled the ban. This is what the wise man did. When he arrived, they were observing the ten days of penitence. The teachers and head of the school urged him to stand before the ark, and, with ardent devotion, lead them in prayer to Him that is revered in the great assembly of the righteous.

In his modesty, he complied with their request. With the fear of God in his heart, he began with the penitential prayers, then melodiously chanted a poem of R. Silanus to show that he was a man of sound faith; that, although he was at first false and sinful and godless, when he remembered the former teachers, he followed them as his masters, who shattered the power of heretical teachings over him, so that he turned away from the heretics. When the sage had finished the prayers, they asked him who that lover of the great teachers was, so consecrated with power to utter prayer, who loved and honored the masters, and turned away and shunned the heretics. He answered, "That beloved one is R. Silanus, who has been denounced as unworthy among you." They immediately arose and annulled the ban which they had declared against him, and, invoking upon him abundant, enduring and substantial good, all of them said, "May R. Silanus ever be blessed."

In those days a king reigned over the Romans, a wicked man, elevated to the throne through treachery and murder, who determined to make an end of the acknowledgement of God whose work is perfect, among the descendants of the upright and holy.

In the 800th year after the destruction of the Holy City and of the Temple, the seat of glory, and of the exile of the people of Judah and of Israel, there arose a king whose name was Basil, a worshipper of images, seeking to destroy the people of Israel ever under God's protection, to lead them astray, to exterminate the remnant of Israel root and branch, to compel them to abandon the Law and to accept the worthless doctrine [of Jesus]. He sent couriers and horsemen to the provinces and all parts of his kingdom, to force the Jews out of their religion, and make them adopt his senseless faith.

The agents of the king went through the land as far as the harbor of Otranto; there they embarked and passed over into the province of Apulia. When the report of their coming reached the inhabitants, the people were thrown into consternation. They traversed the province from end to end. Finally, they came to the city of Oria, bringing a letter, officially stamped with the royal seal—the seal was the bulla of gold—that the king had sent to R. Shephatiah.

And these are the words that were written in the letter, "I, King Basil, send word to thee R. Shephatiah, to have thee come to visit me. Come to me, do not refuse, for I have heard of thy wisdom and thy vast learning. I long to see thee; I swear by my life and by the crown on my head, that thy coming shall be in peace, and that I will send thee back safe to thy home. I will receive thee with honor, as I would one of my own kin, and any boon thou mayest ask of me, I will grant in grateful affection."

R. Shephatiah then embarked to go to Constantinople, which Constantine had built—may God shatter its splendor and the power of all its people. And God let him find favor in the presence of the king and of his court.

The king led him into a discussion of the Law, and then questioned him regarding the building of the Temple, and that of the church called Sophia, asking him to tell in which structure the greater wealth had been used. The king firmly contended that it was Sophia, for in its construction uncounted treasure had been used.

But R. Shephatiah answered, in well-chosen words, "Let the King command that the Scriptures be brought to him. There thou wilt find the truth as to which structure is the more costly." He immediately did so and he found that the quantity used by David and Solomon was in excess of the amount counted out for Sophia, by 120 talents of gold and 500 talents of silver.

Thereupon the king exclaimed, "R. Shephatiah, by his wisdom, has prevailed against me."

But R. Shephatiah answered, "My Lord, not I, but the Scriptures have prevailed against thee."

Then the king asked him to be seated with him at the royal table, to partake of refreshing delicacies and fruits. Golden dishes were placed before him that he might eat in the cleanliness required by the Law. The dishes were drawn up and down by costly chains of silver, but no one could see the place from which they were let down before him.

And Basil had a daughter whom he loved as the apple of his eye. An evil spirit tormented her. He could not find a cure for her. He spoke to Shephatiah in secret and with earnest entreaty said, "Help me, Shephatiah, and cure my daughter of her affliction."

And Shephatiah answered, "With the help of the Almighty, I will surely do so." He then asked the king, "Hast thou any secluded place in which there is no uncleanness?"

The king answered: "I have the beautiful garden of the Bukoleon." After looking about in it, he agreed to make use of the Bukoleon, which literally means the mouth of the lion. He took the maiden into it and exorcised the evil spirit in the name of Him that dwelleth on high, the Creator of height and depth, that founded the earth in His wisdom, the Maker of the mountains and seas, that hangeth the world over nothing.

The evil spirit cried out, "Why dost thou help the daughter of the man who rules in wickedness and heaps affliction upon the people of the redeemed. She has been delivered to me by God, that I should humble and crush her. Therefore, let me be, for I will not come forth from my place."

But Shephatiah answered the evil spirit, "I will not heed thy words; come forth in the name of God, that he may know there is a God in Israel."

It came forth at once and tried to escape; but he seized it and put it into a leaden chest; he then covered the chest on all sides and sealed it in the name of his Maker, dropped it into the sea, and let it sink into the depth of the mighty waters. The maiden, quieted and cured, then returned to the king and queen.

Shephatiah now went to the king for his dismissal. The king came forth to meet him, placed his arm about his neck, brought him into his chamber, and began to tempt him to abandon his religion, and, with the promise of large reward,. to induce him to accept the senseless error of his heathen belief. He walked about with him, and insistently urged him; he approached him with a bribe and appointed companions for him.

When Shephatiah, the master, noticed the fanatic zeal and presumption, he exclaimed in a loud voice, "Mighty Master, Thou overwhelmest me with violence." Thereupon the king arose from his throne, took him from among the people, and gave him permission to go. He sent him to the queen that she might give him her gift and blessing. And the queen questioned him about his affairs saying, "Hast thou any daughters or sons?" He accordingly answered, "Thy servant has one son and two daughters." She then gave him the rings in her ears and the girdle on her loins, and urged them upon him, saying, "As my tribute to thy learning, give them to thy two daughters; in costliness there are none to be compared to them." The weight of the rings was a litra of gold and the girdle was of equal value.

When he was about to go, the king again called him and said to him, "Shephatiah, ask a boon of me and I will give it to thee from my treasures; and if thou dost not desire money I will give thee an inheritance of towns and cities, for I said in my letter to thee, that I would grant thy wish."

He answered in sorrow and bitter weeping, "If thou, my lord, wouldst favor Shephatiah, let there be peace for those engaged in the study of Law. Do not force them to abandon the Law of God, and do not crush them in sorrow and affliction. But if thou be unwilling thus to fulfil my wish, grant for my sake that there be no persecution in my city."

The king exclaimed in anger, "Had I not sent a letter with my seal, and taken an oath, I would this very instant punish thee. But how can I harm thee, since I have bound myself in writing to thee, and cannot retract what I have said in my letter." So he issued for him an edict, sealed with a costly seal of gold, commanding that no persecution take place in the city of Oria, and therewith sent him in peace and honor to his home and people.

Then the wicked king continued to send emissaries into all the provinces and ordered his agents to fall upon them; to force them out of their religion and convert them to the errors and folly of his faith. The sun and moon were darkened for twenty-five years, until the day of his death. Cursed be his end. May his guilt and wickedness be remembered, and his sin not be forgotten. May the recompense for his vileness and cruelty be visited upon the kingdom of Rome, that his royal power may be cast down from its high places and his dominion be removed from the earth, to bring cheer to the afflicted and comfort to the mourners, that, in mercy, we may soon see the time of fulfilment.

After his reign, his own son, Leo, came to the throne; the Lord God had chosen him. May his memory be blessed. He annulled the cruel edict that had been enacted in the days of his father, and permitted the Jews to return to the laws and statutes of their religion, to observe their Sabbaths, and all the requirements of their commandments, and the ordinances of their covenant, as of old. Praised be the name of their Rock that did not abandon them in the hands of their enemies, that saved them from their despoilers, and delivered them from their oppressors. Praised be the name of God from the heights forever and ever.

About this time the Arabians began to invade the Land with their armies, to overrun the borders of the kingdom of the uncircumcised, the country of the idolators; they carried destruction into Calabria, threw their cities into confusion, devastated their provinces, razed their walls of defense. They advanced into Apulia; there they grew in power, attacked the inhabitants in force, shattered their strength and captured many cities, and destroyed and plundered.

In those days there was in Bari, Saudan, the chieftain of the Arabians at the time, who held sway over the entire country. He sent messengers to the famous city of Oria, to make a treaty of peace with its inhabitants, promising not to deliver their land to destruction, only to exact tribute of them. But this was just a ruse, by which he planned to fall upon the city suddenly and overthrow it, and lay it waste.

The governor of Bari sent R. Shephatiah to him, to hear his proposal, to receive his pledge, the document bearing his seal, that the negotiations might be properly completed with his official mark. Saudan, the commander, received him with honor, spoke to him cordially, and lavished attentions upon him in the presence of all the princes that had assembled to welcome him; and he detained him until it was almost Sabbath. He did it purposely; for he could not return to his city on the Sabbath. He would not let him go, so that he might not inform his master of the enemy's plan.

When R. Shephatiah became aware of his ruse he exclaimed, "Give me permission to go, for thou hast deceived me with thy cunning."

But Saudan answered, "Whither wilt thou go at this hour, the Sabbath is about to begin."

Again he said to him, "Let me go, my lord, do not be concerned about me."

So he permitted him to leave, and he went. And when he set out, invoking the help of the Almighty, trusting in the Name of his Creator, and confident that God would aid him, he wrote some letters on the horse's hoof, so that his journey might be quickly made; he rapidly repeated the Ineffable Name and the ground miraculously yielded before him.

And when he reached the outskirts of his city, he called to the people on every hand, "Come forth in haste; flee from the outer city, for Saudan, the commander of the Arabians, with all his forces, is coming to take our possessions, to kill, to rob and plunder." And as he drew near the governor of the city went out to meet him; R. Shephatiah told him what had happened to him, and they took counsel about the matter. So he arrived in the city before nightfall; he washed and bathed, and welcomed the Sabbath as was fitting, with rejoicing, with food and drink, with study of the Law, robed and adorned in festive garments, partaking of all its delights and at ease among them.

And Saudan and all his host, arrogant and insolent, came by forced marches to attack them. He found the country deserted to the very gates of the city; and on the Sabbath, at the time of the afternoon prayer, having found no satisfaction, he asked for R. Shephatiah, saying, "Give me the man who violated his law, and profaned his Sabbath; their law ordains that he be put to death."

And R. Shephatiah answered fearlessly, by the power of his God that was in him, "Why dost thou speak thus? There is no truth in thy words. My witness is in heaven, and all the people of my city can testify that I arrived while it was day; while the sun was up I returned and went to the bath; I washed and bathed and returned to my house, and welcomed the Sabbath with proper sanctification, in obedience to the command of my King and my Redeemer, the Holy One of Israel, my God."

And Abu Aaron, the Aaron mentioned before, was still in the city at the time; he had come to the city of Bari situated on the seacoast, built facing the sea; and Saudan came forth to meet him and bestowed great honor upon him. Aaron remained with him about six months. Saudan's love of him was more wonderful than the love of women. While he remained with him, Saudan did not swerve from his good counsel. Aaron informed him clearly on everything that he asked of him, as though he were consulting the Urim. The wisdom of his instruction was acknowledged during all the time he remained there.

But one day as Aaron awoke from sleep, the spirit of God began to urge him to return to his native land. He went to the seacoast and looked about and found a ship ready to sail for Egypt. He immediately embarked upon it. The ship began to move at great speed. In anguish Saudan sent out ships to overtake it; but the master, by the power of the Great Hand, uttered the Name, and the ships could not approach it. The sailors tried to return to the place from which they had set sail, but the ship could not reach the shore. When the commander saw this, his anger subsided, for he perceived and understood that miracles were being performed by the master's power.

Thereupon the commander exclaimed, "O my master, my master; my father, my father! my horseman and my chariots, why hast thou left and forsaken me? Accept my prayer, return my lord, take my wealth and treasures, do not leave me alone!"

Aaron fittingly answered, "My way is plainly ordained by Him that excelleth in power; I cannot change it. Inquire of me and I will tell thee what thou desirest to know, before I leave thee."

So he questioned him about many things, and Aaron gave answer in keeping with his questions. Finally he asked, "Will I enter Beneventum?"

And Aaron answered, "Thou wilt enter; not in joy, but through sad compulsion."

As he foretold, so it happened. And Aaron went rejoicing to the quiet of the inheritance which he had left in his native land; he reached his home to live in abundance and content, in prosperity and joy, and gave thanks and praise to his Guardian and Creator that had brought him back, safe and happy, to his home.

I will now proceed to tell of the wonderful things that were done by R. Hananeel. He had a cousin, named Papoleon, who died very young. On the day of his death, the brothers of R. Hananeel were away at Beneventum on business. So he delayed burying him in the tomb of his fathers, waiting for his brothers to come and weep over their dead kinsman and to give him proper burial. To prevent the body from decomposing and becoming putrid, he wrote upon a piece of parchment the Name of God, his Master, and placed the parchment under the dead man's tongue. The Name brought him to life, and raised him, and he sat up in bed. He repeated the Name, and gazed at it.

During the night preceding the day on which the brothers returned, they had an astonishing dream: an angel of God seemed to come in a vision and speak the mysterious words, "Why do you vex the Lord God, and do things which are not right? God putteth to death and you bring to life. You should not do so. You should not tempt the Lord your God." But they did not know what R. Hananeel had done. When they reached their house he came out to meet them; they went in to see their cousin and found him sitting on his bed; they knew nothing of what had occurred, of the Name that was under his tongue.

When they heard what had been done, they wept bitterly and said to their brother, "Thou wast able to bring him to life, and thou canst put him to death."

In sadness and anguish R. Hananeel then approached his cousin and said, "Raise thy mouth, that I may kiss thee." The boy opened his mouth. R. Hananeel, kissing him, put his hand under his tongue, and took therefrom the Name written on the parchment. As soon as the Name was taken from him, his body fell back upon the bed. So the body returned to dust and decay, and the soul returned to God who gave it.

I will give thanks to God and declare His works, and speak of that which should be told, which happened in the city of Oria in the palace called Hegemonia, to R. Hananeel, the brother of Shephatiah, who was on the verge of death, and whom the Exalted One brought forth to deliverance, from darkness to light. It is the duty of his descendants, pillars of nobility, to give praise and grateful recognition to his Name, and at all times say before Him Hallelujah.

One day the archbishop questioned him regarding various matters recorded in the official archives, and eventually entered into discussion of the calculations that were prescribed for determining the appearance of the new moon. On the morrow of that very day there was to be New Moon day, which, according to Israel's custom, was to be held sacred. He asked him in how many hours the new moon would appear. R. Hananeel answered by naming a certain hour. But he was mistaken. The archbishop disputed his opinion and said, "If that is thy calculation on the appearance of the moon, thou art not skilled in calculation."

R. Hananeel had not given thought to the time of the appearance of the New Moon, but the archbishop had calculated it and knew; he had cast his net for R. Hananeel, and would have caught him in his snare had not the God of his salvation come to his aid. And the archbishop said to him, "O wise Hananeel, if the new moon appear as I have calculated, thou shalt do my will and adopt my religion, as my gospel teaches, abandon thy faith, and the ordinances of thy law, and accept my religion, my empty doctrine of error. If it be as thou hast calculated, I will do thy will. I will give thee my horse, assigned to me at the ceremonies of New Year's day, the value of which is 300 pieces of gold; and if thou care not for the horse, thou mayest take its value instead."

They accepted the conditions and agreed to abide by what they had spoken, before judges and magistrates and before the prince that ruled over them. That night the archbishop ordered men to go to the top of the wall and towers, to note the exact moment of the moon's first appearance, and observe the portion that appeared.

When R. Hananeel returned to his house, he went over his calculation and found his error, by which he had failed in his reckoning; his heart grew faint and melted within him, no strength was left in him. But he roused himself to entreat God and His favor, the Ancient Help, from the beginning of time, to show His marvelous power in his need, to lift him from the walls of the pit. He went to his brothers and all of his kin and told them of the trouble that had come upon him, that they might make earnest supplication to God; perhaps He would hear their cry, and would intervene with all his signs and wonders, as He had marvelously done in Egypt for his forefathers.

When it grew dark, he went to the roof of his house, looking to Him on high, to Whom praise and exultation are due. As the time of waxing approached, and the moon was about to shine, he called, in distress and tears, upon Him that heareth the supplication of His beloved, saying, in his prayers to the God of his hope, "O God, Ruler of the universe, nothing is hidden from Thee, my thoughts are revealed to Thee. I have not been presumptuous; I have innocently erred and committed folly. And now, O God of my praise, may my prayer come before Thee; arise, to help me, O God of my salvation; forgive my error and pardon my wrong doing, so that I shall not suffer punishment; else my death is better than my life. Do not destroy the work of Thy hands, and do not withdraw Thy kindness from Thy servant; overlook the transgression according to Thy measure of grace and mercy; in Thy great goodness pardon my iniquity; give ear to my prayer and supplication; accept my plea and cry of affliction; hear my entreaty for Thy sake, O God, and I will extol Thee in the assembly of the elders, and give homage to Thee in the company of the upright."

And He that is enthroned amid the praises of Israel heard his prayer. The moon was obscured and did not appear until the next night. In the morning he went to hear the decision; the archbishop summoned him in the presence of all the people, and said to him, "Thou knowest as well as I that the new moon appeared as I had determined in my calculations; I was not mistaken; I had given much thought to it, and knew I had the correct answer. But who can inflict punishment on thee? Thou hast found exemption from thy Master like a son that escapes punishment by caressing and coaxing his father." So he gave him the 300 pieces of gold.

R. Hananeel distributed them among the poor and did not take any of the money to his own house. Then his brothers and friends assembled and gave praise and thanks to the Eternal One, that saveth His servants from affliction, and bringeth them from darkness to light, at all times their Help, mercifully sustaining His people with shield and place of refuge. . . .

R. Shepatiah had a daughter named Cassia, of rare beauty, of genial and charming disposition, and he loved her devotedly. Her father wished to have her marry but her mother did not wish it. Whenever anyone came to ask her in marriage, her mother would turn him away by saying, "My daughter is a woman of high station, and her father is a distinguished man; if we do not find one like him, I will not let her come out of the house. If there be one like her father in mastery of the Law, of tradition and scripture, in the interpretation of Talmudic practice and in the knowledge of decisions, in the understanding of Sifre and Sifra, in ability to explain and apply the principle of major and minor, in familiarity with the mysteries of Binah and Hokmah, and all secret lore, in wealth and eminence, in influence and authority, in his grasp of the statutes and commandments, in reverence and modesty, if he have every good quality, I will give her in marriage to him, as we should."

One night, while R. Shephatiah was about to recite his prayers, it happened that his daughter arose from her bed, and, in her sleeping gown, stood before him, to pour the water for him, that he might wash his hands; he noticed that she had arrived at the time of maturity for marriage. At the conclusion of his prayer, he returned to his wife, to rebuke her, to shame her, to emphasize the truth of his words, saying with great vehemence:

"I have a precious dove, without blemish. She has arrived at maturity to be a crown to her husband, and my brother seeks her in marriage for his son Hasadiah. I have followed your advice and have not found happiness for her; I have violated the ordinance of the Scripture and disregarded the words of the sages."

The next morning as he was leaving his house to go to the house of prayer, he called to his brother R. Hananeel. He quickly came to him and heard him say, "It is my intention and earnest desire to give my daughter to Hasadiah thy son, for it is best that I give her to him." When they concluded their prayers, he invited the congregation to come to his house, and gave his daughter in marriage to R. Hasadiah, son of R. Hananeel the brother of R. Shephatiah. R. Amittai, the brother of the distinguished bride, wrote, in her honor, the poem, "The Lord that from the beginning telleth the end," to crown her with charm and beauty, when this bride and groom were united in marriage.

R. Shephatiah had grown old; God had blessed him with all good qualities; He that dwelleth on high had endowed him with learning, distinguished him with wealth and large possessions; and had favored him with a worthy, upright son; father and son were without fault. And R. Hananeel was equal to them in eminence and uprightness. . . .

R. Shephatiah died in peace; he closed his life in happy devotion to the Judge of the widow and the Father of the orphan; leader among the wise, he tasted of the cup of the first parents, which the first serpent brought upon the first and last generations.

On New Year's day R. Shephatiah alone was thought worthy of the honor of sounding the Shofar, for the glory of God through His people. On that day he was weak, prostrated by sickness. But the whole congregation urged him insistently, saying: "Our master, arrayed in light, the radiance of our glory, the light of our eyes, blow the Shofar for us; as long as God spared you, no one else shall blow the Shofar for us."

They continued to urge him and he arose to blow it. But he did not have sufficient strength and could not produce the proper sounds. The good man calmly accepting the judgment against him said to them, "My children, may this be a sign for good unto you; because of my transgression time has turned against me." He left the house of worship and went to his home and lay upon his bed. The entire congregation followed him and entered his bedchamber. Turning his face to them, he said, "I am going to my eternal rest, to my portion among the fathers of old, and I tell you dear children, my three beloved sons, that Basil the oppressor and persecutor is dead. He passes on before me, bound in chains of fire, delivered to the demons of destruction. My God, whose name is the Lord of Hosts, has sent me to go forth to meet Basil and to stand in judgment against him, for all the evil that he has committed against His people, to blot out his name and the name of his posterity, to destroy him root and branch."

So they noted the day and hour. Soon afterward the report reached them, announcing that Basil the oppressor had died; the letter came just as the good man had foretold. It was the custom of the emperors of Constantinople, whenever an emperor died, to make proclamation by letter, in Bari, giving the time and the day when he had passed away. "Praised be He Who alone doeth wonders, Who destroyed him in this world and shut him out of the world to come. Praised be His name and the name of His Glory. I shall be gathered to my people and shall go to my place and as for you my children, my devoted ones, the assembly of my people, may God be with you."

After the death of Shephatiah, who had served God without deceit, and, with constant devotion, studied the mysteries of the Highest, faithfully loved the Lord and obeyed Him with all his soul and might, and with all his heart had magnified Him, there arose R. Amittai his beloved son, who eagerly adhered to the ways of his father, and did not stray from the statutes of his Creator. The God of his father was his help. He continued his school, to promote, with the sages of his company, the study of the Law of God.

The day before he died, his father had demanded this of him, that he should maintain the assembly of teachers, and direct it properly, so that the teachers and pupils might not be disbanded. He held the assembly together, carried on instruction with the help of the rabbis and sages, and expounded the Torah, systematically, in its length and breadth; his principles of interpretation of the Commandments of God and His covenant were those of his ancestors. His soul lamented the destruction of the Temple, and grieved deeply over the persecution, so long as he lived. . . .

R. Amittai was gathered to his people. He left a son named Abdiel. And Abdiel had a son whose name was Baruch, who was not learned in the Law as his fathers had been. . . . The memory of Baruch perished, his lamp was extinguished; so that he left no one to engage in the study of the Law; he had no sons; only one daughter.

R. Hasadiah, son of R. Hananeel, had a son whose name was Paltiel. And R. Paltiel begat a son, R. Hananeel, and a daughter, Cassia, who was distinguished for piety; she begat a son, R. Paltiel, who was a master of astrology.

In those days the Arabians with their armies, with Al Muizz as their commander, overran Italy; they devastated the entire province of Calabria, and reached Oria, on the border of Apulia; they besieged it, defeated all its forces; so that the city was in dire distress; its defenders had no power to resist; it was taken by storm; the sword smote it to the very soul. They killed most of its inhabitants, and led the survivors into captivity. And the commander inquired about the family of R. Shephatiah. He sent for them and had them appear before him. And God let them find grace in his eyes. He bestowed His kindness upon R. Paltiel, His servant, and let him have favor before him. And Al Muizz brought him to his tent, and kept him at his side, to retain him in his service.

One night the commander and R. Paltiel went out to observe the stars. As they were gazing at them, they saw the commander's star consume three stars, not all at one time, but in succession. And Al Muizz said to him, "What meaning dost thou find in that?"

R. Paltiel answered "Give thy interpretation first."

The commander replied, "The stars represent the three cities, Tarentum, Otranto and Bari, that I am to conquer."

R. Paltiel then said, "Not that, my Lord; I see something greater; the first star means that thou wilt rule over Sicily; the second, that thou wilt rule over Africa; and the third, that thou wilt rule over Babylonia."

Al Muizz at once embraced him and kissed him, took off his ring and gave it to him, and took an oath saying, "If thy words come true, thou shalt be master of my house and have authority over all my kingdom."

Before seven days had passed, a message was brought to Al Muizz. The princes of Sicily sent messengers to him saying, "Know that the Emir is dead. Come thou in haste and assume authority and dominion over us." He thereupon gathered his troops; with all the captains of his army he embarked on his ships and crossed over into their country, and became their ruler. Then he had faith in the words of R. Paltiel, and did not depart from his advice, either to the left or to the right; he appointed him master over his house and domain. R. Paltiel entered his service as his vizier.

Some time after, Al Muizz went to Ifrikiya, leaving his brother as ruler over Sicily; and R. Paltiel went with him. There he grew in eminence, and added to his fame; he was second in power to the Caliph, his renown spread through all the cities.

At that time, the emperor of Greece sent an embassy with a gift to seek audience with the Caliph of Ifrikiya. The ambassador came in state as was the custom of the Greeks. He asked who was warden of the palace and master of the royal ceremonies. An Arabian said to him, "It is a Jew that gives permission to enter and leave; he is in authority over all the Caliph's dominion; and the Caliph always follows his advice. No one can see him or enter the palace to appear before him without the order and consent of the Jew."

But the Greek, in his insolence and pride, in his folly and stupidity, replied, "I would rather leave this city and return to Constantinople, to my master who has sent me hither, than deal with the Jew for permission to let me speak to the Caliph."

These words reached the ear of R. Paltiel; he was informed of all that had occurred. He then commanded throughout the royal court that no one approach the envoy with a sign of greeting or respect, and that no one take notice of him where he had set up his tent. For about ten days he kept aloof, in anger and raging fury. Then, he meekly came up to ask mercy and pardon, begging that he forget his senseless conduct, and forgive the offense which he had committed in his stupidity, and the words he had spoken in his folly.

R. Paltiel granted that he might come, but not on that day. On the third day, he admitted him into his presence; he received him with honor and splendor, and overwhelmed him with lavish gifts, entertained him with music, and dances, and an abundance of perfumes, with precious stones, onyx and opal, and with the costly and beautiful treasures of the realm. He received him in state, from the gate of his palace, to his dining hall; he adorned the entire hall with hangings of silk and wool; the floor of the court and the walls of the palace were beautified with tapestry of scarlet and fine linen and costly ornaments; he walked in upon rugs of silk.

The Greek saw R. Paltiel sitting upon a couch, and, for himself, he found a chair of gold. He took his seat and entered into conversation with him, questioned him about the law of the Hebrews, about his kin, and family and native land; R. Paltiel answered him properly and intelligently. And he gave order that water be brought to wash his hands and mouth, in a dish and bowl of onyx and jasper. Secretly he commanded the servant to break them, after he had washed. The servant carried out the command of his master; he brought the bowl, and its dish; he poured the water over his master's hands, and then fell at his feet, and broke the dishes. Thereupon the Greek arose in amazement and grew pale.

But R. Paltiel laughingly turned to him and said before all gathered about him, "Why art thou disturbed; why dost thou rise from thy seat in amazement?"

The Greek envoy replied, "Because I have seen great damage done. There is no way of replacing the priceless bowl and dish that have been broken."

R. Paltiel then questioned him about the king of the Greeks, as to whether dishes of gold or of precious stone were used in his palace, and the Macedonian ambassador said, "Dishes of gold are used in my master's house."

To which R. Paltiel replied, "Thy master is a man of limited means. Dishes of precious stones and gems are more costly than dishes of gold; for those that are made of precious stone, cannot be restored when broken, but those of gold, when damaged, can be mended without loss; many dishes of rare stone and gems such as thou hast just seen broken in my house, are broken in the palace of my master, the Caliph." Thereupon he dismissed him with honor, to the King of Greece who had sent him.

R. Hananeel, the son of Paltiel, asked permission of the Caliph of If-rikiya to cross the sea and go to Italy, for at the time of the captivity of

Oria, those that were spared sought refuge in Bari and Otranto, bringing their household goods with them, and saving the money of others with their own. So R. Hananeel went to Constantinople, and, sorely depressed and afflicted, entreated the King to receive him with favor, to grant him the authority, under royal seal, to travel through all cities of his kingdom and, with his will and consent, enter any place in which he might find property belonging to him.

He took the sealed letter of authority and went to the city of Bari. There he found an old copy of the Scriptures that had been his, and ornaments of the clothes of women, and sewed garments that they wore. The teachers and sages of Bari disputed their possession with him, in accordance with the principle that he who saves anything from an invading army, from the water or the fire, may claim it as his own; for this was the teaching of Rab, in the interpretation of the Mishna.

He replied, "It is as you say, but our sages have also taught that 'the law of the land is the binding law'; here is the written edict with the seal, which the Emperor issued for me."

So they divided with him. They gave him the robes and the copy of the Scriptures, and he left them the remainder as a compromise. He went down to Beneventum and the entire community respectfully welcomed him. He remained there an entire year. Then he made his home there, and married one of its women, Esther, daughter of R. Shabbethai, of the family of R. Amittai.

In His mercy He turned in kindness, and bestowed His compassion and visited His favor and truth upon the house of R. Shephatiah and R. Hananeel, men of His choice, who, serving Him as long as they lived, did not stray from His law. For it is His promise to do good to those who look to His salvation and wait for His help. He favored him in his old age with worthy sons, R. Samuel, his first born, the beginning of his strength, and R. Shabbethai, and Papoleon, and Hasadiah. Hasadiah went to Ifrikiya with R. Paltiel, the son of his sister Cassia. R. Samuel came to the city of Capua and there married a woman named Albavera. Some time after, R. Shabbethai and Papoleon set out with the gift which was sent by the prince of Amalfi to R. Paltiel. After the manner of young men, they entered into conversation with the pilot of the ship, and said, "Let us write the Name, so that we may move at great speed, and reach the coast of Ifrikiya tonight."

So they wrote and pronounced the Name of Him that dwelleth on High, and cast the writing into the waters, and they said to the sailors, "Keep very close watch on us, that we do not fall asleep." But their sin brought calamity upon them and deep sleep fell upon them; a storm wind tossed them about on the water; the ship capsized and the men sank in deep waters. The power of the Name took the ship to Spain and Narbonne and to the sea of Constantinople; then brought it back to the sea of Ancona, and finally wrecked it before the city of Amalfi.

Upon the death of the ruler of Egypt, the elders of Egypt, through reliable couriers, wise and chosen messengers, sent a letter authorized by the princes and nobles and the people of the cities and villages to Al Muizz, Caliph of the Arabians, in which they said "We have heard of thy mighty deeds, the violence of thy wars, which thou hast waged in thy wisdom, of thy sagacity in which thou excellest the princes that formerly ruled over the kingdom of Egypt. Now, come to us, be king over us, with the consent of our princes and all the eminent men of our country; we will be thy subjects, thou shalt be our king."

He considered the proposal; R. Paltiel was summoned; and they took counsel together as to what they should do, for it was a long journey through a barren and desolate land; all the way there was no water; no supplies of food; no tents or places of shelter. R. Paltiel set out in advance and established the camps; he erected bazaars and places for lodging, appointed merchants for them, and supplied them with bread, water, fish, meat, garden produce, and everything necessary for soldiers coming from the distant cities. Then the Caliph and princes and courtiers set out; they pitched the tents of their encampment three miles from Egypt [Cairo].

All the nobles of Egypt joyfully came forth to greet them, their chiefs and governors, their officials and princes and the masses of the people as well. They came up to him and prostrated themselves. He made them take an oath of allegiance, by their law, and accepted their hostages, princes of the people. Then R. Paltiel entered Egypt with a division of the forces, detailed them on the walls and towers, that they might guard the city, the palace and public buildings, and appointed sentinels to be on guard, day and night, on the outskirts and the borders. And then the Caliph with all his army marched in. The nobles and all the people gathered about him, and again swore allegiance to him. He walked into the court and took his seat in his palace, on the throne of his dominion and majesty. They put the sceptre into his hand, and the royal crown upon his head, and he reigned over the kingdom of the South after his heart's desire.

Once, on the Day of Atonement, when R. Paltiel was called to read from the Torah, the whole assemblage arose and remained standing in his presence, the sages, the scholars that were in the school, the young students and the elders, the lads and children; the entire community was standing. He called to them saying, "Let the old be seated, and the young stand. If you refuse, I will sit down and refuse to read, for this does not seem right to me." When he finished reading, he vowed to the God of his praise 5000 dinars of genuine and full value; 1000 for the head of the academy and the sages, 1000 for the mourners of the sanctuary, 1000 for the academy of Geonim at Babylon, 1000 for the poor and needy of the various communities, and 1000 for the exaltation of the Torah, for the purchase of the necessary oil.

In the morning he arose early and hurried, for he was always zealous in observing the law, that his evil inclination might not prevail over him to prevent his carrying out his good intention; he engaged men and horses and mules, and provided guards, and sent them forth with the caravans that travelled through the deserts. And they delivered the gold pieces, as R. Paltiel their master had ordered, and distributed them among the schools and synagogs, and the mourners of Zion and the poor of the communities of Israel.

The growth of his authority which the king, through his bounty, had bestowed upon him over his royal domain, having appointed him ruler over the kingdom of Egypt and of Syria as far as Mesopotamia, and over all [that had once been] the land of Israel as far as Jerusalem, his eminence and power and wealth with which the king had honored and distinguished him, are recorded in the chronicles of the kingdom of Nof and Anamim [Egypt].

When Al Muizz was stricken with the sickness of which he was to die, he placed his son on the throne and entrusted him to R. Paltiel, his beloved minister, that he might be his adviser and helper and guardian, that he might govern the kingdom with vigor and success. The Caliph died and slept with his fathers and his son reigned in his stead. All his days had been passed in happiness and security, in peace and contentment.

When the young caliph sat upon the throne of his kingdom, the officials appointed to conduct the affairs of Egypt told him lying stories about R. Paltiel, continually striking at him with the sharp sword of their tongues, and covertly slandering him. The Caliph's fury raged against them; he repeatedly rebuked them. He told R. Paltiel, the prince, all they said. So together they devised a plan of dealing with them. R. Paltiel and his wife, and friends and all his family went out to his estate, the royal garden that the Caliph had presented to him.

In words of affection the Caliph asked, "Whither has our beloved R. Paltiel, the interpreter of mysteries, gone?"

The attendants assembled in the court answered "He has gone out for recreation, with his friends and all his kin, to the estate which the king has given him."

Thereupon the king summoned his magistrates, princes and courtiers, and said to them, "We will go and pay our respects to the venerable scholar in my service, R. Paltiel, so highly esteemed and worthy of honor at my hands."

He set out in his chariot and took with him all his lords and princes. The king did this with set purpose; all of this being done as a ruse, ordered by the word of the king, that he might find opportunity to show R. Paltiel his intense love for him, in the presence of the courtiers and princes of the people, to confound his accusers, and cover them with shame and confusion. And as the king drew near the tent of R. Paltiel, he commanded that no one should inform him until he reached the tent.

The king descended from the chariot and R. Paltiel approached him.

The king, out of his love for him, embraced, caressed and kissed him, and took hold of his hands. They walked away together and took their seats apart from the company. The others remained where they were. Then the jesters and players appeared; they took up the harps and timbrels and made merry before them with the pipes, with stringed instruments and songs, playing upon timbrels, cymbals and harps, from morning until the decline of the day in the afternoon, until evening when the shadow begins to move backward. The king then rode off and returned to Egypt [i.e., to the city]. So the face of the accusers was covered with confusion, the enemies and slanderers of R. Paltiel were put to shame. On that day their tongues were silenced, and they did not again speak ill of him. Praised be He that protecteth His saints, that redeemeth and saveth the soul of His servants. Praised be He and praised be His name; praised be the glory of God from His place.

One night R. Paltiel and the king were walking in the open and they saw three bright stars disappear; in an instant their light had vanished. And R. Paltiel said, "The stars that have been eclipsed represent three kings who will die this year; and they will soon be taken off. The first king is John the Greek, the second, the king of Bagdad, in the north"; then the king hastening to interrupt him said, "Thou art the third, the King of Teman," but he replied to the king, "No, my Lord, for I am a Jew; the third is the king of Spain." But the king said, "Thou art in truth the third, as I say."

And in that year R. Paltiel died, the leader of the community of the people of God, settled in Egypt and Palestine, in Palermo [Sicily] and in Africa, and in all the territory of the Arabians [Ishmael], for he ruled over the ancient kingdom of the Hebrews, over that of the Syrians and Egyptians, over the domain of the Arabians and the land of Israel. May his soul be bound in the bundle of life, secure in Eden, enclosed in the Garden of God, reposing by the side of the Patriarchs.

In his stead arose his son R. Samuel, a great man, highly esteemed in his day, worthily filling the place of his father. He brought the remains of his father and mother in caskets to Jerusalem, also the casket containing the bones of R. Hananeel, his father's uncle, which had been embalmed. He devoted to the Most High, that it might be counted as righteousness unto him, by Him that rideth upon the clouds, 20,000 drachmae for the poor and afflicted, for the sages and teachers giving instruction in the law, for the instructors of the children and the readers [of prayer]; and for the oil of the sanctuary, at the western wall of the inner altar, and for the synagogs and communities, far and near; for those who mourned the loss of the Temple, those who grieved and sorrowed for Zion; for the academy of the disciples and the teachers [in Palestine], and for the sages of Babylon in the academy of the Geonim. Blessed be his memory. May his life be prolonged, partaking of the feast of the living, sustained through the treasures of God. . . .

They had lived in Oria, in prosperity, for seventeen Jubilee [periods], when the king of the Arabians fell upon them, and expelled them from the land. . . . When their descendants came to Capua, God let them win the favor of their rulers; the rulers of the city took R. Samuel to their palace and appointed him supervisor of their treasury, that he should have jurisdiction in their realms, over the ports of the harbor, over the income of their markets, and over the finances of the various departments of the city. And the God of our fathers helped him. And he visited R. Paltiel at times to exchange greetings, and remained several days each time. God granted him rest on every hand and made him happy with the knowledge of the law of delight and enriched him with property. He was engaged with all his means in having Torah scrolls written and he erected houses of prayer. God gave him a worthy son, whom he named Paltiel, walking in the ways of God, devoted to the law of Israel. He did not stray from the ways of his father, and was steadfast in the fear of God, in wisdom and understanding; his home did not lack any of the blessings of God.

The prince appointed him governor and director of all the affairs of the city; over prince, noble, counsellor, judges, officials, and all administrators, over all of them he was chief magistrate. His was the authority to receive and dismiss, to direct and command. But he held fast to the statutes of God and His Law, and loved His commandments and ordinances, serving Him with all his heart; declaring His unity with all his soul. He restored the synagog of his grandfather as a house of prayer, for the glory of Him that dwelleth above.

He had no children; for those that had been born to him had died when they were but two or three years of age. In his anguish and affliction he prayed in fervent supplication to Him that inhabiteth the heavens. And God from the heavens of His splendor heard his prayer and cry, and in His mercy and kindness gave him an only son. He named him Ahimaaz. He sent him to school to be instructed in the Law, to give thought to the Scriptures, the unfailing testimony, to their wholesome teaching, their sublime commandments, to learn to observe their precepts.

And I, Ahimaaz, son of R. Paltiel, son of R. Samuel, son of R. Hananeel, son of R. Amittai, the servant of God; in the first month of the year 4814 (1054 C.E.) since the heavens were made, asked a boon of Him, that He might enlighten me in the mysteries of the everlasting delight, that He might confirm me in His perfect Law, handed down thousands of years ago; that He might lead me in the right path and help me; that He might hearken to my prayer, to let me succeed in finding the genealogy of my fathers. I looked to Him and trusted in His holy name and besought His grace and mercy.

He has granted the wish I have so ardently asked of Him. I have pondered and examined and have found what my heart desired, the lineage of my family. With God's help I have arranged and written it in poetic form. I have begun at the very beginning; from the captivity of Jerusalem and the destruction of the house of our glory, through the captivity of the city of Oria, in which I have settled, I have come down to the arrival of my fathers in Capua; and have ended with my own time and that of my children.

In the year 4814 of the creation of the world (1054 C.E.) which God has created, I compiled this book of my genealogy with the help of God, my Refuge, not by any wisdom that is in me, or intelligence of my own, but by the grace of the Lord God my Master.

Praised be He that giveth power to the faint and deliverance to him that hath no might.

Completed by Menahem son of Benjamin. May the Creator of the left and the right, be their help.

The Crusades of 1096

From the point of view of Western (in essence, Christian) literature, the Crusades were a glorious and romantic chapter in European history, as indicated by the plethora of literary material—in poetry and prose—lauding the achievements of single heroic knights and of the crusades as a whole. An entirely different picture is presented by the Jewish chroniclers of the First Crusade. The wanton massacres of Jews—and with few exceptions, the silence of the Pope and Church—as described by Jewish eyewitnesses, makes all the romanticism turn to ash.

Solomon bar Simson's report is one of the few Jewish primary sources for a history of the crusaders' effect on the Jews, and is among the first and most informative portrayals of the First Crusade. This is Solomon bar Simson's only work—nothing else is known of him—and it is extant only in a single manuscript; however, most of the facts are confirmed by non-Jewish accounts. The author states that he wrote his chronicle in 1140—some 44 years after the First Crusade—upon reports of elders who were eyewitnesses to the events.

The martyrdom in the chronicle is representative of one of two polar (but equally noble and saintly) reactions toward violence in the long history of Israel. One is the acceptance of martyrdom for the sanctification of God's name *(kiddush ha-shem)*, as seen in Masada (see "The Fall of Masada," p. 59) in Solomon bar Simson's account, and in the singing of "I Believe" by defenseless Jews on their way to the gas chambers. The other, which has an equally long history, is the spirit of revolt as is evidenced by the Maccabees, Bar Kochba, and in modern times, the ghetto and death-camp revolts, the underground fighters in Europe, and the battles of survival in the State of Israel.

THE CRUSADES OF 1096

And now I shall begin to relate how destruction came upon the congregations who let themselves be slain for the sake of the name of the Eternal, and how with their whole souls they clung to the Eternal, the God of their fathers, and acknowledged Him, the One, with their last breath.

It came to pass in the year 4856, which is the year 1096 according to the calendar of the nations. In that year, trusting the prophecies of Jeremiah, we were expecting consolation and help in our exile. Joy was turned into sorrow and into mourning and lamentation. All the terrors with which we are threatened in the books of the Torah descended upon us, all that is written came to pass with that which is not written; over us and our sons and our daughters, our old men and boys, the great among us and the humble, came desolation.

It was the impious Pope [Urban II] of Rome who arose and issued a call to all the peoples, the sons of Edom [Christians], who believe in the Christ bidding them to gather and fare forth toward Yerushelaim [Jerusalem] and conquer the city in order that they might freely go on pilgrimage to the grave of Him whom they have made their God. The command was obeyed; the nations gathered. Their numbers were as the sands of the shore and their voice like the roar of the storm.

It was now that there arose that Duke Godfrey of Bouillon—may his bones be crushed!—a ruthless man, driven by the spirit of evil to join him with these dissolute hordes. For he swore a great oath that wherever he came he would revenge the blood of his God upon the blood of Israel and leave of the seed of our people neither remnant nor fugitive.

Among us was raised up one who sought to stem the danger, one who feared God and was worthy of eternal joy, Rabbi Kalonymos, who presided over the congregation of Mainz. Swiftly he despatched messengers to Heinrich, the emperor, who had been lingering in Italy for nine years. The emperor was wroth and sent letters to all the provinces of the empire commanding the princes and viceroys and above all, Duke Godfrey, to keep the peace and to protect the Jews and to grant them help and refuge against the rabble. The impious Duke swore that it had never been in his soul to so much as pluck a hair from a Jew's head. Moreover, the congregation of Cologne gave him five hundred marks of fine silver and the congregation of Mainz as much again, and he pledged his honor to protect them and keep the peace . . .

But He whose name is Peace had departed from us; He hid His eye from

His people and delivered it up unto the sword. No prophet nor seer nor any man however wise or learned, can fathom why the sins of our people weighed so heavily that the holy congregations had to suffer as though blood-guiltiness were upon them. But He is a just Judge; ours, ours must have been the guilt . . .

First came an insolent rabble of Christians, a raging mob of Frenchmen and Germans who had taken it into their minds to fare forth to the Holy City and to drive out from thence the sons of Ishmael [Mohammedans]. They fastened a cross upon their garments, both men and women, and they were numerous as locusts upon the earth.

Whenever upon their way they came into cities in which Jews had their dwellings, each said to the other, "Here we are setting out on so long a journey toward the grave of the Lord and meaning to be revenged upon the Ishmaelites. And behold, in our very midst dwell the Jews who hung Him innocent upon the cross and slew Him. Let us be up and doing the revenge ourselves first upon them; let us stamp them out from among the peoples so that the name of Israel be no more remembered. Or else let them become even as ourselves and accept our faith."

When the congregation heard such speech they did after the manner of our fathers, exercising themselves in penitence and prayer and charitable deeds. But the hands of the holy people wearied and their hearts misgave them and their strength went out of them. They hid themselves from the sword in their innermost chambers and mortified themselves with penitential fasts. Three days they fasted, both day and night until their skin clung to their bones and they were thin as faggots. They cried aloud and wept in the bitterness of their hearts, but their Father heard them not. He rejected the tents of Israel; a cloud was round about His countenance; for this matter was fated and a punishment for old sins. And He had chosen this generation because it had the strength to bear witness in His temple, to fulfill His word, to sanctify the ineffable Name. It is concerning such that David spoke: Praise the Lord, ye messengers, ye heroes who are mighty to fulfill His word.

It came to pass on the day of the new moon of the month of Sivan that Count Emicho, the oppressor of all Jews—may his bones be ground in a mill of iron!—came with mercenaries and Crusaders and villagers and set up his tents outside the walls of the city, for the gates had been barred. He was our sorest enemy who had mercy neither on old men nor virgins nor suckling babes nor the sick, who was bent on stamping the people of God into the mire and he put our youths to the sword and ripped open the bellies of our women who were with child. He wore the Crusader's cross and was a leader of armies. He feigned that a messenger of the Crucified had appeared to him and set a sign upon his flesh and promised to wait for him in Sicily, there to crown him with the crown of empire in token that all his enemies were overcome. For two days he besieged the city.

Learning of the arrival of this impious one, the elders of the congregation of Mainz hastened once more to the bishop and bribed him with three hundred marks of fine silver, beseeching him to remain in the city, for it had been his plan to visit the villages of his diocese. He invited all the congregation into the great hall of his palace and vowed to stand by them. The count of the citadel too declared that he would protect the Jews until the crusaders should have fared onward, but stipulated that the Jews were to bear the costs. To this the Jews agreed and both the bishop and the count declared that they would, if need be, die with them. Furthermore, the congregation determined to give money to the impious Emicho as well, and to assure him in a writing that the other congregations upon his way would pay him equal honors. "Perhaps," they said, "God will still show us mercy." Thus to the bishop and his officers and to divers of the townspeople they gave four hundred marks of silver and to the impious Emicho they sent seven pounds of pure gold. But it was all of no avail.

It was on that third day of Sivan which once, when the Torah was given us, was a day of sanctification and separateness for Israel; upon this day it was also granted to the saints of the congregation of Mainz, separated and purified, to ascend unto God together. In their death they were not divided. All were in the bishop's great hall when the wrath of God arose against them like a flame. In one place they were gathered together. With them were the Torah and greatness of soul, wealth and honor, wisdom and humility, charity and faith. All were mown down. They were destroyed as were the sons of Yerushelaim when the Temple and the city fell.

At the hour of noon the cruel Emicho moved against the city with his hordes, and the citizens opened the gates. "Behold, the gates are opened of their own accord," said our enemies. "Thus doth the Crucified to be revenged upon the blood of the Jews." With fluttering banners the army drew up before the bishop's castle. But the sons of the holy covenant knew no trembling in the face of these mighty numbers of the enemy. All of them strong or weak, put on armor and girded on swords. Rabbi Kalonymos ben Meshullam led them. And Rabbi Menachem ben David Halevi, one of the great men of his age, said, "Do you sanctify the ineffable Name in perfect devotion!" Thereupon they proceeded towards the gate in order to fight against the Crusaders and the townsmen. Cruelly the combat raged. But by reason of our sins our enemies prevailed against us and streamed into the castle. The bishop's men, pledged to help us, fled and delivered us into the hands of the wicked. The bishop himself fled into his church, for they threatened him because he had spoken in favor of the Jews.

May darkness devour the memory of that dread day! May God forget the name of that day and let no light shine upon it forever! Why were ye not extinguished, O constellations, ere ye lit the earth for our foes?

When the sons of the holy covenant saw that their fate was about to be fulfilled since their murderers swarmed into the court, they lifted up their voices—old men and youths, virgins and children, men servants and maid servants—and wept. But they submitted to the decrees of the Eternal and urged each the other to take upon him the yoke of Israel's martyrdom. And their one deep fear was that the weakness of the human flesh under the extremity of torture might keep any from sanctifying the ineffable Name. Therefore they all cried, cried even as one man and with a loud voice, "We dare delay no longer, for the enemy is upon us. Let us hasten and sacrifice ourselves to the Lord. Whoever has a knife, let him first slay us and then himself."

The first upon whom the enemies came in the courtyard were some of the most devout, among them that great scholar, Rabbi Yitzchak ben Moshe. These pious men had disdained to flee into the inner chambers in order to buy one more hour of life. Nay, they sat wrapped in their praying shawls ready to fulfill the will of their Maker. The enemies first overwhelmed them with stones and arrows and then hewed them down with their swords. When those in the inner chambers saw the great patience of these saints they cried, "The time has come!" The women girded their loins with strength and slew first their sons and their daughters and then themselves. Many men, too, plucked up courage and slew their wives and their children and their servants. Gentle and delicately nurtured women slew each her favorite child. Men and women slew each other. And girls and young men and women who were betrothed looked out of the windows and cried, "Behold, O God, what we do to sanctify Thy holy Name and to avoid being forced to acknowledge the Crucified!" Some slew and some were slain; the streams of their blood flowed and the blood of men was commingled with that of their wives, of fathers with that of their children, of brothers with that of their sisters, of teachers with that of their pupils, of children and babes with that of their mothers. All were slaughtered upon that day for the sake of the Oneness of the dreadful Name of God. He who hears thereof, is not his very soul shaken? For what has man seen in all ages like unto this thing? Ask whether since the days of Adam there was a martyrdom like this? Eleven hundred were sacrificed on one day. Each was like the sacrifice of Isaac, the son of Abraham, which made the foundations of the universe to tremble. Why then did not the heavens grow dark and the light of the stars go out and the sun and the moon die in their stations on that third day of Sivan when eleven hundred souls were slain in martyrdom—children, among them, oh so many, and the little babes, the poor innocents who had not yet sinned? Canst Thou let such things be, O Lord? Were they not slain for the sake of Thee? Avenge, O Lord, the blood of Thy servants soon, in our days, for our eyes to behold! Amen.

Has human ear heard a tale like unto that of the deeds of that young woman named Rachel, the daughter of Rabbi Yitzchak ben Asher and the wife of Rabbi Yehuda? "I have four children," she said to her friends. "Spare them not for the Christians to catch them alive and make renegades of them. Let them, too, sanctify the Name!" But when one of her friends took up the knife to slay one of the children, the young mother cried aloud and beat her head and breasts. "Where is Thy loving kindness, O Lord?" she cried. And in her despair she spoke to her friend, "Oh, do not kill Isaac before the eyes of Aaron. He must not see his brother's death!" But when little Aaron ran away, she nevertheless took Isaac, who was the younger and fair to look upon, and killed him and caught his blood in her sleeves as in a ewer. Aaron, seeing this, nevertheless, tried to hide behind a chest. The woman also had two very lovely young daughters, Bella and Madrona. These took up the knife of their mother and bent back their white throats and besought her to sacrifice them. When now she had slain three of her dear children, Rachel called to her last child, to Aaron, "Where are you, my son? I dare not spare you!" And by his foot she drew him forth from behind the chest where he was hidden and sacrificed him unto the God. When her husband saw the death of his four lovely children he went and cast himself upon a sword and his entrails oozed forth from his quivering body. But the mother hid her dead children two in each of her wide sleeves, and sat her down and lamented. When the enemies came into the room they roared, "Give us the gold, Jew wench, which is doubtless hidden in thy sleeves!" But when they saw the dead children they struck down Rachel, the mother, with one blow, so that she perished without a moan. . . .

In that year the Passover fell upon a Thursday and the first day of the new moon of the month of Iyar on a Friday. It was on the Sabbath, on the eighth of Iyar that the judgment came upon us. The Crusaders, joining themselves with the townsfolk, arose first against the holy and pious congregation of Speyer, thinking to catch all in the house of prayer. But the Jews, getting word of this, rose early on the morning of the Sabbath, prayed hurriedly, and left the house of prayer. The enemies, seeing that their plan had failed, fell upon the Jews and slew eleven of them. Thus the fatality began.

When the evil news came to Worms that eleven men of Speyer had been slain, the people of Worms cried to the Lord and raised a great and bitter weeping, for they saw that Heaven had determined their destruction and that there was no way out, neither forward nor backward. The congregation divided itself into two parts; one part fled for refuge in the bishop's castle; the other part remained in their houses because the townsmen had promised them protection. But these promises were false and treacherous and like a broken reed. The townsmen had an understanding with the Crusaders that our name and our remnants were to be obliterated. "Fear them not," they spoke to us, "for whoever slays one of you will have to answer us with his life." By fair speeches they made all flight impossible. Relying on their faith, the Jews put into their hands all their goods and precious things, for the sake of which the townsmen betrayed them afterwards.

On the tenth day of Iyar those wolves of the desert attacked those who had remained in their houses and exterminated them—men, women, and children, young and old; they hurled them down the stairs and hacked down the houses and plundered and looted; they stole the scrolls of the Torah and stamped them into the mud and plundered and burned them and left death and horror behind them where the children of Israel had dwelled.

On the twenty-fifth of Iyar the terror came over those who had taken refuge in the house of the bishop. The enemies tortured them like the others and delivered them over unto the sword. But they had been fortified by the example of their brethren and accepted death and sanctified the Name. They stretched forth their heads to be hewn off in the Name of their Creator; and many too laid hands of violence upon themselves and their most dear. One slew his brother; another his kinsman or his wife and his children; bridegrooms slew their brides and tender mothers their little ones. All accepted from the depth of their hearts the judgment of God and commending their souls to their Maker, cried in a loud voice: Hear O Israel, the Eternal is our God, the Eternal is One. The enemies stripped them naked and dragged and hurled them about; they left none save a few whom they forced to accept baptism. Eight hundred was the number of the slain on these two days; naked they were thrown into a common grave. They fell by the hand of God. He brought them to their rest, to the great light in the Garden of Eden. Behold their souls are in the covenant of life with the Eternal Who made them even unto the end of days.

Now when the pious men of the great congregation of Mainz, shield and refuge of our exile, famous through many lands—when they heard of the slaughter of the saints in Speyer and in Worms, they were at first stricken and their hearts turned to water and they cried to God with a great cry. Thereafter they met together and chose wise men out of their midst to take council how the evil might be averted. Those chosen men determined to ransom the lives of the congregation by giving their entire fortunes as bribes to the princes, the governors, the bishops, and the counts. The heads of the congregation who were well seen at the bishop's court went thither and spoke to him and to the officers of his household and asked them what they should do to escape the fate of their brethren in Speyer and Worms. The answer was, "Take our advice. Bring all your fortunes into our treasuries and do you, with your wives and sons and daughters and all who are with you come into the house of the bishop and stay there until the Crusaders have passed by. Thus you will be secure." They spoke thus, but their words were lies. They brought us into their power; they caught us as fishermen catch fishes in a net in order to rob us of our money, as afterwards they did. Thus the event explained the beginning. Only the bishop was honestly inclined to put forth his power in our favor. But had we not given great gifts to him and his servitors for their promise to protect us? But neither bribes nor pleas availed in the end nor guarded us when the day of wrath came. . . .

Responsa

Responsa (from the Hebrew, *she'elot u'teshuvot*—literally, "questions and answers"), one of the oldest and most widespread genres in Hebrew religio-literary creativity, are questions addressed to scholars and rabbinic authorities either by individuals or communities who sought resolution of difficult problems in line with Jewish law. Although the responsa literature is basically a post-Talmudic development, there is evidence in the Talmud of the existence of responsa or some similar form of written communication. The Talmud (*Sanhedrin* 11b) states that R. Gamaliel told his scribe to "write an epistle" to three communities to inform them of the leap year. The same tractate (29a) relates that in the midst of a debate in Babylonia, one of the disputants declared "we can produce a letter from the West [Palestine] that the halakha does not rest with R. Judah." Further, the Jerusalem Talmud (*Kedoshin* 83:12) states that R. Tanhum bar Poppe sent two questions concerning the lineage of two families in Alexandria to R. Yose.

The responsa may be seen as an extension of the halakhic activity that began with the Torah and continued with the Mishnah and Gemara. In writing their responsa rabbis based their decisions on Torah and Talmud passages and other extant legal literature; and, in turn, their decisions were considered precedents by later authorities. The questions were mainly practical ones for which there was no precise statute in either the Talmud or the codes of law, and for which a legal decision was necessary; at other times they were not directly juridical, but touched upon science, the development of tradition (see "The Letter of Sherira Gaon"), mathematics, geography, and textual interpretation.

The early stage of responsa literature developed during the period of the Gaonim in Babylonia; thereafter, responsa became widespread in the European centers of Jewish scholarship, France, Germany, Spain and Italy, and were written by such famous rabbis as Alfasi, Rashi, Rabbenu Gershom, Maimonides and Nachmanides. (The rabbis' disciples usually kept a copy of their masters' remarks and thus helped to preserve them.) Most responsa were written in Hebrew, although some appear in Arabic; but only a fraction of the vast number of extant responsa manuscripts have been published.

Besides describing religious life, responsa also offer a portrait of the times, as well as the life and mind of the writer. Not intentionally historiographic, the responsa in their detailed remarks often present vivid facts about their communities and eras. Responsa are still being written in our own day, and contemporary ones include such futuristic questions as prayer in a spaceship (the criteria for determining therein time and direction, so mandatory for prescribed prayers).

The responsa that follow, written by the most illustrious rabbis and scholars of their day, cover several centuries and deal with various social, economic, intellectual and ethical problems.

LETTER OF SHERIRA GAON (986 C.E.)

[HEADING FROM THE OXFORD MANUSCRIPT:]
Isaac, son of Nissim, son of Josiah, turned with a question to our lord Sherira, head of the Yeshiva; [he asked it] in the name of the sacred congregation of Kairawan; and he [i.e., Sherira] ordered that the response be written here, in the year [986 C.E.] . . .

QUESTION:

As for your question, namely: How was the Mishna written? Did the men of the Great Synagogue begin to write it and the sages of succeeding generations write part of it until Rabbi Judah the Prince came and completed it? But if this is so, and since most of its text is anonymous, why are we taught that the anonymous parts of the Mishna were written by Rabbi Meir [Sanh. 86a]? Besides, most of the rabbis who are mentioned in the Mishna—Rabbi Meir, Rabbi Judah, Rabbi Yose and Rabbi Simeon—all of them were pupils of Rabbi Akiba, and the rules that the rabbis of the Talmud taught us that the law is according to Rabbi Akiba when he disagrees with his colleagues, and according to Rabbi Judah the Prince in preference to his colleagues. All of these lived at the end of the time of the Second Commonwealth. If so [if all the authors mentioned lived so late,] why did the more ancient rabbis leave so much to the later rabbis; and all the more [it is significant] if nothing of the Mishna was written until the end of the days of Rabbi Judah the Prince.

[The question implies that since the rabbis mentioned in the Mishna are all late and since the Mishna was not written down until the day of Rabbi Judah the Prince, it would be difficult indeed to answer the charge of the Karaites that the Mishna is not ancient tradition at all.]

Furthermore [the question continues], although the arrangement of the six main Orders of the Mishna are logical, what reason is there for the [seemingly illogical] arrangement of the tractates within these six Orders? Why, for example, was the tractate Yoma [dealing with the Day of Atonement] placed before the tractate Shekalim [which should precede discussion of the Passover]? And why does Sukkah come before the tractate Yom Tov? And why do both of them precede Rosh Hashanah? Thus [our question covers] all the tractates which are not in sequential relationship with the other tractates according to content.

274

Furthermore, as to the Tosefta, which we have heard was written by Rabbi Hiyyah, was it written after the sealing of the Mishna or was it written at the same time as the Mishna? And why did Rabbi Hiyya write it since it contains, though generally in a fuller form, the same material which expounds the material in the Mishna, why did Rabbi Judah himself omit it and fail to include it in the Mishna? Is not all of this material [in the Tosefta] quoted in the names of the same rabbis who are mentioned in the Mishna?

And similarly, how were the baraitot [material similar to Mishna and Tosefta, but quoted only in the Talmud] written? And also, how did the Talmud come to be written? And so the saboraim? What was their order after Rabina? (Saboraim were the first post-talmudic rabbis, and Rabina was among the last talmudic rabbis.) And who bore authority after them? And how many years was each of them in authority from that time up to today?

(In other words, the community of Kairawan asked for a complete history of the development of the talmudic literature from its beginning and also, by implication, for the proper defense of its antiquity and its authenticity.)

ANSWER:

Our view is as follows: The saintly Rabbi Judah certainly arranged the six Orders of the Mishna so that we might study the laws one after the other, without intending to add or to diminish. For thus it is said in the Talmud [Yeb. 64b]: "When was the Mishna fixed? In the days of Rabbi (Judah the saintly Prince)." As for your question: Why did the earlier rabbis leave so much to the later rabbis? [As is evidenced by the fact that the rabbis mentioned in the Mishna were all contemporaries or pupils of Rabbi Akiba, which might imply that the Mishna is not ancient at all.]

The earlier rabbis did not leave much for the later rabbis to do [i.e., to innovate], but all of the later rabbis studied and interpreted the words of the earlier rabbis [i.e., they merely expounded; they did not create the tradition]. For when Hillel the Elder was appointed by the B'nai Bathera as prince over them, he said to them [Pes. 66a]: "What led to my being chosen prince over you? It was your own laziness, in that you did not serve sufficiently under the two great men of your generation, Shemaya and Abtalyon" [i.e., the knowledge had already been available in an earlier generation, but they did not take advantage of it].

The reason that the older rabbis are not mentioned by name, except for their prince and the head of the court, was that there never was any controversy among them. They knew thoroughly all the reasons for the teachings of the Torah and they knew the whole Talmud completely, and all the arguments, and they were careful in their study of every subject; for we see [B.B. 134a] that there were eighty disciples of Hillel the Elder, thirty of them were worthy that the Divine Presence should rest upon them as it did upon Moses our teacher; and thirty of them were worthy that the sun should stand still for them as it did for Joshua; and twenty were average.

The greatest of them was Jonathan the son of Uziel and the least of them was Yohanan ben Zakkai. And they said about Yohanan ben Zakkai (the least of them all) that there was not a single text of Scripture that he did not know, nor Mishna, nor Talmud, nor laws, nor narratives, nor text details of the Torah or of the scribes, of all the arguments a fortiori and analogies and proverbs, etc., all matters great and small, and even the arguments of Abbaye and Rava (who lived four hundred years after his time). This tells us that even the arguments of Abbaye and Rava were not original with them, but were all well known to the ancients.

(Thus Sherira indicates that the total tradition recorded now in the rabbinic books was all known to the ancients; and the tradition, therefore, is authentic. If their names are not mentioned, it was because there was no need to record their names. In later times the names of various rabbis were recorded in order to explain who took one side of a controversy and who took the other. But among the ancients there was no controversy; they all possessed full knowledge. Now Sherira goes on to explain why it was necessary for Rabbi Judah the Prince to reorganize this vast material which presumably was perfect from the very beginning. He proceeds as follows:)

When the Temple was in existence, each one of the great teachers would explain to his disciples the reasons for the laws of the Torah, Mishna, and Talmud. Each teacher would put it in the words that appealed to him at the time, and thus taught it to his disciples so that they could understand. Abundant wisdom was then available and they needed no other effort [than just to explain the Law, each in his own words]. The dispute as to the laying on of hands was the only dispute among them [i.e., hands laid upon the sacrifice on the holidays, whether such action was permitted on the holidays or not, that is, whether or not it was a violation of the requirements of rest on the festivals].

When Shammai and Hillel arose there were only three matters that they disagreed on [Shab. 14b]. Then came the time of Bethar [i.e., the Bar Kokhba revolt] and Bethar was destroyed and the rabbis were scattered in every direction. Because of these disturbances and persecutions and confusions, there were many disciples who never studied long enough with their teachers. Hence controversies arose among them.

(Sherira then proceeds to mention other controversies due to other persecutions and confusions, resulting in lack of time for sufficient study, and hence the increase of disputes. He continues down to the destruction of the thousands of pupils of Rabbi Akiba and continues from there, as follows:)

Rabbi Meir was more learned and more keen than all of them and Rabbi Akiba ordained him even though he was still young . . .

[He continues with the generation of Rabbi Meir and the following one, coming down to Rabbi Judah the Prince; and he writes:]

After the great calamity of the destruction of the Temple and the doubts that arose due to all the confusions of the time and all the divisions that arose in those three generations when the Law was not settled among the rabbis, there became known among the rabbis the words of individuals and the words of the majority. The rabbis went to great trouble to gather the exact wording of the Mishna; but they did not add anything to the words of the men of the Great Synagogue. They toiled and searched to bring to light what those ancients had said and what they had done, until all those doubts [which had arisen in the three generations of confusion] were finally cleared up for them.

Not one of the ancients had written down his own original opinion, until the end of the days of Rabbi Judah [when it was recorded]. Nor had they all taught in the same phraseology, but they all gave the reasons for the laws which were well known to them and all were unanimous as to the meaning. They knew what was the word of the majority and what were the opinions of the individuals, but the wording was not fixed so that all might study in the same language. It was the meanings and the explanations that were known to them.

[He proceeds to show how each rabbi taught in his own words and how much greater was the mentality of the ancients than that of their successors. Since they all knew all of the material, there was no real controversy among them. And then he continues:]

The rabbis found peace in the days of Rabbi Judah the Prince because of the friendship between Antoninus [Pius, the Roman emperor] and Rabbi Judah; and he decided to arrange the laws so that thereafter all the rabbis would use the same phraseology and no longer teach each in his own phrasing. The ancient rabbis did not need this [uniformity of phrasing] since it was all Oral Law, and its explanations were not given to them in fixed language, as was the Written Law. They knew the reasons [of the Oral Law] by heart, and each taught them to his disciples in any language he wished to use, as a man converses with his neighbour. In the days of Rabbi, help came [i.e., from Heaven] and they arranged and wrote down these words of the Mishna just as Moses had done at the dictation of God as a sign and a miracle. Not of his own invention did he [Rabbi] compose it; for the words that had been taught by the ancients were all before him.

[The rest of the responsum goes on to discuss the development of the other rabbinic books, leading to the development of the Talmud and to the post-talmudic era of the gaonim. And he concludes with a benediction extended to the congregation of Kairawan for its deliverance and blessing.]

The process and the justification and the grounds for authority of the Oral Law were thus made by Sherira Gaon in his answer to the community of Kairawan substantially as follows:

The entire talmudic tradition as we have it was already in its totality known to the ancients. Their names are not mentioned because they had no substantial disagreements. However, each one taught his disciples orally in his own language. In the centuries of confusion due to persecutions and national misfortunes, the various disciples would cite the words of their respective rabbis as they remembered them; but they had not studied sufficiently to recognize that, in spite of the difference of language, all the ancients agreed with one another. Therefore special work was needed to rediscover the true tradition; and when this was finally achieved, Rabbi Judah arranged the material in the fixed text which is the Mishna.

RABBENU GERSHOM BEN JUDAH (960–1040)
A RABBI'S LIVELIHOOD

QUESTION:

As for your question which is as follows: "Reuben" had a *maarufia* [a customer who was his alone] with certain priests for many years.

This Reuben was a scholar. He taught Torah to the public without pay. His students, becoming aware of the profit that he made through his *maarufia*, trespassed into it, to his loss. [They sought to take these private customers away from him.] Complaint was made against the students and the community forced them, by ban and decree, to break off all contact with the *maarufia*. But the question that was in doubt was whether they [the community] had the right to exclude the rest of the people who were not his disciples [from trespassing into this business].

ANSWER:

From your question it is possible to infer that in your locality you do not have the general custom of *maarufia*. [In those localities where the custom prevailed, there would have been no question of anyone trespassing on anybody else's *maarufia*.] Since you do not have that custom in your community, no one can compel the community to allow him (Reuben) to keep this business to himself.

Rab Huna said in the Talmud [B.B. 21b]: "If one who lives in a gateway and sets up a mill and another one comes into that gateway and sets one up by his side, the law is that he can be prevented from doing so, for the first one can say to him, 'You are cutting off my livelihood.'" Yet [though Huna said that the law is not according to him, because they [the other scholars] raised the following objection to him [in the same talmudic passage]: "If a man establishes a store beside the store of his fellow, etc.," and in that discussion they traced the dispute to earlier scholars and concluded that it was Simon ben Gamaliel who said originally that one can prevent even one's neighbor (from opening a competitive store next door); nevertheless the law in that earlier dispute is not according to Simon ben Gamaliel, but according to the preceding scholar who said that one cannot prevent the competitor from opening the store. (Thus the law is in general that you cannot prevent a competing neighbor from opening a store next to yours.)

Nevertheless (although that is the law), it applies only in localities where they do not have the custom of allowing a man to have a monopoly; but in places where they do have the custom [he may prevent a competitor from opening the store, since] everything depends upon the customs of the province.

Furthermore, the right of free competition applies to men in general, but not to a scholar who engages in the Torah and in the affairs of Heaven. It is proper to give such a person special status in order that he may not be distracted from his study. For Rabbi Nahman said [ibid., 22a] that you may not prevent peddlers from opening a stall. Even the citizens of a city where the peddlers are strangers may not prevent them, since Ezra the Scribe arranged for peddlers to travel from city to city (the Talmud says Ezra arranged it so that the daughters of Israel might be able to buy ornaments). The peddlers may not be prevented from traveling about, but they can be prevented from establishing a settled business [next to a store that already exists. This applies to ordinary peddlers], but if the traveling merchant is a scholar, then he is permitted to establish even a fixed [competing] business.

Also we are told [ibid.] that Rab Dimi of Nahardea brought a shipment of dried grapes to Mahusa by ship and the exilarch said to Rava: "If Rab Dimi is a scholar, give him a monopoly." Further it is said [Yoma 72b] Rabbi Yohanan compared two verses: Make for thyself an ark of wood [Ex. 25:10 (i.e. that Moses should make the Ark of the Covenant himself)]. But another verse [Deut. 10:1] says: Let them make an ark of acacia wood [here, using the plural, the verse indicates that the people should make it for Moses]. This proves [said Rabbi Yohanan] that the people of a city are commanded to do a scholar's work for him. Therefore Rabbi Yohanan concludes as follows: How do we describe a scholar? One whose townsmen are commanded to do his [secular] work for him; which means that the scholar is one who neglects his own secular affairs and engages in the affairs of Heaven.

For all these reasons we can conclude that the community is in duty bound to make a special arrangement for this scholar whose work is the work of Heaven and who teaches the Torah in public without pay. They must make arrangements so that he should not be disturbed from his studies. They should decree against the entire community (not only against his own pupils, who owe him a special debt) that they must abstain from interfering with his *maarufia*. They will receive a reward for this and enjoy a long life. As it is written [Prov. 3:18]: It is a tree of life for those who take hold of it and those who support it are happy.

ISAAC ALFASI (1013–1103)
CONTRACT WITH A TEACHER

QUESTION:

Reuben and his wife and sons originally dwelt in eastern France, many days journey from Spain.

He [Reuben] left his wife and his sons in their native place and was content to wander through the communities in the land of Spain. He came to a certain province [in Spain] and preached in public. When five of the leaders of the community met him, they urged him to bring his wife and his sons to that province and dwell among them [i.e., to become their teacher]. But Reuben hesitated because his wife was far away [and the expense of bringing his family would be great]. But they continued to try and persuade him, and he ultimately agreed. They contracted with him, by formal contract.

They agreed to give him 24 gold pieces, maravedis, every year for a term of three years; and he agreed to read before them Halakhah [i.e., some legal compendium or the Talmud], the Mishna and Scriptures, to expound the weekly portion, and to do whatever else they agreed upon, in writing, and in the presence of witnesses. Reuben further agreed, formally, that he and his wife and his sons would come to the community by the festival of Sukkot. When the time fixed upon came, he arrived and they welcomed him joyously. Some of them said: Let us begin by studying the Mishna; others said: let us begin by studying the Talmud. Finally they all agreed [on the course of study]: they began with the tractate Berakhot ["Blessings," the first tractate of the Talmud] which they would study for four days out of the seven; on the fifth day, Scriptures; on the sixth day, interpretation of the weekly portion.

[It was customary to study the weekly portion on Friday, to be prepared for the public reading of it the next day in the synagogue.]

But after that, one of them, Issakhar, quarreled with his neighbor and said to him, "I cannot understand the profound Halakhah and I do not want it." And instead [of four full days of Talmud], he suggested, let there be read out to them [to the class] three lines of Talmud and then three lines of Mishna. But his companions said, "We do not want that" [scaling down our course of study]. Thereupon Issakhar arose and said, "I do not desire to read [i.e., to study] and I will not pay my share." Thereupon Reuben [the teacher] answered and said, "I have a formalized written contract in my hands, and witnesses. I may do no other than fulfill what is in my contract and what I had agreed upon with you."

ANSWER:

We studied this question and investigated all the conditions set forth in it. We see that they are strong and valid and that it is obligatory upon you to fulfill all the conditions that you made between you. As for Issakhar, who changed his mind and does not wish to fulfill the conditions which he agreed to together with his fellows, he has not done right. He is obligated to give Reuben all that he has taken upon himself as his part of the pay. If [when he has paid his share] he wishes to sit and study on the conditions that he had made, then all is well. If not, he has no complaint against Reuben, for note that he, Reuben, did not present an obstacle [to the fulfilment of the contract].

Now, although we learn in the Mishna: "He who hires workmen and they deceive one another [as to wages, etc.] they have against each other nothing but murmurings."

[i.e., they have no legal recourse, except that they can grumble about it. Of course, each of them the workmen or the employer, is free to abandon the contract. In other words, under these circumstances, the contract can be voided. But there can be no suit. All they have against each other are complaints.]

But where does this apply [i.e., that they can void the agreement if they feel they have been misled]? It applies only when the workmen have not yet begun their work, but if they have already begun to work, the employer cannot withdraw from the arrangement. As we learn: "Where does this apply [that they can do no more than complain and withdraw], only where the workmen have not gone down to work?"

"If, for example, the donkey-drivers have started out, but did not find the grain [which they were to transport], or the farm-laborers went out and found the field wet [so that they could not work], then he must pay them their wages." So here in the case of this Reuben [the teacher], if they had changed their mind before he had transplanted his family, they would be able to do so. Since, however, he has brought them from their native place and spent his money to bring them and furthermore, has actually begun his new employment, now they can no longer retract and are in duty bound to pay him according to all the conditions.

And, in fact, even if he had not yet gone [to fetch his family], since he has the contract they are no longer permitted to change their minds, as it is said [Zeph. 3:13]: The remnant of Israel will not do wrong nor speak falsehood, nor will deception be found in their mouth. [This verse is frequently quoted in the legal literature when an appeal is made to conscience and decency, beyond the strict requirements of the Law]. Of course, the court cannot rely merely upon their words; but if it is explained [to a court] that he has already gone [to his native town] and sold his chattels and spent money because of them, they are not permitted to deceive him, but are in duty bound to fulfill all the conditions that they had made with him.

As for Issakhar, if they wish, they can do him a kindness, provided Reuben agrees with them [they might make a special arrangement for Issakhar]. This would be doing a great kindness, since they are not in duty bound to go beyond the law by setting aside a special time for him alone. Also, Reuben is not in duty bound to teach him individually, for he had only contracted to teach all of them together, but not to teach each one separately. Therefore, if Issakhar wishes to sit and learn, let him sit and learn. If not, let him give his share of the pay for the teaching.

RABBENU TAM (JACOB BEN MEIR——1100–1171)

DIVORCE FROM AN APOSTATE

[The responsum here cited deals with the troublesome question of obtaining a divorce for a Jewish woman from a husband who had become an apostate. Since by Jewish Law the marital rights of a husband are his by virtue of having been born a Jew (or by conversion to Judaism), the fact that he had abandoned Judaism does not diminish his power to grant a divorce to his wife. The responsum reveals a number of important circumstances. First, it demonstrates Rabbenu Tam's strongmindedness: with characteristic forthrightness he addresses an older scholar (his kinsman, Rabbi Yom-Tov) and does not hesitate to correct him sharply. Secondly, it reveals his firm stand (which was enacted as a decree in one of the synods which he summoned) that a divorce should not be invalidated upon minor technical grounds, especially a divorce so difficult to obtain as one from an apostate. Finally, the responsum reveals the persecution which existed in those days, when many of the Jews were driven (or chose) to abandon the religion of their fathers.]

The opinion which you adopted seems far-fetched to me and forced. You cause a daughter of Israel to become an *agunah* [a chained woman— a woman who, not being able to obtain a divorce from her husband, can never remarry] and rest your decision upon an exaggerated or meaningless reason. That which you, my kinsman Rabbi Yom-Tov, are doing with regard to the divorce is not good. You said that it [the writ] was signed [by the witnesses] *after* it had been placed in the hands of the woman (and therefore was invalid on the ground that it should have been signed before it was given to her).

For, you see, we consider the law to be according to Rabbi Eliezer [Git. 4a]. According to Rabbi Eliezer, the signing on a bill of divorcement [is not indispensable, but] is only for the sake of proper procedure. Such "proper procedure" can apply both after she received the divorce document [the *get*] and before she receives it. Or, perhaps just because the husband said to the scribe, "Write a *get*," and he then said to the witnesses, "Sign it," you are inclined to invalidate the *get* on the theory that he did not mean her to be divorced until the *get* was actually signed. Were then the witnesses who signed identical with the messengers who delivered the *get?*

[He then proceeds to an analysis of three or four passages in the Talmud, tractate Gittin, as to the various ways in which the husband may have given the order to write the *get* and the variety of possible signatories, etc. He then proceeds to discuss the crucial objection of Rabbi Yom-Tov to the divorce, namely, that the new Christian name of the apostate was not included in the divorce. This was precisely the kind of technical objection which Rabbenu Tam abhorred, and he therefore discusses it rather sharply.]

You declare the *get* invalid because they did not write the [Christian] name of the apostate. It is evident that you are as one who is gathering sheaves in the valley of the shades [a verse from Isa. 17:5, by which he meant to say that Yom-Tov was making idle and worthless objections]. For, in fact, had it included the present name of the convert, it would have been still more open to objection. You and I both know that these apostates are nicknamed mockingly among the Jews, Judah being called Judach (implying "recreant") and Abraham being called Abran (implying "sinner") and Asher, Ashera (meaning "an idolatrous grove"). Menahem (the apostate whose divorce is now under discussion) is nicknamed Melahem (meaning "quarrelsome"). For all who knew him from his childhood called him Menahem, but none at all recognize him by his name William (Guillaume). Even if they *did* know that new name, they would not care to mention it.

How many apostates have divorced their wives and never was there anything written in the *get* other than their Jewish names; for thus most of the Jews called them. Certainly their Jewish name is of no less standing than a nickname [which should be mentioned or recorded in the *get*]. We have similar experiences every day. When [for example] my kinsman Eliezer divorced Madame Rachel, our aunt, his name was Vesselin and her name was Belle-Assez; and yet they wrote "Eliezer" and "Rachel," their Jewish names, and ignored the names which the Gentiles called them. The fact that the majority of the Christians use the new name does not constitute a majority in Jewish Law. It is the name which is used by the majority of Jews that counts, since the man who is giving the divorce is of the children of Israel (by origin).

[Rabbenu Tam then goes into an analysis of the various laws in the Talmud dealing with the names and by-names of husband and wife, which names or by-names need or need not be used. Then he concludes with an exhortation to the older teacher to retract his decision.]

I plead with you most earnestly to reverse yourself, for many men have raised objection to a divorce and have been unable to repair the harm that they have done. Now there is really no flaw in this divorce. You are overcareful about things that have no reality. In fact, it seems to me that there is some hidden rancor in your heart against the parties. I sent to the signers of the document. They asked me to write out my arguments and send them to you. They signed my statement and are astonished at your insistence that the Christian name be written as the essential name. More than twenty divorces from apostates were made in Paris and they wrote only the Jewish names in them; so, too, in Lorraine. All these documents were prepared by great scholars.

I saw with my own eyes the divorce of the son-in-law of the noble Rabbi Jacob Parnes, of blessed memory, who [the son-in-law] became an apostate. The name in the divorce was written Shemaya, surnamed Waldman, whereas his new Christian name was Gottschal, and it was not mentioned in the document at all. For God forbid that it should be mentioned [in a document written] under the Law of Moses and Israel. If [you] my relative had not told me that [this apostate's] name was William [neither I nor any] of the men of our kingdom would know any other than his Jewish name. They nicknamed him Melahem ("quarrelsome").

[He concludes the responsum, addressing the father of the divorced wife, as follows:]

You, noble father of the girl, marry your daughter to someone worthy of her, for one should pay no attention to the words of those who mock [i.e., who object to the divorce], for they cannot find their hands and their feet [i.e., they do not know what they are doing] and they stumble in their minority [i.e., there are not enough of these objectors to matter]. The arguments on which they depend are of no account. The matter is settled that she is permitted to remarry. Also the witnesses, of whom my relative said that they testified before him [against the divorce], deserve to be banned. Let him find out who they are and I will know what the end of them will be. Peace!

ISAAC BEN SHESHET (1326–1408)
ARISTOTLE OR THE TALMUD

You ask what is meant by "the wisdom of the Greeks" from which [according to the Talmud] a man must keep himself far away? Does this refer to those world-famous books [Aristotle's] *Physics* and *Metaphysics?*

[The questioner refers to the fact that the Talmud, in a number of parallel passages prohibits the teaching of "Greek wisdom." In the first part of the responsum, Bar Sheshet indicates that this "Greek wisdom" which the Talmud prohibits, does not refer to philosophy but is a special prohibition of certain secret allusive slang which the Greeks used to conceal thought. He cites Rashi, who has a different though similar interpretation of "Greek wisdom." Rashi says that it refers to a secret method of communicating thoughts by winks and gestures. Having explained the talmudic prohibition of the Greek wisdom in this special way, he proceeds with the main intent of the question.]

The famous [Aristotelian] books on Nature are therefore not meant to be prohibited. Nevertheless, it is better to avoid them, because they strive to uproot the essentials of our holy Torah, especially the two central pillars upon which the Torah rests, namely the creation of the world out of nothing and God's providence over individual human beings. These books bring what they believe is proof to demonstrate the [uncreated] eternity of the world, and that it [the world] is a necessary [i.e., an automatic, an unwilled] derivative from God, just as light comes automatically from the sun and shade from a tree. Therefore [they say that] God, blessed be He, could not change a single thing of Nature, neither to lengthen the wing of a fly nor shorten the leg of an ant, just as the sun cannot change the light which comes from it, nor the tree its shade. So God's providence cannot apply to anything below the sphere of the moon.

They write further in their books that there is no perfect knowledge [attainable by man] except through investigation; but [it does not come] from tradition. Whereas we, who are the recipients of the truth, believe that our Torah is perfect, that it came to us from God when we stood at

Mount Sinai, through [Moses] the chief of the prophets, upon whom be peace. We believe that it is above all other knowledge and that all their "investigations" are as nothing compared to its value.

In chapter 10 of Mishna Sanhedrin, we learn as follows: Among those who have no portion in the world-to-come are those who say that resurrection is not proved in the Torah, those who say that the Torah is not revealed, and the Epicurean. To which Rabbi Akiba adds: also he who reads the external books; and the Talmud says that that means the books of the *minim* [i.e., of the sectarians and the unbelievers].

Now can there be books of greater heresy than those that bring proofs to deny the fundamental doctrines of the Torah? Note, too, that Rabbi Akiba did not say those who *believe* in the "external books," but even those who *read* them, lest the books lead his heart away to credit their words. This indeed happened to Elisha [ben Abuya, the famous heretic in the Talmud]. They say of him that when he stood up in the house of study, many heretical books dropped from his bosom.

[Bar Sheshet then cites a responsum sent by the Gaon Hai to Samuel ha-Nagid, the famous eleventh century Spanish statesman, poet and scholar, declaring that it is not proper to study these "external books." Then he also quotes the older opinion of Solomon ben Adret against the study of Greek philosophy. And he continues:]

Now you cannot cite the case of Maimonides [who did study Aristotle] as a proof to the contrary. He [before he began to study Greek philosophy] had learned first of all the entire Torah completely, the laws and the narratives, the Tosefta, the Sifra and the Sifre, and the whole Talmud, Babylonian and Palestinian, as can be seen from his book *Mishneh Torah*. Furthermore, in order to answer the non-believer, he wrote his book, *Guide to the Perplexed*. His purpose was to refute the arguments and the proofs adduced by the philosopher [Aristotle] who tried to prove the eternity of the world and to deny God's providence. [Maimonides wrote his *Guide*] because in his time there were many Jews perplexed over the essential doctrines of the Torah, because of what they had learned from Greek wisdom. We can say [of Maimonides] as the rabbis said of Rabbi Meir [who was a friend and disciple of the heretic Elisha ben Abuya]: the rabbis asked how could Rabbi Meir learn Torah from his [Elisha's] mouth?

[He then cites the Talmud quotation of the verse in Proverbs 22:17, *Incline thine ear, and hear the voice of the wise,* and shows that the Talmud decided that a great man like Rabbi Meir is permitted to have contact with these heresies because he is able to select the "fine flour and throw away the bran"; as they say in the Talmud, "Rabbi Meir found a pomegranate. He ate its pulp and threw away the shell."

Therefore the teacher Moses son of Maimon, blessed be his memory, cited this very verse at the beginning of his *Guide: Incline thine ear,* etc. [i.e., to study these matters critically and throw away what is not worth keeping].

Nevertheless, this great teacher did not escape entirely from being drawn after the Greek wisdom in some of the proofs that he brings.

[Then Bar Sheshet considers another great rabbinic scholar, Levi ben Gershon (Gersonides), who also had great rabbinic knowledge and therefore could be trusted to study the Greek wisdom selectively. Yet even he was somewhat misled by what he studied.]

The sage Rabbi Levi [Gersonides] of blessed memory, even though he was a great scholar in the Talmud and wrote a beautiful commentary to the Torah and the prophets, and followed in the footsteps of Moses ben Maimon, even his heart was somewhat led astray by those wisdoms.

[Bar Sheshet cites some of the rationalistic explanations which Gersonides gives for the sun's standing still for Joshua, and such others. Then Bar Sheshet concludes:]

Now, then, let every man draw an argument *a fortiori (kal vahomer)* with regard to himself, since those two monarchs of the mind could not keep their footing in certain matters (because of the influence of their Greek studies), nevertheless their honor is unimpaired. But if the great ones of the world had this happen to them, how can we keep our footing, who never saw the light as they did? In fact, many [because of their studies of Greek philosophy] have broken off the yoke of regular prayer and of the Torah and the commandments, because they studied these wisdoms, as the Gaon Hai wrote [in the responsum to Samuel haNagid referred to above].

SIMON BEN ZEMAH DURAN (1361–1444)
THE RABBINATE AS A PROFESSION

[He phrases the question himself and refers to the fact that, in the past generations, some fees and advantages were always given to rabbis. He then concludes, in effect, that since various fees and honors were always permitted, a regular salary should likewise be permitted.]

Since I have noted that many people grumble at the fact that it was customary in all the congregations of Israel for many generations to give some reward to their sages, and that [these complainers] base their argument on what Maimonides said in his commentary to the Ethics of the Fathers, IV.5 [i.e., not to make the Torah a spade to dig with], therefore

I shall set forth my thoughts in this matter, insofar as they will enlighten me from Heaven, and my researches in the Talmud and other places. I shall discuss whether this matter [to give rewards to the scholars] is merely a permissive one, or a commanded one, or an actual obligation, and whether there is in it the slightest scintilla of sin. I am confident that, with the help of the earlier scholars who permitted themselves [to receive such fees], I shall not stumble in the Law and that the matter of this moot subject will be clarified.

[In six responsa he then analyzes all the talmudic references that have to do, first, with the rewards and privileges of priests (kohanim); secondly, of sages and of scholars and of teachers, their right to receive pay for teaching their pupils, their right to be freed from taxes, their right to receive respect and honor. After all this careful analysis, he sums up the matter as follows:]

Having removed from the sages ancient and recent, of blessed memory, the complaints of the children of Israel, and of the great teacher Maimonides and those who followed him, I shall sum up the matter as it has come into our hands from the scattered places in the Talmud.

The community of Israel is in duty bound to elevate anyone who is most worthy in his generation, as Rab Ami was in his generation; but also the sage can take these privileges on his own initiative, as is proved in the Talmud in Hullin 134b.

[This first reference deals with the rights of a priest (kohen) to take what duly belongs to him. Rab Ami was not only a great sage, he was also a kohen.]

If he is a sage, of whom they can ask questions from the *entire* Talmud, and he can answer, it is proper to appoint him chief of all Israel and the head of the yeshiva, and all Israel must exalt him.

If they ask a man the law in a specific tractate (not in the whole Talmud) and he can answer, he may be appointed chief in his own city, and he must be treated with respect. If he is not even at that level, but he engages in studies and neglects his own business affairs, the people of his city are in duty bound to help him gain his livelihood, as is shown in the Talmud [Shab. 114a]. If there is already a rabbinical head in the city who merits all this honor but he happens to be rich in his own right, but there is in the city another sage who needs to be elevated [to the position of the rabbinate], he must in modesty and goodness say that that other [the poverty-stricken sage] should be the one who should teach in the yeshiva until he is elevated, as is proved from the Talmud.

[Duran then proceeds to speak of the other privileges of the rabbis: to be free from taxes, and the like. Then, after completing an enumeration of the duties of the community to the scholars, he continues with the duties which the individual members of the community owe him.]

Thus it is a duty incumbent upon every individual to benefit the scholar from his possessions; and if such persons help him and create business for him, there is no greater virtue than this and they merit a place in the heavenly academy. This is the duty of the individual. Of course, if the sages refrain from accepting such benefits, except what they receive from their pupils, their action is right and proper, as is proved in the Talmud.

Also, if a donor desires to be honored by contact with the sage or [helps the scholar] in order that the sage can engage in Torah and not have to neglect it because of his livelihood [he should do so], as Simon the brother of Azariah and Rabbi Yohanan did, who were supported by the Nasi [the patriarch] in order that they might engage in the study of the Torah. Thus Issakhar did with Zebulon his brother [i.e., Zebulon did business so that Issakhar might have time to study the Torah]; and Zebulon merited to be blessed along with Issakhar; not only that, but Zebulon is mentioned first in Scriptures, for it is said [Deut. 33:18]: Rejoice, O Zebulon, in thy going forth, and Issakhar, in thy tents.

This is what occurs to me on this subject. May He who has given me the merit to defend the earlier scholars, of blessed memory [for accepting the fees and privileges], give me the merit of those who are worthy of the crown of the Torah and the crown of a good name as they [the earlier scholars] were. Thus writeth Simon, the son of Zemah of blessed memory.

[In his commentary to the ethics of the Fathers, IV. 5, he refers to the long treatise which he wrote on the subject, i.e., the one which we have just summarized. He reviews the same arguments, and ends with a biographical note in which he says that he is justified in accepting the position of rabbi and taking a salary. Although justified, he feels the need to explain that he was forced to do this by the necessity of his exile which prevented him from practicing medicine. His words are:]

For all these reasons we resolved to make a practical decision with regard to ourselves [i.e., myself] to take a salary from the congregation and to be appointed as rabbi and judge over them. We did not permit ourselves to do this before we had debated this matter, as we wrote in our long treatise, and before the great scholars of our generation saw it and said it was correct. Thus we have seen that this permission [to take rewards] was customary with the great scholars before us, the highest men and men of action, scholars and rabbis who are far greater than we.

[Then he explains that, of course, he holds to the talmudic principle that a man must not study in order to obtain honor or reward. He must study for the love of it.]

But let it be known that the aim of our studies with the sages [his teachers] was not for this purpose, namely, to sit at the head [of the community]. Because we owned property and we had learned the art of medicine. Medicine is a wisdom which honorably supports its practitioners in the Christian lands. But for the sins of this generation, persecution was decreed in all those lands, and we were left with only our lives. We abandoned all our possessions there, and whatever we could save we gave to the idolators in order that we might survive and not come to harm. It is enough for us to have this door of permission [the talmudic arguments cited above] which we have used in order that Torah shall be our work and we will *not cease from it day and night.*

If the profession of medicine could have supplied us a livelihood, in this land in which we have settled [i.e., Algiers], we would not have come to this state. But it is of low status here; and we do not wish to return to the Christian land because of the confusion in those places where every day new persecutions are decreed; and, as the Midrash says: "Whoever was once bitten by a snake, is frightened by a rope."

Maimonides

*R*abbi *M*oses *b*en *M*aimon (1135–1204), known also as Rambam and Maimonides, was born in Cordova, Spain, where he continued in the path of secular and Jewish studies traditional to the Jews of Spain. In 1148 the fanatic Almohades, a Muslim sect that sought to destroy every other religion, came from North Africa to Spain, conquered Cordova and razed the synagogues. Maimonides' family, along with many other Jews of Cordova, preferred exile to conversion or martyrdom. Between 1148 and 1160 Maimonides studied philosophy and science; with the aid of his father, a *dayan* (rabbinic judge) and author, Maimonides began to master the Talmud.

After a brief visit to Palestine, then under Christian domination, in 1185 the family settled in Fostat, Egypt—a land that had a large Jewish population, its own *nagid* or national Jewish leader, and just treatment and freedom under the Caliph Saladin. Like many of his literary forbears, Maimonides was a physician, and in time became court physician to the Caliph's Vizier.

Maimonides' first major work (written in Arabic) was the *Commentary on the Mishnah* (1168). Herein Maimonides appended his famous thirteen principles of the Jewish faith, perhaps the closest formulation of a creed in Judaism. These principles were poetically condensed by Daniel ben Judah in 1404 (two centuries after Maimonides' death) in the famous hymn *Yigdal*, which appears at the beginning of every Siddur (see Siddur, p. 133)

The *Commentary on the Mishnah* made Maimonides world famous. Four years after the publication of this work, the Jewish community of Yemen turned to him with a crucial question of national survival. Many Yemenite Jews were being forced to convert; others were falling under the influence of a false Messiah. The leader of Yemenite Jewry, then, turned to Maimonides for counsel and encouragement. Maimonides' reply, the *Epistle to Yemen* (1172), is a lengthy responsum to the community. The letter, circulated among the various congregations, gave hope and determination to a beset Jewry. Such was their gratitude that they made the exceptional gesture of including Maimonides' name in the *Kaddish:* "May salvation come in our days and in the days of our teacher Moses." (Another instance of a living person included in the prayers of Israel may be found in "The Installation of an Exilarch," page 156)

From 1170 to 1180, Maimonides worked on his fourteen-volume code, the *Mishne Torah,* a logically arranged Hebrew compilation of new and existing laws (covering both Talmuds, the Midrash, and Gaonic decisions) that embraced the religious, ritual, ethical and social aspects of Jewish life. The first section, the "Book of Knowledge," tells of man's fundamental duty of recognizing God as the universal Creator, and discusses the holidays, proper care of the body, the study of Torah, and repentance.

The work was almost universally acclaimed; still, there were critics who blamed Maimonides for setting forth new legal decisions, and for including his opinions without reference to any former rabbinic authorities (this Maimonides sought to correct in a projected revised edition, but he never had enough time for this task). Others accused him of intending to supplant the Talmud with his own work—for in his introduction he had asserted that his book would enable a reader to know the law on any subject without having to consult any other text. But despite these criticisms, Maimonides' *Mishne Torah* was widely circulated and soon became a classic of Hebrew literature.

Other works by Maimonides include the famed *Guide to the Perplexed* (written in Arabic), which sought to reconcile philosophy with religion and influenced later Christian and Muslim thinkers and theologians; and many responsa, like the one to Obadiah the proselyte, which reveals his erudition and humanity.

A general picture of Maimonides' life as doctor, rabbi and leader is vividly presented in his letter to one of his translators, Samuel ibn Tibbon.

MISHNE TORAH—BOOK OF KNOWLEDGE

LAWS CONCERNING THE STUDY OF THE TORAH

Chapter I.

1. Women, slaves and the young (under the age of puberty) are exempt from the obligation of studying Torah. But it is a duty of the father to teach his young son Torah; as it is said, "And ye shall teach them, to your children, talking of them" [Deut. 11:19]. A woman is under no obligation to teach her son, since only one whose duty it is to learn has a duty to teach.

2. Just as it is a man's duty to teach his son, so it is his duty to teach his grandson, as it is said, "Make them known unto thy children and thy children's children" [Deut. 4:9]. This obligation is to be fulfilled not only towards a son and grandson. A duty rests on every scholar in Israel to teach all disciples (who seek instruction from him), even if they are not his children, as it is said, "And thou shalt teach them diligently unto thy children" [Deut. 6:7]. On traditional authority, the term "thy children" includes disciples, for disciples too are called children, as it is said "And the sons of the prophets came forth" [II Kings 2:3]. This being so, why does the precept (concerning instruction) specifically mention [Deut. 4:9] a man's son and son's son? To impress upon us that the son should receive instruction in preference to a grandson, and a grandson in preference to another man's son.

3. A father (who cannot teach his son) is bound to engage a paid teacher for him. But the only obligation one owes to a neighbour's son is to teach him when it involves no expense. If a father has not had his son taught, it is the duty of the latter, as soon as he realises his deficiencies, to acquire knowledge for himself, as it is said, "That ye may learn them and observe to do them" [Deut. 5:1]. And so too, you will find that study in all cases takes precedence of practice, since study leads to practice, but practice does not lead to study.

4. If a man needs to learn Torah and has a son who needs instruction, his own requirements are to be satisfied first. But if his son has better capacity and greater ability to grasp what he learns, then the son's education takes precedence. Still, even in this case, the father must not wholly neglect the study of the Torah. For, just as it is incumbent on him to have his son taught, so is he under an obligation to obtain instruction for himself.

5. A man should always first study Torah and then marry; for if he takes a wife first, his mind will not be free for study. But if his physical desires are so overpowering as to preoccupy his mind, he should marry and then study Torah.

6. When should a father commence his son's instruction in Torah? As soon as the child begins to talk, the father should teach him the text "Moses commanded us a law" [Deut. 33:4], and the first verse of the *Shema* ("Hear O Israel, the Lord our God, the Lord is One") [Deut. 6:4]. Later on, according to the child's capacity, the father should teach him a few verses at a time, till he attains the age of six or seven years, when he should take him to a teacher of young children.

7. If it is the custom of the country for a teacher of children to receive remuneration, the father is to pay the fee, and it is his duty to have his son taught, even if he has to pay for the instruction, till the child has gone through the whole of the Written Law. Where it is the custom to charge a fee for teaching the Written Law, it is permissible to take payment for such instruction. It is forbidden however to teach the Oral Law for payment, for it is said "Behold, I have taught you statutes and ordinances, even as the Lord, my God, commanded me" [Deut. 4:5]. This means: "Even as I [Moses] learnt (from God) without payment, so have ye learnt from me, gratuitously. And throughout the generations, whenever you teach, do so gratuitously, even as you learnt from me". If a person cannot find any one willing to teach him without remuneration, he should engage a paid teacher, as it is said "Buy the truth" [Prov. 23:23]. It should not however be assumed that it is permissible to take pay for teaching. For the verse continues "And sell it not", the inference being, that even where a man had been obliged to pay for instruction (in the Oral Law), he is nevertheless forbidden to charge, in his turn, for teaching it.

8. Every Israelite is under an obligation to study Torah, whether he is poor or rich, in sound health or ailing, in the vigour of youth or very old and feeble. Even a man so poor that he is maintained by charity or goes begging from door to door, as also a man with a wife and children to support, are under the obligation to set aside a definite period during the day and at night for the study of the Torah, as it is said "But thou shalt meditate therein day and night" [Joshua 1:8].

9. Among the great sages of Israel, some were hewers of wood, some, drawers of water, while others were blind. Nevertheless, they devoted themselves by day and by night to the study of the Torah. They are included among the transmitters of the tradition in the direct line from Moses.

10. Until what period in life ought one to study Torah? Until the day of one's death, as it is said, "And lest they (the precepts) depart from thy heart all the days of thy life" [Deut. 4:9]. Whenever one ceases to study, one forgets.

11. The time allotted to study should be divided into three parts. A

third should be devoted to the Written Law; a third to the Oral Law; and the last third should be spent in reflection, deducing conclusions from premises, developing implications of statements, comparing dicta, studying the hermeneutical principles by which the Torah is interpreted, till one knows the essence of these principles, and how to deduce what is permitted and what is forbidden from what one has learnt traditionally. This is termed Talmud.

12. For example, if one is an artisan who works at his trade three hours daily and devotes nine hours to the study of the Torah, he should spend three of these nine hours in the study of the Written Law, three in the study of the Oral Law, and the remaining three in reflecting on how to deduce one rule from another. The words of the Prophets are comprised in the Written Law, while their exposition falls within the category of the Oral Law. The subjects styled *Pardes* (Esoteric Studies), are included in *Talmud*. This plan applies to the period when one begins learning. But after one has become proficient and no longer needs to learn the Written Law, or continually be occupied with the Oral Law, he should, at fixed times, read the Written Law and the traditional dicta, so as not to forget any of the rules of the Torah, and should devote all his days exclusively to the study of Talmud, according to his breadth of mind and maturity of intellect.

Chapter II.

1. Teachers of young children are to be appointed in each province, district and town. If a city has made no provision for the education of the young, its inhabitants are placed under a ban, till such teachers have been engaged. And if they persistently neglect this duty, the city is excommunicated, for the world is only maintained by the breath of school children.

2. Children are to be sent to school at the age of six or seven years, according to the strength of the individual child and its physical development. But no child is to be sent to school under six years of age. The teacher may chastise his pupils to inspire them with awe. But he must not do so in a cruel manner or in a vindictive spirit. Accordingly, he must not strike them with whips or sticks, but only use a small strap. He is to teach them the whole day and part of the night, so as to train them to study by day and by night. And there is to be no holiday except on the eve of the Sabbath or festival, towards the close of the day, and on festivals. On Sabbaths, pupils are not taught a new lesson, but they repeat what they had already learnt previously, even if only once. Pupils must not be interrupted at their studies, even for the re-building of the Temple.

3. A teacher who leaves the children and goes out (when he should be teaching them), or does other work while he is with them, or teaches lazily, falls under the ban "Cursed be he that doeth the work of the Lord with a slack hand" [Jer. 48:10]. Hence, it is not proper to appoint any one as teacher unless he is God-fearing and well versed in reading and in grammar.

4. An unmarried man should not keep school for the young because the mothers come to see their children. Nor should any woman keep school, because the fathers come to see them.

5. Twenty-five children may be put in charge of one teacher. If the number in the class exceeds twenty-five but is not more than forty, he should have an assistant to help with the instruction. If there are more than forty, two teachers must be appointed.

6. A child may be transferred from one teacher to another who is more competent in reading or grammar, only however, if both the teacher and the pupil live in the same town and are not separated by a river. But we must not take the child to school in another town nor even across a river in the same town, unless it is spanned by a firm bridge, not likely soon to collapse.

7. If one of the residents in an alley or even in a court wishes to open a school, his neighbors cannot prevent him. Nor can a teacher, already established, object to another teacher opening a school next door to him, either for new pupils or even with the intention of drawing away pupils from the existing school, for it is said, "The Lord was pleased for His righteousness' sake, to make the Torah great and glorious" [Is. 42:21].

LAWS RELATING TO MORAL DISPOSITIONS AND TO ETHICAL CONDUCT

CHAPTER I.

1. Every human being is characterised by numerous moral dispositions which differ from each other and are exceedingly divergent. One man is choleric, always irascible; another sedate, never angry; or, if he should become angry, is only slightly and very rarely so. One man is haughty to excess; another humble in the extreme. One is a sensualist whose lusts are never sufficiently gratified; another is so pure in soul that he does not even long for the few things that our physical nature needs. One is so greedy that all the money in the world would not satisfy him, as it is said, "He who loveth silver shall not be satisfied with silver" [Eccles. 5:9]. Another so curbs his desires that he is contented with very little, even that which is insufficient, and does not bestir himself to obtain that which he really needs. One will suffer extreme hunger for the sake of saving, and does not spend the smallest coin without a pang, while another deliberately and wantonly squanders all his property. In the same way, men differ in other traits. There are, for example, the hilarious and the melancholy, the stingy and the generous, the cruel and the merciful, the timid and the stout-hearted, and so forth.

2. Between any moral disposition and its extreme opposite, there are intermediate dispositions more or less removed from each other. Of all the various dispositions, some belong to one from the beginning of his existence and correspond to his physical constitution. Others are such that a particular individual's nature is favourably predisposed to them and prone to acquire them more rapidly than other traits. Others again are not innate, but have been either learnt from others, or are self-originated, as the result of an idea that has entered the mind, or having heard that a certain disposition is good for him and should be cultivated by him, one trained himself in it till it became part of his nature.

3. To cultivate either extreme in any class of dispositions is not the right course nor is it proper for any person to follow or learn it. If a man finds that his nature tends or is disposed to one of these extremes, or if one has acquired and become habituated to it, he should turn back and improve, so as to walk in the way of good people, which is the right way.

7. How shall a man train himself in these dispositions, so that they become ingrained? Let him practise again and again the actions prompted by those dispositions which are the mean between the extremes, and repeat them continually till they become easy and are no longer irksome to him, and so the corresponding dispositions will become a fixed part of his character. And as the Creator is called by these attributes, which constitute the middle path in which we are to walk, this path is called the Way of God and this is what the patriarch Abraham taught his children, as it is said, "For I love him, because he will charge his children and his household after him, that they may keep the way of the Lord" [Gen. 18:19]. Whoever walks in this way secures for himself happiness and blessing, as the text continues, "In order that the Lord might bring upon Abraham that which He spoke concerning him" [Gen. 18:19].

CHAPTER II.

3. There are some dispositions in regard to which it is forbidden merely to keep to the middle path. They must be shunned to the extreme. Such a disposition is pride. The right way in this regard is not to be merely meek, but to be humble-minded and lowly of spirit to the utmost. And therefore was it said of Moses that he was "exceedingly meek" [Num. 12:3], not merely that he was "meek." Hence, our sages exhorted us, "Be exceedingly lowly of spirit" [Ethics of the Fathers 4:4]. They also said that any one who permits his heart to swell with haughtiness has denied the essential principle of our religion, as it is said, "And thy heart will be proud, and thou wilt forget the Lord, thy God" [Deut. 8:14]. Again they have said, "Under a ban be he who is proud, even in the smallest degree." Anger too, is an exceedingly bad passion, and one should avoid it to the last extreme. One should train oneself not to be angry even for something

that would justify anger. If one wishes to arouse fear in his children and household, or in the members of a community of which he is the head, and desires to exhibit anger, so that they may amend their ways, he should make a show of anger before them, so as to correct them, but in reality, his mind should be composed like that of a man who simulates anger and does not really feel it. The ancient sages said, "He who is angry—it is the same as if he worshipped idols." They also said, "One who yields to anger—if he is a sage, his wisdom departs from him; if he is a prophet, his prophetic gift departs from him." Those of an irate disposition—their life is not worth living. The sages therefore, charged us that anger should be avoided to such a degree that one should train oneself to be unmoved even by things that naturally would provoke anger; and this is the good way. The practice of the righteous is to suffer contumely and not inflict it; to hear themselves reproached, not retort; to be impelled in what they do by love, and to rejoice in suffering. Of them Scripture said, "And they that love Him are like the going forth of the sun in his strength." [Judges 5:31].

5. "A fence to wisdom is silence" [Ethics of the Fathers, 3:17]. Hence, a man should not be hasty in reply, nor talk much. He should teach his pupils gently and calmly, not shouting, and avoiding prolixity. Solomon said, "The words of the wise, spoken quietly, are heard" [Eccles. 9:17].

6. It is forbidden to accustom oneself to smooth speech and flatteries. One must not say one thing and mean another. Inward and outward self should correspond; only what we have in mind, should we utter with the mouth. We must deceive no one, not even an idolater. A man, for example, must not sell to an idolater flesh from a beast that has died naturally, as if it were meat of an animal ritually slaughtered. Nor should one sell a shoe, the leather of which came from the hide of a beast that met with a natural death, allowing it to be believed that the leather had come from the hide of a ritually slaughtered animal.

One must not urge another to join one at a meal, when one is aware that the invitation will not be accepted. Nor should one press upon another any marks of friendship which one knows will be declined. So too, casks of wine, which must be opened for sale, should not be broached in such a way as to deceive a guest and make him believe that they had been opened in his honor, and so forth. Even a single word of flattery or deception is forbidden. A person should always cherish truthful speech, an upright spirit and a pure heart free from all forwardness and perversity.

CHAPTER IV

1. Since, by keeping the body in health and vigour, one walks in the ways of God—it being impossible during sickness to have any understanding or knowledge of the Creator—it is a man's duty to avoid whatever is injurious

to the body, and cultivate habits conducive to health and vigour. These are as follows: One should not take food except when one is hungry; nor drink unless one is thirsty. One should not neglect the calls of nature for a single moment, but respond to them immediately.

2. Food should not be taken to repletion; during a meal, about one-third less should be eaten than the quantity that would give a feeling of satiety, and only a little water should be drunk—and that mixed with wine. After the process of digestion has commenced, water may be taken as needed. But even after food has been digested, it should not be drunk copiously. Before eating, careful attention should be paid to the functions of excretion. No meal should be taken without previously walking till the body begins to get warm, or engaging in manual labour, or tiring oneself with other activities. In short, strenuous exercise should be taken every day in the morning, till the body is in a glow. Then, there should be an interval of rest till one has recovered composure. The meal may then be taken. If the exercise is followed by a bath of warm water, so much the better. In this case too, there should be an interval of repose before the meal.

3. During a meal, one should sit or recline on the left side; but not walk, ride, take violent exercise, sway the body, or engage in sport, till the food is digested. Any one who engages in sport or violent exercise immediately after a meal, subjects himself to grave disorders.

4. The day and night consist of twenty-four hours. It is sufficient to sleep for a third of that period, namely eight hours. And these hours should be in the latter part of the night; that is to say, the period from retirement to dawn should be eight hours so that one will rise from his bed before dawn.

5. One should not sleep face downwards, nor on one's back, but lying on the side; at the beginning, on the left side, and at the close of one's rest, on the right side. One should not go to sleep immediately after a meal, but only when three or four hours have elapsed. One should not sleep during the day.

8. In the summer time, cold food should be consumed; one should be sparing with condiments; vinegar should be used. During winter, warm foods should be eaten; condiments should be liberally used with a little mustard and asafoetida. A similar plan should be followed in cold and warm countries. The diet, in every district, should be chosen to suit the climate.

14. Another great principle of hygiene, physicians say, is as follows: As long as a person takes active exercise, works hard, does not over-eat and keeps his bowels open, he will be free from disease and will increase in vigour, even though the food he eats is coarse.

15. But if one leads a sedentary life and does not take exercise, neglects the calls of nature, or is constipated—even if he eats wholesome food and takes care of himself in accordance with medical rules—he will, throughout his life, be subject to aches and pains and his strength will fail him. Over-eating is like a deadly poison to any constitution and is the principal cause of all diseases. Most maladies that afflict mankind result from bad food or are due to the patient filling his stomach with an excess of food that may even have been wholesome. Thus, Solomon, in his wisdom, said, "He who keeps his mouth and tongue, keeps his soul from troubles." [Prov. 21:23]—which text can be applied to the individual who guards his mouth from bad food and over-eating, and keeps his tongue from all speech except that which is necessary to obtain his needs.

23. No disciple of the wise may live in a city that is unprovided with the following ten officials and institutions, namely: a physician, a surgeon, a bath-house, a lavatory, a source of water supply such as a stream or a spring, a synagogue, a school teacher, a scribe, a treasurer of charity funds for the poor, a court that has authority to punish with stripes and imprisonment.

CHAPTER VI.

1. It is natural to be influenced, in sentiments and conduct, by one's neighbours and associates, and observe the customs of one's fellow citizens. Hence, a person ought constantly to associate with the righteous and frequent the company of the wise, so as to learn from their practices, and shun the wicked who are benighted, so as not to be corrupted by their example. So Solomon said "He that walketh with the wise, shall be wise; but the companion of fools shall smart for it" [Prov. 13:20]. And it is also said, "Happy is the man that hath not walked in the counsel of the wicked [Psalms 1:1]. So too, if one lives in a country where the customs are pernicious, and the inhabitants do not go in the right way, he should leave for a place where the people are righteous and follow the ways of the good.

If all the countries of which he has personal knowledge, or concerning which he hears reports, follow a course that is not right—as is the case in our times—or if military campaigns or sickness debar him from leaving for a country with good customs, he should live by himself in seclusion, as it is said, "Let him sit alone and keep silence" [Lam. 3:28]. And if the inhabitants are wicked reprobates who will not let him stay in the country unless he mixes with them and adopts their evil practices, let him withdraw to caves, thickets or deserts, and not habituate himself to the ways of sinners, as it is said, "O that I were in the wilderness, in a lodging place of wayfaring men" [Jer. 9:1].

2. It is an affirmative precept to attach oneself to sages and their disciples, so as to learn from their example; as it is said, "And unto Him shalt thou cleave" [Deut. 10:20]. But can a human being cleave to the *Shechinah* [Divine Presence]? Our wise men explained this text thus: "Attach thyself to sages and their disciples." A man should, accordingly, strive to win a scholar's daughter for a wife, and should give his daughter in marriage to a scholar. He should eat and drink in the company of scholars; give them opportunities to do business, and cultivate their society in every relation, as it is said "And to cleave unto Him" [Deut. 11:22]. So too, our sages exhorted us, "Sit in the dust of their feet, and drink their words thirstily" [Ethics of the Fathers 1:4].

3. It is incumbent on every one to love each individual Israelite as himself, as it is said, "Thou shalt love thy neighbour, as thyself" [Lev. 19:18]. Hence, a person ought to speak in praise of his neighbour and be careful of his neighbour's property as he is careful of his own property and solicitous about his own honour. Whoever glorifies himself by humilitating another person, will have no portion in the world to come.

4. To love the proselyte who comes to take refuge beneath the wings of the *Shechinah* is the fulfilment of two affirmative precepts. First, because he is included among neighbours [whom we are commanded to love] [Lev. 19:18]. And secondly, because he is a stranger and the Torah said, "Love ye therefore the stranger" [Deut. 10:19]. God charged [us] concerning love of Himself, as it is said "Thou shalt love the Lord, thy God" [Deut. 6:5]. The Holy One, blessed be He, loves strangers, as it is said, "And He loveth the stranger" [Deut. 10:18].

5. Whoever entertains in his heart hatred of any Israelite, transgresses a prohibition, as it is said, "Thou shalt not hate thy brother in thy heart" [Lev. 19:17]. . . .

6. When a man sins against another, the injured party should not hate the offender and keep silent, as it is said concerning the wicked, "And Absalom spake to Amnon neither good nor evil, for Absalom hated Amnon" [2 Sam. 13:22]. But it is his duty to inform the offender and say to him "Why did you do this to me? Why did you sin against me in this matter?" And thu it is said, "Thou shalt surely rebuke thy neighbour" [Lev. 19:17]. If the offender repents and pleads for forgiveness, he should be forgiven. The forgiver should not be obdurate, as it is said, "And Abraham prayed unto God" [for Abimelech] [Gen. 20:17].

7. If one observes that a person committed a sin or walks in a way that is not good, it is a duty to bring the erring man back to the path and point out to him that he is wronging himself by his evil courses, as it is said,

"Thou shalt surely rebuke thy neighbour" [Lev. 19:17]. He who rebukes another, whether for offences against the rebuker himself or for sins against God, should administer the rebuke in private, speak to the offender gently and tenderly, and point out that he is only speaking for the wrongdoer's own good, to secure for him life in the world to come. If the latter accepts the rebuke, well and good. If not, he should be rebuked a second, and a third time. And so one is bound to continue the admonitions, till the sinner assaults the admonisher and says to him, "I refuse to listen." Whoever is in a position to prevent wrongdoing and does not do so, is responsible for the iniquity of all the wrongdoers whom he might have checked.

8. He who rebukes another must not at first speak to the offender harshly so as to put him to shame, as it is said, "And thou shalt not suffer sin because of him" [Lev. 19:17]. Our Rabbis explained this text as follows: Since it might have been supposed that you are to rebuke the sinner till he changes colour, therefore it is said, "And thou shalt not bear sin because of him." Hence the inference that it is forbidden to put an Israelite to shame, especially in public. Although one who puts another to shame is not punished with stripes, still it is a grave offence. And thus the sages said, "He who shames another in public has no portion in the world to come."

One ought therefore to beware of publicly shaming anyone, whether he be young or old. One should not call a person by a name of which he feels ashamed, nor relate anything in his presence which humiliates him. This applies to matters between man and man. But in regard to duties to God, if an individual, after having been privately rebuked, does not repent, he should be shamed in public; his sin should be openly declared; he is to be reviled, affronted and cursed till he returns to the right course. This was the method followed by all the prophets of Israel.

9. If one who has been wronged by another, does not wish to rebuke or speak to the offender because the latter is a very common person or mentally defective, and if he has sincerely forgiven him, and neither bears him ill-will nor rebukes him—he acts according to the standard of saints. All that the Torah objects to is harbouring ill-will.

10. A man ought to be especially heedful of his behaviour towards widows and orphans, for their souls are exceedingly depressed and their spirits low. Even if they are wealthy, even if they are the widow and orphans of a king, we are specifically enjoined concerning them, as it is said, "Ye shall not afflict any widow or fatherless child" [Ex. 22:21].

How are we to conduct ourselves towards them? One must not speak to them otherwise than tenderly. One must show them unvarying courtesy; not hurt them physically with hard toil, nor wound their feelings with harsh speech. One must take greater care of their property than of one's own. Whoever irritates them, provokes them to anger, pains them, tyrannizes over them, or causes them loss of money, is guilty of a transgression, and still more so, if one beats them or curses them. Though no stripes are inflicted for this transgression, its punishment is explicitly set forth in the Torah [in the following terms], "My wrath shall wax hot, and I will slay you with the sword" [Ex. 22:23].

He who created the world by His word made a covenant with widows and orphans that when they will cry out because of violence, they will be answered; as it is said, "If thou afflict them in any wise—for if they cry at all unto Me, I will surely hear their cry" [Ex. 22:22]. This only applies to cases where a person afflicts them for his own ends.

But if a teacher punishes orphan children in order to teach them Torah or a trade, or lead them in the right way—this is permissible. And yet he should not treat them like others, but make a distinction in their favour. He should guide them gently, with the utmost tenderness and courtesy, whether they are bereft of a father or mother, as it is said, "For the Lord will plead their cause" [Prov. 22:23]. To what age are they to be regarded in these respects as orphans? Till they reach the age when they no longer need an adult on whom they depend to train them and care for them, and when each of them can provide for all his wants, like other grown-up persons.

CHAPTER VII.

1. Whoever tells tales about another person violates a prohibition, as it is said, "Thou shalt not go up and down as a talebearer among thy people" [Lev. 19:16]. And although no stripes are inflicted, it is a grave offence, and leads to the death of many souls in Israel. Hence, this precept is followed immediately by the sentence, "Neither shalt thou stand idly by the blood of thy neighbour" [Lev. 19:16]. For an example of the tragic consequences of this transgression, read what happened after Doeg's report concerning the priests of Nob. [I Sam. 22:6–19].

2. Who is a talebearer? One who carries reports, and goes about from one person to another and says, "So-and-so said this"; "Such and such a statement have I heard about so-and-so." Even if what he says or repeats may be true, the talebearer ruins the world. There is a still graver offence that comes within this prohibition, namely, the evil tongue. This means talking disparagingly of anyone, even though what one says is true; but he who utters falsehood is called a slanderer. A person with an evil tongue is one who, sitting in company, says, "That person did such a thing"; "so and so's ancestors were so and so"; "I have heard this about him"; and then proceeds to talk scandal. Of such a person, Scripture says, "May the Lord cut off all smooth lips, the tongue that speaketh proud things." [Ps. 12:4].

3. The sages say, "There are three offences for which one is punished in this world and forfeits his portion in the world to come. These are idolatry, incest and murder; but the evil tongue is equal to all the three put together." The sages further said, "To indulge in evil speech is like a denial of the fundamental principle of religion, as it is said, "Who said, With our tongue will we prevail; our lips are our own: Who is lord over us?" [Ps. 12:5]. The sages also said, "The evil tongue slays three persons: the utterer of evil, the listener, the one spoken about; and the listener will be punished worse than the speaker."

4. There are modes of speech that may be styled "dust of the evil tongue." Such are remarks like the following: "Who would have thought of so-and-so that he would be as he is now." Or, "be silent about so-and-so. I do not wish to tell what happened, etc." To speak in a person's favor in the presence of his enemies, savours of the evil tongue. For it will provoke them to speak of him disparagingly. Referring to this, Solomon said, "He that blesseth his friend with a loud voice, rising early in the morning, it shall be counted a curse unto him" [Prov. 27:14]. For out of what had been said to his good, proceedeth evil.

Such too is the case of one who indulges in evil speech jokingly and frivolously, and not out of hatred. And so, Solomon, in his wisdom, says, "As one who mockingly casteth firebrands, arrows and death, and saith, am I not jesting?" [Prov. 26:18]. Equally reprehensible is one who indulges in evil speech deceitfully, that is, speaks as it were in all innocence, as if unaware that what he says is an evil utterance, and when a protest is made, replies, "I do not know that this is evil speech, or that such is the conduct of so-and-so."

5. Whether one indulges in evil speech about a person in his presence, or in his absence, or makes statements which, if repeated, would tend to hurt him physically or injure him financially, distress or alarm him—all this is evil speech. If a statement of this character had been made in the presence of three persons, the subject matter is regarded as public and generally known, and if one of the three repeats it, he is not guilty of evil speech, provided he had no intention of giving the story wider currency.

6. All such persons are scandalmongers in whose neighborhood it is forbidden to reside; and still more is it forbidden to cultivate their society and listen to them. The sentence passed upon our forefathers in the wilderness was confirmed only because they were guilty of the sin of the evil tongue.

7. He who takes revenge, violates a prohibition, and it is said, "Thou shalt not take vengeance" [Lev. 19:18]. And although he is not punished with stripes, still such conduct indicates an exceedingly bad disposition. One should rather practise forbearance in all secular matters. For the

intelligent realise that these are vain things and not worth taking vengeance for. What is "taking vengeance"? The following is a case.

A neighbour says to one, "Lend me your axe," He replies, "I will not lend it to you." The next day, the latter needs a similar favour from the neighbour and says to him, "Lend me *your* axe," and receives the reply "I will not lend it to you, for you did not lend me your axe when I asked it of you." Any one who acts in this way is taking vengeance. But when he comes to borrow aught, one should give what is asked cheerfully and not repay discourtesy with discourtesy. And so in similar cases. Thus David, expressing his excellent sentiments, said, "If I have requited him that did evil unto me, or despoiled mine adversary" . . . [Ps. 7:5].

8. So too, one who bears a grudge against a fellow-Israelite violates a prohibition, as it is said, "Nor bear a grudge against the children of thy people" [Lev. 19:18]. What is "bearing a grudge?" A said to B, "Let this house to me, or let me borrow this ox." B refuses. After a time, B comes to A to borrow or hire something. A replies, "Here it is. I lend it to you. I am not like you. I will not treat you as you treated me." One who acts thus, transgresses the commandment, "Thou shalt not bear a grudge." One should blot the thing out of his mind and not bear a grudge. For as long as one nurses a grievance and keeps it in mind, one may come to take vengeance.

The Torah, accordingly, emphatically warns us not to bear a grudge, so that the impression of the wrong shall be quite obliterated and be no longer remembered. This is the right principle. It alone makes civilized life and social intercourse possible.

RESPONSUM
MAIMONIDES TO OBADIAH, THE PROSELYTE

QUESTION:

The question which Obadiah, the righteous proselyte, asked of our teacher, Moses, of blessed memory, and his answers. [Since his father was not a member of the house of Israel, he wants to know if in his prayers he may say "God of our fathers."]

ANSWER:

Says Moses the son of Maimon of the children of the exile of Jerusalem in Spain [as a compliment to Obadiah the Proselyte, Maimonides describes himself in a phrase taken from the prophet Obadiah 1:20], may his memory be a blessing [the responsum was copied after the death of Maimonides].

There has come to us the questions of our teacher and rabbi, Obadiah, the learned and intelligent proselyte. May God repay him and may his reward be perfect from the God of Israel, since he came to seek shelter under his wings. You ask concerning procedure with regard to benedictions and prayers. When you pray privately or with the congregation, may you say, "God of *our* fathers, who has sanctified *us* by His commandments, and Who has separated and chosen *us* and has given inheritance to *our* fathers and brought *us* out of the land of Egypt and did miracles to *our* fathers," and all such similar phrases [i.e., that appear frequently in the prayer book]? You must say all of these as they are; and you must not change a single word; but just as a born Israelite prays and blesses, so must you bless and pray whether you are praying privately or are the cantor of the congregation.

The essence of the matter is this: Abraham, our father, taught all people and brought them wisdom and told them of the true faith and the unity of God and rejected idols and made void their service and brought many under the wings of the Divine Presence; he instructed them and commanded his sons in his household after him to guard the path of God, as it is written in the Torah [Gen. 18:19]: "For I know him [God says], that he will command his sons and his household after him to guard the way of God." Therefore, every one to the end of all generations [i.e., at all times in the future], who becomes a proselyte and whoever declares the name of God as One, as it is written in the Torah, is a disciple of Abraham, our father, upon whom be peace, and they are all children of his household. It is he who turned them to the good path, just as he [Abraham] turned the men of his generation by his own word of mouth and by his teachings. Thus is he the one who converts all who are destined to become proselytes through his mandate which he commanded his sons and his household after him. Thus we see that Abraham our father is the father of his worthy descendants who walk in his paths, the father of his disciples and of every proselyte who comes to join Israel.

Therefore, you must say [in your prayers], "Our God and God of our fathers"; for Abraham, on whom be peace, he is your father and you can say [in the prayers] "who has given as inheritance to our fathers . . .'; for to Abraham was given the Land, as it is said [Gen. 13:17]: "Arise, walk through the land through its length and its breadth, for to thee I give it." However, as to the phrases, "who has brought us out of Egypt," or "who has performed miracles to our fathers," if you wish to change them and say, "who has brought Israel from Egypt," or "has done miracles to Israel," you may say it that way.

> [Maimonides means that the proselyte is direct kin to Abraham but perhaps cannot be described as being kin to the later generations who were in Egypt. But he does not stress this distinction, since he continues as follows:]

But if you do not change the phrase, no harm has been done at all; for, since you have entered under the wings of the Shekhina [The Divine Presence] and are joined with Him, there is no difference at all between us and you, and all the miracles that were done are as if they were done for you as well as for us. Thus Scripture says: "Let not the stranger who is joined unto the Lord say, 'God has set me apart from His people.'" [Isa. 56:3]. There is no difference at all between us and you in any matter. There is no question but that you must read the blessing: "who has chosen us," and "who has given us an inheritance," and "who has set us apart," because the Creator has already chosen you and set you apart from the Gentiles and given *you* the Law; for the Torah was given both to us and to the proselytes, as it is said:

"As for the congregation, one statute there is for you and for the proselyte, an eternal law for your generations, for you and for the proselyte before the Lord; one law and judgment shall be for you and for the proselyte." [Nu. 15:15, 16]. Know thou that our fathers who came out of Egypt were, the majority of them, idolators. In Egypt they intermingled with the Gentiles and learned their ways, until the Holy One, blessed be He, sent Moses, on whom be peace, the teacher of all prophets, and set us apart from the other peoples and brought us under the wings of the Shekhina, for us and for all the proselytes, and gave us all one Law.

Let not your genealogy be deprecated in your own sight. If we [born Jews] trace our genealogy to Abraham, Isaac, and Jacob, you are related to Him who created the world, for thus it is clearly said in Isaiah [44:5]: "One will say I am the Lord's and another will call himself with the name of Jacob."

And all that we have said to you with regard to the benedictions, that you should not change their form [i.e., that you should not omit the words, "God of our fathers," etc.], for all of it there is a proof in the tractate Bikkurim [1:4]. There we learn that the proselyte who brings [first fruits] does not read the statement prescribed, because he cannot say, [the Land] "which God swore to give to our fathers;" but when he prays privately, he must say, "Our God and the God of the fathers of Israel," and when he is in the synagogue, he says, "Our God and the God of our fathers."

This is the anonymous Mishna and is the opinion of Rabbi Meir [this is according to the general principle stated in the Talmud [Sanh. 86a], that all anonymous parts of the Mishna are to be ascribed to Rabbi Meir]. But this is not the law, as is made clear in the Jerusalem Talmud [Bik., end of ch. 1], where it is said, "It is taught in the name of Rabbi Judah; the proselyte himself can bring and do the reading. Why? (i.e., why is he permitted to say, 'God of our Fathers'?)"

For (God said to Abraham) "I have made thee into a multitude of nations" [Gen. 17:5]. In the past you were father to Aram [as in the Palestinian Talmud text]; from now on you will be father to all living creatures. Rabbi Joshua son of Levi says that the law is according to Rabbi Judah [i.e., that a proselyte may say "God of our fathers"]. An actual case came before Rabbi Abbahu and he decided it according to Rabbi Judah [thus far the quotation from the Palestinian Talmud].

Hence it is made clear to you that you must say, "Which God swore to our fathers to give us," that Abraham is your father and ours, and of all the righteous who walk in his way. The same applies to all the other benedictions and prayers. Do not change any of them at all.

Thus writeth Moses the son of Maimon.

EPISTLE TO YEMEN

THIS IS THE TEXT OF THE EPISTLE OF R. MOSES B. MAIMON, RABBI AND DAYYAN OF BLESSED MEMORY, IN REPLY TO A LETTER FROM R. JACOB OF YEMEN.

To the honored, great, and holy Master and Teacher, Jacob, wise and genial, dear and revered sage, son of the honored, great, and holy Master and Teacher, Nathaniel Fayyumi, distinguished Prince of Yemen, president of its congregations, leader of its communities, may the spirit of God rest upon him, and upon all his associates and upon all the scholars of the communities of Yemen. May the Lord keep and protect them. From a loving friend who never saw him but knows him only by reputation, Moses b. Maimon b. Joseph b. Isaac b. Obadiah of blessed memory.

Just as plants bear testimony to the existence of real roots, and waters are evidence for the excellence of springs, so has a firm shoot developed from the roots of truth and righteousness, and a huge river has gushed forth from the spring of mercy in the land of Yemen, to water therewith all gardens and to make the flowers blossom. It flows gently on to satisfy the needs of the weary and thirsty in the arid places; wayfarers and folks from the isles of the sea satisfy their needs with it.

Consequently it was proclaimed from Spain to Babylonia, from one end of heaven to the other: "Ho, ye every one that thirsteth come for water." [Isaiah 55:1]. Men of business and traffic unanimously declare to all inquirers that they have found in the land of Yemen a beautiful and delightful plantation, and a rich pasture with faithful shepherds wherein every lean one shall wax fat.

They strengthen the indigent with bread and greet the opulent hospitably and generously; even the Sabaean caravans look forward to their generosity. Their hands are stretched out to every passer-by, and their homes are wide open to every traveler. With them all find tranquillity; sorrow and sighing flee.

They continually study the Law of Moses, walk in the way of R. Ashi, pursue justice, repair the breach, uphold the principles of the Torah, bring back the stray people of God by encouraging words, observe the religious ceremonies punctiliously in their communities; "there is no breach, no going forth, and no outcry in the broad places [Psalms 144:14]."

Blessed be the Lord that He has allowed Jews to remain who observe the Torah and obey its injunctions in the most distant peninsulas, as we were graciously assured through Isaiah, His servant, for it is you the people of Yemen he was alluding to when he prophesied, "From the uttermost part of the earth have we heard songs." [24:16].

When we departed from the West to behold the pleasantness of the Lord and to visit His holy place, we learnt that your father has gone to his eternal rest. May God bestow His Justice and Goodness upon him. May he enter unto peace and rest upon his bed. May He send him Angels of Mercy. May he rest and rise up for his reward at the end of days.

This is the token, dearly beloved friend, that God was pleased with your father's deeds, and that He will compensate him doubly, and grant him peace. For you, his son, have risen in his stead to promote religion and observance, to further justice and righteousness, to obey His precepts and laws, and to abide by His covenant. May the Lord thy God be with you as He was with your fathers. May He not forsake you, nor abandon you. May He give you broad understanding to judge His people. May His words never depart from your mouth nor the mouth of your seed as it was written [Isaiah 59:10]. May you succeed your father as leader of his people, and God grant that your fame be greater than his.

When your communication arrived in Egypt, dearly beloved friend, our ears were pleased at hearing it read, and the mere view of it was a feast to the eyes. It revealed that you were one of the ministers of the Lord who dwell in His fans, and are pitched at His standard; that you pursue the study of the Torah, love its laws, and watch at its gates. May the Lord divulge unto you its secrets, and stock you abundantly with the knowledge of its treasures, make its crown your chief crown, place its necklace upon your neck, and may its words be a lamp unto your feet, and a light unto your path, and through them may you become celebrated. "When all the people of the land will see that the name of the Lord is upon you they shall fear you." [Deut. 28:10].

You write in your letter, dear friend, of a report that some of our co-religionists in the diaspora, may the Lord keep and protect them, praise and extol me very highly and compare me to the illustrious Geonim. But they have spoken thus about me out of mere tenderness for me, and written about me out of pure goodness. However, hearken to a word fitly spoken by me, and give no heed to the sayings of others. Verily, I am one of the humblest of scholars from Spain whose prestige was lowered in exile.

Although I always study the ordinances of the Lord, I did not attain to the learning of my forebears, for evil days and hard times overtook us; we did not abide in tranquillity. We labored and had no rest. How could we study the law when we were being exiled from city to city, and from country to country. I pursued the reapers in their paths and gathered ears of grain, both the rank and the full ones, as well as the withered and the thin ones. Only recently have I found a home. Were it not for the help of God, I would not have culled the store I did and from which I continually draw.

Furthermore you write in your letter that our friend and disciple, R. Solomon, a princely priest and scholar of understanding, is profuse in praising me, and lavish in lauding me. But truth to say, he has indulged in hyperboles because of his affection for me, and has spoken extravagantly because of his tender feelings for me. May the Lord guard him, and may he be like a blossoming vineyard, and may he return to us hale and hearty.

As for the other matters concerning which you have requested a reply, I deemed it best to respond in the Arabic tongue and idiom. For then all may read it with ease, men, women, and children, for it is important that the substance of our reply altogether be understood by every member of your community.

You write that the rebel leader in Yemen decreed compulsory apostasy for the Jews by forcing the Jewish inhabitants of all the places he had subdued to desert the Jewish religion just as the Berbers had compelled them to do in Maghreb. Verily, this news has broken our backs and has astounded and dumbfounded the whole of our community. And rightly so. For these are evil tidings, "and whosoever heareth of them, both his ears tingle." [I Samuel 3:11].

Indeed, our hearts are weakened, our minds are confused, and the powers of the body wasted because of the dire misfortunes which brought religious persecutions upon us from the two ends of the world, the East and the West, "so that the enemies were in the midst of Israel, some on this side, and some on that side." [Joshua 8:22]. The prophet upon learning of such difficult and dreadful times prayed and interceded in our behalf, as we read, "Then said I, O Lord God, cease, I beseech Thee: how shall Jacob stand? for he is small." [Amos 7:5]. Indeed, this is a subject which no religious man dare take lightly, nor any one who believes in Moses put aside.

There can be no doubt that these are the Messianic travails concerning which the Sages invoked God that they be spared seeing and experiencing them. Similarly the prophets trembled when they envisioned them as we learn from the words of Isaiah, "My heart panteth, fearfulness affrighteth me, the twilight I have longed for hath been turned for me into trembling." [21:4]. Note also the divine exclamation in the Torah expressing sympathy for those who will experience them, as we read, "Alas, who shall live when God doeth this!" [Numbers 24:23].

You write that the hearts of some people have turned away, uncertainty befalls them and their beliefs are weakened, while others have not lost faith nor have they become disquieted. Concerning this matter we have a divine premonition through Daniel who predicted that the prolonged stay of Israel in the Diaspora, and the continuous persecutions will cause many to drift away from our faith, to have misgivings, or to go astray, because they witnessed our feebleness, and noted the triumph of our adversaries and their dominion over us, while others would neither oscillate in their belief, nor be shaken in their convictions.

This may be gathered from the verse, "Many shall purify themselves, make themselves white, and be refined, but the wicked shall do so wickedly, and none of the wicked shall understand; but they that are wise shall understand." [Daniel 12:10]. Further on he foretells that even men of understanding and intelligence who would have brooked milder misfortunes and remained firm in their belief in God and in His servant Moses, will yield to distrust and will err, when they are visited by sterner and harsher afflictions while only a few will remain pure in faith as we read, "And some of them that are wise shall stumble." [Daniel 11:35].

And now, my co-religionists, it is essential for you all to give attention and consideration to that which I am going to point out to you. You should impress it upon the minds of your women and children, so that their faith which may be enfeebled and impaired may be strengthened, and that they be reestablished in an unceasing belief. May the Lord deliver us and you from religious doubt!

Remember, that ours is the true and authentic Divine religion, revealed to us through Moses, the master of the former as well as the later prophets, by means of which God has distinguished us from the rest of mankind, as Scripture says, "Only the Lord had a delight in thy fathers to love them and He chose their seed after them, even you above all peoples." [Deut. 10:15]. This did not happen because of our merits, but rather as an act of Divine grace, and on account of our forefathers who were cognizant of God and submitted to Him as we read, "The Lord did not set His love upon you, nor choose you, because ye were more in number than any people . . . but because the Lord loved you, and because He would keep the oath which He swore unto your fathers." [Deut. 7:7].

God has made us unique by His laws and precepts, and our preeminence is manifested in His rules and statutes, as Scripture says, in narrating God's mercies to us, "And what great nation is there, that hath statutes and ordinances so righteous as all this law, which I set before you this day?" [Deut. 4:8]. Therefore all the nations instigated by envy and impiety rose up against us, and all the kings of the earth motivated by injustice and enmity applied themselves to persecute us.

They wanted to thwart God, but He cannot be thwarted. Ever since the time of Revelation, every despot or slave that has attained to power, be he violent or ignoble, has made it his first aim and his final purpose to destroy our law, and to vitiate our religion, by means of the sword, by violence, or by brute force, such as Amalek, Sisera, Sennacherib, Nebuchadnezzar, Titus, Hadrian, may their bones be ground to dust, and others like them. This is one of the two classes which attempt to foil the Divine will.

The second class consists of the most intelligent and educated among the nations, such as the Syrians, Persians, and Greeks. These also endeavor to demolish our law and to vitiate it by means of arguments which they invent, and by means of controversies which they institute. They seek to render the Law ineffectual and to wipe out every trace thereof by means of their polemical writings, just as the despots plan to do it with the sword.

But neither the one nor the other shall succeed. We possess the divine assurance given to Isaiah concerning any tyrant that will wish to undermine our Law and to annihilate it by weapons of war, that the Lord will demolish them so that they will have no effect. This is only a metaphorical way of saying that his efforts will be of no avail, and that he will not accomplish his purpose. In like manner whenever a disputant shall attempt to demonstrate the falsity of our Law, the Lord will shatter his arguments and prove them absurd, untenable and ineffective. This divine promise is contained in the following verse, "No weapon that is formed against thee shall prosper; and every tongue that shall rise against thee in judgment thou shalt condemn." [Isaiah 54:17].

Although the exponents of both methods persuade themselves that this is a structure which can be demolished, and they exert themselves to undermine its firmly established foundations, they only increase their pain and toil. The structure remains as firmly planted as ever, while the God of Truth mocks and derides them, because they endeavor, with their feeble intelligence, to achieve a goal that is beyond the powers of mortal man.

The inspired writer describes their attempt and God's scorn of them in the following verses: "Let us break their bands asunder, and cast away their words from us. He that sitteth in heaven laugheth, the Lord hath them in derision." [Psalms 2:3–4]. Both of these parties have harassed and afflicted us incessantly throughout the epoch of our political independence, and partly during the period of our dispersion.

After that there arose a new sect which combined the two methods, namely conquest and controversy, into one, because it believed that this procedure would be more effective in wiping out every trace of the Jewish nation and religion. It, therefore, resolved to lay claim to prophecy and found a new faith, contrary to our Divine religion, and to contend that it was equally God-given. Thereby it hoped to raise doubts and to create confusion, since one is opposed to the other and both supposedly emanate from a Divine source, which would lead to the destruction of both religions. For such is the remarkable plan contrived by a man who is envious and querulous. He will strive to kill his enemy and to save his own life, but when he finds it impossible to attain his objective, he will devise a scheme whereby they both will be slain. . . .

Likewise a person ignorant of the secret meaning of Scripture and the deeper significance of the Law, would be led to believe that our religion has something in common with another if he makes a comparison between the two. For he will note that in the Torah there are prohibitions and commandments, just as in other religions there are permitted and interdicted acts. Both contain a system of religious observances, positive and negative precepts, sanctioned by reward and punishment.

If he could only fathom the inner intent of the law, then he would realize that the essence of the true divine religion lies in the deeper meaning of its positive and negative precepts, every one of which will aid man in his striving after perfection, and remove every impediment to the attainment of excellence. These commands will enable the throng and the elite to acquire moral and intellectual qualities, each according to his ability. Thus the godly community becomes preeminent, reaching a two-fold perfection. By the first perfection I mean, man's spending his life in this world under the most agreeable and congenial condition. The second perfection would constitute the achievement of intellectual objectives, each in accordance with his native powers.

The tenets of the other religions which resemble those of Scripture have no deeper meaning, but are superficial imitations, copied from and patterned after it. They modelled their religions upon ours in order to glorify themselves, and indulge the fancy that they are similar to so and so. However, their counterfeiting is an open secret to the learned. Consequently they became objects of derision and ridicule just as one laughs and smiles at an ape when it imitates the actions of men. . . .

Though they shall appear to be triumphant for a while, and be in the ascendancy for a longer or shorter period of time, they shall not last nor endure. We have a divine assurance from time immemorial that whenever a decree of apostasy is passed against us, God will ultimately terminate it. When King David inspired by the Holy Spirit and speaking in the name of the community reflected, how many peoples ruled over Israel in the past, and how many trials and tribulations they had undergone from the beginning of their history, and nevertheless were not exterminated, he was moved to exclaim, "Much have they afflicted me from my youth up; but they have not prevailed against me." [Psalms 129:2].

My brethren, you all know that in the time of Nebuchadnezzar the Wicked, the Jews were compelled to worship idols and none was spared save Hananiah, Mishael and Azariah. Ultimately God destroyed Nebuchadnezzar, and put an end to his laws, and the religion of Truth came back to its own.

Similarly during the Second Commonwealth when the wicked Greek rulers gained control of Palestine, they instituted severe persecutions against Israel in order to abolish the Torah. The Jews were compelled to profane the Sabbath, and were forbidden to observe the rite of circumcision. Every Jew was forced to write on his garment the words "we have no portion in the Lord God of Israel," and also to engrave this sentence on the horns of his ox and then plough with it. This state of affairs lasted about fifty-two years. Finally, God brought to an end simultaneously their empire and their laws.

The sages, of blessed memory, frequently allude to persecutions in the following manner: "once the wicked government passed the following

decree of persecution," or, "they decreed so and so." After a while God
would make the decree null and void by destroying the power which
issued it. It was this observation that led the rabbis of blessed memory to
affirm that persecutions are of short duration. [Ketubot 3b].

The divine assurance was given to Jacob our father, that his descendants
would survive the people who degraded and discomfited them as it is written: "And thy seed shall be like the dust of the earth." [Genesis 28:14].
That is to say, although his offspring will be abased like dust that is trodden
under foot, they will ultimately emerge triumphant and victorious, and as
the simile implies, just as the dust settles finally upon him who tramples
upon it, and remains after him, so shall Israel outlive its persecutors.

The prophet Isaiah has long ago predicted that various peoples will
succeed in vanquishing Israel and lording over them for some time. But
that ultimately God will come to Israel's assistance and will put a stop to
their woes and affliction as is suggested in the following verse:

A grievous vision is declared unto me; the treacherous one will deal
treacherously, and the spoiler will spoil; Go up, O Elam, besiege, O
Media! But ultimately the sighing thereof I shall make to cease.
[Isaiah 21:2].

We are in possession of the divine assurance that Israel is indestructible
and imperishable, and will always continue to be a preeminent community.
As it is impossible for God to cease to exist, so is Israel's destruction and
disappearance from the world unthinkable, as we read, "For I the Lord
change not, and ye, O sons of Jacob, will not be consumed." [Malachi 3:6].
Similarly He has avowed and assured us that it is unimaginable that He
will reject us entirely even if we disobey Him, and disregard His behests,
as the prophet Jeremiah avers, "Thus saith the Lord: If heaven above can
be measured, and the foundations of the earth searched out beneath, then
will I also cast off all the seed of Israel for all that they have done, saith
the Lord." [Jeremiah 31:36].

Indeed, this very promise has already been given before through Moses
our Teacher who says, "And yet for all that, when they are in the land of
their enemies, I will not reject them, neither will I abhor them, to destroy
them utterly, and to break My covenant with them; for I am the Lord their
God." [Lev. 26:44].

Put your trust in the true promises of Scripture, brethren, and be not
dismayed at the series of persecutions or the enemy's ascendency over us,
or the weakness of our people. These trials are designed to test and purify
us so that only the saints and the pious ones of the pure and undefiled
lineage of Jacob will adhere to our religion and remain within the fold, as
it is written, "And among the remnant are those whom the Lord shall call."
[Joel 3:5].

This verse makes it clear that they are not numerous, being the descendants of those who were present on Mount Sinai, witnessed the divine Revelation, entered into the covenant of God, and undertook to do and obey as is signified in their saying, "We will do, and obey." [Exodus 24:7]. They obligated not only themselves but also their descendants as it is written, "to us and to our children forever." [Deut. 29:28]. We have been given adequate divine assurance that not only did all the persons who were present at the Sinaitic Revelation believe in the prophecy of Moses and in his Law, but that their descendants likewise would do so, until the end of time, as it is written, "Lo, I come unto thee in a thick cloud, that the people may hear when I speak with thee, and may also believe thee forever." [Exodus 10:9].

Consequently it is manifest that he who spurns the religion that was revealed at that theophany, is not an offspring of the folk who witnessed it. For our sages of blessed memory have insisted that they who do entertain scruples concerning the divine messages are not scions of the race that were present on Mount Sinai. [Nedarim 20a]. May God guard us and you from doubt, and banish from our midst confusion, suspicion, which lead to it.

Now, my co-religionists in the Diaspora, it behooves you to hearten one another, the elders to guide the youth, and the leaders to direct the masses. Give your assent to the Truth that is immutable and unchangeable, and to the following postulates of a religion that shall never fail. God is one in a unique sense of the term, and Moses is His prophet and spokesman, and the greatest and most perfect of the seers. To him was vouchsafed by God what has never been vouchsafed to any prophet before him, nor will it be in the future. The entire Torah was divinely revealed to Moses of whom it was said, "with him do I speak mouth to mouth." [Num. 12:8]. It will neither be abrogated nor superseded, neither supplemented nor abridged. Never shall it be supplanted by another divine Revelation containing positive and negative duties.

Keep well in mind the Revelation on Sinai in accordance with the divine precept to perpetuate the memory of this occasion and not to allow it to fall into oblivion. Furthermore we were enjoined to impress this event upon the minds of our children, as it is written, "Only take heed to thyself, and keep thy soul diligently, lest thou forget the things which thine eyes saw, and lest they depart from thy heart all the days of thy life; but make them known unto thy children and thy children's children." [Deut. 4:9].

It is imperative, my fellow Jews, that you make this great spectacle of the Revelation appeal to the imagination of your children. Proclaim at public gatherings its momentousness. For this event is the pivot of our religion, and the proof which demonstrates its veracity. Evaluate this phenomenon at its true importance for Scripture has pointed out its significance in the verse, "For ask now of the days past, which were before thee, since the day that God created man upon the earth, and from the one end of heaven unto the other, whether there hath been any such thing as this great thing is, or hath been heard like it?" [Deut. 4:32].

Remember, my co-religionists, that this great, incomparable and unique historical event, is attested by the best of evidence. For never before or since, has a whole nation witnessed a revelation from God or beheld His splendor. The purpose of all this was to confirm us in the faith so that nothing can change it, and to reach a degree of certainty which will sustain us in these trying times of fierce persecution and absolute tyranny, as it is written, "for God is come to test you." [Ex. 20:17]. Scripture means that God revealed Himself to you thus in order to give you strength to withstand all future trials. Now do not slip nor err, be steadfast in your religion and persevere in your faith and its duties.

Solomon, of blessed memory, has compared our people to a beautiful woman with a perfect figure, marred by no defect, in the verse, "Thou are all fair, my love; and there is no spot in thee." [Song of Songs 4:7]. On the other hand, he depicted the adherents of other religions and faiths, who strive to entice and win us over to their convictions, as courtesans who lure virtuous women for lewd purposes.

Similarly, they seek devices to trap us into embracing their religions, and subscribing to their doctrines. To these who endeavor to decoy her into avowing the superiority of their creed, our nation deftly replies, "Why do you take hold of me, can you confer upon me something like the felicity of the two companies?" She reasons thus, "If you can furnish us with something like the Revelation on Sinai, in which the camp of Israel faced the camp of the Divine Presence, then we shall espouse your doctrines."

This is metaphorically expressed in the verse, "Return, return, O Shulammite; return, return, that we may look upon thee. What will you see in the Shulammite? As it were a dance of two companies." [Song of Songs 7:1]. . . .

Note well the apt imagery and the deeper significance of the aforementioned verse. The fourfold occurrence of the word "return" is an allusion to the four empires, each of which will endeavor to coerce us to abandon our faith and embrace theirs. Incidentally, it may be mentioned that we are now living under the aegis of the Fourth Empire. A prediction to this effect is found in the Torah, that our enemies will force us to accept their faith, for we read, "And there shall ye serve god, the work of men's hands." [Deut. 4:28].

However, it will not be general throughout the world and God will never deprive us of His Law. As he assured us saying: For it shall not be forgotten from the mouth of His seed. Indeed, Isaiah, the herald of the national redemption, has already stated that Israel's indestructibility is the result of a Divine pact betokened by the perpetuation of the Torah in our midst, and our devotion to its tenets and teachings, as he says, "And as for Me, this is My covenant with them, saith the Lord; My spirit that is upon thee, and My words which I have put in thy mouth, shall not depart out of thy mouth, nor out of the mouth of thy seed, nor out of the mouth of thy seed's seed, saith the Lord, from henceforth and for ever." [Isaiah 59:21].

Our nation speaks with pride of the virulent oppression it has suffered, and the sore tribulations it has endured, to quote the words of the Psalmist, "Nay, but for Thy sake are we killed all the day." [44:23]. The rabbis, of blessed memory, in Midrash Hazita, remark that the verse "nay, but for Thy sake" alludes to the generation that undergoes persecution. [Midrash Song of Songs I:3, ed. Vilna, f. 13a]. Let those persons exult who suffered dire misfortunes, were deprived of their riches, forced into exile and lost their belongings. For the bearing of these hardships is a source of glory and a great achievement in the sight of God. Whoever is visited by these calamities is like a burnt offering upon the altar. We may apply in commendation the verse to them, "Consecrate yourselves today to the Lord, that he may also bestow upon you a blessing this day." [Ex. 32: 29].

It behooves the victim for the sake of his religion to escape and flee to the desert and wilderness, and not to consider separation from family or loss of wealth. For they are a slight sacrifice and a paltry offering due to God, King of kings, possessor of all things, the Lord thy God, whose Name is glorious and awful. God may be trusted to compensate you well in this world and in the world to come.

We have noted that godly and pious folk who are animated by a desire to get acquainted with the truth and those who are engaged in its pursuit, rush to the divine religion and wend their way from the most distant parts to the homes of scholars. They seek to gain increased insight into the law with the concomitant hope that God will amply reward them. How much more is it one's duty to go into exile, if the question of observing the whole Torah is at stake.

When a man finds it arduous to gain a livelihood in one country he emigrates to another. All the more is it incumbent upon a Jew who is restricted in the practice of his religion, to depart for another place. If he finds it impossible to leave that locality for the time being, he must not become careless and indulge with abandon in the desecration of the Sabbath and the dietary laws on the assumption that he is exempt from all religious obligations. It is the eternally inescapable duty, willy-nilly, of every one belonging to the stock of Jacob to abide by the Law. Nay, he exposes himself to punishment for the violation of each and every positive or negative precept.

Let no man conclude that he may freely disregard the less important ceremonies without liability to penalty because he has committed under duress some major sins. For Jeroboam, son of Nebat, may his bones be ground to dust, was chastised not only for the sin of worshipping the calves and inciting Israel to do the same, but also for his failure to construct a booth on the Feast of Tabernacles. This is one of the fundamental principles of our religion. Understand it aright, teach it, and apply the principle widely.

In your letter you mention that the apostle has spurred on a number of people to believe that several verses in Scripture allude to the Madman [i.e., Mohammed], such as "bimeod meod"* [Gen. 17:20], "he shined forth from Mount Paran" [Deut. 33:1], "a prophet from the midst of thee" [Deut. 18:15], and the promise to Ishmael, "I will make him a great nation" [Gen. 17:20].

These arguments have been rehearsed so often that they have become nauseating. It is not enough to declare that they are altogether feeble; nay, to cite as proofs these verses is ridiculous and absurd in the extreme. For these are not matters that can confuse the minds of anyone. Neither the untutored multitude nor the apostates themselves who delude others with them, believe in them or entertain any illusions about them.

Their purpose in citing these verses is to win favor in the eyes of the Gentiles by demonstrating that they believe the statement of the Koran that Mohammed was mentioned in the Torah. But the Muslims themselves put no faith in their arguments, they neither accept nor cite them, because they are manifestly so fallacious.

Inasmuch as the Muslims could not find a single proof in the entire Bible nor a reference or possible allusion to their prophet which they could utilize, they were compelled to accuse us saying, "You have altered the text of the Torah, and expunged every trace of the name of Mohammed therefrom." They could find nothing stronger than this ignominious argument the falsity of which is easily demonstrated to one and all by the following facts.

First, Scripture was translated into Syriac, Greek, Persian and Latin hundreds of years before the appearance of Mohammed. Secondly, there is a uniform tradition as to the text of the Bible both in the East and the West, with the result that no differences in the text exist at all, not even in the vocalization, for they are all correct. Nor do any differences effecting the meaning exist. The motive for their accusation lies therefore, in the absence of any allusion to Mohammed in the Torah.

The phrase "a great nation" cited above does not connote a people in possession of prophecy or a Law, but merely one large in numbers just as in reference to idolaters Scripture says, "nations greater and mightier than yourselves." [Deut. 11:23]. Similarly, the phrase "bimeod meod" simply signifies "exceedingly." Were there any allusion in the verse to Mohammed, then it would have read, "and I shall bless him bimeod meod," and whoever likes to hang on to a spider's web might then discover a reference to Mohammed therein. As it is, since Scripture says, "I shall increase him bimeod meod," it can only denote an extravagant increment in numbers.

There is no question that the Divine assurance to Abraham to bless his descendants, to reveal the Torah to them, and to make them the Chosen

---

*The numerical value of Mohammed in Hebrew orthography is 92, and equals that of the Hebrew words "bimeod meod." [Tr.]

People, refers only to the offspring of Isaac. For Ishmael is mentioned as an adjunct and appendage in the blessing of Isaac, which reads, "and also of the son of the bond-woman will I make a nation." [Gen. 21:13]. This verse suggests that Isaac holds a primary position and Ishmael a subordinate place.

This point is made even more explicit in the blessing which ignores Ishmael entirely. "For in Isaac shall seed be called in thee." [Gen. 21:12]. The meaning of God's promise to Abraham is that the issue of Ishmael will be vast in numbers but neither preeminent nor the object of divine favor, nor distinguished for the attainment of excellence. Not because of them will Abraham be famed or celebrated, but by the noted and illustrious scions of Isaac. The phrase "shall be called" simply means, shall be renowned, as it does in the verse, "Let thy name be called in them, and the name of my fathers Abraham and Isaac." [Gen. 48:16]. . . .

To sum up, the Divine covenant made with Abraham to grant the sublime Law to his descendants referred exclusively to those who belonged to the stock of both Isaac and Jacob. Hence the prophet expresses his gratitude to God for "the covenant which He made with Abraham, and His oath unto Isaac, which He established unto Jacob for a statute, and to Israel for an everlasting covenant." [Ps. 105:9; I Chr. 16:16]. . . .

The argument from the phrase "He shined forth from Mount Paran" [Deut. 33:2] is easily refutable. Shined is past tense. Had Scripture employed the future tense "he will shine forth from Mount Paran," then the impostors might have had a semblance of truth on their side. However the use of the past tense "he shined forth" demonstrates that this phrase describes an event that has taken place, namely the theophany on Sinai. When the Deity was about to reveal Himself on Sinai, the heavenly light did not descend suddenly like a thunderbolt, but came down gently, manifesting itself gradually first from the top of one mountain, then from another, until He reached His abode on Sinai.

This notion is implied in the verse, "The Lord revealed Himself at Sinai, after His light had radiated to them from Seir and glimmered from Mount Paran." [Deut. 33:2]. Mark well, that the phrase "unto them" refers to Israel. Note also how Scripture indicates the various graduations in the intensity of the Divine Splendor. It speaks of the light that *glimmered* from Mount Paran which is further removed from Sinai, but of the light that *radiated* from Mount Seir, which is nearer to it, and finally of the revelation of the full splendor of God on Sinai which was the goal of the theophany as is related in the verse "And the glory of God abode on Mount Sinai" [Ex. 24:16], "and the Lord came from Sinai." [Deut. 33:2].

Similarly, the idea that the light descended gradually from mountain to mountain is conveyed in Deborah's description of the grandeur of Israel at the Revelation on Sinai when she exclaimed "Lord when Thou didst go forth out of the field of Edom" [Judges 5:4]. Our sages, of blessed memory, tell us that God, may He be praised and exalted, charged a prophet before the time of Moses to go to the Romans and another to go to the Arabs with the purpose of presenting them the Torah, but each of them in turn spurned it.

When Moses was later sent to us we signified our acceptance in the words, "All that the Lord hath spoken will we do, and obey." [Ex. 24:7]. The aforementioned event happened before the Sinaitic Revelation, consequently Scripture speaks in the past tense: "He came, radiated forth, and shone," which proves that no prophecy is intended in these words.

You write in your letter, that some people were duped by the argument that Mohammed is alluded to in the verse "A prophet will the Lord thy God raise up unto thee, from the midst of thee, of thy brethren" [Deut. 18:15], while others remained unconvinced because of the phrase "from the midst of thee." It is most astonishing that some folks should be deluded by such specious proof, while others were also persuaded, were it not for the phrase "from the midst of thee."

Under these circumstances it is incumbent upon you to concentrate and understand my view in the matter. Remember that it is not right to take a passage out of its context and to draw inferences from it. It is imperative to take into consideration the preceding and following statements in order to fathom the writer's meaning and purpose before making any deductions. Were it otherwise, then it would be possible to assert that Scripture has prohibited obedience to any prophet, and interdicted belief in miracles, by quoting the verse, "Thou shalt not hearken unto the words of that prophet," [Deut. 13:4]. It could likewise be affirmed that a positive command exists requiring us to worship idols, by citing the verse "And ye shall serve other gods" [Deut. 11:16]. Other illustrations could be multiplied ad libidinem. To sum up, it is wrong to interpret any given verse apart from its context.

In order to comprehend unequivocally the verse under discussion, namely, "A prophet will the Lord thy God raise unto thee, from the midst of thee, of thy brethren," it is necessary to ascertain its context. The beginning of the paragraph whence the verse is taken, contains prohibitions of the acts of soothsaying, augury, divination, astrology, sorcery, incantation and the like.

The Gentiles believe that through these practices they can predict the future course of events and take the necessary precautions to forestall them. The interdiction of these occult proceedings was accompanied by the explanation that the Gentiles believe they can depend upon them to determine future happenings. But you may not do so. You will learn about the time to come from a prophet who will rise up among you, whose predictions will come true without fail.

You will thus arrive at a foreknowledge of circumstances without being obliged to resort to augury, divination, astrology and the like, for he will spare you that. Matters will be facilitated for you by the fact that this prophet will live within your borders. You will not be compelled to go in search after him from country to country, nor to travel to distant parts, as is implied in the phrase "from the midst of thee."

Moreover, another notion is conveyed in the words "from the midst of thee, of thy brethren, like unto me," namely, that he will be one of you, that is, a Jew. The obvious deduction is that you shall be distinguished above all others for the sole possession of prophecy. The words "like unto me" were specifically added to indicate that only the descendants of Jacob are meant. For the phrase "of thy brethren" by itself might have been misunderstood and taken to refer also to Esau and Ishmael, since we do find Israel addressing Esau as brother, for example, in the verse, "Thus saith thy brother Israel" [Numbers 20:14].

On the other hand, the words "like unto me," do not denote a prophet as great as Moses, for this interpretation is precluded by the statement "And there hath not arisen a prophet since in Israel like unto Moses." [Deut. 34:10]. The general drift of the chapter points to the correctness of our interpretation and will be confirmed by the succession of the verses, to wit, "There shall not be found among you any one that maketh his son or his daughter to pass through the fire, etc.," [Deut. 18:10], "For those nations that thou are to dispossess, hearken unto soothsayers, and unto diviners; but as for thee, the Lord thy God hath not suffered thee so to do." [verse 14]. "A prophet will the Lord thy God raise up unto thee, from the midst of thee, of thy brethren, like unto me." [verse 15].

It is obviously clear that the prophet alluded to here will not be a person who will produce a new law, or found a new religion. He will merely enable us to dispense with diviners and astrologers, and will be available for consultation concerning anything that may befall us, just as the Gentiles confer with soothsayers and prognosticators. Thus we find Saul advising with Samuel concerning his lost asses, as we read, "Beforetime in Israel, when a man went to inquire of God, thus he said: 'Come and let us go to the seer'; for he that is now called a prophet was beforetime called a seer." [Samuel 9:9].

Our disbelief in the prophecy of Omar and Zeid is not due to the fact that they are non-Jews, as the unlettered folk imagine, and in consequence of which they are compelled to justify their standpoint by the Biblical statement "from thy midst, out of thy brethren." For Job, Zophar, Bildad, Eliphaz, and Elihu are all considered prophets and are non-Jews. On the other hand, although Hananiah, the son of Azur was a Jew, he was deemed an accursed and false prophet.

Whether one should yield credence to a prophet or not depends upon the nature of his doctrines, and not upon his race, as we shall explain presently. Our ancestors have witnessed Moses, our Teacher, foremost among the prophets, holding a colloquy with the Divinity, reposed implicit faith in him when they said to him, "Go thou near and hear," [Deut. 5:24]. Now he assured us that no other law remained in heaven that would subsequently be revealed, nor would there even be another Divine dispensation, as the verse, "It is not in heaven," [Deut. 30:12] implies.

Scripture prohibits us from making any amendments to the Law or eliminating anything, for we read, "Thou shalt not add thereto, nor diminish from it" [Deut. 13:1]. We pledged and obligated ourselves to God to abide by His Law, we, our children, and our children's children, until the end of time, as Scripture says, "The secret things belong to the Lord our God, but the things which are revealed belong unto us and to our children forever." [Deut. 29:28].

Any prophet, therefore, no matter what his pedigree is, be he priest, Levite, or Amalekite, is perfidious even if he asserts that only one of the precepts of the Torah is void, in view of the Mosaic pronouncement, "unto us and unto our children forever." Such a one we would declare a false prophet and would execute him if we had jurisdiction over him. We would take no notice of the miracles that he might perform, just as we would disregard the wonder-working of one who seeks to lure people to idolatry, as we are enjoined in the verse "And the sign or wonder came to pass . . . thou shalt not hearken unto the words of that prophet" [Deut. 13:3].

Since Moses, of blessed memory, has prohibited image worship for all the time, we know that the miracles of a would-be seducer to idolatry are wrought by trickery and sorcery. Similarly, since Moses has taught us that the Law is eternal, we stamp definitely as a prevaricator any one who argues that it was destined to be in force for a fixed duration of time, because he contravenes Moses. Consequently we pay no attention to his assertions or supernatural performances.

Inasmuch as we do not believe in Moses because of his miracles, we are under no obligations to institute comparison between his miracles and those of others. Our everlastingly firm trust and steadfast faith in Moses is due to the fact that our forebears as well as he had heard the Divine discourse on Sinai, as it is intimated in Scripture, "and they will also believe thee forever" [Ex. 19:9]. This event is analogous to the situation of two witnesses who observed a certain act simultaneously. Each of them saw what his fellow saw and each of them is sure of the truth of the statement of his fellow, and does not require proof or demonstration, whereas other people, to whom they would report their testimony, would not be convinced without confirmation or certification.

Similarly, we of the Jewish faith, are convinced of the truth of the prophecy of Moses, inasmuch as our ancestors in common with him witnessed the Divine revelation on Sinai, and not merely because of his miracles. He performed all of these only as the occasion demanded and as is recorded in Scripture.

We do not give credence to the tenets of a miracle worker in the same way we trust in the truth of Moses our Teacher, nor does any analogy exist between them. This distinction is a fundamental principle of our religion, but seems to have fallen into oblivion, and has been disregarded by our co-religionists. . . .

If a Jewish or Gentile prophet urges and encourages people to follow the religion of Moses without adding thereto or diminishing therefrom, like Isaiah, Jeremiah, and the others, we demand a miracle from him. If he can perform it we recognize him and bestow upon him the honor due to a prophet, but if he fails to do so, he is put to death. We require only a miracle as his credentials, although it may be wrought by stratagem or magic, just as we accept the evidence of witnesses although there is a possibility of perjury. For we are divinely commanded through·Moses to render judgment in a suit at law in accordance with the testimony of two witnesses, the possibility of false swearing notwithstanding.

Similarly we are enjoined to yield obedience to one who asserts that he is a prophet provided he can substantiate his claims by miracle or proofs, although there is a possibility that he is an impostor. However, if the would-be prophet teaches tenets that negate the doctrines of Moses, then we must repudiate him. This point was made abundantly clear in the introduction to our large work on the commentary of the Mishnah, where you will find some useful information concerning principles which form the foundation of our religion and the pillars of our faith.

It is incumbent upon you to know that the rule that nothing may ever be added to or diminished from the Laws of Moses, applies equally to the oral law, that is the traditional interpretation transmitted through the sages of blessed memory. Be cautious and on your guard lest any of the heretics —may they speedily perish!—mingle among you, for they are worse than apostates. For although this country is, as you know, a place of scholars, students and schools, they indulge in bombastic talk and we warn our people against their occasional errors, heresies and mistakes. As for you, in this distant country, although you are scholars, learned in the law, and pious, you are few in number, may God increase your number and hasten the time of gathering you all together.

If any of the heretics rises up to corrupt the people, they will undermine the faith of the young folks and they will not find a saviour. Beware of them and know that, in our opinion, it is permitted to slay them, for they repudiate the statement in the prophecy of Moses who commanded us to act "According to the law which they shall teach thee, and according to the judgment which they shall tell thee thou shalt do." [Deut. 17:11]. They assert in wicked defiance that they believe most firmly in the prophecy of Moses, as the Arabs and Byzantines say, yet they destroy and nullify his law and kill the adherents thereof. Whoever joins them is just like his seducer. We deemed it imperative to call your attention to these facts, and to raise the young generation on these tenets, because they are a pillar of faith. . . .

Remember that a blind person submits to an individual having power of sight for intelligent direction, knowing that he lacks the vision to guide him safely; and an ailing person, unskilled in the art of medicine, and uninformed as to matters detrimental to or beneficial for his health, defers to a physician for guidance and obeys him implicitly. Just so is it indispensable for the laity to yield unswervingly to the prophets, who were men of true insight, and to confide in them in respect to matters affecting the truth or the error of a given teaching. Next in importance are the sages who have studied day and night the dogmas and doctrines of our faith and have learned to distinguish between the genuine and the spurious.

After this exposition you may trust me that the statements you have previously quoted are inaccurate and this applies equally to similar views which you heard expressed in conversation or met with in books. For the author of such sayings is either ignorant, a mountebank, or seeks to destroy the law and to demolish its bulwarks. . . .

Whatever happens in this world through Divine intervention, they say is the inevitable consequence of planetary conjunctions. They have affirmed the truth of their propositions in order to undermine the principles of our religion, and to give free reign to their animal instincts and passions, as do the beasts and the ostriches. We were divinely admonished against those views in Scripture to the following effect: "If you rebel against Me so that I bring disaster upon you as a punishment for your misdeeds, but you ascribe your reverses to chance rather than to your guilt, then shall I increase your afflictions and make them more grievous."

This is the intent of the verse in the Chapter of Admonition, "If you will walk with me 'bekeri' I shall walk with you in the wrath of 'keri' " [Lev. 26:21, 24]. Now "keri" signifies chance, hazard. Scripture means to say if you regard My chastisement as a fortuitous event, then shall I bring the most severe calamities upon you "sevenfold for your sins." [Lev. 26:24]. These foregoing remarks have made it abundantly clear that the advent of the Messiah is in no way subject to the influence of the stars.

Indeed one of our keen minds in the province of Andalusia calculated by means of astrology the date of the final redemption and predicted the coming of the Messiah in a particular year. Every one of our distinguished scholars made little of his declaration, discounted what he did, and censured him sharply for it. But grim fate dealt with him more sternly than we could have. For at the very time when the Messiah was supposed to arrive, a rebel leader appeared in Maghreb who issued an order of conversion as you are well aware. The event proved to be a great debacle for the partisans of this prognosticator. Indeed the hardships experienced by our people in the diaspora are responsible for these extravagances, for a drowning man catches at a straw.

Therefore, my co-religionists, "be strong and let your heart take courage, all you that wait for the Lord." [Psalms 31:25]. Strengthen one another, affirm your faith in the Expected One, may he speedily appear in your midst. "Strengthen ye the weak hands and make firm the tottering knees." [Isaiah 35:3]. Remember! Isaiah, the herald of Israel's redemption, predicted that the prolongation of the adversities of exile will impel many of our people to believe that God has relinquished and abandoned us (far be it from Him), as we read, "But Zion said: 'the Lord hath forsaken me, And the Lord hath forgotten me.' " [49:14].

But he was given the Divine assurance that such is not the case, to quote the following, "Can a woman forget her sucking child, that she should not have compassion on the son of her womb? Yea, these may forget, yet I will not forget thee." [49:15]. In truth, this Divine promise had already been divulged by the First Prophet, who declared: "For the Lord thy God is a merciful God. He will not fail thee, neither destroy thee, nor forget the covenant of thy fathers which He swore unto them." [Deut. 4:31]. "Then the Lord thy God will turn thy captivity, and have compassion on thee, and will return and gather thee from all the peoples whither the Lord thy God hath scattered thee." [Deut. 30:3].

It is, my co-religionists, one of the fundamental articles of the faith of Israel, that the future redeemer of our people will spring only from the stock of Solomon son of David. He will gather our nation, assemble our exiles, redeem us from our degradation, propagate the true religion, and exterminate his opponents, as it is clearly stated in Scripture, "I see him but not now, I behold him but not nigh, there shall step forth a star out of Jacob, and a sceptre shall arise out of Israel. And shall smite through the corners of Moab, and break down all the sons of Seth. And Edom shall be a possession, Seir also, even his enemies, shall be a possession, while Israel doeth valiantly." [Num. 24:17–18]. He will be sent by God at a time of great catastrophe and dire misfortune for Israel as was predicted in the verse, "There will be none remaining, shut up or left at large" [Deut. 32:36]. And when he appears, he will fulfill the promises made in his behalf. A later prophet, too, was alluding to the Messianic tribulations when he declared, "But who can endure the day of his coming" [Malachi 3:2]. This is the proper understanding of this article of faith. . . .

You mention that a certain man in one of the cities of Yemen pretends that he is the Messiah. As I live, I am not surprised at him or at his followers, for I have no doubt that he is mad and a sick person should not be rebuked or reproved for an illness brought on by no fault of his own. Neither am I surprised at his votaries, for they were persuaded by him because of their sorry plight, their ignorance of the importance and high rank of the Messiah, and their mistaken comparison of the Messiah with the son of the Mahdi [the belief in] whose rise they are witnessing.

But I am astonished that you, a scholar who has studied carefully the doctrines of the rabbis, are inclined to repose faith in him. Do you not know, my brother, that the Messiah is a very eminent prophet, more illustrious than all the prophets after Moses? Do you not know that a false pretender to prophecy is liable to capital punishment, for having arrogated to himself unwarranted distinction, just as the person who prophesies in the name of idols is put to death, as we read in Scripture, "But the prophet that shall speak a word presumptuously in My name, which I have not commanded him to speak, or that shall speak in the name of other gods, that same prophet shall die." [Deut. 18:20]. What better evidence is there of his mendacity, than his very pretensions to be the Messiah.

How odd is your remark about this man, that he is renowned for his meekness and a little wisdom, as if these were indeed the attributes of the Messiah. Do these characteristics make him a Messiah? You were beguiled by him because you have not considered the preeminence of the Messiah, the manner and place of his appearance, and the marks whereby he is to be identified.

The Messiah, indeed, ranks after Moses in eminence and distinction, and God has bestowed some gifts upon him which he did not bestow upon Moses, as may be gathered from the following verses: "His delight shall be in the fear of the Lord." [Isaiah 11:3]. "The Spirit of the Lord shall rest upon him." [11:2]. "And Righteousness shall be the girdle of his loins." [11:5]. Six appellations were divinely conferred upon him as the following passage indicates: "For a child is born unto us, and a son is given unto us, and the government is upon his shoulder, and he is called Pele, Yoetz, El, Gibbor, Abiad, Sar-Shalom." [Isaiah 9:5]. And another verse alluding to the Messiah culminates in the following manner, "Thou art my son, this day have I begotten thee." [Psalms 2:7]. All these statements demonstrate the preeminence of the Messiah.

Transcendent wisdom is a *sine qua non* for inspiration. It is an article of our faith that the gift of prophecy is vouchsafed only to the wise, the strong, and the rich. Strong is defined as the ability to control one's passions. Rich signified wealthy in knowledge. Now if we dare not put trust in a man's pretensions to prophecy if he does not excel in wisdom, how much less must we take seriously the claims of an ignoramus to be the Messiah.

That the man in question is an ignoramus is evident from the order he issued, as you state, to the people to give away all their possessions for charitable purposes. They did right in disobeying him, and he was wrong inasmuch as he disregarded the Jewish law concerning alms-giving. For Scripture says, "If a man will devote anything of all that he has" and the rabbis explain in their comment on this verse, "part of all that he has, but not all that he has."

The sages accordingly set bounds to the bounty of the beneficent in an explicit statement which reads, "He who is inclined to be liberal with the poor, may not part with more than a fifth of his possessions." [Ketubot 50a]. There is no doubt that the process of reasoning which led him to claim that he is the Messiah, induced him to issue a command to his fellowmen to give away their property and distribute it to the poor. But then the affluent would become destitute and vice versa. According to his ordinance, it would be necessary for the *nouveaux riches* to return their recently acquired property to the newly impoverished. Such a regulation, which would keep property moving in a circle, is the acme of folly.

As to the place where the Messiah will make his first appearance, Scripture intimates that he will first present himself only in the Land of Israel, as we read, "He will suddenly appear in His Temple" [Malachi 3:1]. As for the advent of the Messiah, nothing at all will be known about it before it occurs. The Messiah is not a person concerning whom it may be predicted that he will be the son of so and so, or of the family of so and so.

On the contrary he will be unknown before his coming, but he will prove by means of miracles and wonders that he is the true Messiah. Scripture in allusion to his mysterious lineage says, "His name is the Shoot, and he will shoot up out of his place." [Zechariah 6:12]. Similarly, Isaiah referring to the arrival of the Messiah implies that neither his father nor mother, nor his kith nor kin will be known, "For he will shoot up right forth as a sapling, and as a root out of the dry ground." [53.2].

After his manifestation in Palestine, Israel will be gathered in Jerusalem and the other cities of Palestine. Then will the tidings spread to the East and the West until it will reach you in Yemen and those beyond you in India as we learn from Isaiah, "That sendeth ambassadors by the sea, even in vessels of papyrus upon the waters, go, ye swift messengers, to a nation that has been pulled and plucked to a people that suffered terribly from their beginning onward." [18:2]. The process of the final redemption will not be reversed so that it will first appear in distant lands, and ultimately reach Palestine.

What the great powers are, which all the prophets from Moses to Malachi ascribe to the Messiah, may be inferred from various statements in the twenty-four books of Scripture. The most significant of them all is the fact that the mere report of his advent will strike terror into the hearts of all the kings of the earth, and their kingdoms will fall, neither will they be able to war or revolt against him. They will neither defame nor calumniate him, for the miracles he will perform will frighten them into complete silence. Isaiah refers to the submission of the kings to the Messiah in the verse, "Kings shall shut their mouths because of him." [52:15]. He will slay whom he will, none will escape or be saved, as it is written, "And he shall smite the land with the rod of his mouth." [Isaiah 11:4]. Revolution and war in the entire world, from East to West, will not cease at the beginning of the Messianic era, but only after the wars of Gog and Magog, as was indicated by Ezekiel. I do not believe that this man who has appeared among you possesses these powers. . . .

In sum, had this man acted presumptuously or disdainfully, I would deem him worthy of death. The truth seems to be that he became melancholy and lost his mind. In my opinion, it is most advisable, both for your good and for his that you put him in iron chains for a while, until the Gentiles learn that he is demented. After you have blazoned and bruited abroad the intelligence concerning this man among them, you may release him without endangering his safety. If the Gentiles gain knowledge about him after he has been locked up by you, they will taunt him, and pronounce him irrational and you will remain unmolested by them. If you procrastinate until they learn of this affair of their own accord, then you will most likely incur their wrath.

Remember, my co-religionists, that on account of the vast number of our sins, God has hurled us in the midst of this people, the Arabs, who have persecuted us severely, and passed baneful and discriminatory legislation against us, as Scripture has forewarned us, "Our enemies themselves shall judge us." [Deut. 32:31]. Never did a nation molest, degrade, debase and hate us as much as they.

Therefore when David, of blessed memory, inspired by the holy spirit, envisaged the future tribulations of Israel, he bewailed and lamented their lot only in the Kingdom of Ishmael, and prayed in their behalf, for their deliverance, as is implied in the verse, "Woe is me, that I sojourn with Meschech, that I dwell beside the tents of Kedar." [Psalms 120:5]. . . .

I shall now narrate to you succinctly several episodes subsequent to the rise of the Arabic kingdom, from which you will derive some benefit. One of these refers to the Exodus of a multitude of Jews, numbering hundreds of thousands, from the East beyond Isphahan, led by an individual who pretended to be the Messiah. They were accoutered with military equipment, and drawn swords, and slew all those that encountered them. They reached, according to the information I received, the vicinity of Bagdad. This happened in the beginning of the reign of the Umayyads.

The king then said to all the Jews of his kingdom: "Let your scholars go out to meet this multitude and ascertain whether their pretension is. true and he is unmistakably your Expected One. If so, we shall conclude peace with you under any conditions you may prefer. But if it is dissimulation, then I shall wage war against them." When the sages met these Jews, the latter declared: "We belong to the children of the district beyond the River." Then they asked them: "Who instigated you to make this uprising?" Whereupon they replied: "This man here, one of the descendants of David, whom we know to be pious and virtuous. This man, whom we knew to be a leper at night, arose the following morning healthy and sound." They believed that leprosy was one of the characteristics of the Messiah, for which they found an allusion to the verse: "stricken, smitten of God, and afflicted" [Isaiah 53:4], that is by leprosy. Whereupon the sages explained to them that this interpretation was incorrect, and that he lacked even one of the characteristics of the Messiah, let alone all of them.

Furthermore, they advised them as follows: "O, brethren, you are still near your native country and have the possibility of returning thither. If you remain in this land you will not only perish, but also undermine the teachings of Moses, by misleading people to believe that the Messiah has appeared and has been vanquished, whereas you have neither a prophet in your midst, nor an omen betokening his oncoming." Thereupon they were persuaded by these arguments. The Sultan turned over to them so and so many thousand of dinars by way of hospitality in order that they should leave his country. But after they had returned home, he had a change of heart with respect to the Jews upon whom he imposed a fine for his expenditures. He ordered them to make a special mark on their garments, the writing of the word "cursed," and to attach one iron bar in the back and one in the front. Ever since then the communities of Khorasan and Ispahan experienced the tribulations of the Diaspora. This episode we have learned from oral reports.

The following incident we have verified and know to be true because it occurred in recent times. About fifty years ago or less, a pious and virtuous man and scholar by the name of Moses Al-Dar'i came from Dar'a to the province of Andalusia to study under Rabbi Joseph ha-Levi, of blessed memory, ibn Migash, of whom you very likely have heard. Later he left for Fez, the center of Maghreb. People flocked to him because of his piety, virtue and learning. He informed them that the Messiah had come, as was divinely revealed to him in a dream. Yet he did not pretend on the basis of a divine communication, as did the former lunatic, that he was the Messiah.

He merely affirmed that the Messiah had appeared. Many people became his adherents and reposed faith in him. My father and master, of blessed memory, endeavored to dissuade and discourage people from following him. However only a few were influenced by my father, while most, nay, nearly all clung to R. Moses, of blessed memory. Finally he predicted events which came true no matter what was going to occur.

He would say: "I was informed yesterday—this and this would happen," and it did happen exactly as he foretold. Once he forecast a vehement rain for the coming Friday and that the falling drops would be blood. This was considered a sign of the approaching advent of the Messiah, as was inferred from the verse, "And I will show wonders in the heavens and in the earth, blood and fire, and pillars of smoke." [Joel 3:3].

This episode took place in the month of Marheshvan. A very heavy rain fell that Friday and the fluid that descended was red and viscous as if it were mixed with clay. This miracle convinced all the people that he was undoubtedly a prophet. In itself this occurrence is not inconsistent with the tenets of the Torah, for prophecy will return to Israel before the Messianic advent, as I have previously explained. When the majority of the people put their trust in him, he predicted that the Messiah would come that very year on Passover eve. He advised the people to sell their property and contract debts to the Muslims with the promise to pay back ten dinars for one, in order to observe the precepts of the Torah in connection with the Passover festival, for they will never see them again, and so they did.

When Passover came and nothing transpired, the people were ruined as most of them had disposed of their property for a trifling sum, and were overwhelmed with debt. When the Gentiles in the vicinity and their serfs learned of this hoax they were minded to do away with him, had they located him. As this Muslim country no longer offered him protection he left for Palestine where he died, may his memory be blessed. When he left he made predictions, as I was informed by those who saw him, concerning events both great and little in Maghreb which were later fulfilled.

My father of blessed memory, told me that about fifteen or twenty years before that episode, there lived respectable folks in Cordova, the center of Andalusia, some of whom were given to the cult of astrology. They were all of one mind that the Messiah would appear that year. They sought a revelation in a dream night after night, and ascertained that the Messiah was a man of that city. They picked a pious and virtuous person by the name of Ibn Aryeh who had been instructing the people. They wrought miracles and made predictions just as Al-Dar'i did until they won over the hearts of all the people.

When the influential and learned men of our community heard of this, they assembled in the synagogue and had Ibn Aryeh brought there and had him flogged in public. Furthermore they imposed a fine upon him, and put him into the ban, because he gave assent by his silence to the professions of his adherents, instead of restraining them and pointing out to them that they contradict our religion. They did the same thing to the persons who assembled about him. The Jews escaped the wrath of the Gentiles only with the greatest difficulty.

About forty years preceding the affair of Ibn Aryeh in Andalusia, there appeared a man in Linon [Lyons?], a large center in the heart of France, which numbered more than ten thousand Jewish families. He pretended that he was the Messiah. He was supposed to have performed the following miracle: On moonlit nights he would go out and climb to the top of high trees in the field and glide from tree to tree like a bird. He cited a verse from Daniel to prove that such a miracle was within the power of the Messiah: "And behold, there came with the clouds of heaven One like unto a son of man . . . And there was given him dominion." [7:13–14]. Many who witnessed the miracle became his votaries. The French discovered this, pillaged and put many of his followers to death, together with the pretender. Some of them maintain, however, that he is still in hiding until this very day.

The prophets have predicted and instructed us, as I have told you, that pretenders and simulators will appear in great numbers at the time when the advent of the true Messiah will draw nigh, but they will not be able to make good their claim. They will perish with many of their partisans.

Solomon, of blessed memory, inspired by the holy spirit, foresaw that the prolonged duration of the exile would incite some of our people to seek to terminate it before the appointed time, and as a consequence they would perish or meet with disaster. Therefore he admonished and adjured them in metaphorical language to desist, as we read, "I adjure you, O daughters of Jerusalem, by the gazelles and by the hinds of the field, that ye awaken not, nor stir up love, until it please." [Song of Songs 2:7, 8:4]. Now, brethren and friends, abide by the oath, and stir not up love until it please. [Ketubot 111a].

May God, Who created the world with the attributes of mercy grant us the privilege to behold the return of the exiles, to the portion of His inheritance, to contemplate the graciousness of the Lord, and to visit early in His Temple. May He taken us out from the Valley of the Shadow of Death wherein He put us. May He remove darkness from our eyes, and gloom from our hearts. May he fulfill in our days as well as yours the prophecy contained in the verse, "The people that walked in darkness have seen a great light." [Isaiah 9:1]. May He darken our opponents in His anger and wrath, may He illuminate our obscurity, as it is written, "For behold darkness shall cover the earth . . . but upon thee the Lord will shine." [Isaiah 60:2]. Greetings unto you, my dear friend, master of the sciences, and paragon of learning, and unto our erudite colleagues, and unto all the rest of the people. Peace, peace, as the light that shines, and much peace until the moon be no more. Amen.

I beg you to send a copy of this missive to every community in the cities and hamlets, in order to strengthen the people in their faith and to put them on their feet. Read it at public gatherings and in private, and you will thus become a public benefactor. Take adequate precautions lest its contents be divulged to the Gentiles by an evil person and mishap overtake us, God spare us therefrom.

When I began writing this letter I had some misgivings about it, but they were overruled by my conviction that the public welfare takes precedence over one's personal safety. Moreover, I am sending it to a personage such as you, "and the secret of the Lord may be entrusted to those who fear Him." Our sages, the successors of the prophets, assured us that persons engaged in a religious mission will meet with no disaster [Pesahim 8b]. What more important religious mission is there than this.

Peace be unto all Israel. Amen.

A LETTER TO R. SAMUEL IBN TIBBON

"A man shall be commended according to his wisdom." [Prov. 12:8]. All the letters of the worthy scholar and excellent sage R. Samuel, son of the learned R. Jehuda ibn Tibbon, the Sephardi [from Spain] have duly reached me, Moses the son of Maimûn, the Sephardi. Already many years ago the fame of the honoured prince, the wise R. Yehuda, your father, had reached me; I had heard of his great learning and the elegance of his style, both in Arabic and Hebrew, through well-known and learned men of Granada. Also one of the learned men of Toledo came here and told us of his reputation. Likewise when the honoured R. Meir, a disciple of R. Abraham, the son of R. David, the great Rabbi of Posquières, who had also studied under the learned R. Abraham ibn Ezra came to me, he [R. Meir] spoke concerning your honoured father, and gave me an account of the works on Grammar and other sciences he had translated. I did not however know that he had left a son. But, when your letters in Hebrew and Arabic reached me, and I learned from them your mode of thought and elegance of composition; when I read your remarks both on those passages in my *magnum opus, The Guide for the Perplexed,* concerning the right signification of which you entertain doubt, and on those in which you had discovered errors made by the transcriber, then I said with the ancient poet [Moses ibn Ezra]:

> "Had they known his parentage, they would say,
> The father's excellence has passed over to his son."

Blessed be He who has granted a recompense to your learned father and granted him such a son; and indeed not to him alone, but to all wise men. For in truth unto us all a child has been born, unto us all a son has been given. "This offspring of the righteous is a tree of life," a delight of our eyes and pleasant to look upon. I have already tasted of his fruit, and, lo, it was sweet in my mouth even as honey.

All your questions were just, and all your conjectures with respect to the omission of a word, or words, were correct. At the end of this epistle, I explain everything in Arabic, and give you all the information you desire, and mention the works you should study or neglect. You are thoroughly fitted for the task of translation, because the Creator has given you an intelligent mind to "understand parables and their interpretation, the words of the wise and their difficult sayings." I recognise from your words that you have entered thoroughly into the depth of the subject, and that its hidden meaning has become clear to you. I shall explain to you in Hebrew, how you shall manage with the entire translation. "Give instruction to a wise man, and he will be yet wiser; be wise my son, and my heart also will rejoice."

Be assured, that when I saw the beauty of your style and remarked the depth of your intellect and that your lips utter knowledge clearly, I greatly rejoiced. I was the more surprised that such should be the talents, such the thirst for knowledge, such the acquaintance with Arabic (which I believe to be a partially corrupt dialect of Hebrew) displayed by one who has been born among "stammerers." I also admired your being so well versed in the niceties of that language in abstruse subjects; this is indeed like "a tender plant springing out of a dry ground." May the Lord enlighten your eyes with the light of His law, so that you may be of those that love Him, who are even as the sun when he goes forth in his strength. Amen.

I have carefully examined all the passages concerning the translation of which you entertain any doubt, and have looked into all those passages in which the transcriber has made any mistake, and into the various preliminary Propositions and Chapters which were not perfectly clear to you, and of which you sought the elucidation.

Let me premise one rule. Whoever wishes to translate, and purposes to render each word literally, and at the same time to adhere slavishly to the order of the words and sentences in the original, will meet with much difficulty; his rendering will be faulty and untrustworthy. This is not the right method. The translator should first try to grasp the sense of the subject thoroughly, and then state the theme with perfect clearness in the other language. This, however, cannot be done without changing the order of words, putting many words for one word, or vice versa, and adding or taking away words, so that the subject be perfectly intelligible in the language into which he translates. This method was followed by Honéin ben Is'hâk with the works of Galen, and his son Is'hâk with the works of Aristotle. It is for this reason that all their versions are so peculiarly lucid, and therefore we ought to study them to the exclusion of all others. Your distinguished community ought to adopt this rule in all the translations undertaken for those honoured men, and the heads of the congregation. And may God grant that the spread of knowledge among other communities of Israel be promoted by such works.

I now proceed to reply to your questions *seriatim,* to explain all those points which needed explanation, to give the correct reading according to which you may amend the faults in your copy, arranged in the order of your epistle, and embracing the three books of my work. . . .

Now God knows that in order to write this to you, I have escaped to a secluded spot, where people would not think to find me, sometimes leaning for support against the wall, sometimes lying down on account of my excessive weakness, for I have become old and feeble.

But with respect to your wish to come here to me, I cannot but say how greatly your visit would delight me, for I truly long to commune with you, and would anticipate our meeting with even greater joy than you. Yet I must advise you not to expose yourself to the perils of the voyage, for beyond seeing me, and my doing all I could to honour you, you would not derive any advantage from your visit. Do not expect to be able to confer with me on any scientific subject for even one hour, either by day or by night, for the following is my daily occupation:—I dwell in Mizr [Fostat], and the Sultan resides at Kahira [Cairo]; these two places are two Sabbath days' journeys [about one mile and a-half] distant from each other.

My duties to the Sultan are very heavy. I am obliged to visit him every day, early in the morning; and when he or any of his children, or any of the inmates of his harem, are indisposed, I dare not quit Kahira, but must stay during the greater part of the day in the palace. It also frequently happens that one or two of the royal officers fall sick, and I must attend to their healing.

Hence, as a rule, I repair to Kahira very early in the day, and even if nothing unusual happens, I do not return to Mizr until the afternoon. Then I am almost dying with hunger; I find the antechambers filled with people, both Jews and Gentiles, nobles and common people, judges and bailiffs, friends and foes—a mixed multitude, who await the time of my return.

I dismount from my animal, wash my hands, go forth to my patients, and entreat them to bear with me while I partake of some slight refreshment, the only meal I take in the twenty-four hours. Then I go forth to attend to my patients, write prescriptions and directions for their several ailments. Patients go in and out until nightfall, and sometimes even, I solemnly assure you, until two hours and more in the night. I converse with and prescribe for them while lying down from sheer fatigue; and when. night falls, I am so exhausted, that I can scarcely speak.

In consequence of this, no Israelite can have any private interview with me, except on the Sabbath. On that day, the whole congregation, or, at least, the majority of the members, come unto me after the morning service, when I instruct them as to their proceedings during the whole week; we study together a little until noon, when they depart. Some of them return, and read with me after the afternoon service until evening prayers. In this manner I spend that day. I have here related to you only a part of what you would see, if you were to visit me.

Now, when you have completed for our brethren the translation you have commenced, I beg that you will come to me, but not with the hope of deriving any advantage from your visit as regards your studies; for my time is, as I have shown you, so excessively occupied. . . .

Be careful not to study the works of Aristotle except by the help of his commentators, the commentary of Alexander Aphrodisius, Themistius, or Ibn Roschd. Among the works which you mention as being in your possession, you name *De Pomo,* and *The Golden House.* These two treatises are spurious, and entirely valueless: they are among those which are ascribed to Aristotle, but which are not genuine. The work on theology composed by Alrasi is genuine, but it is without value, as Alrasi was a mere physician. So also the *Book of Definitions,* and *Book on the Elements,* which Isaac Israeli composed, are altogether worthless, for he also was only a physician. It is true I have not seen the *Microcosmos,* which Rabbi Joseph Zadik has written, but I know the author and his method of philosophy, and I am acquainted with his worth, and the worth of his book; for no doubt he has followed in that treatise the system of those who ascribe attributes to the Deity. As a general rule I may tell you, study only the works on Logic. . . .

The writings of Aristotle are the foundations upon which all these philosophical works are based, and, as I have said above, they can only be understood by help of their commentaries—the Commentary of Alexander, or Themistius, or Ibn Roschd. But other works, besides those here enumerated . . . it is not right to waste time upon them. He, Aristotle, indeed arrived at the highest summit of knowledge to which man can ascend, unless the emanation of the Divine Spirit be vouchsafed to him, so that he attains the stage of prophecy, above which there is no higher stage. And the works of Ibn Sina, although they contain searching investigations and subtle thought, do not come up to the writings of Abunazr Alfarabi. Still they are useful, and it is right that you should study them diligently.

I have now indicated to you the works you should study, and to which you should devote your intellect. May your happiness, my son and pupil, increase, and salvation be granted to our afflicted people. Written by Moses, the son of Maimûn, the Sephardi, on the 8th of Tishri, 1511, according to the Seleucide era [corresponding to September 30th, 1199].

Benjamin of Tudela

As may be seen by his precise observations on trade and commerce, the twelfth-century Spanish traveler, Benjamin of Tudela, was evidently a merchant. However, trade was not the only purpose of his journey. He was also deeply concerned with the state of his fellow Jews in their lands of dispersion and in the Land of Israel; moreover, like others before him, Benjamin wanted to make a pilgrimage to the land of his fathers (then under Crusaders' rule). Whatever were his actual motives, Benjamin wrote a remarkable account of the medieval world of his period, and, to the delight of modern historians and physical and social geographers, offers invaluable details about trade and customs.

Benjamin's journeys, from 1160 to 1173, took him to some 300 cities. After leaving Spain he visited Provence, northern and southern Italy, Greece and its islands, Constantinople, Cyprus, Syria and Palestine. He toured the length and breadth of Palestine, traveled via Syria to Bagdad (the residence of the Jewish Exilarch) to which he devotes more space than any other city, visited Yemen, Egypt, Sicily, and then returned home. Not everything listed in the travelogue, however, is based on an eyewitness account. For instance, it is unlikely that he reached India or China, but probably related facts told him by traveling merchants. Since in his visits to Jewish communities in the Mediterranean basin he lists the names of communal elders and omits them in places east of Bagdad—it is a logical conclusion that he did not set foot in the latter areas.

The travels of Benjamin are more valuable for their interesting contents than their style. His Hebrew diction and method of composition are not that of a professional man of letters, but rather that of a keen-eyed, intelligent observer. The various repetitions and the narrative's matter-of-fact tone show Benjamin to be a man untutored in the art of writing. Nevertheless, what he lacked in style he made up in perspicacious observation and insight into conditions, personalities and history. Benjamin's travels give us an interesting and accurate description of what then comprised three-fourths of the known world. He is the first European to describe the assassins' sect in Syria and Persia, and the first to mention China and commerce with India. His travelogue offers the best source material for the history of trade in Europe, Asia and Africa during the twelfth century, and, with his full account of the number and the condition of Jews in various lands, is an important source for the history of the Jews in that era. Besides portraying Jewish occupations and the physical condition of Jewish communities, Benjamin also dwells on their spiritual state. Although not a scholar, he was interested in learning and in learned men; he mentions more than two hundred scholars and communal leaders, many of them known to Jewish history. In addition, he describes Jewish sects like the Karaites, the Samaritans, and the pseudo-Messiah, David Alroy.

The first publication of these oft-reprinted travels was in 1543; several translations appeared in Latin, English, Yiddish and Dutch in the seventeenth century, as well as later in French, German and other languages.

Of Benjamin of Tudela no other facts are known, except what is revealed in his travelogue (written up by an anonymous scribe); thus Benjamin is one of those enigmatic figures in literary history who make their mark with one work and then are heard no more.

THE ITINERARY OF BENJAMIN OF TUDELA

This is the book of travels which was compiled by Rabbi Benjamin, the son of Jonah, of the land of Navarre—his repose be in Paradise.

The said Rabbi Benjamin set forth from Tudela, his native city, and passed through many remote countries, as is related in his book. In every place which he entered, he made a record of all that he saw, or was told by trustworthy persons—matters not previously heard of in the land of Sepharad [Spain]. Also he mentions some of the sages and illustrious men residing in each place. He brought this book with him on his return to the country of Castile, in the year 4933 [1173 c.e.]. The said Rabbi Benjamin is a wise and understanding man, learned in the Law and the Halacha, and wherever we have tested his statements we have found them accurate, true to fact and consistent; for he is a trustworthy man.

His book commences as follows:

I journeyed first from my native town to the city of Saragossa, and thence by way of the River Ebro to Tortosa. From there I went a journey of two days to the ancient city of Tarrogona with its Cyclopean and Greek buildings. The like thereof is not found among any of the buildings in the country of Sepharad. It is situated by the sea, and two days' journey from the city of Barcelona, where there is a holy congregation, including sages, wise and illustrious men, such as R. Shesheth, R. Shealtiel, R. Solomon, and R. Abraham, son of Chisdai. This is a small, beautiful city, lying upon the seacoast. Merchants come thither from all quarters with their wares, from Greece, from Pisa, Genoa, Sicily, Alexandria in Egypt, Palestine, Africa and all its coasts.

Thence it is a day and a half to Gerona, in which there is a small congregation of Jews. A three days' journey takes one to Narbonne, which is a city preeminent for learning; thence the Torah goes forth to all countries. Sages and great and illustrious men abide here. . . . At the present day 300 Jews are there.

Thence it is four parasangs* to the city of Beziers, where there is a congregation of learned men. At their head is R. Solomon Chalafta, R. Joseph, and R. Nethanel. Thence it is two days to Har Gaash which is called Montpellier. This is a place well situated for commerce. It is about a parasang from the sea, and men come for business there from all quarters,

---

*A parasang is about 3.4 miles. Ten parasangs make a day's journey.

from Edom, Ishmael, the land of Algarve, Lombardy, the dominion of Rome the Great, from all the land of Egypt, Palestine, Greece, France, Asia and England. People of all nations are found there doing business through the medium of the Genoese and Pisans. In the city there are scholars of great eminence, at their head being R. Reuben, son of Todros, R. Nathan, son of Zechariah, and R. Samuel, their chief rabbi, also R. Solomon and R. Mordecai. They have among them houses of learning devoted to the study of the Talmud. Among the community are men both rich and charitable, who lend a helping hand to all that come to them.

From Montpellier it is four parasangs to Lunel, in which there is a congregation of Israelites, who study the Law day and night. Here lived Rabbenu Meshullam the great rabbi, since deceased, and his five sons, who are wise, great and wealthy, namely: R. Joseph, R. Isaac, R. Jacob, R. Aaron, and R. Asher, the recluse, who dwells apart from the world; he pores over his books day and night, fasts periodically and abstains from all meat. He is a great scholar of the Talmud. At Lunel live also their brother-in-law, R. Moses, the chief Rabbi, R. Samuel the elder, R. Ulsarnu, R. Solomon Hacohen, and R. Judah the Physician, the son of Tibbon, the Sephardi. The students that come from distant lands to learn the Law are taught, boarded, lodged and clothed by the congregation, so long as they attend the house of study. The community has wise, understanding and saintly men of great benevolence, who lend a helping hand to all their brethren both far and near. The congregation consists of about 300 Jews —may the Lord preserve them. . . .

Marseilles is a city of princely and wise citizens, possessing two congregations with about 300 Jews. One congregation dwells below on the shore by the sea, the other is in the castle above. They form a great academy of learned men. It is a very busy city upon the seacoast. . . .

Thence to the great city of Rome. Rome is the head of the kingdoms of Christendom, and contains about 200 Jews, who occupy an honourable position and pay no tribute, and amongst them are officials of the Pope Alexander, the spiritual head of all Christendom. Great scholars reside here, at the head of them being R. Daniel, the chief rabbi, and R. Jechiel, an official of the Pope. He is a handsome young man of intelligence and wisdom, and he has the entry of the Pope's palace; for he is the steward of his house and of all that he has. He is a grandson of R. Nathan, who composed the *Aruch* and its commentaries. . . .

Rome is divided into two parts by the River Tiber. In the one part is the great church which they call St. Peter's of Rome. The great Palace of Julius Caesar was also in Rome. There are many wonderful structures in the city, different from any others in the world. Including both its inhabited and ruined parts, Rome is about twenty-four miles in circumference. In the midst thereof there are eighty palaces belonging to eighty kings who lived there, each called Imperator, commencing from King Tarquinius down to Nero and Tiberius, who lived at the time of Jesus the Nazarene, ending with Pepin, who freed the land of Sepharad from Islam and was father of Charlemagne.

There is a palace outside Rome (said to be of Titus). The Consul and his 300 Senators treated him with disfavour, because he failed to take Jerusalem till after three years, though they had bidden him to capture it within two.

In Rome is also the palace of Vespasianus, a great and very strong building; also the Colosseum, in which edifice there are 365 sections, according to the days of the solar year; and the circumference of these places is three miles. There were battles fought here in olden times, and in the palace more than 100,000 men were slain, and there their bones remained piled up to the present day. The king caused to be engraved a representation of the battle and of the forces on either side facing one another, both warriors and horses, all in marble, to exhibit to the world the war of the days of old.

In Rome there is a cave which runs underground, and catacombs of King Tarmal Galsin and his royal consort who are to be found there, seated upon their thrones, and with them about a hundred royal personages. They are all embalmed and preserved to this day. In the church of St. John in the Lateran there are two bronze columns taken from the Temple, the handiwork of King Solomon, each column being engraved "Solomon the son of David." The Jews of Rome told me that every year upon the 9th of Ab they found the columns exuding moisture like water. There also is the cave where Titus the son of Vespasianus stored the Temple vessels which he brought from Jerusalem. There is also a cave in a hill on one bank of the River Tiber where are the graves of the ten martyrs. In front of St. John in the Lateran there are statues of Samson in marble, with a spear in his hand, and of Absalom the son of King David, and another of Constantinus the Great, who built Constantinople and after whom it was called. The last-named statue is of bronze, the horse being overlaid with gold. Many other edifices are there, and remarkable sights beyond enumeration. . . .

From Sidon it is half a day's journey to Sarepta [Sarfend], which belongs to Sidon. Thence it is a half day to New Tyre [Sur], which is a very fine city, with a harbour in its midst. At nighttime those that levy dues throw iron chains from tower to tower, so that no man can go forth by boat or in any other way to rob the ships by night. There is no harbour like this in the whole world. Tyre is a beautiful city. It contains about 500 Jews, some of them scholars of the Talmud, at their head being R. Ephraim of Tyre, the Dayan, R. Meir from Carcasonne, and R. Abraham, head of the congregation. The Jews own sea-going vessels, and there are glassmakers amongst them who make that fine Tyrian glassware which is prized in all countries.

Acre, the Acco of old, is on the borders of Asher; it is the commencement of the land of Israel. Situated by the Great Sea, it possesses a large harbour for all the pilgrims who come to Jerusalem by ship. A stream runs in front of it, called the brook of Kedumim. About 200 Jews live there, at their head being R. Zadok, R. Japheth, and R. Jonah.

From there it is three parasangs to Haifa, which is Hahepher on the seaboard, and on the other side is Mount Carmel, at the foot of which there are many Jewish graves. On the mountain is the cave of Elijah where the Christians have erected a structure called St. Elias. On the top of the mountain can be recognized the overthrown altar which Elijah repaired in the days of Ahab. The site of the altar is circular, about four cubits remain thereof, and at the foot of the mountain the brook Kishon flows. From here it is four parasangs to Capernaum, which is the village of Nahum, identical with Maon, the home of Habal the Carmelite. . . .

From there it is three parasangs to Jerusalem, which is a small city, fortified by three walls. It is full of people whom the Mohammedans call Jacobites, Syrians, Greeks, Georgians and Franks, and of people of all tongues. It contains a dyeing-house, for which the Jews pay a small rent annually to the king, on condition that besides the Jews no other dyers be allowed in Jerusalem. There are about 200 Jews who dwell under the Tower of David in one corner of the city [other MS says 4 Jews]. The lower portion of the wall of the Tower of David, to the extent of about ten cubits, is part of the ancient foundation set up by our ancestors, the remaining portion having been built by the Mohammedans. There is no structure in the whole city stronger than the Tower of David. The city also contains two buildings, from one of which—the hospital—there issue forth four hundred knights; and therein all the sick who come thither are lodged and cared for in life and in death.

The other building is called the Temple of Solomon; it is the palace built by Solomon the king of Israel. Three hundred knights are quartered there, and issue therefrom every day for military exercise, besides those who come from the land of the Franks and the other parts of Christendom, having taken upon themselves to serve there a year or two until their vow is fulfilled. In Jerusalem is the great church called the Sepulchre, and here is the burial place of Jesus, unto which the Christians make pilgrimages.

Jerusalem has four gates—the gate of Abraham, the gate of David, the gate of Zion, and the gate of Gushpat, which is the gate of Jehoshaphat, facing our ancient Temple, now called Templum Domini. Upon the site of the sanctuary Omar ben al Khataab erected an edifice with a very large and magnificent cupola, into which the Gentiles do not bring any image or effigy, but they merely come there to pray. In front of this place is the western wall, which is one of the walls of the Holy of Holies. This is called the Gate of Mercy, and thither come all the Jews to pray before the wall of the court of the Temple.

In Jerusalem, attached to the palace which belonged to Solomon, are the stables built by him, forming a very substantial structure, composed of large stones, and the like of it is not to be seen anywhere in the world.

There is also visible up to this day the pool used by the priests before offering their sacrifices and the Jews coming thither write their names upon the wall. The gate of Jehoshaphat leads to the valley of Jehoshaphat, which is the gathering place of nations. Here is the pillar called Absalom's Hand, and the sepulchre of King Uzziah.

In the neighborhood is also a great spring, called the Waters of Siloam, connected with the brook of Kidron. Over the spring is a large structure dating from the time of our ancestors, but little water is found, and the people of Jerusalem for the most part drink the rainwater, which they collect in cisterns in their houses. From the valley of Jehoshaphat one ascends the Mount of Olives; it is the valley only which separates Jerusalem from the Mount of Olives. From the Mount of Olives one sees the Sea of Sodom, and at a distance of two parasangs from the Sea of Sodom is the Pillar of Salt into which Lot's wife was turned; the sheep lick it continually, but afterwards it regains its original shape. The whole land of the plain and the valley of Shittim as far as Mount Nebo are visible from here.

In front of Jerusalem is Mount Zion, on which there is no building, except a place of worship belonging to the Christians. Facing Jerusalem for a distance of three miles are the cemeteries belonging to the Israelites who in the days of old buried their dead in caves, and upon each sepulchre is a dated inscription, but the Christians destroy the sepulchres, employing the stones thereof in building their houses. These sepulchres reach as far as Zelzah in the territory of Benjamin. Around Jerusalem are high mountains.

On Mount Zion are the sepulchres of the House of David, and the sepulchres of the kings that ruled after him. The exact place cannot be identified, inasmuch as fifteen years ago a wall of the church of Mount Zion fell in. The Patriarch commanded the overseer to take the stones of the old walls and restore therewith the church. He did so, and hired workmen at fixed wages; and there were twenty men who brought the stones from the base of the wall of Zion. Among these men there were two who were sworn friends. On a certain day the one entertained the other; after their meal they returned to their work, when the overseer said to them, "Why have you tarried to-day?"

They answered, "Why need you complain? When our fellow workmen go to their meal we will do our work." When the dinner-time arrived, and the other workmen had gone to their meal, they examined the stones and raised a certain stone which formed the entrance to a cave.

Thereupon one said to the other, "Let us go in and see if any money is to be found there."

They entered the cave, and reached a large chamber resting upon pillars of marble overlaid with silver and gold. In front was a table of gold and a sceptre and crown. This was the sepulchre of King David. On the left thereof in like fashion was the sepulchre of King Solomon; then followed the sepulchres of all the kings of Judah that were buried there. Closed coffers were also there, the content of which no man knows.

The two men essayed to enter the chamber, when a fierce wind came forth from the entrance of the cave and smote them, and they fell to the ground like dead men, and there they lay until evening. And there came forth a wind like a man's voice, crying out: "Arise and go forth from this place!" So the men rushed forth in terror, and they came upon the Patriarch, and related these things to him. Thereupon the Patriarch sent for Rabbi Abraham el Constantini, the pious recluse, who was one of the mourners of Jerusalem, and to him he related all these things according to the report of the two men who had come forth.

Then Rabbi Abraham replied, "These are the sepulchres of the House of David; they belong to the kings of Judah, and on the morrow let us enter, I and you and these men, and find out what is there." And on the morrow they sent for the two men, and found each of them lying on his bed in terror, and the men said: "We will not enter there, for the Lord doth not desire to show it to any man." Then the Patriarch gave orders that the place should be closed up and hidden from the sight of man unto this day. These things were told me by the said Rabbi Abraham.

From Jerusalem it is two parasangs to Bethlehem, which is called by the Christians Beth-Leon, and close thereto at a distance of about half a mile, at the parting of the way, is the pillar of Rachel's grave, which is made up of eleven stones, corresponding with the number of the sons of Jacob. Upon it is a cupola resting on four columns, and all the Jews that pass by carve their names upon the stones of the pillar. At Bethlehem there are two Jewish dyers. It is a land of brooks of water and contains wells and fountains.

At a distance of six parasangs is St. Abram de Bron, which is Hebron; the old city stood on the mountain, but is now in ruins; and in the valley by the field of Machpelah lies the present city. Here there is the great church called St. Abram, and this was a Jewish place of worship at the time of the Mohammedan rule, but the Gentiles have erected there six tombs, respectively called those of Abraham and Sarah, Isaac and Rebekah, Jacob and Leah.

The custodians tell the pilgrims that these are the tombs of the Patriarchs, for which information the pilgrims give them money. If a Jew comes, however, and gives a special reward, the custodian of the cave opens unto him a gate of iron, which was constructed by our forefathers, and then he is able to descend below by means of steps, holding a lighted candle in his hand. He then reaches a cave, in which nothing is to be found, and a cave beyond, which is likewise empty, but when he reaches the third cave behold there are six sepulchres, those of Abraham, Isaac and Jacob, respectively facing those of Sarah, Rebekah and Leah.

And upon the graves are inscriptions cut in stone; upon the grave of Abraham is engraved, "This is the grave of Abraham"; upon that of Isaac,

"This is the grave of Isaac, the son of Abraham our Father"; upon that of Jacob, "This is the grave of Jacob, the son of Isaac, the son of Abraham our Father"; and upon the others, "This is the grave of Sarah," "This is the grave of Rebekah," and "This is the grave of Leah." A lamp burns day and night upon the graves in the cave. One finds there many casks filled with the bones of Israelites, as the members of the house of Israel were wont to bring the bones of their fathers thither and to deposit them there to this day.

Beyond the field of Machpelah is the house of Abraham; there is a well in front of the house, but out of reverence for the Patriarch Abraham no one is allowed to build in the neighborhood. . . .

Thence to Tiberias, which is situated upon the Jordan, which is here called the Sea of Kinnereth [Sea of Galilee]. The Jordan at this place flows through a valley between two mountains, and fills the lake, which is called the Lake of Kinnereth; this is a large and broad piece of water like the sea. The Jordan flows between two mountains, and over the plain which is the place that is called Ashdoth Hapisgah, and thence continues its course till it falls into the Sea of Sodom, which is the Salt Sea [Dead Sea]. In Tiberias there are about fifty Jews, at their head being R. Abraham the astronomer, R. Muchtar, and R. Isaac. There are hot waters here, which bubble up from the ground, and are called the Hot Waters of Tiberias. Nearby is the Synagogue of Caleb ben Jephunneh, and Jewish sepulchres. R. Johanan ben Zakkai and R. Jehudah Halevi are buried here. All these places are situated in lower Galilee.

From here it is two days to Tymin or Timnathah, where Simon the Just and many Israelites are buried, and thence three parasangs to Medon or Meron. In the neighborhood there is a cave in which are the sepulchres of Hillel and Shammai. Here also are twenty sepulchres of disciples, including the sepulchres of R. Benjamin ben Japheth, and of R. Jehudah ben Bethera. From Meron it is two parasangs to Almah, where there are about fifty Jews. There is a large Jewish cemetery here, with the sepulchres of R. Eleazar ben Arak, of R. Eleazar ben Azariah, of Chuni Hamaagel, of Raban Simeon ben Gamaliel, and of R. Jose Hagelili. . . .

Thence to Bagdad, the great city and the royal residence of the Caliph Emir al Muminin al Abbasi of the family of Mohammed. He is at the head of the Mohammedan religion, and all the kings of Islam obey him; he occupies a similar position to that held by the Pope over the Christians. He has a palace in Bagdad three miles in extent, wherein is a great park with all varieties of trees, fruit-bearing and otherwise, and all manner of animals. The whole is surrounded by a wall, and in the park there is a lake whose waters are fed by the river Hiddekel. Whenever the king desires to indulge in recreation and to rejoice and feast, his servants catch all manner of birds, game and fish and he goes to his palace with his counsellors and princes.

There the great king, Al Abbasi the Caliph [Hafiz] holds his court, and he is kind unto Israel, and many belonging to the people of Israel are his attendants; he knows all languages, and is well versed in the law of Israel. He reads and writes the holy language [Hebrew]. He will not partake of anything unless he has earned it by the work of his own hands. He makes coverlets to which he attaches his seal; his courtiers sell them in the market, and the great ones of the land purchase them and the proceeds thereof provide his sustenance. He is truthful and trusty, speaking peace to all men. The men of Islam see him but once in the year.

The pilgrims that come from distant lands to go unto Mecca which is in the land El-Yemen, are anxious to see his face, and they assemble before the palace exclaiming "Our Lord, light of Islam and glory of our Law, show us the effulgence of thy countenance," but he pays no regard to their words. Then the princes who minister unto him say to him, "Our Lord, spread forth thy peace unto the men that have come from distant lands, who crave to abide under the shadow of thy graciousness," and thereupon he arises and lets down the hem of his robe from the window, and the pilgrims come and kiss it, and a prince says unto them "Go forth in peace, for our Master the Lord of Islam granteth peace to you." He is regarded by them as Mohammed and they go to their houses rejoicing at the salutation which the prince has vouchsafed unto them, and glad at heart that they have kissed his robe.

Each of his brothers and the members of his family has an abode in his palace, but they are all fettered in chains of iron, and guards are placed over each of their houses so that they may not rise against the great Caliph. For once it happened to a predecessor that his brothers rose up against him and proclaimed one of themselves as Caliph; then it was decreed that all the members of his family should be bound, that they might not rise up against the ruling Caliph. Each one of them resides in his palace in great splendour, and they own villages and towns, and their stewards bring them the tribute thereof, and they eat and drink and rejoice all the days of their life.

Within the domains of the palace of the Caliph there are great buildings of marble and columns of silver and gold, and carvings upon rare stones are fixed in the walls. In the Caliph's palace are great riches and towers filled with gold, silken garments and all precious stones. He does not issue forth from his palace save once in the year, at the feast which the Mohammedans call El-id-bed Ramazan, and they come from distant lands that day to see him. He rides on a mule and is attired in the royal robes of gold and silver and fine linen; on his head is a turban adorned with precious stones of priceless value, and over the turban is a black shawl as a sign of his modesty, implying that all this glory will be covered by darkness on the day of death.

He is accompanied by all the nobles of Islam dressed in fine garments and riding on horses, the princes of Arabia, the princes of Togarma and Daylam [Gilan] and the princes of Persia, Media and Ghuzz, and the princes of the land of Tibet, which is three months' journey distant, and westward of which lies the land of Samarkand. He proceeds from his palace to the great mosque of Islam which is by the Basrah Gate. Along the road the walls are adorned with silk and purple, and the inhabitants receive him with all kinds of song and exultation, and they dance before the great king who is styled the Caliph.

They salute him with a loud voice and say "Peace unto thee, our Lord the King and Light of Islam!" He kisses his robe, and stretching forth the hem thereof he salutes them. Then he proceeds to the court of the mosque, mounts a wooden pulpit and expounds to them their Law. Then the learned ones of Islam arise and pray for him and extol his greatness and his graciousness, to which they all respond. Afterwards he gives them his blessing, and they bring before him a camel which he slays, and this is their Passover sacrifice. He gives thereof unto the princes and they distribute it to all, so that they may taste of the sacrifice brought by their sacred king; and they all rejoice.

Afterwards he leaves the mosque and returns alone to his palace by way of the river Hiddekel, and the grandees of Islam accompany him in ships on the river until he enters his palace. He does not return the way he came; and the road which he takes along the riverside is watched all the year through, so that no man shall tread in his footsteps. He does not leave the palace again for a whole year. He is a benevolent man.

He built, on the other side of the river, on the banks of an arm of the Euphrates which there borders the city, a hospital consisting of blocks of houses and hospices for the sick poor who come to be healed. Here there are about sixty physicians' stores which are provided from the Caliph's house with drugs and whatever else may be required. Every sick man who comes is maintained at the Caliph's expense and is medically treated. Here is a building which is called Dar-al-Maristan, where they keep charge of the demented people who have become insane in the towns through the great heat in the summer, and they chain each of them in iron chains until their reason becomes restored to them in the wintertime.

Whilst they abide there, they are provided with food from the house of the Caliph, and when their reason is restored they are dismissed and each one of them goes to his house and his home. Money is given to those that have stayed in the hospices on their return to their homes. Every month the officers of the Caliph inquire and investigate whether they have regained their reason, in which case they are discharged. All this the Caliph does out of charity to those that come to the city of Bagdad, whether they be sick or insane. The Caliph is a righteous man, and all his actions are for good.

In Bagdad there are about 40,000 Jews, and they dwell in security, prosperity and honour under the great Caliph, and amongst them are great sages, the heads of Academies engaged in the study of the law. In this city there are ten Academies. . . .

The heads of these academies are the ten Batlanim, and they do not engage in any other work than communal administration, and all the days of the week they judge the Jews their countrymen, except on the second day of the week, when they all appear before the chief rabbi Samuel, the head of the Yeshiva Gaon [Jacob], who in conjunction with the other Batlanim judges all those that appear before him.

At the head of them all is Daniel the son of Hisdai, who is styled "Our Lord the Head of the Captivity of all Israel." He possesses a book of pedigrees going back as far as David, King of Israel.

The Jews call him "Our Lord, Head of the Captivity," and the Mohammedans call him "Saidna ben Daoud," and he has been invested with authority over all the congregations of Israel at the hands of the Emir al Muminin, the Lord of Islam. For thus Mohammed commanded concerning him and his descendants; and he granted him a seal of office over all the congregations that dwell under his rule, and ordered that every one, whether Mohammedan or Jew, or belonging to any other nation in his dominion, should rise up before him [the Exilarch] and salute him, and that any one who should refuse to rise up should receive one hundred stripes.

And every fifth day when he goes to pay a visit to the great Caliph, horsemen, Gentiles as well as Jews escort him, and heralds proclaim in advance, "Make way before our Lord, the son of David, as is due unto him," the Arabic words being "Amilu tarik la Saidna ben Daud." He is mounted on a horse, and is attired in robes of silk and embroidery with a large turban on his head, and from the turban is suspended a long white cloth adorned with a chain upon which the cipher of Mohammed is engraved.

Then he appears before the Caliph and kisses his hand, and the Caliph rises and places him on a throne which Mohammed had ordered to be made for him, and all the Mohammedan princes who attended the court of the Caliph rise up before him. And the Head of the Captivity is seated on his throne opposite to the Caliph, in compliance with the command of Mohammed to give effect to what is written in the law—"The sceptre shall not depart from Judah nor a lawgiver from between his feet, until he come to Shiloh: and to him shall the gathering of the people be." [Gen. 49:10].

The authority of the Head of the Captivity extends over all the communities of Shinar, Persia, Khurasan and Sheba which is El-Yemen, and Diyar Kalach [Bekr] and the land of Aram Naharaim [Mesopotamia], and over the dwellers in the mountains of Ararat and the land of the Alans, which is a land surrounded by mountains and has no outlet except by the iron gate which Alexander made, but which were afterwards broken. Here are the people called Alani. His authority extends also over the land of Siberia, and the communities in the land of the Togarmim unto the mountains of Asveh and the land of Gurgan, the inhabitants of which are called Gurganim who dwell by the river Gihon, and these are the Girgashites who follow the Christian religion. Further it extends to the gates of Samarkand, the land of Tibet, and the land of India.

In respect of all these countries the Head of the Captivity gives the communities power to appoint Rabbis and Ministers who come unto him to be consecrated and to receive his authority. They bring him offerings and gifts from the ends of the earth. He owns hospices, gardens and plantations in Babylon, and much land inherited from his fathers, and no one can take his possessions from him by force. He has a fixed weekly revenue arising from the hospices of the Jews, the markets and the merchants, apart from that which is brought to him from far-off lands. The man is very rich, and wise in the Scriptures as well as in the Talmud, and many Israelites dine at his table every day.

At his installation, the Head of the Captivity gives much money to the Caliph, to the Princes and the Ministers. On the day that the Caliph performs the ceremony of investing him with authority, he rides in the second of the royal equipages, and is escorted from the palace of the Caliph to his own house with timbrels and fifes. The Exilarch appoints the Chiefs of the Academies by placing his hand upon their heads, thus installing them in their office. The Jews of the city are learned men and very rich.

In Bagdad there are twenty-eight Jewish Synagogues, situated either in the city itself or in Al-Karkh on the other side of the Tigris; for the river divides the metropolis into two parts. The great synagogue of the Head of the Captivity has columns of marble of various colours overlaid with silver and gold, and on these columns are sentences of the Psalms in golden letters. And in front of the ark are about ten steps of marble; on the topmost step are the seats of the Head of the Captivity and of the Princes of the House of David. The city of Bagdad is twenty miles in circumference, situated in a land of palms, gardens, and plantations, the like of which is not to be found in the whole land of Shinar. People come thither with merchandise from all lands. Wise men live there, philosophers who know all manner of wisdom, and magicians expert in all manner of witchcraft. . . .

Thence to Babylon, which is the Babel of old. The ruins thereof are thirty miles in extent. The ruins of the palace of Nebuchadnezzar are still to be seen there, but people are afraid to enter them on account of the serpents and scorpions. Near at hand, within a distance of a mile, there dwell 3,000 Israelites who pray in the Synagogue of the Pavilion of Daniel, which is ancient and was erected by Daniel. It is built of hewn stones and bricks. Between the Synagogue and the Palace of Nebuchadnezzar is the furnace into which were thrown Hananiah, Mishael, and Azariah, and the site of it lies in a valley known to all. . . .

Thence to the Tower of Babel, which the generation whose language was confounded built of the bricks called Agur. The length of its foundation is about two miles, the breadth of the tower is about forty cubits, and the length thereof two hundred cubits. At every ten cubits' distance there are slopes which go round the tower by which one can ascend to the top. One can see from there a view twenty miles in extent, as the land is level. There fell fire from heaven into the midst of the tower which split it to its very depths.

Thence it is half a day to Kaphri, where there are about 200 Jews. Here is the Synagogue of R. Isaac Napcha, who is buried in front of it. Thence it is three parasangs to the Synagogue of Ezekiel, the prophet of blessed memory, which is by the river Euphrates. It is fronted by six turrets, and between each turret there is a minor Synagogue, and in the court of the Synagogue is the Ark, and at the back of the Synagogue is the sepulchre of Ezekiel. It is surrounded by a large cupola, and it is a very handsome structure. It was built of old by King Jeconiah, king of Judah, and the 35,000 Jews who came with him, when Evil-merodach brought him forth out of prison.

This place is by the river Chebar on the one side, and by the river Euphrates on the other, and the names of Jeconiah and those that accompanied him are engraved on the wall: Jeconiah at the top, and Ezekiel at the bottom. This place is held sacred by Israel as a lesser sanctuary unto this day, and people come from a distance to pray there from the time of the New Year until the Day of Atonement. The Israelites have great rejoicing on these occasions. Thither also come the Head of the Captivity, and the Heads of the Academies from Bagdad. Their camp occupies a space of about two miles, and Arab merchants come there as well. A great gathering like a fair takes place, which is called Fera, and they bring forth a scroll of the Law written on parchment by Ezekiel the Prophet, and read from it on the Day of Atonement. A lamp burns day and night over the sepulchre of Ezekiel; the light thereof has been kept burning from the day that he lighted it himself, and they continually renew the wick thereof, and replenish the oil unto the present day.

A large house belonging to the sanctuary is filled with books, some of them from the time of the First Temple, and he who has no sons consecrates his books to its use. The Jews that come thither to pray from the land of Persia and Media bring the money which their countrymen have offered to the Synagogue of Ezekiel the Prophet. The Synagogue owns property, lands and villages, which belonged to King Jeconiah, and when Mohammed came he confirmed all these rights to the Synagogue of Ezekiel. Distinguished Mohammedans also come hither to pray, so great is their love for Ezekiel the Prophet; and they call it Bar [Dar] Melicha [the Dwelling of Beauty]. All the Arabs come there to pray.

At a distance of about half a mile from the Synagogue are the sepulchres of Hananiah, Mishael, and Azariah, and upon their sepulchres are large cupolas; and even at times of disturbance no man would dare touch the Mohammedan or Jewish servants who attend at the sepulchre of Ezekiel.

Thence it is three miles to the city of Kotsonath, where there are 300 Jews. Here are the sepulchres of Rab Papa, Rab Huna, Joseph Sinai, and Rab Joseph ben Hama; and before each of them is a Synagogue where the Israelites pray every day. Thence it is three parasangs to Ain Siptha, where there is the sepulchre of the prophet Nahum the Elkoshite. Thence it is a day's journey to Kefar Al-Keram, where are the sepulchres of Rab Chisdai,

R. Azariah, R. Akiba, and R. Dosa. Thence it is a half-day's journey to a village in the desert, where there are buried R. David and R. Jehuda and Abaji, R. Kurdiah, Rab Sechora, and Rab Ada. Thence it is a day's journey to the river Raga, where there is the sepulchre of King Zedekiah. Upon it is a large cupola. Thence it is a day's journey to the city of Kufa, where there is the sepulchre of King Jeconiah. Over it is a big structure, and in front thereof is a synagogue. There are about 7,000 Jews here. At this place is the large mosque of the Mohammedans, for here is buried Ali ben Abu Talib, the son-in-law of Mohammed, and the Mohammedans come hither. . . .

Thence it is a day and a half to Sura, which is Mata Mehasya, where the Heads of the Captivity and the Heads of the Academies dwelt at first. Here is the sepulchre of R. Sherira, and of R. Hai his son of blessed memory, also of R. Saadiah Al-Fiumi, and of Rab Samuel the son of Hofni Hacohen, and of Zephaniah the Prophet. . . .

Thence to Samarkand, which is the great city on the confines of Persia. In it live some 50,000 Israelites, and R. Obadiah the Nasi is their appointed head. Among them are wise and very rich men.

Thence it is four days' journey to Tibet, the country in whose forests the musk is found.

Thence it takes twenty-eight days to the mountains of Naisabur by the river Gozan. And there are men of Israel in the land of Persia who say that in the mountains of Naisabur four of the tribes of Israel dwell, namely, the tribe of Dan, the tribe of Zebulun, the tribe of Asher, and the tribe of Naphtali, who were included in the first captivity of Shalmaneser, king of Assyria, as it is written: "And he put them in Halah and in Habor by the river of Gozan and in the cities of the Medes." [II Kings, 18:11].

The extent of their land is twenty days' journey, and they have cities and large villages in the mountains; the river Gozan forms the boundary on the one side. They are not under the rule of the Gentiles, but they have a prince of their own, whose name is R. Joseph Amarkala the Levite. There are scholars among them. And they sow and reap and go forth to war as far as the land of Cush by way of the desert. They are in league with the Kofar-al-Turak, who worship the wind and live in the wilderness, and who do not eat bread, nor drink wine, but live on raw uncooked meat. They have no noses, and in lieu thereof they have two small holes, through which they breathe. They eat animals both clean and unclean, and they are very friendly towards the Israelites.

Fifteen years ago they overran the country of Persia with a large army and took the city of Rayy; they smote it with the edge of the sword, took all the spoil thereof, and returned by way of the wilderness. Such an invasion had not been known in the land of Persia for many years. When the king of Persia heard thereof, his anger was kindled against them, and he said, "Not in my days nor in the days of my fathers did an army sally forth from this wilderness. Now I will go and cut off their name from the earth."

A proclamation was made throughout his Empire, and he assembled all his armies; and he sought a guide who might show him the way to their encampment. And a certain man said that he would show him the way, as he was one of them. And the king promised that he would enrich him if he did so. And the king asked him as to what provisions they would require for the march through the wilderness. And he replied, "Take with you bread and wine for fifteen days, for you will find no sustenance by the way, till you have reached their land."

And they did so, and marched through the wilderness for fifteen days, but they found nothing at all. And their food began to give out, so that man and beast were dying of hunger and thirst. Then the king called the guide, and said to him, "Where is your promise to us that you would find our adversaries?" To which the other replied, "I have mistaken the way." And the king was wroth, and commanded that his head should be struck off. And the king further gave orders throughout the camp that every man who had any food should divide it with his neighbour. And they consumed everything they had including their beasts. And after a further thirteen days' march they reached the mountains of Naisabur, where Jews lived.

They came there on the Sabbath, and encamped in the gardens and plantations and by the springs of water which are by the side of the river Gozan. Now it was the time of the ripening of the fruit, and they ate and consumed everything. No man came forth to them, but on the mountains they saw cities and many towers. Then the king commanded two of his servants to go and inquire of the people who lived in the mountains, and to cross the river either in boats or by swimming.

So they searched and found a large bridge, on which there were three towers, but the gate of the bridge was locked. And on the other side of the bridge was a great city. Then they shouted in front of the bridge till a man came forth and asked them what they wanted and who they were. But they did not understand him till an interpreter came who understood their language.

And when he asked them, they said, "We are the servants of the King of Persia, and we have come to ask who you are, and whom you serve."

To which the other replied: "We are Jews; we have no king and no Gentile prince, but a Jewish prince rules over us."

They then questioned him with regard to the infidels, the sons of Ghuz of the Kofar-al-Turak, and he answered: "Truly they are in league with us, and he who seeks to do them harm seeks our harm."

Then they went their way, and told the king of Persia, who was much alarmed. And on a certain day the Jews asked him to join combat with them, but he answered: "I am not come to fight you, but the Kofar-al-Turak, my enemy, and if you fight against me I will be avenged on you by killing all the Jews in my Empire; I know that you are stronger than I am in this place, and my army has come out of this great wilderness starving and athirst. Deal kindly with me and do not fight against me, but leave me to engage with the Kofar-al-Turak, my enemy, and sell me also the provisions which I require for myself and my army."

The Jews then took counsel together, and resolved to propitiate the king on account of the Jews who were in exile in his Empire. Then the king entered their land with his army, and stayed there fifteen days. And they showed him much honour, and also sent a dispatch to the Kofar-al-Turak their allies, reporting the matter to them. Thereupon the latter occupied the mountain passes in force with a large army composed of all those who dwelt in that desert, and when the king of Persia went forth to fight with them, they placed themselves in battle array against him. The Kofar-al-Turak army was victorious and slew many of the Persian host, and the king of Persia fled with only a few followers to his own country.

Now a horseman, one of the servants of the king of Persia, enticed a Jew, whose name was R. Moses, to come with him, and when he came to the land of Persia this horseman made the Jew his slave. One day the archers came before the king to give a display of their skill and no one among them could be found to draw the bow like this R. Moses. Then the king inquired of him by means of an interpreter who knew his language, and he related all that the horseman had done to him. Thereupon the king at once granted him his liberty, had him clad in robes of silk, gave him gifts, and said to him, "If thou wilt embrace our religion, I will make thee a rich man and steward of my house," but he answered, "My lord, I cannot do this thing." Then the king took him and placed him in the house of the Chief Rabbi of the Ispahan community, Sar Shalom, who gave him his daughter to wife. This same R. Moses told me all these things. . . .

Thence to cross over to the land of Zin [China]. Zin is in the uttermost East, and some say that there is the Sea of Nipka [Ning-po?], where the star Orion predominates and stormy winds prevail. At times the helmsman cannot govern his ship, as a fierce wind drives her into this Sea of Nipka, where she cannot move from her place; and the crew have to remain where they are till their stores of food are exhausted and then they die. In this way many a ship has been lost, but men eventually discovered a device by which to escape from this evil place. The crew provide themselves with hides of oxen. And when this evil wind blows which drives them into the Sea of Nipka, they wrap themselves up in the skins, which they make waterproof, and, armed with knives, plunge into the sea. A great bird called the griffin spies them out, and in the belief that the sailor is an animal, the griffin seizes hold of him, brings him to dry land, and puts him down on a mountain or in a hollow in order to devour him. The man then quickly thrusts at the bird with a knife and slays him. Then the man issues forth from the skin and walks till he comes to an inhabited place. And in this manner many a man escapes. . . .

Thence to the land of Assuan through the desert. This is Seba on the river Pishon [Nile] which descends from the land of Cush. And some of these sons of Cush have a king whom they call the Sultan Al-Habash. There is a people among them who, like animals, eat of the herbs that grow on the banks of the Nile and in the fields. They go about naked and have not the intelligence of ordinary men. They cohabit with their sisters and any one they find. The climate is very hot. When the men of Assuan make a raid into their land, they take with them bread and wheat, dry grapes and figs, and throw the food to these people, who run after it. Thus they bring many of them back prisoners, and sell them in the land of Egypt and in the surrounding countries. And these are the black slaves, the sons of Ham.

From Assuan it is a distance of twelve days to Heluan where there are about 300 Jews. Thence people travel in caravans a journey of fifty days through the great desert called Sahara, to the land of Zawilah, which is Havilah in the land of Gana. In this desert there are mountains of sand, and when the wind rises, it covers the caravans with the sand, and many die from suffocation. Those that escape bring back with them copper, wheat, fruit, all manner of lentils, and salt. And from thence they bring gold, and all kinds of jewels. This is in the land of Cush which is called Al-Habash on the western confines. From Heluan it is thirteen days' journey to Kutz which is Kus, and this is the commencement of the land of Egypt. At Kutz there are 300 Jews; and unto this very day one can see the ruins of the buildings which our forefathers erected there.

Thence to Mizraim is a journey of four days.

This Mizraim is the great city situated on the banks of the Nile, which is Pison or Al-Nil. The number of Jewish inhabitants is about 7,000. Two large synagogues are there, one belonging to the men of the land of Israel and one belonging to the men of the land of Babylon. The synagogue of the men of the land of Israel is called Kenisat-al-Schamiyyin, and the synagogue of the men of Babylon is called Kenisat-al-Irakiyyin. Their usage with regard to the portions and sections of the Law is not alike; for the men of Babylon are accustomed to read a portion every week, as is done in Spain, and is our custom, and to finish the Law each year; whilst the men of Palestine do not do so, but divide each portion into three sections and finish the Law at the end of three years.

The two communities, however, have an established custom to unite and pray together on the day of the Rejoicing of the Law, and on the day of the Giving of the Law. Among the Jews is Nethanel the Prince of Princes and the head of the Academy, who is the head of all the congregations in Egypt; he appoints Rabbis and officials, and is attached to the court of the great King, who lives in his palace of Zoan al-Medina, which is the royal city for the Arabs. . . .

Twice in the year the Egyptian monarch goes forth, once on the occasion of the great festival, and again when the river Nile rises. Zoan is surrounded by a wall, but Mizraim has no wall, for the river encompasses it on one side. It is a great city, and it has marketplaces as well as inns in great number. The Jews that dwell there are very rich. No rain falls, neither is ice or snow ever seen. The climate is very hot.

The river Nile rises once a year in the month of Elul; it covers all the land, and irrigates it to a distance of fifteen days' journey. The waters remains upon the surface of the land during the months of Elul and Tishri, and irrigate and fertilize it.

The inhabitants have a pillar of marble, erected with much skill, in order to ascertain the extent of the rise of the Nile. It stands in the front of an island in the midst of the water, and is twelve cubits high. When the Nile rises and covers the column, they know that the river has risen and has covered the land for a distance of fifteen days' journey to its full extent. If only half the column is covered, the water only covers half the extent of the land. And day by day an officer takes a measurement on the column and makes proclamation thereof in Zoan and in the city of Mizraim, proclaiming: "Give praise unto the Creator, for the river this day has risen to such and such a height"; each day he takes the measurement and makes his proclamation.

If the water covers the entire column, there will be abundance throughout Egypt. The river continues to rise gradually till it covers the land to the extent of fifteen days' journey. He who owns a field hires workmen, who dig deep trenches. Then, when the waters have receded, the fish remain behind in the trenches, and the owners of the fields take them and either eat them or sell them to the fishmongers, who salt them and deal in them in every place. These fish are exceedingly fat and large, and the oil obtained from them is used in this land for lamp oil. Though a man eat a great quantity of these fish, if he but drink Nile water afterwards they will not hurt him, for the waters have medicinal properties.

People ask, what causes the Nile to rise? The Egyptians say that up the river, in the land of Al-Habash [Abyssinia], which is the land of Havilah, much rain descends at the time of the rising of the river, and that this abundance of rain causes the river to rise and to cover the surface of the land. If the river does not rise, there is no sowing, and famine is sore in the land. Sowing is done in the month of Marheshwan [Oct.–Nov.], after the river has gone back to its ordinary channel. In the month of Adar [March] is the barley harvest, and in the month of Nisan [April] the wheat harvest.

In the month of Nisan they have cherries, pears, cucumbers, and gourds in plenty, also beans, peas, chickpeas, and many kinds of vegetables, such as purslane, asparagus, pulse, lettuce, coriander, endive, cabbage, leek, and cardoon. The land is full of all good things, and the gardens and plantations are watered from the various reservoirs and by the river water.

The River Nile, after flowing past [the city of] Mizraim, divides into four heads: one channel proceeds in the direction of Damietta, which is Caphtor, where it falls into the sea. The second channel flows to the city of Reshid [Rosetta], which is near Alexandria, and there falls into the sea; the third channel goes by way of Ashmun, where it falls into the sea; and the fourth channel goes as far as the frontier of Egypt. Along both banks of these four riverheads are cities, towns and villages, and people visit these places either by ship or by land. There is no such thickly-populated land as this elsewhere. It is extensive too and abundant in all good things.

From New Mizraim unto Old Mizraim is a distance of two parasangs. The latter is in ruins, and the place where walls and houses stood can be seen to the present day. The storehouses also of Joseph of blessed memory are to be found in great numbers in many places. They are built of lime and stone, and are exceedingly strong. A pillar is there of marvellous workmanship, the like of which cannot be seen throughout the world.

Outside the city is the ancient synagogue of Moses our master, of blessed memory, and the overseer and clerk of this place of worship is a venerable old man; he is a man of learning, and they call him Al Sheik Abu al-Nazr. The extent of Mizraim, which is in ruins, is three miles.

Thence to the land of Goshen is eight parasangs; here is Bilbais. There are about 300 Jews in the city, which is a large one. Thence it is half a day's journey to Ain-al-Shams or Ramses, which is in ruins. Traces are there to be seen of the buildings which our forefathers raised, namely, towers built of bricks. . . .

Thence to Alexandria of Egypt, which is Ammon of No; but when Alexander of Macedon built the city, he called it after his own name, and made it exceedingly strong and beautiful. The houses, the palaces, and the walls are of excellent architecture. Outside the town is the academy of Aristotle, the teacher of Alexander. This is a large building, standing between other academies to the number of twenty, with a column of marble between each. People from the whole world were wont to come hither in order to study the wisdom of Aristotle the philosopher. The city is built over a hollow by means of arches. Alexander built it with great understanding. The streets are wide and straight, so that a man can look along them for a mile from gate to gate, from the gate of Reshid to the gate by the sea.

Alexander also built for the harbour of Alexandria a pier, a king's highway running into the midst of the sea. And there he erected a large tower, a lighthouse, called Manar al Iskandriyyah in Arabic. On the top of the tower there is a glass mirror. Any ships that attempted to attack or molest the city, coming from Greece or from the Western lands, could be seen by means of this mirror of glass at a distance of twenty days' journey, and the inhabitants could thereupon put themselves on their guard.

It happened once, many years after the death of Alexander, that a ship came from the land of Greece, and the name of the captain was Theodoros, a Greek of great cleverness. The Greeks at that time were under the yoke of Egypt. The captain brought great gifts in silver and gold and garments of silk to the King of Egypt, and he moored his ship in front of the lighthouse, as was the custom of all merchants.

Every day the guardian of the lighthouse and his servants had their meals with him, until the captain came to be on such friendly terms with the keeper that he could go in and out at all times. And one day he gave a banquet, and caused the keeper and all his servants to drink a great deal of wine. When they were all asleep, the captain and his servants arose and broke the mirror and departed that very night. From that day onward the Christians began to come thither with boats and large ships, and eventually captured the large island called Crete and also Cyprus, which are under the dominion of the Greeks. [The other MSS. add here: Ever since then, the men of the King of Egypt have been unable to prevail over the Greeks.] To this day the lighthouse is a landmark to all the seafarers who come to Alexandria; for one can see it at a distance of 100 miles by day, and at night the keeper lights a torch which the mariners can see from a distance, and thus sail towards it.

Alexandria is a commercial market for all nations. Merchants come thither from all the Christian kingdoms . . . and the land of the Arabs, and India, Abyssinia, Lybia, and El-Yemen . . . also Javan, whose people are called the Greeks, and the Turks. And merchants of India bring thither all kinds of spices, and the merchants of Edom buy of them. And the city is a busy one and full of traffic. Each nation has an inn of its own.

By the seacoast there is a sepulchre of marble on which are engraved all manner of beasts and birds; an effigy is in the midst thereof, and all the writing is in ancient characters, which no one knows now. Men suppose that it is the sepulchre of a king who lived in early times before the Deluge. The length of the sepulchre is fifteen spans, and its breadth is six spans. There are about 3,000 Jews in Alexandria.

Thence it is two days' journey to Damietta which is Caphtor, where there are about 200 Jews, and it lies upon the sea. Thence it is one day's journey to Simasim; it contains about 100 Jews. From there it is half a day to Sunbat; the inhabitants sow flax and weave linen, which they export to all parts of the world. Thence it is four days to Ailam, which is Elim. It belongs to the Arabs who dwell in the wilderness. Thence it is two days' journey to Rephidim where the Arabs dwell, but there are no Jews there. A day's journey from thence takes one to Mount Sinai. On the top of the mountain is a large convent belonging to the great monks called Syrians. At the foot of the mountain is a large town called Tur Sinai; the inhabitants speak the language of the Targum [Syriac]. It is close to a small mountain, five days distant from Egypt. The inhabitants are under Egyptian rule. At a day's journey from Mount Sinai is the Red Sea, which is an arm of the Indian Ocean. We return to Damietta. From there it is a day's journey to Tanis, which is Hanes, where there are about 40 Jews. It is an island in the midst of the sea. Thus far extends the empire of Egypt. . . .

The following are the cities in the land of Alamannia [Germany], which have Hebrew congregations: Metz, Treves on the river Moselle, Coblenz, Andernach, Bonn, Cologne, Bingen, Munster, Worms.

All Israel is dispersed in every land, and he who does not further the gathering of Israel will not meet with happiness nor live with Israel. When the Lord will remember us in our exile, and raise the horn of his anointed, then every one will say, "I will lead the Jews and I will gather them." As for the towns which have been mentioned, they contain scholars and communities that love their brethren, and speak peace to those that are near and afar, and when a wayfarer comes they rejoice, and make a feast for him, and say, "Rejoice, brethren, for the help of the Lord comes in the twinkling of an eye."

If we were not afraid that the appointed time has not yet arrived nor been reached, we would have gathered together, but we dare not do so until the time for song has arrived, and the voice of the turtledove [is heard in the land], when the messengers will come and say continually, "The Lord be exalted." Meanwhile they send missives one to the other, saying, "Be ye strong in the law of Moses, and do ye mourners for Zion and ye mourners for Jerusalem entreat the Lord, and may the supplication of those that wear the garments of mourning be received through their merits."

In addition to the several cities which we have mentioned, there are Strassburg, Wurzburg, Mantern, Bamberg, Freising, and Regesnburg at the extremity of the Empire. In these cities there are many Israelites, wise men and rich.

Thence extends the land of Bohemia, called Prague. This is the commencement of the land of Slavonia, and the Jews who dwell there call it Canaan, because the men of that land [the Slavs] sell their sons and their daughters to the other nations. These are the men of Russia, which is a great empire stretching from the gate of Prague to the gates of Kiev, the large city which is at the extremity of that empire. It is a land of mountains and forests, where there are to be found the animals called vair, ermine, and sable. No one issues forth from his house in wintertime on account of the cold. People are to be found there who have lost the tips of their noses by reason of the frost. Thus far reaches the empire of Russia.

The kingdom of France, which is Zarfath, extends from the town of Auxerre unto Paris, the great city—a journey of six days. The city belongs to King Louis. It is situated on the river Seine. Scholars are there, unequalled in the whole world, who study the Law day and night. They are charitable and hospitable to all travellers, and are as brothers and friends unto all their brethren the Jews. May God, the Blessed One, have mercy upon us and upon them!

Finished and completed.

Petachia of Ratisbon

Juxtaposed with his contemporary, Benjamin of Tudela, the travels of Petachia offer an interesting comparison. It is important to remember that Benjamin was a representative of the Sephardic tradition, with its more tolerant attitude to secular culture, and that Petachia was a product of Ashkenazic Jewry, which devoted itself almost exclusively to Jewish scholarship and attempted to avoid contact with outside culture.

Petachia, born at Ratisbon (Regensburg) Germany, began his travels (1170–1180) in Prague. The third person narrative depicts his travels through Poland, southern Russia, Armenia, Persia, Babylonia, Syria and Palestine. He dwells on descriptions of graves, sepulchers of saints and famous personalities, and describes the miracles they performed. He writes from personal knowledge—when his reports are based on hearsay, he carefully apprises the reader of this. Like Benjamin's journey, the motive for his trip may have been a desire to visit his coreligionists in other parts of the world; but, as the narrative indicates, since Petachia was a wealthy man, the possibility of a commercial voyage should not be ruled out. Otherwise unknown to Jewish history and literature, Petachia, too, did not write his own travelogue, but entrusted his notes to another person, Rabbi Judah the Pious, author of the *Book of the Pious* (see page 378).

The travelogue was first printed in 1595 with a German translation, and was also translated into Latin, French and other languages.

THE TRAVELS OF PETACHIA OF RATISBON

These are the travels undertaken by Rabbi Petachia, who travelled through many lands. He set out from Prague, which is in Bohemia, going to Poland, and from Poland to Kiev in Russia. From Russia he went for six days on the River Dnieper. On the other side of the river he commenced his travels in the land of Kedar [Ukraine]. There they have no ships, but sew together ten extended horse hides, with a thong round the border; they then seat themselves on the hides, placing thereon also the wagons and all the luggage. They then tie the thong which is on the border of the hides to the tails of the horses, who start swimming, and thus they pass over the water. They eat no bread in the land of Kedar, but rice and millet boiled in milk, as well as milk and cheese. They also put the pieces of flesh under the saddle of a horse, which they ride and, urging on the animal, cause it to sweat. The flesh getting warm, they eat it. They only travel in the land of Kedar under escort.

This is the manner in which the sons of Kedar pledge their faith to each other. One man thrusts a needle into his finger and invites the intended companion of his journey to swallow the blood of the wounded finger. He and that other person become, as it were, the same blood and flesh. They have another fashion of entering into this bond. They fill a vessel of cast copper of the shape of a human face and the traveller and his escort drink thereout, after which they never prove faithless. They have no king, but only princes and nobles.

Rabbi Petachia passed through the whole length of the land of Kedar in sixteen days. The inhabitants live in tents; they are farsighted and have beautiful eyes, because they eat no salt and live among fragrant plants. They are good archers, bringing down birds whilst on the wing. They perceive and recognize objects at more than a day's distance. There are no mountains in their country, but all is level. And a day's journey behind the land of Kedar extends a gulf [the Black Sea], intervening between the land of Kedar and the land of Khozaria [Crimea]. There it is customary for women the whole day and night to bemoan and lament their deceased fathers and mothers. This they continue until any of their sons or daughters or other members of the family die, and the last survivors lament those that preceded them in death. They teach their daughters lamentation. In the night they groan and howl. The dogs also whine and bark at their voices. . . .

In the land of Kedar there are no Jews but only Karaites. And Rabbi Petachia asked them: "Why do you not believe in the words of the sages?" They replied: "Because our fathers did not teach them to us." On the eve of the Sabbath they cut all the bread to be eaten on the Sabbath. They eat in the dark and sit the whole day on one spot. Their prayers consist only of psalms. And when Rabbi Petachia imparted to them our ritual and prayer after meals they were pleased. They also said: "We have never heard of the Talmud." . . .

R. Petachia fell sick at Nineveh, and the king's physicians said that he would not live. It is the custom there that when a Jew on his travels dies the sultan takes half of his property; and because R. Petachia was dressed in beautiful clothes they thought that he was rich; therefore the scribes of the sultan came thither to take possession of his property should he die. But Rabbi Petachia gave directions, sick as he was, to carry him over the river Tigris. The river is broad and not crossed over in boats, for the current is swift and impetuous and would upset the boat. Therefore, they make rafts of reeds, which we call floss, upon which they put man and luggage. The waters being healing, he recovered immediately. . . .

The rabbi then embarked on the Tigris and went with the current of the river, in fifteen days, to the garden of the head of the academy in Babel. The journey would otherwise take one month. From Nineveh, and further on, there are congregations in every city and village. He came to the garden of the head of the academy. In the garden there are all kinds of fruit. The garden is very large and there are mandrakes in it. These have the face of a human being and their foliage is broad. From thence he travelled in one day to Baghdad, in Babylon. Nobody ascends the River Tigris because its waters are swift and impetuous, but they employ camels and mules on dry land, tying inflated skins on the backs of the camels.

Baghdad is a metropolis. It is the seat of the Caliph or sultan. This is the great king who rules and governs nations. Baghdad is very large, more than a day's journey from end to end. To go round it is more than three days' journey. In the city of Baghdad there are a thousand Jews. They walk about wrapped in cloth. Nobody there looks upon any woman, nor does anybody go into the house of his friend lest he should see the wife of that neighbour, who would immediately say unto him: "Insolent man, wherefor art thou come?" But he knocks with a tin knocker; when the other comes forth, he speaks to him.

They all walk about wrapped in their praying shawls of wool with fringes. The head of the academy at Baghdad is R. Samuel, the Levite, son of Eli, head of the academy. He is the superior, full of wisdom both in the written and oral law and in all the wisdom of Egypt. Nothing is hidden from him. He knows the holy names [the secrets of the Kabbalah], and is profoundly versed in the Talmud. There is no one so ignorant in the whole of Babylon, Assyria, Media, and Persia, but knows the twenty-four books, punctuation, grammar, the superfluous and omitted letters, for the preceptor does not recite the scripture lesson, but he that is called up to the Torah recites it himself.

The head of the academy has about two thousand disciples at once, and more than five hundred sit round him, and they are all well-informed. But before they are ripe for the academy, they study in the city under other teachers, and when ripe they are brought before the head of the academy. The *Rosh Gola* [Exilarch] is Rabbi Eleazar, and under him is the head of the academy. The head of the academy occupies a large house, which is covered with tapestry; he himself is clothed in garments adorned with gold. He is seated above and the disciples sit on the ground. He expounds to the interpreter, and the interpreter to the disciples. The disciples address their queries to the interpreter, and if the interpreter does not know the answer he addresses himself to the head of the academy. An interpreter expounds Tractate of the Talmud on one side, and another interpreter expounds another Tractate on the other side. The treatise to be expounded is first intoned, and afterwards the interpreter expounds it. . . .

In Baghdad he was shown a flying camel [a dromedary]. It is low, and its legs are slender; and if anybody wishes to ride on it he must tie himself to it lest he should fall off. The rider traverses in one day the ground over which a man on foot would have to take fifteen. It would be possible to go even swifter if the rider could only stand it. In one second the flying camel gallops a mile.

They also showed him the gates of Baghdad. They are a hundred cubits high and ten cubits wide. They are of polished copper and ornamented with figures so fashioned that no one can produce the like. A nail once fell out and no artificer is able to fix it again. Formerly the horses used to be startled back at the sight of the gates for, seeing the brightness of the gates, they perceived, as it were, other horses running towards them, whereby they took fright and started off. They, therefore, poured boiling vinegar over the gates, and thus deadened the brightness of the polished copper, so that the horses should enter. However, the polish of the copper is still partly to be perceived at the top, where no vinegar was poured. These gates were once the gates of Jerusalem.

The head of the academy has many servants. They flog anyone not immediately executing his orders; therefore people fear him. He, however, is righteous, humble, and full of knowledge of the law. He is clothed in golden and coloured garments like the king; his palace also is hung with costly tapestry like that of the king.

Rabbi Petachia travelled in two days from Baghdad to the boundary of Old Babylon. The house of Nebuchadnezzar is all desolate. Near his house is a pillar, and the house of Daniel looks as if it were new. On the place where Daniel used to sit there is a stone, and where his feet rested a marble stone. There is also a stone at the top upon which the book lay out of which he used to write. In the wall between the house of Daniel and that of Nebuchadnezzar is a small window through which he threw writings.

There are steps below, upon which three pious sages used to sit before him. On his right, by his seat, a stone is fixed, and they declared that there was a tradition that there the vessels from the holy temple were hidden. One day rulers who had heard of it came for the purpose of digging there but when they laid hold on the stone they all fell down dead, therefore they removed nothing. They then went from that room, and took the rabbi through the thickness of the wall to an upper room, wherein Daniel used to offer up his prayers. The entrance is so inclined that it is exactly opposite Jerusalem, and so cunningly contrived that nobody could point out where it was.

He then returned. He stated that he did not see any woman whilst staying in Babylon because they were all veiled and modest. Everyone has a bath in his courtyard; and no one offered up his prayer before he had bathed. All travellers there travel in the night on account of the heat. Everything grows there in winter as here in summer. Most of their labours are performed during the night. Babylon is, in fact, quite a different world. The Jews are devoted to the study of the law and the fear of God. The Ishmaelites also are trustworthy. When a merchant arrives there he deposits his goods in a house and goes away. The goods are then offered for sale in the marketplaces. If the price demanded by the merchant is given, it is good. If not, the goods are shown to all the brokers. Should they become spoiled they are sold. All this is done with honesty.

In Babylon there are thirty synagogues besides that of Daniel. However, there is no minister there, and he whom the head of the academy bids to do so acts as precentor. It is done in this manner. Someone recites the hundred benedictions, and those present say Amen; then someone recites the prayer of *Baruch She'amar* with a loud voice, another rises and recites all the Praises and in this is joined by the whole congregation, his voice, however, being heard above them all, that they should not recite too fast, and they all follow him. He recites the prayer of *Yishtabach* before *Vayosha,* and then goes on with the other prayers. Thus the prayer is divided between several precentors.

No one talks to his neighbour at synagogue; all stand decorously, and they all appear at synagogue without shoes, barefooted. If, whilst practising, they should be mistaken in a tune, the head of the academy gives them a sign with his finger; they then understand what is the tune. If there be any young man having a pleasing voice he recites a psalm. On the half-holidays they recite the psalms to the accompaniment of musical instruments, and they know by tradition the appointed tunes. For the *Asor* they have ten tunes, and for the *Sheminith* eight tunes; they have several tunes for each psalm. When Rabbi Petachia was in the room of Daniel they showed him a very deep lions' den, and also a furnace half filled with water. Whoever is attacked by fever bathes therein and is healed. . . .

Rabbi Petachia said that the mountains of Ararat are five days' journey from Babylon. The mountains of Ararat are high. There is one high mountain, behind which there are four others, two of which are opposite the two others. The ark of Noah was carried between these mountains and could not get out. However, the ark is not there, for it has decayed. The mountains are full of thorns and other herbs; when the dew falls, manna is rained down upon these, but when the sun shines warm the manna melts. Whatever portion of it is gathered in the night, if it be kept, likewise melts. They, therefore, carry off the manna together with the thorns and herbs on which it has fallen, and which they are obliged to cut off, so very hard are they. The manna is white like snow. However, when boiled together with the manna they become sweeter than honey or any other sweet stuff. Were it boiled without the nettles the limbs of the partaker thereof would become disjointed for excessive sweetness. They look like small grains. They gave the rabbi a few to taste; they melted in his mouth; they were sweet; penetrating into all his limbs, so that he could not bear the sweetness. . . .

The rabbi then came to Tiberias; at which place there is a congregation, for there are also congregations in the land of Israel, numbering, however, only one hundred, two hundred, or three hundred families. At Tiberias there is a synagogue which Joshua, son of Nun, built. At Sepphoris there is buried our Holy Rabbi, R. Judah the Prince. A pleasing odour ascends from his grave. This odour is smelt at the distance of a mile from his grave. The graves in the land of Israel are in hollows, but not those of Babylon. For in Babylon water appears and, therefore, they cannot dig deep caves. Of the posterity of Rabbi Judah a descendant exists, whose name is Rabbi Nehorai. He has a son whose name is Judah, after Rabbi Judah, the Prince. He possesses a book of genealogy going back to Rabbi Judah. Rabbi Nehorai is a physician and sells spices in the market. His children are with him in the shop. They are kept secluded that they may not look about. He is a disciple of the wise and righteous.

Tiberias, Sepphoris, and all the cities in the plain belong to lower Galilee. The rabbi also saw Usha and Shifrem, where Rabbi Gamaliel lived at the seat of the Sanhedrin. There are Jews at Acre.

At Jabneh there is a spring which flows for six days of the week, but on the Sabbath not a single drop is found in it. In Lower Galilee there is a cave which is spacious and high within. On one side of the cave are buried Shammai and his disciples; and on the other Hillel and his disciples. In the middle of the cave there is a large stone, hollow like a cup, which is capable of containing more than forty seah. When worthy men enter, the stone appears full of sweet water; these may then wash hands and feet, and pray, imploring God for what they desire. The stone, however, is not hollowed out right through, for the water does not come up from beneath; it only appears in honour of a man who is worthy, and to an unworthy man the water does not appear. Though men were to draw from the stone a thousand jugs of water its quantity would not be diminished, but it would remain full as before.

Rabbi Petachia then went to Upper Galilee and stayed among the mountains. Nittai, the Arbelite, is buried there at Arbela. Har Gaash is very high; on it Obadiah the prophet is buried. The mountain is ascended by means of steps formed in it. In the midst of the mountain Joshua, son of Nun, is buried, and by his side Caleb, son of Jephunneh. Close by, a spring of good water gushes from the mountains; there are beautiful palaces erected near the graves.

Every building in the land of Israel is of stone. Near one of the palaces a footprint is perceptible, like that of a human being treading on snow. This is that which the angel imprinted after the death of Joshua, son of Nun, when the land of Israel was shaken. Rabbi Petachia said that a compass round the whole land of Israel might be made in three days.

From thence he went to the grave of Jonah, son of Amittai. There is a beautiful palace built over it. Near it is a pleasure garden, wherein all kinds of fruit are found. The keeper of the pleasure garden is a Gentile. Nevertheless, when Gentiles come there he gives them no fruit, but when Jews come he gives them a friendly reception, saying: "Jonah, son of Amittai, was a Jew, therefore, it is due to you to partake of what is his," and then gives to the Jews to eat thereof.

The rabbi then came to Rachel's grave, at Ephrath, half a day's journey from Jerusalem. Upon her grave are eleven stones, according to the number of the eleven tribes; and because Benjamin was only born at her death, there is no stone erected for him. They are of marble. The stone of Jacob, however, consisting of one piece of marble, above all of them, is very large, a load for many persons. A mile from hence are the priests who took away the large stone from the grave and placed it in a building for strange service [monastery or church]. In the morning, however, it was seen on the grave as before. This was repeated several times, until at last they abstained from carrying it away. On the stone is engraved the name of Jacob. He also saw the stone over the well near Haran. Forty persons could not move it from its place. The well is about thirty cubits deep; there is, however, no water in it.

Rabbi Petachia then went to Jerusalem. The only Jew there is Rabbi Abraham, the dyer, and he pays a heavy tax to the king to be permitted to remain there. They showed him Mount Olivet, and he saw that the pavement was three cubits high, which is the breadth thereof. There is also a beautiful palace which the Ishmaelites built in ancient times when Jerusalem was still in the hands of the Ishmaelites. Then came worthless persons who brought to the king of the Ishmaelites a slanderous report, saying: "There is an old man among us who knows the locality of the temple and the court."

Then the king urged that old man until he pointed it out. The king was a friend of the Jews, and said: "I will build here a temple, and none but Jews shall pray therein." He built the temple of marble stone, a beautiful structure consisting of red, green, and variegated marble. Then came

Gentiles and put images in it, but they fell down. They then fixed the images in the thickness of the wall, but in the Holy of Holies they could not place any. The hospice where the poor are is on another side. The ground is cleft, and is called Valley of the Son of Hinnom, where their burial place is.

The circuit of the land of Israel may be made in about three days. The rabbi saw the Salt Sea of Sodom and Gomorrah. There is no herb there. As to the pillar of salt, he said that he did not see it and that it no longer existed. Nor did he see the stones which Joshua erected.

He then went to Hebron. He saw over the cave a large palace, which Abraham, our father, built. There are in it large stones of twenty-seven or twenty-eight cubits. Every corner stone is about seventy cubits. He gave to the keeper of the key of the cave a gold piece to take him to the graves of the fathers; and the keeper opened the door, and behold there was over the entrance an image, and inside three cells.

The Jews of Acre had told him previously: "Beware, for they have placed three corpses at the entrance of the cave and say that these were the patriarchs, but they are not."

But the keeper of the cave said that they were. The rabbi, therefore, gave him another gold piece to take him inside the cave. The keeper then opened the inner door, saying, "I never permitted a Gentile before to enter this doorway."

The keeper then brought lights and they went inside and had to descend steps; before they entered the inner cave they had to descend fifteen steps outside it. They then came to a very spacious cave. In the midst of the cave there is an entrance in the ground. The ground consists all of rock, and all the graves are in the hollow of the rock; and over that entrance, in the middle, are placed very thick iron bars, the like no man can make by earthly means but with heavenly help only. And a storm wind blows from between the holes between bar and bar. He could not enter there with lights. Then he understood that the fathers were there and he prayed there. Whenever he bent towards the mouth of the cave a storm wind went forth and cast him backwards.

At Jerusalem there is a gate: its name is Gate of Mercy. The gate is piled up with stone and lime. No Jew is permitted to go there, and still less a Gentile. One day the Gentiles wished to remove the rubbish and open the gate, but the whole land of Israel shook and there was a tumult in the city until they abstained. There is a tradition amongst the Jews that the Divine glory appeared through this gate and through it would return. It is exactly opposite Mount Olivet. Mount Olivet is lower in height. Nevertheless, whoever stands on that mountain may see it. His feet will stand that day on Mount Olivet. They shall see distinctly when the Eternal will return to Zion through that gate. Prayers are offered up there. The Tower of David still exists.

At Damascus there is a synagogue which Elisha built, also one built by Rabbi Eleazar, son of Azariah. It is large, and divine service is performed in it.

Among the oaks of Mamre, at a distance from there, dwelt an old man, who was near death when Rabbi Petachia arrived there, and he told his son to show Rabbi Petachia the tree under which the angels rested. He also showed him a fine olive tree cleft into three parts with a stone in the middle. They have a tradition that when the angels sat down the tree was cleft into three parts, each resting under one part whilst sitting on the stone. The fruits of the tree are very sweet. By the tree is the well of Sarah; its waters are clear and sweet. By the well is the tent of Sarah. Close by Mamre is a plain, and on the other side it is about a hundred cubits from the well of Sarah to the well of Abraham; its water is very agreeable. They also showed him a stone of twenty-eight cubits upon which Abraham, our father, was circumcised. The old man affirmed with an oath, now that he was quitting the world and would not utter a falsehood, that one day, on the fast of the Day of Atonement, he had seen a fiery angel who was offering up his devotions and a fiery horse by the well of Sarah.

In Greece the Jews are subject to great oppression; and even compelled to perform menial work in their own persons. There are youths among them who are expert in the use of the Divine name and can conjure evil spirits, but who are compelled to serve the Greeks like slaves. There are so many congregations in Greece, that the land of Israel could not contain them were they settled therein.

In the village of Usha is buried Jonah, son of Amittai; in that of Bosra, of Babylon, is buried Ezra, the scribe. Rabbi Chana, the Baghdadi, who is mentioned in the Talmud, was of Baghdad, the great city mentioned before. At Babylon there are no stones, but everything is of brick.

End of the words of Rabbi Petachia, brother of Rabbi Isaac, Halavan, author of the Tosephoth, and of Rabbi Nachman, of Ratisbon.

The Book of Yashar

The *Book of Yashar (Sefer ha-Yashar)*, an anonymous compilation written in Spain in the second half of the twelfth century, is in essence a midrashic amplification of the Pentateuch and some parts of Joshua and Judges. Since one of the lost books of the Bible is *Sefer ha-Yashar* (Joshua 1:13 and II Samuel 1:18), the author evidently titled his book thus to give the impression that it is one of these books.

Although the thirty-nine books of the Bible are the only ones to have survived from ancient Israel, they are obviously not the only literary products of that long and fruitful period, as is evidenced by mention of *Sefer ha-Yashar,* and, among others, the *Chronicle of Solomon* (I Kings 11:41) and the *Book of the Wars of the Lord* (Numbers 21:14).

Thomas Ilive, who published the first English version of the book (1750), stated that the *Book of Yashar* is the lost text mentioned in the Bible. Despite this pseudepigraphic attempt, the book reveals itself to be not at all ancient but quite contemporary with the medieval world: it is influenced by medieval epics like the *Song of Roland,* especially in its depiction of individual combat in the tournaments.

The language of the *Book of Yashar* is an accurate and fluent imitation of Biblical Hebrew. But whereas the Biblical narrative style is usually terse and suggestive, the *Book of Yashar* contains extensive dialogue, psychological details, and expanded story line. About three-fourths of the book deals with stories from

Adam to Moses, while the remainder with tales of Moses and (briefly) his successors. The sources that the author utilized and filtered through his vivid imagination were the Babylonian Talmud, Genesis *Rabbah,* the *Chronicles of Moses, Yosippon,* and Arabic legends.

The author's inventiveness is particularly focused on the life of Abraham and his family, and Joseph, where the world-famous narrative is expanded. Especially fascinating is the finger-pricking motif that appears when Potiphar's wife's friends peel oranges and, cutting themselves, bleed in the presence of Joseph. Thomas Mann made use of this erotic symbol in *Joseph in Egypt,* the finest artistic expression of this primal story; and critics who were aware of Mann's mastery of Freudian psychology considered this a brilliant narrative invention (Mann had at his disposal a German translation of the *Book of Yashar,* as well as other German versions of midrashic sources). Taken as a unit, the Joseph sequence in the *Book of Yashar* is a perfect novella, the precursor of the modern artistic story in Hebrew.

The *Book of Yashar* was translated into Yiddish and Latin, and has often been reprinted since its first edition (Naples, 1552).

JOSEPH IN EGYPT

The sons of Ishmael who had bought Joseph from the Midianites (who had bought him from his brethren), went to Egypt with Joseph, and they came upon the borders of Egypt. When they came near Egypt, they met four men of the sons of Medan the son of Abraham, who had gone forth from the land of Egypt on their journey.

The Ishmaelites said unto them, "Do you desire to purchase this slave from us?" They said, "Deliver him over to us," and they delivered Joseph over to them, and they beheld him, that he was a very comely youth and they purchased him for twenty shekels.

The Ishmaelites continued their journey to Egypt, and the Medanim also returned that day to Egypt. The Medanim said to each other, "Behold we have heard that Potiphar, an officer of Pharaoh, captain of the guard, seeketh a good servant who shall stand before him to attend him, and to make him overseer over his house and all belonging to him."

"Now therefore come let us sell him to him for what we may desire, if he be able to give unto us that which we shall require for him."

These Medanim went and came to the house of Potiphar, and said to him, "We have heard that thou seekest a good servant to attend thee. Behold we have a servant that will please thee, if thou canst give unto us that which we may desire, and we will sell him unto thee."

Potiphar said, "Bring him before me, and I will see him, and if he please me I will give unto you that which you may require for him."

The Medanim went and brought Joseph and placed him before Potiphar, and he saw him, and he pleased him exceedingly, and Potiphar said unto them, "Tell me what you require for this youth?"

They said, "Four hundred pieces of silver we desire for him," and Potiphar said, "I will give it you if you bring me the record of his sale to you, and will tell me his history, for perhaps he may be stolen, for this youth is neither a slave, nor the son of a slave, but I observe in him the appearance of a goodly and handsome person."

The Medanim went and brought unto him the Ishmaelites who had sold him to them, and they told him, saying, "He is a slave and we sold him to them."

Potiphar heard the words of the Ishmaelites in his giving the silver unto the Medanim, and the Medanim took the silver and went on their journey, and the Ishmaelites also returned home.

Potiphar took Joseph and brought him to his house that he might serve him, and Joseph found favor in the sight of Potiphar, and he placed confidence in him, and made him overseer over his house, and all that belonged to him he delivered over into his hand.

The Lord was with Joseph and he became a prosperous man, and the Lord blessed the house of Potiphar for the sake of Joseph.

Potiphar left all that he had in the hand of Joseph, and Joseph was one that caused things to come in and go out, and every thing was regulated by his wish in the house of Potiphar.

Joseph was eighteen years old, a youth with beautiful eyes and of comely appearance, and like unto him was not in the whole land of Egypt.

At that time whilst he was in his master's house, going in and out of the house and attending his master, Zelicah his master's wife lifted up her eyes toward Joseph and she looked at him, and behold he was a youth comely and well favored.

She coveted his beauty in her heart, and her soul was fixed upon Joseph, and she enticed him day after day, and Zelicah persuaded Joseph daily, but Joseph did not lift up his eyes to behold his master's wife.

Zelicah said unto him, "How goodly are thy appearance and form, truly I have looked to all the slaves, and have not seen so beautiful a slave as thou art." And Joseph said unto her, "Surely He who created me in my mother's womb created all mankind."

She said unto him, "How beautiful are thine eyes, with which thou hast dazzled all the inhabitants of Egypt, men and women. He said unto her, "How beautiful they are whilst we are alive, but shouldst thou behold them in the grave, surely thou wouldst move away from them."

She said unto him, "How beautiful and pleasing are all thy words; take now I pray thee, the harp which is in the house, and play with thy hands and let us hear thy words."

He said to her, "How beautiful and pleasing are my words when I speak the praise of my God and his glory. She said unto him, "How very beautiful is the hair of thy head, behold the golden comb which is in the house, take it I pray thee and curl the hair of thy head."

He said to her, "How long wilt thou speak these words? cease to utter these words to me, and rise and attend to thy domestic affairs."

She said unto him, "There is no one in my house, and there is nothing to attend to but to thy words and to thy wish." Yet notwithstanding all this she could not bring Joseph unto her, neither did he place his eye upon her, but directed his eyes below to the ground.

Zelicah desired Joseph in her heart, that he should lie with her, and at the time that Joseph was sitting in the house doing his work, Zelicah came and sat before him, and she enticed him daily with her discourse to lie with her, or even to look at her, but Joseph would not hearken to her.

She said unto him, "If thou wilt not do according to my words, I will chastise thee with the punishment of death, and put an iron yoke upon thee."

Joseph said to her, "Surely God who created man looseth the fetters of prisoners, and it is he who will deliver me from thy prison and from thy judgment."

When she could not prevail over him, to persuade him, and her soul being still fixed upon him, her desire threw her into a grievous sickness.

All the women of Egypt came to visit her, and they said unto her, "Why are thou in this declining state? Thou that lackest nothing; surely thy husband is a great and esteemed prince in the sight of the king, shouldst thou lack any thing of what thy heart desireth?"

Zelicah answered them, saying, "This day it shall be made known to you, whence this disorder springs in which you see me," and she commanded her maid servants to prepare food for all the women, and she made a banquet for them, and all the women ate in the house of Zelicah.

She gave them knives to peel the citrons to eat them, and she commanded that they should dress Joseph in costly garments, and that he should appear before them, and Joseph came before their eyes and all the women looked on Joseph, and could not take their eyes from off him, and thy all cut their hands with the knives that they had in their hands, and all the citrons that were in their hands were filled with blood.

They knew not what they had done but they continued to look at the beauty of Joseph, and did not turn their eyelids from him.

Zelicah saw what they had done, and she said unto them, "What is this work that you have done? behold I gave you citrons to eat and you have all cut your hands."

All the women saw their hands, and behold they were full of blood, and their blood flowed down upon their garments, and they said unto her, "This slave in your house has overcome us, and we could not turn our eyelids from him on account of his beauty."

She said unto them, "Surely this happened to you in the moment that you looked at him, and you could not contain yourselves from him; how then can I refrain when he is constantly in my house, and I see him day after day going in and out of my house? how then can I keep from declining or even from perishing on account of this?"

They said unto her, "The words are true, for who can see this beautiful form in the house and refrain from him, and is he not thy slave and attendant in thy house, and why dost thou not tell him that which is in thy heart, and sufferest thy soul to perish through this matter?"

She said unto them, "I am daily endeavoring to persuade him, and he will not consent to my wishes, and I promised him every thing that is good, and yet I could meet with no return from him; I am therefore in a declining state as you see."

Zelicah became very ill on account of her desire toward Joseph, and she was desperately lovesick on account of him, and all the people of the house of Zelicah and her husband knew nothing of this matter, that Zelicah was ill on account of her love to Joseph.

All the people of her house asked her, saying, "Why are thou ill and declining, and lackest nothing?" and she said unto them, "I know not this which is daily increasing upon me."

All the women and her friends came daily to see her, and they spoke with her, and she said unto them, "This can only be through the love of Joseph"; and they said unto her, "Entice him and seize him secretly, perhaps he may hearken to thee, and put off this death from thee."

Zelicah became worse from her love to Joseph, and she continued to decline, till she had scarce strength to stand.

On a certain day Joseph was doing his master's work in the house, and Zelicah came secretly and fell suddenly upon him, and Joseph rose up against her, and he was more powerful than she, and he brought her down to the ground.

Zelicah wept on account of the desire of her heart toward him, and she supplicated him with weeping, and her tears flowed down her cheeks, and she spoke unto him in a voice of supplication and in bitterness of soul, saying,

"Hast thou ever heard, seen or known of so beautiful a woman as I am, or better than myself, who speak daily unto thee, fall into a decline through love for thee, confer all this honor upon thee, and still thou wilt not hearken to my voice?

"If it be through fear of thy master lest he punish thee, as the king liveth no harm shall come to thee from thy master through this thing; now therefore pray listen to me, and consent for the sake of the honor which I have conferred upon thee, and put off this death from me, and why should I die for thy sake?" and she ceased to speak.

Joseph answered her, saying, "Refrain from me, and leave this matter to my master; behold my master knoweth not what there is with me in the house, for all that belongeth to him he has delivered into my hand, and how shall I do these things in my master's house?

"For he hath also greatly honored me in his house, and he hath also made me overseer over his house, and he hath exalted me, and there is no one greater in this house than I am, and my master hath refrained nothing from me, excepting thee who art his wife, how then canst thou speak these words unto me, and how can I do this great evil and sin to God and to thy husband?

"Now therefore refrain from me, and speak no more such words as these, for I will not hearken to thy words." But Zelicah would not hearken to Joseph when he spoke these words unto her, but she daily enticed him to listen to her.

It was after this that the river of Egypt was filled above all its sides, and all the inhabitants of Egypt went forth, and also the king and princes went forth with timbrels and dances, for it was a great rejoicing in Egypt, and a holiday at the time of the inundation of the sea Sihor, and they went there to rejoice all the day.

When the Egyptians went out to the river to rejoice, as was their custom, all the people of the house of Potiphar went with them, but Zelicah would not go with them, for she said, "I am indisposed," and she remained alone in the house, and no other person was with her in the house.

She rose up and ascended to her temple in the house, and dressed herself in princely garments, and she placed upon her head precious stones of onyx stones, inlaid with silver and gold, and she beautified her face and skin with all sorts of women's purifying liquids, and she perfumed the temple and the house with cassia and frankincense, and she spread myrrh and aloes, and she afterward sat in the entrance of the temple, in the passage of the house, through which Joseph passed to do his work, and behold Joseph came from the field, and entered the house to do his master's work.

He came to the place through which he had to pass, and he saw all the work of Zelicah, and he turned back.

Zelicah saw Joseph turning back from her, and she called out to him, saying, "What aileth thee Joseph? come to thy work, and behold I will make room for thee until thou shalt have passed to thy seat."

Joseph returned and came to the house, and passed from thence to the place of his seat, and he sat down to do his master's work as usual, and behold Zelicah came to him and stood before him in princely garments, and the scent from her clothes was spread to a distance.

She hastened and caught hold of Joseph and his garments, and she said unto him, "As the king liveth if thou wilt not perform my request thou shalt die this day," and she hastened and stretched forth her other hand and drew a sword from beneath her garments, and she placed it upon Joseph's neck, and she said, "Rise and perform my request, and if not thou diest this day."

Joseph was afraid of her at her doing this thing, and he rose up to flee from her, and she seized the front of his garments, and in the terror of his flight the garment which Zelicah seized was torn, and Joseph left the garment in the hand of Zelicah, and he fled and got out, for he was in fear.

When Zelicah saw that Joseph's garment was torn, and that he had left it in her hand, and had fled, she was afraid of her life, lest the report should spread concerning her, and she rose up and acted with cunning, and put off the garments in which she was dressed, and she put on her other garments.

She took Joseph's garment and she laid it beside her, and she went and seated herself in the place where she had sat in her illness, before the people of her house had gone out to the river, and she called a young lad who was then in the house, and she ordered him to call the people of the house to her.

When she saw them she said unto them with a loud voice and lamentations, "See what a Hebrew your master has brought to me in the house, for he came this day to lie with me.

"For when you had gone out he came to the house, and seeing that there was no person in the house, he came unto me, and caught hold of me, with intent to lie with me.

"I seized his garments and tore them and called out against him with a loud voice, and when I had lifted up my voice he was afraid of his life and left his garment before me, and fled."

The people of her house spoke nothing, but their wrath was very much kindled against Joseph, and they went to his master and told him the words of his wife.

Potiphar came home enraged, and his wife cried out to him, saying, "What is this thing that thou hast done unto me in bringing a Hebrew servant into my house, for he came unto me this day to sport with me; thus did he do unto me this day."

Potiphar heard the words of his wife, and he ordered Joseph to be punished with severe stripes, and they did so to him.

Whilst they were smiting him, Joseph called out with a loud voice, and he lifted up his eyes to heaven, and he said, "O Lord God, thou knowest that I am innocent of all these things, and why shall I die this day through falsehood, by the hand of these uncircumcised wicked men, whom thou knowest?"

Whilst Potiphar's men were beating Joseph he continued to cry out and weep, and there was a child there eleven months old, and the Lord opened the mouth of the child, and he spake these words before Potiphar's men, who were smiting Joseph, saying, "What do you want of this man, and why do you do this evil unto him? my mother speaketh falsely and uttereth lies; thus was the transaction."

The child told them accurately all that happened, and all the words of Zelicah to Joseph day after day did he declare unto them.

All the men heard the words of the child and they wondered greatly at the child's words, and the child ceased to speak and became still.

Potiphar was very much ashamed at the words of his son, and he commanded his men not to beat Joseph any more, and the men ceased beating Joseph.

Potiphar took Joseph and ordered him to be brought to justice before the priests, who were judges belonging to the king, in order to judge him concerning this affair.

Potiphar and Joseph came before the priests who were the king's judges, and he said unto them, "Decide I pray you what judgment is due to a servant, for thus has he done."

The priests said unto Joseph, "Why didst thou do this thing to thy master?" and Joseph answered them, saying, "Not so my lords, thus was the matter"; and Potiphar said unto Joseph, "Surely I entrusted in thy hands all that belonged to me, and I withheld nothing from thee but my wife, and how couldst thou do this evil?"

Joseph answered, saying, "Not so my lord, as the Lord liveth, and as thy soul liveth, my lord, the word which thou didst hear from thy wife is untrue, for thus was the affair this day.

"A year has elapsed to me since I have been in thy house; hast thou seen any iniquity in me, or anything which might cause thee to demand my life?"

The priests said unto Potiphar, "Send, we pray thee, and let them bring before us Joseph's torn garment, and let us see the tear in it, and if it shall be that the tear is in front of the garment, then his face must have been opposite to her and she must have caught hold of him, to come to her, and with deceit did thy wife do all that she has spoken."

They brought Joseph's garment before the priests who were judges, and they saw, and behold, the tear was in front of Joseph, and all the judging priests knew that she had pressed him, and they said, the judgment of death is not due to this slave for he has done nothing, but his judgment is, that he be placed in the prison house on account of the report, which through him has gone forth against thy wife.

Potiphar heard their words, and he placed him in the prison house, the place where the king's prisoners are confined, and Joseph was in the house of confinement twelve years.

Notwithstanding this, his master's wife did not turn from him, and she did not cease from speaking to him day after day to hearken to her, and at the end of three months Zelicah continued going to Joseph to the house of confinement day by day, and she enticed him to hearken to her, and Zelicah said unto Joseph, "How long wilt thou remain in this house? but hearken now to my voice and I will bring thee out of this house."

Joseph answered her, saying, "It is better for me to remain in this house than to hearken to thy words, to sin against God." And she said unto him, "If thou wilt not perform my wish, I will pluck out thine eyes, add fetters to thy feet, and will deliver thee into the hands of them whom thou didst not know before."

Joseph answered her and said, "Behold the God of the whole earth is able to deliver me from all that thou canst do unto me, for he openeth the eyes of the blind, and looseth those that are bound, and preserveth all strangers who are unacquainted with the land."

When Zelicah was unable to persuade Joseph to hearken to her, she left off going to entice him; and Joseph was still confined in the house of confinement. And Jacob the father of Joseph, and all his brethren who were in the land of Canaan still mourned and wept in those days on account of Joseph, for Jacob refused to be comforted for his son Joseph, and Jacob cried aloud, and wept and mourned all those days.

In those days Joseph was still confined in the prison house in the land of Egypt.

At that time the attendants of Pharaoh were standing before him, the chief of the butlers and the chief of the bakers which belonged to the king of Egypt.

The butler took wine and placed it before the king to drink, and the baker placed bread before the king to eat, and the king drank of the wine and ate of the bread, he and his servants and ministers that ate at the king's table.

Whilst they were eating and drinking, the butler and the baker remained there, and Pharaoh's ministers found many flies in the wine, which the butler had brought, and stones of nitre were found in the baker's bread.

The captain of the guard placed Joseph as an attendant on Pharaoh's officers, and Pharaoh's officers were in confinement one year.

At the end of the year, they both dreamed dreams in one night, in the place of confinement where they were, and in the morning Joseph came to them to attend upon them as usual, and he saw them, and behold their countenances were dejected and sad.

Joseph asked them, "Why are your countenances sad and dejected this day?" And they said unto him, "We dreamed a dream, and there is no one to interpret it"; and Joseph said unto them, "Relate, I pray you, your dream unto me, and God shall give you an answer of peace as you desire."

The butler related his dream unto Joseph, and he said, "I saw in my dream, and behold a large vine was before me, and upon that vine I saw three branches, and the vine speedily blossomed and reached a great height, and its clusters were ripened and became grapes.

"I took the grapes and pressed them in a cup, and placed it in Pharaoh's hand and he drank"; and Joseph said unto him, "The three branches that were upon the vine are three days.

"Yet within three days, the king will order thee to be brought out and he will restore thee to thy office, and thou shalt give the king his wine to drink as at first when thou wast his butler; but let me find favor in thy sight, that thou shalt remember me to Pharaoh when it will be well with thee, and do kindness unto me, and get me brought forth from this prison, for I was stolen away from the land of Canaan and was sold for a slave in this place.

"Also that which was told thee concerning my master's wife is false, for they placed me in this dungeon for naught"; and the butler answered Joseph, saying, "If the king deal well with me as at first, as thou hast interpreted to me, I will do all that thou desirest, and get thee brought out of this dungeon."

The baker, seeing that Joseph had accurately interpreted the butler's dream, also approached, and related the whole of his dream to Joseph.

He said unto him, "In my dream I saw and behold three white baskets upon my head, and I looked and behold there were in the uppermost basket all manner of baked meats for Pharaoh, and behold the birds were eating them from off my head."

Joseph said unto him, "The three baskets which thou didst see are three days, yet within three days Pharaoh will take off thy head, and hang thee upon a tree, and the birds will eat thy flesh from off thee, as thou sawest in thy dream."

In those days the queen was about to be delivered, and upon that day she bare a son unto the king of Egypt, and they proclaimed that the king had gotten his first born son and all the people of Egypt together with the officers and servants of Pharaoh rejoiced greatly.

Upon the third day of his birth Pharaoh made a feast for his officers and servants, for the hosts of the land of Zoar and of the land of Egypt.

All the people of Egypt and the servants of Pharaoh came to eat and drink with the king at the feast of his son, and to rejoice at the king's rejoicing.

All the officers of the king and his servants were rejoicing at that time for eight days at the feast, and they made merry with all sorts of musical instruments, with timbrels and with dances in the king's house for eight days.

The butler, to whom Joseph had interpreted his dream, forgot Joseph, and he did not mention him to the king as he had promised, for this thing was from the Lord in order to punish Joseph because he had trusted in man.

Joseph remained after this in the prison house two years, until he had completed twelve years.

Judah he-Hasid

The Book of the Pious (*Sefer Hasidim*) has come down to us in two versions: an early draft that is long and unmethodic, and a later, well-edited, brief compendium. Some scholars feel that *Sefer Hasidim* is a collective work, one of whose authors is Judah he-Hasid (the Pious) who died in 1217 and was one of the central figures of medieval Ashkenazic Jewry. Others contend that most of the work was written by him. The unified style and the prevalent personality of one man that mark the book seem to support the latter contention. Judah, about whom little information is available, worked on this volume all his life, adding thoughts in an unsystematic fashion; then, to his basic text were added both the writings of his father, Samuel, and those of his pupils.

Reflecting the thoughtways of medieval Jewry, the work is a blend of ethics—social justice, kindness and charity are always highlighted— and superstition. ("If a man has a bad dream or has seen demons and touches fire before telling it to anyone, no harm will come to him.") A striking feature of the work is its wealth of folklore, its plentiful stories of sprites and devils. (The German-Christian demonoloy that had rooted itself in the Jewish thinking of the day demonstrates the close contact that Jews had with Christians.) Among the hundreds of items in *Sefer Hasidim* are aphoristic statements about honoring parents, slander, business and community affairs, prayer, secular books; there are remarks about holiness, the welcoming of guests, purity, taxes, attitude toward gentiles, punishment of children, charity and modesty. Some of the remarks are prefaced by readable anecdotes and tales; others by stories about contemporary personalities.

Judah's purpose was to create a work that would teach the Hasidim the proper path; his book, therefore, is a mirror of the life and thought of German Jews in Judah's age, reflecting their economic, social and theological views, their ideals, their relationship with Christians, their personal habits and many folk beliefs. For instance, a seemingly incidental remark that sacred books may not be bound with the manuscripts of popular romances indicates that these supposedly forbidden "stories about kings and tournaments" were popular among Jews and that their use as binding material was widespread.

Judah the Pious, whose volume of practical ethics made an impact on Jews throughout the centuries and on subsequent writers of ethical tracts, also wrote a commentary on the Torah and on the cycle of prayers, and was editor of the travel notes of his fellow townsman, Petachia (see p. 358). A penchant for modesty prevented him from signing his works, all of which appeared anonymously.

THE BOOK OF THE PIOUS (SEFER HASIDIM)

Be not jealous of the man who is greater than thou and despise none who is smaller than thou.

If thou hast a guest, never speak to him about learned matters unless thou knowest he is able to partake in the conversation.

Never put to shame thy manservant or thy maidservant.

The man who is cruel to animals will have to answer for it on the Day of Judgment, and the very drivers will be punished for applying the spur too often.

Those who constantly fast are not in the good way. Scribes, teachers, and workmen are altogether forbidden to inflict penance upon themselves. If the Holy One, blessed be He, had any particular delight in much fasting, He would have commanded it to Israel; but He only asked of them that they should worship Him in humility.

If a man should ask: "Behold, I have money; shall I buy a Scroll of the Torah for it or shall I distribute it to the destitute poor?" Answer him with the words of Isaiah: "When thou seest the naked, that thou cover him, and hide not thyself from thine own flesh" [Isa. 58:7].

If a man sees a non-Jew committing a sin, let him protest against it if he has the power to do so; for behold, did not the Holy One, blessed be He, send the prophet Jonah to the people of Nineveh that they may do repentance?

The Holy One, blessed be He, executes the judgment of the oppressed, whether Jew or Christian, hence cheat not anybody.

If a man has a book in his hand he must not display his anger by pounding on it or by striking others with it. The teacher who is angry with his student must not hit him with it, nor should the student ward off blows with a book unless the blows are very dangerous.

380

There was once a student who stuttered and it took him quite a while before he managed to get a word out of his mouth, and when the others laughed at him he would become angry. His teacher, therefore, said to him: "Don't ask questions in their presence. Wait until they leave, or write down your difficulties on paper, and I'll answer you."

A man should not rear an orphan who carries tales for he will get no thanks for it, nor should a person tolerate a talebearer among his pupils, for there will never be any peace among them because of his tattling. Nor should one tolerate a male or female servant who tells tales.

It is written in the Bible [Job 22:23 and 11:14]: "If thou return to the Almighty, thou shalt be built up, if thou *put away unrighteousness far from thy tents.*" If this is true, why then is it necessary to repeat: "If iniquity be in thy hand put it far away, and *let not unrighteousness dwell in thy tents.*" It is merely that the Bible wishes to teach us that the teacher shall not say: "I'll let this mean student remain in order that I may make a better person of him, for he can learn from my good example." It will be of no avail! It is more probable that he will teach the other children in the house to do wrong.

When a person teaches children—some of whom are more brilliant than the others—and sees that it is disadvantageous for all of them to study together inasmuch as the brilliant children need a teacher for themselves alone, he should not keep quiet. He ought to say to the parents, even if he loses by making the division: "These children need a separate teacher; and these, a separate teacher."

[Prov. 22:6]: "Train up a child in the way he should go." If you see a child making progress in Bible, but not in Talmud, do not push him by teaching him Talmud, and if he understands Talmud, do not push him by teaching him Bible. Train him in the things which he knows.

There is a kind of humility which inherits Gehenna, and causes the heirs of the humble to inherit a burning fire in Gehenna. In what manner is it? If a man sees that his children, relatives, or pupils are of bad behavior, and it lies within his power to correct them, by reprimanding or by beating them, but he says to himself: "I shall rather be agreeable to them and not reprimand or beat them," he causes them to inherit Gehenna. For they will corrupt their way, and will even do mischief to their father and their mother, so that they will despise them, and curse the day wherein they were born.

It is in connection with such a case that it is written: "He that spareth the rod hateth his son." [Prov. 13:24]. It is also said that he who smites his grown-up son transgresses the injunction: "Put not a stumbling block before the blind." [Lev. 19:14]. But a son that is accustomed to reproofs of instruction and is beaten while small, will not resent it if his father beats him when he is grown up. It is also written: "Unless I had believed to see the goodness of the Lord" [Ps. 27:13]; there are some dots on the word *Unless,* for David said: "Peradventure I caused my sons to sin, and am not able to make amends by repenting"; for it is written: "And his father had not grieved him all his life in saying: Why hast thou done so?" [I Kings 1:6].

There is another kind of humility which likewise brings a man down to Gehenna. For instance, a man sits in a court of justice, and knows that the judges are in error; or a private man knows that the court is in error, but says: "How shall I go and put them to shame?" or a man knows that the judges are not well versed in law, while he is well versed, and when they say to him: "Sit with us that we may not go astray," he replies: "I shall not take a seat, for ye are well versed." It is obvious that if they go astray, the sin is to be attached to him.

Another instance is, when a man hears that the congregation speak falsely, and he says: "Who am I that I should speak before them?" Behold, it is written: "And in thy majesty prosper, ride on, in behalf of truth and humility of righteousness"; [Ps. 45:5]; from this we infer that there is a kind of humility which is not righteousness, as the above and similar cases show. It is also said: "An untutored priest should not say the benedictions in the presence of scholars."

There is a kind of charity which is pernicious. In what manner is it? One who gives alms to adulterers or to a glutton or a drunkard. For it is written: "She shall not fall into harlotry" [Lev. 19:29]; and thou mayest read, "She shall not cause to fall into harlotry"; "Thou shalt not commit adultery." [Ex. 20:14]; and thou mayest read, "Thou shalt not cause to commit adultery"; "Thou shalt not murder" [Ex. 20:13]; and it may be read: "Thou shalt not cause to murder." He who supplies weapons of destruction to murderers is regarded as if he himself had committed murder. For it is written: "He hath also prepared for him the weapons of death" [Ps. 7:14]: He who gives food to robbers is like their accomplice.

Similarly, he who gives alms to adulterers is regarded as though he had aided them and brought them together, for they take the money that is given to them, and offer it as a hire to harlots. It is also said that a man should give no alms at all rather than give it publicly. In a similar sense it is also said that if a man who cannot pay his debts gives alms, it is obvious that his charity is robbery.

There is a kind of piety which is bad. For instance, a man whose hands are unclean sees a holy book fall into the fire, and says: "It is better that it should be burned," and does not touch the book. Another instance has also been cited: a man sees a woman drown in the river, and says: "It is better that she should drown than that I should touch her."

There is also false piety. For instance: a man brings out a Scroll of the Law into the public thoroughfare on the Sabbath on account of a fire; or when a man says: "How shall I save a man's life and profane the Sabbath?" Another instance is: a question about declaring a thing forbidden or lawful is referred to a man who knows that he is well versed in the Law, though there are others like him in the city, and he says: "Address the question to others"; behold, his meekness may lead to sin: peradventure if he had given his decision, he would have forbidden that which others had declared lawful.

There is sometimes a righteous judge that perishes in his righteousness. For instance: he sees two litigants, one being a swindler, and the other a simpleton; the swindler knows how to plead, but the simpleton, who does not know how to plead, is right; concerning him it is written: "Open thy mouth for the dumb." [Prov. 31:8]. Likewise, if he knows that the verdict is unjust, one of the litigants having hired false witnesses, he should not say: "Let the sin be attached to the witnesses."

A favor sometimes turns out to be harmful, and is regarded as an evil for its author and his offspring. In what manner is it? For instance: a man causes that sinners and they that lead others astray should dwell in the city, it is evident that he and his offspring will stumble over them, and they will do mischief to his offspring. It is in connection with such a case that it is written: "And he did that which is not good among his people." [Ezekiel 18:18]. (Another explanation: *And he did that which is not good among his people* refers to him who disgraces his family; he is punished, because he sinned by inflicting shame and injury upon his people). Another instance: he who does a good deed in order to be honored and to praise himself thereby.

Be a man's piety ever so great, he can make no claim to recompense at God's hands, were his life to last even for thousands of years; there is none, no, not the least of the benefits conferred on him by God which he could repay. Therefore let no one serve his Creator merely because he hopes for Paradise, but out of pure love for Him and His commandment. Let man in his solitary hours feel the same repugnant shame of evil to the sight of God, as he would to commit it in the sight of men, and let him lay down life freely for Him; for if we do not so, we are of less account in the scale than hireling soldiers who go into battle at the words of command. That our soul may become perfected in righteousness, needs must that we bear griefs and agonies; and never should it cross our minds for an instant to shrink from boldly declaiming that we are Jews.

Mislead no one through thy actions designedly, be he Jew or not-Jew; be not disputatious and quarrelsome with people, whatever be their faith. Be honorable in thy business dealings; do not say that such or such a price has been offered thee for thy wares when the thing is not true, and not behave as though thou hadst a desire to sell what thou hast, when there is no serious thought of doing so in thy mind: such things are unworthy of an Israelite.

If one, be he Jew or not-Jew, comes to borrow money from thee, and thou wilt not because of doubt of repayment, say not that thou hast no money.

If a contract be made between Jews and not-Jews, binding to mutual observance and performance, the first man must fulfil it even if the last fail to perform that to which they are bound. If a Jew attempt to kill a not-Jew, and the latter only wishes to defend himself, but not in return to kill, we are bound to help him in his self-defense.

Injustice must be done to none, whether he belong to our religion or to another. On the worldly possessions of those who oppress the workman, who buy stolen goods, and keep articles decorated with heathen symbols or figures in their household furniture, rests no blessing. They or their children will surely lose all they have.

In thy intercourse with not-Jews, be careful to be as wholly sincere as in that with Jews: needst not that thou obtrude on him who is no Jew, argument as to his religious errors, and thou wouldst do better to live on charity, than to abscond with money not thine, to the disgrace of the Jewish faith and name. If one not-Jew seek council of thee, tell him where he will find a true man and not one deceiver in the place whither he repaireth . . .

If an assassin take refuge with thee, give him no protection, even though he be a Jew; if one who bears a heavy burden on his shoulders meet thee on a narrow and difficult path, make way for him, even though he be no Jew. If one not a Jew observe the precepts of the natural [Noachian] moral law, restore to him whatsoever he may have lost, hold him in higher honor than the Israelite who neglects the truth given him by God. For the rest, in most places Jews are not unlike Christians in their morals and usages.

If any one offer thee an amulet, alleging it to be useful in helping to favor or wealth, carry it not, but place thy undivided confidence in God alone. If, when thy plans fail, thou wouldst seek any other Lord than the Eternal thy God, it would be apostasy. If thou canst possibly support thyself with the little thou hast, take not aught from another in order that thou mayest be rich; for few of those who take from others have any happiness in life.

No blessing rests on the money of people who clip coin, make a practice of usury, use false weights and measures, and are in general not honest in business; their children and their friends' friends lose their homes at last and have to beg their bread. But many a one falls into poverty because he has looked down upon poor people or has repulsed them with harsh words.

If one is able to work, I give him nothing, nothing. It is better to spend on poor people than to lavish in keeping useless foolish things, as birds or other such trifles.

To him who is merciful and good to men, God is merciful and good: the pitiless man is like the cattle of the field which are indifferent to the suffering of their kind. There are three sorts of people for whom we ought to feel especial pain and sympathy: a reasonable, prudent creature subjected to a crazy fool; a good man who has to take orders from a bad; and a noble being dependent upon one of vulgar nature. There are three to whom we should sternly close our hearts: a cruel person who does pitiless wrong and vile things; the fool who rushes on ruin in spite of warning; and the ingrate. Ingratitude is the blackest of faults; it is not to be endured even towards the dumb creatures whom we use.

Worthy of punishment is he, too, who heaps excessive burdens on the carrying beast, beats and tortures it, twitches a cat by its ears to hurt it, or plunges his spurs too deep into a horse's flank. A sick or breeding beast ought to be tenderly dealt with; if a not dangerous dog runs into thy house, hunt him out with a small whip that hurts not, but see that thou strike him not with a heavy stick or pour boiling water over him, or jam him in the doors, or madden him by any ill-usage. Even worse hath he to answer for, who deals harshly with servingman or woman. If the people are good, yet thou needest money, part with them not to any cruel person who will chastise them with inhuman severity.

Hear not calumny willingly; seek rather to admonish and restrain him who complains bitterly to thee of the doings of another. When thou speakest concerning one, tell the good thou knowest of him; but do not so in presence of his enemies, for they would make it opportunity to vent themselves concerning his faults.

Praise not one rich man in presence of another rich man; one author in presence of another author, and as a rule, never one man of any business in presence of another whose business is the same; only thou mayest freely give all glory to a God-fearing man in presence of another who fears his God.

Make not reply in high-pitched self-asserting tones, but with moderate and sweet, and when thou findest thyself among people who have nothing better to do than to jeer and gibe, leave them as soon and as quickly as thou canst; for mockery leads to want of respect for one's self and others, and that is the high road to an unchaste life. Insist not upon having explanations by word of mouth with one who, as you ought to know, will turn a deaf ear to thy side of the question, or who is likely to become embittered and vengeful owing to such talk.

If a rich man and a poor man be sick, and thou seest all the world going to see the rich man, go thou to the poor one, even though he be ignorant and unlettered. But when thou hast to choose between supplying the needs of a learned man, or counseling the susceptibilities of a poor man, the first case is of the greater urgency; and if it should be that the scholar is also devout and God-fearing, but the poor man not so, then disregard the poor man's feelings altogether, if need be, to mark thy respect for learned piety. Be intimate and work with rather an uneducated man of generous soul than a learned one closefisted.

If thou art in debt, pay thy debts before thou givest alms. If thou requirest one to join with thee in fellowship of study, and knowest of a worthy, reserved and modest disciple of the schools of whom others in reckless high spirits are wont to make mockery, choose and take him to thee, that one who is undeservedly set down may be lifted up to his right place. Make no sign of visible disgust when thou meetest people afflicted with loathsome visible disease; for they are God's creatures, remember, and healthy as well as sick are all alike dependent upon Him.

Say not, "I will avenge that wrong." Place thy trust in God; He will keep thee. If any one hath deceived thee by false weights, stolen from thee, borne false witness against thee, be not so misguided as to avenge thyself by doing the like. When insult is poured on thee, be thou unmoved, and never permit thy pupils, or those of thy household, to assail with injurious words or blows, when they meet him, one who is doing injury to thee. Expel all envy, all hatred from thy breast; if a fund be making up, and thy name be put down for more than thy possessions warrant, so that richer men pay less than they strictly should, breed not quarrel and mortification for thyself and others by remonstrance and reproach; hold thy peace and busy thyself more than ever with the study of divine things. When thy wife makes thy life heavy for thee, and hatred for her threatens to take possession of thee, then implore the Lord not to give thee another wife, but to turn that one's heart once more back to thee in love.

Let no one be troubled in mind or take up wrong ideas because of the prosperity of wicked people or of such as hold parents in little honor; their end is bad. The reason why good men have an ill lot in life is, lest men should fancy that the good man can only then be good when the world goes well with him. If a congregation has bad men at its head, that is a punishment for not valuing as they should the good men among them. The children of noble, righteous converts to the faith are to be preferred for the marriage tie to children of Jews of nature or conduct not so high.

The ancients of our nation composed works and sent them forth without their names; they disclaimed to seek recompensing delight for their labor in this lower earthly life. And if there be any one who of pure vanity is minded to perpetuate the memory of himself in some work, very surely he will miss his aim. There was once a rich man, who would build a beautiful synagogue at his own charge alone, and suffered not the congregation to contribute to the pious work, because he would that the memorial should be of him and his posterity alone. But ere he died his children all were dead.

If a father knows his married daughter to be busy and occupied with her husband's affairs, let him not suggest or order her to attend to his own, unless the husband allow of it, postponing his own interests for a while. If a mother hath enjoined some action on her son, and the father come suddenly and say: "Who gave orders that this thing should be done?" let not the son say that it was the mother. For if it should hap that the father in rage should vent an angry curse against his wife, the fault would be laid at the door of the son rather than his own.

If a son see an opportunity for some transaction of profit, let him rather miss the chance than rouse his sleeping father, unless he is well assured that the father would be more vexed because the gain was sacrificed than because his sleep was broken. He who spends substance in supporting other than parents and relations will reap nothing but ingratitude, while his property will fall to those of his own blood at last. If a father treats one son well, another ill, it is the latter who is very likely to succeed to his possessions. Let one who hath never known parents, but only elder brothers, render the respect and honor due to father and mother unto these.

Parents may not hinder a son's marriage that he may continue to work for them; let him take a wife and remain with them still. If he can find no wife at the place where his parents live, and these be aged and need his care, let him not leave that city: and if, taking a wife, he can no longer care for such helpless father and mother, let him remain unwedded. If he can pay for the support and care of his parents, then he hath a right to seek wife and settle elsewhere, only let him see to it that they are not such as are repugnant to the parents' feelings. If his choice hath fallen on a worthy girl of honorable parentage, but his father or mother wish to force him to take one not worthy, because her relatives offer money, he needs herein by no means yield to his parents' wishes, for their proceeding is blameworthy.

Parents must by no means, on no account whatever, strike a grown-up son, curse him, or so move him to wrath that he forget himself and with whom he is dealing. If children are hopelessly divided in feeling, a father does well if he arrange all things concerning his possessions while he lives, and place property and children alike, if they be minors, with all legal form under guardianship and trust.

Let not a quite young man take to wife one who hath reached forty years; let no girl be married against her will to an elderly man or one whom she cannot love. It is a thing highly to be disapproved that elderly men should dye gray hairs black to deceive young girls as to their years.

In most cases bad parents beget bad children. If parents have no scruples about false coin and false weights, the sons are apt to commit the same crimes. If we see about us so many uneducated and ignorant, but descendants of people of high instruction, this is the fault of parents whom worldly interest hath led to form connections with unlearned persons. There was a man who lived a poor and hard life, to whom a wealthy woman was offered in marriage; he refused her, for her brothers were unworthy and he dreaded lest his children by her might be the same. So far as legal duty goes, a man indeed need not abstain from wedding a wife so connected, just as he may repudiate his wife for reasons that seem trifling and inadequate; but many things are permitted by the law, the doing of which may lay upon a man the rendering of a heavy account some day or other.

On the day of the last judgment those who are of kindred virtue and merit will find themselves in final companionship with each other. The father then ceases to mourn and grieve over the son that had left him; for the joys of Paradise and the rapturous delight felt in meeting the radiance of God's countenance will send into oblivion all the anguish of the earthly life.

The Poetic Picaresque

The popularity of secular poetry, as expressed by the major figures of the Golden Age in Spain, and the concomitant growth of secular life, prompted the development of poetic fiction, based primarily on the Arabic *maqama*. The *maqama* (literally, the marketplace where the people while away the time) was a complex genre in Arabic (and later in Hebrew) literature which has no Western equivalent: it is a dramatic narrative told in rhymed prose which centers on one picaresque protagonist who wanders about the world telling of his adventures, and another (the author himself) who acts as his interlocutor. Accenting word play and wit, the *maqama* is made up of a number of subsections, each an independent story. Although it is a narrative, the short sentences are rhymed and rhythmic, containing parables, epigrams and proverbs. Unlike poetry, however, there is no fixed meter and no prescribed number of feet to the line. Occasionally, poems are added at the end of a *maqama* to sum up the story and point up the moral.

One of the early important Hebrew versions of the *maqama* was the *Book of Delight,* written by Barcelona-born Joseph ibn Zabara (1140–1200) toward the end of the twelfth century. In contrast to previous nonsacred works, the satirical *Book of Delight,* with its miscellany of stories, parables and fables, does not accent morality, nor does it disguise its secularity by urging man to avoid the world's vanities and prepare for the world to come. Based upon real adventures as filtered through the author's imagination, the *Book of Delight* is one of the first Hebrew works constructed as a frame narrative (as are Chaucer's *Canterbury Tales* and Boccaccio's *Decameron*). Stories intertwine and there are tales within tales, some of whose motifs can be traced to Indian, Latin and even Chinese sources. However, the story of Tobit is modelled after its ancient Jewish original (see *Book of Tobit*, p. 27).

The classical exponent of the Hebrew *maqama* was the troubador-poet Judah al-Harizi (1165–1225). Beginning his literary career as a translator, al-Harizi soon gained fame at this art and, along with Samuel ibn Tibbon, rendered Maimonides' *Guide to the Perplexed* into Hebrew; but unlike the former's accurate and scientific translation, al-Harizi's was a simple and popular edition. Before he began to contribute to Hebrew letters with his original poetry and storytelling, he served his apprenticeship in translating an Arabic *maqama*. After he had successfully demonstrated that Hebrew was as capable as Arabic in producing the technically sophisticated form, he turned to original creation. In writing the *Tahkemoni* (composed between 1214–1218), al-Harizi produced the first Hebrew *maqama* wherein the verbal pyrotechnics are as prominent as in the Arabic form.

The *Tahkemoni* contains fifty sections, independent of one another except for the unifying link provided by the two itinerant heroes. The contents are variegated: travel stories, fables, parables, riddles, parodies, prayers and laments. What the Greeks did with Homer, and the Arabs did with the Koran, al-Harizi did with verses from the Bible, often changing a word or even a letter with comical results. The technical skill displayed in *Tahkemoni* is amazing: an epistle that can be read forward as a blessing and backward as a curse, and one section whose rhyming triplets are in Hebrew, Aramaic and Arabic. The poet even includes a section of literary criticism, reviewing and evaluating the poetry of Judah Halevi, Solomon ibn Gabirol and Abraham ibn Ezra. The *Tahkemoni* is also to a degree a personal document—the author praises his patrons, and satirizes pseudo-poets, hypocrites and heartless men of wealth.

The works of Ibn Zabara and al-Harizi are representative of the poetic picaresque in Hebrew literature, and each excelled in a special sphere—the *Book of Delight* in narrative, and *Tahkemoni* in language and variety of subject matter.

THE BOOK OF DELIGHT—JOSEPH IBN ZABARA

CHAPTER I

ZABARA BEHOLDETH IN HIS DREAM A MAN EXCEEDINGLY TALL, WHO DOTH THEN ROUSE HIM OUT OF HIS SLUMBER, AND GIVE HIM VICTUALS TO EAT. BUT FIRST HE DISPUTETH WITH HIM CONCERNING PRAYER AND FOOD AND WINE.

There lived a man in the city of Barcelona whose name was Joseph ben Zabara. From his youth up had he dwelt at ease, in amity with his friends and comrades. All that knew him became his friends, and they that were his friends loved him; among them was he respected and esteemed, bound to all by ties of affection. He for his part honored and exalted them, served them and healed them. For those of them that were sick he compounded suitable remedies, in accordance with his knowledge and his skill. In his love and charity he busied himself with his patients whether old or young, and served them, and ministered to them. Everyone, then, loved Joseph and sought his company eagerly; but as Scripture hath it [Ps. 117:5], Joseph was sold for a servant.

Came then a night when I, Joseph, was sleeping upon my bed. My sleep was sweet upon me, for that alone was my portion of all my labor. Things there are which are for the soul a weariness but for the body restful; other things are weariness for the body but restful for the soul. But sleep bringeth rest at once to body and soul, as all men know well.

Saintly Hippocrates was once asked, "What is sleep?" "In sleep," he replied, "the highest virtues descend into the depths of the being, to provide refreshed vigor for the body." Furthermore, Aristotle hath said, "Natural slumber compriseth a remedy for every malady." And Galen, "Natural slumber increaseth vigor and minisheth the evil humors." And finally hath the wise Jahja ibn Masewieh said, "Sleep in season bringeth the body to healthfulness."

And it came to pass as I slumbered that I saw an appearance before me in my dream, in the likeness of a man exceedingly tall, who did then rouse me as is the wont of a man who arouseth another from his sleep. "Arise, thou son of man," quoth he. "Wherefore slumberest? Awake thee, and look upon the wine as it floweth red. Arise, and recline at my side and eat whereof I have brought thee, as my means did avail."

So I arose in haste, just as dawn brake, and I beheld wine and bread and viands before me and a lamp burning in the man's hand, whereof the light shone into every corner. Then I spake and said, "What may these be, good sir?" "My wine," he replied, "and my bread and my viands. Sit thee down, and eat and drink with me, for I love thee as thou wert of my mother's sons."

But after I had thanked him for the kindness of the honor he did me, for his love and for the generosity of his hand, I said, "Sir, I may neither eat nor drink until I have prayed to Him that discerneth my way and maketh my footsteps firm and vouchsafeth unto me all my needs. For indeed the choicest of the prophets and the chief of them that were called, our teacher, Moses, may he rest in peace, hath said [Lev. 19:26]: 'Ye shall not eat anything with the blood: neither shall ye use enchantment nor observe times.' Thereby did he admonish the children of Israel that they should not eat until that they had prayed for their souls, for in truth the blood signifieth the soul. And so hath Saul said [I Sam. 14:34]: 'Slay them here and eat; and sin not against the Lord in eating with the blood.' Furthermore he that doth eat before he have offered prayer and supplication is called fellow to the Destroyer and a worker of divination.

"Aristotle too was asked whether prayer or victuals should have first place. 'Prayer,' he replied, 'for prayer is the life of the spirit and victuals are but the life of the body.' Furthermore, prayer and study are not possible for a creature that is sated and a paunch that is stuffed. 'Which is better,' a philosopher was asked, 'victuals or prayer?' 'Abundance of prayer is helpful,' he replied, 'abundance of victuals harmful!' And a certain wise man hath said, 'Prayer doth result in victuals.' Lastly a certain sage of the Sages hath said, 'Prayer is like as the spirit which goeth upward, whereas victuals are like as the flesh which descendeth downward, even into the earth.' "

Then said the stranger, "Pray, if such be thy desire; do as is good in thy sight." So I bathed my hands and face, and prayed before the Lord. Then I ate of all that was before me, for his soul was become dear in my sight. In the midst of the food I would drink of the water of the fountain, but he rebuked me and said, "Drink of the wine, for compared to it even pearls are nothing worthy, and it is indeed a delight to the eyes." "But," I said, "I take no delight in it nor do I desire to drink it, for indeed I fear it." And he said to me, "Wherefore dost thou hate it in thine heart? Surely it maketh glad and rejoiceth the heart of man."

And I replied and said, "I cannot drink it; for he that drinketh of it doth become drunken until that he is stranger to his own brethren. Wine blindeth the eyes, darkeneth the whiteness of teeth, causeth forgetfulness, and rendereth the wise soul foolish. It maketh the faithful speechless and robbeth the elders of their wisdom. It weakeneth the powers of the body and paralyzeth the members in their functions, for it doth disturb the sinews which control them. It occasioneth many maladies, such as paralysis and stuttering and apoplexy, which doth corrupt all the members of the body and their functions. It revealeth the secrets of bosom friends and causeth dissension between brothers. Yea, wine is treacherous and doth strip a man's garments upon a cold day. And so hath the poet sung for any man that lusteth after wine:

> Friend, let not thine heart incline
> To the sweet seductive savor
> Of smoothly flowing ruddy wine,
> For bitter is its flavor.

> You may cherish it now above fine gold,
> It is but a treacherous friend;
> It will desert and forsake you in shivering cold,
> Your coat from your back will it rend.

Again:

> Guard thee well, beloved friend,
> Lest to Bacchus thy neck thou bend;
> Else thy competitor will drive thy trade
> While yet thou slumberest in noonday shade.

And also:

> Of pomegranate juice mayst thou sip;
> It is sweet and gentle and mild.
> But keep red wine far from thy lip;
> It is raging and fiery and wild.

"Further, our master Moses, may he rest in peace, forbade the Nazirites all wine and strong drink, in order that they might not become unclean and desecrate the vows by which they were hallowed all the days of their separation. Furthermore the priests were forbidden to drink wine when they came into the sanctuary to minister."

Then did the man's wrath kindle, and he said, "Wherefore and why dost thou reproach wine and revile it and slander it, not slightly but with vehemence, and recall its defects and deny its virtues? Dost thou not know, hast thou not heard, that wine begetteth gladness and banisheth sorrow and sighing? If any one be afflicted in soul, he may drink and forget his misery. Wine assisteth, furthermore, in the digestion of food, and availeth to assuage pain better than doth rest, it causeth diseases of the nose to depart, and is salutary for maladies of the intestines. It causeth the urine to flow, if it be restrained, it maketh a weak heart firm, and riddeth the kidneys and the veins of humors. It is excellent for arousing appetites, and awakeneth generosity in the heart of a niggard. It prolongeth a man's prime and deferreth his old age; it sharpeneth the wits, maketh the face to shine, and brighteneth the senses. And furthermore our sages—may their memory be for a blessing—have said, 'Wine and spices make a man open-minded.' And because of the sin which he sinned against his own soul in vowing abstinence from wine, Scripture commanded the Nazarite to offer two turtles or two young pigeons to expiate for his sin in afflicting his own person. Yea, and the poet hath sung:

Two fires there be of foaming liquids holden,
Of warfare grim the one, the other in chalice golden.
This one compounded of blood and tears,
A hero's glory, a mother's fears.
The other a sweet essence with genial flame
Kindled by friendship and love's great name.

And again:

As rise in heaven the shining planets
So in our hands rise shining goblets;
But setting stars to westward descend
While descending cups in our bellies end.

And also:

They shall miserably moan and grievously sigh
    For despising the fruit of the vine;
The abstaining Rechabites shall wretchedly die
    Of diseases fell and malign.

Like profitless waters shall they be neglected
    This gloomy folk, dour, severe;
In disdain, yea blasphemy, have they rejected
    What God and man doth cheer.

Then said I unto him, "Seeing thou hast freely proffered thy kindness, let not thy wrath be kindled. The ancient physicians, who were wise and prudent, prescribed that water be drunk at the time of eating for that it is heavier than wine, and by its weight causeth the food to descend to the uttermost parts of the stomach, whereby digestion is improved by reason of the proximity of the heat of the liver, which lieth underneath and lendeth its aid. But an hour or two after eating they prescribed that a little wine unmixed with water be drunk, to augment the natural heat and assist the digestive powers."

"Truly hast thou spoken," said he, "and I too adhere to thy discourse, for in truth little availeth little and much harmeth little."

CHAPTER II

THE STRANGER DECLARETH HIS NAME TO BE ENAN HANATAS, THE SON OF ARNAN HADESH, AND SEEKETH TO PERSUADE ZABARA TO FORSAKE HIS OWN COUNTRY AND ACCOMPANY HIM TO A PLACE WHERE HIS WISDOM WILL BE PROPERLY RECOGNIZED. ZABARA FEARETH TO FOLLOW AFTER HIM AND RELATETH MANY PARABLES TO SHOW THE CAUSE OF HIS FEAR. FINALLY, HOWEVER, HE IS CONVINCED AND WILL GO.

And it came to pass after that I had eaten and drunk with him that I asked concerning his place and his name, saying, "Prithee, good sir, now that thou hast honored me and given me to eat of thy bread and victuals and mine heart hath drunk of thy dear love, tell me pray, what is thy purpose and whence comest thou, what is thy country and of what people art thou?" And he answered and said to me, "I come from a distant land, from pleasant and fruitful hills; my wisdom is as thy wisdom, my people as thy people and my laws as thy laws. My name is Enan Hanatas, son of Arnan Hadesh." I said to myself, "Surely this is a wonderful and awful name. Never before have I heard its like."

He said to me, "Thou mayst not know the secret of my name until that thou hast become my guest and comrade. Come with me from this land and I will tell thee all my secret lore; leave this spot, for here they appreciate neither thy worth nor thy skillful wisdom. I will take thee to another place, in which thou wilt find great delight; a place choice and good, like a fruitful garden, and they that people it are lovable and pleasant and exceeding wise."

And I said to him, "But, good sir, how may I forsake my house and abandon my heritage and depart from my native land wherein my abode is fixed, where dwell gentle folk, noble and princely, and wise sages who possess understanding of all matters? The greater among them graciously do me honor, and the lesser attend me for their own honor. As long as I shall live they will bear me on the pinions of their love and when I am dead their physicians will embalm me. And the sage hath said, 'If thou dwellest in a place in peace and security, if the spirit of the ruler rise up against thee, yield not thy place.' The spirit of the ruler is the evil inclination of man, which doth beguile him, and turn him whithersoever it will. Furthermore the Arab hath said, 'He that changeth his place, his fortune too is changed.' "

But he mocked and said, "The sage hath said, 'He that doth lean on his own knowledge and wisdom will stumble by his speech and perish by his counsel.' What will it profit thee after thy death whether they embalm thee skillfully or tear thee in pieces? Why dost thou speak without counsel and without wisdom, being a man of understanding and discernment? Surely thou knowest that thy beginning is of the earth and thy end vermin and corruption. What will myrrh and cinnamon profit thee when thou hast departed to the night of desolation? Thou wilt not ascend to Arcturus but in Sheol thou wilt wither of rot as a garment which hath been eaten of moths. Cease from words of vanity, for neither by withes nor by chains are thy feet bound. Rouse thyself to words of spirit, come with me to security and tranquillity. If thou hast found honor in thine own place and art favored of the many among thine own people, wherefore shouldst thou withhold from coming with me, to show thy pleasantness and to cause thy name to be remembered? They say that the man who dwelleth in his own city, even if it should please the king to do him honor, he will not perceive his glory nor recall his name or fame until that he have removed to another land, and there become honorable and glorious, above the exalted ones of the city. For that man who goeth not forth to journey among his fellow men, his blood is on his own head. Can the flower grow without water [Job 8:11]? But that one is as spilt water which cannot be gathered up again [II Sam. 14:14]. In the course of time worthy men remove to waters more pleasant. Furthermore the Arab hath said, 'Every journey and every change doth cause blessing and salvation.' "

Even as he was speaking to me I sighed deeply and my head was downcast to the earth; neither peace nor calm was mine. Said he to me, "Wherefore dost sigh and why doth not sorrow depart from thy heart? Reveal unto me thy heart's secret and that which is buried in thy bosom; perhaps I can banish the sorrow from within thee. For the Arab hath said, 'He that revealeth his secret sorrow to a comrade dear to his heart banisheth a part thereof, ofttimes the greater part.' " But I replied to him, "That which is in my heart and inmost thoughts I cannot utter with my lips, for I am abashed and ashamed, and therefore am I become silent and speechless for revealing to thee that which is hidden and which weighs upon my heart and my thoughts."

He then said to me, "Lo, I adjure thee by thine own and thy fathers' souls, tell me all thy thoughts."

And I said to him, "After that thou hast adjured me, and satisfied me with the honey of thy speech, I will reveal my secret before thee; let it but not provoke thy wrath." And he said to me, "Speak thy wish to the full, for in my sight thy lips drop myrrh."

I then replied and said, "Wise Plato hath said in his book on Physiognomy, that he whose countenance is ruddy as flame hastes and is hasted and is prone to prevarication. He whose eyes are sunken and quick to behold and perceive, that man is cunning and wily and of many devices. He whose

eyebrows are abundant and shaggy, his speech is heavy and he is a man of
grief and sorrow. And if his nose is in part thin, but his nostrils are full and
large, he is a contentious man, full of dissension and quarrelsome. He
whose forehead is curved and inclines to the sides of his face, that man is
tempestuous in word and deed. If his lips be large and thick he is dull, evil
by nature, and contentious. He whose ears are large is simple and full of
folly. He whose neck is short is a deceiver, every man's adversary and
enemy. He whose abdomen is large and whose ribs are well covered with
flesh, his folly will neither depart nor minish. A thin shoulder is a sign of an
empty spirit. A short palm is a sign of defective knowledge. Every tall
man is a fool, sinful in speech, blind and a follower of lustfulness; for being
over tall his heart cannot be wide but must needs be strait, and since of the
two chambers of the heart one is too strait to contain the blood which is his
ailment and the marrow of the brain is sustained only by the remainder,
both organs are weakened: the discernment of the heart and the understanding of the brain are both diminished. Furthermore, there being a
more distant expanse between the brain and the heart, discernment and
understanding cannot be quickly conjoined and therefore the tall man's
knowledge is ever wanting."

When he heard this matter, that the knowledge of tall men is short, he
uttered a great and bitter cry, saying "Now I know that thou art seeking a
pretext against me and art simulating in all thy speech."

I said, "I have also not forgotten and indeed know very well the characteristics of short men. For since their members are slight and short and
the traits of the soul follow after the nature of the body and the limbs,
short men display this same divergence. Nay, I am well aware of it. But
I perceive that it behooves me to speak only of tall men seeing that thou
art such. And of the indications I have mentioned, I recognize all in thy
face. Therefore do I tremble and fear to go with thee and to follow in thy
footsteps, lest there befall me what befell a certain leopard with a fox."

"What pray," said he to me, "was this happening you speak of?"

I replied: "A leopard once lived in content and plenty: ever he found
easy sustenance for his wife and children. Hard by there dwelt his neighbor
and friend, the fox. The fox felt in his heart that his life was safe only so
long as the leopard could catch other prey. 'If other prey should be wanting
for a single day he will seize me in his might and slay me in the strength of
his wrath, for he is in truth but shameless and he will apportion me unto
himself and his sons as viands. Surely I must bespeak him cunningly and
beguile him with words of deceit; mayhap I shall prevail by wile and cast
from my neck the yoke of his burden. Before the evil cometh, the sage
hath said, counsel is good, but after trouble hath arrived it is but vain.
Therefore will I remove him from my dwelling place and cause him to
depart from my habitation. I will banish him from his place ere he swallow
me, and cast him from his station ere he cast me down and devour me.
Perhaps I can lead him in the path of death, for have not our sages of

blessed memory declared, 'If one come to slay thee, arise thou betimes and slay him?'

"On the morrow then it came about that the fox came to the dwelling of the leopard in order to fulfill his purpose. The leopard addressed him, 'Whence comest thou?' Reynard replied, 'From a place of amazing beauty and goodness, a place of gardens and orchards, of lilies and myrtles, of turtle doves and pigeons, of hinds and does, of conies and wild goats and asses. They bray amongst the bushes and the fatted oxen lie in the grass. And I have come to give thee the tidings and to lead thee unto that place, for this place is despised and rejected and not fat but lean.'

"The leopard spake, 'Show me this place, for I am indeed eager to see it.' And he led him to that place, but the leopard knew not it was to be at the cost of his life. When he saw the comeliness of the place and its delights, the pleasantness of its situation, its approaches and its avenues, its woods, its shrubs, its herbage, its orchards and myrtles, its hinds and does, he rejoiced exceedingly and was filled with gladness and delight. The fox said in his heart, 'How many joys have been turned to sorrows! This, God willing, shall be added to that number.' The leopard said, 'Now do I know that thy soul is bound fast unto mine, and that love of me is cherished in thy heart, for by reason of the love thou hast for me hast thou chosen a place whose like mine eye hath never beheld nor hath mine ear heard report thereof. Be thou richly blessed, good and beloved sir. I will but go and take counsel with my wife and reveal unto her my secrets, for she is my comrade and the wife of my youth.'

"But the fox feared her, for that she was clever, and of sound sense, and subtle. So he said, 'Take heed of a woman's counsel, for woman is evil and bitter in spirit and hard. Her heart is of flint, an accursed plague is she in the house. Wise and understanding men heed not their wives, for they are of light mind. The sage hath said, Guard against their love; ask their counsel and do the opposite. Whoso heeds them and follows after them brings it about that both he and they are consumed in flames.'

"The leopard replied and said, 'Nevertheless it is incumbent upon a man and by statute ordained, that he take counsel of the wife of his bosom. Furthermore the sage hath said, Take counsel with thy brother or with thy friend, and thy paths will be made firm.'

"The fox then said, 'How much have I counseled thee and taught thee and instructed thee and commanded thee, yet have I not found thee one who hearkens! Surely the prophet hath said [Micah 7:5] Keep the doors of thy mouth from her that lieth in thy bosom.'

"The leopard then replied, 'Truth is with thee in all that thou hast spoken, for at times woman makes of sweet bitter and of bitter sweet. But I will go and ask her, and if she forbid me I will not hearken to her counsel.' The fox said, 'So be it then, go in peace and I will wait until thou return hither.'

"Then the leopard went to his house, rejoicing and glad of heart. His wife addressed him, 'What is this joy wherewith thou art rejoiced and this gladness which shines forth in thy countenance?' To her he replied, 'My friend the fox, whose love for me is without let or deceit, has shown me a place spacious and secure for my dwelling. All that see it covet it and all that hear of it speak its praises; it is my purpose to remove hence and to dwell yonder.' 'Why and wherefore?' said his wife. He replied, 'Because our place is strait and our abode scant, and day by day our prey minishes and here bread nor meat suffices us. But there we shall find all our wants; we shall eat according to the pleasure of our hearts.'

"But his wife replied, 'Beware of the fox, of his gifts and his offerings, for he counsels for his own advantage. The sage, furthermore, hath said, Two there be of the little folk of the earth, yet they are great in subtlety and cunning.' He inquired, 'And who may they be?' She replied, 'The serpent and the fox: They are the humblest of creatures, and are yet filled with guile and deceit. Surely thou hast heard what the snake did unto Adam and Eve, how the serpent did beguile them, and dissuade them from the commandments of their Creator, until that he brought them unto the gates of death? And hast thou not heard how the fox bound the lion by his cunning and slew him by his guile?'

"Then said the leopard to his wife, 'And how was the fox so confident as to approach a lion? Did not dread restrain him?' She replied, 'The lion loved the fox with all his heart, and advantaged him and befriended him, but the fox had small faith in him and plotted to slay him, for in truth he feared him greatly. Once on a day then, the fox came to the dwelling of the lion and was in great pain and cried out. The lion addressed him, What ails thee, beloved of my soul? And the fox replied, A great pain hath seized my head. The lion asked, And what may be done for thee, to assuage thy pain? And the fox replied, I have heard it said of the physicians of Araby that they prescribe that they who suffer from aches of the head be bound hand and foot, which doth then relieve them of their pain. Then said the lion, I will bind thee, as thou sayest; mayhap thy pain will be eased by thy bonds. The lion took a forged chain and bound the fox hand and foot. The fox then said that his pain was departed, and the lion loosed him; nor did the pain return. Then it came to pass after a number of days that the lion found a great ache in his head, for so is his custom and wont, and he went to the fox and said to him, Dear brother, my head is seized of a great pain, so that I am like to pray for death. Do thou quickly bind me with thy chain, both hand and foot. Mayhap my ache will be assuaged, even as befell thee. So the fox took fresh withes and bound him well and went from him and forsook him. Then he brought great stones and smote him upon the head and slew him.

'Perhaps that which befell the lion will befall thee also—forfend it Heaven—for his heart is but for guile, for wherefore chose he not that

place for himself, to be his abode and his delight and his pleasure? Therefore do I tremble before him lest he take us in his snare and cause us to
wander from this place to our hurt.'

"But the leopard spoke to her: 'Silence! for thou speakest as one of the
shameful women! Be not bold to answer my words, for full oft have I tried
him, yet never have I found dross in the pure silver of his love.' But she
said, 'Hearken to my voice and abide in thy home, and destroy not thy seat
and thy heritage.' But he would not hearken to her counsel, to her hurt and
to his own.

"And the leopard went and returned to the fox and said, 'Lo, thy counsel
is good and true, and thy love is fragrant with myrrh and frankincense.
But my wife is not willing to follow after me, nor will she hearken to my
words.' And the fox said, 'I tremble for thee, lest that which befell the
silversmith befall thee also.' The leopard inquired, 'What happening was
that?'

"And the fox narrated: 'There was once a silversmith in the land of
Babylonia who was exceedingly skillful in the working of gold and silver.
One day as he was plying his work his wife said to him, If thou wilt but
hearken to my counsel and do as I bid thee I will make thee rich and
increase thy glory and thy repute. He asked her, Prithee, and how?

'She said to him, Lo, our lord the king hath but one daughter, whom he
loveth as his own life and keepeth as the apple of his eye. Every day she
doth come before him and doth sit at his right hand. And now hearken to
my voice and fashion for her a silver image of her dear self; let it be beautiful and of pure silver. I will bestow it upon her as an offering and engage
that there will ensue for thee wealth and honor and tranquillity. And the
silversmith in his folly and want of sense hearkened to the voice of his wife
and made an image comely and precious, and sent it to the princess by the
hand of his wife. And it came to pass when she saw the image that she
rejoiced exceedingly in its beauty, and she clothed the silversmith's wife
with her mantle and gave her earrings and bracelets. The woman returned
to her house, rejoicing and exultant over her plan. When he saw her her
husband asked, What was thy fortune and how did the matter fall out?
And the woman replied, See my mantle, my earrings, and my bracelets; all
this the princess gave me. Her husband said, And where is the wealth and
the honor thou didst speak of? Art thou in want of mantles and earrings
and bracelets? Many and many times the value of these things thou hast
received did I esteem that silver image.

'When morning came the princess showed the silver image to her royal
father. The king then asked, saying, Who made this image and gave it to
the maid? His servants replied, A certain artisan made it, whose skill in
the working of silver and gold is without equal in the land, and he did send
it to the king's honored daughter, that it should become the most precious
of all her ornaments. But the wrath of the king was kindled against the
image which he saw in his daughter's hand, and he said, Hasten and cut

off the right hand of that artisan; for so is the law for everyone who maketh an image or a likeness. And they hastened and cut off his hand and divested him of his glory. The poor man humbled and sorrowing, with head downcast, returned to his house filled with bitterness and wormwood, and mourned. With a soul sore vexed he cried, Unto you, O men, do I call: take ye heed lest ye hearken to the counsel of your wives, and stop your ear against their whispering, lest there befall you what befell me, for the counsel of my wife hath humbled my glory and cut off mine hand and corrupted my splendor. He continued in his crying day by day until that his gall was burst and his liver was spilled to the ground in his passion.'

"When the leopard heard the words of the fox he trembled exceedingly and said, 'Surely it behooves every man to beware the counsel of his wife.'

"The fox continued, 'A man who taketh counsel of his wife may suffer that which befell the woodcutter.' The leopard inquired, 'What, pray, was the story of the woodcutter?'

"The fox said: 'There was once a man in Damascus who was exceedingly skillful in the hewing of wood. One day he was preparing his logs with his two hands, being preoccupied with his affairs, and his wife was spinning beside him. She said to him, My father, may his memory be for a blessing, was much more skillful at this trade than art thou. For he used to plane his logs with both his hands; when the one grew weary he labored with the other. But thou canst plane with thy right hand only. He replied to her, No artisan or laborer may do his work but with his right hand only, except for the left-handed man, for in that case his left hand serves instead of the right. But she answered him, By thy life, do but make trial of it and see whether thou canst not work with thy two hands as my father was wont to do. The simpleton then raised his left hand with his ax in order to smite the log, but smote instead the thumb of his right hand and cut it off. In a great rage he rose up and smote his wife's head with the ax, and her skull was crushed and she died. The matter became known in the court of justice, and they took the woodcutter and they brought him without the city and stoned him with stones.

'Therefore do I declare unto thee that all women are deceitful; they ansnare the lives of all. I shall relate to thee a little of their deceitfulness and their shamefulness.

'There was once a king of the kings of Araby who was wise and understanding and just, and who had sitting before him always wise and understanding counselors. One day they began to speak of the praises of women and of their virtues, and of their great wisdom and their patience. The king said to them, Cut short your talk and restrain your words, for never hath there been seen or reported a woman who was good and virtuous, endowed with understanding and knowledge. Their love is only for their own benefit and their own pleasure; they have no government over their desires and they sin against themselves. Then his wise men said to him, Let not the king say so, for there are indeed women that are wise and understanding, virtuous and faithful. They love and honor their husbands, find covering for their households and sustenance for their sons and daughters; in them there is neither fault nor disrepute. The king replied, I shall give you a sign for my saying and a mark for my speech. Lo, this city is exceeding great: spread ye abroad therein and see whether ye can find a single woman endued with the virtues ye spake of and the qualities ye mentioned.

'And they sought and found in that city a woman of great reputation, modest and virtuous and wise, comely as the moon and clear as the sun. Her husband was a merchant, a man of great substance who pursued favor and sought goodness. The wise men returned their answer before the king, saying to him, Lo, we have found a wise and understanding woman, free from fault or deceit, without wilfulness or guile; and she is married of a husband.

'The king sent to summon the woman's husband and he came before him and made obeisance. The king cleared a place for him and caused him to sit down, and said to him, There is a secret matter I would discuss with thee. He replied, Speak O King, for thy servant hearkeneth to the voice of his lord. The king said to him, I have a daughter lovely and good, mine only child. I do not desire to give her to a prince or noble, for I cherish her in my heart. But I seek for her a good and faithful man who is free from the iniquity of the times, that he may love her and honor her and bear her upon his shoulder, that he may adorn her with garlands, deal with her with a cheerful countenance, and maintain her in gentleness and loving kindness. There have come to mine ears thy many praises, thine excellent qualities and thy good deeds, and I desire to give my daughter to thee. But I cannot give her unto one who hath a wife; do thou slay thy wife this night and on the morrow I shall give thee my daughter to wife. The merchant replied, My lord the king, who am I and what is my life that I should be son-in-law to the king? In good truth, I am not worthy to tend thy sheep. The king said, Thee do I choose, for thou art my desire and my delight and without thee no man shall raise his hand or his foot in all my kingdom. The man replied, But my lord the king, how can I slay my wife when she hath been with me these fifteen years? Of my bread doth she eat and she drinketh of my cup. She is my heart's delight and my joy, She doth love me and honor me, she watcheth over me and doth minister to me; mine honor is augmented in her eyes daily and never minishes, and I am preserved from every evil thing. But the king said to him, Hearken to my voice and slay her, for by her death great honor will accrue to thee, for I will raise thy head above all the nobles of my kingdom and thou wilt rule over all that thy heart desires. The man replied, I will make trial and see whether I may do this base deed.

'And he went out from before the king in sadness and sorrow, and the blood of his liver dropped with his grief.

'So he came to his house, and when he beheld his wife his sighs increased and his sorrow redoubled. His wife addressed him, My good and pleasant lord, wherefore is thy countenance mournful? But he refrained him and said to her, May the Rock ward you from death and destruction: naught doth trouble me and naught but good is in my heart.

'And it came to pass in the night, when she was sleeping upon her bed, that he arose in confusion of heart to slay her. He took his sword in his right hand and a lamp in his left, and removed the covering from upon her. But when he saw her lying asleep, with her two babes at her breast, he took pity upon her and said, Woe is me, how can I slay her, whither can I take my shame, who will bring up my children, who are the very apple of my eye? Surely it is but the multitude of my transgression and of mine iniquity. And he returned the sword to its sheath, and his soul was melted in sorrow, and he said in his heart with his eyes running tears, Lo, my wife is better than all the kingdoms. Cursed be all kings, for they do but pursue after their own desires, and seduce the hearts of men with their vanities and pour waters of sorrow with the wine of their joy. And he ascended her couch and lay by her and kissed her and put his left hand under her head and embraced her.

'And it came to pass in the morning that he rose up and went to his storehouse to transact his business. The king awaited him, and when he tarried, sent messengers to come before him and to cause him to hasten and to know what detained him. When he saw the king's messenger his anxiety was great. He trembled and his heart was sore afraid.

'When he came before the king, the king asked of him, What hast thou done? Hast thou slain her? Nay, my lord, he replied, for my love of her and pity of her overcame me; and he related all that had befallen when he took the sword to smite her. Then did the king rebuke him saying, Get thee from my sight and never look upon my face more, for thou art in no wise a man, but thy heart is as the heart of women. The man went from the king's presence rejoicing greatly in the king's anger and in his rebuke.

'And it came to pass toward evening that the king sent one of his servants to fetch the wife of the man secretly. And he went and brought her unto him and when the king beheld her he marveled at the comeliness of her appearance and the splendor of her face and form. He addressed her saying: Lo, I have heard of thy wisdom and of the comeliness of thy conduct, and from the day of my hearing thy report there hath burned in my heart the fire of thy love, which hath drawn my soul with the bonds of desire. And now it is my pleasure to take thee to wife, and the kingdom shall be thine for a heritage. However, I may not take a woman that hath a husband, lest it be for a reproach. Go thee, and slay thine husband this night, and afterwards will I take thee and do for thee all thy heart may desire. And the woman replied in gladness of heart and in joy, I shall do the king's bidding and I shall become his handmaiden. The king said, But thou shalt be my wife and all my wives shall be thy tirewomen and my concubines thy handmaidens. And the king gave her a sword forged of tin, for he knew the weakness of a woman's wit. He said, Lo, here is my sword, a blade exceeding keen; do thou but smite him once; thou needst not repeat the stroke, for he will nevermore be able to rise. She took the sword and went to her house, all but skipping her joy.

'She prepared her meat and mingled her wine and brought forth her viands and arrayed her board. Her husband returned home to eat and to drink with his sons and with his wife, and at night she caused him to drink of the wine and made him drunk and lifted him to his bed and caused him to lie down. When it was yet night and he was in his drunkenness, slumbering upon his couch, she arose and took the sword and smote his head and thought that the metal had pierced his very life. But the sword of tin bent back, and he awoke from his slumber and was somewhat aroused from his drunkenness, and he cried out and said to his wife, Who hath roused me from my slumber and who hath smitten me upon the head? When the woman saw that he was awake and that her sword had left him uninjured, she was sore dismayed and her heart melted within her with the greatness of her dread and her trembling; her very soul all but left her body. She said, Dear one, beloved of my soul, lie down and return to thy slumber, perhaps it was in thy dream that thou sawest one smiting thee. So he returned to his sleep, and availed not to open his eye, for he had not yet roused him from his wine. But his wife's anxiety increased without measure. She awaited in trembling until the dawn broke, then she arose to go about her tasks and to order her household, to atone for her shame for the evil deed that she had wrought; she set about to prepare the pottage for her husband as had ever been her wont.

'The king awaited her coming, but as she came not he bade that she be fetched. When she came before him the king said to her, Hast thou wrought the deed agreed upon between me and thee, or did thine eye take mercy upon him? She replied, My lord the king, I did thy bidding, but thou hast frustrated thy good plan and made it vain and nothing worth; for when I upraised thy sword against him, lo, thou hadst weakened it. And she related to him that which she had done and the iniquity that she had wrought. Then the king sent to summon her husband and said to him: Do thou declare to these wise men that sit before me all that befell with thy wife; withhold no word. Thereupon he related all that had befallen between him and his wife. Then the king bade the woman tell all that had befallen her with her husband, and she did so. Then did the king speak to his wise men, saying: Surely this is the saying that I spake to you when I bade you restrain your words. They replied, marveling at his wisdom, With thee is the right; what is there for us to say? Surely our lord is wise as an angel of the Most High.

'Socrates, the divine philosopher, also, in the abundance of his wisdom and the greatness of his piety, hated women and loathed to look into their countenances. His own wife was spare and short, and when his disciples asked of him, How came it that such a man as thou art should wed such a woman as this? he replied, I have chosen the least of the evil. One day as he was walking with his disciples in the cool of the day there passed before him a woman of comely figure and beautiful appearance, and one of his disciples gazed at her. Socrates said to him, Woe is thee, wherefore dost thou gaze upon her? The disciple replied, Not for love nor for desire do I gaze, but to behold in her form the craftsmanship of the Creator. The master said, Turn her inside out; then wilt thou understand her ugliness. Another time he was walking upon the way and he saw a woman hanging from a fig tree. He said, Would that all the fruit of this tree were the same. And once he was walking with his disciples by the banks of a river, where a certain woman was washing clothes. She cried out upon him, and cursed him, and reviled him, and heaped him with abuse; then she threw of the water upon him and drenched him. He said, Surely she cast her lightning and hurled her thunder, and now she bringeth forth rain.

'Again, one of the great men built him a new house and wrote over the lintel, Let no evil enter here. Diogenes, the philosopher, passed and saw the inscription, and then wrote underneath, And how will thy wife enter? Further, when one man reported to another, Thine enemy hath perished, he replied, If thou hadst said, He hath taken a wife, I had been better pleased.'

THE STORY OF TOBIT

In the days of the saints of old and the sages of an elder day there dwelt in this city a man upright and righteous and straightforward in all his speech. The man was great and wealthy, and his eyelids looked straight before him. His name was Tobias, son of Ahijah, the Danite. It was his wont to give food and lodging to every poor and needy person. If any died without relatives to bury him, he prepared shrouds out of his own purse, and wrought what was necessary, and buried him.

But the people of this city were exceedingly evil, being wilful and faithless, and they slandered all the Jews before the king, saying, Lord King, these Jews do open our graves, and draw thence the bones of our dead, and burn them daily to make magic remedies. The wrath of the king was kindled when he heard these words, and he commanded that the yoke of the Jews and their bonds be made heavier. Let this, said he, be their reward: Any Jew that shall die in all my kingdom, let him be cast into a great pit which is near the city, and let anyone that doth bury him be hanged upon a tree.

Came a day when a certain proselyte died, and there were none to bury him. Then arose saintly Tobias and washed him, and clothed him, and buried him. But wicked people had seen him, and they seized him and brought him to the judge and said to him, Sir judge, this Jew hath transgressed the ordinance of the king; he hath buried one of the sons of his people. So the judge bade that he be hanged, for that he had transgressed upon the king's ordinance and his statute. So they took him without the city to hang him upon the tree which they had prepared for him.

But when they had come near the tree, lo! they were smitten with blindness from great to small, and could not see him. Then Tobias escaped from them, and returned to his home and invited his loved ones and his relatives and his companions and all that had mourned for his affliction, and he related to them all that had befallen him and the mercy which the Lord had vouchsafed him, and he said unto them [Ps. 106:1], Praise ye the Lord for He is good, for His mercy endureth forever. There is no god, no providence, beside Him; praised be the name of His glory, for that He delighteth in the peace of His servant.

And it came to pass when the king came unto the city, that they related unto him all that had befallen them with the Jew, when they had sought to hang him. The king trembled exceedingly and his heart smote him within him, and he commanded that the order be proclaimed throughout his kingdom, that anyone who wrought hurt to a Jew, whether in his person or in his substance, did in effect injure the apple of his own eye. Every man that harmed them should be hanged upon a tree, even if his person were respected and he were himself a counselor. And he commanded that the Jews bury their dead in honor, and he uplifted them and exalted them all the days of his life. But those wicked men nevermore saw the light all their days.

One day that saintly man was lying upon his bed, and there was a swallow's nest in his house. When he opened his eye to look at the nest there fell into his eyes of the swallow's dung, so that they were dimmed from seeing, for a film of white had covered his eyeball. He had but one son, only child to him and to his mother, and him he called and spake to him and said:

Son, when I was engaged in the business of commerce, I wandered about all lands and traveled in all countries. One day I went to the land of Ind and traded there until that I had accumulated much wealth by my earnings. But because of the terror of the roads I entrusted my riches into the hand of a good and faithful man, whose name was Pride of the Age. And now, my son, hearken to my voice and go and hire me a man of them that travel upon the ways, one that knoweth the paths of the land of Ind. And I will send thee with him to that faithful man to whom I committed my silver and gold. I know that when he shall behold thee, my son, and the sign of the writing which is between him and between me, that he will give thee my wealth; for he is a faithful man and doth love me, and will have pity upon me when he shall hear of my disease and my pain.

So the lad went to the place of the hirelings and found there a certain man who knew all the land of Ind and its paths, the whole country and its diverse places. Him he brought to his father and said, Lo I have found this man, who knoweth all the land of Ind and its ways, even as he knoweth this city and its avenues.

Pious Tobias inquired of him, Dost know a certain city in the land of Ind whose name is Tobat? Worthy Sir, he replied, I do indeed know it, for I dwelt therein two full years; it is a great city for sages. Said Tobias, What shall I give thee, that thou shouldst go thither with my son? Fifty pieces of gold, he replied. The saintly one said, I will give them thee with joy and with gladness of heart.

So he wrote the script to the man of good faith, and made therein the sign, and took his son and embraced him, and fell upon his neck and kissed him, and said to him, Go in peace, and may the God of my fathers keep me alive until thou return hither.

So the lad went with the man that was hired until they came to the city of Tobat. There this man brought him to the faithful one whose name was Pride of the Age. To him the lad spake, My Lord, art thou the faithful man whose name is Pride of the Age? The other replied, Wherefore dost thou inquire after my name? My father Tobias, the Danite, has sent me to thee, said the lad, and lo, he seeks thy peace and the peace of all that are thine; thereupon he gave him the writing of his father.

When the man beheld the script and its sign, he cast his eye over it and believed the lad was in truth Tobias' son, and embraced him and kissed him and sustained him with honey and milk, and said to him: Doth my friend and comrade, my bosom companion and beloved one, enjoy peace? He doth so, was the reply. Then the man rejoiced in his friend's son and messenger, and the nard of his love was fragrant. Abide with me yet a month, said he, and I will rejoice in thee and in thy pleasant speech. But the laid said to him, My lord, send me forth, and let me go to my place and my country, for such is the will of my father and mine own will and pleasure, for from that day that I forsook my elderly father my heart hath trembled and hath been disturbed, for my father hath no son beside me, and therefore do I hasten, with the help of our Rock, to return to my home. Then did the faithful one fulfill his very wish, and deliver up unto him all his father's substance and his wealth, and added yet gifts of his own and garments and diverse other things; two serving lads also did he give him to attend him, and he sent him away with songs and rejoicing.

And it came to pass on the way, as they were going by the shore of the sea, that its waves were roused by a strong and mighty wind, and cast up a fish before them upon the dry land. The hireling hastened to seize it, and when he had opened its belly he took forth its liver and gall. The lad addressed him: As thy soul liveth, wherefore hast thou left the fish behind and taken only its liver and gall? He replied, Know that in these two things lieth great salvation, for of them potent remedies may be made. Into no house in which this liver is burned as incense will ever destroying demon come; never will its masters be endangered, ever will they be at peace. And for the gall, if a blind man should paint his eyes therewith they would be opened, and his eyeballs would become bright. Thereupon the lad besought his companion earnestly that he give him the organs, and he took them and bound them in the skirts of his garment.

So the lad arrived at his home rejoicing and found his father safe and secure. Then did the man rejoice over his son, and moreover over his substance and his riches, and he said unto his son, Go with this hireling unto the banker and give him an hundred pieces of gold, yea more, as he will, and return payment to him as him pleaseth.

So the lad went with the man, and gazed after him but beheld him not, and sought him in all the city but could not find him. Then he came to his father and said, I did go with the man, but when I gazed after him I beheld him not, and though I sought him in all the city I could not find him. Thereupon his father declared unto him, Son, know thou that our God hath sent him before us to preserve us alive; in truth he is the prophet Elijah.

Then the lad related the matter of the liver and gall and gave them to his father, who then painted his eyeballs with the gall, which the Lord then opened, and restored unto them their sight.

Thereafter the man spake unto his son: My son, after that the Lord hath led thee in the path of truth, nor hath spared His eye from watching over thee, but hath delivered thee from all mishap and evil, and hath hearkened to our voice and returned thee unto us in peace—do thou therefore hearken unto my voice and perform a great kindness and a worthy deed. Take thou to wife the lass that is my brother's daughter, for she doth see that all her companions be wedded and is herself covered with shame.

Now regarding this maiden there was a great portent and marvelous, for thrice had she been wedded to men; but by reason of this great portent everyone that lay with her was thereafter found dead, lying prone on his couch. So the lad replied, Father mine, how may I come nigh unto her? I do indeed dread lest I die by reason of her, for already have her three husbands perished.

But he said to him, My son, know of a truth that it is some demon or destroying angel that doth slay them and take from them their souls. Do thou but take the liver which the man hath given thee, and burn it as incense in the house as he hath directed; then trust in the Lord, and thou wilt be warded from all evil.

So the lad took his life in his hand and stiffened not his neck from doing his father's bidding, and he took the maiden, and she became his wife and he did love her.

And it came to pass at even, that he burned the fish's liver as incense throughout the house, from without and within, and his bed also, and his covering and his garments, and the maiden came unto the chamber, and he came in unto her. But his elderly and saintly father wept and prayed before the Lord, and his heart trembled and sighed within him for the fate of his son. But the young man lay until the light of morning, and when they rose early to seek his peace, they found him rejoicing and glad at heart, free from any disease or sorrow. And the two lived on without fright or fear and ended their days in goodness and their years in pleasantness.

TAHKEMONI—JUDAH BEN SOLOMON AL-HARIZI

SELECTIONS

FROM CHAPTER 3 (ON JUDAH HALEVI)

But the songs of the Levite, R. Judah, are a wreath of grace for the head of testimony and a line-circlet of carnelian, topaz, on its neck. He is the righthand pillar for the edifice of Poetry. He sits in the seat of wisdom. He is Adino, the Eznite. He brandishes his spear against the giants and leaves all the heroes of poetry slain. All his poems break the hearts of the scholar. Before him Asaph almost dies and Jeduthun's hand grows slack, and the song of the sons of Korah become wearisome. He came into the Treasury of Poetry and despoiled the treasure-house. He took all its delightful vessels and then he departed and locked the gate after he had gone out.

All who follow in his footsteps in order to learn the art of his song do not even reach the dust of his chariots. All the poets borrow from his compositions and they kiss his literary pearls. For his tongue is a polished and sharpened arrow in the art of the piyyut. In the poems of praises, there is none who can challenge him. In the poems of prayers, he draws and subdues every heart. In his love poems, his expression is as a layer of dew. Glowing coals flame forth from him. In his elegies he causes a cloud of weeping to flow and he breaks it asunder.

If he composes a letter or a scroll, you will find all the rhetoric included in it beautiful, as if it had been stolen from the celestial stars or had emanated from the Holy Spirit. In the tent of Song the gates of the celestial ones were opened for him, for there Divinity was revealed to him. With the breath of his mouth he calms the billows of wisdom. He roars like a lion, yea, he shouts aloud. In all that he does, he prospers.

Then he took up his parable and said:
All excellence to Halevi streams upward and is led.
He is a garland fair for his anointed's head.
And though his brilliance shines from circles of the West

The fragrance of his song fills every cranny of the East.
In poetry's tourneys he has set his praises
As blades to fight—his verse as spears he raises;
And many swift pursue him but despair
To find his path—they cannot know his lair.
Into the room of song alone he came and stood,
And when he left, he closed the door for good.
Though God upon his gate the bars did bind
He broke its fetters with his power of mind.
With dew of his words he makes buds to grow
When watered by his mind the flowers show.
The glory of his genius vexes every heart
As tongues too short cannot his praise impart,
And when the skilful plan for poetry's fray
'Tis Judah who will carry off the day.

FROM CHAPTER 19

SEVEN YOUNG MEN DISCUSS THE MERITS OF THE VARIOUS VIRTUES

Heman the Ezrahite saith: I was in the land of Pethor, the city of Balaam the son of Beor; and while I was walking by the riverside, under the shadows of plants and thickets of flowers, I perceived seven pleasant youths of the choicest society. They sat upon the bank of the river, making their hearts merry with words of rhetoric. One of them called out, and said: Which is the best quality and is the worthiest in the sight of God and man?

One of them said: I know that all qualities are praiseworthy, but there is none as sublime as humility; for it conceals all faults, and reveals all that is beautiful; it causes to forgive transgressions, and makes its possessor associate with the modest; it increases his lovers and friends, and causes him to inherit a precious and pleasant name. And he took up his parable, and said: Amongst man's good traits there is none like meekness: it is graceful and sublime to all the wise; it stirs up love in hearts of enemies, and covers a man's sins and transgressions.

His companion said unto him: From the right path hast thou gone astray, and hast fed the wind. Humility or impudence is esteemed as nought when compared with promptitude; for with it a man conquers souls, and finds favor and good understanding in the sight of God and men, and inherits much honor and greatness in this world and in the next; with it he amasses increasing riches and houses full of all good things. And he took up his parable, and said: It is true that promptitude has no equal, and happy is he who walks in its way; all precious qualities are but handmaids, and promptness is like a queen to them.

His third companion said: Thou has spoken foolishly, for there is no quality as good and precious as courage and bravery; for with it a man subdues all his enemies, and does good to his friends; he joins himself unto the great, and will cry, yea, he will shout, he will prove himself mighty against his enemies. He will ascend the throne of excellence, so that they will proclaim before him: Cast up the highway! And he took up his parable, and said: In truth there is no precious trait in man like courage blended with strength; indeed with it a man subdues his foes, and brings them down with sorrow to the grave.

The fourth one said: Thou hast wandered out of the way, and hast been made to serve folly with rigor; for among all the qualities there is no quality as worthy as faithfulness; for with it a man lifts up his head, his soul becomes precious, and he is honored in the sight of all flesh and blood, and finds favor and good understanding in the sight of God and man. And he took up his parable, and said: Know there is no quality as worthy in God's sight as faithfulness; if prophecy assumed a mortal garb it would appear like faithfulness in form.

The fifth one said: There is no steadfastness in thy mouth, and thy speech is without understanding; for the most sublime quality is wisdom: it lifts up those of its adherents that are low, and raises its banners upon their heads; and wisdom preserves the life of him that has it; if not for wisdom, man would not excel an animal. And he took up his parable and said: In this our world there is no trait so sublime and glorious to man's head as wisdom; with it a man ascends the royal throne, and with it the weary ones will find strength.

The sixth one said: A vain vision hast thou seen, and falsely hast thou testified; for there is no quality as good to any flesh as culture; for it is for his culture that a man is honored by those that know him, and loved by those that hear him; they cover all his transgressions; his memorial is pleasant to all mouths, and his praise is like a tower built for an armory; such a man is a delight to the heart, and his praises endure for ever and ever. And he took up his parable, and said: There is no quality in man like culture; it is majesty and grace unto all flesh; for if a man possesses all charms, but has no culture, know that he lacks honor.

The seventh one said: Thou trustest in vanity, and following the east wind, feedest on wind; for among all the qualities there is none as worthy as a good heart; for through it a man is beloved of all creatures, and is placed at the head of all guests; he is honored in the sight of those that hear him and see him, all that look upon him love him, and even his enemies praise him; men laud him, and the angels of heaven remember him for good. And he took up his parable, and said: In truth there is no quality like a good heart, with it a man will flourish like a watered garden; through it he will be beloved of his Maker, and will find favor and good repute in His sight.

When the old man heard their words, he said unto them: Ye are all perplexed, and walk in darkness; the right thing is hidden from you, and ye know not to choose the truth; for among all the qualities there is no quality as good as generosity; for all other qualities bow down at its feet, and it excels them all; through it all sins are forgiven, and hatred is removed from the heart; with it a man attains desirable things that are far away, even if they are in heaven; through it he is counted among the pious, for with it he does righteous and kind deeds; with it he acquires a good name, and his memorial is like precious oil. But he who lacks generosity, his righteousness is counted as guilt, his kindnesses as errors, and his favors as sins. All his companions despise him, those who know him hate him, his friends remember him for evil, and they that dwell in his house and his maids count him for a stranger.

The bounteous man, however, lifts up his countenance, for generosity covers all his sins, and blots out his transgressions; his adversaries love him and his enemies praise him; they that are jealous of him laud him, and they who would curse him bless him. For by his generosity he conquers their hearts, and attracts their love; through it haughtiness becomes beautiful, and faults turn into merits; through it the fool is counted as wise, and the despised one soars up to the heavens. Thus I have seen wicked men who commit evil deeds, but if they have a generous heart, it conceals all their wickedness and guilt; their bad qualities become good, and love covers all transgressions.

I have likewise seen men of faithfulness, prudence, and understanding, possessing all worthy qualities; but if generosity is not among them, fear of God becomes a sin, and humility haughtiness, promptitude impudence, prudence folly, merit a fault, and understanding lack of knowledge. For all other good qualities bow down at the feet of generosity, and concerning it it is written: Many daughters have done valiantly, but thou excellest them all [Proverbs 31:29]. And he took up his parable, and said: It is true there are precious traits in this world, but highest of all is generosity; for other traits, though they be praiseworthy, stole their excellence from generosity.

The narrator said: When I heard his discourse and the pleasantness of his instruction, I desired to investigate whether his wisdom is in accordance with his rhetoric, and I said unto him: By the life of Him who endowed thee with eloquent speech and a spirit of counsel and might, make known to me the branch of thy planting and the habitation where thou liest down.

And he answered, and said: I am Heber, who compose a pleasant song, and flash forth flames of fire from my tongue. I strengthen hearts with witty sayings which are set with stones of eloquence and metaphors; I cover my friends with a cloak of praise, but clothe my foes with garments of dread.

When I heard his songs and his powerful words, I knew that he was our teacher and master Heber the Kenite our scholar. I stayed for a while with him to enjoy his fragrance and to satiate myself with the sweetness of his speech. Afterwards I bade him peace, and each man of us turned to his tent.

FROM CHAPTER 24

I will tell you, [says Heber] of marvels that my eyes have seen when I journeyed from the land of the Eastern Jordan, Geshur, to Mosul. It was at the time when the hands of its generous leaders were as hard as the flinty rock, with nobody to help or support a poet. But the city itself was beautiful and imposing, very large and spacious. An influential and wealthy population was to be found in its midst and mighty men formerly dwelt in it. Among all lands there is no city so fair as it, naught comparable to its glory and its loveliness. Moreover it flows with milk and honey and this is its fruit. Howbeit, the people that dwell in it are stingy, as are our own people who live within its borders. Not one of them gives freely either to scholars or tramps so much as a thread or a shoe lachet. All of them have their bags of money tied tightly in their hands without an opening or a crack so that not a single grain falls to the ground.

Now when I came to this city, I was weary and it was at the eve of the Sabbath, just at dusk. Though I to myself, Perchance there is a synagogue near to which I can go and worship.

When I came to the House of Prayer along with the congregation, I beheld it lovely as a palace or a mansion. I sat down in the midst of the throng. Sitting beside me were two elderly men with long beards who seemed as sturdy as oaks. They were of those who sell praises but not of those who buy them, of those who overthrow houses of righteousness, but not of those who build them. They were tall and pompous and their fat paunches protruded as heaps of wheat. They had despicable souls and their eyes were haughty.

When I inquired of them about their great men and the rest of their community and who was their Hazzan, their precentor, they replied:

Our city can boast of Exilarchs and men who are precious as pearls or rubies. But besides these, we have a precentor who is also a preacher. He is meek and modest, rotund and sleek as the rams of Bashan. His prayers are sweet, his company is delightful, and his chanting is superb. He instructs in the Torah, is versed in the Scriptures, and gives many fine interpretations of the Prophets. He knows rare liturgical poems [Piyyutim] and is a singer of songs.

When I heard their words, I said, Thanksgiving and praise to God because He has deemed me worthy to behold this famous precentor.

While I was lost in this reverie, behold, the precentor makes his appearance. Frontlets are on his forehead, and on his head there is a shining white turban about two hundred cubits high. The sweep of his beard reached down to his navel. He was covered with a prayer mantle, decorated with fringes. These he dragged along the ground and almost stumbled on his skirts.

When we saw him, we all trembled with excitement to meet him and we prostrated ourselves before him. We were speechless with awe of him until he began his melodies and started to intone his prayers. I counted in his prayers more than a hundred clear and evident blunders besides innumerable others there is no need to mention here. But I did not say anything to him by way of correction, for I thought to myself, perhaps it is an accident, or preoccupation with the Sabbath has confused him, or perchance sleep has overwhelmed him.

So the next morning, at dawn, I went early to the Synagogue. Behold, the precentor comes in and seats himself in the place of honor. He begins with the Hundred Benedictions which trip glibly from his tongue in memorized fashion. He intoned in a shrill, loud voice:

Blessed be He who hath created man a beast. [The benediction says, b'hohmah—in wisdom. He misreads it for behemah, a beast.]

And in the Verse of Psalms he made so many mistakes that they could not be counted. Instead of:

Keep back Thy servant also from presumptuous sins [Ps. 19:14—Mezadim hasoch] he said: Yea, train thy servant away from olives. [Mezasim hanoch]. Instead of He giveth thee in plenty the fat of wheat—[Ps. 147:14—helev hittim] he said: He giveth thee in plenty a sword of sharpness [herev haddim]. Instead of: Who covereth the heaven with clouds —[Ps. 147:8—b'avim], he said: Who covereth the heaven with clothes [B'gadim]. Instead of: Let Israel rejoice in His Maker [Ps. 149:2], he said Let Ishmael rejoice in Esau—[the pun here is on Yisrael and Yishmael and Osov and Esav]. Instead of Praise Him with stringed instruments and the pipe [Ps. 150:4—B'minim v'ugav], he said: Praise Him with cheese and crackers [g'vinim v'ugah].

Nachmanides

In contrast to the turbulent life of Maimonides, the life of Spanish-born *Rabbi Moses ben Nachman* (1194–1270), known as Ramban and Nachmanides, was rather peaceful and secure. The most dramatic event of this physician-scholar's career occurred at the age of sixty-nine when he was summoned to dispute with the apostate Fra Paulo in the presence of King James of Aragon, his court, ecclesiastical representatives and Jews. Paulo had tried to convert Jews in his journeys through Spain, but seeing that he could not convince them that the Messiah had already come, he had the king summon Jewry's most famous personage to a public disputation, confident that he would triumph. In accepting, Nachmanides requested and was granted complete freedom of speech; his courage in defending his religion and his people is seen in his occasionally bold remarks to the king, especially when he addresses him and demonstrates the irrationality of a cardinal tenet in Christianity, Jesus' miraculous conception. For his part, the king was fairminded, as evidenced by his rebuke of the priest who insulted Maimonides and by his gift and parting remark to Nachmanides.

The disputation took place in the capital city, Barcelona, in 1263, and lasted four days. In point after point Nachmanides refuted Fra Paulo and demonstrated the apostate's ignorance and his inability to even read the very sources upon which he based his arguments. When, in reaction to the Dominicans' claim of victory, Nachmanides published his account of the disputation in a pamphlet, his enemies accused him of blaspheming their religion and publicly burned his report. Brought to trial, Nachmanides was found guilty and banished in 1264. After three years of wandering he arrived in Palestine in 1267, and while living in Acco began to spread Jewish learning to a wide circle of disciples. He constantly wrote letters to his family in Spain, and in one of them cites the fact that only two Jewish families lived in Jerusalem.

During his three years in Palestine, Nachmanides established a synagogue and an academy in Jerusalem. He delivered sermons on the Torah and, by living in the land, gained new insights for his *Commentary on the Pentateuch*. Although Nachmanides did not write a philosophical treatise, his views, thoughts and beliefs are contained in his *Commentary*. Nachmanides' exegesis is based partly on the principles of literal exposition akin to that of Rashi (whom he greatly admired and frequently quoted). However, he goes further than Rashi by also accenting the mystic, or esoteric meaning of the Torah. In addition, Nachmanides also wrote poetry, responsa, and books on halakha.

THE DISPUTATION WITH PAULO CHRISTIANI

Our lord the king had commanded me to debate with Fra Paulo in his majesty's palace, in the presence of himself and his council, in Barcelona. To this command I replied that I would accede if I were granted freedom of speech, whereby I craved both the permission of the king and of Fra Raymond of Peñaforte and his associates who were present. Fra Raymond of Peñaforte replied that this I could have so long as I did not speak disrespectfully.

Whereupon I rejoined: "It is not my desire to be at variance with your rule on procedure of this matter but that I should speak as I wish on the subject of debate, as you on your part may speak entirely as you wish. For I know how to speak with self-control, as you insist, on a subject under dispute, but what to say must be within my own discretion."

So all of them gave their consent to my speaking freely. Thereupon I made the statement that disputation between Gentiles and Jews on many points arose out of customs of the Law upon which the substance of the Faith did not depend, but that I did not wish to argue in this honourable court except upon matters upon which religion as a whole depended. To this all present responded: "You have well spoken."

And so we agreed to discuss first of all the subject of the Messiah— whether he had come already as the Christian belief affirms or whether he is yet to come as the Jews believe. Later the topic would be whether the Messiah was really divine or if he was entirely human, born of man and woman. And after this the question whether the Jews maintained the true law or whether the Christians practised it would be debated.

Then Fra Paulo began by saying that he would prove from our Talmud that the Messiah of whom the prophets had witnessed had already come. I replied to that, that before we argued on that, I would like him to show and tell me how this could possibly be true. For since the time that the king had been in the province, and in many places I had heard that he, Fra Paulo, had made this statement to many Jews and I was most astonished at him.

"Let him answer me," I said, "on this point: Did he wish to say that the scholars who appear in the Talmud believed concerning Jesus, that he was the Messiah and that they believed he was completely man and truly God in accordance with the Christian conceptions of him? Was it not indeed a known fact that Jesus existed in the days of the second temple, being born and put to death before the destruction of that temple?

"But the scholars of the Talmud were later than this destruction, for example, Rabbi Akiba and his associates. And those who taught the Mishna, Rabbi Jehudah ha-Nasi and Rabbi Nathan, lived at a time that was many years after the destruction; and much more remote from that event was R. Ashi who composed the Talmud and reduced it to writing, for he belonged to a period of about four centuries later.

"Now, if these scholars had believed in the Messiahship of Jesus and that he was genuine and his religious belief true; and if they wrote those things which Fra Paulo affirms he is going to prove that they wrote; then how was it that they continued to hold by the Jewish faith and their original religious usage? For they were Jews and continued to abide in the religion of the Jews all their days. They died as Jews, they and their children, and their disciples who heard all the words they uttered.

"Why did they not apostatize and turn to the religion of Jesus, as has done Fra Paulo who understands from their sayings that the Christian faith is the true faith? Far be it so! But he has gone and apostatized on the ground of their words while they and their disciples who received the law from their lips lived and died Jews, as we today are!

"Moreover, these were they who taught us the Mosaic law and Jewish custom. For all our religious practices today are in accordance with what the Talmud teaches and with what we have observed of the scholars of the Talmud who have followed and performed its teaching from the time it was composed up to the present. For the whole Talmud has no other end in view than to teach us the practice of Law and Precept. Just as in this regard, when the sanctuary stood, our forefathers were guided by the authority of the prophets and of Moses our teacher, on whom be blessing. So if the scholars who appear in the Talmud had believed in Jesus and his religion, how is it that they did not act as Fra Paulo has acted, who understands their words better than they themselves did?"

Fra Paulo replied: "These statements of yours are lengthy pronouncements designed to make the debate fruitless. But at any rate you will hear what I have to say; and I say to those who are here that of a surety I have complete and clear evidence that there is absolutely nothing in the statements which this man makes. Indeed the attention I pay to them is given solely because such is the wish of our lord the king."

Fra Paulo then began: "This is what we have in scripture, in Genesis 49.10: The sceptre shall not depart from Judah . . . until Shiloh come. It is the Messiah who is here meant, and the prophet asserts that Judah will always possess power until the Messiah who proceeds from him shall come. That being so, today when you Jews have no longer any sceptre or ruler's staff [or lawgiver], it follows that the Messiah who is of the seed of Judah and whose is the rulership, has already come."

My answer to him was: "The prophet's intention was not to declare that the government of Judah should not at all be suspended at any time but he states that it shall not depart or cease entirely from Judah. For his view was that whenever sovereign power should fall to the lot of Israelites it was appropriate that it should reside in Judah. And if their kingdom should be interrupted because of sin, to Judah it would return. But the proof of my words is that already for a long time before Jesus lived the kingdom had lapsed from Judah, though not from Israel, and for long had lapsed both from Israel and from Judah.

"For you must note that during the seventy years of the captivity in Babylon there was no kingdom at all either in Judah or Israel. At the time of the second temple there was no king of Judah—only Zerubbabel and his sons were governors for a short period. And so thereafter for three hundred and eighty years the position remained unchanged until the laying waste of the Temple when the Hasmonean priestly dynasty with their satellites became kings. And so much the more now when the people are in exile does the principle apply that if there be no people there can be no king."

Fra Paulo then said: "Although throughout all those times the Jews had no kings, they nevertheless possessed ruling powers. For the explanation in the Talmud of the words, "the sceptre shall not depart from Judah" is that this refers to the chiefs of the exile in Babylon who ruled the people with the sceptre. Further it is there explained that the ruler's staff [or Lawgiver] from between his feet refers to the descendants of Hillel who were public teachers of the Law [cf. Sanh. 5a].

"But at the present time you Jews have no longer the ordination of scholars [cf. Sanh. 14a] which was known to the Talmud. So even that ruling power has now come to an end. And today there is no one among you fit to be called *Rabbi*. And whatever you yourself may be called nowadays, to designate you as *Master* [lit. Maestro-teacher] is misleading and it is dishonest of you to make use of that title."

To this I replied with some irony: "This point which you have just raised does not belong to the question we are debating. But even so you are not speaking the truth. For it is not *Rabbi* but *Rab* which is the equivalent of *Master* [Maestro] and in the Talmud the title *Rab* is bestowed without ordination having taken place. But I confess I am neither a master nor a good pupil."

This last remark I made by way of correcting him, then, returning to the subject of discussion, observed: "Were it not that you have no understanding of Law and the legal decisions that have been deduced from it [viz. Halakah] but are only versed a little in the homiletic exegesis of scripture [Haggadah, or Agada] with which you have made yourself acquainted, I might convince you that our teachers of blessed memory had no intention of expounding the verse Genesis 49:10 in any other way than as referring to kingdom properly so called.

"And this view which the scholars have recorded is to the following effect, namely: The Law in its strict interpretation lays down that no man can hold court as a single judge [Avot. 4:8] and exempt anyone from the payment of a penalty unless authority to do so be received from the prince who is the factual king.

"Further, they stated that at the time of the captivity, whenever anyone of royal blood appeared to whom some rulership might be committed by the Gentile monarchs, as was the case with the Chiefs of the exile in Babylon and princes in Palestine, there was a [special] bestowal of authority together with ordination. And this was the customary procedure (namely the bestowal of authority through ordination) among the scholars of the Talmud for more than four centuries after the time of Jesus.

"For it was not the opinion of the scholars who appear in the Talmud that there must [always] be one of Judah's lineage [exercising ruling power] —a sceptre and ruler's staff [or Lawgiver] which is Judah's—but on the other hand the prophet who speaks in Genesis 49 did make the promise to Judah that the kingdom of Israel will be his and that promise was made in regard to real kingdom.

"But nevertheless that sovereignty has been suspended for a long time now as I have remarked. For during the period of the Babylonian captivity there was no sceptre or ruler's staff at all in Judah's hands. When the kingdom in the time of the Second Temple fell to the lot of the priests and their officials, no rulership pertained to the tribe of Judah. There was then no chief of the exile, no prince. For the offices of prince and chief belonged to the priest-kings, to their administrators of Justice, to their officers and to whomsoever they deemed proper." . . .

Here Fra Paulo again took up the debate and claimed that in the Talmud it was stated that the Messiah had already come. He brought forward that Haggadic story contained in the Midrash [i.e., commentary] to the Book of Lamentations, about the man who was ploughing when his cow began lowing. An Arab was passing by and said to the man: "O Jew, O Jew, untie your cow, untie your plough, untie your coulter, for the Temple has been destroyed." The man untied his cow, his plough and his coulter. The cow lowed a second time. The Arab said to the man: "Tie your cow, tie your plough, tie your coulter, for your Messiah has been born."

To this I answered: "I do not give any credence at all to this Haggadah but it provides proof of my argument."

At this the fellow shouted: "See how the writings of his fellow-Jews are denied by him!"

I replied: "I certainly do not believe that the Messiah was born on the day of the destruction of the Temple and as for his Haggadah, either it is not true or it has another interpretation of the sort called the mystical explanations of the wise. But I shall accept the story's plain literal statement, which you have put forward, since it furnished me with support.

"Observe then that the story says that at the time of the destruction of the Temple, after it had been destroyed, on that very day, the Messiah was born. If this be so, then Jesus is not the Messiah as you affirm that he is. For he was born and was put to death before the destruction of the Temple took place, his birth being nearly two hundred years before that event according to the true chronology and seventy-three years previous to that event according to your reckonings." At these words of mine my opponent was reduced to silence.

Master Gilles, who was the king's justiciary, then replied to me with the remark: "At the present moment we are not discussing about Jesus, but the question rather is: whether the Messiah has come or not? You say that he has not come, but this Jewish book says that he has come."

To this I said: "You are, as is the practice of those of your profession, taking refuge in a subtlety of retort and argument. But nevertheless I shall answer you on this point. The scholars have not stated that the Messiah has come, but they have said that he has been born. For, for example, on the day when Moses our teacher, on whom be blessing, was born he had not come, nor was he a redeemer, but when he came to Pharaoh by the commandment of the Holy One and said to Pharaoh [Exod. 8:1]. Thus saith the Lord, 'Let my people go,' then he had come.

"And likewise the Messiah when he shall come to the Pope and shall say to him by the commandment of God: 'Let my people go', then he shall have come. But until that day comes, he shall not have come, nor [till then] will there be any Messiah at all. For David the king, on the day when he was born, was not a king nor was he a Messiah, but when Samuel anointed him he was a Messiah. And when Elijah shall anoint one to be a Messiah by the commandment of the deity he [the anointed one] shall be called Messiah and when, afterwards, the Messiah shall come to the Pope to redeem us, then it shall be announced that a redeemer has come."

Hereupon my opponent Fra Paulo urged that the biblical section Isaiah 52:13 beginning with the words "Behold, my servant shall deal wisely" treats of the subject of the death of the Messiah, of his coming into the power of his enemies and that they set him among the wicked as happened also in the case of Jesus. "You do believe," asked Fra Paulo, " that this section is speaking of the Messiah?"

I answered him: "According to the real meaning of the passage the section speaks only of the community of Israel the people. For thus the prophets address them constantly, as in Isaiah 41:8: 'Thou Israel my servant', and as in Isaiah 44:1: 'O Jacob my servant.' "

Fra Paulo then rejoined: "But I can shew you from the statements of the scholars that in their view the biblical section is speaking of the Messiah."

I replied to this as follows: "It is true that our teachers, of blessed memory, in the Haggadic books do interpret the servant, in the biblical section referred to, as indicating the Messiah. But they never assert that he was slain by his enemies. For you will never find in any of the writings of the Israelite people, neither in the Talmud nor in the Haggadic works, that the Messiah the son of David will be slain or that he will ever be delivered into the hands of his foes or buried among them that are wicked. Moreover, even the Messiah whom you have constituted for yourselves was not buried. But I shall give you, if you wish, a sound and clear exposition of the section in question and you will see that there is nothing in it at all about the servant being slain as was the case with your Messiah."

But they did not wish to listen.

My opponent, Fra Paulo, returned again to the point discussed, with the assertion that in the Talmud it was distinctly stated that Rabbi Jehoshua ben Levi had asked Elijah when the Messiah would come and Elijah had given him the reply: "Ask the Messiah himself [cf. Sanh. 98a]." Jehoshua then asked: "And where is he?" Elijah said: "At the gates of Rome among the sick." Jehoshua went there and found him and put a question to him, etc.

"Now," said Fra Paulo, "if what the Talmud here says be so, then the Messiah has already come and has been in Rome—but it was Jesus who was the ruler in Rome."

I said to him in reply to this: "And is it not plain from this very passage you cite that the Messiah has not come? For you will observe that Jehoshua asked Elijah when the Messiah would come. Likewise also the latter himself was asked by Jehoshua: when will the Master come? Thus he had not yet come. Yet, according to the literal sense of these Haggadic narratives, the Messiah has been born; but such is not my own belief."

At this point our lord the king interposed with the question that if the Messiah had been born on the day of the destruction of the Temple, which was more than a thousand years ago, and had not yet come, how could he come now, seeing that it was not in the nature of man to live a thousand years?

My answer to him was: "Already the conditions of discussion have been laid down which preclude me from disputing with you and you from interposing in this debate—but among those who have been in former times, Adam and Methuselah were well nigh a thousand years old, and Elijah and Enoch more than this since these are they who [yet] are alive with God."

"The king then put the question: "Where then is the Messiah at present?" To this I replied: "That question does not serve the purpose of this discussion and I shall not give an answer to it but perchance you will find him, whom you ask about, at the gates of Toledo if you send thither one of your couriers."

This last remark I made to the king in irony. The assembly then stood adjourned, the king appointing the time for the resumption of the debate to be the day after next.

On the day appointed, the king came to a convent that was within the city bounds, where was assembled all the male population, both Gentiles and Jews. There were present the bishop, all the priests, the scholars of the Minorites [i.e., the Franciscans] and the Preaching Friars [i.e., the Dominicans]. Fra Paulo, my opponent, stood up to speak, when I, intervening, requested our lord the king that I should now be heard. The king replied that Fra Paulo should speak first because he was the petitioner. But I urged that I should now be allowed to express my opinion on the subject of the Messiah and then afterwards he, Fra Paulo, could reply on the question of accuracy.

I then rose and calling upon all the people to attend said: "Fra Paulo has asked me if the Messiah of whom the prophets have spoken has already come and I have asserted that he has not come. Also a Haggadic work, in which someone states that on the very day on which the Temple was destroyed the Messiah was born, was brought by Fra Paulo as evidence on his behalf. I then stated that I gave no credence to this pronouncement of the Haggadah but that it lent support to my contention. And now I am going to explain to you why I said that I do not believe it.

"I would have you know that we Jews have three kinds of writings— first, the Bible in which we all believe with perfect faith. The second kind is that which is called Talmud which provides a commentary to the commandments of the Law, for in the Law there are six hundred and thirteen commandments and there is not a single one of them which is not expounded in the Talmud and we believe in it in regard to the exposition of the commandments.

"Further, there is a third kind of writing, which we have, called Midrash, that is to say sermonic literature of the sort that would be produced if the bishop here should stand up and deliver a sermon which someone in the audience who liked it should write down. To a document of this sort, should any of us extend belief, then well and good, but if he refuses to do so no one will do him any harm. For we have scholars who in their writings say that the Messiah will not be born until the approach of the end-time when he will come to deliver us from exile. For this reason I do not believe in this book (which Fra Paulo cites) when it makes the assertion that the Messiah was born on the day of the destruction of the temple. . . ."

My opponent now stood up and said: "I shall bring further evidence that the Messianic age has already been."

But I craved my lord the king to be allowed to speak a little longer and spoke as follows: "Religion, truth and justice, which for us Jews is the substance of religion, does not depend upon a Messiah. For you, our lord the king, are, in my view, more profitable than a Messiah. You are a king and he is a king, you a Gentile, and he (to be) king of Israel—for a Messiah is but a human monarch as you are.

"And when I, in exile and in affliction and servitude, under the reproach of the peoples who reproach us continually, can yet worship my Creator with your permission, my gain is great. For now I make of my body a whole burnt offering to God and thus become more and more worthy of the life of the world to come.

"But when there shall be a king of Israel of my own religion ruling over all peoples, then I would be forced to abide in the law of the Jews, and my gain would not be so much increased. But the core of the contention and the disagreement between Jews and Christians lies in what you Christians assert in regard to the chief topic of faith, namely the deity, for here you make an assertion that is exceedingly distasteful.

"And you, our lord the king, are a Christian born of a Christian and all your days you have listened to priests [and Minorites and Preaching Friars talking of the nativity of Jesus] and they have filled your brain and the marrow of your bones with this doctrine and I would set you free again from that realm of habit and custom.

"Of a certainty the doctrine which you believe and which is a dogma of your faith cannot be accepted by reason. Nature does not admit of it. The prophets have never said anything that would support it. Also the miracle itself cannot be made intelligible by the doctrine in question as I shall make clear with ample proofs at the proper time and place.

"That the Creator of heaven and earth and all that is in them should withdraw into and pass through the womb of a certain Jewess and should grow there for seven months and be born a small child and after this grow up to be handed over to his enemies who condemn him to death and kill him, after which, you say, he came to life and returned to his former abode—neither the mind of Jew nor of any man will sustain this.

"Hence, vain and fruitless is your arguing with us, for here lies the root of our disagreement. However, as it is your wish, let us further discuss the question of the Messiah."

Fra Paulo then said to me: "Then you do believe that the Messiah has come?"

I replied: "No, but I believe and am convinced that he has not come and there never has been anyone who has said concerning himself that he was Messiah—nor will there ever be such who will say so [concerning themselves]—except Jesus. And it is impossible for me to believe in the Messiahship of Jesus, because the prophet says of the Messiah [Ps. 72.8] that 'he shall have dominion from sea to sea and from the River until the ends of the earth.'

"Jesus, on the other hand, never had dominion, but in his lifetime he was pursued by his enemies and hid himself from them, falling finally into their power whence he was not able to liberate himself. How then could he save all Israel? Moreover, after his death dominion was not his. For in regard to the Empire of Rome, he had no part in the growth of that. Since, before men believed in him the city of Rome ruled over most of the world and after faith in him had spread, Rome lost many lands over which it once held sovereign power.

"And now the followers of Muhammad possess a larger empire than

Rome has. In like manner the prophet Jeremiah [31.34] says that in the Messianic age 'they shall teach no more every man his neighbour, and every man his brother, saying, Know the Lord: for they shall all know me,' while in Isaiah [11.9] it is written, that 'the earth shall be full of the knowledge of the Lord, as the waters cover the sea'. Moreover the latter prophet states [2.4] that, in this time, 'they shall beat their swords into ploughshares . . . nation shall not lift up sword against nation, neither shall they learn war any more.'

"But since the days of Jesus up to the present the whole world has been full of violence and rapine, the Christians more than other peoples being shedders of blood and revealers likewise of indecencies. And how hard it would be for you, my lord the king, and for those knights of yours, if they should learn war no more! And yet another oracle of the prophet Isaiah [11:4] is to this effect: 'He shall smite the earth with the rod of his mouth.'

"In the Haggadic work in the hands of Fra Paulo this verse receives the following commentary: 'It was reported to the king Messiah that a certain province had rebelled against him. The king Messiah commanded the locusts to come and destroy the province. He was told that such and such an eparchy had rebelled against him. He commanded a swarm of insects to come and consume it.'

"But it was not thus in the case of Jesus. And you his servants deem to be better for your purposes horses that are clad in armor; and some-times even all this proves to be of no avail for you. But I would yet submit for your attention many other arguments drawn from what the prophets have said."

At this juncture my opponent called out: "Such is always his method—to make a long speech when I have a question to put to him."

The king thereupon told me to cease speaking on the ground that he, Fra Paulo, was asking a question. So I was silent.

Fra Paulo said: "The Jewish scholars say of the Messiah that he is to be more honored than the angels. This cannot apply to any but Jesus who in his one person was both the Messiah and God." Then he adduced the Haggadic interpretation of the words "my servant shall be exalted and lifted up and shall be very high" [Isa. 52:13], namely, that the Messiah is exalted above Abraham, lifted up above Moses and higher than the ministering angels.

My answer to him on this point was: "Our scholars constantly speak in this manner of all the eminently righteous, saying that they are more righteous than the ministering angels. Our teacher Moses said to an angel: 'In the place where I have my dwelling, you have not authority to stand.' And, in general, Israel avers that Israel is more beloved of God than are the angelic ministrants. But what the author of this Haggadic passage on the Messiah proposes to say is that Abraham, our father, on whom be blessing, wrought the conversion of Gentiles, explained to the peoples his faith in the Holy One, and in debate opposed Nimrod without fear.

"Yet, Moses did more than he. For Moses in his meekness stood before the great and wicked king Pharaoh and did not spare him in the mighty plagues with which he smote him, and brought Israel out beyond the range of Pharaoh's power. But exceedingly zealous were the ministering angels in the task of redemption. As is written in the Book of Daniel [10:21]: 'And, now will I return to fight with the prince of Persia.'

"Yet more than these all will the Messiah do. For his courage will be high in the performance of the purposes of the Lord. For he will come and command the Pope and all the kings of the nations in the name of God, saying: 'Let my people go that they may serve me.' And he will do among them many mighty signs and wonders and in no wise will he be afraid of them. He will make his abode in their city of Rome until he has destroyed it." Having spoken thus, I said to Fra Paulo that I would give an exposition of the whole of the Haggadic passage if he cared to have it; but he did not so desire.

Fra Paulo now submitted another Haggadic passage where it is said about the Messiah that he prays for Israel that the Holy One may pardon their iniquities and undertakes to endure sufferings in behalf of others. In his prayer he says to God: "I undertake to endure sufferings on condition that the resurrection of the dead be in my days, and I undertake this not only on account of the dead of my generation but for all the dead who have died from the days of the first men up to the present, and not only those who died [and whom the earth received] but even those who were cast into the sea and drowned or who were devoured by wolves and wild beasts."

"Now," claimed Fra Paulo, "the suffering which the Messiah took upon himself to endure refers to the death of Jesus which Jesus willingly bore."

To that argument I replied: "Woe be to him who is shameless! All that is spoken of in the prayer of the Messiah was not performed by Jesus. Jesus has not raised to life those who have died from the time of Adam up till now, nor has he done anything at all of this sort. Furthermore that a prayer is spoken of in the passage shews that he, the Messiah, is human and not divine and that he has not power to raise from the dead. Moreover those so-named sufferings of the Messiah signify nothing other than the grief he endures because his advent is exceeding long delayed and he sees his people in exile and he has not power [to deliver them]. Also he beholds brought to honour above his own people them that worship that which is not God and who have denied him and make for themselves a Messiah other than himself." . . .

My opponent Fra Paulo again took up the discussion with the statement: "Jewish scholars have asserted that the Messiah has entered into the Garden of Eden, and there in the Haggadah the Messiah explains why, namely because he saw his fathers engaged in idolatry and dissociating himself from their practices he worshipped the Holy One, Blessed be He, who hid him in the Garden of Eden."

I laughed at him and said: "This that you have quoted is for me an argument that the Messiah is a descendant of idolaters and entirely human and when he had dissociated himself from the practices of his fathers and did not worship idolatrously as they had done, the Holy One reckoned this to him as merit. But would this [that is here said about the Messiah] be said about absolute Deity?"

Then I took up the book which Fra Paulo had with him and read out to those present the Haggadah passage from its beginning. The passage says that there have been fourteen persons who have entered the Garden of Eden without first having died and it numbers among these Serah the daughter of Asher and Bithiah the daughter of Pharaoh. "Now," I said, "had the Messiah of this passage been Jesus, and he the Deity as you think he was, then he would not have been the companion of women in the Garden of Eden for assuredly God's throne is in heaven and the earth is His footstool. God forbid that what you suppose should be true! But what I have stated is that the Messiah has his abode in the Garden of Eden which was the place where the first man dwelt before he sinned. For this is the view of the scholars in the Haggadic books as has been explained."

Then our lord the king rose and the assembly dispersed.

Our lord the king had arranged that on the next Thursday the debate should be held in his palace and had commanded that it be in private. So we had our session in the fore-hall of the palace, Fra Paulo beginning with an airy speech in which there was no substance at all.

After this he declared: "I bring the testimony of a great Jewish scholar named Master Moses of Egypt [i.e. Moses Maimonides, 1135–1204] the like of whom has not been in Jewry for the last four hundred years. This scholar says that the Messiah will die and his son and son's son rule in succession. Thus he does not say, as you have said, that the Messiah is not mortal like other men are." Then Fra Paulo asked for the Book of Judges to be brought to him.

Whereupon I said to my audience: "In that book there appears nothing of that sort but I admit that some of our scholars think as has been described. As I mentioned at the beginning, the view of Haggadic authors is that the Messiah was born on the day of the destruction of the Temple and lives for ever, while the view of those who study the literal sense of scripture is that the Messiah will be born when the end-time, the period of redemption, is at hand, and will live for many years and will die in honour bequeathing his crown to his son. And I have already stated that this latter is the opinion I hold. 'For between this world and the days of the Messiah there is no difference except the delivery from servitude to the secular government [cf. R. Samuel in Sanh. 99a].' "

The book which Fra Paulo had asked for was now brought, and he sought for what he wanted in it and could not find it. So I received the book from his hands, and, calling for attention to the statements of the work which he had introduced into the discussion, read aloud from the beginning of the chapter where it is said that the king Messiah is in the future to be designated for Israel and that he will build the Temple and gather together Israel's dispersed.

At these words of Maimonides, Fra Arnol of Segura exclaimed: "He is speaking lies." To which I replied: "Up till now he has been a 'great scholar' that has 'none like him' and now he is a liar!"

But the king rebuked Fra Arnol, observing that it was not seemly to offer insults to the learned.

Addressing my remarks to the king I now continued: "The author of this book is not speaking falsehood, for I could prove from the Law and the prophets that what he says is true. For upon the Messiah rests the duty of gathering the dispersed of Israel, the scattered ones of Judah, the whole twelve tribes. But your Messiah Jesus did not gather a single individual of them, nor was he living at the time of the Exile.

"Further, to the Messiah belongs the task of building the Sanctuary in Jerusalem. But Jesus had nothing to do with that, neither with building it nor with its destruction. Also the Messiah will rule over all peoples. But Jesus did not rule even over himself."

Then I read to all present the Scripture portion [Deut. 30:1 f.]: "And it shall come to pass when all these things are come upon thee, the blessing and the curse which I have set before thee etc. etc., the Lord thy God will put these curses upon thine enemies and on them that hate thee, which persecuted thee."

I explained to them that in this portion the words "thine enemies" referred to the Christians and "them that hate thee" to the Moslems, the two peoples who have persecuted us. No reply was given to this and the assembly rose.

On the morrow on the Friday they marshalled their array in the palace, the king sitting as usual on his chair by the place where was situated the recess with his throne, and with him were the bishop and many nobles . . . numerous knights, all the people of the suburbs as well as of the poorer folk.

Addressing the king I told him that I did not wish to continue the debate and he enquired my reason for this. I said: "There is a large body of people here who have all sought to bring pressure upon me and to make me amenable to taking this step, for they are very apprehensive of those persons, the preaching friars, who are casting the world into a panic. Moreover, the highest and most honoured of the priesthood have sent to me to say that I should proceed no further in this discussion.

"Also, many knights of your own household, my lord the king, have informed me that I am doing an evil deed in speaking in their presence contrary to their faith. Likewise Fra Peire of Genoa, the Minorite scholar, has told me that this is not proper. Besides people from the suburbs have said to certain of the Jewish community that I should desist."

Indeed such was the case. But when those concerned saw what was the kings's wish in the matter, with hesitation they all urged that I should continue. So after much talk between us on the matter I at length said that I would debate on the condition that the court would allow me a day for putting questions, when Fra Paulo would answer me, since for three days he had been the questioner and I had answered. The king [consenting] said: "At any rate answer him [now]." So I thanked him.

Fra Paulo then stood up and put the question: "The Messiah of whom the prophets spoke, do you believe that he was to be both completely man and very God?"

I replied: "From the beginning of this debate we agreed that we should first discuss whether the Messiah had come, as you Christians say he has, and then afterwards address ourselves to the question of whether he was absolute Deity. But you have not proven that he has come; because I have dissolved all the flimsy arguments which you brought. And thus far I have won my case, for the onus has been upon you to bring proof, for so you took upon yourselves to do. Yet, if you will not acknowledge that I have won this case, I take it upon myself to bring valid arguments on the subject under dispute if you will listen to me. But it having been made clear that your Jesus was not the Messiah, it is not for you to argue in regard to the Messiah who in future is going to come to us as to whether he will be a real man or what he will be." The learned lawyers who were present confirmed that the right lay with me on this point. The king, however, said that in any case I should answer the question that had been asked.

I therefore answered thus: "Surely when the Messiah shall come he shall be truly man, born, as I am, of a man and woman who had been married. And he will be of the line and seed of David, as is written in Isaiah 11:1: 'And there shall come forth a shoot out of the stock of Jesse' and as is said in Genesis 49:10: 'Until Shiloh come'—Shiloh here meaning *his son* and deriving from the word *shilyah* which signifies *afterbirth*. For the Messiah is to be born as are all members of the human race in connection with the *afterbirth* [that is with the membrane enveloping the foetus in the womb]. And were it the Spirit of God [through whom] as you say [the Messiah should be conceived] then he would not be of the stock of Jesse, even had the Spirit lodged in the womb of a woman who was of Jesse's seed. Nor in such case would he be the heir to David's kingdom, for by the Law the daughters and their progeny do not inherit so long as direct male issue exists. And in regard to David, in all ages there have been male children of his line." . . .

This is a full account of the discussions. To my knowledge I have made no alteration in the recording of them. Afterwards on the same day (as the discussion in the palace ended) I had audience of the king who remarked: "The debate still remains to be concluded. For I have never seen anyone who was in the wrong argue so well as you have." Then I heard in the palace court that it was the will of the king and of the Preaching Friars [the Dominicans] to visit the synagogue on the Sabbath. So I tarried in the city for eight days.

When they came to the synagogue on the following Sabbath I addressed our lord the king in words that were worthy of the occasion and of his office. When he expounded earnestly to the effect that Jesus was the Messiah, I rose up and said: "The words of our lord the king in my eyes are noble words, exalted and to be held in honour since they proceed from the mouth of a nobleman highly esteemed and honoured, and like of whom is not in our time, but I do not appraise them as the truth in as much as I have proofs and arguments clear as sunlight that the truth does not correspond with his words.

"Though it be not seemly to have controversy with the king, one thing I would like to say, namely that I am very astonished at him, for the arguments we have heard from his persuading us to believe in Jesus that he is the Messiah, Jesus himself employed to persuade our fathers, and himself endeavored to propound this doctrine to them. And to his face they refuted it with a complete and valid refutation.

"Now, since in your opinion Jesus was divine, he was better equipped with knowledge and ability to establish his own claims than is the king, and if our fathers who saw him and were acquainted with him did not listen to him, how then shall we believe and listen to the king who has no knowledge of him in actual experience but only through a remote report which he has heard from men who did not know Jesus and were not Jesus' countrymen as were our fathers who knew him and were witnesses [that they had seen one who was human as they were]."

After I had spoken thus Fra Raymond of Peñaforte rose up and gave a discourse on the subject of the Trinity and asserted that the Trinity was wisdom and will and power. "And had not also the Master," he said, "in a synagogue in Gerona assented to what Fra Paulo had said on this point?"

At this I got to my feet and spoke as follows: "I ask both Jews and Gentiles to give me their attention on this matter. When Fra Paulo asked me in Gerona if I believed in the Trinity, I replied: 'What is the Trinity? Do you mean that three material bodies, of the sort that men have, constitute the Godhead?' He said: 'No.' Then I asked: 'Do you mean that the Trinity consists of three subtle substances such as souls or that it is three angels?' He said: 'No.' 'Or do you mean,' I enquired, 'that the Trinity is one substance which is a compound of three substances such as are those bodies which are compounded of the four elements?' He said: 'No.' 'If that is the case,' said I, 'then what is the Trinity?' He answered: 'Wisdom and will and power.' To which I replied that I acknowledged that the Deity was wise and not foolish, and will without passibility, and powerful and not weak, but that the expression Trinity was entirely misleading. For wisdom in the Creator is not an unessential quality but He and His wisdom are one and He and His will are one and He and His power are one—and, if this be so, the wisdom and the will and the power are one whole. And even if these were unessential qualities of God, the thing which is the Godhead is not three but is one, bearing three unessential qualities." . . .

Then Fra Paulo stood up and said that he believed in the perfect unity of the Deity but that nevertheless there was in that unity a Trinity, and this was a doctrine very profound for neither the angels nor the princes of the upper regions could comprehend it.

My answer to this was: "It is clear that no person believes what he does not know. Hence it is that the angels do not believe in a Trinity." The associates of Fra Paulo made him remain silent. Our lord the king rose up and he and those with him descended from the place where the prayer-desk was, each going their several ways.

On the morrow I had audience of our lord the king whose words to me were: 'Return to your city in safety and in peace." Then he gave me three hundred dinars and I took my leave of him with much affection. May God make him worthy of the life of the world to come. Amen.

Berechiah ha-Nakdan — Fox Fables

Fables—generally considered to be the domain of Aesop, La Fontaine, and Krylov—have also played a role in the Hebrew literary tradition. Jotham's parable of the trees who seek a king (Judges 9:8–16) is a striking example of an ancient Hebrew fable. The prophet Nathan admonishes David with the fable of a rich man who takes a poor man's only lamb (II Samuel 12:1–12:15). King Solomon knew three thousand fables (I Kings 5:12–5:13), none of which the Bible cites. Rabbi Johanan ben Zakkai, the Talmudic sage responsible for the spiritual recovery of Israel after the destruction of the First Temple in 70 C.E., included fox fables and washers' proverbs among his studies *(Baba Batra* 134a), and stated that Rabbi Meir knew three hundred fox fables. Examples of such fables abound in the Talmud.

By the twelfth century, Jewish contact with various cultures was widespread. Jews were active in translating to and from Arabic, Latin and Hebrew, and stories of diverse origin had found their way into Hebrew secular writing. Berechiah ha-Nakdan (*c.* 1300) is a microcosm of this literary ferment and literary cross-fertilization: he lived in England, France and Provence; knew French, Latin and probably English (he anticipates the Clown in *Hamlet* by saying of the English, "In the island of the sea is a congregation bereft of wit."); and produced a Hebrew imitation of Adelhard of Bath's Latin philosophic treatise *Quaestiones Naturales*.

Berechiah, a scribe who punctuated the Bible, was the finest Hebrew fabulist of the Middle Ages, and one of the leading fabulists in Europe. In his collection of 119 fables appear a Noah's Ark of creatures, from the insect to the leviathan, as well as a score of humans, and lesser, inanimate vessels. Some of the fables are original; some stem from the Talmud and the Midrash, but most are probably adapted from Aesop and the twelfth-century fabulist, Marie de France, and are provided with a moral wherein the author satirizes various human failings.

For the English reader, neither the stories, the characters, nor the social satire appear to be particularly Jewish, nor is there any trace of religious didacticism in the book. Actually, the Jewishness of these fables lies in Berechiah's Hebrew, replete with skilfully used Biblical and Talmudic quotations. Berechiah's audience, thoroughly familiar with the Jewish classics, was no doubt delighted by the comic effect and surprise of a Talmudic phrase uttered by a bear or a moralizing cat quoting Isaiah: "Woe unto them that rise early in the morning to pursue strong drink." Only the story remains for the modern reader; the English cannot reproduce either the subtle, multidirectional glances of the allusions, nor the medieval reader's world view and his literary sensibility.

Berechiah's charming rhymed prose—rhythmic but not metrical—would in translation bring forth only monotonous doggerel; hence the prose translation. Although the fox does not play a role in each fable, the author titled his work *Fox Fables* because this is the phrase that the Talmud used as a generic title for all fables.

FOX FABLES

FOX & FISHES

MANY GIVE COUNSEL IN THEIR OWN BEHALF,
TO DRAW OTHERS UP BY THEIR HOOK

A fox walking by a river bank saw one fish hastening to escape while another fish pursued him. Overtaking him, the second fish attacked him with animosity, and the two fought, with none to deliver between them, each charging angrily against the other. The fox said not a word, but approached the water in the hope that he could sink his teeth into them or trap them by the snare of his cunning. But the waters proved a barrier to his lust, so he turned thence to another spot, where he addressed them with no hesitation. When he saw the fish fighting, the great oppressing the small, the gentry snapping at the lowly, and the war between them growing heated, he called out to them:

"Are all of you such fools that quiet is impossible? Is this the covenant among you and the sole statute of your congregation: that each destroy his neighbor, that the larger swallow his companion which is smaller and hew him asunder on the slightest provocation? If all the fish of the sea would assemble and say to me 'Rule over us,' I would not forsake my resolve, for all the day they are in terror and confusion; each fights his brother, every man his neighbor. Perverse is the path before them with their bow-strings drawn and weapons whetted, and on this path they wander astray, knowing naught of the path of peace. Hear now the logic of my discourse; incline your ears and come unto me. Depart from thence and come hither. In joy shall you go forth and in peace, if you hearken to my counsel, and ye shall bless me also. Depart from the sea to dry land, and together we shall inherit the earth. Then shall your tranquillity be increased, and nation shall not lift sword against nation, for none shall cause a breach. Serene and untroubled shall all the world abide, and the joy of wild asses shall be ours. Hearts that are troubled shall be refreshed, and all the inhabitants of earth shall shout for gladness upon their couches of ease, by day and by night without surcease. None shall do evil, none destroy."

But one of the fish replied: "If thou wilt verily rule over us, wilt thou indeed ordain peace for us? Even when we abide in quiet waters, surrounded by our kin and in peace, the robber assails us, the destroyer rises against us, and we live in terror of men's snares. Many fishermen fish for us, many hunters hunt us; we all roar like bears. If you had experience of our plight, your anguish would equal ours. If now by thy cunning thou devourest spoil, when thou hast done spoiling thou shalt thyself be spoiled, for suddenly thy creditors shall rise up against thee and thy ways will not prosper. How dost thou spread a web of deceit against us and count thyself secure in a land of peace? Surely the fowl of the heavens and the fish of the sea and the beasts of the field all are ambushed and hunted, and even humans quarrel for the envy that is between them. But there be higher than they, and He that is higher than the highest regardeth."

This proverb counsels vigilance against those who advise for their own advantage. Beware of their seduction, for by earth's transgression flatterers have multiplied, and the face of this generation is as the face of a dog. Every men must be aware of him that would destroy; but the wise man hath his eyes in his head.

And I plied my poesy:

The face of this generation is the face of a dog;
They speak with two hearts.
Their words are like butter, their thoughts tallow.
They press the breasts for pleasure,
As a nursling drawing milk.
Spies are they, but there is no Joshua nor Caleb among them.

CROW & FOX

GREAT IS THE POWER OF PRIDE
EVEN SURPASSING GREED

A crow mounted a fig tree, carrying a cheese in his mouth. Under the tree stood a fox, devising and scheming how he might bring the cheese down to earth. He called to the crow: "Stately, handsome, and sweet bird, good and agreeable and lovely, happy is he who is paired with thee. If all the beauties were at thy side their comeliness would not equal thine. If thou shouldst essay to sing songs thou wouldst surpass all birds in music and wouldst be sole perfection, for no flaw is to be found in thee. See whether thy voice matches thy stature and the majesty of thy plumage, for thou art free of fault." The crow said to himself: "I shall let him hear my voice, and he shall heap praise upon praise." So he opened his mouth to raise his voice, whereupon the cheese immediately fell and landed near the head of the fox, who said: "Of the precious things of heaven above this hath come to me from him that raiseth his voice; no longer will I listen to the sound of song." So he went to his own place after he had obtained his desire of the crow.

This parable is for the proud and haughty and for the flatterers and falsifiers who deceive them with their lies and honeyed words, and extract their wealth which they had secreted in vain and in utter futility. Beware, therefore, of the seducer, and be not swayed by the aspect of his figure and the loftiness of his stature; let him not trap thee with his eyeballs, with his false lips, with his violent hands.

And I plied my poesy and said:

A friend hath fooled me; 'tis easy to befool a fool;
Easier still it is when one makes himself a fool.

OX, LION, RAM

WHO HATH A LURKING ENEMY SHALL
TREMBLE MORNING AND EVENING

An ox saw a lion and ran away, for the lion roared and bellowed and trumpeted after him, and he hid him in a certain pit beneath thick flaxen cordage, where a ram was hidden. His heart's terror made him tremble in fear of the ram. Said the ram to him: "Why art afraid? Surely thou and I belonged to the same herd." The ox answered: "Every animal I see alive is in my eyes a mighty lion. If I had found thee alone I had not feared thee, but now because of the lion I am confounded and atremble."

The parable is for a man that has an enemy whom he fears always, morning and evening, walking and sitting, rising and lying down. Every man he imagines is his enemy, and says, "Now shall I be pursued"; but it is the sound of a driven leaf that pursues him.

WOLF & CATTLE

WHOSE FEET ARE ACCUSTOMED TO ROBBERY'S PATH,
HIS EYE WILL NOT SPARE ANOTHER'S WEALTH

A wolf who was the king's vizier and a chief made it his goal to destroy all flesh. He robbed and ravaged, plundered and uprooted; all that he found he pierced. And the beasts and the fowl and the cattle upon whose families confusion had been visited went to the lion to complain of him. Said the lion: "Evil it is and rebellious if, as ye say, he hath bared his teeth. Hath he indeed destroyed according as the cry that hath come unto me? I shall judge him, so that he will turn his back from destroying, and I shall cast the prey from his teeth."

And he sent word to the wolf: "Come unto me on the morrow. Hearken and obey, delay not." So he came, and the lion addressed him with sternness and said to him: "Wherefore hast thou done so? No more crush the neck of the cattle, nor rend the beasts for prey. Thine own food are such carcasses and mangled bodies of fowl or cattle as thou wilt find dead in the field. But the living thou shalt not lurk after nor hunt down. If thou canst not keep my words, swear to me that thou wilt not eat meat for two full years, to atone for thy sins, which are inscribed and sealed. This is the sentence that I determine for thee." So the wolf swore this matter: that he would not eat flesh for two years from the day he preyed upon any that dwelt among the beasts.

The wolf departed thence and went upon his way, and the lion was left king in his lair. The wolf ate not of any four-legged creature, in keeping with the oath which he sware, unless he found some mangled body or carcass cast out into the field or upon the road.

One day when he was famished he turned this way and that and saw a fat kid, desirable to look upon and good to eat; and he said: "Who can keep the commandment?" Within him his thoughts were at war whether to set his face against the kid, and he said in his heart: "If my lust vanquish me and I again smite a living creature as I have done aforetime, from that day I must count two full years during which I must not eat flesh. This is the thing I sware to the king; but my heart hath devised a way to fulfill mine oath: The days of the year number three hundred and sixty-five; let the opening of my eyes be reckoned a day, and their closing a new night."

And he opened his eyes after that he had shut them tight, and the evening and the morning were the first day. So doing he counted two years, and his iniquity was removed and his sin atoned.

Then his eyes turned to the kid of their choice and looked upon him and pierced him; and he said: "Lo, I have made atonement before my food." So he seized the kid by the neck and cut it up and ate it, as was his wont in the beginning. Still is his arm stretched out against living things, as in days of old and years gone by.

The parable is for a man wont ever to steal and rob, whose eye spares not the wealth of others. Their wealth and their toil he spoils and plunders; and if he swear in the presence of all, his heart will cunningly circumvent his oath and he will account himself innocent of his curse.

Ethical Wills

Whereas a last will and testament commonly refers to financial and material matters, the ethical will—a unique genre in literature—deals with a spiritual and religious heritage that a father leaves his children. Although ethical wills date from about the eleventh century, deathbed statements that are, in effect, spiritual commandments can be traced back to the Biblical period. Jacob's blessing of his sons may be considered an ethical will, as can Joseph's request that his bones be returned to the Land of Israel. Moses and Joshua speak to the people in the same vein, as elder counsellors or fathers of the nation. The Book of Proverbs, Job, and *The Wisdom of Ben Sira,* all contain such fatherly injunctions, as does the entire *Testament of the Twelve Sons.*

Along with the responsa and the chronicles, the ethical wills are the building blocks of historical texts, revealing social and cultural sidelights: folk beliefs, literary taste, and customs. An interesting contrast may be noted in the varying attitudes to secular culture of Sephardic and Ashkenazic scholars. In Spain, owing to the more tolerant attitude and the freer contacts between Muslim and Jew, the Jew participated in a broad spectrum of learning. However, in Ashkenaz (Germany and northern France), the enmity of the Christian world made the Jew insulate himself; only Jewish lore was permitted; everything else (despite the difficulty of absolutely banning all contact) was proscribed.

In addition to being morally binding upon the heirs, the ethical wills are also revealing human documents, highlighting some facets of the author's personality. In the first we see a father struggling with an independent and occasionally stubborn son; in the second, the blending of social conventions and heartfelt piety in a simple Jew; and in the third, the author's partial blindness and his sense of family tradition and history.

Judah ibn Tibbon (1120–c. 1190), born in Spain, was a physician and a famous translator, rendering into Hebrew the Arabic works of Judah Halevi, Bahya ibn Pakuda and others. He addressed his ethical will to his son, Samuel, the translator of Maimonides' *Guide to the Perplexed.* In his will appear not only the usual citations from the Bible and Talmud, but also references to Hebrew poets and Arab philosophers; moreover, he specifically orders his son to study secular and scientific books, which would have been anathema to Ashkenazim.

In contrast to the other writers, Eleazar of Mayence (died 1357) was a simple Jew with no extraordinary pretensions to learning. His will vividly portrays the social and religious attitudes of his time; and his strictures against gambling and mixed bathing and dancing probably indicate the prevalence of these activities.

Judah Asheri (1270–1349), the son of R. Asher ben Yehiel, was born in Germany and succeeded his father as chief rabbi of Toledo, Spain. Like him he was a son of the two worlds of European Jewry, Ashkenaz and Sepharad. Although he lived many years in Spain, his testament is not influenced much by that land's liberal view of secular culture, and there are no allusions to any literature outside the Bible and Talmud. Judah Asheri died in Spain, but counseled his sons to return to Germany.

JUDAH IBN TIBBON

My son, hearken to my precepts, neglect none of my injunctions. Set my Admonition before thine eyes, thus thou shalt prosper thy days in pleasantness! . . .

Thou knowest, my son, how I swaddled thee and brought thee up, how I led thee in the paths of wisdom and virtue. I fed and clothed thee; I spent myself in educating and protecting thee, I sacrificed my sleep to make thee wise beyond thy fellows, and to raise thee to the highest degree of science and morals These twelve years I have denied myself the usual pleasures and relaxations of men for thy sake, and I still toil for thine inheritance.

I have assisted thee by providing an extensive library for thy use and have thus relieved thee of the necessity of borrowing books. Most students must wander about to seek books, often without finding them. But thou, thanks be to God, lendest and borrowest not. Of many books, indeed, thou ownest two or three copies. I have besides procured for thee books on all sciences. Seeing that thy Creator had graced thee with a wise and understanding heart, I journeyed to the ends of the earth and fetched for thee a teacher in secular sciences. I neither heeded the expense nor the danger of the ways. Untold evil might have befallen me and thee on those travels, had not the Lord been with us!

But thou, my son, didst deceive my hopes! Thou didst not choose to employ thine abilities, hiding thyself from all the books, not caring to know them or even their titles. Hadst thou seen thine own books in the hand of others, thou wouldst not have recognized them; hadst thou needed one of them, thou wouldst not have known whether it was with thee or not, without asking me; thou didst not even consult the catalogue of the library.

All this thou hast done. Thus far thou hast relied on me to rouse thee from the sleep of indolence, thinking that I would live with thee for ever! Thou didst not bear in mind that death must divide us, and that there are daily vicissitudes in life. But who will be as tender to thee as I have been, who will take my place—to teach thee out of love and goodwill? Even if thou couldst find such a one, lo! thou seest how the greatest scholars, coming from the corners of the earth, seek to profit by my society and instruction, how eager they are to see me and my books. . . . May thy God endow thee with a new heart and spirit, and instill into thee a desire to retrieve the past, and to follow the true path henceforward!

Thou art still young, and improvement is possible, if Heaven but grant thee a helping gift of desire and resolution, for ability is of no avail without inclination. If the Lord please to bring me back to thee, I will take upon me all thy wants. For whom indeed do I toil but for thee and thy children? May the Lord let me see their faces again in joy!

Therefore, my son! stay not thy hand when I have left thee, but devote thyself to the study of the Torah and to the science of medicine. But chiefly occupy thyself with the Torah, for thou hast a wise and understanding heart, and all that is needful on thy part is ambition and application. I know that thou wilt repent of the past, as many have repented before thee of their youthful indolence. . . . Devote thyself to science and religion; habituate thyself to moral living, for "habit is master over all things." As the Arabian philosopher holds, there are two sciences, ethics and physics. Strive to excel in both!

Contend not with men, and meddle not "with strife not thine own" [Prov. 26:17]. Enter into no dispute with the obstinate, not even on matters of Torah. On thy side, too, refrain from subterfuges in argument to maintain thy case even when thou art convinced that thou art in the right. Submit to the majority and do not reject their decision. Risk not thy life by taking the road and leaving thy city in times of disquiet and danger.

Show respect to thyself, thy household, and thy children, by providing decent clothing, as far as thy means allow; for it is unbecoming for any one, when not at work, to go shabbily dressed. Spare from thy belly and put it on thy back.

And now, my son! if the Creator has mightily displayed His love to thee and me, so that Jew and Gentile have thus far honored thee for my sake, endeavor henceforth so to add to thine honor that they may respect thee for thine own self. This thou canst effect by good morals and by courteous behavior; by steady devotion to thy studies and thy profession, as thou wast wont to do before thy marriage.

My son! Let thy countenance shine upon the sons of men: tend their sick, and may thine advice cure them. Though thou takest fees from the rich, heal the poor gratuitously; the Lord will requite thee. Thereby shalt thou find favor and good understanding in the sight of God and man. Thus wilt thou win the respect of high and low among Jews and non-Jews, and thy good name will go forth far and wide. Thou wilt rejoice thy friends and make thy foes envious.

My son! Examine regularly once a week thy drugs and medicinal herbs, and do not employ an ingredient whose properties are unknown to thee. I have often impressed this on thee in vain when we were together.

My son! If thou writest aught, read it through a second time, for no man can avoid slips. Let not any consideration of hurry prevent thee from revising a short epistle. Be punctilious in regard to grammatical accuracy, in conjugations and genders, for the constant use of the vernacular sometimes leads to error in this matter. A man's mistakes in writing bring him into disrepute; they are remembered against him all his days. Endeavor to cultivate conciseness and elegance, do not attempt to write verse unless thou canst do it perfectly. Avoid heaviness, which spoils a composition, making it disagreeable alike to reader and audience.

See to it that thy penmanship and handwriting are as beautiful as thy style. Keep thy pen in fine working order, use ink of good color. Make thy script as perfect as possible, unless forced to write without proper materials, or in a pressing emergency. The beauty of a composition depends on the writing, and the beauty of the writing, on pen, paper and ink; and all these excellencies are an index to the author's worth. . . .

[In the past] when thou didst write thy letters or compose thine odes to send abroad, thou wast unwilling to show a word to me and didst prevent me from seeing. When I said to thee, "Show me!" thou wouldst answer: "Why dost thou want to see?" as if thinking that my help was unnecessary. And this was from thy folly, in that thou wast wise in thine own eyes.

If, my son, thou desirest to undo the past, the Creator will grant His pardon, and I shall forgive all without reserve or reluctance. Reject not my word in all that I have written for thee in this, my testament, and wherein thou hast not honored me heretofore, honor me for the rest of my days, and after my death! All the honor I ask of thee is to attain a higher degree in the pursuit of wisdom, to excel in right conduct and exemplary character, to behave in friendly spirit to all and to gain a good name, that greatest of crowns, to deserve applause for thy dealing and association with thy fellows, to cleave to the fear of God and the performance of His commandments—thus wilt thou honor me in life and in death!

My son! I command thee to honor thy wife to thine utmost capacity. She is intelligent and modest, a daughter of a distinguished and educated family. She is a good housewife and mother, and no spendthrift. Her tastes are simple, whether in food or dress. Remember her assiduous attendance on thee in thine illness, though she had been brought up in elegance and luxury. Remember how she afterwards reared thy son without man or woman to help her.

If thou wouldst acquire my love, honor her with all thy might; do not exercise too strict an authority over her; our sages have expressly warned men against this. If thou givest orders or reprovest let thy words be gentle. Enough is it if thy displeasure is visible in thy look, let it not be vented in actual rage.

My son! Devote thy mind to thy children as I did to thee; be tender to them as I was tender; instruct them as I instructed thee; keep them as I kept thee, try to teach them Torah as I have tried, and as I did unto thee do thou unto them! Be not indifferent to any slight ailment in them, or in thyself (may God deliver thee and them from all sickness and plague), but if thou dost notice any suspicion of disease in thee or in one of thy limbs, do forthwith what is necessary in the case. As Hippocrates has said: "Time is short, and experiment is dangerous." Therefore be prompt, but apply a sure remedy, avoiding doubtful treatment.

Examine thy Hebrew books at every new moon, the Arabic volumes once in two months, and the bound codices once every quarter. Arrange thy library in fair order, so as to avoid wearying thyself in searching for the book thou needest. Always know the case and chest where the book should be. A good plan would be to set in each compartment a written list of the books therein contained. If, then, thou art looking for a book, thou canst see from the list the exact shelf it occupies without disarranging all the books in the search for one. Examine the loose leaves in the volumes and bundles, and preserve them. These fragments contain very important matters which I have collected and copied out. Do not destroy any writing or letter of all that I have left. And cast thine eye frequently over the catalogue so as to remember what books are in thy library.

Never refuse to lend books to anyone who has not means to purchase books for himself, but only act thus to those who can be trusted to return the volumes. Cover the bookcase with rugs of fine quality; and preserve them from damp and mice, and from all manner of injury, for thy books are thy good treasure. If thou lendest a volume make a note of it before it leaves thy house, and when it is returned, draw thy pen over the entry. Every Passover and Feast of Booths call in all books out on loan.

Make it a fixed rule in thy home to read the Scriptures and to peruse grammatical works on Sabbaths and festivals, also to read Proverbs and the Ben Mishle [aphorisms by Samuel ha-Nagid, 11th century Spanish Hebrew poet]. Also I beg of thee, look at the chapter concerning Jonadab son of Rechab every Sabbath, to instill in thee diligence to fulfill my commands. . . .

May He who gives prudence to the simple, and to young men knowledge and discretion, bestow on thee a willing heart and a listening ear! Then shall our soul be glad in the Lord and rejoice in His salvation!

THE IDEALS OF AN AVERAGE JEW—
TESTAMENT OF ELEAZAR OF MAYENCE

My grandfather's Testament to his children; and as it is a rule good for every God-fearer, I write it here, that all men may follow it.

A worthy Testament, whose ways are ways of pleasantness; proved and seemly for publishing to all the people.

These are the things which my sons and daughters shall do at my request. They shall go to the house of prayer morning and evening, and shall pay special regard to the Tephillah and the Shema. So soon as the service is over, they shall occupy themselves a little with the Torah, the Psalms, or with works of charity. Their business much be conducted honestly in their dealings both with Jew and Gentile.

They must be gentle in their manners, and prompt to accede to every honorable request. They must not talk more than is necessary, by this they will be saved from slander, falsehood, and frivolity. They shall give an exact tithe of all their possessions; they shall never turn away a poor man empty-handed, but must give him what they can, be it much or little. If he beg a lodging over night, and they know him not, let them provide him with the wherewithal to pay an innkeeper. Thus shall they satisfy the needs of the poor in every possible way.

My daughter must obey scrupulously the rules applying to women; modesty, sanctity, reverence, should mark their married lives. They should carefully watch for the signs of the beginning of their periods and keep separate from their husbands at such times. Marital intercourse must be modest and holy, with a spirit of restraint and delicacy, in reverence and silence. They shall be very punctilious and careful with their ritual bathing, taking with them women friends of worthy character. They shall cover their eyes until they reach their home, on returning from the bath, in order not to behold anything of an unclean nature. They must respect their husbands, and must be invariably amiable to them. Husbands, on their part, must honor their wives more than themselves, and treat them with tender consideration.

If they can by any means contrive it, my sons and daughters should live in communities, and not isolated from other Jews, so that their sons and daughters may learn the ways of Judaism. Even if compelled to solicit from others the money to pay a teacher, they must not let the young, of both sexes, go without instruction in the Torah. Marry your children, O my sons and daughters, as soon as their age is ripe, to members of respectable families. Let no child of mine hunt after money by making a low match for that object; but if the family is undistinguished only on the mother's side, it does not matter, for all Israel counts descent from the father's side.

Every Friday morning, they shall put themselves in careful trim for honoring the Sabbath, kindling the lamps while the day is still great, and in winter lighting the furnace before dark, to avoid desecrating the Sabbath [by kindling fire thereon]. For due welcome to the Sabbath, the women must prepare beautiful candles.

As to games of chance, I entreat my children never to engage in such pastimes. During the leisure of the festival weeks they may play for trifling stakes in kind, and the women may amuse themselves similarly on New Moons, but never for money. In their relation to women, my sons must behave continently, avoiding mixed bathing and mixed dancing and all frivolous conversation, while my daughters ought not to speak much with strangers nor jest nor dance with them. They ought to be always at home, and not be gadding about. They should not stand at the door, watching whatever passes. I ask, I command, that the daughters of my house be never without work to do, for idleness leads first to boredom, then to sin. But let them spin, or cook, or sew.

I earnestly beg my children to be tolerant and humble to all, as I was throughout my life. Should cause for dissension present itself, be slow to accept the quarrel; seek peace and pursue it with all the vigor at your command. Even if you suffer loss thereby, forbear and forgive, for God has many ways of feeding and sustaining His creatures. To the slanderer do not retaliate with counterattack; and though it be proper to rebut false accusations, yet is it most desirable to set an example of reticence. You yourselves must avoid uttering any slander, for so will you win affection. In trade be true, never grasping at what belongs to another. For by avoiding these wrongs—scandal, falsehood, money-grubbing—men will surely find tranquillity and affection. And against all evils, silence is the best safeguard.

Now, my sons and daughters, eat and drink only what is necessary, as our good parents did, refraining from heavy meals, and holding the gross liver in detestation. The regular adoption of such economy in food leads to economy in expenditure generally, with a consequent reluctance to pursue after wealth, but the acquisition of a contented spirit, simplicity in diet, and many good results. Concerning such a well-ordered life the text says: "The righteous eateth to the satisfaction of his desire." Our teachers have said: "Method in expenditure is half a sufficiency." Nevertheless, accustom yourselves and your wives, your sons and your daughters, to wear nice and clean clothes, that God and man may love and honor you. In this direction do not exercise too strict a parsimony. But on no account adopt foreign fashions in dress. After the manner of your fathers order your attire, and let your cloaks be broad without buckles attached.

Be on your guard concerning vows, and cautious as to promises. The breach of one's undertakings leads to many lapses. Do not get into the habit of exclaiming "Gott!", but speak always of the "Creator, blessed be He"; and in all that you propose to do, today or tomorrow, add the proviso, "if the Lord wills, I shall do this thing." Thus remember God's part in your life.

Whatever happiness befall you, be it in monetary fortune or in the birth of children, be it some signal deliverances or any other of the many blessings which may come to you, be not stolidly unappreciative, like dumb cattle that utter no word of gratitude. But offer praises to the Rock who has befriended you, saying: "O give thanks unto the Lord, for He is good, for His mercy endureth for ever. Blessed art Thou, O Lord, who art good and dispensest good."

Besides thanking God for His bounties at the moment they occur, also in your regular prayers let the memory of these personal favors prompt your hearts to special fervor during the utterance of the communal thanks. When words of gratitude are used in the liturgy, pause to reflect in silence on the goodness of God to you that day. And when ye make the response: "May Thy great Name be blessed," call to mind your own personal experiences of the divine favor.

Be very particular to keep your houses clean and tidy. I was always scrupulous on this point, for every injurious condition, and sickness and poverty, are to be found in foul dwellings. Be careful over the benedictions; accept no divine gift without paying back the Giver's part; and His part is man's grateful acknowledgement.

Every one of these good qualities becomes habitual with him who studies the Torah; for that study indeed leads to the formation of a noble character. Therefore, happy is he who toils in the Law! For this gracious toil fix daily times, of long or short duration, for it is the best of all works that a man can do. Week by week read at least the set portion with the commentary of Rashi. And when your prayer is ended day by day, turn ever to the word of God, in fulfilment of the Psalmist's injunction, "passing from strength to strength."

And O, my sons and daughters, keep yourselves far from the snare of frivolous conversation, which begins in tribulation and ends in destruction. Nor be ye found in the company of these light talkers. Judge ye rather every man charitably and use your best efforts to detect an honorable explanation of conduct however suspicious. Try to persuade yourselves that it was your neighbor's zeal for some good end that led him to the conduct you deplore. This is the meaning of the exhortation: "In righteousness shalt thou judge thy neighbor." To sum up, the fewer one's idle words the less one's risk of slander, lying, flattery—all of them, things held in utter detestation by God.

On holidays and festivals and Sabbaths seek to make happy the poor, the unfortunate, widows and orphans, who should always be guests at your tables; their joyous entertainment is a religious duty. Let me repeat my warning against gossip and scandal. And as ye speak no scandal, so listen to none, for if there were no receivers there would be no bearers of slanderous tales; therefore the reception and credit of slander is as serious an offence as the originating of it. The less you say, the less cause you give for animosity, while in the multitude of words there wanteth not transgression.

Always be of those who see and are not seen, who hear and are not heard. Accept no invitation to banquets, except to such as are held for religious reasons: at wedding and at meals prepared for mourners, at gatherings to celebrate entry into the covenant of Abraham, or at assemblies in honor of the wise. Games of chance, for money stakes, such as dicing, must be avoided. And as I have already warned you about that, again let me urge you to show forbearance and humility to all men, to ignore abuses levelled at you, but the indignant refutation of charges against your moral character is fully justifiable.

Be of the first ten in Synagogue, rising betimes for the purpose. Pray steadily with the congregation, giving due value to every letter and word, seeing that there are in the Shema 248 words, corresponding to the 248 limbs in the human body. Be careful too to let the prayer for redemption be followed immediately by the eighteen benedictions. Do not talk during service, but listen to the precentor, and respond, "Amen" at the proper time.

After the morning prayer, read the Chapter about the Manna, the passages associated with it, and the eleven verses, with due attention to clear enunciation. Then recite a Psalm in lieu of a reading in the Torah; though it were well not to omit the latter passing, as I said above, from strength to strength, from prayer to the Bible, before turning to worldly pursuits. Or if ye can perform some act of loving-kindness, it is accounted as equal to the study of the Law.

I beg of you, my sons and daughters, my wife, and all the congregation, that no funeral oration be spoken in my honor. Do not carry my body on a bier but in a coach. Wash me clean, comb my hair, trim my nails, as I was wont to do in my lifetime, so that I may go clean to my eternal rest, as I went clean to Synagogue every Sabbath day. If the ordinary officials dislike the duty, let adequate payment be made to some poor man who shall render this service carefully and not perfunctorily.

At a distance of thirty cubits from the grave, they shall set my coffin on the ground, and drag me to the grave by a rope attached to the coffin. Every four cubits they shall stand and wait awhile, doing this in all seven times, so that I may find atonement for my sins. Put me in the ground at the right hand of my fathers, and if the space be a little narrow, I am sure that he loves me well enough to make room for me by his side. If this be altogether impossible, put me on his left, or near my grandmother, Yuta. Should this also be impractical, let me be buried by the side of my daughter.

THE TESTAMENT OF JUDAH ASHERI

A Saint once indited a Testament in admonition of his sons, bidding them keep the way of God his Master. He thus exhorted them not because they were worse than their contemporaries, but because he desired to direct them into the paths of the ancients. They are called friends [of God] when they imitate the deeds of their fathers. With this example in view, I said: "Better is open rebuke than love that is hidden."

Such rebuke entwines itself in the hearts of the hearers, and to the utterers it is pleasant, for they know that their words will be guarded as the apple of the eye. So it is said: "He that rebuketh a man shall in the end find more favor than he that flattereth with the tongue."

So I will open with a voice of thanksgiving, I, Judah, to the Rock Whose works are awe-inspiring, to Whom appertain glory and greatness transcending man's capacity to express them; Who, ere ever I was born, remembered me for good. My mother dreamed how she was told that she would bear a son, and was asked whether she wished him to be wise or wealthy. She chose wisdom. And though in reality dreams speak vain things, for I learned not wisdom, yet in a certain deceptive sense the dream was fulfilled. The world imagines that I am a scholar, one who giveth goodly words!

Wealth, too, the Lord, blessed be He, hath bestowed on me beyond the ordinary, in that He hath provided me with the measure of mine allotted bread. I rejoice in my portion.

When I was an infant about three months old, my eyes were affected, and were never completely restored. A certain woman tried to cure me when I was about three years of age, but she added to my blindness, to the extent that I remained for a year confined to the house, being unable to see the road on which to walk. Then a Jewess, a skilled oculist, appeared on the scene; she treated me for about two months, and then died. Had she lived another month, I might have received my sight fully. As it was, but for the two months' attention from her, I might never have been able to see at all. Blessed be the Lord, Who exercised marvelous loving-kindness towards me, and opened for me a lattice through which I might behold, with my own eye, the work of His hands.

Thenceforward I studied the tractates which my lord, my father, taught in the College, as far as my capacity went, and without intricate discussion. When I was about thirteen he took me from the land of persecution, and hurled me up and down with a man's throw. I left the German method of study without entering on that of France. For exile confuses the intellect, and I was able neither to write nor speak their language, nor understand their books. Moreover, I could not pore over my books day and night because of my weak eyesight. For this reason I could not write books nor compile treatises.

When I was twenty-eight my lord, my father, of blessed memory, sent me to the city of Toledo, to seek out a place there, and so I did. The Toledo community sent for him, insisted on securing him for their city, and they sent their delegates after I was gone. On my journey back, I was waylaid by bandits who sought my life. But all their purpose was frustrated. My father's God was with me, and His angels encamped round about me, so that I reached my father's house in peace. Twenty-three years later my father died.

Though there were in the city men greater and wiser than I, the Lord, be His name blessed, inclined unto me grace and favor in the eyes of the inhabitants and they installed me in my father's seat. But I had no experience fitting me for such an honor, my scholarship was not enough for such an office. I was a foreigner of no account, with altogether insignificant attainments. I could find no quality in me.

I sat one day pondering in silence, my heart within me appalled. In my hand was the book of Hagiographa, and I said: How will my lot ascend? I will account it as a sign. I opened and there came up in my hand this verse: "And Nathan said unto David, Do all that is in thine, heart, for God is with thee." When this text providentially presented itself, I rejoiced, and said, Though one may not seek an omen, one may read a sign. By the gracious gift of the Merciful, the Faithful God, I have honorably fulfilled all my duties, and thus far the Lord hath helped me.

Likewise my desire for children was not due to my love for them nor expectation of pride in them; my desire was to obey the divine precept, and to raise up offspring to fill my father's place in study and righteousness. For this I often prayed at the graves of the perfect and upright. God in His mercy gave me five sons, and I considered myself through them as a live man among my people and brethren. But for my sins there was taken the one, "the middle bar," on which I thought my house founded; for there passed a smoking furnace and a flaming torch between my pieces. But my courage revived and I call heaven and earth to witness that I deserve this and double from God, for I know that His judgments are correct. Faithfully He afflicted me, He chastened me sore, but gave me not over unto death.

I found consolation in the knowledge that my son was not punished by heaven for any sin of his, for he spent his days, which were few, in the eternal Law. And when the turn of my time comes, I shall go and shall see him, in Beth-El [the house of God] I shall meet him. I rely on the mercy of God that a substitute will be bestowed on me, and my heart's gladness renewed. Then shall both he and his substitute be holy!

Now because of the weakness of my eyesight, my father and mother left me to do whatever was right in my own eyes; they never punished or rebuked me. Wherefore I have never been wont to chide others, for they taught me not how; even my own sons I knew not how to reprove. If they reprove not themselves, they will receive no reproof from me. Nor have I the face to admonish them by word of mouth, lest I put them to the blush, even though evil unto me was the evil of their ways. No joy of mine on earth equals my happiness at their well-doing, no pain or distress can compare with my grief at their misconduct. I have hated life, when I have seen that they went not in the paths of their fathers, in their sitting down, rising up and walking on the way.

But now my heart has impelled me to write for them this Letter of Admonition, conveying a discipline. I command them to read it carefully once a month, that the Lord may renew a clean heart and a steadfast spirit within them. Perhaps they will mend and listen to my voice, so that I may speedily bring salvation unto them.

Now stand ye still that I may plead with you. Why walk ye not in your father's way, nor hold the fear of God ever before your eyes? In His Law ye meditate not continually day and night, nor do ye go morning and evening to your houses of prayer. All your study is below the standard, and when the law is discussed ye are as the dumb, and open not your lips. You associate with those who are unfit to be your companions, for it is unseemly that their ways should be yours.

Again, ye honor not your mother and your father, your conduct is disrespectful in their presence. Know ye not that unto the honor of God is likened the honor of parents? For three are partners in a man [God and his parents]. What have I left undone for you that a father could do for his children? Regularly were your meals provided, and all your wants.

You own many books, and my every thought was directed to you, to equip you and to leave behind me a blessing for you. And if the Law was given to those who ate the manna, surely ye are a similar case. Or if it were a question of marriage, ye are assuredly wed to wives of your own family, who make no extravagant demands on you, but on the contrary seek to encourage you in your study.

What then will you do on the day of visitation, when you give account of all your conduct? And what will ye answer when reproved before Him who trieth your reins, on the day wherein He arraigneth you for all your works? Nay, my children, act for the glory of God and the honor of your progenitors. Improve your ways and your doings, and listen unto Judah your father.

Make the Torah your main object, remember your Creator in the days of your youth, while ye are still in vigor, and take upon you the yoke of the Torah. Let not the Law depart from your mouth, act always with the motive to please God. And the good name which your fathers bequeathed, uphold it and leave it to your children as a heritage.

Now, therefore, ye children, hearken unto me, for happy are they that keep my ways. Come, listen unto me, I will teach you the fear of the Lord. Look unto the rock, whence ye were hewn, and to the hole of the pit, whence ye were digged. Why, forsooth, were ye brought into this world? Not to eat and drink and wear fine linen and embroideries, but for the service of the God who hangeth the earth over nothing. And since His wisdom has ordained that the body cannot be sustained without food and raiment, He permitted man to eat, drink and clothe himself for the sustenance of the body, that body and soul might be associated to perform God's behests so long as their association continues.

Food to a man is like oil to a lamp, if it have much it shines, if little it is quenched. Yet sooner is the lamp extinguished by redundancy than deficiency of oil. Therefore be diligently on your guard against overfeeding. More heinous than homicide is suicide. Gross eating is as dangerous to the body as a sword, besides that it bars one from occupation with the Law of God and the reverence due to Him.

Ever let the fear of God be before you, and accustom yourselves to recite with devotion, that it depart not from your mouths, the text: I have set the Lord always before me; surely He is at my right hand, I shall not be moved. Keep your minds always alert on whatever may induce the fear of heaven; be not diverted by the jibes of others, nor by your own lusts.

Make it your firm custom to study the Torah at fixed times, probe deeply into its contents, and endeavor to communicate daily a portion of the rabbinic law to others; for to accomplish this you will be compelled to make your own knowledge precise, moreover by the exposition orally it will be fixed in your memories. Always repeat, if possible going back to the beginning of the tractate.

Our sages of blessed memory have said [with regard to perfect service]: "He who repeats his chapter a hundred times cannot be compared to him who repeats it a hundred and one times." Read ye, therefore, every rule [halakah] 101 times, and appoint hours for studying halakah from the codifiers every day, and also strive to read a tractate with Rashi's commentary.

In fine, you must consider yourselves as laborers hired by the day to do the work of God, as it is said in the Talmud: "We are day laborers." Much more is this the case with you, for all that you possess comes from the congregation and the trust fund. This support is given to you for the purpose of your studies, so that ye are indeed daily hirelings. See to it that ye do your tasks faithfully, and faithful is your Employer to pay your wage, nay your reward is already with you, for He has paid it in advance.

Think not in your heart that the Torah is an inheritance from your fathers, and needs no personal effort to win it. The matter is not so. If ye toil not therein, ye shall not acquire, and more than ordinary will be your punishment, in that ye forsake your family tradition. So we read it in tractate Nedarim: "Why do not learned fathers invariably beget learned children?" R. Joseph answered: "So that people shall not say, Your Torah is inherited from your fathers. . . .

Also appoint regular periods for studying the Bible with grammar and commentary. As in my childhood I did not so study it—for in Germany they had not the custom—I have not been able to teach it here. Read weekly the Pentateuchal lesson with Rashi and other commentaries. Also make yourselves familiar with homilies and midrashim; this will make you more effective in public preaching, and to bring men back from iniquity. Our Sages said: "He who wishes to become saintly should fulfil the words of the Fathers." So, I, after making my confession, accustomed myself to read a chapter of the Tractate Abot [Ethics of the Fathers] every day. Do ye the same at table, before grace after meals, read a chapter daily till you know the whole tractate by heart. This practice will habituate and attract you to saintliness.

Discourse of matters of Torah at your meals, then will ye be as those who eat at the table of the Omnipresent. Read regularly in the *Duties of the Heart* and in the *Book of the Upright,* and the *Epistle on Repentance* of Rabbenu Jonah, and similar books. Set your hearts on that you read therein with devout intent to apply the lesson in your life. When you read, do so audibly. And reason with yourselves *a fortiori* after this manner: If you had to speak before a king of flesh and blood, how carefully you would clear your hearts of all other thoughts. Your whole endeavor would be to word your speech acceptably, and you would think of nothing else. How much more should this be your method before the King of kings, blessed and sanctified be His Name!

Pray with the congregation in the same place and in the same context. See that you are among the first. Discontinue your present habit of departing as soon as the lesson is over, thus failing to pray where the congregation is collected. Never speak from the passage, "Blessed is He who spake" until you have ended the Eighteen Benedictions. Be silent, too, while the cantor repeats the last-named prayer. For if there be not ten attentive to it, the repetition is not according to law. Be ye always among these ten, and make it your rule to join in prayer so as to enable the many to do their duty. Let the words be softly spoken, for thus is devotion aroused and prayer made acceptable.

See to it diligently that ye be not among the four classes who behold not the divine presence [Shekinah]: liars, scoffers, hypocrites, and slanderers. . . .

Avoid pride, for every one that is proud in heart is an abomination to the Lord. Majesty, indeed, is the garment of God alone, and he that makes use of the crown shall perish. As a certain Sage said: how can a man be proud, considering the way in which he was conceived and born?" But cleave to humility, that best of good qualities. For this virtue Moses our Master was praised, as it is said: "Now the man Moses was very meek." Be very lowly in spirit, say our Rabbis. They said further that [the fear of the Lord] which Wisdom makes a crown to her head, Humility makes the imprint of her foot.

Be punctilious in honoring all men, for therein shall you find your own honor, for God Himself has declared: "Them that honor Me will I honor." People remarked to a Sage: "We have observed that thou ever showest honor to every man," and he replied: "I have never come across one in whom I failed to recognize superiority over myself; therefore have I shown him respect. Were he older, I said he has done more good than I. Were he richer, I said he has been more charitable. Were he younger, I said I have sinned more. Were he poorer, I said he has suffered heavier tribulations. Were he wiser, I honored him for his wisdom. Were he not wiser, I said his fault is the lighter." Take this to heart and understand it.

Take heed to love and respect him that reproves you. For thus we read in Tractate 'Arakin: "R. Johanan said: I call heaven and earth to witness that many a time was Akiba punished through me, for I complained of him before Rabban Gamaliel; all the more did he augment his love for me, to fulfil what is written: 'Reprove a wise man and he will love thee.' As the Sage said: Love thy critic, and hate thy eulogist, the former helps, the latter hurts thee."

Consider also that man is but a sojourner on earth; his days are numbered, though he knows not their tale, nor when he will be summoned before the King of kings, to give judgment and account for all his works. Therefore let him do all that is in his power, nor think any good opportunity small, for there is no limit to the reward.

In the world to come, when God, blessed be He, makes requital to the righteous, the recipient will ask: "Why am I so rewarded?" He will be told:

"On such and such a day thou didst do such and such a mizvah." Then sighing, he will say: "For so little do I receive so much? Alas for the days that I lost wherein I did no good!" Therefore will a wise man be alert lest he waste an hour of his hours, but he will be energetic in well-doing, thinking ever of the fear of God and His service.

I will make mention of the mercies of the Lord according to all that He hath bestowed on me. He has shepherded me from my birth even unto this day. In the way of truth He led me, taking me from my father's house, sending me before them to preserve life. . . .

I left Germany at the age of thirteen, and when fifteen I came to Toledo, in the new moon of Iyar in the year 1305. It is obvious that at my exodus when I married first the daughter of R. Yehiel and later the daughter of R. Solomon, did I receive even enough to pay for the wedding garments and celebrations. From my lord, my father, of blessed memory, I inherited only a trifle as my share of his library. All that he owned at the time of his demise, together with all his household goods, did not suffice to carry out his testamentary bequests. . . .

For from the time of the death of my lord, my father, of blessed memory, that is to say for twenty-seven years and three months—I have not taken from the Congregation (whom may God preserve!) under contract more than 1290 gold pieces. This I accepted for two years and four months, and I ceased to enter into any contract until the ten years mentioned were completed. Thereafter I received up to August [1340] from them 1500 pieces annually for nine years and ten months, a total of 14,750. Thenceforth they contracted to increase the annual payment to 3000 pieces. They agreed that after my death an annual pension of 1000 pieces should be paid for ten consecutive years to my wife and children or to any of them then living in Toledo. During my lifetime each of my sons was guaranteed 300 pieces for ten years, so long as he should pursue his studies and dwell in Toledo. A similar sum was appointed, under similar conditions, to be paid after my death to each of my sons out of the total of 1000 pieces mentioned above. . . .

He who searcheth hearts knoweth that all my yearning desire for children in this world was solely dictated by my wish to raise up offspring which should fill my father's place in the study of the Law, in good works, and in the service of God. And in this sense I besought Him who is enthroned over the Cherubim, entreating God for myself, my children, and all our generations after us, that we may dwell in the house of the Lord all the days of our life, to behold the graciousness of the Lord and to pass our time in the inner shrine of His Law from morn to eve and from eve to morn, in the precious presence of God.

I prayed that He would keep us far from men of vanity and frivolity, that we might maintain the example of our fathers, who, as our tradition assures us, were for many generations before us men of learning, of right-doing, and God-fearers—men from whom the Torah went forth unto Israel. And this has been my constant prayer at the graves of the righteous and perfect:

"Lord of the Universe, King that sittest on the throne of mercy! It is revealed and known before Thee that all my desire for children was not out of my love for them, nor to gain honor through them, but only to perform that duty of continuing the race which Thou hast ordained. May it be Thy will to order us in all our affairs in good counsel before Thee. O may the fear of Thee be with us that we sin not, and may we live in Thy presence in reverence. Grant unto me sons who may grow into maturity, and may fill my fathers' place. And may God in His mercy raise up for us the merit of the righteous one buried in his grave. May my prayer be heard here, and may he too pray on our behalf, blessing us continually and at all hours."

One of the good methods which I desired for maintaining the family record was the marriage of my sons to members of my father's house. I had many reasons for this. First, it is a fair and fit thing to join fruit of vine to fruit of vine. It is indeed an important duty, for as our Sages said: "He who loves his relatives, he who marries his sister's daughter, and he who lends to the poor in the hour of his distress—to him applies the text: 'Then shalt thou call, and the Lord will answer; thou shalt cry and He will say, Here I am.' "

Furthermore, the women of our family have grown accustomed to the ways of students, and the love of the Torah has entered their hearts, so that they are a help to their husbands in their scholarly pursuits. Moreover, they are not used to extravagant expenditure; they do not demand luxuries, the provision of which disturbs a man from his study. Then again, children for the most part resemble the mother's family. Finally, if with changing times a man see fit to seek his livelihood in another city, there will be none to place obstacles in the way of the wife accompanying her husband.

The second plan is for me to write something of the history of my saintly progenitors, for the edification of those that come after us. Seeing that the Lord, blessed be He, hurled us with a man's throw to Toledo, that great and renowned city, and that a little later the Jews were expelled from France, possibly some may think that we were among the exiles, or that we left our country in consequence of some whispered suspicion.

Therefore, it seems desirable to me to disabuse everyone of such an imputation. And further, when our posterity regards the upright lives of our ancestors, they will be ashamed if they walk not in the same paths. Rather will they strive in all things to imitate their fathers, thus finding grace and good favor in the sight of God and man. Otherwise, better were it for them never to be born, like infants who never see the light.

As I left Germany when about thirteen years of age, I did not acquire exact information as to our fathers' righteous lives, except the little which I heard from my lord, my father of blessed memory, and from his sister and my grandmother, who related to me some of the family history. What little I heard of the doings of our first ancestors I set down here.

My grandfather, R. Yehiel b. Asher, was born in the year 1210. When he was ten years old he had a firm friend in R. Solomon ha-Kohen. They entered into a pact that each should share the other's rewards, whether religious or secular. They held to this agreement all their days, and were unique in their generation for saintliness and benevolence. Now on the eve of the Day of Atonement in the year 1264, early in the night, the candle of my grandfather went out in the synagogue. For it was customary in Germany to kindle a wax candle for every male in the synagogue, on the eve of the Fast, and the candle was of a size to burn the whole day and night.

Later (during the middle days of Tabernacles) my grandfather died and great honor was shown unto him at his death from neighboring places attending his funeral. Now it is the practice in Germany to set the coffin on a stone appointed for the purpose near the cemetery, and to open it to see whether the body has been dislocated by the jolting of the coffin.

When they did this to him, R. Solomon ha-Kohen approached up to four cubits, and said in the presence of the assembly, "In your presence I call upon him to remember our covenant." Within the coffin a look of joy lit his face, most of those present saw him smile, and I testify on the evidence of my father and grandmother that this happened.

A day came when R. Solomon ha-Kohen was studying in his college in the daytime, and lo! my grandfather of blessed memory was seated by his side. Amazed, R. Solomon asked how he fared, and he answered, exceeding well, and that a seat was ready at his side for his friend. "I wonder," said R. Solomon, "that thou art permitted to be visible to mortals." He answered: "I have liberty to go to my house as of aforetime, but I am unwilling that they should say: How this saint prides it over other righteous men!"

Six months after his death, at midnight on the Sabbath night, he appeared to his wife and said to her: "Haste and rise, take thy sons and daughters, and remove them hence, for tomorrow all the Jews of this place will be slain. So was it decreed against the whole neighborhood, but we prayed and our petition was successful except as regards this place."

She rose and obeyed, but returning to save her belongings, she was killed with the congregation. She had previously rescued my lord, my father, R. Asher of blessed memory, and his brother, R. Hayyim, fellow-disciple of R. Meir of Rothenburg, teacher of my father, who also was taught by his brother Hayyim. They had another brother, by name of R. Eleazar, who died at the age of twenty-seven. He was reported to be as fine a scholar as his brother R. Hayyim. They had six sisters, the whole family saintly—all bearing deservedly high reputations among their contemporaries. The nine of them escaped on the day and under the circumstances narrated above. All of them had large families of sons and daughters, and I have heard that one of the sons of my uncle R. Hayyim, of blessed memory, married in Germany, and that there were at his wedding about five hundred men and women, all relatives, the relationship reaching to that of third cousins.

The cause of my father's departure from Germany was due to the imprisonment of R. Meir of Rothenburg, of blessed memory. The Count, then head of the government, arrested him, and the congregation of Germany ransomed him for a considerable sum. The Governor refused to accept as guarantor any other person than my lord, my father, of blessed memory. But before the contributions were apportioned to the various congregations, R. Meir died in prison.

The governor unjustly refused to admit my father's plea that as R. Meir died before his release, the guarantee had lapsed. Payment was still demanded from my father and the congregations, and my father escaped to another city; he left Germany altogether because of his fear of the authorities, and settled in the great city of Toledo.

In the first year of his residence there, they sent him a written communication from the town council of the place where he formerly lived, inviting him to return home. They would despatch fifty officers to meet him on the German frontier, and would give him a documentary safe-conduct from the Emperor. For they recognized his wisdom and excellence, and were wont to follow his advice in all matters. But in face of the frequent illtreatment of the Jews there, he was unwilling to go back.

This was the reason of the coming of my lord, my father, of blessed memory, to this country. "This was the Lord's doing," to the end that my father might raise up many disciples on Spanish soil. "He executed the righteousness of the Lord, and His ordinances with Israel." For there were not in these lands any thorough commentaries.

He also wrote commentaries and decisions to the Talmud. Wherever his commentaries, responsa and decisions reached, they made known the statutes of the Lord and His laws. His sons walked in his ways, and maintained his opinions. . . .

And also in what pertained to the affairs and organization of the community, we passed our time together in settlement of causes and judgments. Men of the government also agreed to abide by my decisions, not because of my wisdom or wit, for "I am brutish, unlike a man, and have not a man's understanding," but God filled them with a kindly disposition towards me, so that my words were acceptable to them, in that they deemed me in their thoughts an impartial judge.

As for me, my prayer is made before the Lord of the Universe, that He may requite with a good recompense this holy congregation for their labors, and for all the good which they as a body and as individuals have done unto me in granting all my requests and of their Heart's generosity and not for any selfish motive. And so will it ever continue until I part from them in great love, "and my seed shall be established in their sight, and my offspring before their eyes." And may it be their good will to prepare a way for my progeny to settle among them as they did with my father and me, kindness after kindness. For what has passed and for what is to come, unto the Rock tremendous in His doing, Judah shall lead the thanksgiving. And may the bounty of God and the merit of our fathers cause that there never fail from us in Toledo—until the majestic God establish Jerusalem and a Redeemer come unto Zion—one to fill the seat of my lord, my father, R. Asher of beloved memory; may this be so for all time until Shiloh cometh and people be gathered unto him, and there arise a priest with Urim and with Thummim.

Ended and completed, praise to the God of the Universe!

The Zohar

The Zohar (meaning "splendor" or "radiance"), composed in the last quarter of the thirteenth century, is the chief text of the mystical tradition known as Kabbala. Like the early Midrash, the Zohar is a symbolic and allegorical exegesis of the Torah. The homiletical, discursive style is prominent and stories abound. Tradition has it that the Zohar was composed in the second century C.E. by R. Simeon ben Yohai who supposedly hid in a cave for thirteen years to avoid Roman persecution. However, the many linguistic anachronisms in the work—it is written mainly in Aramaic—and the references to religious and social practises prove that it is basically a medieval composition which modern scholarship attributes to Moses de Leon (1250–1305). For instance, the limited vocabulary, the grammatical errors and, chiefly, the artificial Aramaic that sounds as though it were translated from the Hebrew, indicate that the author was not thoroughly familiar with his chosen language. Moreover, his terrain of Palestine is a familiar one in Hebrew literature, found in the works of writers who never set foot in the Holy Land; it is a Palestine of the imagination, based on literature rather than on personal contact.

Like other pseudepigraphic writers before him, Moses de Leon, too, attributed his text to a famous ancient personality in order to gain greater renown for his work. Nevertheless, there is undoubtedly older material incorporated in the Zohar, some of it going back to ancient times. Moses de Leon's sources were various midrashim, the Babylonian Talmud and the Aramaic translations of the Bible, the latter two providing him with the groundwork for his vocabulary. He also used medieval works, including the philosophic texts of Maimonides and Judah Halevi, and the kabbalistic writings of his own era. But in his desire to put the patina of age on a thirteenth-century document, he is silent about his real contemporary sources and invents a book-shelf of concocted ones (as did other medieval authors, Geoffrey of Monmouth and his "book," and Chaucer in the Troilus story).

During the several centuries following its composition, the Zohar ranked with the Bible and the Talmud as the leading texts of Judaism, and was the first book since the Talmud to achieve canonical status—within fifty years of its appearance it had circulated widely among Jewish communities. The Zohar is not one book, but like the Talmud a vast work with many parts: in addition to the main section, which is arranged according to chapters of the Torah, there are twenty-three other divisions. Like the Talmud it lacks an organized doctrine and is dependent upon free association: if a word or an idea triggers another similar phrase or thought, the discussion moves freely on.

The Zohar focuses on the soul, the nature of God, the symbolic meaning of the Sabbath, the origin of the universe, the future redemption. It particularly accents the divine fusion between man and God, and man's ability to influence the cosmos —by being a better person man prompts the increase of divine grace. Yet, along with the preponderance of ethical teachings and transcendant poetry, there are many superstitions and foreign elements (demons and metempsychosis) in the work. One of the repeated motifs in the Zohar is that the Torah is not to be understood solely in its literal meaning. With the genius of poetry and legend it probes truths beyond those that meet the eye; it posits a level of knowledge and existence above the commonplace. Typical of its allegorical stance is its discussion of the Book of Jonah; although the details differ, the allegorical approach is coincidentally and strikingly similar to Father Mapple's sermon in the opening of Melville's *Moby Dick*. Although the Zohar uses the four traditional methods of Biblical exegesis —the literal, the aggadic or homiletic, the allegorical, and the mystical—the latter is the most important for the author of the Zohar. In line with the kabbalists' desire to find a means of drawing near to God and search for perfect communion with Him, the Zohar seeks to illumine the words of the Torah with a higher, more profound meaning, and seek out the hidden nuances of words and phrases. The concepts of unity, harmony between man and God, spiritual existence, and divine emanations, had their impact on later Hasidism, whose early proponents were devotees of kabbalistic literature.

THE ZOHAR

MICROCOSM AND MACROCOSM

King Solomon, when he "penetrated into the depths of the nut garden," as it is written, "I descended into the nut garden," [Song of S. 6:11], took a nutshell [*klifah*] and drew an analogy from its layers to those spirits which inspire sensual desires in human beings, as it is written, "and the delights of the sons of men [are from] male and female demons." [Eccl. 2:8]. This verse also indicates that the pleasures in which men indulge in the time of sleep give birth to multitudes of demons.

The Holy One, blessed be He, found it necessary to create all these things in the world to ensure its permanence, so that there should be, as it were, a brain with many membranes encircling it. The whole world is constructed on this principle, upper and lower, from the first mystic point up to the furthest removed of all the stages. They are all coverings one to another, brain within brain and spirit within spirit, so that one is a shell to another.

The primal point is the innermost light of a translucency, tenuity, and purity passing comprehension. The extension of that point becomes a "palace" [*Hekal*], which forms a vestment for that point with a radiance which is still unknowable on account of its translucency.

The "palace" which is the vestment for that unknowable point is also a radiance which cannot be comprehended, yet withal less subtle and translucent than the primal mystic point. This "palace" extends into the primal Light, which is a vestment for it. From this point there is extension after extension, each one forming a vestment to the other, being in the relation of membrane and brain to one another. Although at first a vestment, each stage becomes a brain to the next stage.

The same process takes place below, so that on this model man in this world combines brain and shell, spirit and body, all for the better ordering of the world. When the moon was in connection with the sun, she was luminous, but as soon as she separated from the sun and was assigned the charge of her own hosts, she reduced her status and her light, and shells upon shells were created for covering the brain, and all for the benefit of the brain.

THE PRIMAL LIGHT

AND GOD SAID, LET THERE BE LIGHT, AND THERE WAS LIGHT. This is the original light which God created. This is the light of the eye. It is the light which God showed to Adam, and through which he was able to see from one end of the world to the other. It was the light which God showed to David, who, on seeing it, burst forth into praise, saying, "Oh, how abundant is Thy goodness which Thou hast laid up for them that fear Thee." [Ps. 31:20]. It is the light through which God showed to Moses the Land of Israel from Gilead to Dan.

When God foresaw that three sinful generations would arise, namely the generation of Enosh, the generation of the Flood, and the generation of the Tower of Babel, He put it away so that they should not enjoy it, and gave it to Moses for the first three months after he was born when his mother hid him. When he was brought before Pharaoh, God withdrew it from him, and only restored it to him when he stood upon the mountain of Sinai to receive the Torah. From that time he had the use of it for the rest of his life, so that the Israelites could not approach him till he put a veil over his face. [Ex. 34:30].

LET THERE BE LIGHT, AND THERE WAS LIGHT. Anything to which the term *vayehi* [and there was] is applied is found in this world and the next world.

R. Isaac said: "The radiance which God produced at the time of the Creation illumined the world from one end to the other, but was withdrawn, in order that the sinners of the world might not enjoy it, and it is treasured up for the righteous, i.e., for the *Zaddik*, as it is written, 'light is sown for the *Zaddik*' " [Ps. 97:11]; then worlds will be firmly established and all will form a single whole, but until the time when the future world shall emerge this light is hidden and stored up.

This light issued from the darkness which was carved out by the strokes of the Most Recondite; and similarly from that light which was stored away there was carved out through some hidden process the lower-world darkness in which light resides. This lower darkness is what is called "night" in the verse, "and the darkness he called night." [Gen. 1:5].

CREATION OF MAN

R. Simeon arose and spoke thus: "My meditation disclosed to me that when God came to create man, all creatures trembled above and below. The sixth day was proceeding on its course when at length the divine decision was formed. Then the source of all lights shone forth and opened the gate of the East, for thence light issues. The South displayed in full power the light which it had inherited from the commencement, and joined hands with the East. The East took hold of the North, and the North awoke and spread forth and called aloud to the West to come and join him. Then the West went up into the North and united with it, and afterwards the South took hold of the West, and the South and the North, which are the fences of the Garden, surrounded it. Then the East approached the West, and the West was rejoiced and said to the others, 'Let us make man in our image, after our likeness,' embracing like us the four quarters and the higher and the lower. Then the East united with the West and produced him. Hence our Sages have said that man emerged from the site of the Temple.

Further, the words 'let us make man' may be taken to signify that God imparted to the lower beings who came from the side of the upper world the secret of forming the divine name 'Adam,' which embraces the upper and the lower in virtue of its three letters, *aleph, daleth,* and *mem* final. When these three letters descended below, together in their complete form, the name Adam was found to comprise male and female. The female was attached to the side of the male until God cast him into a deep slumber, during which he lay on the site of the Temple. God then sawed her off from him and adorned her like a bride and brought her to him, as it is written, 'And he took one of his sides and closed up the place with flesh.' [Gen. 2:21]. I have found it stated in an old book that the word 'one' here means 'one woman,' to wit, the original Lilith, who was with him and who conceived from him. Up to that time, however, she was not a help to him, as it is written, 'but for Adam there was not found an help meet for him.' Observe that Adam came last of all, it being fitting that he should find the world complete on his appearance."

AND NO PLANT OF THE FIELD WAS YET IN THE EARTH [Gen. 2:5]. R. Simeon said further: "These are the great trees which were planted out later, but as yet were tiny. We have stated that Adam and Eve were created side by side. Why were they not created face to face? Because 'the Lord God had not yet caused it to rain upon the earth' [Gen. 2:5], and the union of heaven and earth was not yet firmly established. When the lower union was perfected and Adam and Eve were turned face to face, then the upper union was consummated.

"We know this from the case of the Tabernacle, of which we have learnt that another tabernacle was erected with it, and that the upper one was not raised till the lower one was raised; and similarly here. Further, since all was not yet in order above, Adam and Eve were not created face to face. The order of verses in the Scripture proves this: for first we read, 'For the Lord God had not caused it to rain upon the earth,' and then 'there was not a man to till the ground,' the meaning being that man was still defective, and only when Eve was perfected was he also perfected.

"This is further indicated by the fact that in the word *vayisgor* [and he closed] the letter *samekh,* which means "support," occurs for the first time in this section, as if to say that they now supported one another, as male and female. Similarly the lower and the upper world mutually support one another. For until the lower world was completed, that other world of which we have spoken was not completed. When this lower world was turned face to face to the upper, it became a support to the upper, for previously the work had been defective, because 'the Lord God had not caused rain to fall upon the earth.'

Next, A MIST WENT UP FROM THE GROUND, to repair the deficiency below, by 'watering the whole face of the ground.' The rising of the mist signifies the yearning of the female for the male. According to another explanation, we supply the word 'not' from the previous clause after 'mist,' the meaning being that God did not send rain because a mist had not gone up, etc., it being necessary for the impulse from below to set in motion the power above. So vapor first ascends from the earth to form the cloud. Similarly, the smoke of the sacrifice rises and creates harmony above, so that all unite, and in this way there is completion in the supernal realm. The impulse commences from below, and from this all is perfected. If the Community of Israel did not give the first impulse, the One above would not move to meet her, for by the yearning from below completion is effected above."

THE SERPENT AND SATAN

AND THE SERPENT.

R. Isaac said: "This is the evil tempter." R. Judah said that it means literally a serpent. They consulted R. Simeon, and he said to them: "Both are correct. It was Samael, and he appeared on a serpent, for the ideal form of the serpent is the Satan. We have learnt that at that moment Samael came down from heaven riding on this serpent, and all creatures saw his form and fled before him. They then entered into conversation with the woman, and the two brought death into the world. Of a surety Samael brought curses on the world through Wisdom and destroyed the first tree that God had created in the world. This responsibility rested on Samael until another holy tree came, namely Jacob, who wrested the blessings from him, in order that Samael might not be blessed above and Esau below. For Jacob was the reproduction of Adam, and he had the same beauty as Adam. Therefore as Samael withheld blessings from the first tree, so Jacob, who was such another tree as Adam, withheld blessings, both upper and lower, from Samael; and in doing so Jacob but took back his own. It is written: AND THE SERPENT WAS SUBTLE. This serpent is the evil tempter and the angel of death. It is because the serpent is the angel of death that it brought death to the world."

MALE AND FEMALE

R. Simeon was once going to Tiberias accompanied by R. Jose and R. Judah and R. Hiya. On the way they saw R. Phineas coming towards them. When they met, they dismounted and sat down under a large tree. Said R. Phineas, "Now that I am sitting here, I should like to hear some of those wonderful ideas to which you daily give utterance."

R. Simeon thereupon opened a discourse with the text, "AND HE WENT ON HIS JOURNEYS FROM THE SOUTH EVEN UNTO BETHEL, UNTO THE PLACE WHERE HIS TENT WAS AT FIRST, BETWEEN BETHEL AND AI . . ." [Gen. 13:3] He said: "The word 'journeys' is used here where we might have expected 'journey,' to indicate that the Shekinah was journeying with him. It is incumbent on a man to be ever 'male and female,' in order that his faith may be firm, and that the Shekinah may never depart from him.

"What, then, you will say, of a man who goes on a journey and, being absent from his wife, is no longer 'male and female?' His remedy is to pray to God before he starts his journey, while he is still 'male and female,' in order to draw to himself the presence of his Master. When he has offered his prayer and thanksgiving and the Shekinah rests on him, then he can depart, for through his union with the Shekinah he has become 'male and female' in the country as he was 'male and female' in the town, as it is written: RIGHTEOUSNESS [ZEDEK, THE FEMALE OF ZADDIK] SHALL GO BE-FORE HIM AND SHALL PLACE HIS FOOTSTEPS ON THE WAY. [Ps. 85:14].

"Observe this. All the time that a man is on his travels he should be very careful of his actions, in order that the celestial partner may not desert him and leave him defective, through lacking the union with the female. If this was necessary when his wife was with him, how much more so is it neces-sary when a heavenly partner is attached to him? All the more so since this heavenly partner guards him on the way all the time until he returns home. When he does reach home again, it is his duty to give his wife some pleasure, because it is she who procured for him this heavenly partner.

"It is his duty to do this for two reasons. One is that this pleasure is a religious pleasure, and one which gives joy to the Shekinah also, and what is more, by its means he spreads peace in the world, as it is written, 'thou shalt know that thy tent is in peace, and thou shalt visit thy fold and not sin.' [Job 5:24]. (Is it a sin, it may be asked, if he does not visit his wife? The answer is that it is so because he thereby derogates from the honour of the celestial partner who was joined with him on account of his wife.) The other is, that if his wife becomes pregnant, the celestial partner im-parts to the child a holy soul, for this covenant is called the covenant of the Holy One, blessed be He.

"Therefore he should be as diligent to procure this gladness as to procure the gladness of the Sabbath, which is the partner of the Sages. Hence 'thou shalt know that thy tent is in peace,' since the Shekinah comes with thee and abides in thy house, and therefore 'thou shalt visit thy house and not sin,' by performing with gladness the religious duty of conjugal intercourse in the presence of the Shekinah.

"In this way the students of the Torah who separate from their wives during the six days of the week in order to devote themselves to study are accompanied by a heavenly partner in order that they may continue to be 'male and female.' When Sabbath comes, it is incumbent on them to gladden their wives for the sake of the honour of the heavenly partner, and to seek to perform the will of their Master, as has been said.

"Similarly again, if a man's wife is observing the days of her separation, during all those days that he waits for her the heavenly partner is associated with him, so that he is still 'male and female.' When his wife is purified, it is his duty to gladden her through the glad performance of a religious precept. All the reasons we have mentioned above apply to this case also.

"The esoteric doctrine is that men of true faith should concentrate their whole thought and purpose on this one [the Shekinah]. You may object that, according to what has been said, a man enjoys greater dignity when he is on a journey than when he is at home, on account of the heavenly partner who is then associated with him. This is not so. For when a man is at home, the foundation of his house is the wife, for it is on account of her that the Shekinah departs not from the house.

"So our teachers have understood the verse, 'AND HE BROUGHT HER TO THE TENT OF HIS MOTHER SARAH,' [Gen. 24:67], to indicate that with Rebecca the Shekinah came to Isaac's house. Esoterically speaking, the supernal Mother is found in company with the male only at the time when the house is prepared, and the male and female are joined. Then the supernal Mother pours forth blessings for them. Similarly the lower Mother is not found in company with the male save when the house is prepared and the male visits the female and they join together; then the lower Mother pours forth blessings for them. Hence the man in his house is to be encompassed by two females, like the Male above. There is an allusion to this in the verse 'Unto ['ad] the desire of the everlasting hills:' [Gen. 49:26]. This 'ad is the object of the desire of the 'everlasting hills,' viz. the supreme female, who is to prepare for him and beatify and bless him, and the secondary female, who is to be conjoined with him and to be supported by him.

Similarly below, when the man is married the desire of the 'everlasting hills' is towards him, and he is beatified by two females, one of the upper and one of the lower world—the upper one to pour blessings upon him, and the lower one to be supported by him and to be conjoined with him. So much for the man in his house. When, however, he goes forth on a journey, while the celestial Mother still accompanies him, the lower wife is left behind: so when he comes back he has to take measures to encompass himself with two females, as we have said."

Said R. Phineas: "Even the angels above would not dare to open their mouths before thee."

INIQUITY AND MORTALITY

. AND IT REPENTED THE LORD THAT HE HAD MADE MAN UPON THE EARTH, AND IT GRIEVED HIM AT HIS HEART. R. Jose illustrated from the verse: *Woe unto them that draw iniquity with cords of vanity, and sin as it were with a cart rope* [Is. 5:18]. He said: "Those who 'draw iniquity' are the men who sin before their Master every day, and in whose eyes the sins they commit are like gossamer threads, which are of no account and are not noticed by God. And so they go on until they make their guilt as strong as a cart rope which cannot be broken. See now, when the time comes for God to pass sentence on sinners, although they have provoked Him every day, He is yet unwilling to destroy them, and though He sees their deeds, He is yet indulgent towards them because they are the work of His hands, and therefore He gives them a respite. When at last He does come to execute judgement upon them, He is, as it were, grieved, since they are the work of His hands, although it is written, 'Honour and majesty are before him, strength and joy are in his place' [Ps. 96:6]."

R. Jose said: "Observe that it says, 'He was grieved to his heart.' The seat of the grief was the heart and no other place, 'heart' having here the same sense as in the verse, 'according to that which is in mine heart and in my mind' [I Sam. 2:35]."

R. Isaac said: "The word 'repented' here has the same sense as in the sentence, 'And the Lord repented of the evil which he had said he would do unto his people' [Ex. 32:14]. R. Yesa says that the word *niham*, used of God, means 'repent,' as has been remarked, implying that God bethinks Himself that the sinners are the work of His hands, and therefore pities them and is grieved because they sin before Him.

"R. Hizkiah says that it means 'is consoled,' implying that when God resolves to destroy the wicked, He comforts Himself for their loss like one who resigns himself to the loss of some article, and once He has done so, justice takes its course and repentance no longer avails; for up to that point the decision may still be reversed. No only so, but judgement is executed with additional rigour, until the sinners are utterly destroyed.

"The text tells us as much; for the words 'the Lord was comforted' indicate that God resigned Himself, and the words 'he was grieved to his heart' that He allowed justice to take its course without mercy."

R. Hiya said: "The words 'God was comforted because he had made man' refer to the time when man was first created on the earth, in the supernal image, and God rejoiced because the angels praised Him saying, 'Thou hast made him [man] little lower than the angels, and crownest him with glory and honour' [Ps. 8:6]. But afterwards when man sinned, then God 'was grieved,' because now the angels could say that they had been right in protesting against his creation, saying: 'What is man that thou art mindful of him and the son of man that thou visitest him?' [*Ibid.* 5]."

R. Judah said: "God was grieved because the execution of judgement is always displeasing to Him. Thus we read that Jehoshaphat when going out to war 'appointed those that should sing. . . . Give thanks unto the Lord, for his mercy endureth for ever' [II Chron. 20:21], and R. Isaac has explained that the reason why the words 'for he is good' do not appear in this chant, as in other passages where it is given, is because He was about to destroy the works of His hands before Israel.

"Similarly, at the time when Israel crossed the Red Sea, when the angels came as usual to chant their praises before God on that night, God said to them: 'The works of my hands are drowning in the sea, and will you chant praises?'; hence it says, 'and this [angel] drew not near to that one all the night' [Ex. 14:20].

"Thus whenever destruction of the wicked takes place, there is grief for them above."

R. Abba said: "God had already been grieved when Adam sinned before Him and transgressed His commandment. He said to him: 'Woe to thee that thou hast weakened the heavenly power, for at this moment thou hast quenched a light'; and forthwith He banished him from the Garden of Eden, saying: 'I put thee in the garden to bring offerings, but thou hast impaired the altar so that offerings cannot henceforth be brought on it; henceforth therefore it is thy doom to labour at the ground.'

"God also decreed that he should die. Taking pity on him, however, God allowed him when he died to be buried near the Garden of Eden. For Adam had made a cave near the Garden, and had hidden himself there with his wife. He knew it was near the Garden, because he saw a faint ray of light enter it from there, and therefore he desired to be buried in it; and there he was buried, close to the gate of the Garden of Eden.

"So it is that when a man is about to depart from life, Adam, the first man, appears to him and asks him why and in what state he leaves the world. He says: 'Woe to thee that through thee I have to die.'

"To which Adam replies: 'My son, I transgressed one commandment and was punished for so doing; see how many commandments of your Master, negative and positive, you have transgressed.' "

R. Hiya said: "Adam exists to this day, and twice a day he sees the patriarchs and confesses his sins, and shows them the place where once he abode in heavenly glory. He also goes and looks at all the pious and righteous among his descendants who have attained to celestial glory in the Garden of Eden. All the patriarchs then praise God, saying: 'How precious is thy loving-kindness, O God, and the children of men take refuge under the shadow of thy wings' [Ps. 36:8]."

R. Yesa said: "Adam appears to every man at the moment of his departure from life to testify that the man is dying on account of his own sins and not the sin of Adam, according to the dictum, 'there is no death without sin.' There are only three exceptions, namely, Amram, Levi, and Benjamin, who were deprived of life through the prompting of the primeval serpent; some add also, Jesse. These did not sin, and no ground could be assigned for their death save the prompting of the serpent, as we have said.

"All the generations contemporary with Noah committed their sins openly, in the sight of all. R. Simeon was one day walking through the gate of Tiberias when he saw some men drawing the bow tight over earthenware pots. He cried: 'What! do these miscreants dare to provoke their Master thus openly?' He scowled at them, and they were thrown into the sea and drowned. Take note that every sin which is committed openly repels the Shekinah and causes her to remove her abode from this world.

"The contemporaries of Noah committed their sins openly and defiantly, and so they drove the Shekinah away from the world, in punishment for which God removed them from the world, in accordance with the maxim, 'Take away the dross from the silver, and there cometh forth a vessel for the finer; take away the wicked from before the king, and his throne shall be established in righteousness' [Prov. 25: 4 and 5]."

THREE GRADATIONS OF SPIRIT

AND NOAH BEGAT THREE SONS. Said R. Hiya to R. Judah: "Let me tell you what I have heard regarding this text.. A man once entered the recesses of a cavern, and there issued two or three children together, who differed from one another in their character and conduct: one was virtuous, a second vicious, and a third average. Similarly we find three strands of spirit which flit about and are taken up into three different worlds. The *neshamah* (spiritual soul) emerges and enters between the gorges of the mountains, where it is joined by the *ruah* (intellectual spirit). It descends then below where the *nefesh* (vital spirit) joins the *ruah,* and all three form a unity."

R. Judah said: "The *nefesh* and the *ruah* are intertwined together, whereas the *neshamah* resides in a man's character—an abode which cannot be discovered or located. Should a man strive towards purity of life, he is aided thereto by a holy *neshamah,* whereby he is purified and sanctified and attains the title of 'saint.' But should he not strive for righteousness and purity of life, he is animated only by the two grades, *nefesh* and *ruah,* and is devoid of a holy *neshamah.* What is more, he who commences to defile himself is led further into defilement, and heavenly help is withdrawn from him. Thus each is led along the path which he chooses."

THE SABBATH

REMEMBER THE SABBATH DAY, TO SANCTIFY IT.
Said R. Isaac: "It is written, 'And God blessed the seventh day' [Gen. 2:3]; and yet we read of the manna, 'Six days ye shall gather it, but on the

seventh day, the Sabbath, in it there shall be none' [Ex. 16:26]. If there was no food on that day what blessing is attached to it? Yet we have been taught that all blessings from above and from below depend upon the seventh day. Why, then, was there no manna just on this day?

"The explanation is that all the six days of the transcendent world derive their blessings from it, and each supernal day sends forth nourishment to the world below from what it received from the seventh day. Therefore he who has attained to the grade of Faith must needs prepare a table and a meal on the Sabbath eve (Friday) so that his table may be blessed all through the other six days of the week. For, indeed, at the time of the Sabbath preparation there is also prepared the blessing for all the six days that shall follow, for no blessing is found at an empty table. Thus one should make ready the table on Sabbath night with bread and other food."

R. Isaac added: "Also on the Sabbath day."

Said R. Judah: "One must regale oneself on this day with three meals, in order that this day may be one of satisfaction and refreshment."

Said R. Abba: "One must do so in order that blessing may spread to those supernal days which receive their blessing from the seventh. On this day the head of the 'Little Face' is filled with the dew which descends from the Holy Ancient One, the Most Hidden One; He causes it to descend into the holy 'Field of Apples' three times after the entrance of the Sabbath, in order that all unitedly may enjoy the blessing. Therefore it is necessary, not only for ourselves that we should have these three repasts during the day, but for all creation, for therein is consummated the true faith in the Holy Ancient One, the 'Little Face,' and the 'Field of Apples' [symbol of the sphere of the divine presence], and we should rejoice and delight in all three." . . .

Said R. Simeon: "Therefore the Sabbath is more precious than all other times and seasons and festivals, because it contains and unites all in itself, whereas no other festival or holy day does so. . . ."

Said R. Hiya: "Therefore one must wholeheartedly rejoice in these meals, and complete their number, for they are meals of the perfect Faith, the Faith of the holy seed of Israel, their supernal Faith, which is not that of the heathen nations: 'A sign between me and the children of Israel [Ex. 31:17]. And mark this. By these meals the children of Israel are distinguished as the King's sons, as belonging to the Palace, as sons of Faith; and he who abstains from one of these meals causes an incompleteness in the regions above; thus such a man testifies of himself that he is not one of the King's sons, not of the Palace, not of the holiness of Israel's seed, and he will be made to bear the burden of a threefold punishment in Gehenna.

"Also mark this. On all festivals and holy days a man must both rejoice himself and give joy to the poor. Should he regale himself only and not give a share to the poor, his punishment will be great. Concerning such a one it is written: 'Behold, I will reprove your seed and spread dung upon your face, the dung of your solemn feasts.' [Mal. 2:3]. This particular verse, however, applies only to festivals, not to the Sabbath. Similarly, the words, 'Your new moons and your appointed feasts my soul hateth:' [Isa. 1:14], do not include the Sabbath. The unique character of the Sabbath is expressed in the words: 'Between Me and the children of Israel.'

"And because the Faith is centered in the Sabbath, man is given on this day an additional, a supernal soul, a soul in which is all perfection, according to the pattern of the world to come. What does the word 'Sabbath' mean? The Name of the Holy One, the Name which is in perfect harmony at all sides."

Said R. Jose: "It is indeed so. Woe to him who does not help to complete the joy of the Holy King! And what is His joy? Those three meals of the Faith, the meals wherein Abraham, Isaac, and Jacob participate, and which express joy upon joy, the perfect Faith from all sides. On this day—so we have been taught—the Fathers crown themselves and all the Children imbibe power and light and joy, such as is unknown even on other festive days. On this day sinners find rest in Gehenna. On this day punishment is held back from the world. On this day the Torah crowns herself in perfect crowns. On this day joy and gladness resound throughout two hundred and fifty worlds. Mark also this. On all the six days of the week, when the hour of the afternoon prayer arrives, the attribute of Justice is in the ascendant, and punishment is at hand. But not so on the Sabbath. When the time of the Sabbath afternoon prayer arrives benign influences reign, the loving kindness of the Holy Ancient One is manifested, all chastisements are kept in leash, and all is satisfaction and joy. In this time of satisfaction and goodwill Moses, the holy, faithful prophet, passed away from this world, in order that it should be known that he was not taken away through judgment, but that in the hour of grace of the Holy Ancient One his soul ascended, to be hidden in Him. Therefore 'no man knows of his sepulcher unto this day.' [Deut. 34:6]. As the Holy Ancient One is the All-hidden One, whom neither those above nor those below can comprehend, so was this soul of Moses hidden in the epiphany of God's good will at the hour of the Sabbath afternoon prayer. This soul is the most hidden of all hidden things in the world, and judgement has no dominion over it. Blessed is the lot of Moses.

"On this day the Torah crowns herself with all beauty, with all those commandments, with all those decrees and punishments for transgressions —in seventy branches of light which radiate on every hand. What it is to behold the little twigs which constantly emanate from each branch—five of which stand in the Tree itself, all the branches being comprised in it! What it is to behold the gates which open at all sides, and through which bursts forth in splendour and beauty the streaming, inexhaustible light! A voice is heard: 'Awake, ye supernal saints! Awake, holy people, chosen from above and from below! Awake in joy to meet your Lord, awake in perfect joy! Prepare yourselves in the threefold joy of the three Patriarchs! Prepare yourselves for the Faith, the joy of joys! Happy are ye, O Israelites, holy in this world and holy in the world to come! This is your heritage over and above that of all heathen nations—'a sign between Me and you!' "

Said R. Judah: "It is indeed thus. Hence: 'Remember the sabbath day to sanctify it'; 'Be ye holy, for I the Lord am holy.' [Lev. 19:2]; 'Call the sabbath a delight, the holy of the Lord, honourable;' [Isa. 58:13].

"All the souls of the righteous—so we have been taught—on this day are feasted on the delights of the Holy Ancient One, the All-hidden. A breath of this rapture is extended through all the worlds; it ascends and descends, and spreads abroad to all the children of the holy, to all the guardians of the Torah, so that they enjoy perfect rest, forgetting all cares, all penalties, all toil and drudgery. It is the day on which 'the Lord giveth thee rest from thy sorrow, and from thy fear, and from the hard bondage wherein thou wast made to serve.' [Isa. 14:3]. Therefore the Sabbath is equal in importance to the whole Torah, and whosoever observes the Sabbath fulfils the whole Torah: 'Blessed is the man that doeth this, and the son of man that layeth hold on it: that keepeth the sabbath from profaning it, and keepeth his hand from doing any evil.' [*Ibid.* 56:2]."

LOVERS OF TORAH

R. Hiya and R. Jose met one night at the tower of Tyrus, and greatly enjoyed one another's company. Said R. Jose: "How glad am I to behold the countenance of the Shekinah! For during the whole of my journey here I was molested by the chatter of an old carrier who pestered me with all sorts of foolish questions; for example, 'Which serpent is it that flies in the air whilst an ant lies undisturbed between its teeth? What is it that begins in union and ends in separation? Which eagle is it whose nest is in a tree that does not yet exist, and whose young ones are plundered by creatures who have not yet been created, and in a place which is not? What are those which when they ascend descend, and when they descend ascend? And what is it two of which are one and one of which is three? And who is the beautiful virgin who has no eyes and whose body is concealed and yet revealed—revealed in the morning and concealed during the day, and who is adorned with ornaments which do not exist?' So he went on plaguing me the whole of the way. But now I shall have peace and quiet, and we can devote ourselves to discussing the Torah instead of wasting time in empty talk."

Said R. Hiya: "Dost thou know anything of the old man?"

R. Jose replied: "I only know that there is nothing in him; for if there were, he would have expounded some text of Scripture, and the time spent on the road would not have been profitless." "Is the old man in this house?" asked R. Hiya. "For sometimes it happens that in vessels that seem empty grains of gold can be discovered." "Yes," replied R. Jose, "he is here, preparing fodder for his donkey." So they called the carrier and he came to them.

The first thing the old man said was: "Now the two have become three, and the three one!"

Said R. Jose: "Did I not tell thee that he only talks nonsense?"

The old man seated himself and said: "Sirs, it is only recently that I have become a carrier. I have a young son whom I send to school, and whom I wish to bring up in the study of the Torah; so whenever I see a scholar on my way I follow him in the hope of picking up some new idea in connection with the Torah; but today I have heard nothing new."

Said R. Jose: "Of all the things I heard you say, one specially surprised me, because it showed exceptional folly in a man of your years, or else you did not know what you were saying."

Said the old man: 'What do you refer to?'

Said R. Jose: "That about the beautiful virgin and so forth." . . .

When the ancient one had reached this point he paused, and the two rabbis prostrated themselves before him, wept and said: "Had we come into this world only in order to hear these thy words from thy mouth it were sufficient."

Said he: "Friends, I did not begin to speak to you merely in order to tell you what I have told up till now, for, surely, an old man like myself would not limit himself to one saying, making a noise like a single coin in a jug. How many human beings live in confusion of mind, beholding not the way of truth whose dwelling is in the Torah, the Torah which calls them day by day to herself in love, but alas, they do not even turn their heads! It is indeed as I have said, that the Torah lets out a word, and emerges for a little from her sheath, and then hides herself again. But she does this only for those who understand and obey her.

"She is like a beautiful and stately damsel, who is hidden in a secluded chamber of a palace and who has a lover of whom no one knows but she. Out of his love for her he constantly passes by her gate, turning his eyes towards all sides to find her. She, knowing that he is always haunting the palace, what does she do? She opens a little door in her hidden palace, discloses for a moment her face to her lover, then swiftly hides it again. None but he notices it; but his heart and soul, and all that is in him are drawn to her, knowing as he does that she has revealed herself to him for a moment because she loves him.

"It is the same with the Torah, which reveals her hidden secrets only to those who love her. She knows that he who is wise of heart daily haunts the gates of her house. What does she do? She shows her face to him from her palace, making a sign of love to him, and straightaway returns to her hiding place again. No one understands her message save he alone, and he is drawn to her with heart and soul and all his being. Thus the Torah reveals herself momentarily in love to her lovers in order to awaken fresh love in them. Now this is the way of the Torah. At first, when she begins to reveal herself to a man, she makes signs to him. Should he understand, well and good, but if not, then she sends for him and calls him 'simpleton,' saying to her messengers: 'Tell that simpleton to come here and converse with me,' as it is written: 'Whoso is a simpleton let him turn in hither' [Prov. 9:4].

"When he comes to her she begins to speak to him, first from behind the curtain which she has spread for him about her words suitable to his mode of understanding, so that he may progress little by little. This is called 'Derasha' [Talmudic casuistry, namely the derivation of the traditional laws and usages from the letter of Scripture]. Then she speaks to him from behind a thin veil of a finger mesh, discoursing riddles and parables—which go by the name of Haggadah.

"When at last he is familiar with her she shows herself to him face to face and converses with him concerning all her hidden mysteries and all the mysterious ways which have been secreted in her heart from time immemorial. Then such a man is a true adept in the Torah, a 'master of the house,' since she has revealed to him all her mysteries, withholding and hiding nothing. She says to him: 'Seest thou the sign, the hint, which I gave thee at first, how many mysteries it contains?' He realizes then that nothing may be added to nor taken from the words of the Torah, not even one sign or letter.

"Therefore men should follow the Torah with might and main in order that they may become her lovers, as has been described."

JONAH AS ALLEGORY

In the story of Jonah we have an allegory of the whole of a man's career in this world. Jonah descending into the ship is symbolic of man's soul that descends into this world to enter into his body. Why is she called Jonah [lit. aggrieved]? Because as soon as she becomes partner with the body in this world she finds herself full of vexation. Man, then, is in this world as in a ship that is traversing the great ocean and is like to be broken, as it says, "so that the ship was like to be broken." [Jonah 1:4].

Furthermore, man in this world commits sins, imagining that he can flee from the presence of his Master, who takes no notice of this world. The Almighty then rouses a furious tempest; to wit, man's doom, which constantly stands before the Holy One, blessed be He, and demands his punishment. It is this which assails the ship and calls to mind man's sins that it may seize him; and the man is thus caught by the tempest and is struck down by illness, just as Jonah "went down into the innermost part of the ship; and he lay, and was fast asleep."

Although the man is thus prostrated, his soul does not exert itself to return to his Master in order to make good his omissions. So "the ship-master came to him," to wit, the good prompter, who is the general steers-man, "and said unto him: What meanest thou that thou sleepest? Arise, call upon thy God," etc.; it is not a time to sleep, as they are about to take thee up to be tried for all that thou hast done in this world. Repent of thy sins. Reflect on these things and return to thy Master.

"What is thine occupation," wherein thou wast occupied in this world; and make confession concerning it before the Master; "and whence comest thou"; to wit, from a fetid drop, and so be not thou arrogant before him. "What is thy country"—reflect that from earth thou wast created and to earth thou wilt return; "and of what people art thou"; that is, reflect whether thou canst rely on merits of thy forbears to protect thee.

When they bring him to judgement before the Heavenly Tribunal, that tempest, that is none other than the judgement doom which raged against him, demands from the King the punishment of all the King's prisoners, and then all the King's counsellors appear before Him one by one, and the Tribunal is set up. Some plead in defence of the accused, others against him. Should the man be found guilty, as in the case of Jonah, then "the men rowed hard to bring it to the land, but they could not"; so those who plead on his behalf find points in his favour and strive to restore him to his world, but they cannot; "for the sea grew more and more tempestuous against them", the prosecution storms and rages against him, and convicting him of his sins, prevails against his defenders.

Then three appointed messengers descend upon the man; one of them makes a record of all the good deeds and the misdeeds that he has per-formed in this world; one casts up the reckoning of his days; and the third is the one who has accompanied the man from the time when he was in his mother's womb. As already said, the doom summons is not appeased until "they took up Jonah," until they take him from the house to the place of burial. Then proclamation is made concerning him. If he was a righteous man, it runs, Render honour to the King's image! "He entereth into peace, they rest in their beds, each one that walketh in his uprightness" [Isa. 57:2].

But when a wicked man dies, the proclamation runs: Woe to that man, it would have been better for him had he never been born! Regarding such a man it is written, "and they cast him forth into the sea, and the sea ceased from its raging," that is, only after they have placed him in the grave, which is the place of judgement, does the judgement summons cease from its raging. For the fish that swallowed him is, in fact, the grave; and so "Jonah was in the belly of the fish," which is identified with "the belly of the under-world [sheol], as is proved by the passage, "Out of the belly of the under-world [sheol] cried I."

"Three days and three nights"; these are the three days that a man lies in his grave before his belly splits open. After three days it ejects the putrid matter on his face, saying: "Take back what thou gavest me; thou didst eat and drink all day and never didst thou give anything to the poor; all thy days were like feasts and holidays, whilst the poor remained hungry without partaking of any of thy food. Take back what thou gavest me."

In regard to this it is written: "and I will spread dung upon your faces," etc. [Malachi 2:3]. Again, after the lapse of three days, the man receives chastisement in each organ—in his eyes, his hands, and his feet. This continues for thirty days, during which time the soul and the body are chastised together. The soul therefore remains all that time on earth below, not ascending to her place, like a woman remaining apart all the days of her impurity.

After that the soul ascends whilst the body is being decomposed in the earth, where it will lie until the time when the Holy One, blessed be He, will awaken the dead. A voice will then resound through the graves, proclaiming: "Awake and sing, ye that dwell in the dust, for thy dew is as the dew of light, and the earth shall cast forth the dead [rephaim]." [Isa. 26:19]. That will come to pass when the Angel of Death will depart from the world, as it is written: "He will destroy death for ever, and the Lord God will wipe away tears from off all faces; and the reproach of his people will he take away from off all the earth" [Ibid. 25:8].

It is of that occasion that it is written: "And the Lord spoke unto the fish, and it vomited out Jonah upon the dry land"; for as soon as that voice will resound among the graves they will all cast out the dead bodies that they contain. The term rephaim [the dead] being akin to the root, rapha [healing], indicates that the dead will be restored to their former physical condition. But, you may say, is it not written elsewhere, "the rephaim will not rise" [Ibid. 26:14]? The truth is that all the dead will be restored to their former state whilst in the graves, but some of them will rise and others will not. Happy is the portion of Israel, of whom it is written, "My dead bodies shall arise" [Ibid. 26:19].

Thus in the narrative of that fish we find words of healing for the whole world. As soon as it swallowed Jonah it died, but after three days was restored to life and vomited him forth. In a similar way the Land of Israel will in the future first be stirred to new life, and afterwards "the earth will cast forth the dead."

Said R. Simeon: "Alas for the man who regards the Torah as a book of mere tales and everyday matters! If that were so, we, even we could compose a torah dealing with everyday affairs, and of even greater excellence. Nay, even the princes of the world possess books of greater worth which we could use as a model for composing some such torah. The Torah, however, contains in all its words supernal truths and sublime mysteries.

"Observe the perfect balancing of the upper and the lower worlds. Israel here below is balanced by the angels on high, of whom it says: 'Who makest thy angels into winds' [Ps. 104:4]. For the angels in descending on earth put on themselves earthly garments, as otherwise they could not stay in this world, nor could the world endure them. Now, if thus it is with the angels, how much more so must it be with the Torah—the Torah that created them, that created all the worlds and is the means by which these are sustained. Thus, had the Torah not clothed herself in garments of this world the world could not endure it.

"The stories of the Torah are thus only her outer garments, and whoever looks upon that garment as being the Torah itself, woe to that man—such a one will have no portion in the next world. David thus said: 'Open thou mine eyes, that I may behold wondrous things out of thy law.' [Ps. 119:18], to wit, the things that are beneath the garment. Observe this. The garments worn by a man are the most visible part of him, and senseless people looking at the man do not seem to see more in him than the garments. But in truth the pride of the garments is the body of the man, and the pride of the body is the soul.

"Similarly, the Torah has a body made up of the precepts of the Torah, called *gufe torah* [bodies, main principles of the Torah], and that body is enveloped in garments made up of worldly narrations. The senseless people only see the garment, the mere narrations; those who are somewhat wiser penetrate as far as the body. But the really wise, the servants of the most high King, those who stood on Mount Sinai, penetrate right through to the soul, the root principle of all, namely, to the real Torah. In the future the same are destined to penetrate even to the supersoul (soul of the soul) of the Torah.

"Observe that in a similar way in the supernal world there is garment, body, soul and supersoul. The heavens and their hosts are the outer garment, the Community of Israel is the body which receives the soul, to wit, the 'Glory of Israel'; and the supersoul is the Ancient Holy One. All these are interlocked within each other.

"Woe to the sinners who consider the Torah as mere worldly tales, who only see its outer garment; happy are the righteous who fix their gaze on the Torah proper. Wine cannot be kept save in a jar; so the Torah needs an outer garment. These are the stories and narratives; but we must penetrate beyond."

The Letters of Obadiah da Bertinoro

Obadiah Yareh da Bertinoro (1450–1520) was born in Italy and served as rabbi in the city of Bertinoro (and hence his name). Although he led a life of ease and wealth in Italy, he was drawn to the Land of Israel, and left his home in 1486. In Obadiah's day a Jew was not permitted to sail from Venice to Palestine, lest he be thrown overboard if his destination became known. The prohibition stemmed from the dispute between the Franciscan monks and the Jews, wherein the former wrongly suspected the latter of wanting to buy the Temple Mount and the grave of Jesus. Obadiah, therefore, proceeded to Rome, Naples, Palermo, Greece and Egypt, where he took a camel caravan to Jerusalem. According to his description, the city was desolate, containing only seventy poor Jewish families out of a total population of four thousand. However, subsequent to the 1492 expulsion of Jews from Spain, the refugees began to arrive in Jerusalem and added to its community.

Arriving in 1488, Obadiah immediately set out to improve the lot of the physically and spiritually impoverished Jews in the Holy Land. Aside from being a religious leader Obadiah was also a political and public figure: he intervened with the governing authorities to abolish an unjust tax that had been imposed on the Jews; established a hospital, a Talmudic academy and charitable institutions; and received contributions for the upkeep of the needy not only from Jewish communities in Turkey, Egypt and other places, but also from his family in Italy as well. Obadiah's reputation as a man of impeccable character spread even to the Muslim community, whose members would come to him to adjudicate disputes.

Obadiah is best known for his *Commentary on the Mishnah,* which by now has achieved the status of a classic. Just as Rashi's *Commentary* is printed with virtually every Pentateuch, Obadiah's *Commentary*—since its first publication in Venice in 1549 —appears in nearly all editions of the Mishnah. His popular, easily-ready commentary is based to a large extent on those of Rashi and Maimonides.

Other works by Obadiah da Bertinoro include a commentary upon Rashi's explication of the Torah, one of the many extant supercommentaries to Rashi's text, and several liturgic poems. His most personal and revealing work, however, is in the non-sacred field—his letters from Palestine wherein he depicts the status of Jews in the various countries he visited, gives an unbiased account of the Karaites and the Samaritans, and provides a picturesque account of the Jews in Palestine.

LETTER TO HIS FATHER

My departure has caused you sorrow and trouble, and I am inconsolable because I have left you at a time when your strength is failing; when I remember, dear father, I cannot refrain from tears. But since I am denied the happiness of being able to serve you as I ought, for God has decreed our separation, I will at least give you an account of my journey from beginning to end in the way which you desired me to do in your letters, which I received in Naples about this time last year, by describing the manners and customs of the Jews in all the places I have visited and the nature of their intercourse with the other inhabitants of these cities.

On the first day of the ninth month [Kislev, 1486], after having arranged all matters in my place of residence, Citta di Castello, I repaired to Rome, and thence to Naples, where I arrived on the twelfth of that month and where I tarried for a long time, not finding any vessel such as I wished. I went to Salerno, where I gave gratuitous instruction for at least four months and then returned to Naples.

In the fourth month, on the fast day [the 17th of Tammuz, 1487], I set out from Naples, in the large and swift ship of Mossen Blanchi, together with nine other Jews; it was five days, however, before we reached Palermo, owing to a calm.

Palermo is the chief town of Sicily, and contains about 850 Jewish families, all living in one street, which is situated in the best part of the town. They are artisans, such as coppersmiths and ironsmiths, porters and peasants, and are despised by the Christians because they wear tattered garments. As a mark of distinction they are obliged to wear a piece of red cloth, about the size of a gold coin, fastened on the breast. The royal tax falls heavily on them, for they are obliged to work for the king at any employment that is given them; they have to draw ships to the shore, to construct dykes, and so on. They are also employed in administering corporal punishment and in carrying out the sentence of death.

The synagogue at Palermo has not its equal in the whole world; the stone pillars in the outer courtyard are encircled by vines such as I have never seen before. I measured one of them and it was of the thickness of five spans. From this court you descend by stone steps into another which belongs to the vestibule of the synagogue. This vestibule has three sides and a porch in which there are large chairs for anyone who may not wish to enter the synagogue, and a splendid fountain. The entrance is placed at the fourth side of the synagogue which is built in the form of a square, forty cubits long and forty cubits wide. On the eastern side there is a stone building, shaped like a dome, the Ark. It contains the rolls of the law which are ornamented with crowns and pomegranates of silver and precious stones to the value of 4,000 gold pieces (according to the statement of the Jews who live there) and are laid on a wooden shelf, and not put into a chest as with us. The Ark has two doors, one towards the south, and one towards the north, and the office of opening and shutting the doors is entrusted to two of the congregation.

In the center of the synagogue is a wooden platform where the readers recite their prayers. There are at present five readers in the community; and on the Sabbath and on the Festivals they chant the prayers more sweetly than I have ever heard it done in any other congregation. On weekdays the number of visitors to the synagogue is very small, so that a little child might count them.

The synagogue is surrounded by numerous buildings, such as the hospital, where beds are provided for sick people, and for strangers who come there and do not know where to pass the night; and again a large and magnificent mansion, where those who are elected sit in judgment and regulate the affairs of the community. There are twelve of these, and they are chosen every year; they are empowered by the king to fix the taxes, to levy fines, and to punish with imprisonment. There is nothing to be said in favor of this arrangement, for men of no name and of bad character frequently prevail upon the governor, by means of gifts, to appoint them members of this body. They then indemnify themselves for their presents by taxing the synagogue and congregation, so that the poor people are overwhelmed with imposts; for this elected body is supported by the governor and has absolute power, and the cry of misery from the oppressed is exceedingly great.

In Palermo I noticed the following customs: When anybody dies, his coffin is brought into the vestibule of the synagogue and the ministers hold the funeral service and recite lamentations over him. If the departed is a distinguished man especially learned in the law the coffin is brought into the synagogue itself, a roll of the law is taken out and placed in the corner of the Ark, while the coffin is placed opposite to this corner, and then the funeral service commences and lamentations are recited: the same thing is done with all the four corners of the Ark. The coffin is then carried to the place of burial outside the town and on arriving at the gate of the town the reader begins to repeat aloud the forty-ninth and other psalms till they reach the burial ground.

I have also noticed the following customs: On the evening of the Day of Atonement and of the Seventh Day of Tabernacles [Hoshana Rabba], after the prayers are finished, the two officials open the doors of the Ark and remain there the whole night; women come there in family groups to kiss the roll of the Law and to prostrate themselves before it; they enter at one door and go out by the other, and this continues the whole night, some coming and others going. . . .

I remained in Palermo from Tammuz 22nd, 5247, till Shabbath Bereshith, 5248 (i.e., from about July to October). On my arrival there the chief Jews invited me to deliver lectures on the Sabbath before the Afternoon Service. I consented, and began on the Sabbath of the New Moon of Ab (5247). My discourses were favorably received, so that I was obliged to continue them every Sabbath; but this was no advantage to me, for I had come to Palermo with the object of going on to Syracuse, which is at the extreme end of Sicily, for I had heard this was the time when Venetian ships going to Beyrut, near Jerusalem, would touch there.

The Jews of Palermo then got many persons to circulate false rumors to dissuade me from my intention, and succeeded in taking me in their net, so that I missed the good crossing for the ships to Syracuse; I therefore remained in Palermo to give lectures to the people, about three hours before the Afternoon Service. In my discourses I inveighed against informers and transgressors, so that the elders of the city told me that many refrained from sin, and the number of informers also decreased while I was there; I do not know if they will go back to their old ways. But yet I cannot spend all my life among them, although they honor and deify me, for indeed they treated me as the Gentiles treat their saints.

The common people said that God had sent me to them, while many wanted a piece of my garments for a remembrance; and a woman who washed my linen was counted happy by the rest. They calculated that I would remain there at least a year, and wanted to assign me an extraordinary salary, which, however, I declined, for my heart longed to reach the Promised Land.

On the eve of Tabernacles, 5248 [1487 C.E.] a French galley came to Palermo, on its way to Alexandria. The worthy Meshullam of Volterra was in it, with his servant, and I rejoiced to travel in his company. The night after the Sabbath we embarked, and on Sunday at midday we left Palermo. All day and night we had a favorable wind, so that in the morning we were close to the Pharos of Messina; we got safely past this and were in Messina on Monday at noon.

This town is a trade place for all nations; ships come here from all parts; for Messina lies in the middle of the Pharos, so that ships from the east and west pass it by, and its harbor is the only one of its kind in the world; the largest vessels may here come close to the shore. Messina is not so large as Palermo, neither has it such good springs; but the town is very beautiful and has a strong fortress.

There are about four hundred Jewish families in it, living quietly in a street of their own; they are richer than those in Palermo, and are almost all artisans; there are only a few merchants among them. They have a synagogue with a porch, open above but enclosed on the four sides, and in the middle of it is a well with spring water. There is an administration consisting of persons who are chosen every year; and this as well as other arrangements resembles that of the Jews of Palermo.

At a wedding which took place near my residence I witnessed the following ceremony. After the seven blessings had been repeated, the bride was placed on a horse and rode through the town. The whole community went before her on foot, the bridegroom in the midst of the elders and before the bride, who was the only one on horseback; youths and children carried burning torches and made loud exclamations, so that the whole place resounded; they made the circuit of the streets and all the Jewish courts; the Christian inhabitants looked on with pleasure and no one disturbed the festivity.

On the eleventh of Marheshvan [October] we left Messina to go to Rhodes. We were joined in the ship by a Jewish merchant from Sucari, with his servant, three Jewish leatherworkers from Syracuse, and a Sephardic Jew with his wife, two sons and two daughters, so that together we were fourteen Jewish souls on board. We passed the Pharos in safety, sailed through the Gulf of Venice, and thus reached the Archipelago. The Archipelago is full of small islands—Corfu, Candia, Negropont, Rhodes and Cyprus—and altogether it is said to contain about three hundred inhabited and uninhabited islands.

For four days we had a favorable wind; on the fourth day towards evening, we were thrown back by a storm and could only escape the fury of the waves by remaining in a little natural harbor in the mountains, into which we were thrown; these mountains are full of St. John's bread and myrtle trees, and here we remained for three days.

After three days, on Sunday, the 18th of Marheshvan, we left this place and came within sixty miles of Rhodes. All the way we saw islands on both sides, and the Turkish mountains were also visible. But we were driven back eighty miles; and the ship had to cast anchor on the shores of the island Longo, which is under the dominion of Rhodes, and there we had to remain ten days, for the wind was unfavorable.

During our stay here, one of the sailors used insolent language to the worthy Meshullam, who complained of it to the master. The master himself went in search of the sailor; the others tried to hide him, but in vain. He commanded him to be tied to the mast and severely flogged, and when the beater seemed to spare him he took the rope himself and continued to punish the insolence of the sailor. He also desired him to make a public apology to the worthy Meshullam. The whole ship's crew were very much annoyed that all this should have happened on account of a few abusive words spoken against a Jew, and from this they began to hate us and no longer treated us as they had done before.

The worthy merchant, Meshullam, took advantage of a small ship that was coming from Rhodes and going to Chios to leave our vessel, intending to go to Chios and thence to Constantinople, for he had given up his intention of accompanying us to Alexandria. On the second day after Meshullam had left us we met a small ship by which we were made aware that a well-armed Genoese man-of-war was coming toward us. This news alarmed the master, for we had no wind; otherwise, if the wind be favorable, the galley does not fear a multitude of other ships, for there is no safer vessel than this.

The master therefore made for a little town, Castel San Giovani, on the Turkish mountains, which is under the supremacy of Rhodes, and is the only place in Turkey that has remained in the possession of the Christians. It is small but very strongly fortified, and its extreme environs already belong to the Turks. We arrived there on Friday, the day of the New Moon, Kislev [November] 5248, and were in safety. On Saturday, towards noon, God caused a favorable wind to blow so that we were able to leave the place and to sail all day and night and on Sunday, Kislev 3rd, 5248, we arrived joyfully at Rhodes, after a twenty-two days' sail.

The inhabitants of Rhodes welcomed us gladly, for the master of our ships was a friend and relative of the governor. The chief men of the Jewish community soon came to our ship, and received us with kindness; for the merchant Meshullam, who had been with us in the ship, was the brother of the physician Rabbi Nathan, the most distinguished man among the Jews of Rhodes.

A fine room, provided with all necessities, was assigned to me, while the other Jews who accompanied me were accommodated as well as it was possible, for the Jewish houses in Rhodes had been almost entirely destroyed by the siege of the Turks, under their first emperor, undertaken by him in the year of his death. No one who has not seen Rhodes, with its high and strong walls, its firm gates and battlements, has ever seen a fortress. The Turkish Emperor in the year of his death sent a besieging army against it, bombarded the town with a multitude of stones, which are still to be seen there, and in this way threw down the walls surrounding the Jewish street and destroyed the houses.

The Jews here have told me that when the Turks got into the town they killed everyone they saw until they came to the door of the synagogue, when God brought confusion among them, so that they began at once to flee and slay one another. On account of this miracle the governor built a church on the spot and gave the Jews another building instead of it. While I was in Rhodes, he granted them a hundred ducats from the revenues of the town to build a new synagogue.

Not many Jews have remained in Rhodes; altogether there are twenty-two families, all poor, who subsist with difficulty on vegetables, not eating bread or meat, for they never slaughter nor do they buy any wine, for fear of getting into disputes with the Greeks who dwell there. When they buy in the market, they touch nothing that belongs to the Greeks; and they observe the law against wine just as strictly as against pork.

The Jews here all are very intelligent and well educated; they speak a pure dialect and are very moral and polite; even the tanners are neatly dressed and speak with propriety. They all allow their hair to grow long and are beautiful in person. Nowhere are there more beautiful Jewesses than in Rhodes; they occupy themselves doing all kinds of handiwork for the Acomodors [the nobles of the land], and in this way support their husbands. The Acomodors hold the Jews in high esteem, often coming into their houses to chat awhile with the women who work there.

When anybody dies there is no coffin made for him; he is buried only in his shroud; an impression of a human form is made in the ground where he is to be buried for the earth there has never been cultivated so that it receives any impression. The dead body is laid in this cavity, a board is placed over it, and then it is covered with earth. The air in Rhodes is purer and more agreeable than I have yet felt in any other place; the water is sweet, the soil is clean but poor, and most of the inhabitants are Greeks who are subject to the Acomodors.

In Rhodes we remained from the 3rd of Kislev to the 15th of Tebet [December], because the governor would not allow the ship to sail to Alexandria, fearing lest the king of Egypt would keep it there. For the governor had accepted 120,000 gold pieces from the Egyptian King, promising to deliver up to him the brother of the Turkish Emperor, Dschem by name, who was detained a prisoner in France; but he had not been able to keep his promise from fear of the Turkish Emperor; for this reason he was afraid that the Egyptian King might seize the ship, which contained a vast amount of treasures, together with all the men in it. When, however, time wore on, the master having consulted with the merchants of the ship, thought better to sail in spite of all the danger.

On the 15th of Tebet, therefore, we left Rhodes and after six days we were before Alexandria; the master would not sail into it until he had learnt how matters stood. We therefore remained at Bukari, a place between Alexandria and Rosetta, on the way to Cairo; the water was not deep here but the place was large, and we cast anchor about four miles from the shore. We had a vessel of two hundred tons with us, as tender, which the master had bought and loaded with grain to sell in Alexandria.

The Emir [the representative of the King of Egypt] who had his seat in Alexandria, sent an assurance to the master that the ship and all that was in it might come there in safety, but the latter placed no faith in this promise, and himself sent ambassadors to the king. He was willing, however, to send the smaller ship with wheat and a small crew to Alexandria on the word of the Emir. The Jews therefore resorted to this ship on Friday, expecting to reach Alexandria on the Sabbath. But the Emir would not allow this because the master had refused to place confidence in him, and so we Jews remained in this ship, about a bowshot removed from the galley.

A considerable time had elapsed and the messengers had not yet returned from Cairo; our victuals began to be exhausted, we had no water, and would already have preferred death to life.

On the 18th of Shebat [January], about midnight, a dreadful storm arose; two anchors of our ship suddenly broke, only the weakest remaining. The sailors were terrified and threw many things overboard to lighten the ship; they signalled to the other ship, by firing guns, to send off the boat with men; but nobody heard and nobody answered, for those in the galley were concerned with their own safety, and, indeed, it would scarcely have been possible for a bark to have approached us, for the sea was too stormy. It drove us, with the damaged anchor which still remained, on to a whirlpool; the waves went over us, we were tossed hither and thither, and the ship threatened to be wrecked every moment, for it was old and damaged, so that the water penetrated on all sides, and the sea in that part was full of rocks.

For about twenty-four hours we were in such danger that we expected death every moment. We each had a pail in our hands to empty out the water which flowed abundantly into the ship; and we tearfully filled our pails and emptied them, till God took mercy on us, and we happily escaped the storm almost miraculously. When the storm was over, the master sent for the people from the damaged vessel and on the morning of the second day we entered into the large ship and remained there until the ambassadors returned bringing a guarantee from the king. There was now again a calm, and the ship could not leave Bukari. The merchants and the Jews in the large ship preferred to go ashore in a bark that their lives might be in safety.

We then traveled on foot (not being able to get asses) for eighteen miles of the way, and we reached Alexandria on the 14th of Shebat, tired and weary. Here God gave us favor in the eyes of a generous man who was very much beloved even by the Arabs, by name Rabbi Moses Grasso, dragoman of the Venetians. He came to meet us and released us from the hands of the Arabs who sit in the gate and plunder foreign Jews at their pleasure. He took me in his house, and there I had to remain while I stayed in Alexandria. I read with him a book on the Kabala, which he had in his possession, for he dearly loved this science. By thus reading with him I found favor in his sight and we became friends. On the Sabbath he gave a dinner, to which he invited the Sephardi who had come with me; his two sons were also there when he brought me into the dining room.

The following is the arrangement of the Sabbath meal customary to Jews in all Arabian countries. They sit in a circle on a carpet, the cupbearer standing near them near a small cloth which is spread on this carpet;

all kinds of fruit which are in season are brought and laid on the cloth. The host now takes a glass of wine, pronounces the blessing of sanctification [Kiddush], and empties the cup completely. The cupbearer then takes it from the host, and hands it successively to the whole company, always refilled, and each one empties it, then the host takes two or three pieces of fruit, eats some, and drinks a second glass, while the company say, "Health and life." Whoever sits next also takes some fruit, and the cupbearer fills a second glass for him, saying, "To your pleasure," the company join in with the words, "Health and life," and so it goes round.

Then a second kind of fruit is partaken of, another glass is filled, and this is continued until each one has emptied at least six or seven glasses. Sometimes they even drink when they smell flowers which are provided for the occasion; these flowers are the "dudaim," which Rashi translates into Arabic by "jasmine"; it is a plant bearing only blossoms which have a delightful and invigorating fragrance.

The wine is unusually strong, and this is especially the case in Jerusalem, where it is drunk unmixed. After all have drunk to their heart's content, a large dish of meat is brought, each one stretches forth his hand, takes what he wants, and eats quickly, for they are not very big eaters. Rabbi Moses brought us confectionery, fresh ginger, dates, raisins, almonds, and confectionery of coriander seeds; a glass of wine is drunk with each kind. Then followed raisin wine, which was very good, then malmsey wine from Candia, and again native wine. I drank with them and was exhilarated.

There is another custom in the country of the Arabs: On Friday all go to bathe, and on their return the women bring them wine, of which they drink copiously; word is then brought that the supper is ready, and it is eaten in the daytime, before evening. Then they all come to the synagogue, cleanly and neatly dressed. They begin with psalms and thanksgiving and evening prayer is read until two hours after dusk.

On their return home they repeat the Kiddush, eat only a piece of bread of the size of an olive, and recite the grace after meals. In this whole district the Afternoon Prayer is read on Friday in private, except in Jerusalem, where the Ashkenazim [Germans] have done away with the custom, and the afternoon and evening prayer are said with minyan as with us, and they eat at night; the evening prayer is not begun, however, until the stars are visible.

In these parts the Sabbath is more strictly kept than in any other; nobody leaves his house on the Sabbath, except to go to the synagogue or to the Bet Hamidrash [house of study]. I need scarcely mention that nobody kindles a fire on the Sabbath, or has a light that has been extinguished rekindled, even by a Gentile. All who are able to read the Holy Scriptures read the whole day, after having slept off the effect of their wine.

In Alexandria there are about twenty-five families and two old synagogues. One is very large and somewhat damaged, the other is smaller. Most pray in the smaller, because it bears the name of the prophet Elijah;

and it is said that he once appeared to somebody in the southeast corner, where a light is now kept constantly burning. I have been told that twenty years ago he again appeared to an old man. God alone knows the truth! In all Arabian countries no man enters the synagogue with shoes on his feet; even in paying a visit the shoes are left outside the door, and everybody sits on the ground on mats or carpets.

Alexandria is a very large town surrounded with a wall and encircled by the sea, though two-thirds of it are now destroyed and many houses uninhabited. The inhabited courts are paved with mosaic; peach and date trees are in the middle of them. All the houses are large and beautiful, but the inhabitants are few on account of the unhealthy atmosphere which has prevailed here for many years. It is said that those who are not accustomed to the air, and remain long here, die or at least fall sick. Most of the inhabitants are subject to the diseases of the eye.

Merchants come from all parts, and at present there are four consuls here: for Venice, Genoa, Catalonia and Ancona, and the merchants of all nations have to treat with them. The Christians are obliged to shut themselves in their houses every evening; the Arabs close up the streets from without, and open them again every morning. It is the same on Friday from noon till the evening; while the Arabs tarry in the house of prayer, the Christians have to stay in their houses, and whoever is seen in the street has himself to blame if he is ill-treated.

The King of Egypt receives an immense sum of money by the export and import duties paid on wares which come to Alexandria, for the tax is very high; even current money that is brought in has to pay two per cent. As for me, by the help of God, I was not obliged to pay entrance duty for my money. Smugglers are not subjected to any special punishment by the Egyptian taxcollectors.

I spent seven days in Alexandria, leaving my effects, which were very few, in the large ship, which was still detained in Bukari by the calm. It happened just at this time that there was a man in Alexandria who had made a vow to celebrate the Passover feast in Jerusalem with his wife and two sons. I joined myself to him, and traveled with him on camels. I commissioned Rabbi Moses Grasso to bring my things from the large ship and send them to Cairo.

At Rosetta, on the Nile, we got into a ship. On both sides of the Nile there are towns and villages which are beautiful, large and populous, but all unfortified. We remained two days in Fuah, because the wind was not favorable; it is a large and beautiful place, and fish and vegetables can be got for almost nothing. We came next to Bulak, which already forms the beginning of Cairo.

On the Nile I saw the large species of frog which the natives call El Timsah [the crocodile]; it is larger than a bear and spots are visible on its skin. The ship's crew say that there are some twice as big. These are the. frogs which have remained from the time of Moses, as Nahmanides mentions in his commentary. The Nile is wide and its waters are very sweet but turbid. The part on which we sailed forms merely a branch, for the other goes to Damietta, where it flows into the sea.

Before coming to Bulak we observed two very old dome-shaped buildings which lay on the same side of the stream; it is said that they are the magazines which Joseph built. The door is above in the roof. Although they are now only ruins, yet it is easy to see that they have once been magnificent buildings; the district is uninhabited.

Twelve days before Purim, towards evening, we came to Cairo; it was the time of the great harvest and the severe famine which had prevailed in the whole district of Cairo was on the decrease. The barley ripens sooner here than elsewhere by the influence of the waters of the Nile, and the harvest appeared to be very good. In the following month there was great plenty, so that there was no more thought of famine. The inhabitants and their fields are to this day subject to the king, who takes a fifth part of the produce, and sometimes more. Egypt is the only place in the world where the fields are thus subject to the king to the present day.

I shall not speak of the grandeur of Cairo and of the multitude of men to be seen streaming there, for many before me have described them, and all that has been said of the town is true. It is not completely surrounded by a wall, though there are several places here and there protected in that way. The town is very animated, and one hears the different languages of the foreigners who inhabit it. It is situated between the Red Sea and the Mediterranean, and all merchants come from India, Ethiopia, and the countries of Prester John [Abyssinia] through the Red Sea to Cairo both to sell their wares, which consist of spices, pearls, and precious stones, and to purchase commodities which come from France, Germany, Italy and Turkey, across the Mediterranean Sea through Alexandria to Cairo.

In the Red Sea there are magnets; hence the ships which come through them have no iron in them, not so much as a nail. The place where the sea was divided for our forefathers is said to have been identified, and many priests go to visit it, but I have heard of no Jew who has been there. The harbor where the ships coming from the Red Sea unload their cargoes, and from whence the wares are brought to Cairo by means of camels, is said to be not far distant from Mt. Sinai, which is only five days' journey from Cairo.

The Christian ecclesiastics live here in a convent and come daily to Cairo, making the journey there and back more frequently than any other people, even than the Arabs, for it is known that they carry no gold with them; the whole way is infested by Bedouin, who rob and plunder at their will in the wilderness; they do no injury, however, to these ecclesiastics who have made an agreement both with the king and with the Bedouin. It is said, indeed, that the Bedouin keep their word to strangers who dwell among them.

In Cairo there are now about seven hundred Jewish families; of these fifty are called Samaritans, called also Cutheans, one hundred and fifty are Karaites, and the rest Rabbanites [Jews who followed the traditional teachings of Judaism: Torah, Talmud, etc.].

The Samaritans have only the five books of Moses, and their mode of writing differs from ours—the sacred writing. Maimonides remarks that this writing was customary among the Israelites before the time of the Assyrian exile, as already related in tractate Sanhedrin; but their Hebrew is like ours. Wherever the tetragrammaton occurs in scripture they write Ashima; they are an abomination to the Jews because they offer up sacrifices and frankincense on Mt. Gerizim. Many of them left Cairo with us to bring the Passover offering to Mt. Gerizim, for they have a temple there; they celebrate the Sabbath from the midday of Friday till the midday of Saturday. There are very few of them in existence now: it is said scarcely five hundred families in all the world.

The Karaites, as you know, do not believe in the words of our sages, but they are familiar with all the Bible. They fix the day of the new moon according to the appearance of the moon; consequently the Karaites in Cairo keep different days for Rosh Hashana [New Year] and the Day of Atonement, from those in Jerusalem, maintaining that there is nothing wrong in this. Every year they send to Jerusalem to observe the month of spring; and when they see that it is necessary to have a leap year they add an intercalary month. They do not think it any harm if the Karaites in Cairo add a month and those in Constantinople do not, for every place fixes its calendar according to its own judgment: they fast on the 7th and 10th of Ab.

It is well known that they always celebrate Shabuot [Pentecost] on Sunday; they hang the lulab [palm branch] and the other plants in the midst of the Synagogue; they all look upon them, and this they consider sufficient; they have no fire in their houses on the Sabbath, either by day or night; the five rules respecting shehita [slaughtering animals for food] are the same with them as with us, although not expressly mentioned in the Torah; they also observe the regulations to kill with a very sharp knife, free from all notches, and the law respecting wine they keep even more strictly than the Rabbanites.

In all the districts through which I passed, I have noticed that the law respecting wine is most strictly kept; there is even a doubt as to whether the honey may be used which the Arabs prepare from the grapes; it is very good, and in preparing it the grapes are not trodden in the same way as in making wine. I was asked to allow the use of it, for there are so many arguments in its favor, but my predecessors had not done it, and I did not wish to make innovations. There is not a single man who would drink wine that had been touched by an Arab, much less by an idolator.

The Karaites observe all the laws of purification; if anybody dies they all leave the house and hire poor Rabbanites to carry away their dead, for they will not touch a corpse. I have seen some of their commentaries, such as that of Japhet, which is quoted by Ibn Ezra, and those of Rabbi Aaron, the Karaite. Every day they make new explanations of the Torah, and maintain that even a fundamental law which has been established by the ancients may be altered if it does not appear to one of their wise men now living to agree with the text of the Bible, and they decide everything by the letter of the Torah. In all this they do not consider that either old or living scholars do any wrong.

They have a synagogue in Cairo; most of their prayers consist of psalms and other biblical verses; in recent times they have made a rule to read from the Torah on Mondays and Thursdays, which was not done formerly; they have priests and Levites, and it is said of a very rich and honorable Karaite in Cairo, Zadakah by name, that he is really descended from the family of David; he wanted to lay before me his genealogy, attested by witnesses of every generation, but I had not time to meet him.

The Samaritans are the richest of all the Jews in Cairo, and fill most of the higher offices of state; they are cashiers and administrators; one of them is said to have a property worth 200,000 pieces of gold. The Karaites are richer than the Rabbanites, but there are opulent men even among the latter. The custom of the Jews is always to represent themselves as poor in the country of the Arabs; they go about as beggars, humbling themselves before the Arabs; they are not charitable towards one another; the Karaites mix among the Rabbanites and try to become friendly with them.

In Cairo there are about fifty families of forced apostates [Maranos] from Spain, who have all done penance; they are mostly poor, having left their possessions, their parents, their relatives, and come here to seek shelter under the wings of the Lord God of Israel. Among the Jews in Cairo there are moneychangers and merchants, for the country is large, and some branch of industry is open to everyone.

For trade there is no better place in the world than Cairo; it is easy to grow rich. Hence one meets there with innumerable foreigners of all nations and languages. You may go out by night as well as by day, for all the streets are lighted with torches; the people sleep on the ground before the shop. The Jew can buy everything that is necessary, such as meat, cheese, fish, vegetables, and in general all that he requires, for everything is sold in the Jews' street; this is also the case in Palermo, but there it is not the same as in Cairo, for in the latter place the Jews cook at home only for the Sabbath, since men as well as women are occupied during the whole week and can therefore buy everything in the market.

Wood is very expensive; a load of wood, not so large as the load of a pair of mules, costs upwards of two-thirds of a ducat, and even more; meat and fruit are also expensive; the former is very good, however, especially the tail of the sheep. The Karaites do not eat this, for according to them it belongs to that kind of fat which the Torah has forbidden. I have seen nothing cheap in Cairo except onions of the Nile, leek, melons, cucumbers, and vegetables. Bread is cheap in years of plenty: it is made in the form of a cake and kneaded very soft.

The Jewish Nagid [Prince] who has his residence in Cairo is appointed over all the Jews who are under the dominion of the King of Egypt. He has all the power of a king and can punish and imprison those who act in opposition to his decrees; he appoints the dayyanim [judges] in every community. The present prince lived formerly for a long time in Jerusalem but was obliged to leave it on account of the Elders, the calumniators and informers who were there. He is called Rabbi Nathan HaCohen; he is rich, wise, pious, old and is a native of Barbary.

When I came to Cairo he showed me much honor, loved me as a father loves his son, and tried to dissuade me altogether from going to Jerusalem on account of the informers there; all scholars and rabbis formerly in Jerusalem left the city in haste in order to preserve their lives from the oppression of the Elders. The Jews who were in Jerusalem, about three hundred families, disappeared by degrees on account of the great taxes and burdens laid upon them by the Elders, so that the poor only remained, and women: and there was scarcely one to whom the name of man could justly be given.

These grey-haired criminals went so far as to sell the scrolls of the law with their covers, the curtains, the pomegranates, and all the sacred appurtenances which were in Jerusalem, to Gentiles, who were to carry them away into foreign lands; they sold the numerous books, such as the Talmud and Codes, which were deposited by the Ashkenazim in Jerusalem, so that nothing of value was left there.

The Nagid told me he could not well put a stop to this because he feared that the Elders would speak evil against all the Jews to the King, and "the throat of the King is an open sepulchre, and his eyes are not satisfied." About the same time disturbances took place in Egypt; for the King wanted to raise money to give to his generals who were to fight against the Turkish Emperor in Aleppo; and he imposed the heavy tax of seventy-five thousand pieces of gold on the Jews in Cairo, viz. the Samaritans, Karaites, and Rabbanites, and the same on Christians and Arabs, for he wanted to raise an immense sum of money. In Purim of that year there was, therefore, sorrow, fasting and weeping among the Jews; yet I did not lose my courage, my heart was fixed on God.

On the 20th of Adar, I left Cairo in company with the Jew who came from Alexandria, and we came to Chanak which is about two miles distant from Cairo. Before I left New Cairo I went to Old Cairo, called Mizraim Atika, which is also inhabited, though not so closely as New Cairo, and both are quite close together. On the way thither we saw the place where the King sends people every year to prepare a dam against the rising of the Nile, which takes place in the month of Ab [August]. I have heard many things about the rising of the Nile, which, however, would be too wearisome to write down, especially as I have not seen it with my own eyes. I saw rain in Cairo, but not much; and while there I felt severe cold at the time of Purim. The people, indeed, wondered and said it had not been so cold for many years, for according to all accounts Egypt is very warm.

In Old Cairo there is a very beautiful synagogue built on large and splendid pillars; it is also dedicated to the prophet Elijah, who is said to have appeared there to the pious in the southeast corner, where a light is kept continually burning. In the northeast corner is a platform where the scroll of Ezra used to be placed.

It is related that many years ago a Jew came from the West, and bought it from the temple servant; he set sail from Alexandria, carrying with him the roll of the law, but the ship was not far from Alexandria when it sank, and he was lost, together with the roll of the law. The temple servant, who had sold it to him for a hundred gold pieces, became an apostate and died shortly afterwards. The case of this roll is still in the synagogue and a light is always kept burning before it.

Last year the King wanted to take the pillars on which the synagogue is built for his palace because they are large and very beautiful, but the Jews redeemed them for a thousand gold pieces. According to the date on the wall of the synagogue, it was built thirty-eight years before the destruction of the Second Temple. Near to it there is another fine large synagogue, but not equal to the former; prayers are offered up here every Sabbath, and the Jews hire a person to watch over it.

I was not so fortunate as to get to Dimo, a place outside Cairo, where Moses is said to have prayed; here there are two synagogues, one belonging to the Rabbanites and one to the Karaites; Divine Service is often held here on Sabbaths and feast days. I was told that the mamelukes of the King feed their horses on the way to it, and that it would therefore be dangerous for a Jew to go there, for the mamelukes were at this time in the habit of beating and plundering Jews as well as Arabs.

In Chanak we remained two days, and there hired five camels, for two men and two women had joined us in Cairo. It is said that this is Goshen, where the Jews sojourned in Egypt. We then came to Salahia where we remained over the Sabbath, waiting for a passing caravan, since the way through the wilderness begins here and it is not safe to make the journey with only five camels. Not a Jew lives on the way from here to Gaza.

We were three days in Salahia when an Arab caravan of eight camels arrived, with which we travelled as far as Katiah, a town in the middle of the wilderness, where no vegetation is to be seen except date trees. The wilderness between Egypt and Palestine is not large, for from one day's journey to another there are places of encampment for the camels, erected principally for travellers; yet it is all sand, and no vegetation whatever is to be seen except date trees in well-known places. Water is found after two days' journey, sometimes even after one day's journey, but it is rather brackish.

In the wilderness we came to Arish, said to be the former Succot. The caravans going through the wilderness either encamp at midday and journey in the evening till midnight, or travel from midnight into the first third of the day; this depends on the will of those who have charge of the caravans. Generally speaking, they travel by night rather than by day. Thus we journeyed from place to place in the wilderness, till we came to Gaza without misadventure.

Gaza is the first town on coming out of the wilderness leading to the land of the Philistines. It is a large and beautiful city, of the same size as Jerusalem, but without walls, for among all the places under Egyptian dominion, which now extends over Palestine, the country of the Philistines and Syria, Alexandria and Aleppo alone are surrounded by walls. If the account of the Jews living there be correct, I saw in Gaza the ruins of the building that Samson pulled down on the Philistines.

We remained four days in Gaza; there is now a Rabbi from Germany there, by name, Rabbi Moses, of Prague, who fled thither from Jerusalem; he insisted on my going to his house, and I was obliged to stay with him all the time that I was in Gaza. On the Sabbath all the wardens were invited to dine with us. Cakes of grapes and fruit were brought; we partook of several glasses before eating and were joyful.

On Sunday, the 11th of Nisan [April], we journeyed from Gaza on asses; we came within two miles of Hebron, and there spent the night. On Monday we reached Hebron, a small town on the slope of the mountain, called by the Turks Khalil. It is divided into two parts, one beside the Cave of the Patriarchs; the other opposite, a bowshot farther away. I was in the Cave of Machpelah, over which the mosque has been built; and the Arabs hold the place in high honor. All the kings of the Arabs come here to repeat their prayers, but neither a Jew nor an Arab may enter the cave itself, where the real graves of the Patriarchs are. The Arabs remain above, and let down burning torches into it through a window, for they keep a light always burning there.

All who come to pray leave money, which they throw into the cave through the window; when they wish to take the money out they let down a young man who is unmarried by a rope, to bring it up—so I have been told by the Jews who live there.

All Hebron, with its field and neighborhood, belongs to the cave; bread and lentil, or some other kind of pulse, is distributed to the poor every day without distinction of faith, and this is done in honor of Abraham. Without, in the wall of the cave, there is a small opening, said to have been made just after the burial of Abraham, and there the Jews are allowed to pray, but none may come within the walls of the cave. At this little window I offered up my prayers.

On the summit of the opposite mountain is a large cave, said to be the grave of Jesse, the father of David. We went there also to pray on the same day. Between the grave of Jesse and the Cave of the Patriarchs is a well, which the Arabs call the well of Isaac, said to have belonged to the patriarch Isaac. Near to Hebron, between rocks, there is a spring of fresh water, distinguished as the well of Sarah. Hebron has many vineyards and olive trees, and contains at the present time twenty families, all Rabbanites, half of whom are the descendants of the forced apostates who have recently returned to their faith.

On Tuesday morning, the 13th of Nisan, we left Hebron, which is a day's journey distant from Jerusalem, and came on as far as Rachel's tomb, where there is a round, vaulted building in the open road. We got down from our asses and prayed at each grave, each one according to his ability. On the right hand of the traveller to Jerusalem lies the hill on which Bethlehem stands; this is a small village, about half a mile from Rachel's grave, and the Catholic priests have a church there.

From Bethlehem to Jerusalem is a journey of about three miles. The whole way is full of vineyards and orchards. The vineyards are like those in Romagna, the vines being low but thick. About three quarters of a mile from Jerusalem, at a place where the mountain is ascended by steps, we beheld the famous city of our delight, and here we rent our garments, as was our duty.

A little farther on, the sanctuary, the desolate house of our splendor, became visible, and at the sight of it we again made rents in our garments. We came as far as the gates of Jerusalem, and on the 14th of Nisan, 5248, at noon, our feet stood within the gates of the city. Here we were met by an Ashkenazi who had been educated in Italy, Rabbi Jacob Calmann; he took me into his house, and I remained his guest during the whole time of Passover.

Jerusalem is for the most part desolate and in ruins. I need not repeat that it is not surrounded by walls. Its inhabitants, I am told, number about four thousand families. As for Jews, about seventy families of the poorest class have remained; there is scarcely a family that is not in want of the commonest necessities; one who has bread for a year is called rich.

Among the Jewish population there are many aged, forsaken widows from Germany, Spain, Portugal and other countries, so that there are seven women to one man. The land is now quieter and happier than before; for the Elders have repented the evil they have done, when they saw that only the poorer portion of the inhabitants remained; they are therefore very friendly to every newcomer. They excuse themslves for what has happened, and assert that they never injured anyone who did not try to obtain the mastery over them. As for me, so far I have no complaint to make against them; on the contrary, they have shown me great kindness and have dealt honorably with me, for which I give daily thanks to God.

The Jews are not persecuted by the Arabs in these parts. I have traveled through the country in its length and breadth, and none of them has put an obstacle in my way. They are very kind to strangers, particularly to anyone who does not know the language; and if they see many Jews together they are not annoyed by it. In my opinion, an intelligent man versed in political science might easily raise himself to be chief of the Jews as well as of the Arabs; for among all the inhabitants there is not a wise and sensible man who knows how to deal affably with his fellowmen; all are ignorant misanthropes intent only on gain. . . .

The synagogue here is built on columns; it is long, narrow, and dark, the light entering only by the door. There is a fountain in the middle of it. In the court of the synagogue, quite close to it, stands a mosque. The court of the synagogue is very large, and contains many houses, all of them buildings devoted by the Ashkenazim to charitable purposes, and inhabited by Ashkenazi widows. There were formerly many courts in the Jewish streets belonging to these buildings, but the Elders sold them, so that not a single one remained. They could not , however, sell the buildings of the Ashkenazim, for they were exclusively for Ashkenazim, and no other poor had a right to them.

The Jews' street and the houses are very large; some of them dwell also on Zion. At one time they had more houses, but these are now heaps of rubbish and cannot be rebuilt, for the law of the land is that a Jew may not rebuild his ruined house without permission, and the permission often costs more than the whole house is worth. The houses in Jerusalem are of stone, none of wood or plaster.

There are some excellent regulations here. I have nowhere seen the daily service conducted in a better manner. The Jews rise an hour or two before daybreak, even on the Sabbath, and recite psalms and other songs of praise till the day dawns. Then they repeat the Kaddish; after which the two of the Readers appointed for the purpose chant the Blessing of the Law, the chapter on Sacrifices, and all the songs of praise which follow with a suitable melody, the "Hear, O Israel" being read on the appearance of the sun's first rays. The Kohanim [descendants of the Priests] repeat the priestly benediction daily, on weekdays as well as on the Sabbaths; in every service this blessing occurs. At the morning and afternoon service this blessing occurs. At the morning and afternoon service supplications are said with great devotion, together with the Thirteen Attributes of God; and there is no difference between Mondays and Thursdays, and the other days of the week except that the Law is read on the former.

Jerusalem, notwithstanding its destruction, still contains four very beautiful, long bazaars, such as I have never before seen, at the foot of Zion. They have all dome-shaped roofs, and contain wares of every kind. They are divided into different departments, the merchant bazaar, the spice bazaar, the vegetable market, and one in which cooked food and bread are sold.

When I came to Jerusalem there was a dreadful famine in the land. A man of moderate means could have eaten bread the weight of a drachma at every meal, which in our money makes a bolognino of old silver, and he would not have been satisfied. I was told that the famine was less severe than it was at the beginning of the year. Many Jews died of hunger; they had been seen a day or two before asking for bread, which nobody could give them, and the next day they were found dead in their houses. Many lived on grass, going out like stags to look for pasture.

At present there is only one German Rabbi here who was educated in Jerusalem. I have never seen his equal for humility and the fear of God; he weaves night and day when he is not occupied with his studies, and for six months tasted no bread between Sabbath and Sabbath, his food consisting of raw turnips and the remains of St. John's bread, which is very plentiful here, after the sugar has been taken out of it. According to the account of a trustworthy man, Jericho, the "city of palms," is only half a day's journey from Jerusalem, and there are at the present day scarcely three palm trees in the town.

Now, the wheat harvest being over, the famine is at an end, and there is once more plenty, praise be to God. Here, in Jerusalem, I have seen several kinds of fruits which are not to be found in our country. There is one tree with long leaves, which grows higher than a man's stature and bears fruit only once; it then withers, and from its roots there rises another similar one, which again bears fruit the next year; and the same thing is continually repeated.

The grapes are larger than in our country, but neither cherries, hazelnuts, nor chestnuts are to be found. All the necessities of life, such as meat, wine, olives, and sesame oil can be had very cheap. The soil is excellent, but it is not possible to gain a living by any branch of industry, unless it be that of a shoemaker, weaver, or goldsmith; even such artisans as these gain their livelihood with great difficulty. Persons of various nationalities are always to be found in Jerusalem from Christian countries, and from Babylonia and Abyssinia. The Arabs come frequently to offer up prayers at the temple, for they hold it in great veneration.

I made enquiries concerning the Sambatyon, and I hear from one who has been informed that a man has come from the kingdom of Prester John and has related that there are high mountains and valleys there which can be traversed in a ten days' journey, and which are certainly inhabited by descendants of Israel. They have princes or kings, and have carried on great wars against the Johannites [Abyssinians] for more than a century, but, unfortunately, the Johannites prevailed and Ephraim was beaten. The Johannites penetrated into their country and laid it waste, and the remembrance of Israel had almost died away in those places, for an edict was issued against those who remained prohibiting the exercise of their religious duties as severe as that which Antiochus issued in the time of the Hasmoneans.

But God had mercy. Other kings succeeded in India who were not so cruel as their predecessors; and it is said that the former glory of the Jews is now in a measure restored; they have again become numerous, and though they still pay tribute to the Johannites they are not entirely subject to them. Four years ago, it is said, they again made war with their neighbors, when they plundered their enemies and made many prisoners.

The enemy, on the other hand, took some of them prisoners, and sold them as slaves; a few of these were brought to Cairo; they were black but not so black as the Negroes. It was impossible to learn from them whether they belonged to the Karaites or the Rabbanites. In some respects they seem to hold the doctrine of the Karaites, for they saw that there is no fire in their houses on the Sabbath; in other respects they seem to observe Rabbanism. It is said that the pepper and other spices which the Negroes sell come principally from their country.

It is universally known here that the Arabs who make pilgrimages from Egypt to Mecca journey through a large and fearful desert, forming caravans of at least ten thousand camels. Sometimes they are overtaken in the wilderness by a people of gigantic stature, one of whom can chase a thousand Arabs. They call this people El-Arabes, that is, children of the Almighty, because in their battles they always invoke the name of Almighty God. The Arabs assert that one of these people is able to bear the burden of a camel in one hand, while in the other he holds the sword with which he fights; it is known that they observe the Jewish religious customs, and it is affirmed that they are descendants of Rechab.

No Jew may enter the enclosure of the Temple. Although sometimes the Arabs are anxious to admit carpenters and goldsmiths to perform work there, nobody will go in, for we have all been defiled [by touching bodies of the dead]. I do not know whether the Arabs enter the Holy of Holies or not. I also made enquiries relative to the Eben Shethiah where the Ark of the Covenant was placed, and am told that it is under a high and beautiful dome built by the Arabs in the court of the Temple. It is enclosed in this building, and no one may enter. There is great wealth in the enclosure of the Temple. We hear that the monarchs build chambers there inlaid with gold, and the king now reigning is said to have erected a building, more splendid than any other ever built, adorned with gold and precious stones.

The Temple enclosure still has twelve gates. Those which are called the "Gates of Mercy" are of iron, and are two in number; they look towards the east of the Temple and are always closed. They only reach halfway above the ground, the other half is sunk in the earth. It is said that the Arabs often tried to raise them up but were not able to do so.

The western wall, part of which is still standing, is composed of large, thick stones, such as I have never before seen in an old building, either in Rome or in any other country. At the northeast corner is a tower of very large stones. I entered it and found a vast edifice supported by massive and lofty pillars; there are so many pillars that it wearied me to go to the end of the building. Everything is filled with earth which has been thrown there from the ruins of the Temple. The temple building stands on these columns, and in each of them is a hole through which a cord may be drawn. It is said that the bulls and rams for sacrifice were bound here. Throughout the whole region of Jerusalem, in fields as well as vineyards, there are large caves connected with one another.

In all these districts, in the valleys and mountains, there are tollcollectors, who represent themselves as overseers for the security of the way, and are called "Naphar" in Arabic. These men take as many taxes as they like from the Jews with perfect impunity. From Cairo there are twenty tollbars; and I for my part paid them altogether about a ducat. The Jews who come from Cairo to Jerusalem have only to pay ten silver denarii at the city gate, while, on the other hand, those who come by way of Jaffa have to pay a ducat. The Jews in Jerusalem have to pay down every year thirty-two silver pieces per head. The poor man, as well as the rich, has to pay this tribute as soon as he comes to the age of manhood.

Everyone is obliged to pay fifty ducats annually to the Nipeo [the Governor of Jerusalem] for permission to make wine, a beverage which is an abomination to the Arabs. This is the whole amount of annual taxation to which the Jews are liable. But the Elders go so far in their iniquity that, in consequence of alleged deficits, they every week impose new taxes, making each one pay what they like; and whoever refuses is beaten by order of a non-Jewish tribunal until he submits.

As for me, so far God has helped me, they have demanded nothing from me as yet; how it may fare with me in the future I cannot tell.

The Christians in Jerusalem are divided into five sects—Catholics, Greeks, Jacobites, Armenians and Johannites [Abyssinians]; each one declares the faith of the others to be false, just as the Karaites do with respect to the Rabbanites. Each sect has a separate division in the Church of the Sepulchre, which is very large and has a tower surmounted by a cupola, but without a bell. In this church there are always two persons of each sect who are not allowed to leave it.

On Mount Zion, near the Sepulchre of the Kings, the Franciscans have a large Church. The Sepulchre of the Kings also belonged to them a long time ago, but a rich Ashkenazi, who came to Jerusalem, wished to purchase the graves from the King, and so involved himself in strife with the ecclesiastics, and the Arabs then took the graves away from them and have ever since retained them in their own keeping. When it became known in Venice that the graves had been taken from the Catholics through Jews who had come from Christian lands, an edict was published that no Jew might travel to Jerusalem through Venice; but this edict is now repealed, and every year Jews come in the Venetian galleys and even in the pilgrim ships, for there is really no safer and shorter way than by these ships. I wish I had known all this while I was still in those parts, I would not then have remained so long on the journey. The galleys perform the voyage from Venice here in forty days at the most.

I have taken a house here close to the synagogue. The upper chamber of my dwelling is even in the wall of the synagogue. In the court where my house is there are five inhabitants, all of them women. There is only one blind man living here, and his wife attends on me. I must thank God, who has hitherto vouchsafed me His blessing, that I have not been sick, like the others who came at the same time with me. Most of those who come to Jerusalem from foreign countries fall ill, owing to climatic changes and the sudden variations of the wind, now cold, now warm. All possible winds blow in Jerusalem. It is said that every wind before going where it listeth comes to Jerusalem to prostrate itself before the Lord. Blessed be He that knoweth the truth.

I earnestly entreat that you will not despond nor suffer anxiety on account of my having travelled so far away, and that you will not shed tears for my sake. For God in His mercy has brought me to this holy dwelling, which rejoices my heart and should also delight you. God is my witness that I have forgotten all my former distresses, and all remembrance of my native country has passed away from me.

All the memories which I still retain of it centre in your image, revered father, which is constantly before my eyes. Mine eyes are dimmed when I remember that I have left you in your old age, and I fear that lest your tears will recall the sins of my youth.

Now, I beseech you, bestow your blessing upon your servant. Let this letter atone for my absence, for it will show you the disposition of your son and you will no longer be displeased with him. If God will preserve me, I shall send you a letter every year with the galley, which will comfort you. Banish all sorrow from your heart. Rejoice with your dear children and grandchildren who sit around your table. They will nourish and sustain your old age. I have prayed for their welfare and continue to do so, in the sacred places of Jerusalem, the restoration of which, by means of the Messiah, God grant us to witness, so that you may come joyfully to Zion. Amen.

Finished in haste in Jerusalem, the Holy City. May it soon be rebuilt in our days.

From your son,

OBADIAH YAREH

on the 8th Ellul, 5248 [1488].

LETTER TO HIS BROTHER

How precious are your words to me, my brother. They are sweeter than
sweet spices. Your three letters came to me on the 15th Ellul, through the
master of the pilgrim ship, together with the long letter from the worthy
Signor Emanuel Chai of Camerino. I shall answer them generally, and in
a few points more explicitly.

First of all I praise the Almighty and thank you for the good news that
our aged father, whom I never cease to love tenderly, still lives. May God
continue His mercy and preserve him to us in strength and health for a
long time to come. But my joy was very much saddened by the death of
your eldest daughter and of your son who was born to you after I had left
you. What God determines is ever for the best, however, and there is
nothing left for us to do but to pray for those who still remain to us, that
God would grant them His blessing and preserve them.

You ask me about the miracles which are said to take place at the
Temple mountain and graves of the pious. What can I tell you, my
brother, about them? I have not seen them. As for the lights on the site
of the Temple, of which you have heard that they always cease to burn on
the 9th of Ab, I have been told that this is the case, but I cannot speak with
certainty respecting it; I need not say that the story about the Sephardi is all
deception and falsehood; but intelligent men like you, my brother, must
inquire into such stories and not trust to false reports.

I have not yet had time to go anywhere since I came here, therefore I
can only tell you by hearsay of the environs of the Holy City and the other
adjoining districts. It is said that the Jews live quietly and peaceably with the
Arabs in Safed, in the village of Cana, and in all Galilee, yet most of them
are poor and maintain themselves by peddling, and many go about the
village seeking scanty means of subsistence. In Damascus, on the other
hand, I hear the Jews are rich merchants and in every respect there is no
place so blessed as Damascus. It has beautiful houses and magnificent
gardens, such as are scarcely to be seen elsewhere. The air, however, is not
very pure, and strangers going there become sick. People come hither from
Egypt, Damascus, Aleppo, and other places to prostrate themselves before
the Lord.

Jews have come here from Aden. Aden is said to be the site of the
garden of Eden: it lies southeast of Ethiopia, but the Red Sea separates
them. These Jews say that in their country there are many large Jewish
communities. The king is an Arab and is very kindly disposed to the Jews,
and that country is very large and beautiful, bearing many splendid fruits,
of kinds which are not to be found among us. Where Paradise was actually
situated they do not know; they sow in the month of Adar [March] and
reap in Kislev [December]. The rain season there is from Passover to the

month of Ab [August]. It is in consequence of the great quantity of rain that falls there that the Nile rises in the month of Ab. Its inhabitants are somewhat black.

The Jews do not possess the books of the Talmud; all that they have are the works of R. Isaac Alfasi, together with commentaries on them, and the works of Maimonides. They are all, from great to small, well versed in the works of Maimonides, for they occupy themselves principally with studying them.

The Jews told us also that it is now well-known through Arabian merchants that the river Sambation is fifty days' journey from them in the wilderness, and like a thread, surrounds the whole land where the descendants of Israel dwell. This river throws up stones and sand and rests only on the Sabbath, therefore no Jew, who is travelling in that country is likely to violate the Sabbath. It is traditional among them that the descendants of Jacob dwell there.

It is traditional among them that they are all descendants of Moses, all pure and innocent as angels, and no evildoer in their midst. On the other side of the Sambation the children of Israel are as numerous as the sand of the sea, and there are many kings and princes among them, but they are not so pure and holy as those who are surrounded by the stream. The Jews of Aden relate all this with a certain confidence, as if it were well-known, and no one ever doubted the truth of their assertations.

An old Ashkenazi Rabbi, who was born and educated here [Jerusalem], tells me that he remembers how even in his youth Jews came from Aden, and narrated everything literally as these do. The Jews of Aden also say that the Israelites dwelling on the borders of their territory, of whom I wrote in my first letter, are now at war with the people of Prester John (the Abyssinian), and that some of them have been taken prisoners and brought to Cairo. I have seen some of these with my own eyes; these Jews are a month's journey in the wilderness from the others who live on the Sambation. The Christians who come from the territory of the Johannites relate that the Jews there, who are at war with the people of Prester John, have suffered great defeats, and we are very anxious to know if these accounts are really true, which God forfend. May the Lord always protect his people and his servants!

I live here in Jerusalem in the house of the Nagid, who has appointed me ruler of his household, and twice a month I hold discourses in the Synagogue in the Hebrew tongue, which most of the people here understand. My sermons sound in their ears like a lovely song, they praise them and like to listen to them, but they do not act in accordance with them. Yet I cannot say that anybody has done me an injury: even the Elders have done me no wrong; they have not yet burdened me with any tax, as is generally done here every week. They even would not have me pay the poll tax the first year, from which no one is exempt. So I remain here as by a miracle. God knows how it will go with me in the future!

The honoured Emanuel Chai of Camerino sent me one hundred Venetian ducats at my request, the profits on the capital I left with him, and he has promised to do so every year. I give ten per cent to the master of the ship who brings me the money. The worthy Emanuel also added twenty-five ducats, partly for oil for the synagogue lamps and partly to give to the poor.

As for me I live contentedly in Jerusalem wanting nothing from anyone. Every morning and evening we meet together to study Halacha [law]. Two Sephardic pupils take uninterrupted part in my instruction and we have now also two Ashkenazic Rabbis here. And perchance the Promised Land may now be rebuilt and inhabited, for the king has issued a decree of lasting validity, that the Jews in Jerusalem shall pay only the poll tax imposed on them.

Formerly the Jewish inhabitants had to pay four hundred ducats annually, without reference to their number, and thus all suffered. Now each one pays his own poll tax, and has nothing to pay for the others. This is a decree such as has not been made in Jerusalem for fifty years. Hence many who left Jerusalem are returning. May it please God that the city and the temple be rebuilt, and that the scattered of Judah and Ephraim may come together here and prostrate themselves before God at the holy mountain. I must now conclude for the present, for I am much occupied.

Sent in haste from Jerusalem, Ellul the 27th, 5249 [1489].

From Your Brother,

OBADIAH YAREH

David Reubeni

David Reubeni (1480–1532) is one of the most intriguing and enigmatic figures of the Middle Ages. Besides his own partly autobiographical diary there is little outside information available about him. He claimed to have been born in Arabia, where his brother, King Joseph, ruled over 300,000 members of the tribe of Reuben, Gad and half of Manasseh. Reubeni's account of his travels in the East and in Palestine prior to his arrival in Italy has the same legendary-romantic quality as the narrative of Eldad the Danite; indeed, Reubeni's work, a fusion of vivid imagination, extant folk stories, travelers' tales and real events, is influenced by Eldad's travelogue. Ninth-century Jews were no less enchanted by Eldad and his tales of the lost tribes (see p. 148), than sixteenth-century Jews were by David Reubeni.

Short of stature, dark-skinned, clad in striking oriental garb, Reubeni appeared in Rome on a white horse (symbolically suggestive of the Messiah's white donkey). His entourage, his flag, his personal magnetism, and above all, his plan to recapture the Holy Land, impressed all his listeners, and he was soon granted an audience by the philo-Semitic Pope Clement VII. The emissary of a far-off Jewish nation of warriors, Reubeni wanted the Pope's aid in securing weapons to drive the Muslims from the Holy Land—a request to which any Christian spiritual and temporal leader would be favorably disposed. Although the Pope was cautious, he sent Reubeni to the King of Portugal with letters of recommendation.

In post-expulsion Portugal, where the only Jews were Marranos, the story of David Reubeni takes a dramatic and crucial turn. Where it had hitherto been a historic adventure, a political gamble with some Jewish nationalistic overtones, in Portugal it took on the guise of an apocalyptic and messianic mission. The Marranos in Portugal gathered about Reubeni and considered him a redeemer. This ferment naturally irritated the king, who began to suspect that Reubeni had come to bring the Marranos back to Judaism. When one of Reubeni's adherents in Portugal, Shlomo Molkho (the noted pseudo-Messiah) formally reembraced Judaism, Reubeni was ordered to leave the land.

Although the events in Portugal have some historic confirmation, the details are enveloped in novelistic exaggeration and fabrication. Reubeni asserted that Hebrew was his mother tongue; however, an analysis of his vocabulary, grammar and syntax shows that many of his Hebrew phrases were translated from one of the European languages, most probably German; hence the supposition that David Reubeni may actually have been an Ashkenazic Jew who resided for a time in the East. It is noteworthy that Reubeni's travel diary is silent concerning his origin and his life prior to his European mission; the same silence and air of mystery surrounds much of his activity—to the extent that modern scholarship is still not sure what to make of him, whether to regard him as a charlatan or a visionary. In any event, Reubeni was certainly a sensitive Jew who bore in mind his fellow-Jews' plight and sought to alleviate their suffering and degradation; and his coreligionists in Italy and Portugal saw him precisely in this light. Naive to political considerations, Reubeni was a dreamer who sought salvation in terms beyond the realistic—*i.e.,* the miraculous. Unfortunately, his end was bitter. When he came to Emperor Charles V in Germany with his new-found disciple, Shlomo Molkho, both were put in chains and returned to Italy. There Molkho was burned at the stake; and Reubeni was incarcerated in Spain, where he later died.

THE TRAVEL DIARY OF DAVID REUBENI

I am David, the son of King Solomon (may the memory of the righteous be for a blessing), and my brother is King Joseph, who is older than I, and who sits on the throne of his kingdom in the wilderness of Habor [Khorgbar], and rules over thirty myriads of the tribe of Gad and of the tribe of Reuben and of the half-tribe of Manasseh. I have journeyed from before the King, my brother and his counselors, the seventy Elders. They charged me to go first to Rome to the presence of the Pope, may his glory be exalted.

I left them by way of the hills, ten days' journey, till I arrived at Jeddah, where I was taken with a great sickness and remained five weeks, until I heard that a ship was going to the land of Ethiopia. I embarked on the ship in the Red Sea and we went three days, and on the fourth day we arrived at the city of Suakim, in Ethiopia. I took a house and stayed there two months, but I was ill, and being cupped lost fifty pounds of blood; for in order to get better I had more than one hundred applications of hot nails.

Afterwards I met many merchants who were travelling by way of Mecca to the Kingdom of Sheba, and I called the chief of them, a descendant of the Prophet of the Ishamelites named Omar Abu Kamil. I took two camels to journey with them, and they were a great multitude with more than three thousand camels. I improved in health daily, and we passed through great deserts and forests and fields in which there are many good herbs and good pasturage and rivers, a journey of two months, until we arrived at the capital of the kingdom of Sheba in Ethiopia, where resides King Omara, who dwells on the Nile. He is a black king and reigns over black and white, and the name of his city is Lamula, and I stayed with him ten months. The King travels in his countries, every month a different journey. I travelled with the King and had as my servants more than sixty men of the sons of the Prophet riding on horses, and they honoured me with great honour.

All the time that I stayed in the country of Ethiopia with the King I fasted daily, when I lay down and when I got up, and I prayed day and night and I stayed not in the company of scoffers or of merrymakers. On every journey they prepared for me a wooden hut near the King's house.

The King has maidservants and menservants and slaves, most of them naked, and the Queen and the concubines and the ladies are dressed in golden bracelets, two on the hands and two on the legs; and they cover their

505

nakedness with a golden chain, hand-embroidered, and a cubit wide round their loins closed before and behind. But their body is quite naked and bare, and they wear a golden wreath in their noses. The males and females eat elephants and wolves, leopards, dogs, and camels, and they eat human flesh.

The King called me every day before him and said, "What askest thou of us, thou son of the Prophet; if thou desirest slaves, camels, or horses, take them"; and I replied to him, "I want nothing of thee, but I have heard of the glory of thy kingdom and I have brought thee this gift with love and pleasure, and behold, I give thee a garment of silk and seven hundred ducats, florins of gold," and I said, "I love thee and I grant thee pardon and forgiveness and a full title to paradise to thee and to thy sons and daughters, and all thy household, and thou shalt come to us next year to the city of Mecca, the place for the atonement of sins."

After these things an Ishmaelite came from the city of Mecca and slandered me before the King, and said, "This man in whom thou believest is not of the sons of the Prophet, but from the wilderness of Habor." When the King heard this and sent for Abu Kamil and told him the words and the slander, and Abu Kamil answered and said, "I know neither one man nor the other, but I have seen that the first man is honourable and fasts every day and fears God, and does not go after merriment nor after women and does not love money. But the other man loves money and does many evil things and talks a great deal". And the King said, "Thy words are true," and Abu Kamil left him and told me these matters.

After that the king's wife heard the words of the slanderer and sent for me and said to me, "Do not remain in this country for this new man who has come from Mecca has slandered thee to the King in words unfitting and he is taking counsel with many men to seek from the King to slay thee." And I said to her, "How can I go away without the King's permission?" But the Queen replied, "The King comes tonight to my house and I will send for thee, and thou shalt come before me and before the King and thou shalt ask permission from the King, and I shall help thee and thou shalt go tomorrow on thy way in peace."

So when I came before the King I burst forth and said, "What is my transgression, and what is my sin? Have I not come before thee with gifts and love and kindness, and desired not to receive from thee, either silver or gold or slaves or maidservants or menservants; but this knave who has slandered me to thee loves money and speaks falsehood, and behold, I have been with thee ten months. Call thy servants and thy lords and let them tell thee if they have found in me any sin or transgression or any fault. Therefore, in thy kindness and for God's sake, give me permission to go on my way and I shall pray for thee and bless thee."

And the Queen also said, "Give him permission that he may go on his way, for he is honourable and trusty and we have found no blemish in him, but only good report."

And the King answered and said to me, "What needest thou, slaves, or camels, or horses? Take them and go in peace."

And I said to the King, "I want nothing but permission from thee that I may go to-morrow at dawn, for I know that I have wicked enemies against me; therefore may it be good in thy sight to send with me one of thy honoured servants to the place of the house of Abu Kamil."

Then the King called one of his servants and ordered him to go with him and gave us two horses and we rode to the house of Abu Kamil, and on the way we crossed many rivers and the feeding ground of elephants. There was one river of mud and water in which horses, when crossing it, sank in the mire up to their bellies, and many men and horses had been drowned in this place. But we crossed it on horseback, and thanked God we were safe. We travelled eighteen days until we arrived at Senaar, and next morning I and my servant journeyed on further five days on the River Nile until I reached the city of Sheba, but it is in ruins and desolate, and there are wooden huts in it, and Abu Kamil came to me and said, "How art thou come from the King and he did not give thee slaves? I know that the King loves thee, therefore stay in my house and I will go up to the king and will beg him for thee"; and I said, "I will do so."

But that night I dreamt in the house of Abu Kamil, and I saw my father, on whom be peace, and he said to me, "Why hast thou come to this far land? Go hence tomorrow in peace and no evil will come upon thee, but if thou waitest until Abu Kamil returns, know that thou wilt die"; and when I woke from my sleep I said to Abu Kamil, "Let me go, I do not wish thee to go to the King for me," and in the morning I journeyed from Sheba, and Abu Kamil sent his brother with me, and we went . . .

I entered Jerusalem on the 25th Adar, 283 [1523], and that day I entered the house of the Holy of Holies, and when I came to the sanctuary all the Ishmaelite guardians came to bow before me and to kiss my feet, and said to me, "Enter, Oh blessed of the Lord, our lord, the son of our lord," and the two chief among them came and took me to the cavern which is under the *Eben Shethia* [the foundation rock of the Temple] and said to me, "This is the place of Elijah the prophet, and this the place of King David, and this King Solomon's place, and this the place of Abraham and Isaac, and this the place of Mahomet."

I said to the guardians, "Now that I know all these places go ye on your way, for I wish to pray, and in the morning I will give you charity."

They went away and I knew at once that all their words were false and vain. I prayed until all the Ishmaelites came to prayer. They left the Temple court after their prayer two hours after dark. I went below the *Eben Shethiah.* Then the guards extinguished all the lights in the Court except four, and before they closed the gates they searched to see if any man were sleeping in the cavern, so as to turn him out.

They found me, and said, "Leave this place, for we are the guards and may allow no one to remain to sleep here. We have so sworn to the King, and if thou wilt not go we shall ask the Governor to remove thee against thy will." When I heard these words, I came out of the court and they shut the doors, and I prayed outside the court all night, and fasted, and this was my fourth day.

In the morning, when the Ishmaelites came to pray in the court, I entered with them, and when they had finished their prayer, I called out with a loud voice, "Where are the guards? Let them all come before me"; and I said to them, "I am your lord, and the son of your Lord, the Prophet. I have come from a distant country to this holy house and my soul desireth to remain therein to pray and not to sleep."

And after that four of the guards came to expel me, and I said to them, "I am your lord, the son of your Lord, if you wish peace wish me well and I will bless you; but if not I will be avenged of you and will write to the King of Turkey your evil deeds."

They replied, "Forgive us this time for we wish to serve thee and to be thy slaves as long as thou remainest in the holy house, and will do thy will."

Then I gave them ten ducats for charity, and stayed in the sanctuary and fasted in the Holy of Holies five weeks. I ate no bread and drank no water except from Sabbath eve to close of Sabbath, and I prayed below the *Eben Shethiah* and above it. Afterwards ten messengers from King Joseph, my brother, and his elders came before me, and they recognized and stood before me in the sanctuary.

The Ishmaelites have a sign on the top of the cupola of the court, and this sign is like a half moon turned westward; and on the first day of Pentecost of 283 [1523], it turned eastward. When the Ishmaelites saw this they cried out with a loud voice, and I said, "Why do you cry?" and they replied, "For our sins, this sign of the half moon is turned eastwards, and that is an evil sign for the Ishmaelites"; and the Ishmaelite workmen went on the Sunday to restore the sign to its place, and on Monday the sign again turned eastward while I was praying, and the Ishmaelites were crying and weeping, and they sought to turn it round but they could not; and our Elders had already told me, "When thou seest this sign go to Rome," and I saw the gates of mercy and the gates of repentance, and walked in the sanctuary.

It is a big structure like the upper buildings, and I did that which the Elders ordered me underneath the sanctuary, out of man's reach, and the turning of the sign took place after I had done what the Elders commanded beneath the sanctuary. I went up the Mount of Olives, and I saw two caves there and returned to Jerusalem and ascended Mount Zion. There are two places of worship there in the town; the upper place is in the hands of the Christians and the lower in that of the Ishmaelites. This the Ishmaelites opened for me and showed me a grave, and told me that it was the grave of King David, on whom be peace, and I prayed there.

Then I left and went to the upper place of worship, which the Christians opened for me. I entered it and prayed there and returned to Jerusalem, and went to the house of a Jew called Abraham Hager. He was smelting near the synagogue, and there were women there cleaning the candlesticks of the Synagogue. I asked him his name and he said, "Abraham"; and I sent the Ishmaelites away and said to them, "I have work to do with the smelter."

They went away and I asked him, "At this season do you pray for rain or dew?" and he said, "Dew," and was astonished, and I spoke a good deal with him but did not tell him I was a Jew. But on the third time that I went to his house before leaving Jerusalem, I said to him, "Make me a model showing Venice, Rome, and Portugal." He made me such a model, being a Sefardi, who had come from there and I said I wished to go to Rome, and he said, "Why?" and I answered, "I am going for a good cause, but it is a secret which I cannot reveal, and I want thee to advise me how I should go"; and I then gave him a letter which I had written to Jerusalem and said to him, "Give this letter into the hand of R. Isaac the Nagid." . . .

I and my servant, Joseph, travelled from Alexandria in the middle of Kislev, 5284 [November, 1523], and I fasted all day and prayed day and night, and took with me from Alexandria all kinds of food for Joseph. But it was no use, for all became mixed up with the food of the Christians. He ate from their utensils, and I cried out against him, but he cared not. When I reached Candia I bought many kinds of food, and the Christians and the Captain complained to me of Joseph that he stole bread and wine from the people on the ship. I was ashamed of him but could not speak with him, for he regarded not my word.

When I reached Venice I went to the Captain's house, where he gave me room, and I fasted in his house six days and six nights, and when I had finished prayers I saw a man behind me, and said to him in Hebrew, "Who art thou?"

He replied, "I am a Jew," and I asked him who told him I was here.

He replied, "Thy servant Joseph says that thou art a holy envoy." . . .

R. Simon ben Asher Meshullam came to me and said, "I hear that you are a holy envoy from the seventy Elders and going to Rome; tell me wherefore they have sent you and I will send two Jews with you and pay all the expenses."

I said to him, "I am going to the Pope and can say nothing more than that I am going for the good of Israel. If thou wilt send two men with me to Rome, thou wilt have a share in the good deed, and they will bring you back good tidings." . . .

I, David, the son of King Solomon, of righteous memory, from the wilderness of Habor, entered the gate of the City of Rome on the 15th day

of Adar, 1524 [c.e.], and a Gentile from Venice came to me and spoke
with me in Arabic, and I was angry with him. I went to the Pope's palace,
riding on horseback, and my servant before me, and the Jews also came
with me, and I entered the presence of Cardinal Egidio; and all the
Cardinals and Princes came to see me, and with the said Cardinal was R.
Joseph Ashkenazi, who was his teacher, and the physician Rabbi, Joseph
Sarphati.

I spoke to the Cardinal, and said that to the Pope I would complete my
message. I stayed with the Cardinal all day till the eve of Sabbath, and he
promised to bring the matter before the Pope on the morrow.

I went away with R. Joseph Ashkenazi and with R. Raphael, the old
man who lived in the same house, and we took our Sabbath meal and slept
till the morning; and I went with them to the Synagogue in order to pronounce the blessing of deliverance from peril before the scroll of the Law.
Men, women, and children came to meet us all the way until we entered
the house of the said R. Raphael, and I fasted on that Sabbath day. All
day long men and women, Jews and gentiles came to visit me until evening.

Cardinal Egidio sent for R. Joseph Ashkenazi to tell me that the Pope
was very pleased, and wished to see me on Sunday before eleven. And so
in the morning, before prayers, they gave me a horse and I went to Bor-
ghetto Santo Gile to the house of an old man, the brother-in-law of R.
Joseph Sarphati, before morning prayer; and I prayed there, and many
Jews came to me, may God keep them and multiply them a thousand fold!

At eight o'clock I went to the house of the Pope and entered Cardinal
Egidio's room, and with me were about twelve old and honoured Jews.
As soon as the Cardinal saw me, he rose from his chair and we went to
the apartment of the Pope. I spoke with him and he received me graciously
and said, "The matter is from the Lord"; and I said to him, "King Joseph
and his elders ordered me to speak to thee that thou shouldst make peace
between the Emperor and the French King, by all means, for it will be well
with thee and them if thou makest this peace, and write for me a letter to
these two Kings, and they will help us and we will help them; and write
also for me to King Prester John [i.e. the King of Abyssinia].

The Pope answered me, "As to the two Kings between whom thou askest
me to make peace, I cannot do it, but if thou needest help the King of
Portugal will assist thee, and I will write to him and he will do all. His
land is near to thy country and they are accustomed to travel on the great
sea every year, more than those in the lands of those other Kings."

And I replied to the Pope, "Whatever thou wishest I will do, and I will
not turn to the right or left from what thou biddest me, for I have come for
God's service, and not for anything else, and I will pray for thy welfare and
good all the days of my life."

And the Pope asked the Cardinal, "Where does the Ambassador lodge?"
and he answered, "The Jews asked him to go with them." The honourable

Jews who were there with the Pope told him, "Let the Ambassador stay with us, for we will honour him for the sake of thy honour."

The Pope said to them, "If you will do honour to him I will pay all your expenses."

I said to the Pope, "I wish to come before thee once every two days, for to see thee is as seeing the face of God."

The Pope answered that he ordered Cardinal Egidio to come with me every time I came to see him. I took leave of the Pope and went from him. I went with the Jews and rejoiced and was glad of heart. . . .

After that I sent a letter to the Cardinal to tell him that I had left the house of Joseph Sarphati because of the illness that had come upon me in that house, and that I was now staying in a house which was not fitting nor proper; and immediately he sent to the wardens and requested them to prepare a good and proper house for the needs of myself and four servants.

The wardens hired or rented for me four rooms and paid six months rent, and my servants prepared all the rooms nicely with a nice bed, and in the big room they made a synagogue with a scroll of the law and thirty lamps lighted therein. The servants waited on me for the love of God, and asked no wage of me and vowed to come with me anywhere that I should go, and my scribe, R. Elijah, the teacher, the son of Joab, and his brother, Benjamin, the Cantor, remained with me and waited on me all the time that I remained in Rome.

To the servant who came with me from Candia, that wicked Joseph, I gave clothes and money and sent him to his father in Naples, because every day he made quarrels and strife with the other servants and wanted to rule over them. He also slandered me to Don Miguel, the Ambassador of the King of Portugal, saying that I had come hither to bring the Marrano Jews back to their Judaism. The Marranos in Rome heard this and sought to slay him, but I begged them to do him no harm and sent him away. I stayed in this house until the new year.

Cardinal Egidio went to Viterbo and I wondered who would help me and stand between me and the Pope. I saw a man whose name was R. Daniel of Pisa, who used to frequent the Pope, and lived in a house near the Pope's, a very rich man and a Kabbalist, and I decided to ask him.

I said to him, "I see that you are honoured and considered by the Pope and all the Cardinals. I want you to be interpreter between me and the Pope, and to advise me and show me the good way, for the love of God and the love of the house of Israel and the love of King Joseph, my brother, and his elders of the wilderness of Khabor; and God will show you more honour than you have yet had if you do this in His service. I have come from the East to the West, for the sake of God's service and the love of Israel, who are under the dominion of Edom and Ishmael."

I then told him all the secrets of my heart and the hints and the secrets told me by my brother King Joseph; there was nothing I did not tell him, because I saw that he was good and upright in the eyes of man and God; and then I said to him, "God's secret is to them that fear him."

The said R. Daniel vowed that he would not journey or move from Rome until he had received letters from the Pope for me, and he would be interpreter between us; and he also vowed not to leave me on the road, but to go with me on the ship I was to enter; and he forthwith wrote a letter to the Pope, and I sent him by Chaim, my servant, to Ratieri, and he said to him, "The Ambassador gives thee a thousand greetings and sends this letter to you to hand to the Pope, and he wishes to know at what hour he can get an answer to the letter." He took the letter and said to Chaim, "Go in peace, and come back for the answer in eighteen hours."

Next day I sent Chaim to the Ratieri, and as soon as he entered he said, "Go call thy lord, the ambassador, and let him come speedily before the Pope, because he summons him." Then Chaim, my servant, returned with the servant of R. Daniel of Pisa, brought me a horse, and I went to the Pope with all my servants. They opened all the rooms for me, and I entered the room nearest the Pope, and said to the guards of the Pope's rooms that I did not wish to appear before the Pope until R. Daniel of Pisa should come, because he was interpreter between us.

When R. Daniel came I said to him, "Go thou first before the Pope". He entered and returned to me and I went with him and spoke to the Pope as follows, "I have stood before thee for nearly a year and it is my will for God's sake and thy honour that thou shouldst write me the letters which I asked of thy Holiness for Prester John, and also all the Christians whose lands I shall traverse, whether great or small."

R. Daniel spoke to the Pope, who said, "I will do all that the ambassador desires."

Then I and R. Daniel of Pisa left the Pope, happy and of good courage, and we went in peace to my home; but there were then in Rome four or five slanderers, and God put repentance in their hearts that they should return from their evil way; and there were also strong Jews in Rome and Italy, mighty and lionhearted for all work, and suitable for war, but the Jews who are in Jerusalem and Egypt and Iraq, and all the Moslem countries, are fainthearted and prone to fear and fright and not fitted for war like the Italian Jews. May the Almighty increase them a thousand fold, and bless them! . . .

Within a few days the letters came from the Pope and R. Daniel gave them to me. That night many Jews came to my house in order to rejoice with me that I had received the letters. Four notables, the heads of the Roman congregation, R. Obadiah of Sforno, and R. Judah of Ascoli, the Physician, and two others came to me. But there were in my house slanderers and spies whom I did not recognize, and they wished to read the brief and the letters which the Pope had written, that they might profit by remembering them. I was very angry with them, for men told me that they were spies and would go before the scribes of the Pope repeating the words, in order to spoil my business. They caused me much worry and thought.

Afterwards the Pope sent for R. Daniel of Pisa and spoke with him about me whether I wished to go, for he would give me leave, and ordered that I should come before him at eighteen o'clock on the 24th of the first Adar, and I and R. Daniel went before him, and I stayed with him about two hours.

He spoke to me saying, "I have given you a letter to King Prester John, and I have also written to the King of Portugal, and I have written to the Christians whose country thou wilt pass so that they should help thee, and honour thee for God's sake and my sake"; and he further said, "Be strong and of good courage and fear not, for God is with thee."

I said to him, "There is none before me but the Almighty and thou, and I am prepared to serve thee all the days of my life, and also King Joseph my brother and all my people's sons are inclined to thee."

The Pope ordered that they should give me a sign and shield to show to King Joseph my brother, and he also gave me one hundred golden ducats. I would not take the money, but only under compulsion when he said, "Take it for thy servants," and I left the Pope and returned home in peace and joy and a good heart.

Then I went to Don Miguel, the King of Portugal's Ambassador, in order to get a safe conduct from him for the journey, and he said, "If thou wishest to go to Pisa, I will write and send thee to Pisa the safe conduct." But he did this by way of trick, and I left his house in anger. The Pope heard the matter and said to Don Miguel, "Write for him a safe conduct, for I too have written to the King of Portugal."

But he did not obey the Pope, and left Rome for hunting and stayed away a week and returned. I asked a second time for a safe conduct, and he said that he would send it after me to Pisa at any rate, and I believed his words and I went home and R. Daniel went with me. I said to him that it was my desire to leave Rome tomorrow, in the middle of the month of Nisan, as our fathers left Egypt.

I stayed in Rome till midday of the 15th of Adar to arrange my matters and see who of all my servants should go with me. Two went, one called R. Raphael ha-Cohen, who sang in my home from the day I arrived in Rome, a strong man and warlike, and the second, Jacob ha-Levi, even stronger than Raphael Cohen, and he was my servant from the day I arrived in Rome; and I gave each of them in Rome five ducats in order that they should arrange all their affairs, and R. Daniel was with me and promised to give me other servants, and he gave me a third servant, Tobias.

We left Rome at midday, the 15th of the Second Adar, just as we entered Rome at midday on the 15th of Adar, so that we stayed in Rome a full year. The Jews of Rome come to accompany me on thirty horses for five miles, and I found at Roncelin an army of the King of France with five hundred horses, thank God; they showed us great honour. At last I arrived at Viterbo, and with me were my servants Raphael Cohen and Joseph Levi and Tobias; but R. Daniel stayed on in Rome, saying he would follow us, and ordered Joab to go with me to Pisa to the house of R. Jechiel of Pisa, and we stayed in Viterbo at the house of R. Joseph Cohen. . . .

When I left Viterbo, Jews on ten horses accompanied me and we stayed at Bolsena over Sabbath in the house of the said R. Joseph, and remained there until Sunday, and they showed us great honour, more than proper. Thence we journeyed to Siena and came to the house of the honourable Ishmael of Rieti, who took us and made room in his house, and prepared for me a bed and separate room.

He has a large dwelling and is very rich, and I said to him, "What desirest thou more, Jerusalem or thy own place?" and he answered, "I have no desire in Jerusalem but only in Siena"; and I was much surprised at him that he cannot do meritorious deeds with the wealth that God has given him. "He that loveth silver shall not be satisfied with silver." He promised to do kindness unto my servants, but repented and did not keep his promise and did not desire to earn a good name before all Israel.

We journeyed from Siena on the Monday and arrived at Pisa in the house of R. Jechiel, may he be remembered with a thousand times a thousand blessings, he and his mother Signora Laura and his grandmother Signora Sarah, may they be blessed among women. Amen!

He was like an angel of God, wise in the Torah and Talmud, humble, pious and charitable; his heart cleaves to Jerusalem, the holy city, and his house is open to all the poor of Israel, and all who come to his house eat at his table. Every day he does charity to the poor and likewise his mother and grandmother do charity, for they all do kindness and truth; and, with my own eyes, I saw all their good deeds, more than I saw throughout Italy.

We stayed in their house seven months and I sent my servants back to Rome because they had been slandering, but only Tobias, who was my cook, remained as my servant. Don Miguel did not send me the safe conduct he had promised, but wrote to me that the King does not wish me to come to him in Portugal this year. This was false and a lie, and I had great pain from it, and fasted six times six days and nights, and I also fasted three days and nights in forty days.

The household of R. Jechiel gave me all kinds of food and spices and flowers and apple water, and served me with all the delicacies of the world, and did all kindnesses and truth with me and sent me great presents and silk robes, and gave money to all my servants and, on the great fast, they came to me with honour to the house of R. Jechiel. His wife, called Diamante, the daughter of R. Asher Meshullam, of Venice, and the mother of R. Jechiel, Signora Laura, and her mother, Signora Sarah, and other young women used to dance in the room where I was and the wife of R. Jechiel played the harp, and they said to me, "We are come here for your honour's sake, and in order that the sorrow may go from the fast and that you may rejoice."

They asked me if I had any delight in the sound of the harp and in dancing and I answered, "You are very kind"; but God knows my thoughts that I did not wish to listen to the sound of the harp and the flute and rejoicings. The gentiles of Pisa came to me to R. Jechiel's house and blew trumpets and made great sounds in order to get money.

The said R. Jechiel wrote a scroll of the law with his own hand, and I made the blessing over that scroll several Sabbaths. It was very well written and the Signora Benvenida, the wife of Samuel Abarbanel, sent me from Naples to Pisa a banner of fine silk on which the ten commandments were written in two columns, with golden embroidery old and antique. She also sent me a Turkish gown of gold brocade to wear for her sake, besides having sent me money three times when I was in Rome. I heard that she fasts every day, and had also heard of her fame when in Alexandria and Jerusalem; how she used to ransom the captives, and had ransomed more than a thousand captives, and gave charity to everyone that asked of her, may she be blessed before the Lord!

Signora Sarah, of Pisa, gave me a golden signet ring and said to me, "Let this be a witness between me and thee." She also gave me a big manuscript of Psalms, Job, Proverbs, and the five Scrolls on parchment, and she wrote with her own hand at the beginning of the book her advice "Never be angry or hasty." She also gave me a prayer book, saying, "Pray with this for my sake."

After a few days the King of Portugal sent to Rome as Ambassador Don Martin instead of Don Miguel, and as soon as Don Martin arrived in Rome he wrote to me to Pisa that "The King of Portugal has heard about thee that thou has come to serve him; he is glad and will do thee kindness, therefore prepare and go with this ship." . . .

Thence we went with a good wind westward to the King of Portugal through the great sea [Mediterranean]. We arrived close to Cadiz, in the Kingdom of the Emperor, and I sent Tobias to the magistrate with the Pope's letter to ask him to allow us to leave the ship and stay in his city for one day, but the magistrate was not willing.

Tobias said that the men of the city spoke evil things of us to the magistrate and said that the Jewish King had sent to the King of Portugal, who was of small account [compared with the Emperor]. They thought we were going against the Emperor and advised him to come and arrest me and get horses to send me before the Emperor, but I was emboldened in my mission and rejoiced in all that God had done, for it would be for my good and the good of Israel to appear before the Emperor. But my servants were afraid and terrified. I said to them, "Do not fear or be terrified."

After that the ship captain came to me and said, "Better that you should leave this ship for another ship belonging to the King of Portugal," so we left that ship at midnight and left all our belongings in the cabin and closed it, and got into a little boat, which took us to the King of Portugal's ship, on which we embarked. . . .

When all the people of the city heard that I had reached the shore, notables came to me, Christians and Marranos, with women and children, and I rode to that city on a mule. All the road was full of men and women, too numerous to count, and we arrived at the city of Tavira at the house of a Marrano, and they prepared the house for us, and beds and tables.

The Marrano is an honorable man and his wife very honorable and the magistrate of the city came to me and rejoiced over us greatly, and said to me, "I am ready and prepared to do anything thou wishest at thy command and for thy service." He came twice to see me and that magistrate wrote to the King to tell him that we had arrived in Tavira and I wrote a letter to the King of Portugal and sent it by the hand of David the Rumanian, and I stayed in the house of the Marrano to wait for the King's answer.

The Marrano and his wife showed me much kindness and would not allow us to spend anything from our pocket, for they wished to pay all expenses, and we stayed in their house forty days until the messenger from the King of Portugal reached me in Tavira.

In those days a priest came from Spain, who spoke with R. Solomon Cohen Da Porto, and R. Solomon was angry with him for the priest said that there was no Jewish King and that we had no sons of royal seed. He was standing before a big window, and I was zealous for God's sake and took hold of him and threw him from the window on to the ground outside before all the gentiles, and they laughed at the priest and feared to speak against me, and the great magistrate heard of this and was greatly rejoiced.

When the messenger returned to me, he brought two letters from the King and in one he wrote that I should come to him in all honour and that he would do my will, and the second he wrote to all the magistrates in his kingdom that they should honour me an advance me from city to city, that they should prepare for me a bed, a table and a light in every place to which we came.

The said messenger said that the King had commanded that I should set out to visit him tomorrow, and he gave me five hundred ducats and a scribe of the King's scribes, who should superintend the expenditure. In the morning they gave me horses for me and my servants to ride to the King. We journeyed from Tavira, and the magistrate and all the notables of the city went out with me and returned, but I went on with two notables and the King's scribe and a number of men who came with me from Tavira, and at every place the King's Scribe went to the magistrates so that they should prepare for me a house and a table and a chair and candle according to the King's command.

We arrived at a city called Beja and came before the magistrates on horseback, and all the notables of that city, Marranos and Christians, came out three parasangs to meet me, and when we approached the city, men, women and children also came. We arrived at the city and entered the house of a Marrano and stayed there that night and, in the morning, we journeyed on and came to a great city, Evora. On Friday, the eve of Sabbath, the magistrates and many men came to meet me two parasangs outside the city; and I entered the city, and it is very big, and the King's palace is there and also a community of many honoured Marranos. We stayed at the house of a Marrano on the Sabbath and Sunday.

And in every city we entered Marranos came, men and women, great and small, and kissed my hand, and the Christians were jealous of me, and said to them, "Show him great honour, but do not kiss his hand, but only the hand of the King of Portugal alone." Some were of stout heart, because they believed in me with a perfect faith, as Israel believed in our Master, Moses, on whom be peace! And I said to them in every place we came to that I am the son of King Solomon, and that I have not come to you with a sign or miracle or mystery, but I am a man of war from my youth till now, and I have come to help your King and to help you and to go in the way he shall lead me to the land of Israel.

I journeyed from Evora and the magistrates came to escort me, and with them were many honoured nobles and many men, too numerous to count, and they went with me two parasangs and returned. In every road that I passed, Marranos came to me from every side and every corner to accompany me, and they gave me presents, and some righteous Gentiles also, until I arrived two parasangs distance from the King.

Now the King was residing in Almeda, for he had fled because of the plague in Lisbon, and I wrote to the King as follows: "Behold, I have arrived at this place, and I will stay until thou dost let me know that I may come before thy honour." I sent an honourable old gentile to the King and also the King's scribe who had come with me from Tavira and was appointed over the expenses of the journey. They returned to me and said that the King has called his counsellors before him and are taking counsel over this matter.

Some say this and some say that; some of them said, "Show him honour and send all the honoured notables before him to accompany him, for he has come from a distant land to seek thee and serve thee."

But Don Miguel, my enemy, because I wished to slay him with a sword in Rome, stood and spoke against me before the King and the notables and the messengers I had sent to the King. They inquired of the scribe if the Marranos showed me more honour than the Christians, and he replied that they honoured me with great honour and kissed my hand, and all the way honoured me and kissed my hand in all the way that I journeyed.

Then said Don Miguel to the King, "Did I not say to thee that he is come to destroy thy kingdom and to restore the Marranos to the faith of the Jews? If thou wilt send before him notables to honour him, all the Marranos in thy country will follow him and will take counsel how the Christians are to be made Jews."

All these things said the wicked Don Miguel to the King and to his counsellors and messengers, and the King asked his counsellors what to reply to the Jewish King, and they said to him, "Reply that thy grandmother is dead and that thou art in mourning and canst not show him honour this year as is our custom, and ask pardon of the Ambassador who wishes to come before you with his servants from Tavira."

And when I heard the word of the King and his counsellors I rode with all my servants and the men who had come with me on horses, and we went before the King. We were about fifty men and fifteen horses besides mules which carried my belongings, and we reached Almeda and came to the palace and court of the King. I had been fasting from Sunday to Wednesday when I came to the King and stood before him with all my servants, each one with his sword upon his thigh.

I said to the King and to his wife, the Queen, "I am weary and fatigued from the journey, and have been fasting four days, and cannot speak to thee today, but if it seems good in thy eyes I will go to my house today and tomorrow we shall speak, I and thou." I was not willing to kiss his hand either when I came or when I left, because of the anger in my heart which the wicked Don Miguel had caused me. . . .

The King sent to summon me on Wednesday, eight days after I had arrived here, and I went before him; I and old Solomon Cohen and Benzion, my servants, and we came before the King, and the King called a Marrano, an old physician, who was interpreter between me and the King in Hebrew. That old man was somewhat deaf and, when he spoke to the King and to me he was in fear and terrified.

The King said, "I have heard of thee that thou speakest Arabic well, and I have an old servant who can speak Arabic well, and he will hear your words from beginning to end and tell them to me." The King called that lord and said, "Speak with that Ambassador in Arabic."

I spoke in Arabic to that lord, and he interpreted my words to the King. I placed in the King's hand all the letters and spoke with him on the matter of my mission. I told him all my journey, which I had travelled from the wilderness, until I came before him. I also said to the King, "King Joseph, my brother, asks me with reference to the artificers of weapons for his kingdom."

The King was greatly pleased with my words and his heart rejoiced within him, and he said, "The matter is of the Lord. I am willing to do so and it shall be my desire." The matter was good in his eyes, and in the eyes of all his lords. Then said the King to me, "Return from Santarem to Almeda, which is near me." The King ordered the old lord to prepare for me a house near to the Palace, and so the old man did, and I sent all that I had in my house, beds and linen and all household furniture, from Santarem to the house which they prepared for me in Almeda, near to the Palace.

Afterwards a great Moslem lord, a Judge of the King of Fez, came to me. He had been sent by this King to the King of Portugal, and is an honourable man, a friend of the Jews. He has ten servants. This Judge came to my house because the King of Fez had heard about me and ordered him to go first to the King of Portugal, and then to come and see me, and he gave me letters from the Jews of Fez and from R. Abraham ben Zimori of Asfi-Safi and a third letter from the Captain of Tangier. Then the Judge asked me about my country, whether many Jews were there.

I answered that it was the wilderness of Habor, and that there are thirty myriad Jews in my country, and King Joseph, my brother, rules over them and has seventy counselors and many lords, and I am a military lord over ways and war. The Judge said to me, "What seekest thou from this kingdom that thou hast come from the East to the West?"

I answered that from our youth we are trained in war, and our war is with the sword and lance and bow, and we wished to go, with God's help, to Jerusalem to capture the land of Israel from the Moslems, for the end and salvation has arrived, and I have come to seek wise handicraftsmen who know how to make weapons and firearms that they should come to my land and make them and teach our soldiers.

The Judge was much amazed at this, and said to me, "We believe that the kingdom will return to you this time, and if you return will you do kindness to us?"

I said to him, "Yes, we will do kindness to you and to all who do kindness to Israel, which is in captivity under Ishmael and Edom"; and I said to the Judge, "Do you also believe that the kingdom of the land of Ishmael will return to us?"

And he replied to me, "In all the world they believe this."

I said to him, "We are kings, and our fathers were kings from the time of the destruction of the Temple till this day, in the wilderness of Habor. We rule over the tribes of Reuben and Gad, and the half-tribe of Manasseh in the wilderness of Habor, and there are nine and a half tribes in the land of Ethiopia and other kings. The nearest to us are the tribe of Simeon and the tribe of Benjamin, and they are on the River Nile, above the kingdom of Sheba . . ."

The Judge said to me, "Dost thou wish to write for me a letter to the King of Fez?"

I answered, "I need not write, but you can say all this to him by word of mouth and give him from me a thousand greetings and say to him that the Jews under his rule should be protected by him, and that he should honour them and this will be the beginning of peace between us and him, between our seed and his seed."

The Judge also asked me, "What will you do with the Jews in all the lands of the west, will you come to the west for them and how will you deal with them?"

I replied that we shall first take the Holy Land and its surroundings and that then our captains of the host will go forth to the west and east to gather the dispersed of Israel, and whoever is wise among the Moslem Kings will take the Jews under his rule and bring them to Jerusalem, and he will have much honour, greater than that of all the Moslem Kings, and God will deliver up all the kingdoms to the King of Jerusalem.

Further, the Judge asked me, "Is it true that the Jews in Fez and its neighborhood say, and the Moslems also, that you are a prophet and the Messiah?"

I answered, "God forbid, I am a sinner before the Lord, greater than any one of you, and I have slain many men, and on one day I killed forty enemies. I am neither a prophet nor the son of a prophet, neither a wise man nor a Kabbalist, but I am a captain of the host, the son of Solomon the King, the son of David, the son of Jesse, and my brother the King rules over thirty myriads in the wilderness of Habor. Moreover, the Marranos in the Kingdom of Portugal, and all the Jews in Italy and all the places that I passed also thought me to be a prophet, wise man, or Kabbalist, and I said to them, 'God forbid, I am a sinner and a man of war from my youth till now.' "

Afterwards the Judge began to write to the Jews of Fez, and to R. Abraham ben Zimori of Asfi-Safi, and I wrote to them and handed the letters to him and he went on his way in peace. . . .

Joseph Caro — The Shulhan Arukh

Joseph Caro (1488–1575) was born in Toledo, Spain, and was only four years old when the expulsion of the Jews in 1492 made his family refugees. Stemming from a long line of scholars, Caro early proved his brilliance. In 1520, after he wrote a commentary on Maimonides' *Mishne Torah*, he was appointed chief rabbi of Adrianople, Turkey, and had students from all over the world. In 1525, Caro arrived in Safed, Palestine, mountain city of scholars and mystics, and lived and taught in the midst of a brilliant circle of colleagues, which included Solomon Alkabez, the author of the Friday night hymn, *Lecha Dodi* (see Siddur, p. 141), and the kabbalist Rabbi Isaac Luria.

One of Caro's important works is *Bet Joseph*, a collection of Jewish laws, to which he devoted twenty years of his life (1522–1542). Soon after its publication in Venice in 1551, it was hailed as the greatest extant legal code, and showed Caro to be the most profound scholar of Talmudic learning of his age. With *Bet Joseph* Caro sought to provide a code that would aid rabbis adjudicate matters of law, and also trace the origin and development of halakha from the Talmud through the Gaonic period and down through the responsa of his own day. In contrast to the method utilized by Maimonides (and for which the latter was severely criticized) Caro did append sources to support his decisions which sought to resolve conflicting views.

Although Caro considered his *Bet Joseph* his *magnum opus*, he was destined to be immortalized by the *Shulhan Arukh*, a digest and more popular version of *Bet Joseph*. The *Shulhan Arukh* is divided into four major sections:

1) *Orah Hayim* ("Path of Life") deals with the duties that a Jew performs daily and on Sabbaths and holidays.

2) *Yoreh Deah* ("Teacher of Knowledge") focuses on the dietary laws, family purity, charity, prohibition against idolatry, respect for parent and teacher, circumcision and mourning.

3) *Even ha-Ezer* ("Stone of Help") treats all aspects of marriage and divorce.

4) *Hoshen Mishpat* ("Breastplate of Judgment") deals with civil and criminal law, inheritance, loans, and appointment of judges.

With the publication of the *Shulhan Arukh* in 1564, Caro became the most famous teacher and scholar of his day, and had questions addressed to him from all over the world. Although the work contains many medieval superstitions, some of which Caro himself notes (stating that he found them in other texts), the *Shulhan Arukh* saved Judaism from schisms by uniting—as Caro hoped it would—the religious practise of the Sephardim and Ashkenazim. Caro's code soon replaced all previous compilations and became the official standard code for Jewry. Rabbi Moses Isserles additions (1578) to the *Shulhan Arukh* made its use even more widespread. Numerous commentaries have also been appended to it, and it has been continuously reprinted. Found in most observant Jewish homes, the *Shulhan Arukh* sums up the ideal conduct for the individual throughout his lifetime.

THE LAW OF HONORING PARENTS

CHAPTER 240

THE FIFTH COMMANDMENT—HONOR THY FATHER AND MOTHER: THAT THY DAYS MAY BE LONG UPON THE LAND WHICH THE LORD THY GOD GIVETH THEE [EX. 20].
YOU SHALL FEAR FOR YOUR MOTHER AND FATHER [LEV. 19].

1. What is fear? It is forbidden to stand or to sit in the seat which belongs to the father at the time when he has a meeting with his members or at the time when he is at prayer in the synagogue or when he is sitting in his home, and shall not contradict or second his words and shall not call their parents by their first names either if they are alive or dead but only "My dear Father or Mother."

2. If another man is called by the same name as the father if it is a nickname it is forbidden to call the other in the presence of the father, if it is an ordinary name it is permitted to call the other by his name in the absence of the father.

3. If the children were sitting in a great assembly with honorable, highly educated people, and very nicely dressed, and the parents come in and tear their clothes, and spit on them, and smite them on the head or face, the children must be silent, and have fear for the Lord who is the King of all the kingdoms and he commands them to honor their parents.

4. What is honor? To honor is to give the parents drink, food, clothes cover them and assist them in going and coming, wait on them, and do it all cheerfully and happily and gladly. If these things are done for the parents with a sour face then the children are subject to receive great punishment.

5. If the parents are able to bear the expense of the food and drink, etc., they must pay for same themselves, if not and the children are able to bear the expense they must pay it, but anyway the children must bear the trouble themselves for waiting on the parents.

6. If the children are unable to support their parents they are not bound to beg from door to door to support their parents, but they are bound to honor the parents with their personal services, even if they have to hinder their work and will be forced to beg from door to door afterwards for themselves.

7. These above rules apply only when the children have enough support for the day. If, however, they have not enough support for the day they are not bound to give their time for the service for the parents.

8. If the children are all rich the expenses of treating the parents must be borne by each of them according to the amount of their wealth. If part of them are rich and part poor the expenses of the treatment of the parents must be borne by the ones that are rich, but the personal services must be shared by all the children.

8a. If a son needs a favor from the members of his city and he can receive the favor either on account of his own respect or the respect of his father, he shall not request it account of the respect of himself but he shall request it on account of the respect of the father.

9. It is the duty of the children to stand up when the parents come into their presence.

10. If the son is the teacher of the father each one must stand up for the other, in other words both must stand up.

11. Even if the parents throw a pocket of gold denarim in the river the children shall not slander them nor cause them pain, nor feel incensed against them, only they must be silent. It is an opinion if the money was of the fortune of the son the son can forbid the father to throw it away. If, however, it is destroyed it is forbidden to slander the parents, but the son has the right to claim for the debit in the court.

12. If the father has a claim against the son and they live in different cities the son must be tried in the city of the father, but the father must pay the son the expenses of the trip.

13. The child is bound to honor the parents even after they are dead. For example, if he quotes something in his father name, he must say, "My beloved father and teacher said so."

14. If the parents become insane the children must provide for them treatment with doctors and nurses until they recover.

15. If the son sees that the father violates a command of the Torah he shall not say, "Father you violate a command of the Torah," only he must say, "Father it is written in the Torah so"; and then he understands his mistake and will correct it himself.

16. If a father ask for services from the son and at the same time the son has another command to fulfill, *i.e.,* the son has to attend a burial at the same time, if the other command can be done through others the son is bound to attend to his parents. If the other command cannot be done through others then the son must attend to the other command first and after he will attend to the services of the father.

17. The command of learning the Torah has the preference over services to the parents.

18. If the parents both of them ask the children for service at one time, *i.e.,* the father and mother ask for a drink at one time, the preference belongs to the father.

20. If the father commands his son not to talk to or forgive R until a certain length of time, and the son would like to forgive R immediately the son need not obey the father.

21. Both son and daughter are equally bound to honor the parents, but a married daughter is not able to attend to her parents because she must attend her family; however, if she become divorced she must attend to her parents like the son.

22. It is the duty of the parents not to trouble their children too much, to pardon them if they neglect to honor them, and not cause them to sin.

23. If a father smite his grown son after 22 years of age, the father can be excommunicated by the Court because he violates the law not to place a stumbling-block in front of a blind man.

24. It is the duty of a man to honor the wife of his father even though she is not his mother; to honor the husband of his mother even though he is not his father.

25. A man is bound to honor his oldest brother even if he is a half-brother, and even if he is more educated than the oldest one.

26. A man is bound to honor his father-in-law or mother-in-law.

27. If the father desires to serve the son the son is permitted to receive the services; but if the father is a scholar then it is not permitted.

28. If a student wishes to go to another place to study because of better opportunity and his father forbids him on account of the dangers in the city, the son need not obey the father.

29. If the parents are against their child's marriage to a certain party, the right is with the child, provided the marriage is not against religion.

CHAPTER 241

He that smiteth his father or his mother, shall purely be put to death [Ex. 21].

He that curseth his father, or his mother, shall purely be put to death [Ex. 21].

1. Children are forbidden to curse their parents even after their death.

2. It is forbidden to smite one's parents, and if children violate this law and they shed their blood they are subject to execution.

3. If a man smites his father on his ear and makes him deaf the son is liable to execution, because it is impossible to become deaf without shedding a drop of blood from the ears.

4. If a father gets a splinter in his hand the son is forbidden to take it out if there is anyone else nearby to do so, for fear that he might wound his father.

5. If the son is a doctor and the father needs an operation the son is forbidden to perform it even if he does it for the welfare of his father. If, however, there is no other doctor to do this and the father is suffering great pain the son is permitted to do whatever the father permits.

6. If a man slanders his parents, with words or actions, the son will receive curses from the Lord, and the Court has the right to punish the son with flagellations.

THE LAW OF HONORING TEACHERS
AND LEARNED MEN

CHAPTER 242

1. It is the duty of a man to honor and respect his teacher. Honor to the teacher comes before honor to the parents, when the parents are ignorant, because the parents support the children materially in this world and the teacher supports them spiritually and prepares them for the future world.

2. He who strives with his teacher is like one striving with the Lord and he who complains of his teacher is like one complaining of the Lord.

3. It is forbidden for a scholar to answer questions of law in the presence of his teacher without the teacher's permission, and he who violates the law is liable to punishment.

4. It is forbidden to call the teacher by the first name even after his death. He must only be addressed "My dear teacher."

5. It is forbidden to occupy the teacher's seat.

6. If a teacher dies the scholar is bound to tear his coat as he is bound to tear his coat when his father dies.

7. If the father and the teacher lose anything, and it is impossible to look for both of them at once, the preference belongs to the teacher.

8. If the father and the teacher carry a heavy load, and need some assistance, and it is impossible to help them both at once, the preference of assistance belongs to the teacher.

9. If the teacher and the father are in captivity or detention the preference in helping to release them is given to the teacher.

10. The above rules of preference for the teacher hold good only when the scholar has received the majority of his education from this teacher; if, however, he has not received so much learning from the teacher, then the preference belongs to the father.

11. If the scholar and the teacher each lose an article and it is impossible to look for both at the same time, then the preference belongs to the scholar.

12. The teacher is bound to honor the scholar as the scholar is bound to honor him.

13. It is the duty of the scholar to stand up as soon as he sees the teacher.

CHAPTER 243

The judges thou shalt not revile; and a ruler among thy people thou shalt not curse. [Ex. 22].

1. It is the duty of the people to honor and to fear the ruler and the judges and all the learned men.

3. Clergymen are free from all kinds of taxation.

4. It is the duty of the people to provide funds to support the judges and the learned men, that they may have enough to live in a good manner.

5. It is a great sin to slander and to hate learned men. He who does so has no part in the world to come.

6. It is forbidden to ask a service of a learned man.

7. The court has the authority to punish the man who slanders a learned man.

8. The learned man has a right to excuse the slanderer.

CHAPTER 244

Before the hoary head shalt thou rise up, and honor the face of the old man; and thou shalt be afraid of thy God: I am the Lord (Lev. 19).

1. One must rise in the presence of a learned man, even if he is not an old man, and stand up in the presence of an old man, seventy years of age, even if he is not learned, providing he is less than four yards away. It is forbidden to close one's eyes and pretend not to see him.

2. A working man, when he is on duty, is not bound to stand up in the presence of a learned man, because his work must not be hindered.

3. It is the duty of the learned man to go in a different way if he can, to avoid troubling the people to stand up for him.

CHAPTER 245

1. It is the duty of every man to teach his son and his grandchildren the learning of the Torah; and if the father did not teach them, the children are bound to obtain learning themselves.

2. If the father and the son desire to learn and the father cannot afford the expenditure for both, the father comes first; however, if the son is clever in learning, and he can make quicker progress, then the son comes first.

3. The residents of each city can compel one another to cover the expenses of a school for children.

4. A teacher is supposed to teach not more than 25 children, and if there are from 25 to 40, he must have an assistant, if there are 50 they need two teachers.

5. The teacher is not allowed to whip his students with a rod or with a stick, only with a little strap.

6. Each neighborhood must have a school so that the child will not have to go a great distance to reach the school, and shall not have to pass bridges, rivers, or dangerous places.

7. If a teacher leaves his scholars alone during school hours and goes out to look for other business, or if he neglects the children and is lazy in the teaching, he is cursed by the Lord and can be discharged without notification.

8. It is forbidden for the teacher to be up at night, and attend the school in the day time, or to fast at the time of teaching, or to overeat, because these things impair his health and result in neglect in the teaching of the children.

CHAPTER 246

1. Every man, rich or poor, healthy or sick, young or old, even a beggar who goes from door to door who has a wife and children to support, must devote some time during the day to studying the Torah. If he has no time to study the Torah on account of his business, he must support the poor students, and when they study with his assistance, it is as if he studied himself.

2. A man can make a verbal agreement with a poor student to support him and he shall share with him the rewards of future studies.

3. The student should not be ashamed to ask the teacher what is doubtful to him even one hundred times. The wise ask everything they do not understand, the fools are ashamed to ask.

4. A man must study the Torah until he dies; if he stops studying he surely will forget what he has already learned, because the Torah is like gold and glass, that is, it is as hard to get as gold; and it is as easy to forget, as it is to break glass.

5. If the teacher does not conduct himself properly, even if he has a good education, he shall not be appointed as teacher.

6. If the teacher goes over the lesson and the student does not understand, the teacher shall not be angry with him, but shall continue going over the lesson, even a hundred times, until the student does understand, and if the teacher feels angry with the student the student must ask the teacher to excuse him, and tell him he is learning and desires to learn but that his mind cannot grasp all the learning at once.

7. If a woman learns the Torah even if she is not commanded to, she

fulfills a command, and she is bound to learn the law of the three commands which belong to her, and if she helps her husband by attending to the children, bringing them up well and educating them, she will receive a great compensation in the world to come.

8. A man should study before he marries, because after marriage family burdens prevent him from studying.

9. If a man has another command to attend to, and he must study the Torah, the Torah studying has preference provided that the other commandment can be attended to by others.

10. If a man violates the command to study the Torah on account of the burden of his riches, as punishment he will become poor and he will be forced to violate the command of studying the Torah owing to his poverty.

11. It is forbidden to study the Torah in an unclean place, as for example, in a bath house, lavatory, etc.

12. It is commanded to make a celebration or party after finishing a part of the Torah.

LAW OF CHARITY

CHAPTER 247

If there be among thee a needy man, any one of thy brethren within any of thy gates in thy land which the Lord thy God giveth thee, thou shalt not harden thy heart, nor shut thy hand from thy needy brother.

But thou shalt open wide thy hand unto him, and thou shalt surely lend him sufficient for his need, which his wishing want requireth.

Thou shalt surely give him, and thy heart shall not be grieved when thou givest unto him; for because of this thing the Lord thy God will bless thee in all thy work, and in all the acquisition of thy hand.

For the needy will not cease out of the land; therefore do I command thee, saying, "Thou shalt open wide thy hand unto thy brother, to thy poor, and to thy needy, in thy land" [Deut. 15].

CHAPTER 248

1. One must give charity according to one's means; it is forbidden to refuse the poor because it may lead to the shedding of the blood of the poor man, because he may die of hunger.

2. A man cannot become poor from giving charity.

3. If a man feels pity for the poor the Lord will feel pity for him and save him from all dangers and risks, and will even save him from sickness and death.

4. There are eight steps in the command of giving charity. Each one is higher than the other.

> a. When a man is in financial straits, it is a command to help him with a loan, with a present, or with work, so that he will be saved from beggary.
>
> b. When a man gives charity and he doesn't know to whom he is giving it; for instance, when he gives to a charity organization.
>
> c. When a man gives charity and he knows to whom he is giving it, but the poor man doesn't know where it comes from. For instance, one learned man puts money under the door of a poor man who finds it in the morning when he opens the door, so that the poor man would not feel ashamed. This way is very good in case the man knows that the leaders of the charity are not so trustworthy.

d. The poor man knows from whom he is taking, but the giver doesn't know to whom he is giving. For instance, a learned man puts money in his back pocket and goes among the poor, so the poor could take the money from his pocket and need not feel ashamed.

e. To give to a poor man before he asks for it.

f. If the poor man requests it, give it.

g. To give the poor man less than he asks for, but with a happy face.

h. To give to the poor man, but with a sour face.

5. It is forbidden to praise and announce oneself when giving charity. If one does so, he will not receive good returns from the Lord, but great punishment.

6. A man who presents an article to a synagogue may put his name on it stating that he donated it to the synagogue.

7. It is a great command to influence others to give charity by going around among people and collecting for charity.

8. If a man turns his back on a poor man and refuses him, he is called a bad man and can sometimes cause the poor man's death. For example: Nahum Gamzu was walking on a road with three asses heavily loaded, one with food, one with drink, and the other with spices. A poor man met him and said, "Feed me." Nahum Gamzu answered, "Wait until I unload my asses." Before he finished unloading them, the poor man died of starvation. Nahum Gamzu fell upon the body and said, "May my eyes which did not feel pity for your eyes become blind, and my hands, which did not feel pity for your hands, be taken off, and my feet, which didn't feel pity for your feet, become crooked and may my whole body become covered with blisters." And all this punishment happened to him because he refused the poor man; he was satisfied with this punishment which he received in this world, so that he be forgiven for this sin in the other world.

10. A man never gets poor by giving charity, the more he gives the richer he becomes because if he feels pity for the poor the Lord will have pity on him and he will be supplied with long life, health and riches.

11. If a man is taxed a certain amount for charity, and he refuses to pay, the court and the leaders of the charity have the right to compel him and take some of his property as a pledge for it.

12. It is forbidden to put a tax on orphans for charity, except when it is for the welfare of the orphans.

13. It is forbidden to receive a large amount of charity from a married woman, or from a minor who has a father, without the consent of the husband or father; because, perhaps, the father or the husband will be against this amount.

14. However, if a woman is active in her husband's business it is permitted to receive any amount of charity from her.

15. The charity leaders are forbidden to demand charity from a man

who has a good character, but who cannot afford to give it on account of support of his family.

16. If you must refuse the poor man because you cannot afford to give him charity do not slander him, but ask him to excuse you in a nice, polite manner and give him as much as you can.

17. The charity leaders are permitted to use the collected charity money for the purpose of assisting poor girls for wedding expenditures.

CHAPTER 250

1. The leaders of charity must give the poor man enough for his needs. When a rich man becomes poor charity must supply him with all kinds of food he was used to before, even a fat chicken and a bottle of good wine.

2. If the poor man is single and desires to get married and possesses no means, the charity must help him.

3. The contributions for the support of the poor men of each city must be divided according to the proportion of the wealth of the inhabitants. For example, the man who has 50,000 must pay twice as much as the man who has 25,000.

4. A man must support himself and his family first, then if he is able he must support his parents, followed by support of his oldest children, and his brothers and relatives; his neighbors and the poor of his own city come before the support of the poor of an outside city; and the poor of Palestine have preference over the poor of other countries.

5. When a man gives a sum of money to the charity officers he or his heirs have no right to command to whom it shall be given.

6. If a man and a woman both ask for assistance of the charity, either for food or for clothing, and there is not enough money in treasury for both, the woman has the preference in receiving charity.

7. If the male and female orphans ask for assistance of charity for the purpose of marrying, and there is not enough money for both, the orphan girl has preference in receiving the assistance for marriage expenditures.

8. If a man asks for food he must be believed, without investigation as to its truth, but if he asks for clothing, then he must be investigated to see if he needs it.

9. If two poor men make a promise to give a certain amount for charity this promise can be fulfilled if each one gives the amount to the other.

10. If a community needs to hire a Rabbi and Cantor and the funds in the treasury are insufficient for hiring both, the hiring of the Rabbi has the preference.

11. It is forbidden for the charity officers to support the Rabbi of a city with charity money, because it is a great disgrace for him and for the

city for him to be supported with such money. He must be supported through a separate fund with great honor. However, it is permitted for anyone to send him a gift of money.

CHAPTER 252

1. The command to release a man from captivity has the preference over the command of support; therefore, if there are two demands for the charity leaders one to support a poor man and another for the purpose of releasing a man from captivity, and the treasury has not enough for both, the preference is given to releasing the man in captivity.

2. The man who violates the command to release a man from captivity is liable to punishment by God and by mankind; denying release from captivity is equal to shedding the man's blood.

3. It is forbidden to assist a prisoner to escape because the laws of the government are like the law of the Lord, and must not be violated.

4. If a man and a woman both are in captivity and the charity has not enough funds to release them both, the woman has the preference because it is a shame to leave a woman in such a place.

5. If they both declare that if they are not released they will commit suicide, the preference of release is given to the man.

6. If the man in captivity can be released by means of his own fortune, but refuses and desires to be released from the charity fund, he can be released but is bound to return the expenses.

7. If a son is in captivity and is unable to release himself, and the father possesses means he must release his son from captivity; the same rule applies to other relatives.

8. If a wealthy man is on a journey and becomes short of money he can obtain same from charity.

9. If a rich man is a miser and does not feed himself properly the charity is not bound to assist him.

10. If a man receives charity for support, his debtor cannot attach this money for his debt.

11. It is forbidden for a poor man to depend on charity, he must try to find manual labor and live by his own work by the sweat of his brow; if he does this he will become rich and will be able to give charity to others.

12. A man is forbidden to pretend that he is blind, lame or deaf in order to beg; if he does this he will really become blind as a punishment.

13. If a man goes to another city for business and is taxed for charity he must pay it in the city where he is taxed; he cannot fulfill his promise by paying the same amount in the city where he resides.

14. If a poor man receives charity and afterward becomes rich he need not repay the amount to the charity.

15. If a leader of a charity claims that he made a loan of a certain amount for the use of the charity he is believed, but if the claim is made after his term of office has expired he is not believed.

Leon of Modena

Leon of Modena (1571–1648) was a son of the Italian Renaissance, who, like the residents of Arab Spain, combined both Jewish and secular learning. His father gave him a comprehensive Jewish education; in addition, he was taught philosophy, natural sciences, mathematics and classical literature, and, like his gentile contemporaries, was trained in singing and dancing. A precocious child and youth, Modena is said to have chanted the *Haftorah* in the synagogue at the age of two and a half, and at three read the Torah and translated each verse. At twelve he rendered into Hebrew the first canto of Ariosto's *Orlando Furioso;* a year later he wrote his famous tract on cardplaying and produced a tour de force, an elegy that could be read both in Hebrew and Italian.

Although Modena did not make his imprint on Hebrew literature with a major work, his versatility is evident in a number of spheres. In 1616 he wrote a book in Italian about Jewish religious practise *(Historia dei Riti Hebraici)* for James I of England, later translated into English (1650), French (1671), Latin (1693), and Hebrew (1867). As a lover of music, Modena had a special interest in musical accompaniment to prayers. He wrote poetry and liturgic hymns which were included in the services of Ashkenazic and Sephardic communities, and he favored compositions that could easily be understood and sung. He also wrote some of the rare parodies in sixteenth-century Hebrew literature. Taking some verses against gambling (ascribed to Abraham ibn Ezra) he reversed their spirit and produced a poem in praise of gambling—a weakness that was to beset him the rest of his life. Another parody was a witty epitaph; based on the hymn *Adon Olam,* it faithfully mimicked its meter, rhyme, and, to a large extent, even its vocabulary. For instance, instead of *Adon Olam* ("master of the universe"), Modena declared, *Adon Ne'elam* ("the master has vanished").

For his liberal views, Modena was disliked by the orthodox rabbis of his day. However, royalty, laity, and Christian clergy were in constant contact with him and came to hear him preach. He found as many friends at the pulpit as at the gaming table. In 1625 he was appointed official preacher in Venice, and he was also the reader of the Italian congregation. The post of professional rabbi being nonexistent in seventeenth century Venice, he had to earn his money at various occupations: among others he gave private lessons, received royalties from books, wrote poems, speeches and letters on order, and composed comedies. His autobiography, which provides us with much of the information about his life, is one of the earliest in Hebrew. Superstitious and enlightened, rabbi and gambler, interpreter of halakha and writer of jingles and amulets, Leon of Modena was no giant of Hebrew letters, but one of the most fascinating personalities in the early modern Jewish period, and perhaps a classic symbol of a man torn between two cultures.

ON GAMBLING

IN WHICH ELDAD ENDEAVORS TO PROVE THAT THE GAMBLER TRESPASSES EACH ONE OF THE TEN COMMANDMENTS, AND MEDAD RETORTS.

ELDAD: If with all human effort you draw out words and arguments to institute a comparison between gaming and commerce, in order to prove that one is similar to the other, inasmuch as they both equally tend to increase or diminish one's possessions, wealth, and the coveted things of this world; I would still ask, how you could possibly defend this pursuit when it is understood that they who walk in its ways are workers of iniquity? Each commits thereby an act of rebellion toward his Maker, and gradually estranges himself from Him, since he takes money from his fellowman by wicked and thievish methods without giving him a *quid pro quo,* and without any labor on his own part.

If you go into the matter thoroughly, you will see that the gambler trespasses all the Ten Commandments, the very foundation of the Law of Moses and of his Prophecy, acknowledged not alone by the people of Israel, holy unto the Lord, but also by those nations among whom we dwell. First, with regard to those Commandments from the words [Ex. 20:2,8] "I am the Lord thy God" unto the fourth, "Remember the Sabbath Day." These all warn against the sin of idolatry; and beyond doubt he trespasses against each one of them. For, as soon as his star is unlucky, and he loses everything, he will be beside himself, will grow full of fury and anger; and it is clear to us that our Rabbis were right when they said that "the man of anger is like the idolator [in forgetting his God, Zohar, Gen. 27b]." They have expressed the same idea even more clearly when they remarked: "A gambler is an idolator," basing their dictum on the Scriptural phrases: "And Sarah saw the [idolatrous] son of Hagar . . . playing [gambling]"; "And the people [after they made the golden calf, an idol,] sat down to eat and drink, and they rose up to gambol [gamble]" [Gen. Rabbah 53:15].

As regards the Third Commandment [Ex. 20:7]: "Thou shalt not take the name of the Lord thy God in vain," ets., it is self-evident to all, that at every moment during play, at every opportunity for sinning, or differences among players, a man will commit perjury; he will swear thousands of vain and false oaths, dragging his soul down to earth—a dark and dreary outlook.

And how easily the Commandment referring to the Sabbath Day is broken! A man is playing on Sabbath Eve, near dusk; the loser, in the forlorn hope of winning back what he has lost; the winner, whose greed for gain is not satisfied, hoping to make more, suddenly find that the Sabbath has overtaken them, and they have infringed the sanctity of the day. In many other ways, too, this can happen to players.

The honoring of father and mother is equally jeopardized by this pursuit. Properly speaking, it is the duty of father and mother to correct and chastise the son who is addicted to gambling, in the endeavor to bring him back; but the son who is steeped in this sort of thing, which has become to him as second nature, will give them no ear. He answers them harshly, and this is a source of bitterness to their lives, for he has ignored the command [Lev. 19:3]: "A man shall fear his mother and his father."

Furthermore, when a man realizes that he has lost his money, the fire of envy and hatred will burn within him against his fellowman; or he will seek a pretext to quarrel with him, remarking, "The game was not so," calling him a wicked scoundrel, anxious to rob him of his own. The other will retort, and the discussion, having become heated—we cannot predict where it will end. It may even be that each will draw his sword, so that one gets killed, and the command of the Lord [Ex. 20:13], "Thou shalt not murder," be transgressed.

A gambler will mix with loose women. In his rage he will utter obscene and filthy expressions, and concerning such a sin our Rabbis have said [Shabbat 33a]: "The one who defiles his mouth with unhallowed words has no share in the bliss of the World to Come."

Words are the index to actions; the mouth makes the first move, and the organs of action do the rest. This is all contained in the prohibition [Ex. 20:13]: "Thou shalt not commit adultery."

Now, when he has been left destitute, left entirely without money, it is natural that all his thoughts are misdirected the livelong day. He broods upon how he may steal secretly, or rob his fellow creatures openly, hoping by this means to make up for his deficiencies, with the result that he will be like the chief baker, Pharaoh's servant, hanging between heaven and earth, for not having observed the warning [Ex. 20:13]: "Thou shalt not steal."

It may happen, too, in the course of a game with his friend, that they may form a compact to share the profits equally and a misunderstanding arising, a third party is called in to arbitrate; but he, being a friend of one of the players, gives the decision in favor of that friend, to wit, unjustly; what becomes now of the command [Ex. 20:13]: "Thou shalt not bear false witness against thy neighbor"? It is thrown overboard.

And it stands to reason that, if a man is not particular with regard to the law of stealing, he will be less careful as regards the prohibition [Ex. 20:14]: "Thou shalt not covet"; for whatever his eyes see, his heart will desire with a longing which will never satisfy the eye of covetousness.

Consider and answer now, whether the evil of this wicked pastime is not monstrous enough to reach unto Heaven. . . . Surely the one who touches such a diversion cannot go unpunished!

MEDAD: You have employed many words to condemn this sport, but you have nevertheless said nothing effectual to cast a stigma upon it which might not apply equally to every other human pursuit. For [Eccl. 7:9] "anger resteth in the bosom of fools" even in trivial matters, but the sensible man is patient at all times.

This is my experience. I saw a man yesterday losing 400 goldpieces, and he never uttered a word by way of cursing his luck; only once he exclaimed: "Thou, O Lord, art righteous!" On the other hand, I knew a man who, on receipt of the news that corn had depreciated in value—he was a corn and wine dealer—went up to the roof, threw himself down, and was killed.

And where will you find the occasion for more wicked and perplexing oaths than among merchants, which they employ to confirm their statements in the course of buying and selling?

And with regard to your apprehension as to the violation of the Sabbath, this may apply as well to the tailor, shoemaker, and every other workman who is desirous of increasing his profits.

There are, furthermore, many other diversions which might lead to the breaking of the command to honor father and mother, or to the commission of murder and adultery.

And the same is the case with stealing, which a poor fellow in straitened circumstances justifies by saying, it is not for stealing that he is hanged, but owing to his unlucky star and hard times.

As far as concerns false swearing, this may occur in any form of partnership; and covetousness, even outside gaming, is well known to reside naturally in the heart of man.

To sum up the matter: a perfectly righteous person will be as upright in commercial pursuits as in sport or anything else; whilst a wicked person will act wickedly in the one matter as in the other.

And now, finally, I say, go and reflect upon this one point. If, as you insist, gambling is such robbery and an intolerable sin, why did not our Rabbis of old prohibit it to us and our descendants in a clear decisive, and expressive manner? Considering, too, as is well known, that their object was ever to keep us aloof, not alone from transgression and wickedness itself, but even from that which in a remote degree might lead to its commission, and they, therefore, in their exalted and perfect wisdom, instituted one fence and safeguard upon another to protect the law—what conclusion can we arrive at from the consideration that they never lifted up their voice against this diversion, but that they found therein nothing of vice or vanity, as you would have us believe? . . .

JEWS AND MUSIC—RESPONSUM

QUESTION:

We have among us some who know the art of music. Six or seven knowledgeable young men of our congregation lift up their voices in the synagogue on holidays and festivals and chant the songs and praises "Ein Kelohenu," "Alenu," "Yigdal," "Adon Alam" and the like, to honor the Lord by orderly arrangement of the voices in accordance with the musical art [i.e., in harmony]. There arose a man to drive them out with the speech of his lips. He said that it is not proper to do so, for, since the Temple was destroyed, rejoicing is forbidden, songs are forbidden, and even praise of God through singing is forbidden. [They are forbidden] because of the verse: "Rejoice not, O Israel, among the nations" [Hos. 9.1]. He made of these singers a mockery in the eyes of the multitude who heard their voice, even though most of them were learned in the Torah. Now let the "royal" word come forth from the teachers of the Torah as to whether there is any prohibition in the matter, whether the voice of the objector is right, or the voice that is "pleasant to praise the Lord."

ANSWER:

This matter is discussed in the Talmud [Git.7a]. We read there as follows: "They send [this question] to Mar Ukba: Is music forbidden? He drew a line [on paper] and wrote to them: 'Rejoice not, O Israel, among the nations.' [Hos. 9.1]. Why did he not send them the verse: 'Drink not wine with singing.' [i.e., and instrumental accompaniment, as is implied in Isa. 24.9]?" [The answer is] if he had sent them the latter verse, I might suppose that only instrumental music is forbidden but vocal music is permitted (therefore he sent them the first verse to indicate that *both* are prohibited). From the fact that he did not send them the second verse mentioned, we learn then that the oral music is also forbidden. Therefore the man who [here in Venice] prohibited the choir, did so because it is vocal music. Also he saw what is written in the *Tur*, "Orah Hayyim" 560: "They forbade all kinds of singing, both by instrument and by mouth." And also Maimonides explains in responsum [no.370, ed. Frèimann]: "That even by mouth it is forbidden and even at a banquet, and it makes no difference whether the song is in Hebrew or in Arabic." Perhaps also he has not seen the opinion of the other scholars.

[Modena cites all the objections to music in the Talmud and among the later scholars, in order that the negative case be fully stated. Then he analyzes the legal status of music among the Jews as follows:]

Now consider: he who examines carefully, in their respective places, all that has here been cited, will find that there are six distinctions to be made in this matter. Two of them have to do with the production of the music and four with its intention and its occasion. One is music by instrument; two, music by mouth; three, music at a wine banquet; four, to pamper oneself as kings do [who rise and retire to music]; five, to rejoice bride and groom, or for any other mitzvah. I add here still another [i.e., the sixth], namely, learning the art or engaging in it so as to remember it when the time comes to perform a mitzvah.

The first classification, instrumental music, is as all agree, the most serious. With regard to that, Mar Ukba, cited above, knew that no one would disagree, and therefore he did not feel it necessary to quote a verse to prove it. Instead, he quoted that which would be proof of the prohibition of vocal music. So, too, Maimonides wrote [*Yad,* "Laws of Fasting," V.14]: "They decreed that we are not to play on instruments; all singing for the sake of enjoyment is forbidden; and it is forbidden to hear it, because of the destruction of the Temple."

Now we must understand the intention and the occasion of music. It is now clear that vocal music, which is not at a wine festival, is permitted. We see this from what Rashi wrote, when commenting on the statement of Mar Ukba, that it is forbidden to sing at wine festivals: from which we derive (says Leon) that we must not assume that singing is prohibited everywhere and under all circumstances.

[He analyzes all these opinions to show that they do not mean a general prohibition, but only music under special circumstances, namely, at wine festivals, to pamper oneself as kings do, etc. Then he continues:]

Vocal music, not at a festival nor for self-pampering as kings do, but to rejoice in the Law or.to learn the art, or at the command of princes and rulers and the like, and of course for a mitzvah—all of the authorities will grant that it is permitted.

[The reference in the phrase "at the command of princes and rulers" is to Solomon dei Rossi, to whose book this responsum was a preface. Solomon dei Rossi was official singer and musician at the ducal court of Tuscany.]

[Our decision] depends upon the reason for the music. The prohibition was due to the destruction of the Temple and to the exile in which we find ourselves. How can we rejoice when our Temple is desolate and we are in exile? It is with this in mind that they said in the Talmud [Sang. 101a]. "The ear that hears song will be uprooted, and song in the house means destruction in the end, etc." But if the music is for a mitzvah, such as bringing joy to bride and groom, and the like, "even a lad can write" [a reference to the verse in Isa. 10.19 that it is completely permitted].

In fact, even instrumental music and music at a banquet of wine, which are the two gravest subdivisions of the law, are permitted for the sake of bride and groom. Thus the *Tur*, "Orah Hayyim" 338, says in the name of Abi HaEzri [Eliezer ben Joel haLevi, 13th century] that it is permitted on the Sabbath to tell a Gentile to play, on instruments, songs at wedding parties; for if a mitzvah is involved, asking a Gentile is permitted. So, you see [says Leon] he actually calls it a mitzvah to play on instruments at a wine banquet.

In fact, Maimonides, in the "Laws of Fasting," V.14, also concludes: "Already it is an established custom among all of Israel to sing praises to God at banquets of wine." The *Tur, ibid.*, says that it is permitted to utter songs and praises over wine at a banquet; and Caro quotes the *Semag* [*Sefer Mitzvot Gadol* a 13th century code by Rabbi Moses of Coucy, France] that to rejoice bride and groom is song of mitzvah and permitted. So does Joseph Caro say in his short book (*Shulkhan Arukh*, "Orah Hayyim" 560.3) and Moses Isserles adds there: "Thus for the needs of a mitzvah, as in the house of bride and groom, it is all permitted." Isaac Alfasi [Ber., beginning of ch.5] said that the statement of Mar Ukba about vocal music being prohibited applies only to human love songs, rejoicing in human beauty, what the Arabs call *Ashar*; but no Israelite need refrain from words of song and praise and recollection of the kindness of God.

[Modena continues citing the authorities which indicate that music is permitted for a worthy purpose. He continues more specifically:]

Of course, it is a duty incumbent upon the cantor to make his voice beautiful in prayer. If he can make his voice as impressive as these ten singers [well and good]. But if he cannot, then it is good that, by his side, to help him, should stand those whom God has graced with a pleasant voices. This need not be organized but can be in the nature of an aria, as is customary all the time among the Ashkenazi congregations. They sing with him. It happens sometimes that they organize their voices [into a choir]. Can this be counted against them as sinful? For it is written, "Honor the Lord with thy riches." [Prov. 3.9], which the rabbis interpret to mean: if God has enriched you with a beautiful voice . . . [*Pesikta d'Rav Kahana*, Buber, p. 97a]. Should we then say that, because God has graciously given these people the knowledge of organizing music and they come to honor the Lord with it, they have committed a mortal sin? God forbid! For if it were a sin, then we should decree that the cantors should bray like donkeys and sing in unpleasant voices, and then one could apply to them the verse: "They raise their voice against Me . . .". [Jer. 12.8]. If you are going to say that music is forbidden, then you will have to say that it is forbidden also for an individual to sing, as the Talmud says: "The voice of a sheepherder is forbidden" [Sota 48a], and he is an individual. Then those of us who know music and use it in our prayers and praises would be a mockery among the nations who would say that we no longer have any wisdom, but make noises at God like dogs and ravens.

> [After this sarcasm, Leon of Modena continues to mention the dancing performed by great scholars, as recorded in the Talmud. Then he explains the verse in Psalm 137: "How can we sing the songs of the Lord in a strange land?" as referring specifically to the special songs sung by the levites in the Temple in Jerusalem. It was only these Temple songs which were referred to in the psalms. He concludes as follows:]

There is no place for complaint, except possibly against those who learn this art, not for singing in the synagogue or for a mitzvah, but for its own sake. Yet even this is surely permitted, for we have indeed proved above that Rashi and the Tosafot and Maimonides and all the great ones of the world forbade vocal singing only for self-indulgence, as with wine or as kings do; but that in every other way it is permitted. All the more is it permitted to learn it, for it is a right and proper thing to do, in order to rejoice bride and groom, and in order to praise God in the synagogue, and for every other such mitzvah. How can people do these [worthy] things if they do not first learn the skill? If they know a little of the art and want to perfect it and fix it in their minds so that it should not be forgotten, all this is permitted.

This is how the matter is seen by the humblest of the pupils; and he has taken it to heart. Now his eye turns to the "rivers of honey and wisdom" [i.e., to the rabbis] to confirm or to annul what he has set down. The lion speaketh and seeketh good [a double pun on the verse in Prov. 28.15, which in the original has an entirely different meaning; he uses the verse to refer to himself because his name is "Aryeh" which means "a lion"].

Signed the young one,

Judah Aryeh of Modena

[Following this responsum there are four paragraphs, each one an endorsement of Leon Modena's decision by one of the rabbis of Venice.]

LIFE IN LOMBARDY

In the year 1569 Mistress Penina, my father's wife, died; and in the same year at the Feast of Weeks he took to wife Mistress Rachel, daughter of Johanan Halevy of blessed memory, who came from Apulia but was of German stock. At the time she was the widow of Mordecai, known as Gumpeln Parenzo, the brother of Meir Parenzo, who is mentioned by name in sundry printed books. She had one son from the aforesaid Master Mordecai, whose name was Abraham and who was then about nine years old. Before the marriage my father asked Rabbi Abraham da Rovigo, who was well versed in many wisdoms, whether he would succeed if he took this woman, and the Rabbi told him that he would not succeed with her in property, and if he took her, she should change her name; so she changed her name to Diana. And the said Mistress Diana conceived from him in the year 1571.

Now there was a very great and wonderful earthquake in the city of Ferrara, the like of which had not been known in any country, just as is written in the book *Light of the Eyes* by the sage Azariah dei Rossi. And my father and his household fled for their very lives to Venice.

While they were there I, the bitter and hasty, was born on Monday between the eighteenth and nineteenth hour on the 23rd of April, 1571. Well-nigh like Job and Jeremiah may I curse that day, for wherefore did I come forth to see toil and wrath, distress and straits and evil alone all the while?

The birth was extremely hard for my mother, and when I came forth I was doubled over with my breech facing outwards, even then having to do with reverses. At the end of eight days I was circumcised with great joy by the renowned scholar and kabbalist, Rabbi Menaham Azariah of Fano, and my father and Mistress Sarah, daughter of my uncle Shemaiah, were my godparents; and my Hebrew name was called Judah Aryeh. May the Lord have mercy on my soul and may the upsets of my life be an atonement for my sins and transgressions.

They dwelt in Venice for about eight months and then returned to Ferrara. While they were on the way to Francolino, near Ferrara, they left the ship and gave me to a gentile porter, who fled and bore me away in his bosom. As soon as they saw that I had vanished, his honor Master Samson Meshullam of blessed memory, who was my father's guide, pursued him about two miles, and caught up with him and took me. Then he thrashed him thoroughly, and brought me back to my parents; and we came to Ferrara and dwelt there.

I began to learn the alphabet from a certain teacher known as Hazaneto, afterwards from Rabbi Isaac Supino, and afterwards from the Rabbi Azriel Basola. And though it is said, "Let a stranger praise thee but not thine own mouth," I may admit since I am now fully grown and it is no longer praise that in truth I did well with my studies from the very beginning. When I was two and a half years old, I said the Haphtarah [the selection from the Prophets chanted after the Torah reading] in the synagogue, and when I was three I recognized my Creator and the value of study and knowledge, and I would explain the portion of the week and understand it. [There appears to have been an ancient custom of this kind in the Italian Jewish Community, and other sources also refer to it.] And so I passed from class to class.

One day I was walking about in the garden and fell from a stone and twisted my hand and was sick for some time, to say nothing of the worms which troubled me. A certain woman gave me rock oil, and I fainted, and almost remained in that faint. A little later I became sick with smallpox; and these were all things that happened to me before I was four, yet are as clear in my mind and memory as if they happened yesterday; for I still know what my thoughts were then.

In 1575 we left Ferrara and went to live in Colonia, a small town belonging to Venice, to conduct a pawnshop. My father went to a great deal of trouble to prepare a ritual bath for the womenfolk in his house and to draw suitable water there. At the end of 1576 it was declared fitting, and at the time I was studying Mishna together with Rabbi Gershon Cohen, who is now the head of a Yeshivah in Poland, and was then a boy like me.

The teacher went somewhere, and both of us went down to the bath to play, as boys do; and I fell in to it when it was full to the brim, and the other boy ran away shouting, and the housefolk heard him and came dashing with my father and mother and looked for me here and there and did not know where I had fallen. And meanwhile an hour passed while I kept hold of a ledge round the bath until the housefolk came. Then a servant girl jumped into the water and took me out; and they carried me to bed as though I had been dead of dread and fear.

There at Colonia my brother Samuel was married to Mistress Giuditta, daughter of Angelo della Faggiani of Pesaro, with feasting and festival, and I spoke Torah at the table as my teacher had instructed me, so that everybody there was astonished. As teacher I had Malachi Gallico of blessed memory, a rabbi, a physician and a kabbalist. In those days a certain gentile named Priamo had been beaten and wounded and people were discussing in the presence of my father and various guests of our house, whether he would die or not. I jumped up and said that he certainly would, making a pun on a Bible verse in this connection which set them all laughing.

In the month of Elul [August-September] 1578, we left Colonia for Montagnana about five miles away, and father made a synagogue in his house, where it can still be found in the home of Master Zerah Halevy, long life to him. For during many years the men of the spot had not prayed in congregation, because of quarrels among themselves. But we put the matter in order.

Rabbi Malachi left us, and for a year my teacher was Rabbi Eliakim da Macerata of blessed memory, a kabbalist and holy. Soon after, Rabbi Malachi was murdered in Piedmont on the way by the servant of a horse-owner for the sake of his money. And since he took his red vest and put it on, the Jew whom he had left understood what had happened and the servant was arrested and executed. May the Lord avenge the blood of Rabbi Malachi.

In Nisan, 1580, my father sent me to Ferrara to the house of his grand-son, Mordecai de Modena, to study books and wisdom, and there I spent a year. For four months I studied with Rabbi Yehiel Taureolo, and for eight months with Rabbi Hezekiah Finzi. It was his practice that every Sabbath all the pupils who studied *Alfasi* [a talmudic compendium] should prepare a discourse of their own on the portion of the week. And at the house of study on the Sabbath Day he would gather a quorum and the boy would deliver his discourse to him. When it came to my turn it was the portion on heave offerings, and I took as my subject the words "gold and silver and copper," and the saying "Rabbi Simeon ben Gamliel says the world depends on three things: on the Torah, and on the temple service, and on mutual aid." And I compared the first three with the second three, these being the things which the Lord desires of men and wherein He let His Presence rest on Israel.

When I had finished Rabbi Hezekiah said to two old men who were there, "I am convinced that this boy will preach sermons in Israel, for his manner shows that he will succeed with them."

Later, in 1605, 1606, and 1607, when I delivered sermons at the Great Synagogue every Sabbath by order of the community, he would always come to hear me; and when they used to praise my words he would say, "I prophesied twenty-five years ago that he would be a preacher."

I also learnt to play instruments, to sing, to dance, to do fine penmanship, and a little Latin. But on account of two servant women who hated me and embittered my life, I returned home when the year was over. So in the spring of 1581 my father of blessed memory sent me to Padua to the house of Rabbi Samuel Archivolti of blessed memory, to board with him and learn Torah from him. From him I learnt the craft of versifying and how to write prose, and he loved me very much until the day of his death; for he used to say that I was one of the pupils who was his very likeness and image in wisdom.

I was there for a whole year and then my father summoned me home. Now since my parents wanted to keep me there, the Lord provided us in the spring of 1582 with a young man from Italy who, however, came at the time from Safed. His name was Moses, son of Benjamin della Rocca, a grandson of the scholar Rabbi Moses Basola and a knowledgeable and understanding man. During two years he was with me, after which he left for Cyprus where he married. While still a fine young man, he was sum-moned to the Upper Assembly. When I heard this sad news, I wrote laments for him and particularly the Hebrew and Italian *ottava rima* which is printed in my volume of sermons *Midbar Yehudah;* at the time I was thirteen years old. All the poets saw it and praised it, and up to the present it is a wonder for Christian and Jewish sages alike. Thereafter I ceased to study with any regular teacher, but only on my own, though I was not in a large city where comrades might have helped me to maintain my studies. Alas that I dwelt during the best period for study without a teacher and rabbi!

At that time my father began to send me from time to time to Ferrara to supervise business affairs and collect debts. There our affairs were conducted by Samson Meshullam of blessed memory and I would come in and go out and have nothing to do. In the month of Tishri, 1587, when my father Isaac was growing old, his eyes grew dim. For about six months he was blind, groping in the dark. After many treatments everybody said that there was no hope any longer. All the same he did not cease praying day and night unto the Lord, until the Lord heard his voice and set it in the heart of a certain physician to give him an easy water to put in his eyes; and he returned to his strength, and the light came back to his eyes.

What was even more miraculous, previously he had been accustomed to read with spectacles and afterwards he read and saw everything without them for the five years that he still lived. But all that time we were growing steadily poorer, eating and doing nothing: for my father was disturbed and affrighted and in dread from the constellations which fought against him; and his heart would not raise him to any decision to leave this unlucky spot and to travel elsewhere, or anything similar.

At that time my brother, my mother's son Abraham Parenzo, who had grown up in my father's house in childhood and youth, came into bad company who incited him to gaming, and he lost both his own and my father's money, yet my father always had for him a father's mercy for his son and always treated him well. But when this said brother saw how badly he had behaved, he went to Ancona, where there were many families that were kin to my mother of blessed memory, and he found favor in their eyes, for he was handsome, good-looking and intelligent.

So they gave him a wife and trained him for the right path, while he too repented and went the proper way without going wrong any more. He was beloved and esteemed by all the gentile merchants of the city and by the whole Jewish community, who honored him; and he succeeded and earned very much, gaining more than he had lost. He wrote to my father several times that the time had come to repay him for all the good he had done, and entreated him to remove thither, since he would be doing him a favor. In addition he promised to train me in business because he loved me very much. Despite his entreaties father did not wish to listen until he saw nothing but evil all the time and had lost all hope. Then he sent property there with flax and silk and household goods and synagogue requirements, and agreed to send me in advance.

Now that year there was a great plague at Ancona in which many householders died; and my brother lost two sons, and the two brothers of his wife also died, married men and fathers of children. In the month of Iyar, 1588, I left Montegnana for Ancona; when I reached Venice I heard that my brother's mother-in-law had also died while his wife was very sick.

But I went on, made a very stormy passage by water, and reached Ancona on the new moon of Sivan, 1588, where I found that the Lord had held my brother's wife, but he was very bitter in spirit at all the mishaps which had befallen him. Still, when he saw me he rejoiced very much and felt a little better, esteeming me exceedingly, as the townsfolk also did.

But on the day after the Feast of Weeks, his head pained him and he went to bed; and from day to day his sickness grew worse though nobody knew what it was. While from the time that he took to his bed, he said that he was going to die and told dreams he had dreamt. And when flies buzzed round his bed, he used to say that they were death flies. Finally he lost his mind, and after fifteen days, on the eve of Sabbath, the 18th of June, 1588, as the morning star arose, he passed away, at the age of twenty-eight years. And the whole community honored me exceedingly at his death with sermons and laments. And they all bewailed him because he had been acceptable to all his brethren and acquaintances. I wrote a lament for him in rhyme with an echo. It is found among my poems and writings.

Then I remained perplexed and at a loss, for they warred against me from Heaven; and I went on a ship alone without any Jews with me, and I came to Venice and then returned home to Montegnano. Here I cannot describe the pain and grief which my mother suffered, for she had loved him with all her soul and did not forget him till the day of her death. My father of blessed memory also wept for him as a father weeps for his son. And in truth from that time all the well-being of our house vanished and our hope and support came to an end. Since that time the stars have decided that I shall not see anything good.

On the New Moon of Tammuz, 1589, in order that I should not remain idle, I began to teach Torah to the son of Manasseh Levy of blessed memory and to Joseph the son of Zerah Halevy; an employment with which I continued until 1612 in my own despite, for it was not proper in my own eyes.

After this my mother spoke to me every day, saying,

"If only you were to listen to me and comfort me in my grief! Take the daughter of my sister, namely Esther, daughter of Mistress Gioja, wife of Isaac Simha, for she is fitting for you in my opinion; then I shall have found a match for you among my kin, and there will be peace in our home."

And she also begged my father of blessed memory with all her might, and wrote to her sister about it; and her sister also replied suitably, and it came about.

Meanwhile I had undertaken a Query to Heaven by process of dream, by prayer, but without conjuration, to see the woman who was intended as my match. And I dreamt: a certain old man took me by the hand and led me to a wall where there was a picture painted with a curtain in front of it. He removed the cover and I saw the likeness of Mistress Esther, daughter of my said aunt, and the very color and fashion of her clothes. Yet while I looked at her, that likeness was changed, and in its place there came another which my eyes could not clearly distinguish. Next morning I told the dream to my father and mother, but they did not believe it.

In the month of Elul, 1589, my mother and I came to Venice to journey to Ancona in order to recover the property and goods which had been in the hands of my brother of blessed memory; for his wife had taken them and we did not see as much as a shoelace. Still, afterwards we decided not to go and stayed in Venice. While we were there, my mother and her sister and the kinsfolk again took up the matter of the match; and we came to an agreement and gave our hands on it, and I took possession at the betrothal with great joy, and to my mother I pointed out the color of the clothes and ornaments which I had described to her more than a year earlier, when I had seen her in my dream. She was indeed a beautiful woman and wise, and I said that the words of Proverbs would apply about her and not the words of Ecclesiastes. [In Proverbs there is a verse "He who finds a wife finds something good." In Ecclesiastes, however, there is a verse, "A woman more bitter than death I have found."]

When the time of the wedding came, which was on the 13th day of Sivan, 1590, I wrote to my father who was then in Bologna, and he came. And I summoned all my friends and relations and we went immediately after Shebuoth, all of us rejoicing and merry at heart, to Venice. When we got there, we found the bride in bed; but everybody said that there was nothing more serious than a little diarrhea, which would soon be cured. But from day to day the sickness grew worse, till she was on the verge of dying; but her heart was as the heart of a lion, and she was not frightened.

On the day of her death she called me and embraced and kissed me, saying, "I know that this is shamelessness. But God knows that during the whole year of our match we have not touched one another, even with the little finger. And now at the hour of death, the right of death is permitted me. I did not merit to be your wife. What shall I do if it is decreed from on high? Let the Lord do His Will."

Then she requested that a sage be called for her to confess; and he came and she said the death confession and requested the blessing of her parents and my mother. And on the eve of Sabbath, the 24th of Sivan, 1590, almost the anniversary of the time my brother died, my bride departed as the bride Sabbath came in, with a life of vanity to a life of eternity; and she passed away to her own place. There was much weeping in and out of the house among all who knew her; and she was laid to rest in all honor.

Immediately after she was buried all the kinsfolk came to my mother and me and said, "The sister who follows her is as good as she is. Why should we not maintain the kinship and give comfort to the father and mother of the girl?"

And they pressed me unceasingly to take her sister Rachel as my wife. So I wrote my father, who replied to me as he always replied regarding this matter, as follows: "Do what you wish, for you have to make the choice. Today or tomorrow I shall be taken from you, but you and your children will stay with her. Therefore understand what lies before you and do as the hand of the Lord doth show you."

So in order to give satisfaction to my mother and the dead girl after the fashion she had hinted in her words, I agreed and took the aforesaid Mistress Rachel as my wife. And we immediately wrote the contract and made the wedding on Friday, the 5th of Tammuz, 1590, under a good star.

On the 10th of Tishri, 1615, my son Mordecai went away because a godless man troubled us; and he ceased to teach the pupils of the society. In the month of Kislev he returned and began to engage in the art of alchemy, together with the priest Joseph Grillo, a great sage; and he toiled therein exceedingly. He grew so wise in this art that all the followers of it, who had grown gray and aged thereat, were astonished that a lad like him should know so much.

Finally in the month of Iyyar he prepared himself a house in the Old Ghetto and himself made all the preparations necessary for the work. Then he repeated a certain experiment which he had learnt and tried at the house of the priest; namely, to take nine onkias of lead and one of silver and transform them into ten onkias of pure silver. This I saw and tested on two occasions it was done by him. I myself sold this silver for six and a half pounds the onkia. It stood the test of the *coppella* [a small instrument used at the period for testing gold and silver]. And I knew that it was really so, although this work involved great labor and toil and took two and a half months each time.

It should finally have brought in about a thousand ducats a year. And this is not all; for I also devoted my life to understanding things like that and was not likely to deceive myself. But thanks to our sins, at the festival of Tabernacles, 1616, much blood suddenly descended from his head to his mouth. After that he ceased to engage in this work, for people said that this might be due to the vapors and smokes of the arsenic and the salts which entered his head and harmed him. So he remained engaged in trifles for two years until he died.

Here I wish to write down for a memorial the number of ways I sought to earn my living; and I tried and did not succeed:
1. Jewish pupils. 2. Gentile pupils. 3. Teaching how to write. 4. Sermons. 5. Sermons written for others. 6. Acting as cantor. 7. Secretary of charitable and other societies. 8. Officiating as rabbi. 9. Decisions in ritual law. 10. Officiating as judge. 11. Daily lessons in the synagogue. 12. Conferring rabbinical diplomas. 13. Letters written in the names of others. 14. Music. 15. Verses for weddings and tombstones. 16. Italian sonnets. 17. Writing comedies. 18. Producing them. 19. Drawing up legal documents. 20. Translation. 21. Printing my own writings. 22. Proofreading. 23. Teaching the writings of charms and talismans. 24. Selling books of charms. 25. Commercial agent. 26. Matchmaker.

Moses Hayim Luzzatto —
The Path of the Upright

Moses Hayim Luzzatto (1707–1747) occupies a unique niche in the history of Hebrew literature. With his belletristic works he is considered to be the founding father of modern Hebrew literature, and with his ethical compositions he is the last great exponent of a genre developed in the Middle Ages. Born in Padua to a wealthy Italian-Jewish family, Luzzatto studied the Jewish classics, became a devotee of Kabbala, and had knowledge of the secular learning of the day. He wrote plays, poetry and kabbalistic tracts, but his most popular work was *Path of the Upright,* which people accepted as the finest book on practical ethics since Bahya's *Duties of the Heart.*

Luzzatto's eighteenth century work is in direct line with the most ancient ethical works in Hebrew—from the Bible through the Talmud and Midrash, *Duties of the Heart,* the *Book of the Pious,* and ethical wills—all of which aim to improve man's conduct in this world. As a master stylist, dramatist and poet, Luzzatto had—in striking contrast to the turgid Hebrew prose of his day—a dynamic, lucid diction. His text on rhetoric, *Leshon Limmudim* (written when he was seventeen) discusses the theory of style and includes excerpts from his play about Samson and Delilah. He also wrote his version of the Book of Psalms, but of the 150 poems only a few survive.

Luzzatto's first full-fledged secular composition was an allegorical drama *Migdal Oz* (1727), based on Guarini's *Pastor Fido*. This metrical verse drama has a pastoral theme, one fitting the archetypal occupation of Israel's heroes (Abraham, Jacob, Moses, David, Amos, *etc.*). Soon thereafter Luzzatto developed a lifelong passion for mysticism; he imagined himself to be the Messiah, wrote an imitation of the Zohar, and other works on the kabbala. His third and final drama was *la-Yesharim Tehilla*.

Luzzato believed (as did Joseph Caro) that a heavenly messenger had transmitted divine revelations to him. After a controversy with regard to his kabbalistic activity, the rabbis obliged Luzzatto to leave Italy in 1735; he moved to Amsterdam, where, like Spinoza, he supported himself by grinding lenses. There, in 1840, he published his famous ethical work *Path of the Upright*. New in organization, it reflects nine stages of spiritual ascent (based on the statement of a fourth-century sage, Pinhas ben Yair), from watchfulness, zeal, cleanness, to abstinence, purity, saintliness, humility, fear of sin, and finally to holiness; a chapter is devoted to each of these attributes. Luzzatto's love for his fellow man suffuses the book, and without admonishing his reader he gently shows him how to be fully devoted to God and man.

Towards the end of his life, Luzzatto left for Palestine, but died soon after his arrival.

THE PATH OF THE UPRIGHT

I have not written this book to teach the reader anything new. Rather is it my aim to direct his attention to certain well known and generally accepted truths, for the very fact that they are well known and generally accepted is the cause of their being overlooked. Hence, this book, if it is to be of any benefit, has to be read more than once. A single reading may give the impression that it does not enlarge one's stock of ideas. Therefore, to derive any benefit from the book, it should be read and reread time and again. Only then will it lead us to reckon with those truths which we naturally forget, and to take seriously the performance of those duties which we usually try to avoid.

If you will observe the present state of affairs, you will note that most of those who possess a quick mental grasp and keen intellect, concentrate all their study and thought upon the subtleties of the sciences, each according to the bent of his mind and natural taste. Some devote themselves to the physical sciences; others turn all their thoughts to astronomy and mathematics; others, again, to the arts. Finally, there are those who penetrate into the innermost sanctuary of knowledge, which is the study of the holy Torah. Of these latter, some pursue the study of dialectics, some study Midrash, and others study the Codes. There are but few who study the nature of the love and the fear of God, of communion, or any other phase of saintliness.

Yet the neglect of these studies is not due to their being regarded as inessential. On the contrary, every one would admit that these subjects are of cardinal importance, and that a man cannot be considered learned unless he finds himself thoroughly at home in them. But the reason they are neglected is that they are regarded as so familiar and commonplace as not to deserve that anyone should spend much time on them. Consequently, the pursuit of these studies is confined to people of limited mentality. These mainly are the people you see eagerly and continually occupied with these subjects. Indeed one who is saintly is inevitably suspected of being a dullard.

This fact has its evil consequences both for the learned and the unlearned. It will be exceedingly hard to find saintliness among us, since neither the learned nor the ignorant are likely to cultivate it. The learned will lack saintliness because they do not give it sufficient thought; the ignorant will not possess it because their powers of understanding are limited, so that the majority of men will conceive saintliness to consist in reciting numerous

Psalms and long confessionals, in fasting and ablutions in ice and snow. Such practices fail to satisfy the intellect, and offer nothing to the understanding. We find it difficult properly to conceive true saintliness, since we cannot grasp that to which we give no thought.

Although saintliness is latent in the character of every normal person, yet without cultivation it is sure to remain dormant. Bear in mind that such qualities of character as saintliness, fear and love of God, and purity of heart are not so innate as to enable men to dispense with the effort needed to develop them. These traits are not so natural as being asleep or awake, being hungry or thirsty, or experiencing any other physical want. They can be developed only by means of special effort. Though there are many obstacles to the cultivation of these traits, there are various ways of overcoming those obstacles.

Should we not, therefore, devote some time to this study in order to find out all that is to be known about the virtuous traits of character, and learn how to acquire and cultivate them? How shall a man obtain wisdom if he do not look for it? Every sensible person will understand that piety must be whole-souled, pure, and without taint; otherwise, it is not only unacceptable, but disgusting and abhorrent. "For the Lord searcheth every heart and understandeth all the imaginations of the mind" [I Chron. 28:9].

What shall we answer for ourselves on the Judgment Day, if we are too indolent to engage in this study, and so neglect one of the principal duties prescribed to us by God? Is it proper that we should exert our minds to the utmost upon subjects which we are under no obligation to pursue, or that we should engage in the study of dialectics which have no practical value, or of laws that have no relevance to our needs, while we leave to habit and blind custom that which constitutes our main duty to our Creator?

If we make no effort to understand what true fear of God means, or to comprehend its various aspects, how can we acquire it, or how can we escape the worldly vanities that distract us from it? Will we not disregard it altogether, though we know it to be a duty? How can we discover the love of God within us, if, instead of using every possible means to become imbued with such love, we make no effort whatever to cultivate it? Whence shall come to us the ecstatic communion with God and His Torah, if we give no thought to the greatness of God? For without comprehending God's greatness it is impossible to enter into communion with Him. How can our thinking be pure, if we do not strive to cleanse it of the impurities with which our physical nature taints it? And as for those traits of our character which require training, who will cultivate them for us, if we ourselves pay no attention to them nor scrutinize them carefully?

If, however, we shall apply ourselves earnestly to this subject, we shall not only master it ourselves, thereby promoting our own good, but we may also be able to teach others and thus promote their good. In speaking of wisdom, Solomon said, "If thou seekest her as silver and searchest for her as for hidden treasures, then shalt thou understand the fear of the Lord"

[Prov. 2.4,5]. He did not say, "then shalt thou understand philosophy, astronomy, medicine, the codes, the halakhot [laws]," but "then shalt thou understand the fear of the Lord." We infer from that verse that to understand what the fear of God is, one must search for it as for hidden treasures. Both tradition and common sense confirm the truth of that inference. Shall we find time for all other studies, and no time for this study? Though we are compelled to spend the greater part of our time on all kinds of subjects, why should we not set aside at least some time for the consideration of matters that pertain to our spiritual life?

We read in Scripture, "The fear of the Lord, that is wisdom" [Job 28.28]. The fear of the Lord is thus identified with wisdom, and declared to be the only true wisdom. The term "wisdom" presupposes the use of the intellect. The truth is that the fear of God, to be properly understood, requires profound study, especially if one wants to comprehend it with the thoroughness necessary to make it part of oneself. Whoever pursues this inquiry realizes that saintliness has nothing to do with what foolish pietists consider to be essential, but rather with wisdom and true perfection.

This is the teaching of Moses in the following verse, "And now, Israel, what doth the Lord thy God require of thee, but to fear the Lord thy God, to walk in all His ways and to love Him, and to serve the Lord thy God with all thy heart and with all thy soul, to keep the commandments of the Lord and His statutes which I command thee this day for thy good" [Deut. 10:12, 13]. Herein are included all the elements of perfect piety, which are considered acceptable to the Holy One, blessed be He, namely, fearing God, walking in His ways, loving Him, acting sincerely, and keeping all the mitzvot.

To fear God is to be moved by a sense of awe, like that which one experiences in the presence of a great and awe-inspiring king. In every move that one makes, one ought to feel self-abased before the greatness of God. This is especially true when one addresses Him in prayer, or engages in the study of His Torah.

To walk in His ways includes everything that makes for uprightness and for the improvement of character. This is what our Sages meant when they said, "As He is merciful and gracious, so be thou merciful and gracious." [Shab. 133b]. What they wish to point out is that all of a man's habits and actions should be regulated in accordance with the standard of uprightness and morality. According to our Sages, "The right course which a man should choose for himself is that which he feels to be honorable to himself, and which also brings honor from mankind." [Ab.2.1]. It is that course which leads to the achievement of the true good, namely, zeal for the Torah and the improvement of social relationships.

To love God is to be so imbued with the love of God that we are impelled, of our own accord, to give Him pleasure, so to speak, in the same way as a child sometimes feels moved to give pleasure to his father and mother. On the other hand, we should feel distressed whenever we, or others, are the cause of His being deprived of such pleasure. Every opportunity to further it ought to be greeted by us with joy and enthusiasm.

To be wholehearted is to serve God with pure motive, that is, for the sake of the worship itself, and without any ulterior aim. The service of God demands wholeheartedness. That excludes both hesitancy and mechanical observance.

To keep the mizvot is scrupulously to observe the mizvot in all their minutiae.

All of the foregoing principles require considerable explanation. I find that our Sages have followed a different arrangement and a more detailed classification of the virtues, giving at the same time the order in which those virtues should be cultivated. Thus we read in the oft quoted *baraita* [statement or tradition not included in the Mishna] of R. Phinehas ben Yair, "The knowledge of Torah leads to watchfulness, watchfulness to zeal, zeal to cleanness, cleanness to abstinence, abstinence to purity, purity to saintliness, saintliness to humility, humility to the fear of sin, and the fear of sin to holiness" [Ab. Zarah 20b].

In planning this book, which is intended as a reminder both to myself and to others of the prerequisites to perfect piety, I have followed the order laid down in that *baraita*. I shall point out the different phases and details that belong to each of these prerequisites, the way to fulfill each of them, the hindrances that beset them, and how to be on one's guard against those hindrances. I, or anyone else who may be interested in this book, will read it with the view of learning to fear the Lord our God, and not to be remiss in our duty to Him. Reading this book and meditating upon it will recall to us those duties of which our physical nature tends to make us forgetful. And may the Lord be our confidence and keep our feet from being taken. [Cf. Prov. 3:26.] And may the prayer of the Psalmist, the beloved of God, "Teach me Thy way, O Lord; I will walk in Thy truth; unite my heart to fear Thy name." [Ps.86:11], be fulfilled in us. Amen, may it be His will.

OF MAN'S DUTY IN THE WORLD

CHAPTER I

It is fundamentally necessary both for saintliness and for the perfect worship of God to realize clearly what constitutes man's duty in this world, and what goal is worthy of his endeavors throughout all the days of his life.

Our Sages have taught us that man was created only to find delight in the Lord, and to bask in the radiance of His presence. But the real place for such happiness is the world to come, which has been created for that very purpose. The present world is only a path to that goal. "This world," said our Sages, "is like a vestibule before the world to come." [Aboth 4.16]. Therefore has God, blessed be His Name, given us the mizvot. For this world is the only place where the mizvot can be observed. Man is put here in order to earn with the means at his command the place that has been prepared for him in the world to come. In the words of our Sages, "This day is intended for the observance of the mizvot; the morrow, for the enjoyment of the reward earned by means of them." [Er. 22a].

If you were to give this matter thought, you would, no doubt, conclude that true perfection lies only in communion with God. In the words of David, "But for me, the nearness of God is my good" [Ps.73.28]. And elsewhere he said, "One thing have I asked of the Lord, that I will seek after, that I may dwell in the house of the Lord all the days of my life, to behold the graciousness of the Lord." [Ps.27:4]. For that is the only good, and all else that men consider good is vanity and illusion. Only by arduous effort can man earn that good; only through works, that is, through the observance of the mizvot, can men enter into communion with God.

The Holy One, blessed be He, has placed man in a world where there are many things to keep him aloof from God. If a man follows the promptings of his physical desires, he gradually departs from the true good, and soon finds himself engaged in a desperate battle. Man's circumstances, whether fortunate or unfortunate, are a source of trial. So poverty and so wealth. "Lest I be full and deny, and say, 'Who is the Lord?; or lest I be poor and steal, and take the name of my God" [Prov.30:9]. Tempted both by prosperity and by adversity, man is in a sore predicament. If he is valorous and conquers his enemies, he becomes the perfect man who earns the privilege of communing with his Creator. Then he will pass from the vestibule of this world into the palace to enjoy the Light of Life. To the extent that a man subdues his evil inclinations, keeps aloof from the things that prevent him from attaining the good, and endeavors to commune with God, to that extent is he certain to achieve the true life and to rejoice in it.

If you will penetrate further into this matter, you will observe that this world has been created for man's use. This is why the fate of the world depends upon man's conduct. If a man is allured by the things of this world, and is estranged from his Creator, it is not alone he who is corrupted, but the whole world is corrupted with him. But if he exercises self-control, cleaves to his Creator and makes use of this world only insofar as it helps him to serve his Creator, he himself rises to a higher order of being and he carries the world along with him. All created things are transfigured when they are made to serve the perfect man who reflects the holiness of God. This is what our sages implied in their saying concerning the light which the Holy One, blessed be He, stored away for the righteous. "When Adam beheld the light which God had stored away for the righteous, he rejoiced [Hag.12a], as it is said, 'The light of the righteous rejoiceth' " [Prov.13.9].

R.Isaac [an *Amora* of the fourth century], said of the stones at Beth-el which Jacob placed under his head before he went to sleep, "When they were gathered together, they strove with one another, each one insisting, 'Upon me shall the righteous one lay his head.' " [Hul.91b]. In commenting upon the verse, "Consider the work of God; for who can make that straight which He had made crooked?" [Eccl.7:13], our Sages added, "When the Holy One, blessed be He, created Adam, He led him about and showed him all the trees of Paradise, and said to him, 'Beautiful and glorious as My works are, they have all been created for thy sake. Take heed not to corrupt or destroy My world.' " [Koheleth R. to 7.13].

In sum, the purpose for which man was created is realized not in this world, but in the world to come. Man's existence in this world is a preparation for his existence in the next world, which is his goal. You will find that our sages, in many of their sayings, compare this world to a place where the food is prepared, and the world to come to a place where the food is enjoyed. This contrast is also implied in their comparison of this world to a vestibule. "Only he who toils on the eve of the Sabbath has food to eat on the Sabbath day" [Ab.Zarah 3a]. Elsewhere, they say "This world may be compared to the land, and the world to come to the sea. If a man lay not up provisions while on land, what will he eat when at sea?" [Koheleth R. to 1.15].

No reasonable person can believe that the purpose for which man was created is attainable in this world, for what is man's life in this world? Who is really happy here, and who content? "The number of our years is three-score and ten, or even by reason of strength fourscore years, yet is their pride but travail and vanity . . ." [Ps. 90.10], because of the suffering, the sickness, the pain and vexations which man has to endure, and finally death. Hardly one in a thousand finds that the world yields him true pleasure and contentment. And even that one, though he live a hundred years, passes away and is as though he had never been.

Moreover, if the purpose for which man was created is attainable in this world, why was he imbued with a soul which belongs to an order of existence higher than that of angels, especially since the soul cannot enjoy any of the worldly pleasures? In commenting on the verse, "Neither is the soul filled . . ." [Eccl.6:7], our Sages add, "The soul may be compared to a princess who is married to a commoner. The most precious gifts that the husband brings to his princess fail to thrill her. Likewise, if thou wert to offer the soul all the pleasures of the world, she would remain indifferent to them, because she belongs to a higher order of existence." [Koheleth R. to 6.7].

In a similar vein, the Rabbis said, "Perforce thou wast formed, and perforce thou wast born" [Ab.4.29], because the soul does not love this world, but, on the contrary, spurns it. Yet we know that the Creator, blessed be He, could not have created a being for an end which is so contrary to its nature as to be repellent. Hence it must be assumed that man has been endowed with a soul, because he has been created for the world to come. The soul alone is capable of serving God and of enabling man to receive his reward at the proper time. Thus, the things of this world, instead of being repellent to the soul of man may, on the contrary, prove worth while and desirable.

As soon as we know this, we can forthwith appreciate the importance of the mizvot, and the value of the piety which it is in our power to cultivate. For these are the means whereby we can attain true perfection; without them, perfection is inconceivable. No end is achieved except through an aggregate of means; the character of the end depends upon the character and function of the means employed. The slightest variation in the use of the means is sure to be perceived in the outcome. It therefore follows that we should be as scrupulous with regard to the mizvot and the worship of God as though we had to weigh gold or precious stones, for they are means to true perfection and eternal worth. Hence, what should be more precious than the mizvot and the worship of God?

We thus see that the chief function of man in this world is to keep the mizvot, to worship God, and to withstand trial. The pleasures of this world should be only the means of affording that contentment and serenity which enable man to apply his mind to the fulfillment of the task before him. All of man's strivings should be directed toward the Creator, blessed be He.

A man should have no other purpose in whatever he does, be it great or small, than to draw nigh to God and to break down all separating walls, that is, all things of a material nature, between himself and his Master, so that he may be drawn to God as iron to a magnet. He should pursue everything that might prove helpful to such nearness, and avoid everything that is liable to prevent it, as he would avoid fire. In the words of the Psalmist, "My soul cleaveth to Thee; Thy right hand upholdeth me fast." [Ps.63:9]. Since man came into the world only for the end of achieving nearness to God, he should prevent his soul from being held captive by the things which hinder the realization of that end.

Now that we are convinced of the truth of this proposition, we should examine it in detail and analyze it in accordance with the scheme laid down by R. Phinehas ben Yair in the *baraita* quoted in our introduction, namely, under the headings of watchfulness, zeal, cleanness, abstinence, purity, saintliness, humility, fear of sin, and holiness. We shall now, with the help of God, proceed to explain each of them in turn.

DETAILS AS TO THE QUALITY OF CLEANNESS

CHAPTER XI

The quality of cleanness finds expression in manifold ways. It assumes, indeed, as many forms as there are negative commandments, since to be clean means to be clean of transgression in all its forms.

Although the evil *Yezer* [inclination] endeavors to lead man into sin by all sorts of temptations, there are certain temptations which are stronger than others. Those are the ones to which the evil *Yezer* always helps us find a reason for yielding. Hence, it is against them especially that we must fortify ourselves, if we would overcome the *Yezer* and be free from sin. Thus have the Sages said, "The human being has a natural inclination for theft and licentiousness." [Hag.11b]. We see that although most people are not outright thieves, that is, do not actually seize their neighbor's property and transfer it to their own premises, yet in their dealings with one another they have a taste of the sin of theft, insofar as they permit themselves to profit at their neighbor's expense, claiming that profit has nothing to do with theft.

There are, indeed, many laws against theft.

"Thou shalt not steal" [Ex.20:15].

"Thou shalt not rob" [Lev.19:13].

"Thou shalt not oppress" [ibid].

"Ye shall not deal falsely, neither lie to one another" [Lev.19:12].

"Ye shall not wrong one another" [Lev.25:14].

"Thou shalt not remove thy neighbor's boundary" [Deut.19:14].

All these laws against theft apply to many of the dealings that generally take place in commercial transactions. Each law in itself embraces a number of prohibitions. Not only are those deeds forbidden which are manifestly rapacious and fraudulent, but also those which in the end must lead to fraud.

Our Sages liken the act of underbidding the labor of another to adultery [San.81a]. We find that R. Judah forbids a merchant to distribute parched corn and nuts among children as an inducement to buying. If the other Sages permitted such practice, it is only because it gives no advantage to the trader over his competitors, since they do the same [B.M.60a]. "To defraud a human being," said our Sages, "is a graver sin than to defraud the Sanctuary" [B.B.88b]. They have even exempted the laborer who works on his employer's premises from reciting the benediction when breaking bread, and from all but the first benediction after meals. A laborer may interrupt his work to recite only the first paragraph of the *Shema'* [Hear, Oh Israel] [Ber.16a].

All the more is it forbidden to have any matter of a secular character interrupt the work that one is hired to do. To transgress this law is to commit theft. When Abba Hilkiah was hired to do work, he refused to answer the greetings even of men of learning. He considered it a sin to use for his own purpose the time that belonged to his employer [Ta'an.23 a,b]. Our father Jacob said explicitly, "Thus I was; in the day the drought consumed me, and the frost by night; and my sleep fled from mine eyes" [Gen.31:40]. What excuse can they give who look after their own pleasures, and attend to their own interests, when they should be doing the work for which they are paid?

When a man is paid to do a day's work, his time is not his own for that day. "One who hires himself out to do a day's work," said the Rabbis, "sells himself for that day" [B.M.56b]. Therefore, whatever time he uses in any way for his own purposes is stolen; and if his employer waive not the claim against him, he is not absolved from his sin. As it is said, "The Day of Atonement absolves no man from sins committed against his neighbor, unless his neighbor be conciliated" [Yoma 85b]. Even if a man perform a mizvah during the time when he should be engaged in work, it is not accounted to him as a meritorious deed but as a transgression; for an act initially a transgression cannot be transformed into a mizvah.

We read in Scripture, "I hate robbery for burnt offering" [Isa 61:8]. Similarly, our Sages have said [B.K.94a], "If a man steal a measure of wheat, and grind it, and bake it, and recite a benediction over it, he only blasphemes, as it is written, 'The covetous, though he bless, contemneth the Lord' " [Ps.10:3]. Concerning such a man it is said, "Woe unto him; for the very angel that should have been his defender becomes his accuser" [Lev.R.30.6). In similar terms they described one who recites the benediction over a stolen *Lulab* [Lev.R.30.6]. It is obvious that just as it is wrong to steal anything that is tangible so is it wrong to steal time. The principle of the defender becoming the accuser applies equally whether one performs a mizvah with a stolen thing or with stolen time.

The Holy One, blessed be He, wants us to be absolutely honest. Thus we read in Scripture, "The Lord preserveth the faithful" [Ps.31:24]. "Open ye the gates that the righteous nation which keepeth the truth may enter in" [Isa.26:2]. "Mine eye shall be upon the faithful of the land, they that dwell with me" [Ps.101:6]. "O Lord, are not Thine eyes upon truth?" [Jer.5:3].

It was Job who, in defending himself against imputation of guilt, exclaimed, "Hath my step turned out of the way, or hath my heart walked after mine eyes, or hath any spot cleaved to mine hands?" [Job 31:7]. See how apt is the last remark. He describes a minor theft as something that cleaves to the hand. There are things which come into a man's possession because they happen to cling to his hand, although he does not mean to take them. So, many a man, without actually intending to steal, finds it hard to be absolutely cleanhanded. This is the case because, instead of the heart controlling the eyes so that they should not desire what belongs to others, the eyes seduce the heart to condone wrong committed for the sake of owning beautiful and desirable things. Hence, Job protested that he had not in this wise erred; his heart followed not his eyes, and therefore nothing cleaved to his hands.

Consider the trait of cleanness in relation to deceit. How we are liable to yield to the temptation of acting deceitfully! For example, it is evidently proper for a man to praise his wares, or, by resorting to persuasion, to earn for his labor as much as he can. We say of such a man that he is ambitious and will succeed [Pes.50b]. "The hand of the diligent maketh rich" [Prov. 10:4]. But, unless he is very careful to weigh his actions, the outcome is bound to be evil instead of good. He will sin and act dishonestly in violation of the precept, "Ye shall not wrong one another" [Lev.25:17]. Our Sages said, "It is forbidden to deceive even a non-Jew" [Hul.94a], and in Scripture we read, "The remnant of Israel shall not do iniquity, nor speak lies; neither shall a deceitful tongue be found in their mouth" [Zeph.3:13].

"It is not permitted," the Rabbis added [B.M.60a], "to vamp up old things to make them appear new. It is not permitted, in the sale of one kind of produce, clandestinely to introduce any other kind into it, though what is introduced is as fresh as the rest, and even worth more. Whoever does such things is called an evildoer. Scripture terms him 'iniquitous, odious, abominable and obnoxious' " [Sifra to Lev.19:35].

"They said further, "One who despoils his neighbor, even of a farthing's worth, is as though he had deprived him of his life" [B.K.119a]. You see, therefore, how grave is this sin even when only a small amount is involved. "The rains are withheld," our Sages said, "mainly for the sin of robbery" [Ta'an.7b]. "When the sins are gathered into a heap, the sin of robbery is placed on top" [Lev.R.33 .3]. "The decree against the generation of the flood would not have been sealed, were it not for their rapacity" [San.108a].

"But," you will say, "how, in the course of bargaining, can we avoid trying to convince our neighbor that the article we want to sell him is worth the price we are asking?" There is an unmistakable distinction between fraudulent and honest persuasion. It is perfectly proper to point out to the buyer any good quality which the thing for sale really possesses. Fraud consists in hiding the defects in one's wares and is forbidden. This is an important principle in the matter of business honesty. . . .

Now we shall speak of the common sins that we commit in our social life, as when we taunt, or insult, or mislead, or slander, or hate our neighbor, or nurse revenge, or swear, or lie, or act sacrilegiously. Who can say, "I am free from such sins; I am clear of all such guilt"? These are sins that take on so many various and subtle forms that only by great effort may we be on our guard against them.

Do not taunt your neighbor. This means that you must neither do nor say to him that which might shame him, though there be no one else present. "If a man has repented of his sins," says the Talmud [B.M.58b], "no one should say to him, 'Remember thy former doings.' " A man who has been afflicted with disease must not be spoken to as was Job by his friends, who said, "Remember, I pray thee, whoever perished, being innocent?" [Job 4:7].

When a person is asked whether he has any grain to sell, he must not refer the applicant to his neighbor if he knows that his neighbor never dealt in grain. Our Sages said [B.M.58b] that to taunt one's neighbor is worse than to deceive him, as is shown by the fact that the admonition, "And thou shalt fear thy God" [Lev.25:17], comes immediately after the law against taunting, and not after the law against deceiving one's neighbor.

To insult one's neighbor in the presence of others is an even graver sin. We are expressly taught, "He that insults his neighbor in public has no share in the world to come" [Ab.3.12]. Rab Hisda said, "All the gates of heaven are finally closed, except the gate through which passes the outcry of the one whose feelings have been hurt by a taunt" [B.M.59a]. R. Eleazar said, "The Holy One, blessed be He, exacts punishments for all sins through an intermediary, except for the sin of taunting one's neighbor" [ibid].

The Rabbis said, further, "God draws the curtain over all sins except three, one of which is that of taunting one's neighbor" [ibid.]. Even when a man neglects the performance of a mizvah, so that we are in duty bound to rebuke him, as it is said, "Thou shalt rebuke thy neighbor" [Lev.19:17], it is necessary to give heed to the warning of the Rabbis, "Lest you think that this behest gives you the right to put your neighbor to shame, Scripture adds, 'But thou shalt not bear a sin on his account' " [Arak.16b]. From all these dicta you may see how widely ramified is the prohibition, and how severe the penalty for violating it . . .

SAINTLINESS

CHAPTER XVIII

In truth, the nature of saintliness requires considerable explanation. There are numerous habits and practices which pass with many people for perfect saintliness, but which are in reality nothing more than the rude and inchoate forms of this trait. This is the case because those of whom these habits are characteristic lack the power of true understanding and reflection. They have neither troubled nor toiled to understand clearly and correctly the way of the Lord. They have practiced saintliness according to the course of conduct which they hit upon at first thought. They have not delved deeply into things nor have they weighed them in the scales of wisdom. Such people render the very savor of saintliness repellent to the average person, as well as to the more intelligent. They give the impression that saintliness depends upon foolish practices that are contrary to reason and common sense, like reciting numerous supplicatory prayers and long confessionals, or weeping and genuflections, or afflicting oneself with strange torments that are liable to bring one to death's door, such as taking ablutions in ice and snow.

Though some of these practices may serve as an expiation for certain sins, while others may be fit for ascetics, they cannot form the basis of saintliness. The best of these practices may be associated with saintliness; nevertheless, saintliness itself, properly understood, is something far more profound. Saintliness should be reared upon great wisdom and upon the adjustment of conduct to the aims worthy of the truly wise. Only the wise can truly grasp the nature of saintliness; as our Sages said, "The ignorant man cannot be saintly" [Ab. 2.5].

The fundamental principle of saintliness is implied in the saying of the Sages, "Blessed is the man who labors in the study of the Torah and who affords joy to his Creator" [Ber.17a]. We know what mizvot are equally binding upon every Israelite, also how much one should exert himself in fulfilling them. But the man who truly loves the Creator, blessed be He, does not content himself only with the fulfillment of the duties that are binding upon every Israelite. He takes the attitude of the son who loves his father. If there is anything the father desires, he has only to suggest it, and his son makes every possible effort to secure it for him.

The father may have mentioned the matter only once, and only hintingly; yet that is enough to enable the son to infer the trend of his father's thoughts and to impel him to carry out his father's unexpressed wish, because it would afford his father pleasure, without waiting to be told a second time more expressly what he should do. We see this occurring usually between friends, between husband and wife, and between father and son. In fact, all who are bound to each other by true love never say, "I have not been asked to do more," or, "It is enough that I do what I am expressly told." From the merest suggestion, they try to reason out the implied wish behind it, and then they do whatever they think will give the beloved one pleasure.

The same is true of the man who loves his Creator faithfully, for such a man is, in a sense, a lover. The mizvot which are explicitly commanded are to him merely an indication of the purpose which is willed and desired by God, blessed be His Name. Such a man will not say, "It is enough that I do what I am expressly commanded," or, "I will fulfill only those duties which have been imposed upon me." On the contrary, he will say, "Now that I have discovered what God's purpose is, it will guide me in going beyond the prescribed commandment, and in cultivating those phases of the commandments which, so far as I may judge, are pleasing to Him." This is what is meant by affording happiness to the Creator.

Accordingly, the principle of saintliness is that the scope of the observance of the mizvot should be enlarged. This applies to every possible aspect of the mizvot, and to the circumstances under which they are to be observed.

You thus see that saintliness is only another form of abstinence, except that abstinence finds expression in negative precepts whereas saintliness expresses itself through positive precepts. Yet the same principle is implied in both, namely that it is necessary to do much more than what we are explicitly commanded, and to do that which we believe will afford happiness to God, blessed be He. This is the nature of true saintliness. We shall now treat of its different aspects.

THE ASPECTS OF SAINTLINESS

CHAPTER XIX

There are three aspects of saintliness. One concerns the act itself; the second, the manner in which the act is performed; the third, the motive of the act. The act itself is subject to further classification: the act pertaining to the relation between man and God, and the act pertaining to the relation between man and his fellow. The saintly rule with regard to religious acts is to observe as far as possible every minutiae of what we have been commanded. The sages designate these minuitiae as the "surplus" of the mizvot. "The surplus of the mizvah," they say, "has the power to stay punishment." [Suk. 38a]. Though the average Jew fulfills his duty, insofar as he observes the main content of the mizvot, the duty of the saint is to fulfill the mizvot in all of their particulars and to omit nothing pertaining to them.

With regard to moral conduct, the principle that a man must always act benevolently towards his neighbor and never cause him harm, applies to his neighbor's body, possessions, and feelings. Regarding the body, a man should strive to be of as much help as possible to those who are weighted down with some burden. "Bearing the yoke with one's fellow" [Ab.6.6], the Mishna declares to be a duty. Moreover, a man should spare no effort to prevent his neighbor from suffering bodily injury. Regarding possessions, a man should be of as much service as possible to his neighbor and do all he can to prevent the likelihood of damage. And he himself must surely be careful not to cause damage to private or public property. Anything that might in time cause damage must be removed at once. Our Sages said, "Let the possessions of thy neighbor be as dear to thee as thine own" [ibid. 2.12]. Regarding feelings, a man should strive to please his neighbor as much as possible, whether it be by showing him respect, or in any other way. That a man should do whatever he knows will afford pleasure to his neighbor, is a mizvah which belongs to the category of saintliness. As to causing any one any kind of pain, that, certainly, is forbidden to the saint. This is the ethical precept of "lovingkindness" which our Sages never tire of lauding and emphasizing as obligatory. Under this heading comes also the pursuit of peace or mutual benevolence.

Though these truths are too self-evident to require demonstration, I shall nevertheless mention various dicta of our Sages in support of them. R. Zakkai was once asked by his disciples, "Whereby hast thou merited long life?" He replied, "I have never called my neighbor by a nickname, and I have never failed to recite the Sabbath *Kiddush*." [Meg.27b]. Here we have an instance of saintliness in the scrupulous observance of the mizvot. Legally, he was exempt from having wine for *Kiddush*, since he was so poor that his mother had to sell her very hood [ibid]. It was his saintliness, however, that led him to obtain the wine for *Kiddush*. And as regards his neighbor's honor, R. Zakkai was so careful that he refrained from calling his neighbor by any nickname, even though it had nothing derogatory about it.

We are told also concerning R. Huna that he wore a girdle made of bast, having sold his linen one in order to be able to buy wine for the Sabbath *Kiddush* [ibid.]. When R. Eleazar ben Shammu'a was asked by his disciples, "Whereby hast thou merited long life?" he replied, "I have never used the synagogue as a thoroughfare, nor have I ever stepped over the heads of the holy people" [ibid.]. This is the way to show respect for a synagogue, or to people. To walk among a company of people when they are seated on the ground in Oriental fashion is a mark of disrespect.

R. Pereda was asked by his disciples, "Whereby hast thou merited long life?" He replied, "I have always been the first one in the house of study, I have never preceded a *Kohen* in the reading of the Torah, and I have never eaten of an animal before the portions that belong to the *Kohen* were given to him" [ibid]. R. Nehunia was asked the same question by his disciples. He replied, "I have never allowed my neighbor's curse to follow me to bed" [ibid.28a]. This saying is illustrated by the following incident. R. Huna was carrying a spade on his shoulder, when he was met by R. Hanina ben Hanilai, who wanted to carry the spade for him. "If thou art accustomed to carry a spade in thine own city," said R. Huna, "I shall let thee carry it here. Otherwise, what would be an honor to me would be a cause of dishonor to thee" [ibid.]. It is true that the literal meaning of the rule that a man should not look for honor at his neighbor's expense is that a man should not deliberately put his neighbor to shame. But a saint goes further. He refuses to accept any honor, however willingly conferred, that might embarrass his neighbor.

Similarly, R. Zera said, "I have never been domineering in my home; I have never walked in front of one older than I; I have not meditated in unclean places on anything sacred; I have never walked four ells without thought of Torah and without *Tefillin;* I have never slept in the house of study, nor even napped; I have never rejoiced when a mishap occurred to my neighbor; and I have never called any one by a nickname" [ibid.]. Such are the deeds of saintliness as expressed in the various ways mentioned above.

We read further, "R. Judah said, 'Whoever would be a saint should fulfill the laws with regard to the benedictions' [B.K.30a]. These refer to man's duties toward his Creator. Others say, 'Let him fulfill the laws contained in the treatise of *Nezikin*.' These refer to the duties of man toward his neighbor. Still others, 'Let him live up to the principles contained in *Abot*, for those principles include both religious and moral duties.' "

The practice of lovingkindness is essential to saintliness. The Hebrew word which denotes saintliness is derived from the same root as that which denotes kindness. The practice of lovingkindness is one of the three things upon which, according to our Sages, the world is based. Our Sages have also included deeds of lovingkindness among the meritorious deeds, the interest of which a man enjoys in this world, while the principal remains for him intact in the world to come. [Peah 1.1].

R. Simlai preached, "The Torah begins and ends with loving kindness as a divine act." [Sotah 14a]. Raba preached, "There are three traits, the possession of which characterizes one as a descendant of our patriarch Abraham, namely, the sense of compassion, the sense of shame, and lovingkindness." [Cf.Yeb.79a and Bezah 32b.] R. Eleazar said, "Greater than almsgiving is lovingkindness, for the former is called 'sowing,' and the latter 'reaping.' When a man sows he is in doubt whether he will enjoy what he has sown, but what he reaps he will surely enjoy." [Suk. 49b].

Elsewhere our Sages said, "Lovingkindness is superior to almsgiving in the following three respects: When a man gives alms, he gives merely of his possessions, whereas lovingkindness involves giving of one's self. Alms is given only to the poor; lovingkindness may be shown both to the poor and to the rich. Alms can be given only to the living; lovingkindness can be shown both to the living and to the dead" [ibid.].

Our Sages said furthermore, "We read in Scripture, 'He will show thee mercy and have compassion upon thee' [Deut.13:18]. This teaches that God is compassionate to him who is compassionate to his fellowman" [Shab. 151b.] This is self-evident, since the Holy One, blessed be He, metes out measure for measure [San.90a]. He, therefore, who has compassion upon his fellowmen and who is merciful to them will be dealt with mercifully on the Day of Judgment; his sins will be forgiven because of the mercy which he practiced while on earth. This forgiveness is due him as a reward for his deeds. Thus said our Sages, "Whose iniquity doth God forgive? That of the man who shows forbearance to others" [R.H.17a, based on Micah 7.18].

He who neither shows forbearance nor is willing to act kindly should by right be dealt with in strict justice only. But who shall endure being dealt with by the Holy One, blessed be He, in accordance with strict justice? King David prayed, "Enter not into judgment with Thy servant; for in Thy sight shall no man living be justified" [Ps.143:2]. But he who acts mercifully will receive mercy, and the more mercifully a man acts toward others, the more will God grant him mercy. David gloried in that he possessed the trait of treating kindly even his enemies. He said, "But as for me, when they were sick, my clothing was sackcloth; I afflicted my soul with fasting" [ibid. 35:13]. Elsewhere he said, "If I have requited him that did evil unto me," etc. [ibid.7:5].

Loving kindness requires that we shall not inflict pain upon any living being, even an animal. We should be merciful and compassionate toward animals, as it is said, "A righteous man regardeth the life of his beast" [Prov. 12:10]. Some are of the opinion that cruelty to animals is prohibited even by the Torah. In any case, it is certainly prohibited by the Rabbis [Shab.

128b]. The sum of the matter is that in the saint's heart compassion and benevolence must be firmly rooted. His striving must be always to increase the happiness of the world's creatures, and never to cause them any pain.

The second aspect of saintliness pertains to the manner in which the deed is performed, and this aspect may be treated under the categories of reverence and love, the two indispensable pillars of true piety. Reverence denotes the feeling of humility in the presence of God, the feeling of shame when approaching Him in worship, the feeling of respect toward the precepts of God and toward His Torah. Love denotes joy, devotion, or zeal . . .

Reverence includes also the duty of respecting the synagogue and the house of study. Nor should a man merely refrain from frivolous conduct while he is there. In all his actions there he should conduct himself with respect and awe. Whatever he would not do in the palace of a great king, he must not do in a synagogue or in a house of study.

We will now treat of the love of God. Its elements are three: joy, devotion, and zeal. To love God is to long passionately for His near presence, blessed be He, and to follow in the wake of His holiness, as we follow after anything which we passionately desire. To mention His name, or to discourse concerning His wonderful deeds, or to busy oneself in the study of His Torah, or in the study of His divine nature, is then as real a source of pleasure as the intense love of a husband for the wife of his youth, or of a father for an only son. Such is the love which renders communion a delight. In the words of Scripture, "For as often as I speak of Him, I do earnestly remember Him" [Jer.31:19] . . .

In the worship of God joy is one of the great essentials. "Serve the Lord with gladness," exhorted David, "come before His presence with singing" [Ps.100:2]. Elsewhere, "Let the righteous be glad: let them exult before God: yea, let them rejoice with gladness" [ibid.68:4]. "The Shekinah," said our Sages, "rests only upon one who finds joy in the performance of a mizvah." [Shab. 30b]. In commenting upon the verse, "Serve the Lord with gladness," R. Aibu said, "Whenever thou art about to pray, let thy heart rejoice that thou art about to pray to a God Who is without a peer" [Shoher Tob to Ps.100:2].

Here, indeed, is cause for true rejoicing, that we are privileged to serve the Lord, blessed be He, who is incomparable, and to busy ourselves with His Torah and His mizvot, which are means to the attainment of perfection and eternal glory. In the words of Solomon, "Draw me to Thee, we will run after Thee; the King hath brought me into His chambers; we will be glad and rejoice in Thee" [Cant.1:4]. The farther a man is permitted to penetrate into the innermost recesses of the knowledge of God's greatness, the greater will be his joy, and the more will his heart exult within him.

"Let Israel rejoice in his Maker," sings the Psalmist, "let the children of Zion be joyful in their King" [Ps.149:2]. David, who in a great measure attained this goal, said, "Let my musing be sweet unto Him; as for me I will rejoice in the Lord" [ibid.104:34]. And elsewhere, "Then will I go unto the altar of God, unto God my exceeding joy; and praise Thee upon the harp, O God, my God" [ibid.43:4]. And again he said, "My lips shall greatly rejoice when I sing praises unto Thee; and my soul which Thou hast redeemed" [ibid.71:23]. So overcome was David by his inward joy, that his lips moved of their own accord and uttered praises while he was meditating on the glories of God, blessed be He. So far was his soul in ecstatic rapture; and hence the concluding words, "And my soul which Thou hast redeemed."

We find that the Holy One, blessed be He, reproaches Israel for failing to attain that state of mind in their worship, as it is said, "Because thou didst not serve the Lord thy God with joyfulness, and with gladness of heart" [Deut.28:47]. On the other hand, when David saw that Israel, upon bringing their free will offerings for the building of the Temple, reached this high degree of joy, he prayed that they might retain it forever. He said, "And now have I seen with joy Thy people that are present here, offer willingly unto Thee. O Lord, the God of Abraham, of Isaac and of Israel, our fathers, keep this forever, even the imagination of the thoughts of the heart of Thy people, and direct their heart unto Thee" [I Chron. 29:17f].

Nachman of Bratslav

Nachman of Bratslav (1772–1810), the charismatic Hasidic leader and storyteller, was a great-grandson of the Baal Shem Tov, the founder of Hasidism. Nachman was born in the small Ukrainian town of Medzhibezh, settled in Bratslav in 1802, and died in Uman, where his gravesite has been the site of pilgrimages.

Nachman was so revered by his Hasidim that they (unlike other Hasidic sects who choose a son of the rebbe as their next leader) did not choose a successor. For the Bratslavers, Reb Nachman is still the rebbe, and hence they have been called *"di toite Hasidim"*—the dead Hasidim.

Toward the end of his short life, Nachman composed 13 tales of varying lengths (1806–1810). As he and his Hasidim sat around a long table as the Sabbath or a holiday waned, he narrated his stories between the *Mincha* and *Maariv* prayers.

These parables/fairy tales for grownups have become holy texts for the Bratslaver Hasidim. They study and ponder them and seek out their hidden meanings, especially since they are laced with kabbalistic motifs and Nachman's vision of himself as *"tzaddik hador"*—the tzaddik of his generation. Composed in the folktale style and flirting with the surreal, the magical, the mystical and the supremely make-believe, these stories influenced two great 20th-century Jewish writers, who themselves wrote surreal tales: Franz Kafka (1883–1924) of Prague, who wrote in German and studied Hebrew late in his life, and

S. Y. Agnon of Israel (1888–1970), who won the Nobel Prize in 1966.

It should be noted that Nachman did not write his stories; he told them. They were written down at the conclusion of the Sabbath (or holiday) by his faithful scribe and disciple, Nathan of Nemirov, who transcribed Nachman's Yiddish and translated the stories into Hebrew. Nachman himself edited some but not all of his tales. Through the generations his stories have been passed down in bilingual editions.

"The Rabbi and His Only Son" is the only one of Nachman's stories that overtly deals with the struggle between Hasidim and their opponents, the Misnagdim. Although in Hebrew "tzaddik" means a saintly or righteous man, in Hasidic terminology "the tzaddik" refers to the leader of a Hasidic sect.

As in true fables, individuals have no names, and details of the characters' lives are lacking. Note that the youth is married—but no mention is ever made of his wife; neither does his mother play a role in the story. The driving force in the tale is the longed-for meeting of the rabbi's son with the tzaddik, which will bring about a momentous event, the equivalent in the physical world of stars colliding.

Like other stories in Jewish literature that deal with the fruitless attempt to bring down the Messiah—for instance, the anonymous "The Awesome Tale of Rabbi Joseph de la Reina" (c. 17th century)—this one too must reflect reality, and so the attempt of the hero is obviously doomed to failure.

In the Talmud and Midrash, Samael is the Angel of Death, or Satan, *i.e.*, the evil inclination, and he plays that destructive role in this story.

I have translated "The Rabbi and His Only Son" from the classical Hebrew version.

THE RABBI AND HIS ONLY SON

This is the story of a rabbi who had no children and then had an only son. He raised him and married him off. The youth then sat in an attic chamber and studied Torah, as was customary among the rich. However, despite constant prayer and study he felt a certain lack within himself, but did not know what it was. And he felt no satisfaction, neither in study nor in prayer.

He told this to two friends; they advised him to go and see a certain tzaddik. Now this only son performed a mitzva that caused him to attain the level of the Lesser Light. He then approached his father and told him he was getting no satisfaction from his holy work, as mentioned above. He felt a lack but did not know what it was. And that's why he wanted to go and see that tzaddik.

"How can you go to see him?" his father replied, "You are more learned than he and you come from a better family. It would be beneath your dignity for you to go to him. Desist from this."

Thus the father prevented him from going. The youth returned to his Torah studies, but still felt a lack. Once again he consulted the two friends to whom he had previously spoken. They repeated their earlier suggestion to see the tzaddik.

Once more he approached his father, who discouraged him and prevented him from going, as we have seen.

This happened several times. The son felt that something was missing. He had a great yearning to fill the void within him, but did not know what it was.

Again he turned to his father and pleaded until he was obliged to travel with him, for since he was an only son, he didn't want to let him travel by himself.

"You see, I'm going with you," said the father, "but I'll show you there is no substance to that tzaddik."

They harnessed the carriage and began their journey.

"I'm going to make a test," the father told his son. "If everything goes well, it's a sign from heaven. But if not, then it's not from heaven and we will turn back."

They proceeded until they came to a little bridge. One of the horses fell, the carriage overturned, and they nearly drowned.

"See?" his father said. "Things are not going well. Heaven does not approve of this journey."

572

They returned home. The son resumed his studies.

Again he felt an emptiness within him and didn't know the cause. Once more the son importuned his father as he had done before. And the father was obliged to travel with his son once more.

During the journey the father imposed his previous condition. If things go well it's a sign from heaven; if not . . .

It so happened that as they were travelling the two axles of the carriage broke.

"You see?" his father said. "Our trip isn't going well. Is it natural for two axles to break? Haven't we often travelled in this carriage without anything ever happening?"

They returned home.

The son went back to his studies and once more felt that void within him. His friends advised him to take that journey to the tzaddik.

He turned to his father, importuned him as he had done previously, and the father was obliged to accompany his son once more.

"This time," the son told his father, "we won't impose any conditions on the journey, for it's in the natural order of things for a horse to fall or axles to break—unless of course something extraordinary occurs."

And so they began their journey, and at night they stopped at an inn. There they met a merchant with whom they had the sort of conversation common among businessmen.

However, they did not tell him whom they were going to see, for the rabbi himself was ashamed to say he was going to see that tzaddik. They spoke about worldly matters until in the course of talking they began discussing tzaddikim and where one could find them. The merchant mentioned places where a tzaddik could be found. Then they began to talk about the tzaddik they were going to see.

"That tzaddik?" the merchant said in astonishment. "But he's a libertine! I've just come from him. I was there when he committed a sin."

"You see what the merchant has said in all innocence?" the father said to his son. "He has just come from there."

They returned home and the son died.

Then the son appeared to his father, the rabbi, in a dream. He saw his son standing there incensed.

"Why are you so angry?" the father asked him.

"Go to the aforementioned tzaddik," the son replied, "and he will tell you why I'm so angry."

The father woke up and said, "It's only a dream."

When the rabbi dreamed the same dream again he said, "This too is a false dream."

When it continued for a third time, he realized there was something to the dream and he journeyed to the tzaddik. On the way, he encountered the merchant whom he had met previously when he had travelled with his son.

He recognized the merchant and said:

"You're the man I saw at the inn."

"Of course you saw me," the man replied. And he opened up his mouth and said, "If you want I will swallow you."

"What are you talking about?" the father said.

"Do you remember," the merchant replied, "when you travelled with your son and at first the horse fell on the bridge and you turned back? Then the axles broke and then you met me. And I told you the tzaddik he was a libertine. And now that I have done away with your son, you are free to go. For he had reached the level of the Lesser Light, and the tzaddik whom he wanted to see has reached the level of the Great Light. If they had met, the Messiah would have come. And now that I did away with him, you are free to go." While saying this he disappeared and there was no one to talk to.

The rabbi went to the tzaddik and shouted, "Ah woe, woe—woe unto those who are gone and will never be seen again."

May the Holy Blessed One soon bring back our dispersed brethren.

This merchant was Samael himself, who disguised himself as
a merchant to deceive them. Then, when he met the
rabbi a second time, he teased him for
listening to his advice, for such is
his way, as is well known.
May God save us!

ERRATA

The following are corrected versions of misprints in text. A short bar before the line indicates that the line should be counted from bottom of page, not from the top, as the others. For example, –line 13 means the 13th line from the bottom of the page.

p. xi	line 4	postbiblical Hebrew creativity
p. 274	line 4	Kairawan, in Tunisia
p. 367	line 5	Josh. 10:13
p. 391	line 14	Ps. 105:17
p. 394	line 9	two turtledoves
p. 414	–line 10	*Mizaydim*
p. 414	–line 9	*Mizaytim*
p. 421	line 14	Exod. 7:26
p. 426	line 7	10:20
p. 432	line 10	Second Temple
p. 478	line 11	easily read
p. 523	line 8	shall not contradict, or even corroborate
p. 525	top	(add missing section 19) If a father tells his son to violate either a positive or a negative commandment, even if it is a rabbinic injunction, he shall not listen to him.
p. 577	bottom	32. *Sefer Sippurey Ma'asiyos*, Nachman of Bratslav, Jerusalem, 1975, pp. 58–61.

SOURCES

1. *Apocrypha*, Edgar J. Goodspeed, New York, 1959. *The Story of Susanna*, pp. 349–353; *The Song of the Three Children*, pp. 357–361; *The Wisdom of Ben Sira*, pp. 223–243; *The Book of Tobit*, pp. 109–130.

2. *Pseudepigrapha*, R. H. Charles, Oxford, 1913. *The Testament of the Twelve Sons*, pp. 325–332, 339–342, 346–354.

3. *The Great Roman-Jewish War*, Flavius Josephus, tr. William Whiston, New York, 1960, pp. 264–273.

4. *The Mishnah*, tr. Herbert Danby, Oxford, 1933. *Rosh ha-Shanah*, pp. 188–194; *Pirke Avot*, pp. 446–461.

5. *The Babylonian Talmud, Tractate Berakhot*, tr. Maurice Simon, London, 1960, pp. 30b–33a.

6. *Mekilta*, ed. Jacob Z. Lauterbach, Philadelphia, 1933, pp. 229–266 (slightly abridged); *Midrash Rabbah*, tr. S. M. Lehrman, London, 1951, pp. 25–39, 52–63, 156–159.

7. *Sabbath and Festival Prayerbook*, ed. Morris Silverman, New York, 1946, pp. 15, 28, 37, 42–45, 87–88, 96–101 (slightly revised by C. L.), 118. "L'cha Dodi" and "Prayer for the State of Israel," tr. by C.L. "Grace After Meals," in *Grace, Hymns and Blessings*, tr. C. M. Brecher, New York, 1960, pp. 25–49.

8. *Jewish Travellers*, ed. E. N. Adler, London, 1930, pp. 5–15.

9. *Post-Biblical Hebrew Literature*, ed. B. Z. Halper, Philadelphia, 1921, pp. 64–69.

10. *Miscellany of Hebrew Literature*, vol. I, London, 1872, pp. 92–112, tr. A.I.K.D.

11. Poems by Samuel Ha-Nagid: *Hebrew Poems from Spain*, tr. David Goldstein, New York, 1963, pp. 33–35, 39–43, 45, 55–59.
    Poems by Solomon ibn Gabirol: *Ibid.*, "An Apple for Isaac," p. 63, "In the Morning I Look for You," p. 69; *Treasures of Oxford*, tr. M. H. Bresslau, London, 1851, "Epitaph on the Death of Rabbi Yekuthiel," p. 25, "To a Friend," p. 18, "Prayer," p. 29; "The Royal Crown," (selections), tr. E. David, *Jewish Quarterly Review*, vol. 7, 1895, pp. 461–464, and tr. Alice Lucas, *JQR*, vol. 8, 1896, pp. 71–73.
    Poems by Moses ibn Ezra: *Selected Poems of Moses ibn Ezra*, tr. Solomon Solis–Cohen, Philadelphia, 1934, pp. 10–15, 23, 40–45, 47, 52, 115–116, 120–121, 130–131; *Treasures of Oxford, op. cit.*, "Lines," p. 27.
    Poems by Judah Halevi: "Where Shall I Find Thee?" *JQR*, vol. 10, 1898, pp. 117–118, "A Longing," "A Love Song," *Ibid.*, p. 628, tr. Nina Davis; "Back My Soul," "God's Still With Me," *JQR*, vol. 16, 1904, pp. 206–208, tr. M. Simon; "The Lord Is My Portion," "Song of the Oppressed," *JQR*, vol. 10, 1898, p. 627, tr. M. Simon; "Wedding Song," *JQR*, vol. 11, 1899, pp. 300–301, tr. Nina Davis; "To Zion," "The Voyage," "A Prayer," *JQR*, vol. 7, 1895, pp. 464–469, tr. E. G. King; "To Rabbi Moses ibn Ezra," "Spring," *Treasures of Oxford, op. cit.*, pp. 12, 44–45; "My Heart is in the East," "Physician's Prayer," *Selected Poems of Jehuda Halevi*, tr. Nina Salaman, Philadelphia, 1928, pp. 2, 113.

12. *Duties of the Heart*, Bahya ibn Pakuda, tr. M. Hyamson, New York, 1925, vol. II, pp. 30–44.

13. *Pentateuch with Rashi's Commentary*, ed. A. M. Silbermann, London, 1946, Genesis, pp. 179–185, 190–193; Exodus, pp. 102–106; Leviticus, pp. 86, 86a–86b, 87, 87a–87b.

14. *Chronicle of Ahimaaz*, ed. M. Salzman, New York, 1924, pp. 60–102, abridged.

15. *The Island Within*, Ludwig Lewisohn, New York, 1928, pp. 327–339. In Lewisohn's text the selection is erroneously attributed to Ephraim of Bonn.

16. *A Treasury of Responsa*, ed. S. Freehof, Philadelphia, 1963, pp. 6–12, 14–16, 24–27, 37–40, 74–77, 79–83.

17. *Book of Knowledge*, Maimonides, ed. M. Hyamson, Jerusalem, 1962, pp. 47a–52b, 54b–59a; "Maimonides to Obadiah," *Treasury of Responsa, op. cit.*, pp. 31–34; *Epistle to Yemen*, tr. B. Cohen, New York, 1952, pp. i–xx, abridged; "Letter to Samuel ibn Tibbon," *Miscellany of Hebrew Literature, op. cit.*, pp. 219–228, tr. A. I. K. D.

18. *Itinerary of Benjamin of Tudela*, ed. M. N. Adler, Oxford, 1907, pp. 1–14, 19–29, 35–45, 59–67, 69–81.

19. *The Travels of Rabbi Petachiah*, tr. A. Benish, London, 1856, abridged.

20. *The Book of Yashar*, tr. M. M. Noah, New York, 1840, pp. 136–147.

21. *The Jew in the Medieval World*, ed. J. R. Marcus, New York, 1938, pp. 337–378; *Faith and Knowledge*, ed. N. N. Glatzer, Boston, 1963, pp. 102–103; *Post-Biblical Hebrew Literature, op. cit.*, pp. 162–166; *Hebrew Characteristics*, L. Zunz, New York, 1875, pp. 18–26.

22. *The Fourteenth Gate of Judah al-Harizi's Tahkemoni*, tr. V. E. Reichert, Cincinnati, 1963, pp. 32–35, 39–40; *Post-Biblical Hebrew Literature, op. cit.*, pp. 156–161. *The Book of Delight*, Joseph ibn Zabara, tr. Moses Hadas, New York, 1932, 47–67, 90–95.

23. *Jewish Religious Polemic*, "The Disputation with Paulo Christiani," O. S. Rankin, Edinburgh, 1956, pp. 178–210 (abridged).

24. *Fables of a Jewish Aesop: Translated from the Fox Fables of Berechiah ha-Nakdan*, Moses Hadas, New York, 1966, pp. 16–18, 31–32, 62, 69–70.

25. *Ethical Wills*, ed. I. Abrahams, Philadelphia, 1948, pp. 54–89 (abridged); 164–200, 207–218.

26. *The Zohar*, tr. Harry Sperling and Maurice Simon, London, 1949, vol. I, pp. 83–84, 119–120, 115–116, 129–132, 133–134, 157–160, 182–186, 203; Vol. II, pp. 268–273, 284–285, 301–302; vol. IV, pp. 173–176; vol. V, pp. 211–212.

27. *Miscellany of Hebrew Literature, op. cit.*, pp. 113–150.

28. *Jewish Travellers, op. cit.*, pp. 251–328 (abridged).

29. *Jewish Code of Jurisprudence*, tr. J. L. Kadushin, New Rochelle, 1923, Part I, pp. 396a–424a.

30. "On Gambling," *Translations from Hebrew and Aramaic*, tr. Hermann Gollancz, London, 1908, pp. 185–192; "Jews and Music," *A Treasury of Responsa, op. cit.*, pp. 161–166; "Life in Lombardy," *Memoirs of My People*, ed. Leo W. Schwarz, Philadelphia, 1943, pp. 75–83.

31. *Mesillat Yesharim*, M. H. Luzzatto, tr. M. Kaplan, Philadelphia, 1936, pp. 1–19, 71–118, 135–182.